PRE-RAPHAELITISM

A Bibliocritical Study

PRE-RAPHAELITISM

A Bibliocritical Study

WILLIAM E. FREDEMAN

1965

HARVARD UNIVERSITY PRESS

CAMBRIDGE, MASSACHUSETTS

Distributed in Great Britain by Oxford University Press, London

Publication of this book has been aided by a grant from the Ford Foundation

Library of Congress Catalog Card Number 64–21242

Printed in the United States of America

PREFACE

This study is neither a simple enumerative nor a formal descriptive bibliography. As its title states, it is intended as a critical reference guide to the whole subject of Pre-Raphaelitism. Although the term "Bibliocritical" is unconventional, it best describes the tripartite approach employed: first, to suggest a definition of Pre-Raphaelitism which reflects the complexities involved in dealing with the movement critically; second, to reinforce this definition by examining the shifting critical attitudes toward the movement, through a survey of selected scholarship; and third, to provide an annotated check list of both primary and secondary sources, covering all aspects of literary and visual Pre-Raphaelitism. The two major divisions of the study, the Commentary and the Bibliography, are designed to complement one another rather than to stand alone as separate entities.

The Bibliography is divided into four major parts and one-hundred sections. Although necessarily selective, the four parts together comprise the most complete catalogue of Pre-Raphaelite materials yet assembled. Bibliography is always cumulative, and previous lists, such as Ehrsam, Deily, and Smith's *Twelve Victorian Authors* (1936), the standard bibliographical references, and the annual periodical indices, have been freely consulted. With few exceptions, however, all items have been reconfirmed before being included, and the great majority have been personally examined. The intent throughout has been to indicate the extent of the material available rather than to make the compilation meticulously definitive.

In addition to the more conventional categories of bibliographical classification, part I contains two kinds of items with which little has previously been done: first, descriptions of those museums, art galleries, and libraries in the United Kingdom and the United States which are major repositories of Pre-Raphaelite materials, together with descriptions of the most important private collections; second, detailed lists of the principal exhibitions and sales of Pre-Raphaelite interest, as represented by the numerous catalogues which have been issued. Combined, the twenty-one sections of part I offer an inclusive summary of the available bibliographical and provenance sources of the Pre-Raphaelite Movement.

Individual introductions are provided for each of the four parts and for most of the one-hundred sections. Background materials, special problems, critical evaluations, biographical facts, and other elaborative information are contained in these introductions. Nearly half the items in the Bibliography are annotated.

In the annotations an attempt has been made to indicate the relative usefulness of the items included and to offer detailed descriptions of the contents of the more important works. Items discussed in the Survey of Pre-Raphaelite Scholarship are in general unannotated, but cross-references to the Commentary are provided. Many items are duplicated in the Bibliography; when an annotated item appears more than once, a cross-reference to the annotation is provided in subsequent entries. Numbering is consecutive within each section and cross-references are made by section and entry number — for example, 62.12 refers to to Cecil Y. Lang's edition of *The Swinburne Letters,* item 12 in section 62, the section on A. C. Swinburne. The various sections facilitate the convenient location of related items; more precise groupings can be found quickly in the Index. Thus, studies of individual poems or prose works of Dante Gabriel Rossetti are all included in section 28; but to find all the studies of "Hand and Soul" or "The Blessed Damozel," without going through the entire section, would necessitate consulting the Index.

The arrangement of items within the sections is, with very few exceptions, chronological. The formal cut-off date for entries is 1962, but every effort has been made to add items as they appear, to record sales and exhibitions, and to keep track of material added to or withdrawn from the collections of the major repositories. Most sections therefore will be found complete to the early part of 1964.

ACKNOWLEDGMENTS

The indebtedness one accrues while engaged on a project extending over four or five years is staggering. Only when the score is finally struck does it become fully apparent how helpless would be the researcher without the generous assistance of colleagues, specialists, friends, institutions and foundations. Equally humbling is the realization that one can hardly hope even to acknowledge, let alone repay, that assistance. A colleague who made a casual suggestion or who asked a provocative question, a librarian who tracked down an elusive reference or replied to a hasty query, a friend who read a page of copy or proof, or who arranged a vital introduction, a scholar who uncovered a single usable fact, a former teacher who planted the tiniest seed of an idea — all these are the silent partners, the unremarked collaborators who hold the work in fee.

This bibliocritical study had its genesis in my Ph.D. dissertation, directed by the late Alexander Marion Saunders, at the University of Oklahoma in 1956. Little known in the academic world, Professor Saunders was a model scholar who possessed that subtle blend of erudition and precision, skepticism and cynicism that keeps the mind full and the ego starved. He was my mentor and my friend, and I honor his memory and ability in bringing this work to fruition.

I am indebted to the University of Oklahoma for permission to utilize freely materials in my dissertation.

The Wilmington Society of the Fine Arts first commissioned this study in 1957, but owing to various exigencies the publication never went beyond the reading of the manuscript. For their encouragement and aid in the evolution of the present study, I wish especially to thank Mr. Bruce St. John, the Director, and Mr. E. I. Du Pont, who was then President of the Board.

The University of British Columbia has assisted my research in numerous ways. Specifically, a grant from the President's Committee on Research in 1957, and a year's leave of absence in 1959–1960, provided me with the necessary time and funds to travel in the eastern United States and in England to collect materials for the bibliography and to examine the holdings of the leading repositories of Pre-Raphaelite art and literature. Another grant from the President's Committee in 1962 has eased the burden of preparing the manuscript. Finally, the University has granted funds in aid of the publication of this volume.

Special thanks must be extended to the Canada Council, who in 1959–1960 awarded me a Senior Research Fellowship. Without their generous grant, in conjunction with my leave of absence from the University of British Columbia, this study could not have been completed. This work has been published with the help of a grant from the Humanities Research Council of Canada using funds provided by the Canada Council.

Among the many persons who have taken an interest in the project, five in particular deserve special recognition. The late Professor Paull Franklin Baum read the original draft of the manuscript and made many valuable suggestions for its elaboration and improvement. Dr. Dennis Rhodes of the British Museum offered invaluable guidance through the labyrinthine recesses of that library's collection. Miss Helen Willard of the Houghton Library put at my disposal her wide knowledge of visual Pre-Raphaelitism. John Woodward, formerly of the City Museum and Art Gallery, Birmingham, was responsible, more than anyone else, for putting me on the track of materials which I might otherwise have missed. Professor Cecil Y. Lang, a superspecialist in the field, has in a sense served as obstetrix in the preparation of this volume. His careful and precise reading of two drafts of the manuscript has saved me from many blunders, and the incorporation of many of his recommendations has greatly improved the bibliography.

Other persons who have given me aid of all sorts are Signora Helen Rossetti Angeli, her sister, the late Signora Agresti, and her daughter, Mrs. Geoffrey Dennis; John Gere (Department of Prints and Drawings, British Museum), Eugene Le Mire (University of Windsor), A. N. L. Munby (King's College Librarian, Cambridge University), Lona Mosk Packer (University of Utah), W. D. Paden (University of Kansas), and my friend and colleague at the University of British Columbia, Albert E. Piloto. Private collectors have been more than responsive in opening their collections for examination and in allowing them to be described in the Bibliography. Among these I should like to mention William Alwyn, John Bryson, Miss Evelyn M. Courtney-Boyd, the late Sir Geoffrey Mander, Lady Mander, Mrs. J. A. R. Munro, and especially Mrs. Janet Camp Troxell. Correspondents have been too numerous to particularize, but I should like to thank John S. Mayfield and Richard D. Altick, both of whom have been most courteous in supplying information. For their generous assistance in reading proof I am especially indebted to Reginald W. Ingram, Peter A. Quartermain and Mabel L. H. Mackenzie.

So many persons associated with the libraries and art galleries which I have visited have extended gracious assistance to me that I can only resort to a catalogue of the "participating" institutions and gratefully acknowledge the courtesy and hospitality of their staffs. The following institutions have all made their facilities available to me: The Ashmolean Museum (Oxford), the City Museum and Art Gallery, Birmingham, the Berg Collection of the New York Public Library, the British Museum, the Bodleian Library (Oxford), the

Brotherton Library (Leeds), the Fitzwilliam Museum and the University Library, Cambridge University, the Frick Art Reference Library, the Fogg Museum, the Widener Library, and the Houghton Library of Harvard University, the Henry E. Huntington Library, Kelmscott Manor (Lechlade, Gloucestershire, special thanks to the incumbent tenant, Dr. D. C. Wren of London University), the Library of Congress, Manchester City Art Gallery and Museum, the Lady Lever Art Gallery (Port Sunlight), the John Rylands Library (Manchester), the Tate Gallery, the Humanities Research Center of the University of Texas, the Victoria and Albert Museum, the Walker Art Gallery (Liverpool), the Whitworth Art Gallery (Manchester), the William Morris Gallery (Walthamstow), the Wilmington Society of the Fine Arts, and the Sterling Library of Yale University.

It is a pleasure to acknowledge the cooperation and assistance of Pat Hines Fredeman, who did most of the spadework on the Pre-Raphaelite illustrations and who deserves a larger share of the credit for basic researches than can be specified. Mrs. L. J. Kewer, Chief Editor of Harvard University Press, has been generous with her time and with suggestions for a more useful presentation of this material. Also, I should like to thank my editor, Miss Virginia Wharton, of the Press, for her patience and her careful attention to detail. For complete involvement in the manuscript and for willingness to undertake the most onerous tasks in its preparation, I am finally, more than a little indebted to Violet MacInnes.

In a real sense this study has been a cooperative project, though the responsibility for the weaknesses and errors in it remains solely my own. If, as Seneca says, "Qui grate beneficium accepit, primam eius pensionem solvit," my hope is that all those creditors acknowledged above who hold a lien on this volume may feel themselves in some small way recompensed.

CONTENTS

COMMENTARY

BIBLIOGRAPHY

Other Pre-Raphaelite Brothers

Associates and Later Pre-Raphaelites

Minor Pre-Raphaelites, Associates, and Affiliates

III. BIBLIOGRAPHY OF THE PRE-RAPHAELITE MOVEMENT (SECTIONS 66–87)

ILLUSTRATIONS

Solomon, from a photograph in *Five Years Dead*, Bernard Falk (London: Hutchinson, 1937); Algernon Charles Swinburne, portrait by George Frederick Watts, 1865, courtesy of the National Portrait Gallery, London; George Frederick Watts, self-portrait, in *George Frederic Watts*, M. S. Watts, 3 vols. (London: Macmillan, 1912); Theodore Watts-Dunton, from a photograph, 1887, in *Life and Letters of Theodore Watts-Dunton*, Thomas Hake and Arthur Compton-Rickett, 2 vols. (London: Jack, 1916); and William Lindsay Windus, self-portrait, early 1840's, courtesy of the Walker Art Gallery, Liverpool.

PLATE VI. Associates and Later Pre-Raphaelites: William Morris, portrait by George Frederick Watts, 1880, courtesy of the National Portrait Gallery, London; Edward Burne-Jones, at work in his studio, portrait by Philip Burne-Jones (his son), 1898, courtesy of the National Portrait Gallery, London; Christina Georgina Rossetti, from a drawing by Dante Gabriel Rossetti, 1877, in the collection of Signora Helen Rossetti Angeli of Woodstock, Oxfordshire; John Ruskin, portrait by George Richmond, c. 1857, courtesy of the National Portrait Gallery, London; and Ford Madox Brown, portrait by Dante Gabriel Rossetti, 1852, courtesy of the National Portrait Gallery, London.

FOLLOWING PAGE 154

PLATE VII. Decorated Book Covers: Ford Madox Brown for *Gabriel Denver* by Oliver Madox Brown (London: Smith, Elder, 1873); [Joseph Noel Paton?] for his *Poems by a Painter* (Edinburgh: Blackwood, 1861); [Simeon Solomon?] for his book *A Vision of Love Revealed in Sleep* (London: printed for the author, 1871); and Dante Gabriel Rossetti for *Parables and Tales* by Thomas Gordon Hake (London: Chapman and Hall, 1872), design withdrawn after only a few copies had been issued, never before reproduced.

PLATE VIII. Other Pre-Raphaelite Illustrations: *The Choice of Paris: An Idyll*, 1860, a caricature in oil by Florence Claxton, in the collection of Ralph Dutton of London; *The Three Maids of Elfinmere*, an unrecorded Merton Abbey tapestry, design attributed to Maud Beddington, border probably by William Morris, illustrating William Allingham's poem "The Maids of Elfen-Mere," in *The Music Master* (London: Routledge, 1855), tapestry in the collection of W. E. Fredeman; and drawing by John Everett Millais for "Locksley Hall," in *Poems by Alfred Tennyson* (London: Moxon, 1857), drawing in the collection of W. E. Fredeman.

Ubi Sunt?

And we, the young men with long necks, long, fair hair, protruding blue eyes, and red ties, or the young maidens in our blue curtain serge with our round shoulders, our necks made as long as possible to remember Rossetti drawings, uttered with rapt expression long sentences about the Social Revolution that was just around the corner. We thought we were beautiful, we thought we were very beautiful; but Pre-Raphaelitism is dead, aestheticism is dead. Poor William Morris is very dead, too, and the age when poetry was marketable is most dead of all. It is dead, all dead, and that beautiful vision, the Social Revolution, has vanished . . .

What has become of the young men with the long necks and the red ties? What has become of all the young maidens with the round shoulders, the dresses of curtain serge, and the amber necklaces? . . .

Where are all the adorers of the Pre-Raphaelites?

Ford Madox Hueffer
Memories and Impressions

COMMENTARY

ABBREVIATIONS

Anglia	*Zeitschrift für englische Philologie*
CBEL	*Cambridge Bibliography of English Literature* (1.7)
CHEL	*Cambridge History of English Literature*
CW	Library edition of the *Works of John Ruskin*, ed. Cook and Wedderburn (45.3)
DNB	*Dictionary of National Biography*
EB	*Encyclopaedia Britannica.* 11th ed., 1910–1911
ELH	[*English Literary History*]
MLN	*Modern Language Notes*
MLQ	*Modern Language Quarterly*
MP	*Modern Philology*
N&Q	*Notes and Queries*
PMLA	[*Publications of the Modern Language Association*]
PQ	*Philological Quarterly*
SP	*Studies in Philology*
TLS	*The Times Literary Supplement*

INTRODUCTION

Critics and literary historians of the Victorian period have too often been inclined to simplify the term Pre-Raphaelite to denote only those aspects of Victorian romanticism centering on the Pre-Raphaelite Brotherhood. More accurately, the term includes three stages of a congeries of literary and artistic impulse which have been used loosely and interchangeably as synonyms: the Pre-Raphaelite Brotherhood, the Pre-Raphaelite Movement, and Pre-Raphaelitism. Actually, they are not mutually exclusive but sequential terms descriptive of a continuous, if not a unified, aesthetic force.

The Pre-Raphaelite Brotherhood specifically refers to the pleiad who undertook in 1848 to bring about a revolution in English painting and poetry: James Collinson (1825?–1881), William Holman Hunt (1827–1910), John Everett Millais (1829–1896), Dante Gabriel Rossetti (1828–1882), William Michael Rossetti (1829–1919), Frederic George Stephens (1828–1907), and Thomas Woolner (1825–1892). Broader in its implications, the Pre-Raphaelite Movement incorporates not only the Brotherhood but all later aesthetic influences emanating from the doctrines of the Brotherhood and culminating in what may be called, historically and critically, a school. Pre-Raphaelitism, broader still in its applications, is essentially a generic usage, including the more common characteristics of the art and literature of such disparate figures as Rossetti, Hunt, and Millais, Edward Burne-Jones, Ford Madox Brown, and Christina Rossetti, Arthur Hughes, Simeon Solomon, and the early Algernon Swinburne — in short, the whole panoply of artists and writers for whom, roughly between 1848 and 1882, Pre-Raphaelitism was the special kind of romantic common denominator.

Definitions of Pre-Raphaelitism are almost as numerous as the persons attempting to define it. To their contemporaries the Pre-Raphaelites were either the *avant garde* of a long-anticipated artistic renaissance, foreshadowed by such artists as Maclise, Mulready, and Turner, or reactionaries seeking to undermine existing morality and to destroy the noble traditions of English art. Modern critics have distorted the significance of Pre-Raphaelitism in various ways: by attempting to popularize the movement, by depreciating it as another silly manifestation of the twentieth century's most popular scapegoat, Victorianism, or by neglecting it altogether. As an "aesthetic adventure" Pre-Raphaelitism has been dramatized beyond all proportion: it has been staged as both a "comedy" and a "tragedy"; and the Pre-Raphaelites have been etherealized, like Shelley, although admittedly on "poor" but "splendid wings."[1] The resulting incoherence has reduced Pre-Raphaelitism to the oversimplified generalizations of anthology definitions.[2] The failure of critics to distinguish the three phases of Pre-Raphaelitism has almost stripped the term of critical significance.

The Pre-Raphaelites, because of their critical reticence, are partially responsible for the exaggerated views of their aesthetic. Besides their "manifesto," *The Germ*, itself a vague declaration of intent, and a few scattered documents, they left no canon of critical comment by which they can be clearly identified. The numerous reminiscences, memoirs, and autobiographies, written half a century after the demise of the Brotherhood, tend, however interesting and informative they are, to be misleading; for in them old prejudices, clouding memories, and filial concern too often obscure crucial issues. Had the Pre-Raphaelites succeeded in crystallizing their aesthetic assumptions, confusion about the movement would doubtless have been appreciably lessened. Unfortunately, most of them were content to let others speak for them, or negligently to allow misconceptions and misstatements about themselves to be published without refutation.

Also responsible for the aura of confusion surrounding Pre-Raphaelite scholarship is the failure of critics to examine and explain the basic complexity of a movement which, beginning as a reform in painting, had its greatest influence in the field of English letters. In reality, Pre-Raphaelitism, a mid-nineteenth-century flowering of the Romantic Movement, is an important transitional stage between "high Victorianism" and Aestheticism. It had its roots in the reaction against the materialism of the Industrial Revolution, and it affirmed and reasserted the values of individuality in an age dominated by materialistic demands for social and artistic conformity. In art and literature, it was a revolt against the rules of the academicians and a reassertion of faith in the truth of the creative expression of the individual artist as opposed to the stereotyped and conventionalized expression of pseudo-"classical" art. Pre-Raphaelitism emphasized the artist as creator rather than as copyist, and to this end the Pre-Raphaelites insisted that the artist should follow nature, reproducing what he saw rather than what artists before him said he ought to see. Philosophically, the Pre-Raphaelites, like most romantics, were idealists, and their "medievalism," if the conscious employment of medievalisms can ever be so classified, was part of their revolt, a substitution by analogy for the materialism of the civilization around them. But the reforms they advocated were largely aesthetic, and were social only by association; for with the notable exceptions of Ruskin and Morris, whose social theories also rest ultimately on moral-aesthetic foundations, the Pre-Raphaelites were unconcerned with social reform. In stressing the indi-

---

[1] See William Gaunt, *The Aesthetic Adventure* (61.15); Francis Bickley, *The Pre-Raphaelite Comedy* (66.22); William Gaunt, *The Pre-Raphaelite Tragedy* (66.24); and Frances Winwar, *Poor Splendid Wings: The Rossettis and Their Circle* (66.23).

[2] See, for example, the brief definition in George B. Woods, *Poetry of the Victorian Period* (New York: Scott, Foresman, 1930), pp. 1008–1009.

viduality of the artist, they had not abandoned the possibility of reforming public taste, and they were emphatic in their belief that the artist and the poet had positive roles to fulfill, even in a materialistic age. But the projection of these basic attitudes into social reforms was a later extension which did not characterize the movement in its earlier stages.

The major difficulties in arriving at a clear definition of Pre-Raphaelitism stem from seeming and actual inconsistencies in their working aesthetic: the immediate complications of the *ut pictura poesis* concept apparent in Pre-Raphaelite art; the sometimes unclear distinction between "literary" art and genre painting; the contrast between a romantic choice of subject and the realism of technique in their scrupulous depiction of external detail; and, crucially, the unreconciled contradiction between the mimetic — "follow nature"[3] — and the expressive — "fidelity to inner experience"[4] — theories of art. In addition to these more obvious problems in dealing critically with the movement, there is the problem of resolving a wide and divergent range of artistic motivations within the context of the movement's aesthetic continuity: the near-aestheticism of Rossetti, the religiosity of Holman Hunt, the literal realism of Millais (a technique that continued long after his subjects had deteriorated into the sentimentalized tableaux of his Academy work), the moral-ethical sermon-paintings of Ford Madox Brown, and ultimately the medieval-socialism of Morris via Ruskin.

Much of this confusion can be resolved by confining discussion to Pre-Raphaelitism as an historical phenomenon, that is to the Brotherhood phase, or, at most, to the so-called second "Brotherhood" which flourished at Oxford between 1856 and 1859.[5] While convenient for reducing the movement to manageable proportions,

[3] The advertisement in the first and second issues of *The Germ* reads: "The endeavour held in view throughout the writings on Art will be to encourage and enforce an entire adherence to the simplicity of nature." After the title of *The Germ* was changed, with the third issue, to *Art and Poetry*, the advertisement was altered to conform to the new emphasis indicated by the title (though the concern with poetry had been implicit from the beginning): "[The periodical] is intended to enunciate the principles of those who, in the true spirit of Art, enforce a rigid adherence to the simplicity of Nature either in Art or Poetry . . ." (See 72.3, facsimile edition of *The Germ*, nos. I and II, back covers)

[4] While "follow nature" seems to have been the aesthetic crutch upon which the Pre-Raphaelites leaned, the implications of other of their aesthetic pronouncements clearly indicate that nature was not their sole guide. " 'Thoughts towards Nature' [the proposed title and finally the subtitle of *The Germ*] indicated accurately enough," William Michael Rossetti states, "the predominant conception of the Præraphaelite Brotherhood, that an artist, whether painter or writer, ought to be bent upon defining and expressing his own personal thoughts, and that these ought to be based upon a direct study of Nature, and harmonized with her manifestations." (*The Germ:* . . . *A Facsimile Reprint*, 73.7, Preface, pp. 9–10) In outlining the dangers of the Pre-Raphaelite aesthetic, William Michael lists as one possible danger that "detail and accessory should be insisted on to a degree detracting from the importance of the chief subject and action." ("Præraphaelitism," 75.8, p. 173) However, he concludes that the creed of the Pre-Raphaelites is truth, "which in art means an appropriateness in the first place, scrupulous fidelity in the second. If true to himself, he [the artist] will search diligently for the best attainable model; whom, when obtained, he must render as conformably as possible with his conception, but as truly as possible also to the fact before him. Not that he will copy the pimples or the freckles; but transform, disguise, 'improve,' he may not." (75.8, p. 174; see also the annotation to 38.1)

[5] Originally known as the "Birmingham Set," this group, influenced by the poetry of Tennyson and

this theory in reality begs the question, for it is Pre-Raphaelitism in its generic sense with which the aesthetician or art historian must finally concern himself if he is to account for the dynamic role played by the movement in the history of nineteenth-century English art and literature.

The importance of Pre-Raphaelitism as the dominant animating force in English aesthetics through four decades of the nineteenth century is indisputable. The Pre-Raphaelites were not only the arbiters, they were often the instigators of taste — in literature, in art, in clothes, in houses, in book design, in furniture, in wallpapers — the contagion of their enthusiasm creating an atmosphere that fired the imaginations of workers in almost every field of the beautiful. A catalogue of the Movement's devotees and associates includes figures as remote as Charles Reade [6] and William Butler Yeats.[7] Maurice Browning Cramer has traced the influence of the group in furthering Browning's reputation between 1847 and 1856, and in kindling a devotion for Browning at Oxford during the period of the second "Brotherhood."[8] Similarly, G. H. Ford has shown that Rossetti and the Pre-Raphaelites were largely instrumental in keeping alive the reputation and influence of Keats.[9] Whatever else may be said of them, it is characteristic that they championed Whitman in England long before others became aware of his poetry.[10] Dante Gabriel and William Rossetti, Swinburne, and William Bell Scott were all pioneers in the Blake revival;[11] and Rossetti proselytized avidly for the insignifi-

---

the writings of Carlyle and Ruskin, consisted of William Fulford, who edited *The Oxford and Cambridge Magazine*, Charles Joseph Faulkner, Richard Watson (later Canon) Dixon, Cormell Price, Edwin Hatch, Edward Burne-Jones, William Morris, and others. Morris and Burne-Jones, who went up to Exeter College — most of the other members of the "Set" were Pembroke men — in 1853, planned to take orders and for a time the group envisioned founding a monastery. The advent of Rossetti fortuitously tipped the scales in favor of art, and under his tutelage Burne-Jones and Morris, together with a number of Rossetti imports — Arthur Hughes, John Hungerford Pollen, Spencer Stanhope, Valentine Prinsep and even Holman Hunt — occupied themselves with the Oxford Union frescoes (see below, p. 14, for discussion). Swinburne, at Balliol since 1856 and a member of the Old Mortality Society (whose organ was *Undergraduate Papers*, 1857), was not introduced to Rossetti and the Pre-Raphaelites until 1857. The main characteristic of the new Pre-Raphaelite "Brotherhood" was its intense medievalism, a tendency reflected in Rossetti's choosing Arthurian subjects from Malory for the Union murals and in Morris' first volume, *The Defence of Guenevere* (1858).

[6] See Wayne Burns, "Pre-Raphaelitism in Charles Reade's Early Fiction" (77.18).

[7] See footnote 13.

[8] "What Browning's Literary Reputation Owed to the Pre-Raphaelites, 1847–1856" (77.2). See also Ralph Granger Watkin, *Robert Browning and the English Pre-Raphaelites* (77.1).

[9] *Keats and the Victorians* (77.9). For specific articles on Keats and the Pre-Raphaelites see 77.8 and 77.10.

[10] William Michael Rossetti edited the first English edition of Whitman's poetry (London: Hotten, 1868) and he was instrumental in the establishment of the Gilchrist-Whitman relationship. See *The Letters of Anne Gilchrist and Walt Whitman*, ed. Thomas B. Harned (New York: Doubleday, 1918). For William Michael Rossetti's interest in Whitman see the volume of his letters edited by Clarence Ghodes and P. F. Baum (38.11) and the chapter in Harold Blodgett's *Walt Whitman in England* (38.18).

[11] Gilchrist's *Life of Blake* (86.1) was published in 1863 with contributions by both Dante Gabriel and William Michael Rossetti. Swinburne published his *William Blake: A Critical Essay* with Hotten in 1868. William Bell Scott's *William Blake: Etchings from His Works* appeared in 1878. Rossetti early acquired Blake's unpublished notebook (generally known as the *Rossetti Manuscript*,

cant little volume of verse that FitzGerald's publisher had disposed of, thereby retrieving the *Rubáiyát* from possible oblivion.[12]

Not only did the Pre-Raphaelites influence Yeats who, of himself between 1887 and 1891, says, "I was in all things Pre-Raphaelite,"[13] as well they left their mark on Shaw, who in the Preface to *Candida* (1897) specifically states that he is writing a "pre-raphaelite" play.[14] Beyond these — and the obvious attempt of Wilde and others of the *fin de siècle*, rightly or wrongly, to trace the origins of their aesthetic beliefs to the Pre-Raphaelites — the influence of the movement spread further: to Richard Aldington, to Pound, to the early Lawrence, and to the Imagists. In the final analysis, the Pre-Raphaelites must be considered as individual artists and writers, but "in the days of a deep, smug, thick, rich, drab, industrial complacency," Pre-Raphaelitism itself shone, as Max Beerbohm says of Rossetti, "with the ambiguous light of a red torch somewhere in a dense fog"[15] for most of those whose lives it touched, however briefly.

Pre-Raphaelitism, then, represents a middle ground between the extremes of Victorian art morality (with its concomitants of social reform) and the Art for Art's Sake of the *fin de siècle*. More an aesthetic than an ethical movement in art and literature, it maintained, to some degree, the values of both, preserving the principles of beauty and truth so vital to the development and continuation of art in an age that had itself reacted against Romanticism. Complex and contradictory, often inconsistent, as expansive movements in art and literature tend to be, Pre-Raphaelitism seems today remote and vague. A considerable number of capable persons have applied their critical talents to elucidating the tenets of the movement and to relegating it to its proper niche in the history of aesthetics. But the scholarship reflects, in its own complexity and contradictions, the need for a new and fairer critical evaluation of this unique literary and artistic movement.

---

see 86.1), which he kept until his death. For the influence of Blake on Rossetti see Kerrison Preston (33.34).

[12] For an interesting account of the discovery of the *Rubáiyát* see Letters 1680 and 1810A in *The Swinburne Letters* (62.12), VI, 96, 187–188.

[13] *Autobiographies: Reveries Over Childhood and Youth and The Trembling of the Veil* (New York: Macmillan, 1927), p. 141.

[14] *Plays Pleasant and Unpleasant* (New York: Brentano, 1906), p. vii.

[15] *Rossetti and His Circle* (82.9), p. vi.

A SURVEY OF
PRE-RAPHAELITE
SCHOLARSHIP

Pre-Raphaelite scholarship clusters around five salient dates: 1851, when Ruskin's letters to the *Times* (75.1) and his pamphlet, *Pre-Raphaelitism* (66.1), suddenly catapulted the Pre-Raphaelite cause into prominence; 1857, the *annus mirabilis* of the movement; 1882, the year of Rossetti's death; and 1928 and 1948, the respective celebrations of the Rossetti and Pre-Raphaelite centenaries. Other criticism appeared at other times, obviously, such as the flurry of prearranged and spontaneous reviews that attended the publication of the several volumes of Rossetti's poetry. But so central are these dates to the whole sweep of the movement that they provide convenient points of reference in a cursory examination of the history of its scholarship. Because a great deal of Pre-Raphaelite, like Browning, criticism consists of essentially ephemeral articles, pamphlets, and books, much that clutters the bibliography can be dismissed with only a passing recognition of its existence. Collectively, however, the extent and range of the available body of writings on the movement is staggering; and this Survey is designed, primarily, by relating the scholarship to a skeleton history of the movement, to provide a kind of précis or paraphrase of the bibliography which follows.

When Ruskin decided to support the Pre-Raphaelites in 1851, the group had already become a popular subject of critical controversy, and for two years it had come under attack from almost every quarter. Earlier, after the appearance of *The Germ*, critical response had been in the main favorable. The *Critic*, for example, was without serious reserve in its approval. Finding *The Germ* a periodical that commanded "peculiar and uncommon claims to attention," it concluded that the magazine's "affected title" and "unpromising theme really hides a great deal of genius; mingled however, we must admit, with many conceits which youth is prone to, but which time and experience will assuredly tame. *The Germ* has our heartiest wishes for its success; but we scarcely dare to *hope* that it may win the popularity it deserves. The truth is that it is too good for the time. It is not material enough for the age." (72.1, 15 February 1850, pp. 94–95) On 1 June 1850, apparently before it became generally known that the publication had been permanently abandoned, the *Critic* noticed the new *Germ, Art and Poetry*, in a review that was unreservedly enthusiastic. "We cannot," wrote the reviewer, "contemplate this young and rising school in art and literature without the most ardent anticipations of something great to grow from it, something new and worthy of our age, and we bid them God speed upon the path they have ventured." (72.1, p. 278) And the *Guardian*, on 28 August 1850, noted the demise of the publication in an "obituary" that must have suggested possibilities well beyond the dreams of the Pre-Raphaelite sponsors:

We are very sorry to find that, after a short life of four monthly numbers, this magazine is not likely to be continued. Independently of the great ability displayed by some of its contributors, we have been anxious to see the rising school of young and clever artists find a voice, and tell us what they are aiming at, and how they propose to reach their aim. This magazine was, to a great extent, connected with the Pre-Raffaelle Brethren, whose paintings have attracted this year a more than ordinary quantity of attention, and an amount of praise and blame perhaps equally extravagant. . . .

It is a pity that the publication is to stop. English artists have hitherto worked each one by himself, with too little of common purpose, too little of mutual support, too little of distinct and steadily pursued intellectual object . . . Here, at last, we have a *school*, ignorant it may be, conceited possibly, as yet with but vague and unrealised objects, but working together with a common purpose, according to certain admitted principles, and looking to one another for help and sympathy . . . Its aim, moreover, however imperfectly attained as yet, is high and pure. No one can walk along our streets and not see how bebased [sic] and sensual our tastes have become . . . A school of artists who attempt to bring back the popular taste to the severe draperies and pure forms of early art, are at least deserving of encouragement. Success in their attempt would be a national blessing. (72.1, p. 623)

Unfortunately, the sympathetic attitude exemplified by the three articles quoted was uncommon and praise was to become even more a stranger to the Pre-Raphaelites after Rossetti casually divulged to Alexander Munro, the sculptor, what was meant by the letters, "PRB." Munro confided Rossetti's secret to his journalist friend Angus B. Reach, who in turn confided it to the readers of the *Illustrated London News*. (see 71.1) Once the meaning of the letters was made public, Pre-Raphaelitism became anathema to the artistic world. Critics who had seen promise in the pictures of 1849 and who had treated the young artists sympathetically and even encouragingly suddenly were aware that a formal conspiracy was in the offing. The name Pre-Raphaelite, twisted into grotesque, inaccurate definitions, became synonymous with the most scurrilous and depraved tendencies and techniques in art. Thus, when the Pre-Raphaelites, Hunt and Millais, once again entered their works for exhibition in the halls of the Royal Academy,[1] the critics of the various periodicals were almost unanimous in their

---

[1] The first exhibition year for the Pre-Raphaelite Brotherhood was 1849. To the Royal Academy Holman Hunt sent *Rienzi*, and Millais was represented by *Lorenzo and Isabella*. Rossetti chose to send his *The Girlhood of Mary Virgin* to the Free Exhibition (see 18.1). In 1850 Rossetti again exhibited — this time *Ecce Ancilla Domini* — at the Free Exhibition; to the Academy Hunt sent his *Christian*

disapproval. Millais, especially, reaped a harvest of abuse for his *Christ in the House of His Parents.*[2] The *Athenaeum* referred to the picture as "pictorial blasphemy," and to the *Times* critic it was simply "revolting." But the most brutal (and stupid) attack came from the titan Dickens, whose diatribe epitomizes the general animosity which the picture generated:

You come in this Royal Academy Exhibition . . . to the contemplation of a Holy Family. You will have the goodness to discharge from your minds all Post-Raphael ideas, all religious aspirations, all elevating thoughts; all tender, awful, sorrowful, ennobling, sacred, graceful, or beautiful associations; and to prepare yourselves, as befits such a subject — Pre-Raphaelly considered — for the lowest depths of what is mean, odious, repulsive, and revolting . . . Wherever it is possible to express ugliness of feature, limb, or attitude, you have it expressed.[3]

Ruskin's role in supporting the Pre-Raphaelites at this time should not be underestimated, but surely he is often praised as their champion for the wrong reasons. The most immediate members of the Brotherhood could not, in 1851, predict what the long-range effect of Ruskin's alliance might be, but two things seem certain from even the most cursory glance at Ruskin's letters and pamphlet and from the contemporary reactions of the PRB's, especially those recorded in "The P.R.B. Journal" kept by William Michael Rossetti:[4] first, that Ruskin did not fully understand (perhaps not even partially, since he knew none of the Brotherhood personally and the movement itself only through the works of Hunt and Millais) the original aims of the group, but that he was ready to see the whole affair as an offshoot of aesthetic ideas which, if they did not have their origin in, at least were reflections of, those brave tenets that he himself had been for the past few years crystallizing in *Modern Painters*; and, second, that the Pre-Raphaelites, although certainly not in full agreement with Ruskin's appraisal of their motives, were willing, for practical reasons, to suffer in silence, so propitious was Ruskin's patronage. The real importance of the letter to the *Times* and of the later pamphlet, *Pre-Raphaelitism*, however, was not that Ruskin clarified the artistic tenets underlying Pre-Raphaelite art, but that by identifying himself with the movement, and

---

Priests Escaping from Druid Persecution, Millais, *Christ in the House of His Parents*. Both Hunt and Rossetti were ridiculed, but Millais' picture bore the brunt of the season's laughter.

[2] For a complete discussion of the teapot storm stirred up by this picture see D. S. MacColl, "A Picture that Shocked the 1850's" (37.96).

[3] See Dickens' "Old Lamps for New Ones" in *Household Words* (67.1), 15 June 1850, pp. 265–266.

[4] "The P.R.B. Journal" was published in *Præraphaelite Diaries and Letters*, 1900 (72.7). The "Journal" covers a period from 15 May 1849 to 29 May 1853, and was kept by the PRB secretary, William Michael Rossetti, whose note on the "Journal" is of particular interest: "After the Journal had been finally . . . discontinued, it lay by me unnoticed for a number of years. When at last I had occasion to re-inspect it, I found that several pages had been torn out by my Brother, and several others mutilated. I never knew accurately . . . why he did this . . . Thus the P.R.B. Journal is now much more fragmentary than it need have been — for the portion destroyed by my Brother amounted . . . to a fair fifth of the whole . . . The extracts here presented may constitute something like a half of the extant MS. — less rather than more." (72.7, pp. 207–208)

consequently its aesthetic with his own,[5] he unintentionally provided a diversionary maneuver which altered significantly the perspective in which the Pre-Raphaelites were to be examined. In other words, his publications shifted the focus from the principals of the movement to himself and redirected the whole course of the Pre-Raphaelites' critical reception and future reputation.

That "Ruskinism" became associated in the popular mind with Pre-Raphaelitism is convincingly demonstrated by the publications which followed fast upon his own defense of the movement, and by the effect which his teachings had in the development of an American Pre-Raphaelite Movement, a subject that has been extensively, if not imaginatively, treated by David H. Dickason in *The Daring Young Men: The Story of the American Pre-Raphaelites* (80.8). The critical literature of this period is far too extensive to be discussed in detail, but the scope can be indicated accurately by four works which appeared between 1852 and 1860, and which were obviously stimulated by Ruskin's intervention and the transfer of focus effected by his publications.

It is unnecessary to go beyond the title of E. V. Rippingille's *Obsoletism in Art: A Reply to the Author of Modern Painters in his Defence of "Pre-Raphaelitism,"* 1852 (66.2), to perceive his primary target. William Cave Thomas' *Pre-Raphaelitism Tested by the Principles of Christianity: An Introduction to Christian Idealism*, 1860 (66.7), reflects the moral-aesthetic associated with Ruskin's theories of art. Thomas, who is generally credited with suggesting the title for *The Germ*, had moved on the outer fringes of the PRB in the early days. By construing Rossetti's old discussions on the common motives between Pre-Raphaelite and Early Christian art — a kinship which Holman Hunt, for whom, ironically, the spirit of Pre-Raphaelitism always remained essentially religious, was never willing to acknowledge — Thomas sought to examine the movement as purely a religious phenomenon and to identify Pre-Raphaelitism with moral and ethical values, rather than with artistic ones. John Ballantyne, in his 1856 pamphlet, *What is*

---

[5] While Ruskin never ventured to claim himself the founder of Pre-Raphaelitism — a role jealously guarded by Holman Hunt — he often emphasized that many of the artistic tenets of the Pre-Raphaelites had appeared in his writings before the organization of the PRB. In "The Three Colours of Pre-Raphaelitism" (75.11), Ruskin states: "Without claiming, — nay, . . . utterly disclaiming — any personal influence over, or any originality of suggestion to, the men who founded our presently realistic schools, I may yet be permitted to point out the sympathy which I had as [a] . . . spectator with their effort; and the more or less active fellowship with it, which, unrecognized, I have held from the beginning." (*CW*, 45.3, XXXIV, 162) In his own copy of *Modern Painters*, Ruskin wrote in the margin opposite a paragraph treating finish in painting, "Note this as one of the important passages leading to Pre-Raphaelitism." In another marginal note he refers to a passage "having been written years before Pre-Raphaelitism was thought of." (*CW*, 45.3, III, 178n.) In the Preface to his 1886 *Notes on . . . Millais* (21.18), Ruskin tried to check the substitution of Ruskinism for Pre-Raphaelitism: "I must . . . broadly efface any impression that . . . my criticisms . . . [have] been of any service to the Pre-Raphaelite school, except in protecting it against vulgar outcry. The painters . . . rightly resented the idea of misjudging friends that I was either their precursor or their guide; they were entirely original in their thoughts, and independent in their practice." (*CW*, 45.3, XIV, 495) See also Ruskin's letter to Tennyson concerning the illustrations for the Moxon *Tennyson* (24 July 1857), ending, "We P.R.B.'s must do better for you . . ." (*CW*, 45.3 XXXVI, 265)

Pre-Raphaelitism? (66.4), is more direct: "It is impossible," he says, "to speak or write upon this subject without citing the name of the great apostle and advocate of Pre-Raphaelitism, Mr. Ruskin; and that accomplished writer's pamphlet upon it must necessarily furnish us with texts to discourse upon, as it is almost the only, — certainly the most forcible and elaborate, response to the question that has appeared." (p. 3) Ballantyne's pamphlet is plainly a response to Ruskin rather than an attempt to answer adequately the question posed in its title. Pre-Raphaelitism, Ballantyne observes, might well have amounted to very little had it gone unaided by its able interpreter, Ruskin.

The most pompous of all those publications influenced by Ruskin, however, was written by the Reverend Edward Young of Trinity College, Cambridge: *Pre-Raffaellitism: Or, A Popular Enquiry into Some Newly-Asserted Principles Connected with the Philosophy, Poetry, Religion, and Revolution of Art*, 1857 (66.5). In this inordinately long and boring book, the author, who had earlier, taking Ruskin's words out of context, written, "Woe, woe, woe! to 'exceedingly young men of stubborn instinct,' calling themselves Pre-Raphaelites" (71.3), succeeds completely in avoiding the whole issue of Pre-Raphaelitism. In the numerous sections of the book — an introductory discussion of Turner followed by others on "The Philosophy of Art," "The Poetry of Art," and the like — Young examines different aspects of Ruskin's aesthetic theories, carefully and consistently retaining Ruskin, never the Pre-Raphaelites, as his central focus. The relevant point in all this, of course, is that in at least three of these early works, the authors *thought* they were addressing Pre-Raphaelitism directly, when actually, by viewing Ruskin as a kind of nucleus of the movement, they were evaluating not the artistic productions of Pre-Raphaelitism but the moral, critical canon of John Ruskin. What they succeeded in doing was not to elucidate the tenets and ideals of the Pre-Raphaelites but to insure that the confusion between "Ruskinism" and Pre-Raphaelitism, inaugurated by the publication of Ruskin's pamphlet in 1851, would be further perpetuated by later critics, as indeed has been the case.

The effects of Ruskin's writings on American Pre-Raphaelitism are readily ascertainable. William James Stillman,[6] the co-editor of the first Pre-Raphaelite periodical in America, *The Crayon*, 1855–1861 (80.1), had been made aware of the Pre-Raphaelites by Ruskin, and his conception of the movement was molded almost exclusively by Ruskin's attitudes. The founder of the "Society for the Advancement of Truth in Art," Thomas Charles Farrer, an Englishman, had studied art with Ruskin and was his ardent supporter. The organ of the Society, *The New Path*, May 1863–December 1865 (80.2),[7] evoked from Ruskin the follow-

---

[6] Stillman's wife, the beautiful Marie Spartali, was Rossetti's model and a painting student of Ford Madox Brown, whose style she imitated. See William Michael Rossetti's brief note on her art (49.1); see also Stillman's *Autobiography of a Journalist* (25.22).

[7] "We exist," stated the *New Path* in 1864, in "A Letter to a Subscriber," "for the purpose of stirring up strife; of breeding discontent; of pulling down unsound reputations; of making the public

ing comment: "I . . . have too long delayed the expression of my sympathy with
you, both in the labor you have set yourself, and in the feelings with which you
undertake it: — no less than of my thanks for the help you are giving me in carrying forward and illustrating the views which I have hitherto endeavored to main-
tain almost single handed . . ." (May 1864, pp. 2–3) The American group made
Pre-Raphaelitism synonymous with naturalism. Drawing their inspiration largely
from *Modern Painters,* they avowed: "*We do not believe that mere faithful
transcript from nature can ever be the greatest art*: but we believe and positively
affirm, that there can never be any degree of greatness without this as a *basis* . . .
Naturalism is not *all* we believe in, but we know it must come first." (October
1863, pp. 62–63) In their "Articles of Organization," the American Pre-Raphaelites
held that "the right course for young Artists is faithful and loving representations
of Nature, 'selecting nothing and rejecting nothing,' seeking only to express the
greatest possible amount of fact." (May 1863, p. 11)

Ruskin was not the sole inspirer of American Pre-Raphaelitism but he was
certainly its godfather; and his influence continued to be important as the movement became more socialistic and concerned with the reform of institutions other
than art. The Ruskin Commonwealth in Tennessee (1894) and the later Ruskin
Society in Georgia, which combined this group with the American Settlers' Co-
operative Association,[8] were only two external manifestations of Ruskin's regency.
American Pre-Raphaelitism was far less restrictive in its activities and broader in
its scope, however, and it early applied the aesthetic tenets, or what it understood
to be the aesthetic tenets, of Pre-Raphaelitism to literature as well as art. The
mission of the artist according to the "Society for the Advancement of Truth in
Art," the American equivalent of the Brotherhood in England,[9] was "to put into
marble or music or verse or painted form whatever they see imaged on the retina
of their mental vision." (August 1863, p. 39) For, they further declared, "the Poet
and the Artist have the same errand in the world . . ." (January 1864, p. 117)
". . . Pre-Raphaelitism has saved the art of England, and made it the first art of
the modern world, and Pre-Raphaelitism will save our art, yet, if we can but have
the modesty and patience to obey its teachings." (July 1864, p. 47)

The Pre-Raphaelite catechism as recited by most of these American converts
was mainly embedded in the ever-increasing bulk of Ruskin's writings, what might
be called the artistic gospel according to St. John. Other and better teachers —

dissatisfied with the work of most of the artists, and, better still, of making the artists dissatisfied with
themselves. We refuse our respect to popular verdicts . . . and we utterly deny the value of the
greater number of Academic laws, believing that they and the Academies which made and upheld
them have done harm, and only harm, to the sacred cause of true Art." (80.2, January 1864, p. 114)

[8] See the chapter, "The Ruskin Commonwealth," in David Dickason's *The Daring Young Men*
(80.8), pp. 188–192.

[9] The seven original members of the Society for the Advancement of Truth in Art were: Thomas
Charles Farrer, Clarence Cook, Clarence King, Peter B. Wight, Russell Sturgis, Charles Herbert Moore,
and Eugene Schuyler. Listed in Dickason (80.8), pp. 83–124.

Rossetti, Burne-Jones, Morris — were to engender a broader understanding of art among the American Pre-Raphaelites, but the seeds of their very existence were sown by Ruskin. The distinction seems to be that the American, as well as many of the followers of the English, Pre-Raphaelites drank from two tributaries of what in the public mind was the same stream: the *spirit* of Pre-Raphaelitism which animated the original Brotherhood, and the *word* of Pre-Raphaelitism, as interpreted by John Ruskin. If in following the latter they went astray, at least in expressing the spirit of the movement they met the challenge of mid-century America, whose leaders were crying for independence and originality in American art and letters. In its insistence on the complete individuality of the artist and on his rejection of the traditional rules of art (the moral-aesthetic addenda of Ruskin notwithstanding), Pre-Raphaelitism provided American artists with the method, if not the example, for unshackling themselves from the fettering bonds of tradition.

It should be obvious from the above discussion that Ruskin's support of the Pre-Raphaelites in 1851 cannot be lightly weighed, but that certainly as its formal apologist he played a role which was ultimately ambiguous. On the positive side, Ruskin must be given credit for taking the side of the Pre-Raphaelites and for promulgating the ideals of the movement and thereby enhancing its popularity; but Ruskin was also responsible for a considerable confusion regarding the movement's basic aesthetic. In general, Ruskin's understanding of the purposes of the movement as a whole, not just of the PRB, was too literal and suffused with his own moral and didactic concepts of art. But the impact of a strong, messianic critic such as Ruskin perhaps saved Pre-Raphaelitism from an obscurity that its own inarticulate disciples were helpless to prevent.

ii

In the intervening years, while Pre-Raphaelitism, with the help of Ruskin, was undergoing a marked metamorphosis in *word*, the lives of the several PRB's had taken separate courses, which were not to reconverge — and then only with the addition of new faces and new ideas — until 1857, the *annus mirabilis*. The Brotherhood had begun to disperse as early as 1850 when James Collinson resigned. In July of 1852, Woolner sailed for Australia, leaving behind only five of the original band; by December of the same year Holman Hunt had gone to paint the *Scapegoat* in the Holy Land. Only a month before, Millais had defected to the Royal Academy, a reversal that would lead ultimately to the presidency of that dreadful institution against which the Pre-Raphaelite revolt had been primarily directed. Stephens and William Michael Rossetti had settled as art critics, for the *Critic* and *Spectator*, respectively. Rossetti strengthened his bond of friendship with his early teacher, the almost-Pre-Raphaelite, Ford Madox Brown. "So now," Rossetti wrote to his sister Christina on the day of Millais' election to the Royal

Academy, "the whole Round Table is dissolved"; and Christina responded with a
sonnet-epitaph, beginning "The P.R.B. is in its decadence," which mockingly
epitomized the desuetude of the Brotherhood phase.[10]

The disintegration of the PRB served paradoxical ends, however, and the continuation of the *spirit* of the movement, largely as a result of the personality of
Rossetti, amounted to an elaboration and extension of the rather narrow "naturalistic" limits which had defined the movement initially. The activities of the
new "Brotherhood" in 1857 stimulated a noticeable reversal of critical opinion
regarding the significance of Pre-Raphaelitism as a palpable force in English art
and helped to establish its future reputation as a literary movement.

The Oxford and Cambridge Magazine, 1856 (72.4), was immediately recognized as a generic successor to *The Germ*; [11] it was warmly received by Ruskin,
and Tennyson, on whose poetry a series of three articles by William Fulford
appeared, praised the articles he had read for their truthfulness and earnestness.
Although Rossetti's only connection with the publication consisted of three contributed poems, it was during the brief existence of the magazine that the members
of the Oxford coterie were drawn within the Pre-Raphaelite circle. The first result
of this new alliance was the painting of the Oxford Union frescoes, an activity
which, never completed, occupied the group on and off for a period of three years,
between 1857 and 1859. The Oxford Union venture is recorded photographically,
with a short narrative account, in Holman Hunt's volume published in 1906 (79.3),
and need not be reviewed here. The young artists — Rossetti, Burne-Jones, Morris,
Hughes, Pollen, Prinsep, Stanhope, and Hunt — had a surplus of enthusiasm and
a paucity of skill and experience in the work they had undertaken. The murals,
painted on unprepared walls, soon chipped and faded. As late as 1869, the Oxford
Union Committee were still debating a solution and negotiating with Rossetti and
Morris for some kind of help. Fortunately, both proposals made to the committee
were rejected, and the murals were neither whitewashed as Rossetti recommended
in 1870, nor covered with wallpaper designed by Morris. While they lasted, the
murals were nonetheless beautiful and resplendent with a color which Coventry
Patmore, in 1857, writing in the *Saturday Review*, found "sweet, bright, and pure
as a cloud in the sunrise . . . ; so brilliant as to make the walls look like the
margin of an illuminated manuscript." (79.1, p. 584) Beyond the ephemeral
beauty of the work, the painting of the murals brought some of the Pre-Raphaelites
together again — this time with new adherents — in a community effort which was
highly important in determining the later course of their work.

If the Oxford Union murals were a failure and today stand as reminders of the
technical deficiencies of the Pre-Raphaelite artists, the two Pre-Raphaelite exhibi-

[10] For Dante Gabriel's letter to Christina Rossetti, 8 November 1853, see *Family Letters* (24.5), II,
120–121; Christina's sonnet is printed in vol. I, 138.

[11] In a letter to William Allingham (24.6, p. 174), Rossetti said, "Surely this [*The Oxford and
Cambridge Magazine*] cometh in some wise of the *Germ*, with which it might bind up."

tions of 1857 — one in London, the other in New York — were not; rather they provided an excellent index of the accomplishments made by the Pre-Raphaelites since the demise of the PRB. The first of these exhibitions, held at Number 4, Russell Place, Fitzroy Square (see 16.1), was a semipublic showing to which Rossetti contributed numerous water colors, including *Dante's Dream* and *Dante Drawing an Angel in Memory of Beatrice,* and a few pen and ink sketches. Also represented were Millais, Hunt, Brown, Elizabeth Siddal, Hughes, Charles Collins, John Brett, and W. L. Windus. The exhibition aroused excited comment and confirmed the "impression that something was still going on in the country very different from what could be seen in the ordinary picture-shows." (24.5, I, 200) The tone of the criticism engendered by the 1857 exhibition was considerably more favorable than it had been in 1851, reflecting the rising interest in the movement and the recognition of both its merits and its growing influence. Patmore, writing in the *Saturday Review,* found the exhibition "especially interesting as showing what are the real views and aims of the people calling themselves Pre-Raphaelites," and praised the quality of all the paintings exhibited, which he saw as "resulting from the artist's simple and sincere endeavour to render his genuine and independent impression of nature." (21.1) And the *Athenaeum* critic noted that "Pre-Raphaelitism has taught us all to be exact and thorough, that everything is still unpainted, and that there is no finality in art." The errors, eccentricities, and aberrations of early Pre-Raphaelite pictures he found "fast modifying and softening. Its large hands and feet, ugly, hard, mean faces, gaudy colours, and streaky stipplings have subsided into common sense, good taste, and discretion." (16.1, p. 886)

Although the critical reception of the exhibition in New York was less generally favorable, owing primarily to the choice of pictures — neither Rossetti nor Millais was represented — the success of the exhibition with both critics and public indicated that Pre-Raphaelitism had finally overcome the prejudice of critical opinion and had won recognition as a sincere and significant movement.[12]

G. S. Layard's "Book about a Book," as he subtitles his *Tennyson and His Pre-Raphaelite Illustrators,* 1894 (79.9), is a superficial account of the roles of Millais, Hunt, and Rossetti in the preparation of Moxon's 1857 edition of Tennyson's *Poems* (90.3), the last major enterprise of the Pre-Raphaelites during the *annus mirabilis.* Beyond its obvious evidence of Pre-Raphaelite collaboration, the Moxon edition is perhaps the outstanding example of Pre-Raphaelite illustration, exemplifying the essentially literary force which animated the movement. Pre-Raphaelite interest in book illustration had its origin in the etchings of *The Germ,* and its continuance as a permanent interest may be traced through various illustrated editions of the poetry of Christina Rossetti, William Allingham,

[12] For details of the 1857 Exhibition of British Art see 18.4, and the chapter, "British Pre-Raphaelite Art in America: 1857 Exhibition," in Dickason (80.8).

Thomas Woolner, and others, as well as in the delicate and expertly made decorations and illustrations that Burne-Jones and Morris were later to produce at the
Kelmscott Press.[13] In an introductory chapter, Layard discusses in general terms
the status of book illustration in the mid-nineteenth century, relating to that tradition the contributions of the Pre-Raphaelites. Finally, in three separate chapters he
outlines in detail the parts played by the three Pre-Raphaelites in the preparation
of the edition and makes some not very satisfactory observations on the quality of
the illustrations and on the basic resemblances between Tennyson and the Pre-
Raphaelites.

The year 1857, then, represents, both historically and aesthetically, the emergence
of the movement as a recognized artistic school. It is less important for the actual
criticism that the year's activities stimulated than for the recognition of maturity
which those activities evinced. No longer was Pre-Raphaelitism just a revolt
against academic traditions, limited to the meager productions of a group of
seven; no longer was it merely synonymous with "Ruskinism" — though the confusion on this point exists today; no longer was it only a blind, naturalistic devotion
to detail. The movement had been accepted as a serious step in the development of
a distinctly English art, characterized first, in subject matter, by the interests of the
Romantic Movement; second, in treatment, by its emphasis on the literary context
of pictures and by its own literary side; and, third, in technique, by a concern with
visual accuracy and an emphasis on the fidelity of the artist in depicting natural
scenes.[14] The movement was in a constant process of evolution, and the shifting
definitions reflect the essentially organic and vital nature of the movement.

iii

The twenty-five years between 1857 and 1882 were eventful ones for the development of an *idea* of Pre-Raphaelitism. The most important development was the
literary maturity of the movement, which was clearly evinced by the successive
volumes of poetry by Morris, Swinburne, and Rossetti. But these years were also
marked by an ever-increasing tendency to identify Pre-Raphaelitism with Rossetti
and later to see him as the immediate progenitor of the Aesthetic Movement of the
1880's and 1890's. Certainly Pre-Raphaelitism, in its concern with beauty and the
role of art, anticipated the Aesthetic Movement, but with the extremes of Art for
Art's Sake or the fetishism of the *fin de siècle* Pre-Raphaelitism had little to do.

In the year of Rossetti's death, Walter Hamilton published a volume entitled
The Æsthetic Movement in England (78.2) which consisted primarily of discus-

---

[13] Part IV of the Bibliography in this volume is a detailed examination of Pre-Raphaelite illustrations.

[14] Each of these characteristics was caricatured in Florence Claxton's *The Choice of Paris: An Idyll*
which was exhibited at the Portland Gallery in 1860. See 82.3 and my (W. E. Fredeman's) analysis
of this picture in the *Burlington Magazine*, 1960 (76.14).

sions of Rossetti, Ruskin, and the Pre-Raphaelites, with a final chapter on Oscar Wilde, who had recently stirred up considerable comment during his American tour. To Hamilton, Aestheticism had definite and noble functions to perform: "I think," he concluded, that "it may be safely predicted that the poetry of the Æsthetic school will come to be regarded as a distinct growth typical of the later half of the nineteenth century, as the Lake School of Poetry was of the earlier . . . The Lake writers have outlived the scorn of their contemporaries, and in the same way people will live to see how much there is of the good, the beautiful, and the true, in the Æsthetic movement, and to recognize the beneficial influence it has had upon modern life in the cultivation of good taste in art." (p. 125) From the contents and the early date of Hamilton's work, there is little doubt that the principal aesthetic writers to whom he refers are the Pre-Raphaelites.

Like the Lake writers whom Hamilton discusses, the Pre-Raphaelites also felt most acutely the "scorn of their contemporaries," signally in the "Fleshly Controversy" instigated by Robert Buchanan's article in the *Contemporary Review* (29.16) and by his pamphlet, *The Fleshly School of Poetry and Other Phenomena of the Day*, 1872 (82.6). The complications of the "Fleshly Controversy" have been admirably clarified by J. A. Cassidy in his article, "Robert Buchanan and the Fleshly Controversy," which appeared in *PMLA*, March 1952 (76.11). G. G. Storey's "Reply to Cassidy's Article on Buchanan" (76.11) examines Buchanan's critical principles and finds the fleshly attack consistent with aesthetic and moral concepts which Buchanan never altered.

The antecedents and repercussions of Buchanan's article and pamphlet were highly involved. In summary: 1) Buchanan early satirized the Pre-Raphaelites in his novelette, "Lady Letitia's Lilliput Hand." [15] 2) After the publication of Swinburne's *Poems and Ballads* (1866), one of the two major antagonistic reviews was Buchanan's, though it appeared anonymously.[16] 3) Buchanan also attacked Swinburne in "The Session of the Poets." [17] 4) Swinburne's cause was championed by William Michael Rossetti in his pamphlet, *Swinburne's Poems and Ballads*, 1866 (62.13), in which reference was made to Buchanan as a poetaster who "stirs storms in teapots" (p. 7), a slight Buchanan repaid with interest in the *Fleshly* pamphlet when he immortalized William Michael to future bibliographers as the "editor of the worst edition of Shelley which has ever seen the light" (p. 35),

---

[15] Published in *Temple Bar*, 1862.

[16] *Athenaeum*, no. 2023 (4 August 1866), 137–138. Articles in the *Athenaeum* were regularly unsigned, but considering later cases it is probably not unfair to assume that Buchanan capitalized on this anonymity, since the review is scurrilous. In "The Session of the Poets," Buchanan used the pseudonym "Caliban." Cassidy points out that in order to preserve his identity, Buchanan deals with himself more severely than do most writers of anonymous sessions. Since the major portion of the attack is leveled at Swinburne, Buchanan's desire to remain undetected was probably heightened, Cassidy surmises, by his fear of angering Swinburne's friend, Lord Houghton, and by fear of reprisals from the Pre-Raphaelites. (76.11, pp. 66–68)

[17] *Spectator*, XXXIX, no. 1994 (15 September 1866), 1028.

undoubtedly an echo of his own anonymous review of Rossetti's edition of Shelley.[18]

The turning point in the gathering storm came with the publication in 1870 of Dante Gabriel Rossetti's *Poems* (23.8). Buchanan, embittered no less by William Rossetti's championing of Swinburne and the immediate success of Rossetti's *Poems* than by the adverse opinions of the critical press on his own poems in *The Book of Orm* (1870), leveled the sights of his big guns at Dante Rossetti in the *Contemporary Review* article, "The Fleshly School of Poetry: Mr. D. G. Rossetti" (29.16).

The controversy now began in earnest: 1) Centering on the anonymity of the article, a note appeared in the *Athenaeum* [19] announcing the forthcoming appearance of an answer by Sidney Colvin to " 'The Fleshly School of Poetry,' by Thomas Maitland, a *nom de plume* assumed by Mr. Robert Buchanan." 2) A week later, Colvin's subtle disclaimer, designed to draw Buchanan out, was printed.[20] 3) Colvin's ruse resulted in two letters to the *Athenaeum*:[21] one by Alexander Strahan, the publisher of the *Contemporary Review*, denying Buchanan's authorship; the other from Buchanan admitting authorship, denying any involvement in the use of the pseudonym, calling on Strahan for corroboration, and announcing his intent to expand the article into a pamphlet. These contradictory letters appeared simultaneously, together with "The Stealthy School of Criticism" (23.9), D. G. Rossetti's letter answering Buchanan's article.[22] 4) Two other letters of weak defense by Strahan and Buchanan appeared the following week, Strahan's in the *Pall Mall Gazette*,[23] Buchanan's in the *Athenaeum*.[24]

Early in 1872, Buchanan's pamphlet was published. Among the reviews of the pamphlet, most of which were unfavorably disposed toward Buchanan,[25] the two most important were H. Buxton Forman's "The 'Fleshly School' Controversy" (27.2) and an anonymous review in *Fraser's Magazine*.[26] Buchanan followed the pamphlet with one more hit at Rossetti in *St. Paul's Magazine* in March 1872.[27] Swinburne administered the *coup de grace* of this phase of the controversy in

[18] *Athenaeum*, no. 2205 (29 January 1870), pp. 154–156.

[19] In no. 2301 (2 December 1871), p. 724.

[20] *Athenaeum*, no. 2302 (9 December 1871), p. 755.

[21] In no. 2303 (16 December 1871), p. 794.

[22] Rossetti prepared a longer answer to Buchanan, but it was suppressed. "It was a very angry letter and in the opinion of Rossetti's best friends was not worthy of publication — a lawyer who was consulted gave it as his opinion that it was actionable. It was put in type & a slip proof was printed. One copy was sent to Rossetti & one I kept by me for some years, but as it had been the author's wish to suppress it I did not think it right to preserve it & so destroyed it." (From a note by F. S. Ellis, Rossetti's publisher, quoted in 24.16, p. 107)

[23] 23 December 1871, p. 3.

[24] See 23.9.

[25] Other reviews of Buchanan's pamphlet appeared in the *Illustrated London News*, LX (1870), 490; *Athenaeum*, no. 2326 (25 May 1872), pp. 650–651; *Saturday Review*, XXXIII, no. 866 (1 June 1872), 700–701; *Graphic*, V (1872), 606; *Temple Bar*, XXXIV (1872), 99–100.

[26] In n.s. V (May 1872), 588–596.

[27] "Tennyson's Charm," X (March 1872), 282–303. Of Rossetti: "Here is Euphues come again with

Under the Microscope (1872), the most virulent attack of the lot, besides which the cleverness of Buchanan's response, "The Monkey and the Microscope,"[28] is vacuous and pathetic.

As Cassidy clearly shows, the controversy was disastrous to Buchanan's literary career. Nor did the matter end for Buchanan at this point. He became the whipping boy for a variety of literary quarrels, including the later *Jonas Fisher* controversy, instigated by Swinburne and culminating in the litigation of 1876,[29] that once again resuscitated the pains of the seven-year-old fleshly wound. Four years later, Buchanan attempted to mitigate the effects of his original diatribe against Rossetti in the dedication to his novel, *God and the Man* (1881), "To an Old Enemy." In a letter to Hall Caine, written after Rossetti's death, he acknowledged: "I was unjust, . . . most unjust when I impugned the purity and misconceived the passion of writings too hurriedly read and reviewed *currente calamo*." (25.1, pp. 71–72n) His final statement on Rossetti appeared in "A Note on Dante Rossetti" in *A Look Round Literature*, 1887 (27.15), in which he stated that his critical ideas had changed with the times and that he regarded "love, even the fleshly variety," as "the highest human pleasure."[30] But none of Buchanan's efforts assuaged the contempt of many of Rossetti's friends, who unfairly blamed Buchanan personally for the decline of Rossetti in his later years.[31]

Walter Pater had first used the term "aesthetic poetry" to refer to Pre-Raphaelitism in his essay on Morris' poetry in 1868 (43.33). By describing the parallel between medieval asceticism and sensualism which results in the imaginative and psychological paradox whereby the artist can employ the symbols and sentiments of Christianity and at the same time rebel against them to produce an essentially pagan effect, Pater explained in psychological terms what Buchanan could only express in babbling fulminations of moral indignation. This pagan spirit, against which Buchanan protested and which Pater found so prominent in "aesthetic" Pre-Raphaelite poetry, especially in the work of Rossetti, is, Pater observed, "the continual suggestion, pensive or passionate, of the shortness of life. This is contrasted with the bloom of the world, and gives new seduction to it — the sense of

---

a vengeance, in the shape of an amatory foreigner ill-acquainted with English, and seemingly modelling his style on the 'conversation' of Dr. Samuel Johnson."

[28] *St. Paul's Magazine*, XI (August 1872), 240.

[29] *Jonas Fisher* (82.7), a long satirical poem, was published anonymously by James Carnegie, the Earl of Southesk, in 1875. Swinburne took the work to be by Buchanan, and on 11 December 1875 he published in the *Examiner*, "The Devil's Due," signed Thomas Maitland. Buchanan, who had already denied having even read the poem (*Athenaeum*, 4 December 1875), brought a libel suit against Swinburne in 1876, claiming five thousand pounds damages. After a sensational, widely publicized, and often amusing trial which lasted three days, the jury found against Swinburne, and Buchanan was awarded one hundred and fifty pounds. For a thorough and interesting account of the *Jonas Fisher* controversy see Cassidy (76.11), pp. 83–88.

[30] Quoted in Cassidy (76.11), p. 90.

[31] See "The Truth about Rossetti" (25.9) in which Watts-Dunton compares the attack on Rossetti with those upon Keats and Poe. For Cassidy's discussion of this aspect of the whole "Fleshly" controversy see 76.11, pp. 90–93.

death and the desire of beauty: the desire of beauty quickened by the sense of death." [32] Buchanan was too insensitive to comprehend that the two extremes of sensualism and asceticism are almost always fused in art that is primarily mystical, as in the art of Blake and Rossetti. But Pater's explanation of the psychological basis for Pre-Raphaelite medievalism helps to clarify at the same time the distinction between the aestheticism of the Pre-Raphaelites and that of the *fin de siècle*; belonging to the early phase of the aesthetic movement, Pre-Raphaelitism is less closely related to Wilde than to Keats, for whom beauty in art finds its most complete expression in the sentimentalized symbols of Platonic idealism. Max Nordau, [33] for whom any tendency toward medievalism or mysticism was a sign of "degeneration," is correct in saying that Pre-Raphaelitism degenerated into Aestheticism, but one need not agree that the Pre-Raphaelites themselves were necessarily degenerate.

The attitude that made Pre-Raphaelitism synonymous with Aestheticism was one which the aesthetes themselves cultivated from the beginning. At the same time, of course, the satirists were paying the Pre-Raphaelites "the homage which mediocrity pays to genius," as Wilde said, and further cementing the association between the two movements. Reginald Bunthorne [34] is, after all, a "fleshly poet," and the aesthetic type with the poppy or the lily in his medieval hand is obviously a synthesized figure caricaturing Rossetti, Swinburne, and Wilde.

All these involuting definitions could hardly result in the clarification of Pre-Raphaelitism as a meaningful critical term, and by the year of Rossetti's death it had degenerated into either a general term for any of a variety of artistic and literary tendencies, including "Rossettiism," or a synonym for Aestheticism. In fact, so many extensions of meaning had been given the term that one critic, William Sharp in his essay "Pictorialism in Verse," which appeared in the *Portfolio* (27.10), questioned whether it retained any longer a justifiable usage. Some critics took the reverse stand — that, having accomplished what it set out to do, Pre-Raphaelitism had now become so universally accepted that the movement no longer existed as a separate, recognizable entity. Writing in the *Nation* in 1865, Russell Sturgis concluded:

Pre-Raphaelitism has gone through the first phase of its life and has entered on its second. It is hard now to distinguish and draw a line between the new school (made up of the followers of the P.R.B.) and the old. Under the strong and self-confident teaching of the reformers, the art of England has changed its nature, and today, in England, it is inaccurate to call any painter a Pre-Raphaelite, unless the word is used to denote a member of the original P.R.B. For between a crowd of well-meaning and hard-working artists and the great chief Dante Rossetti himself, there is no gulf or visible separation. Realistic, painstaking, purposeful work is the rule with so many painters that set the

[32] See 43.33. Quoted from the reprint in the *Bibelot*, V (1899), 319.
[33] "The Pre-Raphaelites" in *Degeneration*, 1895 (68.6).
[34] The hypersensitive aesthetic type in Gilbert and Sullivan's satirical operetta *Patience*, 1881.

fashion. Pre-Raphaelitism, as it once was exists no longer, having done its work. (67.13, p. 274)

The equating of "Rossettiism" with Pre-Raphaelitism, fostered to a degree by Ruskin, had great currency in the nineteenth century and has continued to the present time. So recent a critic as G. H. Ford, in his *Keats and the Victorians* (1944), concedes that "as used by literary historians, Pre-Raphaelitism really means 'Rossettiism.'" (33.33, p. 108) Between 1857 and 1882, it was perhaps inevitable that Rossetti's art and poetry should usurp the term, so responsible was he for the continuance of the movement. But this is an oversimplification that hardly takes into account the diverse directions of Pre-Raphaelite influence after the dissolution of the PRB. Certainly, the critical literature on Rossetti during these years suggests the primacy of his influence. S. N. Ghose's useful volume, *Dante Gabriel Rossetti and Contemporary Criticism (1849–1882)* (1.2), offers the most convenient survey of this body of criticism.[35] The limitations of Ghose's work are patent, since he is primarily concerned with Rossetti rather than with Pre-Raphaelitism itself. His method is to present in chronological sequence, often with insufficient commentary, excerpts from the critical articles and books on Rossetti which appeared during his lifetime. Ghose includes, however, a vast amount of material on Pre-Raphaelitism, making the book a vital introduction to, and a survey of, the criticism of the movement from its incipience to Rossetti's death, which clearly indicates the critical tendency to subsume under what may be called Rossettiisms, the generic traits of Pre-Raphaelitism.

Concomitant with the later development of Pre-Raphaelitism was the birth and growth in France of the movement which so completely overshadowed the English school, despite superficial similarities between the two in their concern with such technical matters as light and color. Unlike the Impressionists, the Pre-Raphaelites were never able fully to disassociate art from the context of a higher purpose, partially because of the contrasting social milieu in which they lived and worked, but more significantly because in rebelling against the artistic conventions and the materialism of their age, they were almost forced into the self-conscious substitution of values in art, from which English Aestheticism, even amidst the nihilistic cries of the 1890's, never really extricated itself.

In the face of the modern critic's denigration of the Pre-Raphaelites for not being Impressionists, it is especially interesting to examine one or two contemporary accounts of the movement by French writers familiar with the Impressionist revolt.[36] Ernest Chesneau, whose two chapters on the Pre-Raphaelites in *La Peinture anglaise*, 1882 (70.5), appeared the same year as the last Impres-

[35] See also John Bonar Gregory's 1931 University of London Ph.D. dissertation, "A Bibliographical and Reference Guide to the Life and Works of Dante Gabriel Rossetti with a Study of the Pre-Raphaelite Movement" (22.6).

[36] For two studies of the French reaction to the Pre-Raphaelites, see Camille Mauclair (78.12) and Jacques Lethève (78.25).

sionist exhibition, is unmistakably clear about his feelings for the English movement. Offering little new insight to an understanding of the movement, his purpose
being in the main to present it historically for his French audience, Chesneau
considers the moralistic associations with art that he finds characteristic of the
Pre-Raphaelites "a misapprehension of the true vocation of art." Yet he finds the
very error noble:

Although the whole system of pre-Raphaelitism is in direct opposition to the æsthetic
principles of Latin nations, and might possibly lead our artists into sad difficulties were
they seriously to take it up, still — taking into consideration its utter disinterestedness,
and the scrupulous care and thoughtfulness of its followers — I can never join in the
contempt and ridicule which it has awakened in French amateurs and painters. (p. 242)

Nor is his criticism of the Pre-Raphaelites vindicated in Impressionism, for, speaking of these "amateurs and painters," he says:

The first have lost the power of admiring, and the others that of executing works need-
ing careful observation and patient manipulation, while all that is offered in the place of
these are hasty, superficial productions, engendered by indolent minds. (p. 242)

Robert de la Sizeranne in *La Peinture anglaise contemporaine*, 1895 (70.8), makes
even more explicit an unbounded enthusiasm for English Pre-Raphaelitism. His
premise is simply that there is an English school of painting which produces art
distinctive from that of the continent and that "it is time that we should learn to
know this neighbouring art, neglected by us — for, if the English artists seldom
come to us, our artists are beginning to go to them, and the charm of the unknown
operates more surely than any public exhibition would do." (p. xiii) After tracing
the history and theory of Pre-Raphaelitism, La Sizeranne suggests a method from
which the modern critic can learn:

There was something more lasting than the pre-Raphaelite theory. There was an idea,
which united the innovators more closely and guided them for a longer time. To
discover this idea theory must be set aside and practice examined; the collections of
newspapers in which the P.R.B. wrote must no longer be consulted, but their pictures
must be visited in galleries and museums; in short they must no longer be judged by
their words, but by their works. (pp. 64–65)

Nor is La Sizeranne insensible to the actual contributions made by Pre-
Raphaelitism.

Whatever may have been their theories, or those of their friends, whatever the goal
they aimed at, or which was attributed to them, the pre-Raphaelites greatly modified
their countrymen's ideas of line and colour. Unconsciously perhaps, certainly without
any very definite intention, they introduced into England the practice of deepening the
expression of a subject by significant gestures, and of procuring brilliancy of tone by
great simplicity of method. Whether that could furnish England with masterpieces
remains to be seen after the chief productions of English contemporary art have been
examined; but it must certainly produce new work, and a national art. Perhaps the pre-

Raphaelites may not have gained the battle they fought, but they gained another. Perhaps they may not have proved that nature is the final expression of art, but they proved that it was the foundation of it, and that the efforts of a Pleiad of men of talent and resolution are never lost, whatever may have been their object. (pp. 77–78)

La Sizeranne does not really view the movement as extending very far beyond the PRB, but he acknowledges the debt owed the Brotherhood by the Oxford group and the later aesthetes. Unlike Chesneau, who decried the moral concern of Pre-Raphaelite art, La Sizeranne extols this quality above all others in two final panegyrical paragraphs on the results of Pre-Raphaelitism:

> When we look back now, after the lapse of years, to this handful of pre-Raphaelites setting out to conquer the Holy Land of Art, we seem to be gazing on one of the last Crusades. They sallied forth in 1848 all clothed in the same armour, enrolled under the same flag. How many of them have reached 1895?
>
> Some, like Deverell,[37] died by the way, before they saw the shining roofs and towers of the Holy City. Others, like Millais, are kings of some island, and have forgotten the aim of their expedition amidst the honours heaped upon them by the infidels. Others, passing by some convent on a sloping hill side, said to themselves that the road was long, the return uncertain; they entered, attracted by the bells, those sirens of heaven, and no one knows their fate. Some attained to the Jerusalem of art and planted their standard there. But what a standard! Changed indeed is the pre-Raphaelite standard of early days! The battle breeze, the gloss of age has dulled its once startling hues. Such as it is, however, it floats from one of the summits of the century, a token of the noblest attempt, the grandest effort of modern artists. And it may be said of pre-Raphaelitism as was said of the Crusades, that it did not perhaps exactly fulfil its purpose, but that it realised a purpose more lasting and more universal, which has been not unfruitful for the renewing of the old world and for the glory of Christianity. (pp. 78–79)

Thus, in France, the home of the most important competitors of the Pre-Raphaelites, the movement was not ignored, though its significance as a revival of the religious spirit was there, as in England, greatly exaggerated. A sincere French moralist makes his English counterpart seem like the false Duessa, and good, healthy abuse might have done more for the reputation of Pre-Raphaelitism in France than La Sizeranne's identification of it as the handmaiden of Christian morality. When he was preparing his book on English painting, Chesneau corresponded with many of the Pre-Raphaelites in order to document his work; in fact, Rossetti's last letter was probably one dictated to the French author. Rossetti would likely have found Chesneau's volume a satisfactory presentation of the facts in the Pre-Raphaelite case, but had he read La Sizeranne's essay, say in 1880, *The House of Life* might have remained forever a fragment. But Holman Hunt — whom the French author might be parodying were he not serious — would doubt-less have nodded his approval and smiled to himself. After all, had he not sug-

---

[37] Walter Howell Deverell (1827–1854), who was nominated for membership in the PRB after the resignation of Collinson.

gested as much in his article in the *Contemporary Review* not a decade before?[38]
He would make the case stronger when he came to write the full-dress, Holman
Hunt version of the movement's history a decade later.[39] In time, Pre-Raphaelitism
might cease to be regarded as "Rossettiism" after all.

iv

Between the year of Rossetti's death and the centenary of his birth, the reading
world was inundated with historical, critical, and biographical books and articles
on Rossetti and the Pre-Raphaelites. Two biographies of Rossetti, intended to
capitalize on his popularity, appeared in the year of his death: William Sharp's
Dante Gabriel Rossetti: A Record and a Study (25.3) and Hall Caine's *Recollections
of Dante Gabriel Rossetti* (25.1).[40] Neither of these books was scholarly or "official," and both tended more toward undocumented value judgments, generally
adulatory, than toward the objective presentation of fact. But both books are
valuable and interesting as portraits of Rossetti by men who had known him
intimately and had been influenced by him. Joseph Knight's *Life of Dante Gabriel
Rossetti*, 1887 (25.11) has little more to commend it as biography, although the
bibliography by J. P. Anderson contains some items not listed elsewhere.

In the 1890's, three studies of importance appeared: F. G. Stephens' *Dante
Gabriel Rossetti*, 1894 (30.17), Ford Madox Hueffer's *Rossetti: A Critical Essay on
his Art*, 1896 (30.21), and H. C. Marillier's *Dante Gabriel Rossetti: An Illustrated
Memorial of His Art and Life*, 1899 (30.24). Stephens' *Portfolio* monograph,
restricted to Rossetti's art, puts but slight emphasis either on his writing or on
Pre-Raphaelite aspects of his art. The perspective of Hueffer's *Rossetti*, one of
the better of the early studies of Rossetti's art (with biographical background
sketched in), is too narrow, overlooking Rossetti's importance as a writer and in
general de-emphasizing the influence of Pre-Raphaelitism on Rossetti. Marillier's
Memorial—the unabridged folio version of 1899—is still the standard work on
Rossetti's art. With profuse photographic reproductions, an extensive catalogue-
appendix of Rossetti's paintings and drawings, and the text which traces the
development of Rossetti's artistic career, with detailed discussions of his various
pictures, this book has never been superseded, and despite its obvious dating and
the many inaccuracies of fact and errors of taste, it is here that all work on
Rossetti's art must inevitably begin.

[38] Holman Hunt's first published account of the Pre-Raphaelite Movement appeared in the *Contemporary Review*, 1886 (75.13).

[39] Hunt's account of the Pre-Raphaelites in his two-volume history (75.23) was seriously challenged
from many quarters, though there were only two other survivors of the original PRB at the time.
For F. G. Stephens' answer to some of Hunt's statements see 77.4.

[40] Hall Caine was still alive in the Rossetti centenary year, forty-six years later, at which time he
published the revised version of his original *Recollections*, which had been included in 1908 as part II
of his autobiography, *My Story* (25.1).

Between 1882 and 1928, no complete biographies of other members of the original Brotherhood were published, though frequent articles on the individual Pre-Raphaelites appeared in the periodicals. Among the studies of the later and lesser Pre-Raphaelites published during this period, Mackenzie Bell's *Christina Rossetti: A Biographical and Critical Study*, 1898 (44.36), deserves special mention. During this period also were published J. W. Mackail's celebrated biography of William Morris, 1899 (43.45), and Aymer Vallance's and Malcolm Bell's respective studies of Morris, 1897 (43.38), and Burne-Jones, 1892 (42.16), both in the same series as Marillier's *Memorial* of Rossetti. Although many of these early biographical studies contain references to Pre-Raphaelitism, much of the material is duplicative, the primary aim of each volume being historical. Mention should also be made at this point of George Birkbeck Hill's edition of the *Letters of Dante Gabriel Rossetti to William Allingham, 1854–1870*, 1897 (24.6), one of the earliest volumes devoted to Rossetti's correspondence.

Few important monographs on Pre-Raphaelitism were published between 1882 and 1928. Walter Hamilton's *The Æsthetic Movement in England*, 1882 (78.2), has already been discussed in another context, as has G. S. Layard's *Tennyson and His Pre-Raphaelite Illustrators*, 1894 (79.9). Besides these, three other books treating the Pre-Raphaelites influenced the course of Pre-Raphaelite criticism: Esther Wood's *Dante Gabriel Rossetti and the Pre-Raphaelite Movement*, 1894 (77.21), Percy H. Bate's *The English Pre-Raphaelite Painters*, 1899 (75.21), and Ford Madox Hueffer's *The Pre-Raphaelite Brotherhood: A Critical Monograph*, 1907 (66.13).

Esther Wood's book was one of the first attempts to examine the Pre-Raphaelite Movement critically. Kineton Parkes published a small volume entitled *The Pre-Raphaelite Movement* (66.9) five years before Miss Wood's book, but his work was a simple retrospective history that concluded with the acknowledgment that, "Pre-Raphaelitism is now a thing of the past." One metaphor from Parkes's study is worth recalling, however:

It may have been unconsciously, but it was nevertheless surely, that Pre-Raphaelitism did and is doing its work. All our artists have, at one time or another, been "down" with the "Pre-Raphaelite measles," and though they seemed — some of them entirely — to recover, and that rapidly, yet there can be no doubt that it did them good. (66.9, p. 200)

Relying heavily on secondary sources for her information, Miss Wood nevertheless considered the movement with a wider lens than had many critics before her. Her volume contains sections on the historical evolution of art that culminated in the PRB, on the period of the Brotherhood, on the problem of literary and artistic influence, and on the psychological and aesthetic motives and aims of the Pre-Raphaelites. There is also a chapter on the poetry of Rossetti. Miss Wood also recognized, as few earlier critics had, and as many present critics refuse to do, the continuity of the movement beyond the period of the Brotherhood. The weakness of her book — a characteristic one as we have seen — lies in her design "to deal with the Pre-Raphaelite movement more as an ethical than an æsthetic revolution." (p. v) As a result of this ethical concern, Miss Wood places too much emphasis on the religious aspect of Pre-Raphaelite art and literature, and her approach is too sentimental to enable her to sustain a critically objective point of view.

Percy Bate's history of the Pre-Raphaelite painters is an important and pioneer work. In fact, until the appearance of Robin Ironside's *Pre-Raphaelite Painters*, 1948 (83.8), it was the only important illustrated monograph available. Bate limited his relatively short and profusely illustrated book to a study of the painting, considering besides the major Pre-Raphaelites the bevy of minor artists who clustered about them. His chapter headings indicate clearly enough the scope of his work, for in addition to chapters on Hunt ("The Staunch Pre-Raphaelite"), Millais ("The Transitory Pre-Raphaelite"), and Rossetti ("Pre-Raphaelite and Idealist"), and an inclusive chapter on the other PRB's, Bate includes two chapters on "Pre-Raphaelitism as a Modern Influence," one on "Pre-Raphaelitism as a Phase," another on "Pre-Raphaelites as Decorators," two on "The Rossetti Tradition," and a final one on "Pre-Raphaelitism Today." Although he considers Ford Madox Brown the founder of the movement, Bate recognizes the existence of what he calls a "Rossetti tradition" in such painters as Burne-Jones, Spencer Stanhope, and Marie (Spartali) Stillman. His definition of Pre-Raphaelitism is consistently vague, but it is fairly clear that he assumed only those connotations of the term that pertained to the original Brotherhood. He distinguishes, however, between the true and the popular definitions of the term, and his view of the movement is sufficiently broad to avoid excluding the painters he places in the "Rossetti tradition" from the ranks of the movement. If the volume has a major fault, it is that too much is attempted and that the author is somewhat indiscriminate in relegating questionable artists to the Pre-Raphaelite camp. However, the general treatment, the breadth of coverage, and the illustrations more than compensate for whatever weaknesses the volume may possess.

Ford Madox Hueffer's *The Pre-Raphaelite Brotherhood* is perhaps the best of the early studies of the movement, within the limitations imposed by the author at the outset. He does not recognize the existence of the movement beyond the PRB phase, but in attempting to clarify some of the debatable points concerning the history of the Brotherhood, he does succeed in catching the spirit which animated the original group. Of Holman Hunt's and Millais' disparagement of the Brotherhood he is intolerant; and, although he tends to dismiss the problem of the influence of Pre-Raphaelitism on Rossetti, and consequently Rossetti's status as a genuine Pre-Raphaelite, he does not belittle the importance of the role which the mere act of organizing played in enabling the young men of the Brotherhood to translate their ideas into words and their words into action.[41] He censures the Pre-Raphaelites for their inability to catch in their painting "the sense of fleeting light and shadow" that characterized Impressionistic art, but he attributes their sense of permanency not so much to themselves as to the age which nurtured them.

> Pre-Raphaelitism was . . . a return to Nature, in that it led the Arts and followed the tide of humanity in England. And, in so far as it was possible as it were to nail Nature down — to record her most permanent parts — these Pre-Raphaelites succeeded very miraculously in rendering a very charming, a very tranquil, and a very secure England. (p. 164)

Hueffer was an indefatigable writer who produced an impressive number of provocative, if not critical, works relating to the Pre-Raphaelites. His monograph on the Brotherhood fortunately escapes the nostalgic extravagance that permeates his *Memories and Impressions*, 1911 (77.55). Despite his critical strictures on the art of the movement, he is not impervious to the dynamism and personal magic that were so inextricably a part of the Brotherhood. It is much truer, he says, speaking of Holman Hunt's retrospective maligning of the motivations of the PRB's (except of course for himself and Millais), "to believe that the Pre-Raphaelites really were a brilliant young band, created to burn torches, break open closed doors, and wear in their hair the vine leaves of a splendid amity." (p. 66)

Two vast bodies of writings appearing before 1928 form the most important nucleus of any study of the Pre-Raphaelites: the massive tomes which contain the memoirs of almost everyone worth remembering — and forgetting — and the profuse output from the pen of William Michael Rossetti, the critic-amanuensis and self-appointed apostle-historian of Dante Gabriel Rossetti and the Pre-Raphaelites. The memoirs, issuing from more and less prominent Pre-Raphaelites, their friends, enemies, wives, and associates, are no slight obstacle to the student of Pre-Raphaelitism. Indeed this is a dilemma of the student of nineteenth century literature in general. Indispensable are *The Life and Letters of Sir John Everett Millais*, by his son, J. G. Millais, 1899 (37.52), who relied heavily on Holman Hunt for his information; Lady Burne-Jones' *Memorials of Edward Burne-Jones*, 1904 (42.63); William Holman Hunt's *Pre-Raphaelitism and the Pre-Raphaelite Brotherhood*, 1905–1906 (75.23), the most prejudiced of the memoirs; William Michael Rossetti's *Some Reminiscences*, 1906 (38.8); and Amy Woolner's *Thomas Woolner, R.A., Sculptor and Poet*, 1917 (40.14). Each of these memoirs, save Woolner's, is in two volumes, and these are only those of the major figures. William Michael Rossetti's edition of Dante Gabriel's *Family Letters*, 1895 (24.5), and the *Autobiographical Notes* of William Bell Scott, 1892 (56.10), have to be

---

[41] Praising the Pre-Raphaelite revolt against academic authority, Hueffer says: "But, of course, the step from holding revolutionary views to the putting them into execution without any outside aid or the sympathetic contagion that is afforded by such a coterie as was embodied later in the Brotherhood itself — such a step is a great one." (66.13, p. 62)

contended with, as do dozens of other less bulky, but no less formidable memoirs. A list of a few from a seemingly infinite number of volumes might include those of Anne Gilchrist (86.1), Sidney Colvin (25.52), Frederic Leighton (86.5), Murray Marks (86.14), G. F. Watts (63.8), Frederic Shields (58.7), William Sharp (25.40), and the *Diary* of William Allingham (46.22). These patient volumes are not always directly pertinent to a study of the Pre-Raphaelites — Holman Hunt's volumes alone pretend to be a history of the movement as well as a memoir — but they are storehouses of personal information, critical opinions, reminiscences, and anecdotal accounts of the vibrant personalities who moved in the ever-widening Pre-Raphaelite circle.

The publications of William Michael Rossetti are possibly the most valuable single group of writings on Pre-Raphaelitism — certainly on Rossetti — before 1928. Besides his major works,[42] mention should be made of the several prefaces and memoirs which he appended to the succession of editions of Dante Gabriel's and Christina's poetry from 1886 to 1911. William Michael Rossetti also contributed numerous articles to the journals on the individual Pre-Raphaelites and on the movement as a whole. William Michael is an honest, if not always a far-sighted critic, and to him must go the credit for preserving the records of his family and of the movement, as well as for stimulating a continued interest in the literary and artistic productions of the Pre-Raphaelites in a period when their general popularity had begun to wane.

v

By the time of the Rossetti centenary, the bibliography of Pre-Raphaelitism had grown to sizable proportions, although, admittedly, most of the published material was historical and biographical rather than critical, impressionistic rather than scholarly. The majority of the studies since 1928 have not altered significantly scholarly trends prior to the centenary, and the confusion regarding definition is as real today as it was throughout the nineteenth century, perhaps more so since now it is necessary not only to determine what Pre-Raphaelitism *was* but to disentangle what it was from all that it is said to have been during the past century.

Before 1928, there were three volumes of Rossetti's collected letters, all of which have been previously cited. In the past thirty years, three more volumes of letters have been edited: Oswald Doughty's *The Letters of Dante Gabriel Rossetti to His Publisher, F. S. Ellis,* 1928 (24.16); Janet Camp Troxell's *Three Rossettis: Unpublished Letters to and from Dante Gabriel, Christina, William,* 1937 (24.18); and Paull Franklin Baum's *Rossetti's Letters to Fanny Cornforth,* 1940 (24.19). Doughty's volume, which is prefaced with an introduction of commendable clarity and exactness, is a careful, though pedantic, editing of a

[42] For William Michael Rossetti see Section 38.

group of letters, relating to the publication of Rossetti's poetry, principally to the *Poems* 1870, which demonstrate in action many of Rossetti's literary peculiarities, such as his unreasonable fear of adverse criticism by the reviewers, and which reveal at the same time a good deal about his poetic practices, such as his constant reworking of his poems, both in manuscript and printed form. Mrs. Troxell's edition, like so many volumes on the Pre-Raphaelites, is inherently interesting, although the letters are more revealing for the new light they throw on Charles Augustus Howell [43] than for the materials which they contain on the Rossettis. Professor Baum's edition of a series of letters in the Pre-Raphaelite collection of the Wilmington Society of the Fine Arts is exemplary, elucidating an extended episode in Rossetti's life — his relationship with Fanny Cornforth — about which there has been an unfortunate amount of mere speculation. The published letters of Rossetti do not at present offer a continuous or chronologically organized picture of the poet, but this deficiency will no doubt be considerably alleviated by the publication of his collected letters, edited by Oswald Doughty and J. R. Wahl, already catalogued in the 1957 Supplement to the *CBEL*, having been announced for publication by the Clarendon Press. An edition of Rossetti's letters is one of the most urgently needed tools in Rossetti and Pre-Raphaelite scholarship. The admirable six-volume edition of *The Swinburne Letters* (62.12), recently completed by Cecil Y. Lang, has heightened the expectation that a skillfully edited critical edition of Rossetti's letters will, by offering such a wealth of information in a single source, open up whole new areas of research and study.

Amid a spate of articles, reviews, notices, exhibitions, and books occasioned by the Rossetti centenary of 1928, there were two major studies of Pre-Raphaelitism. Laurence Housman's 1929 address to the Royal Society of Literature, "Pre-Raphaelitism in Art and Poetry" (76.5), is still one of the most balanced appraisals that has been made of the movement. Housman considers Pre-Raphaelitism as "the pictorial expression of influences which had already made their mark in literature," that is, as the logical cultural outcropping in painting of romantic tendencies that had found earlier expression in Blake, Coleridge, and especially in Keats, whose "method of getting at things was their method — sensation, openness to impressions, watchfulness, intensity of feeling, were the lines upon which they found themselves." (p. 18) Although Housman tends to follow too closely the directions of the movement indicated by Ruskin — in stating, for example, that they declared their intention to "reject nothing and to select nothing" in nature — his ultimate basis for examining the Pre-Raphaelites is more accurate. In a single metaphor he suggests both the strength and the limitation of the Pre-Raphaelite revolt:

Art was a coffin in which Raphael lay embalmed. Therefore, in order not to remain

[43] See also Helen Rossetti Angeli, *Pre-Raphaelite Twilight*, 1954 (77.66), the only full-length account of Charles Augustus Howell.

mutes at a funeral, the men of the new movement had to become Pre-Raphaelites; get rid, not of the living Raphael, but of his corpse. First and foremost they had to find themselves . . . That mummy chamber into which, at the Royal Academy School, they had been so carefully inducted had no further exit. The grave has only a way in; there is no way of quitting it except by backing out. And the Pre-Raphaelite movement was the backing out process — very swiftly and resolutely effected. (pp. 6–7)

The poetry and painting of the Pre-Raphaelites Housman finds equally characterized by individualism, a "close linking together of nature and romance," a determination to treat romance in terms of natural feeling, and the assumption that, in choosing a romantic subject, its characters were real people; and all of these characteristics were "in flat contradiction to the 'grand manner' as hitherto understood." (p. 8) In short, the Pre-Raphaelites intended "to give a new individualism to romantic art, and to express the ideal in terms of reality." (p. 11) But more important than these observations is Housman's recognition of the central dynamic quality that permeated the lives and work of the Pre-Raphaelites. "They were young and very much alive," he notes, and it is this "alive" quality that is so often lost sight of; in fact, Housman signals the decadence of Pre-Raphaelitism in the later poetry of Morris that no longer contained the "head-strong qualities of enthusiasm and youth." He concludes:

English Pre-Raphaelitism was but a phase, a passing revival, full of weakness and mannerisms in its mode of setting forth. But what it stands for is, I believe, something which, in one form or another, will for ever recur in the evolution both of poetry and painting. You can't shut out romance from the human heart; you can't shut out wonder. And the romance and the wonder of life will always find in Art an instrument ready to hand. It may all be illusion, but if it is, so is life. (p. 29)

Thomas Earle Welby traces, in *The Victorian Romantics, 1850–1870*, 1929 (66.21), the development of English aesthetics from the Pre-Raphaelites to the beginning of the Aesthetic Movement. Although much of the book is purely historical, Welby is a provocative and stimulating critic, blind neither to the faults nor to the virtues of the art and poetry of the movement. He is disturbed, for example, that the reputation of the Pre-Raphaelites should to so great an extent be determined by "misunderstanding, scandal, cult, craze" — all the substitutes for critical concentration; and he recognizes how much Pre-Raphaelitism has lost in reputation by being too closely identified with the aesthetes. "If there was spiritual snobbery in those who got a compendiously condensed 'culture' out of the Pre-Raphaelites, valuing them chiefly for that reason, there is no less in the endeavour to acquire merit by rejecting the Pre-Raphaelites." (p. 153) What Welby is specifically prescribing for Pre-Raphaelite scholarship is that the art and poetry of the movement be once again examined as art and poetry; in other words, that scholarship rescue Pre-Raphaelitism from the obscurity that has overtaken it. While its adherents have talked about what the movement might have become, and its opponents have stigmatized it for not being something else, the main point of its identity — what it really was as is revealed in its art and poetry — has been too often neglected.

Since 1928, two serious biographies of Rossetti have been published, neither of them notably sympathetic. The more controversial of the two, Evelyn Waugh's *Rossetti: His Life and Works*, 1928 (25.59), is primarily a study of Rossetti's development as a painter, interspersed with rather detailed analyses of the actual paintings. Waugh's technique is to examine the successive stages of Rossetti's life in terms of his art, rather than to resort to the usual device of anecdotal analysis. Not really sympathetic with Rossetti as artist or man, Waugh assumed a healthier approach in so far as his book was read by many as an attack on the jargon of modern art criticism by one who was himself an ally of contemporary art. Waugh's concern with Pre-Raphaelitism is negligible [44] since he does not identify Rossetti to any great degree with the movement; but at least Waugh provides the seeds of a method for a critical biography, in contrast to another, formidable type of writing.

Professor Oswald Doughty's *A Victorian Romantic: Dante Gabriel Rossetti*, 1949 (25.92),[45] is disappointing after his earlier edition of Rossetti's letters and his excellent article on "Rossetti's Conception of the 'Poetic' in Poetry and Painting" (32.22). Doughty's biography of Rossetti is extremely readable — and it certainly is, as Howard Mumford Jones says of it, "the most detailed and stable of recent lives" of Rossetti — but deficient in documentation, source acknowledgment, and notes (commensurate with the volume's length), and suffering from an abundance of *errata* (both factual and typographical) and from a most inadequate index, this biography hardly lives up to its pretensions. Nor is it totally devoid of fictional apparatus: the author's desire to "sustain 'local colour'" (p. 10) often leads to a casualness of tone — Janey, Lizzie, Guggums, Topsy, *etc.* — reminiscent of other, less serious biographies of Rossetti. Surely the persistence with which Professor Doughty pursues the paranoia stemming from the death of Elizabeth Siddal and from Rossetti's passion for Mrs. Morris (Doughty's "two almost inescapable conclusions" that the facts "overwhelmingly insisted upon" [p. 8]) is unnecessarily relentless. In fact, so concerned with the Rossetti-Jane Morris relationship is Professor Doughty that Philip Henderson summarizes the volume as "the first attempt to penetrate the mystery surrounding Morris's [!] private life" in the bibliography appended to his pamphlet in the "Writers and Their Work" series (43.137). Since Professor

---

[44] It is not generally known that Evelyn Waugh's first published book was a small pamphlet, privately printed, entitled *P.R.B.: An Essay on the Pre-Raphaelite Brotherhood, 1847–1854*, 1926 (66.19).

[45] A second edition was published by the Oxford University Press in 1960, but considering the paucity of actual revisions and additions it might have been more accurate to describe the edition as a reprinting. Pagination is identical though a few new illustrations have been added.

Doughty is extremely careful in his preface to inform the reader what the book is *not*,[46] it is perhaps unfair to wish that he had chosen either of his first two rejected alternatives. Professor Jones's observation that "one of the present embarrassments of scholarship is that we know too much about the poets and not enough about the poetry" (1.11, p. 183) is, after all, the crucial one in the case of Rossetti and the Pre-Raphaelites. The above strictures notwithstanding, Doughty has succeeded in assimilating an astonishing amount of material, and he does offer genuine insights into an understanding of Rossetti and his poetry.

Only Holman Hunt, of the original Pre-Raphaelites, has had since 1928 a biographer. A. C. Gissing's *William Holman Hunt*, 1936 (36.66), reflects the author's credulous acceptance of everything in Hunt's retrospective memoir-history, *Pre-Raphaelitism and the Pre-Raphaelite Brotherhood* (75.23). Completely sympathetic with Hunt, Gissing presents a distorted view in his examination of Rossetti's role in the Pre-Raphaelite movement. Christina Rossetti, William Morris, and Swinburne have fared much better than many of the other figures affiliated with the Pre-Raphaelites, but their bibliographies are far too extensive for examination in this brief survey.

The texts of four of Rossetti's poems have been carefully edited.[47] However, there is no satisfactory edition of the complete works of either Dante Gabriel or Christina Rossetti. The 1911 edition of Rossetti's *Works* (23.27) edited by William Michael Rossetti is still the nearest thing to a definitive edition, but it has been out of print for years without a suitable replacement. Oswald Doughty's new edition of Rossetti's *Poems*, 1957 (23.37), has the virtue of accessibility, the Oxford edition being limited to the poems of 1870 and the excellent edition of Paull Franklin Baum (23.31) being no longer available, but it hardly satisfies the need for a complete and critical text. No edition of the minor poets has ever been issued, and there is no anthology of Pre-Raphaelite poetry, an omission which seriously inhibits the thorough study of the literary side of the movement.[48]

There has been almost no attempt to provide adequate bibliographical tools for dealing critically with the movement. Ehrsam, Deily, and Smith's *Twelve Victorian Authors*, 1936 (1.5), contains good working bibliographies, though incomplete and often inaccurate, of Dante Gabriel and Christina Rossetti, William Morris, and Swinburne, but Pre-Raphaelitism has found a bibliographer only in Howard Mumford Jones, in his chapter on the poets in *The Victorian Poets: A Guide to Research*, edited by Frederic E. Faverty, 1956 (1.11). Professor Jones's

[46] The book is *not*, Doughty explains in his Author's Note: "1. A history of Preraphaelitism or of the Preraphaelites, 2. A critical study of the Preraphaelites' (or of Rossetti's) painting and poetry, 3. A biography of the Rossetti family." (p. 11)

[47] *The House of Life* (23.28) and *The Blessed Damozel* (23.32), edited by Paull Franklin Baum; *Sister Helen* (23.33), edited by Janet Camp Troxell; *Jan Van Hunks* (23.35), edited by John Robert Wahl.

[48] An anthology of Pre-Raphaelite poetry is now being compiled by Cecil Y. Lang.

chapter is valuable as literally the pioneer work in the field, its only limitation being the scope of the volume in which it is included. Even more pertinent than the books and articles he lists and the comments about them is the fact that the article — and the author deviates substantially from the plan of the other chapters in the volume — is highly provocative in its critical approach, suggesting in some detail both the deficiencies in the scholarly range of Pre-Raphaelite criticism and the direction which future research in the field must take if the movement is to be re-examined.

At the hands of artists and art historians, Pre-Raphaelitism has fared even worse. The movement is more often condemned out of hand as an insignificant (sometimes even pernicious or perverse) episode in the history of English art, a derailing, as it were, of the train of artistic progress. Even representative reproductions of the works of the Pre-Raphaelites are not readily available for the scrutiny of the curious, save in the sometimes invisible black and white and half-tone reproductions in many of the books already discussed. Robin Ironside's *Pre-Raphaelite Painters*, 1948 (83.8), is the only major volume of recent reproductions available; but it contains only four badly registered color plates, and the black and white reproductions are not always discernible. Since the rediscovery of color was one of the main contributions of the Pre-Raphaelites, it is unfortunate that owing to excessive printing costs and the general inferiority of color plates, reproductions of their works are often even darker than the browns and blacks against which the Brotherhood so demonstrably rebelled.

vi

Current attitudes toward Pre-Raphaelitism reflect the critical ambiguity attending any movement that within a single century has vacillated between so many extremes of definition and reputation. Modern critics in both arts, for whom the term has no accepted meaning, have difficulty finding a common area for examining the movement. The vagueness of definition does not, however, prevent marked differences of critical opinion; on the contrary, it is not unlikely that the hazy, amorphous connotations that hover about the term contain within themselves the germ of critical dissidence. The Pre-Raphaelites have experienced a mixed reception among modern critics, some regarding them with suspicion, others with disgust; but in general there has been a revival of interest in the movement in recent years. Stephen Spender's article, "The Pre-Raphaelite Literary Painters," which appeared in *New Writing and Daylight*, 1945 (76.9), is a judicious appraisal of the movement, its limitations and influence, and is especially interesting as coming from a poet who, thirty years ago, was himself involved in a revolt from tradition not totally unlike that of the Pre-Raphaelites a century before.[49] Too often, unhappily, interest in the Pre-Raphaelites is

---

[49] For a summary of the contents of this exemplary article see the annotation to item 76.9.

rooted only in the sensational, and of books of this sort there has been a seemingly endless succession. But if the sensationalizers have done their damage so have the anti-Victorians, those critics for whom anything Victorian is disgustingly vulgar. This *ex cathedra* condemnation of the taste of an entire age places yet another obstacle in the way of a favorable reception of the Pre-Raphaelites, even though — and it seems necessary to reiterate the obvious — these artists and poets refused, as many of their more reputable contemporaries most assuredly did not, to accept what is pejoratively labeled the "Victorian compromise."

The only book published since 1948, devoted entirely to the Pre-Raphaelites, is D. S. R. Welland's *The Pre-Raphaelites in Literature and Art*, 1953 (76.12), an abbreviated handbook and anthology of the movement which makes no attempt at definition, avoiding the issue nicely by tacitly assuming that everyone is in perfect harmony concerning its meaning. The several sections of the Introduction — "Pre-Raphaelite Book Illustration," "Pre-Raphaelitism and Contemporary Society," "Detail in Pre-Raphaelite Description," and "Pre-Raphaelite Medievalism" — consequently begin by begging the initial question, without which there is no referential and no real basis for discussion. Indeed, Mr. Welland does not even avail himself of the most common refuge of restricting Pre-Raphaelitism to the PRB since he includes not only the work of the Brotherhood but that of Christina Rossetti, William Allingham, Morris, and Swinburne as well. Despite the fact that Mr. Welland has constructed a Pre-Raphaelite building, leaving out the cornerstone of definition, at least his sympathy is with the movement; and as an anthology of Pre-Raphaelite creative writing and contemporary critiques, the book is a convenient introduction for the student.

Two examples of recent, sympathetic examinations of Pre-Raphaelitism are Graham Hough's chapters on "Rossetti and the P.R.B." and "William Morris" in *The Last Romantics*, 1949 (77.39), and Humphry House's 1948 BBC centenary broadcast on "Pre-Raphaelite Poetry," reprinted in his collection *All in Due Time*, 1955 (74.13). The latter of these, House's radio address, is more limited in scope and purpose than Hough's survey from Ruskin to Yeats, but House succeeds admirably in articulating some of the principles common to Pre-Raphaelite poetry. He begins by depreciating the triumph of Holman Hunt's particular brand of Pre-Raphaelitism, which locks the door on Rossetti and many of the fellow travelers (a view of the movement that had been espoused by so many speakers on the BBC during the centenary year). The central concern of this short essay is to suggest the ways in which the medievalism of the Pre-Raphaelites is to be examined, and as House follows through his main argument — that Pre-Raphaelitism "was searching through the mixture of modernism and medievalism after deeper purposes" (p. 153) — one can only regret that he never developed further the ideas he here advances.

Graham Hough accurately sees Pre-Raphaelitism as an attempt at a reconciliation of opposites stimulated by conflicting impulses, a "patient naturalism" on the one hand and a "flight from actuality into archaic romance" on the other, both stemming from the extremes inherent in Romanticism itself: "the eager search for new sensations" and a "huge nostalgia for a timeless and unchanging order." (p. 119) Positing that the "basic mistake of the Pre-Raphaelites was in forming a brotherhood at all," Hough nevertheless faces the reality of the Brotherhood — he does not in general subscribe to the continuation of the movement in the Oxford phase, but he recognizes the aesthetic and cultural impact that Pre-Raphaelitism had on English life — with an insight that is clear, critical, and sympathetic. His purpose — to trace the impulse of Romanticism in Victorian letters — precludes a complete discussion of Pre-Raphaelite aesthetics in *The Last Romantics*, but his concluding observation is indicative of the mature view of the movement which he holds:

. . . their most important contribution was to the spirit in which painting was undertaken. "Literary" they may have been; their justification is that they brought English painting again into touch with the most vivid imaginative life of their time; and their "Early Christian" affiliations brought almost the odour of sanctity into the practice of the arts. This may have led to preciosity, but it also led to a real ennobling of the attitude towards the visual arts. If we can see the figure of Bunthorne on the horizon, those of Frith and Landseer at least are disappearing into the shadows. The attitude of the cloistered and devoted aesthete is healthier for art than that of the rank commercial populariser; and if the English people after this date were again to regard art with indifference and sometimes with hostility, at least they were never again to regard it as the comfortable apotheosis of their own commonest tastes and sentiments. To that extent at least the history of the P.R.B. is something more than a chronicle of an unfulfilled promise. (pp. 66–67)

Contrasting with these two works are the unsympathetic, but by no means uninformed, opinions of John Heath-Stubbs and Geoffrey Grigson. In his chapter, "Pre-Raphaelitism and the Aesthetic Withdrawal," in *The Darkling Plain*, 1950 (78.23), Heath-Stubbs sees the Pre-Raphaelite Movement as a withdrawal "into the contemplation of purely decorative beauty"; and, incorrectly, I believe, he sees it as a "movement which primarily affected painting and the arts of decoration, but also found its expression in the sphere of poetry." (p. 149) The Aestheticism of the 1890's (in poetry) he sees as a resumption of Pre-Raphaelitism. In general, Heath-Stubbs reserves his antipathy for Rossetti and Swinburne rather than for Pre-Raphaelitism itself, and for other Pre-Raphaelites — Christina Rossetti, William Morris, Canon Dixon — he has at least faint praise. The basic characteristic of literary Pre-Raphaelitism Heath-Stubbs identifies as a kind of "dream-poetry, rather than the formal peculiarities of their style, or their mediævalism." (p. 157)

In a sense their movement may be regarded as a resumption of the romantic impulse from the point it had reached in the dream poetry of Hood, and Darley . . . But in the poetry of the pre-Raphaelites it has more the quality of reverie. Their very insistence upon visual exactness in their imagery gives to their work a kind of detachment and remoteness. We seem to be gazing at something a long way off, as through the wrong end of a telescope — something, too, which is at a great distance in time, as well as in space. The sense of urgency, of relevancy to the waking world is gone. The symbols . . . seem to be robbed of their significance. (pp. 157–158)

Whereas John Heath-Stubbs is concerned with Pre-Raphaelite poetry and is specifically prejudiced against two of the individual poets rather than against the movement as a whole, Geoffrey Grigson, in "The Pre-Raphaelite Myth" in *The Harp of Aeolus*, 1947 (68.15), treats the painting and the painters of the movement with disgust and distrust. Ostensibly a review of William Gaunt's *The Pre-Raphaelite Tragedy* (66.24), Grigson's article is an open accusation of fraud. The myth in his title is the result of what he considers collusion on the part of the Pre-Raphaelites, a kind of Pre-Raphaelite conspiracy in which the members surrounded "themselves, for posterity, with a set of gigantic magnifying-glasses" that distorts their real importance. His ultimate conclusion, with some reservation for Rossetti: "They were mostly compromisers and cowards, concealing their materialism in a mist of pseudo-spiritual morality, scared of looking at their own souls in sulphur-light." (p. 93) They were, he says, "very English Victorian brethren," illustrating "the big hold of morality and the separation of morality and emotion." (p. 90) However bigoted his strictures, Grigson is dead right on one point: sooner or later criticism must take the "inclusive view" in its analysis of English art of the 1840's and 1850's, and later. The lesser men — C. A. Collins, Walter Deverell, Arthur Hughes, James Smetham, and Godfrey Sykes; R. B. Martineau, W. L. Windus, John Brett, Augustus Egg, Henry Wallis, William Dyce, and William Maw Egley — are really *only* names, artists who still await exhumation from an oblivion they may well not deserve.[50]

Grigson indicates (without saying so) that the myth emanates in part from sources other than the Pre-Raphaelites. What he resents are the sensational popularizations of Pre-Raphaelitism that, during the 1930's and 1940's, substituted fictionalized accounts for scholarship and critical analyses of the movement.[51] In the hands of these sensationalists, the myth of Pre-Raphaelitism became almost a formula. These writers have placed their sights on the commercial market, exploiting the "human interest" appeal of martyrdom, revolution, neuroticism, sexual perversion, drug addiction, tragic or unrequited love, disease, insanity, fornication, adultery, sentimental romanticism, and every lachrymogenic aspect they have been able to distort and squeeze out of the individual Pre-Raphaelites (and their aesthetic successors) to satisfy the tabloidal interests of their readers. Dante Gabriel Rossetti staggers through book after book, plagued and haunted by the consumptive beauty of his exhumed wife, Elizabeth Siddal. All the aberrations

[50] See Grigson's article on James Smetham (60.7).

[51] Violet Hunt's *The Wife of Rossetti* (59.7) was one of the first of the sensationalist volumes on the Pre-Raphaelites. David Larg's *Trial by Virgins* (25.84) belongs essentially to this class of writing. William Gaunt's two volumes (61.15, 66.24) and Frances Winwar's *Poor Splendid Wings* (66.23) are not always wholly innocent of the charge. Two recent novels, Paula Batchelor's *Angel with Bright Hair* (59.12) and Nerina Shute's *Victorian Love Story* (81.7) both capitalize on the sensational attractiveness of the Pre-Raphaelites.

from Ruskin's impotency to Wilde's homosexuality are paraded before the reader, who is reminded periodically that Pre-Raphaelitism is tragic, but that the horror of the Pre-Raphaelites is nevertheless strangely and exotically beautiful. The myth that these popularizers have created warps and twists the real nature of the movement beyond recognition. Almost valueless from a critical or historical, even from a biographical, standpoint, these books have served only to keep the Pre-Raphaelites before the public mind, a mission that is at least partially vitiated by the means of promulgation.

One of the most recent critical evaluations of Pre-Raphaelitism, Vernon Young's "From Pre-Raphaelitism to Bloomsbury," 1957 (68.20), offers a convenient illustration of the "anti-Victorian" attitude and reflects the current disrepute into which Pre-Raphaelitism, as a Victorian manifestation, has descended. Working backward and forward from two symptomatic events of 1885 — the purchase of Millais' *Bubbles* by the Pears Soap Company, and Whistler's "Ten O'Clock" lecture — Young castigates the Pre-Raphaelite "illusion" as an aesthetic force which "led, in one direction, to the 'Decadence,' in the other, to the billboard." (p. 101) He generously allows to most of the Pre-Raphaelites a basic sincerity and varying degrees of competence, but concludes that "none of them was a painter in the creative sense." (p. 105) In their paintings, "they introduced a meretricious light that never was, and shouldn't be, with autonomous color areas and ungraduated backgrounds: but this, with utterly puerile subject matter." (p. 105) Pre-Raphaelitism he summarizes as a "combination of domestic complacency, empirical investigation, and appropriational traditionalism"; the naturalism of the movement he finds "sterile and decorative"; the critical abuse of the 1850's he sees as one with which "we can heartily concur — for modified reasons." (p. 105) Finally, he mitigates his attack by attributing the responsibility for the decadence and commercialism of English art between the Pre-Raphaelites and Roger Fry, not to Ruskin, who aesthetically is the most obvious whipping boy for the modern critic but to the limitations inherent in the moral (puritan) and ethical (mercantile), and hence aesthetically negative, structure of the Victorian environment.

Actually, one has little cause to quarrel with many of Mr. Young's critical strictures. On the contrary, in applying Geoffrey Scott's idea of the "Romantic Fallacy" to the Pre-Raphaelites he succeeds in articulating the principal weakness of the movement and of nineteenth-century English art in general. Pre-Raphaelite art is essentially literary, and in much of their work, certainly, the literary concern enforces an overemphasis of associative experience (perception), but not to the complete exclusion of the direct experience, and seldom to the ultimate exclusion of the object itself. Mr. Young's generalizations would need, I should think, rather extensive qualification to explain the later work of Rossetti, in which the literary context is not infrequently merely a kind of arbitrary programming, quite extraneous to the object itself. Mr. Young's own explanation that the Rossetti "heads" represent his "ambivalent dreams of a fatally passive woman and a fatally cruel woman" (p. 113), despite his psychological dexterity, seems somehow too facile, whatever Swinburne and the aesthetes may have made of them.

But to reiterate, Mr. Young's critical strictures have behind them at least the shrewdness of considered opinion and analysis. The same unfortunately cannot be said for his tone, and in this he weakens and makes vulnerable an otherwise effective critique. The following passage, concluding a catalogue of Pre-Raphaelite anecdotes, is representative of a bias which, perhaps unintentional, permeates the entire article:

> The persistence with which these gentry [the Pre-Raphaelites] were attended by the Comic Muse almost disarms serious criticism; after all, the mid-Victorian years offer us so few genuine delights. (p. 111)

By adopting the supercilious and condescending pose exemplified throughout this article, the critic exposes himself, together with the comfortable superiority that motivates his initial, though tacit premise: that Victorianism in all its manifestations, Pre-Raphaelitism included, is synonymous with grossness, sterility, and bad taste; and that modern art is fortunate indeed to have escaped unsoiled from an era so devoid of aesthetic fecundity. Some years ago, Howard Mumford Jones read the last rites over the corpse of this attitude.[52] Apparently many critics, Mr. Young among them, not only didn't attend the funeral, but failed as well to read the obituary.

vii

Thus, Pre-Raphaelitism remains today little removed from the obscurity and misunderstanding that has haunted it throughout the past century and a decade. The works discussed in this Survey are merely representative, chosen because they illustrate dominant trends in the criticism which have produced the present confusion over definition. It would be impossible in so short an essay to do more than sketch in lightly the major lines in the development of Pre-Raphaelite scholarship, and certainly many good (and bad) works have here gone unnoticed for reasons of brevity. But to do more would be to anticipate too thoroughly the bibliography which follows.

Despite the extensiveness of the Pre-Raphaelite bibliography, research is greatly impeded by the lack of standard tools — editions, letters, biographies, iconographies, collections of reproductions, objective criticism. Because Pre-Raphaelitism, as a movement within the Victorian period, has only in relatively recent years begun to be *seriously* re-examined, much basic scholarship remains to be done. And it must be done if the movement is ever to be properly considered in the critical and historical perspective of its age and balanced against the aesthetic values of our own.

---

[52] Howard Mumford Jones, "Those Eminent Victorians," *Scribner's Magazine*, XCIII (February 1933), 89–93. Reprinted as "The Comic Spirit and Victorian Sanity" in *The Reinterpretation of Victorian Literature*, edited by Joseph E. Baker (Princeton University Press, 1950), pp. 20–32.

BIBLIOGRAPHY

I. SOURCES FOR BIBLIOGRAPHY AND PROVENANCE

The twenty-one sections of this part of the Bibliography are designed both to indicate the wealth of research materials available for the study of Pre-Raphaelitism and to offer some direction through a wilderness hitherto virtually uncharted.

Sections 2 to 4 provide descriptions of the *major* public and private collections of Pre-Raphaelite materials in England and the United States. The descriptions are necessarily brief, the intention being to suggest the scope of a given collection rather than to enumerate in detail the particulars of its holdings. For some repositories, printed descriptions or catalogues are already available, and these are listed in section 5. General descriptions of the several collections or publications treating specific holdings will be found in section 7. Obviously, no attempt has been made to describe every repository with items of Pre-Raphaelite interest; it has been necessary, in fact, to restrict the descriptions to those public and private museums, art galleries, and libraries having significant collections of Pre-Raphaelite paintings, drawings, and manuscripts, and to leave unremarked those with only token holdings.

Private collections have necessitated even more severe restrictions. Most — but by no means all — of the larger and more important private collections have by now found their way into public or privately managed institutions. Others are gradually being acquired by established collections. Most of the descendants of the Pre-Raphaelites and their friends retain in their possession — where entrée is not always possible and seldom easy — items of interest. But private collections, both large and small, are so numerous that it has been possible here only to describe five of the most extensive. The serious student working in the field will eventually find his way to the sources he requires. Sections 2 to 4 can merely facilitate his search by indicating those collections which are likely to prove the most useful.

Over half the sections in part I of the Bibliography are devoted to a listing of pertinent exhibitions and sales, the catalogues of which have much more than a limited, topical interest. In fact, they often contain information unobtainable elsewhere. Since there is at present no means of determining directly the location of a particular painting or drawing or manuscript, an exhibition or a marked sale catalogue may prove the readiest, if not the only means of tracing it; and a succession of such catalogues is one of the most convenient methods of determining provenance. Catalogues of exhibitions not infrequently contain valuable commentaries and notes; and taken with the notices which they invariably stimulate (see section 21), exhibitions and sales offer a reliable and reasonably accurate index to the critical reception of a particular artist or movement at a given time.

Bibliographical Sources

Section 1

BIBLIOGRAPHY OF BIBLIOGRAPHIES

There are no full-length bibliographical studies of the Pre-Raphaelite Movement. Excluded from the following list are bibliographies of individual figures, which will be found in the appropriate sections. Acquaintance with the standard bibliographic sources, the annual periodical indexes, and other literary and art bibliographies is presumed. Notices of bibliographical appendixes of minor importance are provided in the annotations to the volumes which contain them.

*   *   *

1.1 Vaughan, Charles E. *Bibliographies of Swinburne, Morris, and Rossetti* (The English Association, Pamphlet no. 29). [Oxford: Clarendon Press], 1914.

1.2 Ghose, S. N. *Dante Gabriel Rossetti and Contemporary Criticism (1849–1882)*. Dijon: Imprimerie Darantiere, 1929 (diss. Strasbourg, 1929).

More properly a collection of critical excerpts than a bibliography, this volume is an essential aid to the study of Pre-Raphaelitism, though its main emphasis is on Rossetti. For discussion see Survey, p. 21.

1.3 Carter, John, and Graham Pollard. *An Enquiry Into the Nature of Certain Nineteenth Century Pamphlets*. London: Constable, 1934.

This famous exposé of forgeries and suspected forgeries cannot be overlooked by the Pre-Raphaelite scholar. The sections on Rossetti (22.7), Morris (43.5), and Swinburne (62.2) should be consulted. For other works indicted since 1934 and for Wise's legitimate bibliographies, private editions, and piracies see William B. Todd, "A Handlist of Thomas J. Wise," in *Thomas J. Wise: Centenary Studies*. W. B. Todd, ed. (Austin: University of Texas Press, 1959).

1.4 Jones, Howard Mumford, *et al.* "The

Pre-Raphaelite Movement," *Syllabus and Bibliography of Victorian Literature*. 2 vols. Ann Arbor: Brumfield, 1934–1935.

One of the earliest bibliographies of Pre-Raphaelitism. A good, brief general survey of both the art and literature of the movement, with sections on all the major and many of the minor figures. The Pre-Raphaelite section is in volume II, part IV, pp. 298–308.

1.5 Ehrsam, Theodore G., Robert H. Deily, and Robert M. Smith. *Bibliographies of Twelve Victorian Authors*. New York: Wilson, 1936.

Contains valuable and extensive, sometimes unreliable, sections on William Morris (43.7), Christina Rossetti (44.1), Dante Gabriel Rossetti (22.8), and Swinburne (62.3). See also Joseph G. Fucilla, "Bibliographies of Twelve Victorian Authors: A Supplement," *MP*, XXXVII (August 1939), 89–96. Reprinted in 1.9.

1.6 Wise, Thomas James. *The Ashley Library: A Catalogue. . .* 11 vols. London: Printed for private circulation only, 1922–1936.

A catalogue of printed books, manuscripts, and autograph letters collected by Thomas J. Wise and now in the British Museum. Volume IV is of special interest for materials relating to Rossetti and the Pre-Raphaelites.

1.7 Bateson, F. W., ed. *The Cambridge Bibliography of English Literature*, vol. III: 1800–1900. Cambridge University Press, 1940.

Vol. V: *Supplement: 600–1900*, edited by George Watson, should also be consulted. The *CBEL* contains bibliographical accounts of all the literary figures treated in the present work, and the *CBEL* reference is included in the headings of the sections on the various authors.

1.8 Harrold, Charles Frederick. "Recent Trends in Victorian Studies: 1932–1939," *Studies in Philology*, XXXVII (October 1940), 667–697.

Part VI (pp. 692–694) deals with the Pre-Raphaelite Movement.

1.9 Templeman, William D., ed. *Bibliographies of Studies in Victorian Literature for the Thirteen Years, 1932–1944*. Urbana: University of Illinois Press, 1945.

1.10 Wright, Austin, ed. *Bibliographies of Studies in Victorian Literature for the Ten Years 1945–1954*. Urbana: University of Illinois Press, 1956.

The bibliographies reprinted in 1.9 and 1.10 originally appeared in *Modern Philology*, which until 1956 carried the annual bibliography in Victorian literature. Since 1957, the annual bibliography has appeared in *Victorian Studies*.

1.11 Jones, Howard Mumford. "The Pre-Raphaelites," in *The Victorian Poets: A Guide to Research*, edited by Frederic E. Faverty. Cambridge, Mass.: Harvard University Press, 1956.

With a separate section on Swinburne (62.4). For discussion see Survey, pp. 32–33.

Descriptions of Collections

Section 2

PUBLIC COLLECTIONS OF PRE-RAPHAELITE MATERIALS: UNITED KINGDOM

The fifteen collections described in this section comprise the most important, not necessarily the only, collections of Pre-Raphaelite materials in Great Britain. Many other museums and galleries — such as the Watts Gallery, Compton; the Ruskin Museum, Brantwood, Coniston; the Ruskin Galleries, Bembridge School, Isle of Wight; Leighton House, London; and others — contain related materials, but their combined holdings are so diversified that it is impracticable to catalogue them. Cross-references refer in the main either to catalogues issued by the various galleries (section 5) or to descriptions of their particular holdings (section 7).

*   *   *

2.1 Birmingham City Museum and Art Gallery.

The Birmingham collection of visual Pre-Raphaelitism, especially of drawings, is unsurpassed anywhere in the world. Two major groups of drawings, originally in the possession of Charles Fairfax Murray and acquired by the Corporation in 1903 and 1906, form the nucleus of the collection. The first group comprises 260 drawings, studies, and sketches by Rossetti and 220 by Burne-Jones; the second includes over 300 drawings by Millais, Ford Madox Brown, Sandys, and others. Another major bequest in 1927 — pictures and drawings from the collection of J. R. Holliday — added considerably to the Pre-Raphaelite holdings of the museum. Besides the artists already mentioned, Birmingham also has representative drawings and studies, as well as finished works, by Holman

Hunt, Morris, Deverell, Collinson, Simeon Solomon, and Arthur Hughes.

While the principal emphasis of the Birmingham collection is its large and comprehensive group of finished drawings and studies important in tracing the development of certain Pre-Raphaelite pictures, the oils and water colors exhibited in the two permanent rooms devoted to the Pre-Raphaelites offer an interesting balance not often available in other galleries. Birmingham has a number of the more famous paintings associated with the movement. Millais is represented by *The Blind Girl* and many lesser known works. *The Last of England, An English Autumn Afternoon, Pretty Baa-Lambs (Summer's Heat)*, a large version of the small picture in the Ashmolean, and a small version of *Work* provide a comprehensive view of the art of Ford Madox Brown. Apart from *Sir Galahad*, Rossetti is represented in the main by late versions of two of his better known works, *The Lady of Pity (La Donna della Finestra)* and *Beata Beatrix*. By Holman Hunt there are two major pictures, *Two Gentlemen of Verona* and *The Finding of the Saviour in the Temple*, both relatively early; in addition, the smaller version of *The Shadow of Death* is on permanent loan from the Middlemore Trustees. The gallery's three small paintings by Arthur Hughes, *The Annunciation, The Nativity*, and *The Young Poet*, are among his better works and contrast favorably with *The Long Engagement* (also at Birmingham) which resembles the later "sentiment" pictures of Millais. Of special interest also is the reduced-scale version of Wallis' *The Death of Chatterton*, the larger version of which is in the Tate Gallery.

Birmingham's impressive collection of Burne-Jones cartoons, paintings, stained glass, and decorative work is shown in a separate gallery, an innovation in the hanging of Pre-Raphaelite pictures which admirably precludes the inevitable dwarfing of smaller canvases which occurs when they are hung beside the enormous productions of Burne-Jones, and which at the same time shows his work to best advantage. The principal picture in the Burne-Jones Room is the renowned *The Star of Bethlehem*, but the *Pygmalion* series, *The Story of Cupid and Psyche*, and *The Story of Troy* are especially good examples of Burne-Jones' work. There is also in the gallery a select group of Merton Abbey tapestries, including *Love and the Pilgrim* and a partial set of *The Holy Grail* tapestries.

A detailed listing of the holdings of the Birmingham Museum appears in three official publications (5.4 to 5.6). Mention should also be made of the many picture postcards and photographic reproductions of works at Birmingham on sale in the gallery.

2.2 The British Museum.

Pre-Raphaelite material in the British Museum is maintained in three separate departments. The Department of Printed Books has, with few exceptions, the majority of the books, pamphlets, catalogues, and ephemera associated with the movement, together with the most complete group of secondary works and periodicals available. The major gaps stem from losses during the war, in which thousands of books were destroyed. As a consequence, occasional disappointments are to be expected, but the museum is making every effort to replace those volumes which were destroyed. Despite these lacunae, the Department of Printed Books remains for Pre-Raphaelite printed sources the foremost repository.

The Prints Room maintains separate catalogues, and the publications in its reference library are not entered in the *Catalogue of Printed Books*. Concentrating on the fine arts, the Prints Room is particularly important for its materials dealing with all aspects of the visual side of the movement. The collection of drawings and water colors includes works by Rossetti, Burne-Jones, Hughes, Shields, Solomon, Scott, Hunt, Madox Brown, Woolner, Millais, Sandys, and C. A. Collins — in short, nearly all the Pre-Raphaelites are represented, though the holdings in Rossetti and Burne-Jones are the most extensive. Of special interest by Rossetti are the two water colors, *My Lady Greensleeves* and *Writing on the Sand*. It should be pointed out that many of the Rossetti drawings in the Prints Room came originally from Colonel William Gillum, one of the earliest patrons of the Pre-Raphaelites (see 77.65). Besides many other works by Burne-Jones, the Prints Room has the original drawings for *The Flower Book* (42.5). The Dalziel Collection, a large group of proofs, prints, wood blocks, and records is a valuable source for the study of the illustrated books of the 1860's and 1870's. This section of the museum also maintains indexed files of exhibition and sales catalogues. Although no special emphasis is given to Pre-Raphaelitism by the Department of Prints and Drawings, its collection of visual Pre-Raphaelitism is outstanding.

The Department of Manuscripts has two principal collections of Pre-Raphaelite material, the Ashley Library manuscripts and the William Morris Manuscripts. Manuscripts in the Ashley Library — books from which also enrich the printed books collection, although they are separately catalogued — are given Ashley rather than Add. MSS. numbers (for a list and description of these see 1.6). The William Morris Manuscripts are divided into two series, the May Morris Bequest (forty volumes, Add. MSS. 45298–45337) and the William Morris Papers (twenty-two volumes, Add. MSS. 45338–45341; 45407–45411). Combined, the two series of the William Morris Manuscripts include both published and unpublished poems, letters, journals, sketch books, and other items. One volume of Rossetti letters is included in this group, plus the correspondence from Rossetti to Jane Morris (see 24.28 and 24.29). For an account of the contents of the Morris collection see 7.5. Besides the two collections mentioned, the Department of Manuscripts has other groups of miscellaneous letters, including 97 from Rossetti to F. S. Ellis (published in 24.16), sixteen from Christina Rossetti to Ellis concerning the publication of *Commonplace*, and 21 from Millais to the brothers Dalziel relating to the engravings for the *Parables* (see 95.80).

2.3 The Brotherton Library. University of Leeds.

The Brotherton Library has an extensive collection of Pre-Raphaelite correspondence — nearly 600 letters in all from Rossetti, Madox Brown, William Michael and Christina Rossetti, Burne-Jones, Watts-Dunton, and William Bell Scott. Of primary importance is the large group of 319 letters from Rossetti to Watts-Dunton and the three volumes of

121 letters to William Michael Rossetti. Other major groups include 25 letters from Rossetti to William Davies, twenty from Rossetti to Francis Hueffer, and forty from Ford Madox Brown to Watts-Dunton.

2.4 Cambridge University. The Fitzwilliam Museum.

The Fitzwilliam Museum became a leading repository of literary and visual Pre-Raphaelitism largely through the efforts of the former director, the late Sir Sydney Cockerell. The museum's literary holdings include an extremely important group of Rossetti manuscripts — among which are "Jenny," "A Last Confession," sonnets from *The House of Life*, "Dante at Verona," "The King's Tragedy," and "Poems and Sonnets" (poems included in the *Poems*, 1870). There are also four sets of annotated proofs (trial books) of Rossetti's 1870 volume, formerly in the collection of Charles Fairfax Murray. Other literary manuscripts include Christina Rossetti's *Treasure Trove* and a large body of Morris material, with the complete draft of *The Earthly Paradise*, the 1871 "Journal of Travel in Iceland," and a number of volumes of miscellaneous poems and fragments. Of autograph letters in the collection, there are many from Morris, Holman Hunt, Madox Brown, Millais, Burne-Jones, and William Michael Rossetti; and an especially interesting group of thirty letters from Rossetti to Murray Marks. By far the largest single group of manuscripts, however, is the tin box of Burne-Jones papers, presented by Lady Georgiana Burne-Jones. These papers include 23 packets of letters and other items, plus a typescript volume of letters from Burne-Jones to various correspondents. Among the packets are 27 letters from Burne-Jones to Swinburne, eight to Rossetti, and 67 from Ruskin to Burne-Jones (plus 35 to Lady Burne-Jones and seventeen addressed to both). Of special interest are Burne-Jones's account books with Morris and Company and the chronological list of works by Burne-Jones which the artist began in 1872 and continued until his death. In the library also is an unpublished scrapbook of "Photographs from Designs and Sketches by Elizabeth Eleanor Rossetti Given to Charles A. Howell by his Friend D. G. Rossetti, 18th January 1867."

There are fifteen oil paintings in the Fitz-william by Pre-Raphaelite artists, including works by Sandys, Collins, Hughes, Hunt, Millais, Brown, and Rossetti; but far more impressive is the really vast collection of drawings and water colors, many of them from the collections of Fairfax Murray and J. R. Holliday. Drawings and water colors by almost all the Pre-Raphaelites are included in the collection, from which may be mentioned Simeon Solomon's portrait of Swinburne, Holman Hunt's original pen and ink sketch for *Claudio and Isabella*, Brown's "The Death of Tristram," two original studies by Millais for *Lorenzo and Isabella* and *Christ in the House of His Parents*, and a volume of miscellaneous drawings and water colors by Sandys, with seven studies for illustrations. Elizabeth Siddal's *Clerk Saunders* and *Lady Clare* are also in the collection. Burne-Jones and Rossetti are especially well represented. By Burne-Jones there are sixteen sketchbooks, numerous portfolios, notebooks, and series pictures, including all the original drawings for the Kelmscott *Chaucer*, plus more than fifty other drawings, studies, and designs. By Rossetti the Museum has eleven portraits (of Browning, Swinburne, Christina Rossetti, and others), plus portraits and studies of Elizabeth Siddal, Jane Morris, and five other Rossetti models. Also of interest by Rossetti, there are four illustrations and studies for stained glass and nineteen other miscellaneous drawings, water colors, and studies for pictures, including *How They Met Themselves*, *Morning Music*, and *The Annunciation*, all water colors. There is no catalogue of the holdings of this important Pre-Raphaelite collection.

2.5 The Lady Lever Art Gallery. Port Sunlight.

The Lady Lever Gallery contains a number of paintings by Ford Madox Brown, Holman Hunt, Millais, Burne-Jones, and Rossetti. Rossetti's *The Blessed Damozel* (the 1874 version from the Leyland collection — see 6.2 and 6.3), *Sibylla Palmifera*, and *Pandora*, Millais' *The Black Brunswicker* and *Sir Isumbras at the Ford*, Hunt's *The Scapegoat* and *May Morning on Magdalen Tower*, and one version of Madox Brown's *Windermere* comprise the most important pictures in the

gallery. Besides the paintings, there are also various drawings and water colors by Madox Brown, Millais, and Rossetti. For a complete description of the holdings of the gallery see the *Record* (5.8). An *Illustrated Guide* (5.8), sold at the gallery, also gives a brief description of the Pre-Raphaelite pictures. See also 19.36 for works no longer in the collection as a result of the 1958 sale.

2.6 Manchester City Art Gallery.

Particularly strong in the works of Ford Madox Brown, the Manchester Art Gallery is one of the major repositories of Pre-Raphaelite art. Over twenty of Brown's pictures are in this collection, including his famous *Work*, which should be examined in conjunction with Brown's other *tour de force*, the twelve murals in the Manchester Town Hall, illustrating episodes from the history of the city. *Stages of Cruelty*, also in the gallery, is one of Brown's most Pre-Raphaelite pictures. Among the Manchester artists who were closely associated with the movement, Frederic Shields is also strongly represented, principally by a large collection of drawings. Many of the most famous Pre-Raphaelite pictures are in the Manchester Gallery: Millais' *Autumn Leaves*; Hunt's *The Hireling Shepherd* and the small version of *The Scapegoat*, the large version of *The Shadow of Death* and one version of *The Light of the World*; Rossetti's *Joli Coeur*, *Astarte Syriaca*, and *The Bower Meadow*; and *Ophelia* (the large version) by Arthur Hughes.

The gallery has much more extensive holdings than this brief list indicates, particularly in the works of Millais and Hunt. Besides the artists already mentioned, Brett, Burne-Jones, Collins, Sandys, Windus, Prinsep, and Oliver Madox Brown are also represented by one or more works. In addition to pictures and drawings, one group of manuscripts, the notebooks of Oliver Madox Brown, should be noted. There is no catalogue of the collection, but the picture book, *Pre-Raphaelite Paintings* (83.9) contains reproductions and notes on twenty of the most important Pre-Raphaelite pictures.

2.7 The Tate Gallery and the National Portrait Gallery.

The Tate Gallery — the National Gallery

of British Painting and of Modern Foreign Art — contains the most thoroughly representative collection of visual Pre-Raphaelitism. The gallery has works by all of the major and minor Pre-Raphaelites, however obscure, and featured among its holdings are many of the outstanding pictures produced during all stages of the movement. So comprehensive is the Tate's collection that its scope can only be suggested.

By Hughes there is *The Eve of St. Agnes,* *April Love* (the large version), and *The Tryst*; by Rossetti *Ecce Ancilla Domini, Arthur's Tomb, Dr. Johnson at the Mitre,* and more than forty others; by Millais *The Vale of Rest, Ophelia, Christ in the House of His Parents,* and thirty more; by Hunt *Claudio and Isabella* and a later version of *The Triumph of the Innocents*; by F. G. Stephens *The Proposal* and *Mother and Child*; by William Morris *La Belle Iseult* (Morris' only known finished oil); by Burne-Jones *King Cophetua and the Beggar Maid,* and nearly fifty besides; by Ford Madox Brown *Take Your Son, Sir, Lear and Cordelia, Chaucer at the Court of Edward II,* and twenty more — on and on the list might be extended, so comprehensive is the collection. Besides the artists already mentioned, the Tate has works by Elizabeth Siddal, Deverell, Collins, Collinson, Windus, Simeon Solomon, Calderon, G. P. Boyce, Stanhope, Seddon, Smetham, Bell Scott, and that most interesting painter of one Pre-Raphaelite picture — *The Doubt: Can These Dry Bones Live?* — H. A. Bowler. For an excellent and readily available listing of the Tate's holdings see Mary Chamot's *British School: A Concise Catalogue* (5.9).

Not all the pictures in the Tate Gallery are convenient for viewing. One room is devoted exclusively to the Pre-Raphaelites, and pictures not hung can be seen only by advance notice. Also, a portion of the Tate's pictures, including the Pre-Raphaelites, is always on exhibition in the National Gallery in Trafalgar Square, and others are sent out on extended loan to other galleries throughout the country.

Within the context of the national collection are the pictures in the National Portrait Gallery, whose holdings are especially strong in works by Millais, Holman Hunt, and Rossetti. Many other Pre-Raphaelite artists are represented, however, including Ford Madox Brown, Arthur Hughes, and Burne-Jones. Portraits of the Pre-Raphaelites by G. F. Watts should also be noted: portraits of Morris, Rossetti, Swinburne, Walter Crane, and himself. The pictures in the National Portrait Gallery are fully detailed in the official *Catalogue* (5.10).

Both the Tate Gallery and the National Portrait Gallery have for sale a wide assortment of postcards, color slides, and reproductions of Pre-Raphaelite pictures in their collections.

2.8 Oxford University: The Ashmolean Museum. The Bodleian Library.

Oxford, its colleges and environs, contains many fine examples of Pre-Raphaelite works and reflects the remarkably close contact which the Pre-Raphaelites had with the city and the university, especially in the decade of the 1850's. The tapestry at Exeter College (the college of Burne-Jones and Morris), the windows at Christ Church Cathedral, the Woolner statues in the Ruskin Museum, Keble College's *The Light of the World,* and what remains of the Oxford Union murals of 1857 — all these are the incidentals of Oxford's Pre-Raphaelite treasures, the historical remnants, as it were, of Oxford's association with the Pre-Raphaelite past. Major interest, however, attaches to two collections at Oxford — the Ashmolean Museum and the Bodleian Library. Mention should also be made of the group of forty letters from Rossetti to various correspondents in the library of Worcester College. For a general discussion of the Pre-Raphaelites and Oxford see 66.26.

The Pre-Raphaelite collection in the Ashmolean Museum was formed around the nucleus of the Combe Bequest (1894) and therefore includes the only nineteenth-century collection which has been preserved intact. One room in the museum is given over completely to Pre-Raphaelite painting: Millais' *Return of the Dove to the Ark,* Hunt's *The Dovecot* and *Early Britons Sheltering a Missionary from the Druids,* Hughes' oil, *Home from Sea,* Brown's *Pretty Baa-Lambs* (the small version), Rossetti's water color *Dante Drawing an Angel on the Anniversary of Beatrice's Death,* Collins' *Convent Thoughts,* and Burne-Jones's exquisite little oil *The Building of the Brazen Tower.* Other artists represented in the collection are Sandys, Watts, Walter Crane and William Bell Scott. All the oils are listed in the *Catalogue of Paintings* (5.1).

As yet uncatalogued — a catalogue is in preparation — are the many drawings in the Ashmolean. Besides the huge Ruskin collection (catalogued in *CW,* 45.3, XXI), the Ashmolean has drawings by nearly all the figures associated with the Pre-Raphaelite Movement — Morris, Hunt, Sandys, Solomon, Prinsep, Hughes, Deverell, Elizabeth Siddal, Henry T. Dunn — and a really distinguished group of drawings by Rossetti, Burne-Jones, and Millais. There are nearly 100 drawings by Burne-Jones, including two large works and 47 cartoons belonging to various sequences such as "Pan and Psyche." Among Rossetti's works are a number of lovely and typical heads and three finished studies for major pictures: *Reverie, Proserpine,* and *The Day Dream.* Millais is represented by fifteen drawings in all, among them two early Pre-Raphaelite works and five of the original drawings for the Moxon *Tennyson.*

The principal collection of Pre-Raphaelite manuscripts in the Bodleian Library is the Correspondence of Frederic George Stephens (MSS. Don. e.78, d. 116–119, e.57–87). The Stephens correspondence has been partially described in two articles on the collection (see 7.3 and 7.4). Because this collection represents the aggregation of a lifetime, there is much extraneous material which must be sorted; however, there is great interest in the section of "Pre-Raphaelite Correspondence," and in the separate groups of letters from Rossetti, Hunt, Brown, Burne-Jones, Boyce, Street, Tupper, and Woolner. The largest single body of letters is from W. M. Rossetti, covering the period 1849–1906. In all, the Stephens correspondence consists of letters from more than 150 separate persons. Lady Mander's description of the collection is an accurate appraisal: "While there are no 'revelations' in these, they are essential to any future definitive biographies of the personalities concerned" (7.4, p. 232).

2.9 The John Rylands Library. Manchester.

Three principal groups of manuscripts of Pre-Raphaelite interest are contained in the John Rylands Library: the Holman Hunt diaries and correspondence, the papers of Oliver Madox Brown, and the Fairfax Murray collection. Included in the first are two diaries (1855, 1872), kept during Hunt's two visits to Palestine, and four groups of letters — to Thomas Combe (1853–1856), to Edward Lear (1852–1887), family letters (1876–1899), and miscellaneous letters (1843–1910). There is also a long and interesting holograph account of Hunt's visit to the Middle East, written in 1854. The papers of Oliver Madox Brown consist principally of his literary remains, most of them published in 47.2; but also included among the papers are twelve drawings, a number of fragments, and four letters to Ford Madox Brown. A large group of Ruskin letters and papers (1874–1899) is also in the Rylands collection.

Subsequent to the 1961 Sotheby sale of literary materials associated with Fairfax Murray (see 19.37), from which the Rylands Library obtained further letters to add to its extensive collection of Ruskin correspondence, the library has acquired the remaining portions of Murray's literary manuscripts, comprising over 1250 items, many of which are of primary interest to students of the Pre-Raphaelite Movement. Of the more than 400 letters in the Pre-Raphaelite correspondence, over 300 relate to Charles Augustus Howell, nearly half of these being letters to Howell from Frederick Sandys. Smaller groups of letters from other major and minor Pre-Raphaelites are also included.

2.10 The Victoria and Albert Museum.

The Victoria and Albert Museum contains a wide assortment of pictures, drawings, manuscripts, and artifacts relating to the Pre-Raphaelites and their circle. In the library — the National Library of British Art — there is, besides the printed works, an extensive collection of manuscripts, many of which were presented to the museum by Sir Sydney Cockerell. Among the manuscripts are nearly 200 letters from Rossetti to Henry T. Dunn, James Smetham, and Mrs. Morris (one only). Most of the manuscripts relate more to Morris and the arts and crafts side of the movement. In this connection, there are in the museum both the notebook and the day-book of Morris and Company, kept by May Morris (Mrs. Halliday Sparling). There is also a volume of letters from Mrs. Morris and others to Sir Sydney Cockerell and another volume to him from Lady Burne-Jones (1896–1920). There is a volume of letters from Philip Webb to Morris, twenty letters from Wilfred Scawen Blunt to Morris, and a typescript of 61 letters from Morris to Sir Thomas Wardle concerning dyeing and calico printing. An interesting typescript is that prepared by Clara Watts-Dunton in 1930 of letters from Rossetti to Swinburne, Dunn, William Michael Rossetti, and Watts-Dunton, which she was apparently assembling for publication. A few miscellaneous letters from Woolner, Millais, Lady Millais, Holman Hunt, Arthur Hughes, and others; an illuminated manuscript book of verse written and decorated by Morris for presentation to Lady Burne-Jones (1870); and an album of photographs of Jane Morris posed by Rossetti in 1865 with ten additional prints from modern negatives made from the original prints by Emery Walker and Gordon Bottomley in 1933, complete the manuscript holdings of the library.

The Department of Paintings and the Department of Engravings, Illustration and Design contain numerous paintings, water colors, and drawings by most of the Pre-Raphaelites. Among the oils in the Victoria and Albert are Millais' *Pizarro Seizing the Inca of Peru* (1846), Burne-Jones's unfinished *The Car of Love*, Collins' *The Good Harvest*, and Rossetti's *The Day Dream*, the latter from the Ionides Bequest. Rossetti's *The Borgia Family*, Millais' *The Eve of St. Agnes*, Hunt's *The Ponte Vecchio*, Brown's *Elijah Restoring the Widow's Son*, and Burne-Jones's *Dorigen of Bretaigne* are outstanding among the museum's Pre-Raphaelite water colors. The collection of drawings, illustrations, and studies is far too extensive to enumerate, but it includes works by most of the members of the Pre-Raphaelite circle. The Simeon Solomon drawings are of particular interest as are the 45 designs and drawings by John P. Seddon, the eighteen original drawings for illustrations to various books by Arthur Hughes, the collection of designs for book ornaments, carpets, embroideries, tapestries, and stained glass by Morris, and the twelve Burne-Jones sketch books, ten of which were given to the museum by Dr. W. L. Hildburgh. The basic collection of water colors is listed in the *Catalogue of Water Colour Paintings* (5.14); the catalogue of the Constantine Ionides Bequest (5.11) should also be consulted.

The Department of Circulation of the Victoria and Albert has for some time, on the initiative of the late Peter Floud, specialized in the decorative arts, a massive exhibition of which was held in 1952 (see 18.19). In this area the department has accumulated hundreds of examples of tapestries, printed and woven textiles, pottery, tiles, furniture, and the like, which characterize this later development of the Pre-Raphaelite impulse. This practical side of the movement is further exemplified by the William Morris Room. The Green Dining Room, decorated by Morris and Company in 1866–1867, was one of the firm's first large commissions, and it remains today one of the few schemes of secular decoration carried out by the firm that still remains intact. Preserved now as the William Morris Room, it contains various pieces of furniture designed by the Pre-Raphaelites, including King René's Honeymoon Cabinet (see 79.14) and the wardrobe designed by Webb and painted by Burne-Jones, which the latter gave to Morris as a wedding present. During 1961, the centenary year of Morris and Company, the Victoria and Albert, together with the William Morris Society, helped to organize a commemorative exhibition (see 13.12) sponsored by the Arts Council. A museum devoted to both the fine and applied arts, the Victoria and Albert Museum offers a representative and comprehensive selection from all phases and activities of the Pre-Raphaelite Movement.

2.11   The Walker Art Gallery. Liverpool.
Many of the early patrons of the Pre-Raphaelites came from Liverpool, and it was in this city that the Pre-Raphaelites, in the an-

nual competitions, began to receive consistent recognition. The Walker Art Gallery reflects to a great degree the interest that Liverpool has always taken in Pre-Raphaelite art. The gallery contains many of the best known and earliest "pure" Pre-Raphaelite works: Holman Hunt's *Eve of St. Agnes*, Millais' *Lorenzo and Isabella* and *Ferdinand and Ariel*, Brett's *The Stonebreaker*, and Windus' *Burd Helen*. Other pictures of note are Hunt's *The Triumph of the Innocents* and Rossetti's largest canvas, *Dante's Dream*. Other Pre-Raphaelite artists such as Ford Madox Brown, R. B. Martineau, and Burne-Jones are also represented; and the gallery has three of Arthur Hughes's best works, including the triptych of scenes from *As You Like It*. The holdings in Windus, a Liverpool artist, are the largest anywhere. There has been no catalogue of the Walker collection issued since 1929 (see 5.15, now long out of print), but a new catalogue of the permanent collection is now in the planning stage. A subsidiary of the Walker Gallery is Sudley House, at which a number of Pre-Raphaelite works are always on exhibition.

2.12 The Whitworth Art Gallery. Manchester University.

The Whitworth Gallery has many water colors and drawings by the Pre-Raphaelites. The water color collection includes *Romeo and Juliet, Cromwell on his Farm,* and *Byron's Dream* by Ford Madox Brown, together with other works by Millais, Simeon Solomon, Holman Hunt and Frederic Shields. Among the drawings are a chalk version of Rossetti's *La Donna della Finestra* and a study for *Dante's Dream*, sixteen studies of *King Lear* by Madox Brown, a study for *Sir Isumbras* by Millais, and many Burne-Jones drawings, including five cartoons for stained glass.

2.13 Wightwick Manor. The National Trust. The Home of the late Sir Geoffrey, and Lady Mander. Wolverhampton.

Wightwick Manor, a house in the best tradition of Victorian architecture, is a kind of Pre-Raphaelite memorial. Each room is decorated with Morris wallpaper or silk and damask hangings, and throughout the house there are examples of furniture designed by the Pre-Raphaelites, including most of the decorative furniture from the sale of "The Pines" (see 19.30). Many of the fixtures in the house were designed by Morris and Company, and the house contains fine examples of the tiles and pottery of William De Morgan. Three of the upstairs bedrooms and the hall take their names from the Morris wallpapers with which they are decorated: the Pomegranate Passage, the Honeysuckle Room, the Indian Bird Room, and the Acanthus Room.

Of greatest interest at Wightwick, however, are the many Pre-Raphaelite pictures and drawings, including works by Millais, Rossetti, Burne-Jones, Madox Brown, Collinson, Holman Hunt, Hungerford Pollen, Morris, May Morris, H. T. Dunn, Lucy Rossetti, and Elizabeth Siddal, whose *The Eve of St. Agnes* and *The Haunted Wood* are especially delightful. Works by Rossetti and Ford Madox Brown dominate the collection. Pictures of special interest are two portraits of Maria Francesca and Christina Rossetti by James Collinson, the latter signed with the letters "P.R.B."; a portrait of Jane Morris on which both Rossetti and Brown are said to have collaborated; Brown's exquisite portrait of William Michael Rossetti by gaslight; and a small oil picture of Christ with the cross, attributed to Christina Rossetti. Many of the pictures at Wightwick are on loan from Signora Helen Rossetti Angeli. Two brief publications on the collection are available (see 5.16 and 5.17); Lady Mander's recent and profusely illustrated article describing Wightwick (7.14) should also be consulted.

2.14 The William Morris Gallery. Walthamstow.

The William Morris Gallery, situated in the Water House, Morris' boyhood home, contains many examples of Morris' work in his various fields: original designs, wallpapers, ceramics and stained glass, textiles, furniture, and book production. In the library attached to the gallery there are a number of manuscripts and letters by Morris and his circle, as well as most of Morris' published writings, including the socialist pamphlets and many of the Kelmscott Press books. The "Brangwyn Gift," which forms the other half of the William Morris Gallery, has numerous drawings and water colors and a few oils by Burne-Jones, Holman Hunt, Madox Brown, Rossetti, and the minor Pre-Raphaelites, including Oliver Madox Brown. One of Rossetti's most interesting drawings, *Michael Scott's Wooing*, and a study by Morris for "Iseult on the Ship" are also included in the collection. The gallery publishes at nominal cost two catalogues, one of the "Brangwyn Gift" (5.18) and one of the Morris collection (5.19). Combined they offer a detailed account of the holdings of the William Morris Gallery.

2.15 Kelmscott Manor. Kelmscott, near Lechlade.

Set in the rustic village of Kelmscott, near Lechlade, in the cemetery of whose Norman church the Morris family is buried, Kelmscott Manor is much today as it was when Morris and Rossetti became its joint tenants in 1871. Beyond the architectural interest of the house itself and its associations with Morris and Rossetti, Kelmscott still contains Morris' decorations — the tapestries, tiles, and wallpapers of his arts and crafts period — much of the original furniture, and numerous works by Rossetti and Burne-Jones. In the Tapestry Room, which was Rossetti's,

part of Morris' library, with a few presentation copies and Kelmscott Press books, is still preserved. Among Rossetti's works at Kelmscott are the two oil portraits of Morris' daughters, a study of *Water Willow* (1871), and an oil portrait of Jane Morris, dating from 1868. There are also two earlier sketches of Jane, from 1857 and 1861. Other works of interest at Kelmscott are Morris' first-executed tapestry, eleven of the twelve designs for "Months" by Burne-Jones, and a few of Morris' designs for stained glass.

In her will, May Morris, having previously negotiated with officials of the university, bequeathed Kelmscott Manor, its furnishings and contents, to Oxford University, which maintained and administered the estate as an unviable trust from 1939 to 1962. In 1962, after litigation initiated by the university, the bequest was declared void, and the Kelmscott Estate, manor and chattels, devolved upon the Society of Antiquaries as the residuary legatees of May Morris. For a discussion of the background of Kelmscott and the legal maneuver whereby the estate has now passed to the Society of Antiquaries see A. R. Dufty's article (7.19), which reprints the will of May Morris and the memorandum specifying the furniture and effects contained in the manor.

Section 3

PUBLIC COLLECTIONS OF PRE-RAPHAELITE MATERIALS: UNITED STATES AND CANADA

While the Pre-Raphaelite holdings of galleries, museums, and libraries in the United States are substantially less extensive than in Great Britain, there is nevertheless a significant amount of material available in North America. The ten collections described in this section are the most important, but there is material elsewhere. The Rossetti manuscripts in the Duke University Library have been published with a thorough introduction and detailed notes by Paull Franklin Baum (7.6). The Boston Public Library has eight letters and four literary manuscripts by Rossetti. The Boston Museum of the Fine Arts has a number of paintings and drawings by Rossetti, Burne-Jones, and Simeon Solomon; a volume of fifty letters from Millais to various correspondents (1859–1889); and the Hartley Collection in the Boston Museum contains the most extensive body of material on the illustrations of the 1860's to be found in the United States. The University of Kansas Museum of Art has recently purchased Rossetti's *La Pia*, and the catalogue of the 1958 exhibition commemorating the acquisition of the painting (see 16.23, also 31.34) provides a convenient abbreviated check list of minor Pre-Raphaelite holdings in the United States. Doubtless many collections of minor importance have been slighted in this brief survey of American collections, but those included indicate sufficiently the widespread dispersal of Pre-Raphaelite materials on the North American continent.

* * *

3.1 The Samuel and Mary R. Bancroft English Pre-Raphaelite Collection. The Wilmington Society of the Fine Arts. Wilmington, Delaware.

The Bancroft Collection is the only one in the world devoted specifically to Pre-Raphaelitism. Accumulated between 1890 and 1915 by Samuel Bancroft, Jr., and acquired by the Wilmington Society of the Fine Arts in its present location in 1938, the collection consists of both a gallery and a library.

The examples of visual Pre-Raphaelitism in the gallery are selective rather than comprehensive, but the number of oils is unsurpassed in the United States. The emphasis, reflecting Bancroft's own taste, is on Rossetti, and the collection contains some of his most famous paintings: *Bottles* — a still life done while Rossetti was a student of Ford Madox Brown — the unfinished *Found, La Bella Mano, Lady Lilith, Mary Magdalene, Mnemosyne, Veronica Veronese,* and *Water Willow.* Of the original PRB, Stephens, Woolner, and Collinson are not represented, and only one example of Holman Hunt's work is present. But numerous works by the minor Pre-Raphaelites — Brown, Sandys, Shields, Elizabeth Siddal, and Mrs. William J. Stillman (Marie Spartali) — give additional scope to the collection.

The library, comprising nearly a thousand volumes, many of them rare ephemeral or periodical publications, offers a comprehensive survey of both primary and secondary sources. In addition to printed books, there is a sizable body of manuscript material, including approximately ninety letters from Rossetti (many of them to Fanny Cornforth, published in 24.19), plus additional letters from Christina Rossetti, Hall Caine, Shields, and others. Forty-five manuscript poems by Rossetti also form part of the literary holdings (for descriptions see 7.1 and 7.2). The manuscript called "The Debbie Book," officially "The Catalogue of Paintings and Photographs of the Collection of Samuel Bancroft, Jr., Rockford, Wilmington, Delaware" (5.3), prepared by Bancroft's secretary, Deborah J. Peacock, contains many interesting records and letters pertaining to the formation of the collection, among which Bancroft's letters to Fanny Cornforth deserve special mention. For a list of the paintings and drawings in the Bancroft Pre-Raphaelite Collection see 5.2.

3.2 The Berg Collection. New York Public Library.

This collection contains various miscellaneous letters and one volume of 65 letters from Rossetti to his solicitor, James Anderson Rose (1863–1869).

3.3 Harvard University: The Winthrop Collection of the Fogg Museum. The Houghton Library.

A 1943 bequest of the late Grenville Lindall Winthrop, this collection consists of both studies and finished works by most of the Pre-Raphaelites, including a significant group of studies by Rossetti and Burne-Jones, Holman Hunt's earliest oil sketch for *The Triumph of the Innocents,* and representative works by Ford Madox Brown, Millais, Simeon Solomon, and others. Because it primarily lists the works in the permanent collection, the Fogg Museum catalogue of the 1946 Pre-Raphaelite exhibition (16.13) is a reasonably complete listing of the Pre-Raphaelite holdings in the Winthrop Collection. In contrast to the Bancroft Pre-Raphaelite Collection, where the majority of the pictures are permanently hung, little emphasis is given to the Pre-Raphaelites at the Fogg Museum, and few pictures are actually on view in the gallery. For a brief description of this collection see 7.13, and appendix III in Dickason (80.8).

Pre-Raphaelite manuscripts in the Houghton Library include seventeen letters from Rossetti to Mrs. Anne Gilchrist, twelve to C. E. Norton, and five from Rossetti to various correspondents. There is also the manuscript of Rossetti's translation of Bürger's *Lenore* (23.22) and one leaf of the three surviving — the other two are in the British Museum — from the buried poems, together with a manuscript account of the interment and exhumation of the poems, by Thomas J. Wise. Besides Rossetti manuscripts, the Houghton also has twenty letters from William Michael Rossetti to C. E. Norton, more than fifty letters from Burne-Jones to Norton and others, 85 letters from Georgiana Burne-Jones to Norton, and 26 letters from Millais and Holman Hunt to various correspondents. In addition, the Norton papers contain a large group of Ruskin letters.

3.4 The Henry E. Huntington Library. San Marino, California.

Together with rich holdings in the printed sources of Pre-Raphaelitism, the Huntington Library has a valuable group of manuscripts. Of particular interest is an unpublished memoir of Walter H. Deverell by Mrs. Frances E. Deverell, the wife of Walter's brother, Wykeham, entitled "The P.R.B. and Walter Howell Deverell. Letters from Dante Gabriel Rossetti & Others. With a Narrative and Illustrations. Prefaced by William Michael Rossetti." Another volume of letters, miscellaneous drawings, and proofs contains, besides the actual manuscripts incorporated in Mrs. Deverell's memoir (twenty letters and two pages from Deverell's "Journal"), three groups of letters: thirteen from Rossetti to Robert Browning (now published, see 24.24); thirty letters from Millais to various correspondents including the brothers Dalziel; and twenty letters from Holman Hunt to various correspondents. The Library also has miscellaneous letters from Rossetti, Brown, Sandys, and others, and extensive manuscript material by Ruskin, Swinburne, and Morris.

3.5 The Library of Congress.

There are approximately 35 manuscripts of various Rossetti poems in the collections of the Library of Congress. The library also has 46 letters from Rossetti to Theodore Watts-Dunton and scattered letters in other collections and papers, including the Browning papers, which contain letters from several others in the Pre-Raphaelite circle. The Philip

Bourke Marston papers contain, among other items, seventeen letters from Rossetti and the manuscript of his poem "To Philip Bourke Marston."

3.6 The Pierpont Morgan Library. New York City.

Included among the manuscript holdings of the Pierpont Morgan Library are over 160 letters from Rossetti, counting those to William Allingham edited by G. B. Hill (see 24.6), and numerous manuscripts, the most important of which is the disputed draft of "The Blessed Damozel" (see 7.15). The library also has 35 letters to William Holman Hunt, considerable Ruskin material not incorporated in *CW* (45.3), and unpublished portions of Ford Madox Brown's diary. Of special interest are the voluminous "Millais Papers," which were acquired from Sir Ralph Millais in 1953. These papers include over 1300 letters to and from Millais and about 200 other miscellaneous items. In addition to the manuscripts already mentioned, lesser groups of holographs by other figures associated with the Pre-Raphaelite Movement and a rich selection of the rarer printed sources form part of the library's holdings.

3.7 Rutgers University Library. The Symington Collection.

The Symington Collection in the Rutgers University Library has extensive manuscript holdings relating to Swinburne and his circle. Included in this collection are 95 letters from Swinburne to William Michael Rossetti (described in 7.8, all these letters have been published in 62.12), transcripts from Rossetti's letters to Watts-Dunton (1872–1881), letters from Rossetti to his family, and a large number of Swinburne manuscripts (described in 62.11). For a general description of the Symington Collection see 7.7.

3.8 The Humanities Research Center. The University of Texas.

The two famous Wrenn and Henley Collections of the Humanities Research Center contain, among other items, the autograph manuscript of Christina Rossetti's *A Pageant and Other Poems*, Christina's transcript of Rossetti's "My Sister's Sleep," and a volume of Rossetti's manuscripts consisting of drafts of fifteen of his poems, sonnets, and translations, including a seven-page autograph draft of "The White Ship."

The principal recent source of Texas' acquisitions of Pre-Raphaelite material was the Sotheby sale of the property of A. R. Murray in 1961 (see 19.37). From this collection, Texas secured all the lots containing material relating directly to the Rossettis, most of it correspondence to Charles Augustus Howell. One lot of twenty-one letters from Christina Rossetti to Howell and his wife, Kate, was included, and two groups of letters from William Rossetti to Howell, Fairfax Murray, and other correspondents, comprising over eighty letters. By far the most important materials, however, were the properties connected with Dante Gabriel Rossetti, including several drafts of his poems and important series of letters to G. P. Boyce, Frederick Sandys, Mrs. Stillman, Fairfax Murray, and other correspondents. Of particular interest were the letters to Howell and his wife, numbering nearly 500. For a description of Morris materials acquired in the Murray sale see E. E. Stokes, Jr., "The Morris Letters at Texas," *Journal of the William Morris Society*, I, no. 3 (Summer 1963), 23–30. Texas has subsequently acquired from Signora Helen Rossetti Angeli the reciprocal part of the Rossetti-Howell correspondence, much of which was utilized in her biography of Howell (77.66). In addition to the materials already mentioned, Texas had previous to the Murray sale a few miscellaneous Rossetti letters, letters from W. M. Rossetti to T. J. Wise, and a fine selection of the printed books dealing with the movement. Perhaps the most formidable competitor in the field of nineteenth-century material, the University of Texas has by its recent acquisitions become one of the most important public repositories of Pre-Raphaelite manuscripts in North America.

3.9 Yale University. The Beinecke Rare Book and Manuscript Library.

Among the manuscripts in the Beinecke Library at Yale University are 61 letters from Rossetti to Frederic James Shields (most of them published in 58.7) plus nine others to various correspondents; 28 letters from Holman Hunt to Shields, together with eight other miscellaneous letters; nearly thirty letters from William Michael Rossetti to Thomas J. Wise; and small groups of letters from Ford Madox Brown, Burne-Jones, and Lady Burne-Jones, the last consisting of seventeen letters from George Eliot and five to her. Also in the Yale manuscript collection is an interesting holograph abstract (attributed to D. G. Rossetti but almost certainly in the hand of William Michael) giving brief biographical summaries of the artists whose works were shown in the exhibition of British art held in New York in 1857 (see 18.4). For Yale holdings from the library of Chauncey Brewster Tinker see 7.16.

3.10 The University of British Columbia. Special Collections. Vancouver, British Columbia, Canada.

Recently acquired from Penkill Castle, Ayrshire, Scotland is an extensive collection of unpublished manuscript letters relating to William Bell Scott and the Pre-Raphaelites. Included in the collection is the bulk of Scott's letters to Alice Boyd (nearly 500); a small group of letters from Alice to Scott (around forty); and over 400 letters from various writers and artists to Scott and Alice Boyd. Also included are the day-diaries of Alice Boyd, from 1859–1890 (lacking four or five years), and five day-diaries of Scott. Of special interest is a packet of seventy letters from Arthur Hughes to Scott and Miss Boyd, and another packet of seventy letters from Scott and other correspondents relating to the 1872 illness of Rossetti.

Section 4

PRIVATE COLLECTIONS OF PRE-RAPHAELITE MATERIALS

Besides the five private collections described in this section, there are many others worthy of mention; and while these collections cannot be conveniently catalogued, some indication of their holdings should be given.

Manuscripts and artistic works of the Pre-Raphaelites have been widely dispersed among private owners, but considerable material remains in the collections of the surviving heirs of the Pre-Raphaelites. Many items pertaining to the Rossettis — various drawings, family portraits, letters, and manuscripts — remain in the collections of Harold Rossetti, Oliver Rossetti, and Mrs. Roderic O'Conor, all of whom reside in England. A substantial correspondence from Rossetti to Hall Caine belongs to the novelist's son, Sir Derwent Hall Caine. Many of Holman Hunt's works remain in the possession of his granddaughter, Mrs. Michael Burt, from whose collection have been sold in recent years *The Lady of Shalott* (which realized nearly £10,000) and Hunt's portrait of Rossetti, which was acquired by the Birmingham City Museum and Art Gallery. A sizable number of Burne-Jones's works remain in the family, the largest group belonging to Mr. Graham MacInnes of Toronto. Material relating to James Smetham and other Pre-Raphaelites is owned by Dennis Smetham. The descendants of James Leathart, one of the foremost patrons of the Pre-Raphaelites, have retained a number of family portraits and other works by Rossetti, Arthur Hughes, and Ford Madox Brown, together with numerous letters from various Pre-Raphaelite artists, most of them dealing with arrangements for pictures which Leathart commissioned. In America, John S. Mayfield, the Curator of Rare Books and Manuscripts at Syracuse University and a noted Swinburne collector, has brought together many books and manuscripts of Pre-Raphaelite interest, including autograph letters from Holman Hunt, the Rossettis, Woolner, Ford Madox Brown, Burne-Jones, Simeon Solomon, and other members of the Pre-Raphaelite circle.

One extremely interesting smaller collection of Pre-Raphaelite pictures is that belonging to Mrs. Virginia Surtees, a great granddaughter of Ruth Herbert (Mrs. Crabbe), Rossetti's model. Besides numerous portraits of Miss Herbert, the collection includes a pencil drawing of a dancing girl from the *Borgia,* a red chalk drawing of Jane Morris, formerly owned by F. S. Ellis, a drawing of Georgiana Burne-Jones presented by Rossetti as a wedding present in 1860, a small oval water color portrait of Miss Siddal, *King René* (1864), *Rosa Triplex* (1874), and an undated water color, *Ruth and Boaz.* Exclusively focused on Rossetti, and on Miss Herbert, this collection reflects the interest of Mrs. Surtees, who is preparing for publication a *catalogue raisonné* of Rossetti's paintings and drawings.

To locate individual pictures, drawings, and manuscripts in private collections would be a prodigious undertaking. A few owners of important Pre-Raphaelite works are Lord Leverhulme, Lady Makins, Sir Colin Anderson, Kerrison Preston, the Trevelyan family, and John Gere. The collection of printed works and ephemera belonging to William E. Fredeman may also be mentioned as being one of the largest specialized collections in private hands.

This very much abbreviated list of private owners of Pre-Raphaelite literary and artistic materials might be considerably elaborated, but those noticed, taken together with the descriptions of the major private collections which follow, suggest at least the extent of these materials remaining outside the public repositories.

* * *

4.1 Signora Helen Rossetti Angeli — Mrs. Geoffrey Dennis. Woodstock.

The collection of Rossetti and Pre-Raphaelite material belonging to Signora Helen Rossetti Angeli and her daughter, Mrs. Geoffrey Dennis, is the most extensive gathering of both literary and visual materials in private possession in Great Britain, and it is to be equaled only by the collection of literary manuscripts in America belonging to Mrs. Janet Camp Troxell (see 4.5). Part of the collection, mostly pictures and drawings, is deposited at Wightwick Manor (see 2.13).

The literary papers are divided into two main groups: those relating to Dante Gabriel Rossetti and those pertaining to William Michael Rossetti. Among the D. G. Rossetti papers are over 100 letters from Rossetti to his mother, to Ford Madox Brown, and to other correspondents; there are also significant groups of letters to Rossetti from fellow artists and writers, friends and patrons, and family. The papers of William Michael Rossetti are more extensive, as might be expected. Described as a "Fofetic Compilation" — the family's pet name for William Michael Rossetti was "Fofus" — this group of manuscripts consists of approximately 1000 letters to and from members of the Rossetti family, and from various outside correspondents. These papers William Michael Rossetti intended to edit in volumes successive to *Rossetti Papers* (24.9), but they were never published. The collection also includes the complete manuscripts of W. M. Rossetti's Diaries, which are being published by the Oxford University Press. Manuscripts of particular interest to the history of the Pre-Raphaelite Movement are "The P.R.B. Journal," critical sheets from the Cyclographic Club, and the list of proposed titles for *The Germ* prepared by William Cave Thomas. These latter documents are now being edited for publication by William E. Fredeman. The Angeli-Dennis collection is also rich in the printed books of the period. Of special interest among the printed volumes are the "Miscellanies" collected by W. M. Rossetti — tract volumes made up of articles from periodicals and other contemporary ephemera relating to the Rossetti family and to the Pre-Raphaelite Movement. Notice should also be given to the abundance of material, both manuscript and printed, pertaining to Gabriele Rossetti.

Although many of the artistic works in this collection are on loan at Wightwick Manor, the residual collection at Woodstock is still overwhelming, though there are few major works — no large Rossetti oils, for example — represented. It is impossible here to give more than the briefest outline of the artistic side of the collection. There are many family portraits, including a fine oil self-portrait of Elizabeth Siddal, and others by Ford Madox Brown, D. G. Rossetti, Valentine C. Prinsep, Walter H. Deverell, W. M. Rossetti, Frederic Shields, and Holman Hunt. The works of Lucy Madox Brown, Signora Angeli's mother, are fitly represented, as are many drawings by Elizabeth Siddal. Christina Rossetti's artistic abilities are well displayed in her marginal drawings for several of her volumes of poems. Rossetti's *Cassandra* and a fine draught-sketch of Blackfriars Bridge (the background for *Found*), together with two superb portraits of Christina Rossetti, are among the best of his works to be seen, but his early (c. 1840) drawings for Homer are especially interesting. Works by many minor artists fill out the collection; among the miscellaneous oddments, perhaps the most curious is the volume of silhouettes illustrating *Prometheus Unbound* and *Queen Mab*, which William Rossetti commissioned from the now-forgotten artist, James Allen.

This description hardly does justice to the Angeli-Dennis collection which, because it derives from William Michael Rossetti, himself a Pre-Raphaelite, is in some ways the most inherently interesting in the world.

4.2   John Bryson. Oxford.

The collection of John Bryson of Balliol College consists of books, drawings and water colors, and a number of letters from Rossetti and other members of the Pre-Raphaelite circle. Many of his drawings and water colors were lent to the 1947 Birmingham exhibition (16.14) and are described in detail in the catalogue. By Rossetti, Mr. Bryson has two exquisite drawings of Elizabeth Siddal playing musical instruments, a portrait of Christina Rossetti (reproduced as the frontispiece in her posthumously published poems edited by William Michael Rossetti), two other drawings of Elizabeth Siddal and one of Fanny Cornforth, a study for *Bonifazio's Mistress*, a water color of lovers kissing, based on the design for the unused title-page illustration for *The Early Italian Poets*, and a small water color "Madonna and Child." Other artists represented are Millais ("girls in a meadow"), Burne-Jones (*The Knight's Farewell*), Ford Madox Brown (a portrait of Oliver Madox Brown), and Elizabeth Siddal ("Pippa Passes" and "The Lovers").

4.3 Charles Alexander Munro (and Mrs. J. A. R. Munro). Oxford.

This collection, which has remained in the Munro family since the death of the sculptor, Alexander Munro, is one of the most interesting still in private hands. Alexander Munro's close association with the Pre-Raphaelites is reflected in the inscribed pictures and books and in the letters to him which form part of this collection. Most of the works belonging to the Munro family are by Rossetti and Arthur Hughes, but there are also works by Simeon Solomon, G. P. Boyce, and John Brett. By Rossetti, there is a pencil drawing of *Paolo and Francesca*, a pen and ink drawing of *Michael Scott's Wooing* (inscribed to Alexander Munro, 1863), a very early (1848) sketch of *La Belle Dame Sans Merci*, and four early sketches, including one for Poe's "The Raven." There is also a portfolio of nearly seventy early Rossetti drawings and sketches done between 1844 and 1850. By Hughes, who was closely associated with the family, there are several portraits of Annie Munro and other members of the family; an early water color, *The Adoration of the Shepherds*, done when Hughes was seventeen, and an excellent oil, *Prospero*, for which Alexander Munro posed. Books in the collection consist of inscribed presentation copies from Rossetti, Browning, William Bell Scott, William Allingham, and others. Nearly fifty autograph letters — from Hughes, Boyce, Solomon, Millais, Ruskin, and Rossetti — complete the collection.

4.4 Miss Evelyn M. Courtney-Boyd. Penkill Castle. Girvan, Ayrshire, Scotland.

Penkill Castle, the home of Alice Boyd, was for many years the retreat of William Bell Scott, and occasionally of Rossetti. Today, it is the major repository of Scott's literary and artistic remains (see also 4.5 and 19.32). Besides the murals at Penkill for *The King's Quair* (see 56.6 and 56.9), there is also the largest collection of Scott's pictures, relatively few of which have gone into public galleries. The library contains many presentation copies from the Rossettis, Allingham, Hughes, Swinburne, Morris, and others, and a complete collection of Scott's own works. In addition, there are scrapbooks, sketchbooks, and portfolios containing manuscripts, drawings, press cuttings, letters, and other material by (or on) the various Pre-Raphaelites. Alice Boyd's unpublished drawings for Christina Rossetti's *Sing Song*, and Rossetti's manuscript of "The White Ship" are among the most interesting items. Finally, there is a rich group of drawings by Alice Boyd and by David Scott. There is no published catalogue of the contents of Penkill, but there is a typescript catalogue available to those who visit the collection (see 5.7). For a brief description of Penkill Castle and its literary and artistic associations, with numerous photographs of both the interior and exterior of the castle see 7.12. For Pre-Raphaelite material sold from Penkill see 19.38. See also 3.10.

4.5 Mrs. Janet Camp Troxell. New Haven, Connecticut.

The outstanding private Pre-Raphaelite collection in the United States, and with few rivals anywhere else, is that of Mrs. Janet Camp Troxell. Mrs. Troxell's collection is so vast that its contents can only be sketchily indicated; but so important is it to the literary side of the movement that no scholar engaged in textual or biographical research, particularly on the Rossettis, can safely disregard the material which it contains.

The emphasis in Mrs. Troxell's collection is distinctly, though not exclusively, literary. On the visual side of the movement are the water colors and drawings, among which the following are outstanding: Rossetti's *The Gate of Memory* (one of his finest water colors), a pen and ink drawing of *Desdemona's Death Song*, and eleven designs for stained glass; many Rossetti drawings, including several of Miss Siddal, Fanny Cornforth, Annie Miller, and Jane Morris; a small sketch of Ruskin, two heads of Dante, an interesting rough sketch for "Sister Helen," and the unused cover design (in color) for Allingham's *Day and Night Songs* (reproduced in 46.22, p. 74). By other Pre-Raphaelites may be mentioned Simeon Solomon's pencil drawings for Swinburne's *Lesbia Brandon*, two early drawings by William Morris, and a few slight sketches by Burne-Jones. Mrs. Troxell also has one of the very scarce impressions of Sandys' *The Nightmare*.

Besides most of the secondary works on the Pre-Raphaelites, first editions of their published writings, and the more common rarities such as *The Germ*, Christina Rossetti's *Verses*, and Dante Gabriel Rossetti's *Sir Hugh the Heron*, the collection contains many unusual and unique publications, including presentation and association copies: presentation copies of *The Early Italian Poets*, Rossetti to George Meredith, and to Browning; Rossetti's annotated copy of Poe's *The Raven* and Walter Scott's *Tales of a Grandfather*, the latter given him by William Michael Rossetti in 1880 "to guide him in his ballad of the King's Tragedy." One (of many) copies of *The Early Italian Poets* is the prepublication issue without the Smith, Elder imprint (see 22.9 for discussion); another is "extra illustrated" with six original Rossetti drawings. Another rarity is the generally unknown periodical ("The Year's Proceeds to be Devoted to the Royal Patriotic Fund") entitled *Our Paper. Being a Monthly Serial for Private Circulation*, which ran for nine issues between January and September 1855 and to which both Christina and William Michael Rossetti contributed.

Among the printed books is the group of proof copies of Rossetti's poems, the trial books of the 1870 volume. Literally hundreds of separate proof sheets and cancels, together with various copies of the 1869–1870 trial books (including H. Buxton Forman's copy and another given by Rossetti to Miss Losh containing pages from both the first and second states of the 1869 version) make this part of the collection without parallel. The "Penkill proofs" (Rossetti's trial books corrected at Penkill and preserved by William Bell Scott) alone are so heavily annotated as to be almost manuscript copies. For further details of these trial books see 27.89.

Of manuscripts and autograph letters there are no less than twenty volumes in Mrs. Troxell's collection. The Rossetti manuscripts dominate this side of the holdings — original manuscripts of *The House of Life* sonnets, about 25 "Sonnets and Fragments," eleven "Original Sonnets," a volume labeled simply "Lyrics," plus additional manuscripts of minor poems — but as well there are major groups of Christina Rossetti's manuscripts and a number of Swinburne's, including a most intriguing manuscript of the unpublished "The Laird of Waristoun" written in collaboration with Rossetti and in the autograph of both poets. The manuscripts and proofs of various secondary sources — Dunn's *Recollections*, Minto's edition of Scott's *Autobiographical Notes*, and Mackenzie Bell's *Christina Rossetti* — together with the manuscript of an unpublished article on Rossetti by Osbert Sitwell also form part of this collection.

Even more extensive is the wide assortment of letters in the collection, many of them unpublished: nine letters from Rossetti to Robert Browning; a volume of twenty letters from Rossetti to his mother, annotated by William Michael Rossetti; two volumes of Rossetti's letters to various correspondents; Rossetti's Kelmscott letters to William Bell Scott plus a large, uncatalogued group of letters from Rossetti to Scott (see 19.32); Rossetti's letters to Miss Losh (published in 24.18); two volumes of letters and manuscripts of Christina Rossetti; fifteen unpublished letters from Swinburne to C. A. Howell (not included in 62.12); a group of 36 letters from Jane Morris to Rossetti (probably replies to the letters from Rossetti to Jane Morris in the British Museum — see 2.2); and, finally, a scrapbook of miscellaneous letters from Rossetti, William Michael Rossetti (to Frederic Shields), Ruskin, and others, together with a specimen page from the "P.R.B. Journal."

Unfortunately, this magnificent collection has never been fully catalogued, a job that badly wants doing, and for which the present abbreviated description is in no way an adequate or satisfactory substitute.

Section 5
CATALOGUES OF MUSEUMS AND ART GALLERIES
AND PRIVATE COLLECTIONS

5.1 *Catalogue of Paintings in the Ashmolean Museum.* Oxford: Oxford University, n.d.

For a description of the Ashmolean collection see 2.8.

5.2 Rockwell, Jessie C. *The Samuel and Mary R. Bancroft English Pre-Raphaelite Collection.* Wilmington, Delaware: Wilmington Society of the Fine Arts, n.d.

Second edition, 1962, with a Foreword by Bruce St. John and an Introduction by Rowland P. Elzea. For description of the Bancroft Collection see 3.1.

5.3 Peacock, Deborah J. ["The Debbie Book"]. "The Catalogue of Paintings and Photographs of the Collection of Samuel Bancroft, Jr., Rockford, Wilmington, Delaware." Unpublished manuscript, n.d.

5.4 *Catalogue of the Permanent Collection of Paintings in Oil, Tempera, Water-Colour, etc.* Birmingham: City Museum and Art Gallery, 1930.

Three supplements: [1935], 1935–1939, 1939–1950. The descriptions of the oil paintings have now been superseded by 5.6, but this earlier catalogue is still essential for media other than oil. For description of the Birmingham collection see 2.1.

5.5 [Whitely, A. E.]. *Catalogue of the Permanent Collection of Drawings in Pen, Pencil, Charcoal, Chalk, etc., Including Cartoons for Stained Glass.* Birmingham: City Museum and Art Gallery, 1939.

An excellent catalogue with detailed notes on the hundreds of drawings in the Birmingham collection. Supersedes the two earlier catalogues of Pre-Raphaelite drawings: *Catalogue of the Collection of Drawings & Studies by Sir Edward Burne-Jones and Dante Gabriel Rossetti, Presented to the City in 1903* (Birmingham: City Museum and Art Gallery, 1904); *Catalogue of the Collection of Drawings and Studies by Sir Edward Burne-Jones, Dante Gabriel Rossetti, Sir J.*

E. Millais, Ford Madox Brown, Frederick Sandys, John Ruskin, and Others, Exhibited in the Upper Galleries of the Museum (Birmingham: City Museum and Art Gallery, 1913).

5.6 [Woodward, John]. *Catalogue of Paintings.* Birmingham: City Museum and Art Gallery, [1960].

Limited to a description of the oil paintings in the Birmingham collection. For work in other media see 5.4.

5.7 "Catalogue of Books, Etcetera, at Penkill Castle, Ayrshire." Unpublished typescript, n.d.

For description of the collection at Penkill see 4.4.

5.8 Tatlock, R. R. and others. *Record of the Collections in the Lady Lever Art Gallery.* London: Batsford, 1928.

See also Reginald C. Grundy and Sydney L. Davison, *Illustrated Guide to the Lady Lever Collection* (Port Sunlight: Published by the Trustees, 1956). For description of the Lady Lever collection see 2.5.

5.9 Chamot, Mary. *The Tate Gallery. British School. A Concise Catalogue.* London: Printed for the Trustees, 1953.

An excellent catalogue with periodic supplements. See also the *Illustrated Guide: British School* (London: National Gallery, 1925). For description of the Tate collection see 2.7.

5.10 *Catalogue of the National Portrait Gallery, 1856–1947, with an Index of Artists.* London: National Portrait Gallery, 1949.

Bound with *Supplement, 1948–1953* (1954). For description of the collection see 2.7.

5.11 *The Constantine Ionides Bequest.* London: H. M. Stationery Office, 1904.

See also Sir Charles J. Holmes, "The Constantine Ionides Bequest. Article I. The Pre-Raphaelites," *Burlington Magazine,* V (Aug.

1904), 455–462. For description of the Victoria and Albert collection, of which the Ionides Bequest is a part, see 2.10.

5.12 Hardie, Martin. *Catalogue of Modern Wood-Engravings* (Victoria and Albert Museum, Department of Engraving, Illustration and Design). London: H. M. Stationery Office, 1916.

For annotation see 88.7. See also Martin Hardie's *Catalogue of Prints: Wood Engravings after Sir John Everett Millais . . . in the Victoria and Albert Museum* (89.5).

5.13 *Catalogue of Works by William De Morgan.* London: H. M. Stationery Office, 1921.

Catalogue prepared by the Department of Ceramics of the Victoria and Albert Museum. With a biographical note, a "Technical Note on the Wares," a "Note on Marks," a catalogue of pottery and tiles, designs and drawings, and sixteen illustrations.

5.14 *Catalogue of Water Colour Paintings by British Artists and Foreigners Working in Great Britain* (Victoria and Albert Museum).

Revised edition. London: Board of Education, 1927.

5.15 *Walker Art Gallery: Catalogue of the Permanent Collection.* Liverpool: Published by the Corporation, 1929.

For description of the Walker collection see 2.11.

5.16 *Wightwick Manor: A Property of the National Trust.* London: Published by Country Life Ltd. for the National Trust, n.d.

For description of the collection at Wightwick see 2.13.

5.17 "Catalogue of Pictures at Wightwick Manor." Unpublished mimeographed list, 1949.

5.18 *The William Morris Gallery and Brangwyn Gift, Walthamstow.* Walthamstow: Published by the Borough, n.d.

For description of the William Morris Gallery's collection see 2.14.

5.19 *Catalogue of the Morris Collection.* Walthamstow: William Morris Gallery, 1958.

Section 6

DESCRIPTIONS OF RETROSPECTIVE COLLECTIONS

6.1 Monkhouse, Cosmo. "A Pre-Raphaelite Collection," *Magazine of Art*, VI (1883), 62–70.

A description of the collection of Mr. J. Hamilton Trist of Brighton.

6.2 Child, Theodore. "A Pre-Raphaelite Mansion," *Art and Criticism: Monographs and Studies.* New York: Harper, 1892.

Reprinted from *Harper's Magazine*, LXXXII (December 1890), 81–101. A description, with illustrations, of Frederick Leyland's home in London, at 49 Prince's Gate, Kensington, and of its Pre-Raphaelite interior and contents. Leyland's house was a show place, filled with the art of Rossetti and Botticelli. Whistler's famous "Peacock Room," now in the Freer Art Gallery, Washington, D.C., was designed and executed for Leyland's house. The second half of the article discusses the technique employed in

specific paintings by Burne-Jones and Rossetti.

6.3 Prinsep, Valentine C. "The Private Art Collections of London. The Late Mr. Frederick Leyland's in Prince's Gate First Paper — Rossetti and his Friend," *Art Journal*, LIV (May 1892), 129–138.

For Rossetti's letters to Frederick Leyland see 24.4.

6.4 Temple, A. G. "Collection of William Coltart, Esq., of Woodleigh, Birkenhead," *Art Journal*, LVIII (April 1896), 97–101.

Many of the pictures formerly in Coltart's collection are now in the Lady Lever Art Gallery (see 2.5).

6.5 Rossetti, William Michael. "A Pre-Raphaelite Collection," *Art Journal*, LVIII (May 1896), 129–134.

A discussion of Mr. Leathart's collection at the time of the exhibition in the Goupil Gallery (see 16.4). Reprinted in *Fifty Years of Art, 1849–1899* (see 77.52).

6.6 *Catalogue of Mr. George Rae's Pictures.* Redcourt, Birkenhead: [Privately printed], n.d.

Rae was one of the foremost Pre-Raphaelite patrons and collectors. For the details of the acquisition of his pictures by the National Gallery see Roger Fry, "The New Rossettis at the National Gallery," in the "Monthly Chronicle" section, *Burlington Magazine,* XXIX (May 1916), 80–81. See also 30.56.

Section 7

DESCRIPTIONS OF CURRENT COLLECTIONS OR OF THEIR SPECIFIC HOLDINGS

7.1 Wallerstein, Ruth C. "The Bancroft Manuscripts of Rossetti's Sonnets, with the Text of Two Hitherto Unpublished Sonnets," *Modern Language Notes,* XLIV (May 1929), 279–284.

For annotation see 27.81. For description of Bancroft Collection see 3.1.

7.2 Baum, Paull Franklin. "The Bancroft Manuscripts of Dante Gabriel Rossetti," *Modern Philology,* XXXIX (August 1941), 47–68.

For annotation see 27.91

7.3 Taylor, Basil. "F. G. Stephens and the P.R.B.," *Architectural Review,* CIV (October 1948), 171–178.

For annotation see 39.3. For description of the Stephens papers now in the Bodleian Library see 2.8.

7.4 Grylls, R. Glynn [= (Lady) Rosalie Mander]. "The Correspondence of F. G. Stephens," [2 parts], *Times Literary Supplement,* no. 2875 (5 April 1957), p. 216; no. 2876 (12 April 1957), p. 232.

For annotation see 39.4.

7.5 Flower, R. "The William Morris Manuscripts," *British Museum Quarterly,* XIV (1939–1940), 8–12.

For discussion of the Morris manuscripts in the British Museum see 2.2.

7.6 Baum, Paull Franklin, ed. *Dante Gabriel Rossetti: An Analytical List of Manuscripts in the Duke University Library, with Hitherto Unpublished Verse and Prose.* Durham: Duke University Press, 1931.

Manuscripts acquired by the Duke University Library in 1930.

7.7 Marchand, Leslie A. "The Symington Collection," *Journal Rutgers University Library,* XII (December 1948), 1–15.

For description of the Symington Collection see 3.7.

7.8 Lang, Cecil Y. "ALS: Swinburne to William Michael Rossetti," *Journal Rutgers University Library,* XIV (December 1950), 1–8.

Letters in the Symington Collection, all published in 62.12. For Lang's account of Swinburne manuscripts in the Symington Collection see 62.11.

7.9 Hartley, C. G. *Pictures in the Tate Gallery.* London: Seeley, 1905.

For description of the Tate collection see 2.7. The present volume has four illustrated chapters on the Pre-Raphaelite pictures in the Tate.

7.10 Manson, J. B. "The Pre-Raphaelites," *Hours in the Tate Gallery.* London: Duckworth, 1926.

Essentially a catalogue with descriptions of the pictures. "All the works of the Pre-Raphaelite School are interesting, in most cases, on account of the stories they illustrate; but interest of that sort is a cold and limited activity, and may pass with a fashion or a period. Consequently there has been no further growth or development of the Pre-Raphaelite movement; no newer or rarer plant grew from its stem, but it faded away, and ceased to be, forty or fifty years after its inception" (pp. 88–89). The volume also contains a brief section on Burne-Jones and Watts.

7.11 ——— "The Pre-Raphaelites," *The Tate Gallery*. London: Jack, 1930.

7.12 Gaul, Victoria. "Ayrshire's Little Castle," *Scottish Field*, CVIII (January 1961), 55–57.

An illustrated description of Penkill Castle and its Pre-Raphaelite associations. For an earlier description see T. M. Lyon, "Penkill Castle: The Home of Miss E. M. Courtney-Boyd," *Scottish Field*, XLIX (June 1927), 270–273. See 4.4.

7.13 Sweeney, John L. "The Winthrop Collection: Imaginative Design: Blake to the Pre-Raphaelites," *Art News*, XLII (1 January 1944), 18–19, 35–36.

For description of the Winthrop Collection see 3.3.

7.14 Grylls, R. Glynn [= (Lady) Rosalie Mander]. "Wightwick Manor — a William Morris Period-Piece," *Connoisseur*, CXLIX (January 1962), [2]–11.

With two colored illustrations of the interior (the Drawing Room and the Great Parlour) of Wightwick Manor and nine black and white illustrations of the house and its Pre-Raphaelite art contents. For description of the collection at Wightwick see 2.13.

7.15 Sanford, J. A. "The Morgan Manuscript of Rossetti's 'The Blessed Damozel,'" *Studies in Philology*, XXXV (July 1938), 471–486.

For annotation see 28.30. For description of the Pierpont Morgan collection see 3.6.

7.16 *The Tinker Library: A Bibliographical Catalogue of the Books Collected by Chauncey Brewster Tinker*. Compiled by Robert F. Metzdorf. New Haven: Yale University Press, 1959.

With sections on Christina and Dante Gabriel Rossetti, Swinburne, Morris, and many of the minor Pre-Raphaelites. Full collations are provided. All of the books and manuscripts are housed in, and many are part of, the permanent collection of the Beinecke Library, Yale University.

7.17 Thomas, Daniel. "Pre-Raphaelite Works in the Collection of the National Gallery of Victoria," *Annual Bulletin of the National Gallery of Victoria*, II (1960), 21–26.

With reproductions of works by Deverell, Millais, Hunt, Rossetti, and Burne-Jones. The cover illustration, in color, is of Hughes's *Fair Rosamund*.

7.18 Cornforth, John. "Wightwick Manor, Staffordshire: A Property of the National Trust," *Country Life*, CXXXIII, no. 3456 (30 May 1963), 1242–1245; no. 3457 (6 June 1963), 1316–1319.

A two-part article, profusely illustrated.

7.19 Dufty, A. R. "William Morris and the Kelmscott Estate," *The Antiquaries Journal*, XLIII, part I (1963), 97–114.

A discussion of the background and history of Kelmscott Manor and of the recent litigation which culminated in the estate reverting to the Society of Antiquaries, after having been held in trust by Oxford University for nearly a quarter century.

7.20 Stokes, E. E., Jr. "The Morris Letters at Texas," *Journal of the William Morris Society*, I, no. 3 (Summer 1963), 23–30.

Exhibitions of Separate Artists

Section 8

FORD MADOX BROWN

8.1 *Work, and Other Paintings by Ford Madox Brown* [Catalogue of the Exhibition]. London: Gallery at 191 Piccadilly, 1865.

Cover title: *Mr. Madox Brown's Exhibition*. This catalogue, prepared by Brown himself, contains 98 items, including paintings, sketches for stained glass, and furniture. The notes to the pictures, with five pages devoted to *Work*, are also by the artist, and the catalogue contains a sonnet by Brown. For notices of the exhibition see the *Athenaeum*, no. 1950 (11 March 1865), p. 353; and 21.3 to 21.5.

8.2 *Pictures by Living and Deceased Artists. Works by Italian Masters. Pictures by Dante Gabriel Rossetti, Ford Madox Brown, E. Burne-Jones, A.R.A., and R. Spencer Stanhope, etc. Lent by Major Jekyll, R.E.* [Catalogue of the Exhibition]. Nottingham: Museum and Art Gallery, 1892.

Listed in the Victoria and Albert hand list of exhibitions but unavailable for examination.

8.3 "Loan Collection and Other Decorative Work by the Late Ford Madox Brown," *Arts and Crafts Exhibition Society* [Catalogue of the (5th) Exhibition]. London: The New Gallery, 1896.

The small loan exhibition of Brown's works was held in the South Gallery (catalogued pp. 95–106, items 361 to 454A). Ford Madox Hueffer's "A Note on the Work of Ford Madox Brown," originally delivered (in part) as a paper before the Art Workers' Guild, is included in the catalogue (pp. 11–28).

8.4 *The Works of Ford Madox Brown* [Catalogue of the Exhibition]. London: Grafton Gallery, 1896–1897.

Introductory note by Ford Madox Hueffer. The catalogue is taken in large part from Brown's own notes in the 1865 exhibition (8.1). Noticed in *Athenaeum*, no. 3616 (13 February 1897), pp. 220–221; *Nation*, LXIV (18 February 1897), 123–124; *Artist*, XIX (March 1897), 127–129. See also 21.57.

8.5 *Collected Works of Ford Madox Brown* [Catalogue of the Exhibition]. London: Leicester Galleries, June-July 1909.

Preface and Notes by Ford Madox Hueffer. Forty-four works exhibited.

8.6 *Loan Exhibition of Works by Ford Madox Brown and the Pre-Raphaelites* [Catalogue of the Exhibition]. Manchester: City Art Gallery, Autumn (14 September to 30 November) 1911.

For annotation see 16.7.

8.7 *D. G. Rossetti and Madox Brown: Family Portraits* [Catalogue of the Exhibition]. Manchester: City Art Gallery, July 1920.

Prefatory Note by Lawrence Haward.

Section 9
EDWARD BURNE-JONES

9.1 *Handbook with Notes to the Collection of Paintings by G. F. Watts, R. A. and Edward Burne-Jones, A.R.A.* [Catalogue of the Exhibition]. Birmingham: City Museum and Art Gallery, [1885].

9.2 *The Legend of "The Briar Rose": A Series of Pictures by E. Burne-Jones, A.R.A.* [Catalogue of the Exhibition]. London: Thomas Agnew and Sons, 1890.

The descriptive text for the series is by E. J. Milliken; the introductory poem for each picture is by William Morris. The pamphlet also contains three press opinions from 1890. A condensed version of this pamphlet-catalogue was issued by Agnew's Liverpool branch. Both are essentially advertisements for photographic reproductions.

9.3 *Pictures by Living and Deceased Artists. Works by Italian Masters. Pictures by Dante Gabriel Rossetti, Ford Madox Brown, E. Burne-Jones, A.R.A., and R. Spencer Stanhope, etc. Lent by Major Jekyll, R.E.* [Catalogue of the Exhibition]. Nottingham: Museum and Art Gallery, 1892.

Listed in the Victoria and Albert hand list of exhibitions but unavailable for examination.

9.4 *The Works of Edward Burne-Jones* [Catalogue of the Exhibition]. London: The New Gallery, 1893.

Noticed in *Athenaeum*, no. 3403 (14 January 1893), pp. 58–59; no. 3405 (28 January 1893), pp. 127–128.

9.5 *A Small Collection of Pictures, Including the Bath of Venus, by E. Burne-Jones* [Catalogue of the Exhibition]. London: Laurie and Co. Galleries, 1893–1894.

Listed in the Victoria and Albert hand list of exhibitions but unavailable for examination.

9.6 *The Legend of "St. George and the Dragon" by Sir E. Burne-Jones, Bart.* [Catalogue of the Exhibition]. London: Thomas McLean, 1895.

Burne-Jones prepared these seven drawings for Birkett Foster and they were never exhibited prior to this time. The catalogue contains a brief section on "The Story of St. George" together with a short verse on each of the panels by William Morris. For one notice of this exhibition see *Athenaeum*, no. 3513 (23 February 1895), p. 257.

9.7 *Studies and Drawings by Sir Edward Burne-Jones, Bart.* [Catalogue of the Exhibition]. London: Fine Art Society, 1896.

Prefatory Note by Julia Cartwright. One hundred and forty-eight works exhibited, including twenty designs for Kelmscott publications. All items for sale without copyright. For one notice see 21.25.

9.8 *A Selection of Studies by Sir Edward Burne-Jones, Bart.: Also a Number of Drawings and Detail Studies* [Catalogue of the Exhibition]. London: Frederick Hollyer and Frederick T. Hollyer, 9 Pembroke Square, Kensington, 22 April to 28 May 1898.

Foreword by Horace Townsend. The exhibition consisted principally of photographic studies together with a few original drawings. See 42.34.

9.9 *The Works of Sir Edward Burne-Jones, Bart.* [Catalogue of the Exhibition]. London: The New Gallery, 1898–1899.

Noticed in *Nation*, LXVIII (26 January 1899), 65–66; *Athenaeum*, no. 3715 (7 January 1899), pp. 23–24; *Spectator*, LXXXII, no. 3680 (7 January 1899), 17–18. The long Introduction to the catalogue by J. Comyns Carr is reprinted in 25.45.

9.10 *Drawings and Studies by Sir Edward Burne-Jones, Bart.* [Catalogue of the Exhibi-

tion]. London: Burlington Fine Arts Club, 1899.

Introduction by Cosmo Monkhouse. Drawings, studies, and sketches (171 works in all) were exhibited. In addition, the exhibition included many of Burne-Jones's designs for Kelmscott publications, the original drawings for *The Flower Book* (42.5), and nineteen portraits. Some of Burne-Jones's humorous drawings for children, a side of Burne-Jones often overlooked, were also exhibited. Noticed in *Athenaeum*, no. 3719 (4 February 1899), p. 151.

9.11 *Platinotype Reproductions of Works of Sir Edward Burne-Jones, D. G. Rossetti, G. F. Watts, R. A., and Other Masters: Portraits by Various Painters and . . . Frederick Hollyer* [Catalogue of the Exhibition]. London: Egyptian Hall, Piccadilly [Dudley Galleries], 1902.

Listed in the Victoria and Albert hand list of exhibitions but unavailable for examination.

9.12 *Drawings and Studies by Sir Edward Burne-Jones, Bart.* [Catalogue of the Exhibition]. London: Leicester Galleries, April–May 1904.

With an Introductory Note by Sidney Colvin; 114 drawings on view.

9.13 *Drawings by the Late Sir Edward Burne-Jones, Bart.* [Catalogue of the Exhibition]. Manchester: Municipal School of Art, October–December 1905.

Introduction by Charles Rowley. Ninety-five drawings shown, fifteen of which are reproduced in the catalogue.

9.14 *Notes on the Life and Art of Burne-Jones* [Catalogue of the Exhibition]. Birmingham: City Museum and Art Gallery, 1933.

A brochure announcing the acquisition and exhibition of *Phyllis and Demophoön*, from 17 June 1933.

9.15 *Centenary Exhibition of Paintings and Drawings by Sir Edward Burne-Jones, Bart. (1833–1898)* [Catalogue of the Exhibition]. London: National Gallery, Millbank (The Tate Gallery), 17 June to 31 August 1933.

With an Introduction by W. Rothenstein and a note on "Burne-Jones's Medium" by T. M. Rooke. Noticed by Kenneth Clark in *New Statesman and Nation*, VI (22 July 1933), 105–106; by R. A. Bell in *Saturday Review*, CLV, no. 4052 (24 June 1933), 620–621; and in *Apollo*, XVIII (August 1933), 120–121. For two other notices see 21.39 and 21.40.

9.16 *The Decorative Art of Burne-Jones and Morris* [Catalogue of the Exhibition]. Birmingham: City Museum and Art Gallery, 1956–1957.

A traveling exhibition organized by the Midlands Federation of Museums and Art Galleries. With an Introduction on Burne-Jones by John Woodward.

Section 10

ARTHUR HUGHES AND FREDERICK SANDYS

10.1 *Cabinet Pictures Illustrating the By-ways of Cornwall &c. by Arthur Hughes* [Catalogue of the Exhibition]. London: Fine Art Society, July 1900.

Brief Introduction. Eighty works exhibited.

10.2 *A Collection of Pictures by Arthur Hughes* [Catalogue of the Exhibition]. London: Robert Dunthorne's [The Rembrandt Gallery], 1904.

Fifty-nine works shown.

10.3 *The Memorial Exhibition of Some of the Works of the Late Arthur Hughes* [Catalogue of the Exhibition]. London: Walker's Galleries, October 1916.

Foreword by Albert Goodwin. Catalogue contains eight illustrations. Ninety-one drawings, paintings, and studies exhibited. The remaining works of Hughes, most of them late, were sold at Christie's, 21 November 1921.

* * *

10.4 *Drawings by Frederick Sandys and Other Eminent Artists* [Catalogue of the Exhibition]. London: Leicester Galleries, February–March 1904.

With a Prefatory Note by F. G. Stephens entitled "The Higher Art: An Appreciation of Drawings." Among the other artists included were Simeon Solomon and Rossetti.

10.5 *Works by the Late George Frederick Watts, R.A., O.M., and the Late Frederick Sandys* [Catalogue of the Exhibition]. London: Royal Academy of Arts, 1905.

Gallery V was devoted to the works of Sandys, by whom 66 drawings and paintings were exhibited.

Section 11

WILLIAM HOLMAN HUNT

11.1 *May Morning, Magdalen Tower, Oxford. Painted by W. Holman Hunt* [Catalogue of the Exhibition]. London: Gainsborough Gallery, n.d.

A brief description of the ceremony, distributed at the time of the exhibition of the picture.

11.2 *Holman Hunt's Light of the World* [Catalogue of the Exhibition]. London: Florence Gallery, n.d.

11.3 *Mr. Holman Hunt's Picture "The Shadow of Death"* [Catalogue of the Exhibition]. London: Thomas Agnew and Sons, n.d.

An advertisement for the engraving. A brief discussion of the picture with two press notices (dated 1873).

* * *

11.4 *The Pictures in the Holman Hunt Exhibition* [Catalogue of the Exhibition]. London: Fine Art Society, 1886.

For the *Notes* on the exhibition see 21.17. Three notices of the exhibition appeared in the *Spectator*, LIX, no. 3012 (20 March

1886), 387–388; no. 3013 (27 March 1886), 418–420; no. 3014 (3 April 1886), 451–453.

11.5 *The Triumph of the Innocents by William Holman Hunt, R.W.S.* [Catalogue of the Exhibition]. Liverpool: Walker Art Gallery, 1891.

The description of the picture was written by Holman Hunt. Also contains opinions on the picture by Leighton, Watts, Crane, and others. An earlier, nearly identical pamphlet with an epitome and description by Hunt appeared in London in 1885.

11.6 *A Description of the Picture "The Triumph of the Innocents," by W. Holman Hunt, Lent by Mr. John T. Middlemore (Written by the Artist)* [Catalogue of the Exhibition]. Birmingham: City Museum and Art Gallery, 1897.

The "Epitome" of the picture is the same as 11.5, but the opinions are somewhat elaborated.

11.7 *"The Miracle of the Holy Fire in the Church of the Sepulchre at Jerusalem." Painted by W. Holman Hunt* [Catalogue of the Exhibition]. n.p., gallery unknown, [1899].

With a long explanatory text by Holman Hunt.

11.8 *"The Light of the World" by W. Holman Hunt. Now Exhibiting. . . .* [Catalogue of the Exhibition]. London: Fine Art Society, 1904.

11.9 *"The Lady of Shalott" by Holman Hunt. Now on View* [Catalogue of the Exhibition]. London: Arthur Tooth and Sons, 1905.

With a note by Hunt explaining the painting in terms of Tennyson's poem. Included also is the catalogue of Tooth's Spring Exhibition of 1905. See also the slighter pamphlet, *"Tennyson's 'Lady of Shalott'"* by W. Holman Hunt, a brief description of the picture printed with the poem, issued by Tooth's in 1909.

11.10 *The Collected Works of W. Holman Hunt* [Catalogue of the Exhibition]. Manchester: City Art Gallery, 1906. Introduction by J. E. Phythian. Noticed in *Nation*, LXXXIII (25 October 1906), 357–358.

11.11 *The Collected Works of W. Holman Hunt* [Catalogue of the Exhibition]. London: Leicester Galleries, October–November 1906.

Prefatory Note by Sir William Blake Richmond. For one notice see 21.32.

11.12 *Pictures and Drawings by William Holman Hunt, O.M., D.C.L.* [Catalogue of the Exhibition]. Glasgow: Corporation Art Gallery and Museum, 1907.

Listed in the Victoria and Albert hand list of exhibitions but unavailable for examination.

11.13 *The Art of William Holman Hunt* [Catalogue of the Exhibition]. Liverpool: Walker Art Gallery, 2 February to 2 March 1907.

With a note by Holman Hunt. One hundred and twenty-five items exhibited, with generous notes to the pictures. Essentially the same as 11.10.

Section 12

JOHN EVERETT MILLAIS

12.1 *Effie Deans by J. E. Millais, R.A. to be Engraved by T. Oldham Barlow, A.R.A. . . . Now Exhibiting* [Catalogue of the Exhibition]. London: King Street Galleries, n.d.

Catalogue contains extracts from *The Heart of Midlothian* together with a description of Millais' handling of the subject.

12.2 *The Proscribed Royalist: 1651. Painted by John Everett Millais, A.R.A. Engraved by W. H. Simmons* [Catalogue of the Exhibition]. London: Gambart's Gallery, n.d.

A description of the background for the picture and an advertisement for the excellence of the engraving.

*   *   *

12.3 *The Collected Work of John Everett Millais* [Catalogue of the Exhibition]. London: Fine Art Society, 1881.

See Andrew Lang's *Notes* (21.6).

12.4 *The Works of Sir John Everett Millais* [Catalogue of the Exhibition]. London: Grosvenor Gallery, 1886.

With notes by F. G. Stephens. See also the *Notes* on the exhibition (21.18). Two notices appeared in the *Spectator*, LIX, no. 3001 (2 January 1886), 16–17; no. 3006 (6 February 1886), 176–177; a third in the *Art Journal*, XLVIII (February 1886), 62–63.

12.5 *The Woodcut Illustration of Millais* [Catalogue of the Exhibition]. London: Hacon and Ricketts (at the Sign of the Dial, 52 Warwick Street), 16 March 1898.

This private exhibition was designed to supplement the exhibition of Millais' paintings and drawings at the Royal Academy (12.6). The catalogue consists of an Introduction by C. J. Holmes and a list of 32 woodcut designs.

12.6 *Works by the Late Sir John Everett Millais* [Catalogue of the Exhibition]. London: Royal Academy of Arts, 1898.

For notices see Hueffer (21.28), Phillips (21.29), Spielmann (21.26), Beale (21.30), and Pennell (21.27).

12.7 *Pictures, Drawings, and Studies for Pictures Made by the Late Sir J. E. Millais* [Catalogue of the Exhibition]. London: Fine Art Society, April 1901.

Introductory Note by J. G. Millais. One hundred and eight works shown.

Section 13

WILLIAM MORRIS

13.1 *The Morris Exhibit at the Foreign Fair, Boston, 1883–84* [Catalogue of the Exhibition]. Boston: Roberts, 1883.

This pamphlet, which was a handbook to the Morris and Company entries at the Boston Foreign Fair, contains the circular "The Hammersmith Carpets," originally issued by the Firm in 1880, and two other occasional circulars issued by the Firm, including a succinct account of the twelve departments of art work in which Morris and Company indulged, and a brief pamphlet relating to their furniture prints. Most of the pamphlet was written by Thomas Wardle, who accompanied the exhibit to Boston, but H. Buxton Forman, in *The Books of William Morris* (43.1), attributing various sections (including the circular mentioned above) to Morris, says that "the poet's prose works are not complete without that little dissertation" (p. 195).

13.2 "Exhibition of Works by William Morris," *Arts and Crafts Exhibition Society* [Catalogue of the (6th) Exhibition]. London: The New Gallery, 1899.

The Morris exhibit was held in the South Gallery (catalogued pp. 96–111, items 262–398 +). Special emphasis was given in the exhibition to Morris' contribution to the making of books.

13.3 *The Works of William Morris* [Catalogue of the Exhibition]. Manchester: Municipal School of Art, October 1908.

Catalogue contains twelve plates.

13.4 *The William Morris Centenary Exhibition: Drawings, Chintzes, Wall Papers, Manuscripts, First Editions, A Complete Series of the Publications of the Kelmscott Press . . .* [Catalogue of the Exhibition]. San Francisco: Mills College Art Gallery, 4 March to 24 March 1934.

A small brochure distributed at this exhibition contained a brief article entitled "William Morris, 1834–1896. Craftsman, Romancer, Poet, Prophet." No copy of this catalogue has been located.

13.5 *William Morris Bibliography, or the Catalogue of the Exhibition of Morrisiana Held by the Tokio W[illiam] Morris Society at Maruzan Co. Ltd. . . . in Celebration of Morris's Centennial Birthday* [Catalogue of the Exhibition]. Tokyo, Japan: William Morris Society, 24 April to 3 May 1934.

13.6 *Guide to the William Morris Centenary Exhibition* [Catalogue of the Exhibition]. Walthamstow: Walthamstow Museum [now The William Morris Gallery], 5 May to 28 July 1934.

Brief Foreword by G. E. Roebuck, and an article on "The Art of William Morris" by H. C. Marillier. For publications growing out of the Walthamstow centenary celebrations see 43.108, 43.109, 43.111.

13.7 *Exhibition in Celebration of the Centenary of William Morris* [Catalogue of the Exhibition]. London: Victoria and Albert Museum, 9 February to 8 April 1934.

With an Introduction by J. W. Mackail and a note on "William Morris, Craftsman, & the Firm of Morris & Co." A significant exhibition in which all phases of Morris' many activities in the arts were represented.

13.8 *The Decorative Art of Burne-Jones and Morris* [Catalogue of the Exhibition]. Birmingham: City Museum and Art Gallery, 1956–1957.

For annotation see 9.16.

13.9 *The Typographical Adventure of William Morris* [Catalogue of the Exhibition]. London: The William Morris Society, 30 July 1957 to 26 March 1959.

A large and comprehensive exhibition of Morris' place in the history of printing. Beginning with *The Oxford and Cambridge Magazine* and *The Germ* and concluding with examples of printing "After Kelmscott" which evince the long-range impact of Morris' style, the exhibition "looked backward and forward from the brief period of Morris' printing activity." A traveling exhibition, *The Typographical Adventure* opened at the St. Bride Foundation Institute on 30 July 1957 and closed on 26 March 1959 after sixteen separate showings. When the exhibition left Antwerp in May 1958, it was taken over by the British Council, who sponsored the showings in Offenbach, Berlin, Oslo, Stockholm, Berne, Copenhagen, and Vienna. The catalogue of the exhibition, a handsomely designed volume in two separate states, was

published in 1957–1958. Illustrated, the catalogue contains a Foreword by Sir Sydney Cockerell and a long Introduction by R. C. H. Briggs. So many notices, reviews, articles, and separate publications developed out of the exhibition that no attempt has been made to summarize them, but many are included in section 43.

13.10 *William Morris, Designer: An Exhibition of His Works at the Studio Gallery* [Catalogue of the Exhibition]. Isle of Wight: Bembridge School, 23 July to 4 August 1959.

With a brief introduction by John Hodgson, the Art Master of the school.

13.11 *William Morris and the Kelmscott Press* [Catalogue of the Exhibition]. Providence, Rhode Island: Brown University Library, 9 October to 31 December 1959.

Appended to the catalogue is an address by Philip C. Duschnes, given before the Friends of the Library, 7 December 1959. The catalogue contains sixteen plates.

13.12 *Morris and Company, 1861–1940: A Commemorative Centenary Exhibition* [Catalogue of the Exhibition]. London: The Arts Council of Great Britain, 1961.

The exhibition opened at the Victoria and Albert Museum on 11 April, the exact date of the founding of the Company. Other showings were held in the provinces through 30 December. The works on exhibit were selected and catalogued by Mrs. Barbara Morris, Assistant Keeper in the Department of Circulation, who also wrote the Introduction to the catalogue. A hand list of notices of this exhibition was prepared and circulated by the William Morris Society.

13.13 *Designs for Beauty and Use: An Exhibition Commemorating the Founding of Morris & Co. — 1861–1940* [Catalogue of the Exhibition]. New York: The William Morris Society (in cooperation with the Avery Architectural Library and the Department of Art History and Archaeology, Columbia University), October–[December] 1961.

For one notice see "Morris and Co." in "Talk of the Town," *New Yorker*, 25 November 1961, pp. 43–44.

13.14 *The Work of William Morris* [Catalogue of the Exhibition]. London: William Morris Society (at the Times Bookshop, Wigmore Street), 1962.

An exhibition of 76 items presenting Morris, the whole man, designed to complement the coverage and scope of *William Morris: Selected Writings and Designs*, edited by Asa Briggs and Graeme Shankland (London: Penguin Books, 1963). The catalogue was prepared by R. C. H. Briggs.

Section 14

DANTE GABRIEL ROSSETTI

14.1 *Works by the Old Masters, Including a Special Selection from the Works of John Linnell and Dante Gabriel Rossetti* [Catalogue of the Exhibition]. London: Royal Academy of Arts, 1883.

Eighty-four paintings by Rossetti were shown. For notices see 21.9, 21.10, 21.12 to 21.14, 21.16, 21.20. See also 31.12.

14.2 *Pictures, Drawings, Designs, and Studies by the Late Dante Gabriel Rossetti. Born 1828, Died 1882* [Catalogue of the Exhibition]. London: "The Rossetti Gallery." 1A Old Bond Street, 1883.

Most of the works exhibited were owned by Fanny Cornforth (Schott), by whose husband the exhibition was arranged and for whom the catalogue was printed. Thirty-one drawings, oils, and water colors and 27 photographs were shown. The catalogue contains an introductory sonnet on Rossetti. This exhibition seems to have been largely a commercial venture.

14.3 *Pictures, Drawings, Designs and Studies by the Late Dante Gabriel Rossetti* [Catalogue of the Exhibition]. London: Burlington Fine Arts Club, 1883.

The Introduction to the catalogue of this loan exhibition of 153 of Rossetti's works is by H. Virtue Tebbs. For notices see 21.7, 21.11, 21.12.

14.4 *Pictures by Living and Deceased Artists. Works by Italian Masters. Pictures by Dante Gabriel Rossetti, Ford Madox Brown, E. Burne-Jones, A.R.A., and R. Spencer Stanhope, etc. Lent by Major Jekyll, R. E.* [Catalogue of the Exhibition]. Nottingham: Museum and Art Gallery, 1892.

Listed in the Victoria and Albert hand list of exhibitions but unavailable for examination.

14.5 *Pictures Ancient and Modern by Artists of the British and Continental Schools, Including a Special Selection from the Works of Dante Gabriel Rossetti* [Catalogue of the Exhibition]. London: The New Gallery, 1897–1898.

Seventy-three works by Rossetti were shown, all from private collections. For one notice see 21.28.

14.6 *Platinotype Reproductions of Works of Sir Edward Burne-Jones, D. G. Rossetti, G. F. Watts, R.A., and Other Masters: Portraits by Various Painters and . . . Frederick Hollyer* [Catalogue of the Exhibition]. London: Egyptian Hall, Piccadilly [Dudley Galleries], 1902.

Listed in the Victoria and Albert hand list of exhibitions but unavailable for examination.

14.7 *D. G. Rossetti and Madox Brown: Family Portraits* [Catalogue of the Exhibition]. Manchester: City Art Gallery, July 1920.

Prefatory Note by Lawrence Haward.

14.8 *The Art Exhibition at the Central Library (Finchley Rd.) . . . Chiefly of Works by Hampstead Artists, with a Section Relating to Dante Gabriel Rossetti* [Catalogue of the Exhibition]. London: Borough of Hampstead Public Libraries, 18 June to 31 July 1928.

14.9 *The Rossetti Centenary Exhibition at the Central Public Library, Finchley Road, Hampstead* [Catalogue of the Exhibition]. London: Borough of Hampstead Public Libraries, 7 May to 31 July 1928.

A loan collection from Thomas J. Wise's Ashley Library, with notes condensed from

the *Ashley Catalogue.* The illustrated catalogue also contains a brief note on Rossetti
and on "Rossetti and Hampstead." A similar,
though much smaller, centenary exhibition
was held in the Chelsea Public Library and a
brief hand list was issued.

14.10 *Drawings and Paintings by Dante
Gabriel Rossetti, 1828–1882* [Catalogue of the
Exhibition]. London: Beaux Arts Gallery,
24 April to 31 May 1940.

Twenty-six pictures from private collections were shown in this exhibition. Speaking of the persistence with which spurious
"Rossettis" come on the market, Helen Rossetti Angeli notes: "Another set [of forger-
ies] was on exhibition in a West-End Gallery on the eve of World War II and, hap-
pening to meet in the rooms Sir Sydney
Cockerell, then Curator of the Cambridge
Fitzwilliam Museum, we both gazed at the
walls and at each other and stood aghast.
The exhibition included some genuine Rossetti drawings; Cockerell was instrumental in
getting the libellous plagiaries withdrawn."
(*Pre-Raphaelite Twilight,* 77.66, pp. 243–244)

14.11 *Dante Gabriel Rossetti, Pittore* [Cata-
logue of the Exhibition]. Vasto, Italy: Museo
Rossettiano, [November] 1954.

An exhibition of original works and photographs, the latter presented to the city by the
late Signora Olivia Rossetti Agresti. Eighty
photographs and 24 original works, mostly
drawings and studies, were shown. The catalogue contains a critical essay on Rossetti by
Florindo Ritucci-Chinni. The occasion for
this exhibition was the centenary commemoration in Vasto of the death of Gabriele Rossetti, for which a separate catalogue was issued, with various articles on the patriot-
poet, reproductions of three of Dante Rossetti's pictures, and an Introduction by Signora Agresti.

14.12 *Dante Gabriel Rossetti and His Circle: A Loan Exhibition of Paintings and Decorative Objects by the Pre-Raphaelites and
Their Friends* [Catalogue of the Exhibition].
Lawrence, Kansas: The University of Kansas
Museum of Art, 4 November to 15 December
1958.

For annotation see 16.23.

Section 15
FREDERIC JAMES SHIELDS

15.1 *The Shields Exhibition* [Catalogue of
the Exhibition]. Manchester: Royal Institute,
24 February to 3 March 1875.

One hundred and forty-six works exhibited.
Noticed in *Athenaeum,* no. 2470 (27 February 1875), p. 299.

15.2 *A Loan Collection of the Works of
Frederic Shields* [Catalogue of the Exhibi-
tion]. Manchester: The Brasenose Club, May
1889.

Printed for private circulation. Includes a
six-page section entitled "Shields' Autobiography" (see Ewart, 58.3) and selections from
Horace E. Scudder's article in the *Atlantic
Monthly* (58.1). Profusely illustrated with
very bad reproductions.

15.3 *Studies and Drawings by Frederic
Shields* [Catalogue of the Exhibition]. Manchester: Municipal School of Art, 1906.

Ninety-two works shown. Catalogue contains 29 plates.

15.4 *The Collected Works of Frederic J.
Shields* [Catalogue of the Exhibition]. Manchester: City Art Gallery, 1907.

With an Introduction by J. E. Phythian.

15.5 *The Memorial Exhibition of Some of
the Works of Frederic J. Shields, A.R.W.S.*
[Catalogue of the Exhibition]. London: The
Alpine Club Gallery, 30 September to 28 October 1911.

With a Foreword by Ernestine Mills.

General Exhibitions

Section 16

PRE-RAPHAELITE ARTISTS

16.1 [Pre-Raphaelite Exhibition]. [Catalogue of the Exhibition]. London: No. 4, Russell Place, Fitzroy Square, 1857.

The first exhibition devoted entirely to the Pre-Raphaelites. The catalogue, which is merely a "List of Pictures on View," numbers 72 exhibited works. Noticed in the *Athenaeum*, no. 1550 (11 July 1857), p. 886; and by Coventry Patmore (21.1). For a general discussion of this exhibition see Survey, pp. 14–15.

16.2 [The Pre-Raphaelites] *Special Loan Collection of Modern Pictures in Oil and Water Colours* [Catalogue of the Exhibition]. Birmingham: City Museum and Art Gallery, 1891.

Catalogue compiled by Whitworth Wallis and Arthur B. Chamberlain. For notices see "Pictures at Birmingham," *Athenaeum*, no. 3337 (16 October 1891), p. 491; and J. M. Gray (21.22). For Morris' address on the Pre-Raphaelite painters given during the showing of the exhibition see 75.14.

16.3 *Examples of the English Pre-Raphaelite School of Painters, Including Rossetti, Burne-Jones, Madox Brown and Others, together with a Collection of the Works of William Blake* [Catalogue of the Exhibition]. Philadelphia: The Academy of the Fine Arts, 8 December 1892.

This exhibition contained over 100 catalogued items. A few Pre-Raphaelite water colors were lent by Charles Eliot Norton, and Charles L. Hutchinson, the President of the Chicago Art Institute, lent his version of Rossetti's *Beata Beatrix*. Most of the items came from Bancroft's collection (see 3.1). Besides the actual pictures exhibited, Holyer photographs of Rossetti's principal works, unavailable in the United States, were shown. The Blake items were borrowed from the collection of Herbert H. Gilchrist. The exhibition was also shown in New York at the Century Club from 2–9 January 1893. See 21.23.

16.4 *A Pre-Raphaelite Collection: D. G. Rossetti, Ford Madox Brown, Holman Hunt, Burne-Jones, Albert Moore, Simeon Solomon, Inchbold, etc.* [Catalogue of the Exhibition]. London: The Goupil Gallery, June and July 1896.

Exhibition of Pre-Raphaelite pictures from the collection of James Leathart. The introductory note on the Pre-Raphaelite pictures written by William Michael Rossetti, who also published a description of the collection in the *Art Journal* (see 6.5). For one notice of this exhibition see 21.24. The catalogue is illustrated, and most of the pictures shown were for sale.

16.5 *Loan Exhibition of Pictures* [by the Pre-Raphaelites]. [Catalogue of the Exhibition]. London: Leighton House, July 1902.

With an introductory "Family Note" by William Michael Rossetti. Most of the works exhibited were by Rossetti, Holman Hunt, John Hancock, Madox Brown, H. T. Dunn, Elizabeth Siddal, and Lucy Rossetti, and were lent by William Michael Rossetti. A special selection of photographs from Rossetti's paintings, lent by Frederick Hollyer, was also included. The "Large Studio" was given over to the works of Watts and Leighton.

16.6 *The Combe Bequest: Pictures and Drawings of the English Pre-Raphaelite and Allied Schools* [Catalogue of the Exhibition]. Oxford: The Ashmolean Museum, 1909.

The original Combe Bequest was made in 1893, and other items were purchased at Mrs. Combe's sale in the following year. The Burne-Jones studies were presented by Ingram Bywater in 1901. Five items, including the cabinet Burne-Jones gave to Morris as a wedding present (now in the Victoria

and Albert Museum), were lent by Mrs.
Morris. Items presented by other donors were
also exhibited, such as the two pictures of
the graves of Keats and Shelley (recently
shown at the Royal Academy *Italian Art and
Britain* exhibition, 1960) which were given
to the Ashmolean by Alice Boyd in 1893.
Artists represented in the exhibition, the
catalogue of which served as both a guide to
the exhibition and a handbook of the permanent collection, were Rossetti, Bell Scott,
Millais, Burne-Jones, Woolner, Hughes,
Holman Hunt, C. A. Collins, and J. F.
Lewis. For discussion of the Ashmolean
collection see 2.8.

16.7 *Loan Exhibition of Works by Ford
Madox Brown and the Pre-Raphaelites*
[Catalogue of the Exhibition]. Manchester:
City Art Gallery, Autumn (14 September to
30 November) 1911.

Introduction by J. Ernest Phythian. One of
the most extensive Pre-Raphaelite loan exhibitions ever held. Two complete rooms (127
items) were devoted to Ford Madox Brown.
In addition, 68 works of Rossetti, 55 of Millais, 14 of Holman Hunt, 12 of Arthur
Hughes, and many works of other Pre-Raphaelites, including Burne-Jones and Sandys,
were shown. The catalogue also contains
Brown's descriptions of his twelve mural
paintings in the Manchester Town Hall (see
41.3). Illustrated.

16.8 *Works by the English Pre-Raphaelite
Painters Lent by the Art Gallery Committee
of the Birmingham Corporation* [Catalogue
of the Exhibition]. London: National Gallery, Millbank (The Tate Gallery), December 1911 to March 1912.

For notices see 21.34 and 21.35.

16.9 *Works by Pre-Raphaelite Painters from
Collections in Lancashire* [Catalogue of the
Exhibition]. London: National Gallery, Millbank (The Tate Gallery), July-September
1913.

16.10 *Works by Pre-Raphaelite Painters
from Collections in Lancashire Forming a
Portion of Those Recently Exhibited at the
National Gallery, British Art, with Certain
Additions* [Catalogue of the Exhibition].

Bath: Victoria Art Gallery, 10 November to
6 December 1913.

16.11 *A Series of Drawings, "Rossetti and
His Friends" by Max Beerbohm . . . Drawings and Paintings by the Pre-Raphaelites and
Others* [Catalogue of the Exhibition]. London: Leicester Galleries, September 1921.

16.12 *Samuel Bancroft, Jr., Collection of
English Pre-Raphaelite Paintings* [Catalogue
of the Exhibition]. Wilmington, Delaware:
The Wilmington Society of the Fine Arts,
13 April to 15 May 1934.

Since 1938, the Bancroft English Pre-Raphaelite Collection has been on permanent
exhibition (for description see 3.1), For one
notice of this exhibition see 21.42.

16.13 *Paintings and Drawings of the Pre-
Raphaelites and Their Circle* [Catalogue of
the Exhibition]. Cambridge, Massachusetts:
William Hayes Fogg Museum of Art, Harvard University, 8 April to 1 June 1946.

With a Preface by Arthur Pope, an Introduction by Agnes Mongan on the history of
Pre-Raphaelitism, and an important technical
"Note on the Methods and Materials of the
Pre-Raphaelite Painters" (see 76.10) by Rich-
ard D. Buck. The catalogue, prepared by
Mary Wadsworth and others, contains 21
plates. Artists represented were Rossetti,
Brown, Burne-Jones, Hunt, Albert Moore,
Solomon, Stevens, and Watts. Most of the
works shown belong to the Winthrop Col-
lection (see 3.3). Noticed in *Art News*
(21.45) and *Time* (21.44). For other notices
see *Studio*, CXXXII (December 1946), 192;
Art Digest, XX (15 May 1946), 13; *College
Art Journal*, V (May 1946), 376; *Arts*, 19
July 1946, p. 3.

16.14 *"The Pre-Raphaelite Brotherhood"*
(*1848–1862*) [Catalogue of the Exhibition].
Birmingham: City Museum and Art Gallery,
7 June to 27 July 1947.

With an Introduction by Mary Woodall
and biographical notes on the artists shown.
In addition to the members of the Brotherhood, the following artists were included in
the exhibition: Boyce, Brett, Brown, Burton,
Calderon, Collins, Deverell, Dyce, Hughes,
Morris, Sandys, Seddon (both John and

Thomas), Elizabeth Siddal, Smetham, Wallis, Webb, and Windus. A number of special lectures were given in conjunction with the exhibition. For notices see 21.46 to 21.49.

16.15 *Pre-Raphaelite Drawings* [Catalogue of the Exhibition]. London: Roland, Browse and Delbanco, September 1947.

All the pictures exhibited were on loan from the City Museum and Art Gallery, Birmingham. Introduction reprinted from 16.14. For one notice see 21.50.

16.16 *The Pre-Raphaelite Brotherhood, 1848–1948, A Centenary Exhibition* [Catalogue of the Exhibition]. London: National Gallery, Millbank (The Tate Gallery), September 1948.

The catalogue was issued in a limited number on large paper, printed by Guido Morris; there was also a broadside giving a brief description of the works, all of which are in the permanent collection of the Tate. The members of the later movement, including Burne-Jones, were not included in this exhibition. For notices see 21.51, 21.55, and 21.56.

16.17 *Centenary Exhibition of Works by the Pre-Raphaelites — Their Friends and Followers* [Catalogue of the Exhibition]. Port Sunlight: The Lady Lever Art Gallery, 14 June to 29 August 1948.

With a brief introduction. The nucleus of the exhibition was the pictures from the Lady Lever collection, but a large number were on loan, and in all nearly 200 works were exhibited. Among the "friends" whose works were represented were many figures only casually related to the Pre-Raphaelite Movement: H. H. Emmerson, W. P. Frith, T. S. Good, Edward Lear, and James Tissot.

16.18 *Pre-Raphaelite Masterpieces, 1848–1862* [Catalogue of the Exhibition]. Manchester: City Art Gallery, 14 June to 8 August 1948.

Introduction by David Baxandall. A small (22 works) but important exhibition because of its emphasis on the earliest Pre-Raphaelite pictures.

16.19 *The Pre-Raphaelites: A Loan Exhibition of Their Paintings and Drawings Held in the Centenary Year of the Foundation of the Brotherhood* [Catalogue of the Exhibition]. London: Whitechapel Art Gallery, 8 April to 12 May 1948.

Introduction and catalogue of the pictures by John Gere. Many works by the associates of the movement — Deverell, Hughes, Elizabeth Siddal, Smetham, Wallis, and Simeon Solomon — were included. The sections on Rossetti and Millais were particularly strong. Noticed in *Times*, no. 51,041 (9 April 1948), p. 6; and in 21.52 to 21.54.

16.20 *Paintings and Drawings by the Pre-Raphaelites and Their Followers* [Catalogue of the Exhibition]. Bournemouth: Russell-Cotes Art Gallery, 4 June to 7 August 1951.

Organized for the Bournemouth and Wessex Festival. Note and Introduction by Carlos Peacock. Included among the "followers" of the movement were Samuel Butler and W. P. Frith. Burne-Jones' painting, however, is not included because it "tends . . . merely to conjure up the wan ghost of Pre-Raphaelitism under the necromantic influence of Rossetti." In all, 56 oil paintings and fifty water colors and drawings were exhibited.

16.21 *Pre-Raphaelite Drawings and Watercolours* [Catalogue of the Exhibition]. London: The Arts Council of Great Britain, 1953.

This exhibition, originally intended for showing at Cambridge, was also shown at the National Museum of Wales. Introduction and catalogue by John Commander.

16.22 *Some Pre-Raphaelite Paintings and Drawings* [Catalogue of the Exhibition]. Cardiff: The Arts Council of Great Britain, Welsh Committee, July–August, October 1955.

Shown at both the National Library of Wales, Aberystwyth, and at the Glynn Vivian Art Gallery, Swansea. The catalogue contains a brief introduction and four illustrations. Seventy-three works were exhibited.

16.23 *Dante Gabriel Rossetti and His Circle: A Loan Exhibition of Paintings, Drawings, and Decorative Objects by the Pre-Raphaelites and Their Friends* [Catalogue of the Exhibition]. Lawrence, Kansas: The University of Kansas Museum of Art, 4 November to 15 December 1958.

An exhibition commemorating the acquisition of Rossetti's *La Pia* by the University of Kansas Museum of Art (see W. D. Paden's monograph on the picture, 31.34). For one notice of the exhibition see 21.58.

16.24 *The Pre-Raphaelites and Their Contemporaries. Paintings, Drawings and Watercolours.* [Catalogue of the Exhibition]. London: Maas Gallery (15a Clifford Street), 13 November to 8 December 1961.

In this interesting exhibition there were 126 drawings and water colors and fourteen paintings, mostly from private collections, by the major and minor Pre-Raphaelites and by many artists totally outside the movement.

This exhibition and its successor (16.26) stimulated considerable interest and wide notice in the press. Robin Ironside (*Sunday Times*, 12 November 1961) observed: "Pre-Raphaelite art has a specifically English fragrance which, in so far as it may evoke in us a proprietary affection unrelated to its aesthetic quality, may account for the relative immunity of Pre-Raphaelite painters to the vicissitudes of taste."

16.25 *Pre-Raphaelite Art. Paintings, Drawings, Engravings, Sculpture, Tapestries, Chintzes, Wallpapers. An Exhibition Arranged by the State Art Galleries of Australia* [Catalogue of the Exhibition]. Sydney, March–October 1962.

A traveling exhibition, the first of the Pre-Raphaelites to be held in Australia. Ninety-three items were exhibited, emphasis being given to examples of Pre-Raphaelite art in Australian collections. Included among the artists represented were Edward La Trobe Bateman, Brown, Burne-Jones, Deverell, Hughes, Holman Hunt, Millais, Morris, Rossetti, Ruskin, Sandys, Bernhard Smith, J. M. Strudwick, and Thomas Woolner. The catalogue includes eighteen plates, sixteen of which reproduce works in the Australian collections, including a color reproduction of

Hughes's *Fair Rosamund*. The Introduction to the catalogue is by Daniel Thomas.

16.26 *The Pre-Raphaelites and Their Contemporaries. Paintings, Drawings and Water-colours. Second Exhibition* [Catalogue of the Exhibition]. London: Maas Gallery, 5–30 November 1962.

Including 137 items of minor importance but of distinct interest by the Pre-Raphaelites and their contemporaries.

16.27 *The Pre-Raphaelites: A Loan Exhibition of Paintings and Drawings by Members of the Pre-Raphaelite Brotherhood and Their Associates* [Catalogue of the Exhibition]. Indianapolis: Herron Museum of Art, 16 February — 22 March 1964; New York: Gallery of Modern Art, Including the Huntington Hartford Collection, 27 April — 31 May 1964.

An exhibition of 84 pictures and drawings by ten Pre-Raphaelite artists (including William J. Webbe) from public and private collections in the United States and Canada. The catalogue, a handsome one with reproductions of each of the pictures shown, contains an Introduction by Curtis G. Coley and extensive notes on each item exhibited. Presented in conjunction with the Herron showing was "An Exhibition of Literary Material Relating to the Pre-Raphaelites," organized by *Victorian Studies*, Indiana University, for which a four-page brochure listing exhibited items was issued. For one notice see "Raphael Rejected," *Time*, LXXXIII (14 February 1964), 46 (Canadian Edition); with six reproductions in color.

16.28 *Pre-Raphaelites — Art Nouveau: Exhibition of Drawings and Water-colours* [Catalogue of the Exhibition]. London: Maas Gallery, 22 June 1964.

This illustrated catalogue of 150 exhibited items contains an introductory note by Mario Amaya. Burne-Jones, Rossetti, Solomon, and Ruskin — constituting two-fifths of the exhibition — are set against Charles Conder and Edmund Dulac, the major representatives of Art Nouveau here shown.

Section 17

MINOR PRE-RAPHAELITE ARTISTS

17.1 [Special Exhibition of Thomas Seddon's Eastern Subjects]. [Catalogue of the Exhibition]. London: The Society of Arts, May 1857.

For additional information see 57.1. The exhibition was noticed in the *Spectator*, XXX, no. 1506 (9 May 1857), 503. A Committee and Subscription was organized to purchase Seddon's *Jerusalem and the Valley of Jehoshaphat* for the National Gallery, and a circular was issued; but no copy of the catalogue has been located.

17.2 *William Bell Scott's Eight Pictures Illustrative of the History of the English Border, Painted for Sir W. C. Trevelyan, Bart.'s Hall, at Wallington* [Catalogue of the Exhibition]. London: French Gallery, 1861.

The catalogue consists primarily of Scott's descriptions of the pictures. See also 56.6.

17.3 *Three Months on the Scottish Coast: A Series of Sketches and Pictures Painted During the Summer of the Present Year, Accompanied by an Explanatory Essay by John Brett* [Catalogue of the Exhibition]. London: Fine Art Society, 1886.

Another exhibition of Brett's landscapes and seascapes was held at the Fine Art Society in 1893. For a notice of this later exhibition, no catalogue of which has been located, see *Athenaeum*, no. 3424 (10 June 1893), p. 740.

17.4 *Studies of the Late Thomas Woolner, R.A.* [Catalogue of the Exhibition]. London: 29 Welbeck Street, 15 February to [8] March 1893.

Two hundred and eighteen plaster and metal busts, statues, medallions, and reliefs were exhibited.

17.5 *Loan Collection by the Late George Price Boyce* [Catalogue of the Exhibition]. London: Old Water-Colour Society, 1898–1899.

Boyce's work occupied only a small part of this winter exhibition. For another listing of Boyce's pictures in this exhibition see 72.8.

17.6 *Paintings and Drawings by the Late Simeon Solomon* [Catalogue of the Exhibition]. London: The Baille Gallery, 9 December 1905 to 27 January 1906.

Shown were 122 works by Solomon. A collection of sixteen of Solomon's works was shown in the *Old Masters and Deceased Masters of the British School* exhibition at the Royal Academy in 1906.

17.7 *Pictures and Drawings by the Late R. Spencer Stanhope* [Catalogue of the Exhibition]. London: Carfax and Co., March 1909.

Introduction and brief biographical note by William De Morgan. Only thirty works exhibited.

Section 18

REPRESENTATIVE WORKS
BY PRE-RAPHAELITE ARTISTS

18.1 [Catalogue of the Exhibition]. London: The Association for Promoting the Free Exhibition of Modern Art, 1849, 1850.

Both Rossetti and Ford Madox Brown contributed to this exhibition: Rossetti, *The Girlhood of Mary Virgin* (no. 368); Brown, *Portrait of a French Artist* (no. 160) and *King Lear* (no. 82). Special interest is attached to the catalogue because it contains Rossetti's sonnet "This is that Blessed Mary, Pre-elect," his first published poem apart from *Sir Hugh the Heron* (23.1). In 1850, Rossetti contributed *Ecce Ancilla Domini* to the Free Exhibition. Notices of Rossetti's *The Girlhood of Mary Virgin* appeared in the following journals: *Athenaeum*, no. 1191 (7 April 1849), p. 362; *Builder*, VII, no. 321 (31 March 1849), 145; *Literary Gazette and*

Belles Lettres Journal, no. 1680 (31 March 1849), p. 239; *Art Journal*, XI (April 1849), 147; *Observer*, Supplement, 8–9 April 1849, p. 1; *Morning Chronicle*, no. 24,782 (26 March 1849), p. 5. *Ecce Ancilla Domini* elicited the following notices: *Builder*, VIII, no. 376 (20 April 1850), 184; *Athenaeum*, no. 1173 (20 April 1850), p. 424; *Observer*, 14 April 1850, p. 5; *Critic*, X (1 July 1850), 334–335; *Times*, no. 20,463 (15 April 1850), p. 5. For exhibitions of the other Pre-Raphaelites during 1849–1850, the catalogues of the Royal Academy should be consulted, together with Ruskin's *Academy Notes* (45.1). See also 71.2.

18.2 *L'Exposition universelle* [Catalogue of the Exhibition]. Paris, 1855.

The English Pre-Raphaelites were first seen in France during this exhibition. The other two international or universal exhibitions to which the Pre-Raphaelites made significant contributions were those of 1867 and 1878. For a thorough treatment of the French reaction to Pre-Raphaelitism see 78.25.

18.3 *The Art Treasures of the United Kingdom* [Catalogue of the Exhibition]. Manchester, 1857.

One of the most important exhibitions of the 19th century. Most of the Pre-Raphaelites and their associates sent pictures to it — Rossetti of course did not — and a large number of the most famous early pictures of the movement were shown: *Convent Thoughts, Burd Helen, The Death of Chatterton, April Love*, and *Kit's Writing Lesson*. Millais contributed only *Autumn Leaves*, but Holman Hunt was represented by five of his better known works. For J. B. Waring's parody of Pre-Raphaelite pictures in this exhibition see 82.5. For one notice see Prosper Mérimée (21.2).

18.4 [Loan Exhibition of British Art]. [Catalogue of the Exhibition]. New York: National Academy of Design, 1857.

For details of this exhibition see *Præraphaelite Diaries and Letters* (72.7) and the chapter "British Pre-Raphaelite Art in America: 1857 Exhibition" in Dickason (80.8). Announcements and notices of the exhibition appeared in *Crayon* (80.1), IV (August

1857), 251; (September 1857), 280; (October 1857), 314–315; (November 1857), 343–344. A brief abstract of the contributors to this exhibition is in the manuscript collection of the Yale University Library (see 3.9). No catalogue of this exhibition has been located.

18.5 *International Exhibition*. [Catalogue of the Exhibition]. London, 1862.

An extremely important exhibition for Pre-Raphaelite participation. Besides the exhibited pictures, the 1862 International attracted significant groups of sculpture from Munro and Woolner. More important, it was at this exhibition that the firm of Morris and Company first attracted public notice. The official handbook of this International was prepared by Francis Turner Palgrave, as was the official catalogue.

18.6 *Royal Jubilee Exhibition* [Catalogue of the Exhibition]. Manchester, 1887.

Madox Brown, Burne-Jones, Millais, and Holman Hunt were the major artists exhibiting, but most of the minor Pre-Raphaelites, including Simeon Solomon, were represented. Twenty pictures by Rossetti in private collections were also exhibited.

18.7 *International Exhibition: A Loan Exhibition of Painting and Sculpture* [Catalogue of the Exhibition]. Glasgow, 1888.

For Pre-Raphaelite pictures in this exhibition see Henley (21.21). At a later International Exhibition at Glasgow (1901), the Pre-Raphaelites were also represented. See D. S. Riddoch (21.31).

18.8 *British Art Fifty Years Ago* [Catalogue of the Exhibition]. London: Whitechapel Art Gallery, 1905.

In large part a Pre-Raphaelite exhibition, with a special section devoted to the "Liverpool School." In addition to commentaries on individual pictures, the catalogue contains a long introduction treating various phases of the Pre-Raphaelite Movement, including book illustration. Five hundred and twenty works were exhibited, many of which were reproduced in the picture book of the exhibition. A great many major and minor Pre-Raphaelite paintings were also shown in the Spring Exhibition at Whitechapel in 1901.

18.9 *The Historical Exhibition of Liverpool Art* [Catalogue of the Exhibition]. Liverpool: Walker Art Gallery, 23 May to 4 July 1908.

Included 45 works by W. L. Windus. Another historical exhibition of works exhibited at the Liverpool Academy of Arts, 1810–1867 was held at the Walker Art Gallery between 3 June and 3 July 1960.

18.10 *A Century of Art, 1810–1910* [Catalogue of the Exhibition]. London: Grafton Gallery, 1911.

See Charles Ricketts' pamphlet (21.33).

18.11 *International Fine Arts Exhibition* [Catalogue of the Exhibition]. Rome, 1911.

For one notice of this exhibition, including a discussion of Pre-Raphaelite pictures shown, see 21.36.

18.12 *Paintings and Drawings of the 1860 Period* [Catalogue of the Exhibition]. London: National Gallery, Millbank (The Tate Gallery), 27 April to 29 July 1923.

A loan exhibition with a strong Pre-Raphaelite representation. For one notice see 21.37.

18.13 *Book Illustration of the Sixties* [Catalogue of the Exhibition]. London: National Gallery, Millbank (The Tate Gallery), 18 January to 31 December 1923.

Identical with the Whitechapel exhibition the following year. Includes all the Pre-Raphaelite illustrators as well as many who do not belong to the group.

18.14 *Exposition rétrospective de peinture anglaise (XVIIIᵉ et XIXᵉ siècles)* [Catalogue of the Exhibition]. Bruxelles: Musée Moderne, 12 October to 1 December 1929.

Foreword by Baron Moncheur. Catalogue includes three brief prefatory articles on English art: "L'École de peinture anglaise" by Charles J. Holme; "Les Aquarelles anglaises" by Martin Hardie; and "William Blake et les Pré-Raphaélites" by Charles Aitken. Pre-Raphaelite artists represented were Brett, Madox Brown, Burne-Jones, Burton, Hughes, Hunt, Millais, Morris, J. F. Lewis, Sandys, Stanhope, and Rossetti. Of 206 works exhibited, 46 were by the Pre-Raphaelites.

18.15 *British Art c.1000–1860* [Catalogue of the Exhibition]. London: Royal Academy of Arts, 6 January to 17 March 1934.

Gallery IX, XIXth Century Painting, was given over to the Pre-Raphaelites. See the notice by Douglas P. Bliss (21.41) dealing with changes in public taste as exemplified by this exhibition.

18.16 *200 Years of British Art* [Catalogue of the Exhibition]. Amsterdam, 1936.

18.17 *British Art* [Catalogue of the Exhibition]. Paris, 1937.

18.18 *The First Hundred Years of the Royal Academy, 1769–1868* [Catalogue of the Exhibition]. London: Royal Academy of Arts, 1951–1952.

Gallery IX devoted to the Pre-Raphaelites.

18.19 *Victorian and Edwardian Decorative Arts* [Catalogue of the Exhibition]. London: Victoria and Albert Museum, 1952.

An extremely important exhibition on the arts and crafts. Of special interest is section I, "William Morris and His Associates." The exhibition was organized by the late Peter Floud.

18.20 *Masters of British Painting 1800–1850* [Catalogue of the Exhibition]. New York: Museum of Modern Art, 1956–1957.

A traveling exhibition, shown in New York, St. Louis, and California. Pre-Raphaelites represented were Rossetti, Madox Brown, Holman Hunt, and Millais.

18.21 *Exhibition of Victorian Painting* [Catalogue of the Exhibition]. Nottingham: University Art Gallery, 1959.

Foreword by Alastair Smart. The Introduction, by John Woodward, contains a brief section on the Pre-Raphaelites. Included were Brett, Brown, Burne-Jones, Collinson, Hunt, J. F. Lewis, Millais, Wallis, and Rossetti.

18.22 *British Art, 1700–1960* [Catalogue of the Exhibition]. Leningrad: The Hermitage, 1960.

18.23 *Loan Exhibition of Victorian Painting, 1837–1887: In Aid of the Victorian*

Society [Catalogue of the Exhibition]. London: Thomas Agnew & Sons, 22 November to 16 December 1961.

The pictures exhibited came mainly from private collections. Catalogue contains a Foreword by D. E. L. Joll and an Introduction by Graham Reynolds. Eighteen Pre-Raphaelite pictures were included in the exhibition, by Brett, Thomas Seddon, Collinson, Millais, Brown, Hunt, Burne-Jones, Rossetti, Sandys, and Hughes. Also exhibited (for the first time since 1860) was Florence Claxton's satiric picture, *The Choice of Paris: An Idyll* (see 82.3).

Sales

Section 19

AUCTION SALES

19.1 *The Highly Important Collection of English Pictures and Drawings Formed by . . . Thomas E. Plint . . .* [Catalogue of the Sale]. London: Christie's, 7 March 1862.

The first major Pre-Raphaelite sale. See the discussions in W. Roberts, *Memorials of Christie's* (London: Bell, 1897), vol. I, 196–198; and in H. C. Marillier, *Christie's, 1766–1925* (London: Constable, 1926), pp. 40–41. See also the notice in the *Art Journal*, XXIV (April 1862), 105–106.

19.2 *16, Cheyne Walk, Chelsea: The Valuable Contents of the Residence of Dante Gabriel Rossetti . . .* [Catalogue of the Sale]. London: T. G. Wharton, Martin and Co., 5–7 July 1882.

There are two editions of this catalogue. Sale noticed in *Academy*, XXII, no. 532 (15 July 1882), 49.

19.3 *The Remaining Works of the Painter and Poet, Dante Gabriel Rossetti . . .* [Catalogue of the Sale]. London: Christie's, 12 May 1883.

One of the most important of all Pre-Raphaelite sale catalogues; an indispensable source for authenticating many of Rossetti's works, especially later and minor drawings. There are 211 items in all, "comprising a few specimens in oil and water colour and numerous works in crayons, coloured chalks, pen and ink, india ink, pencil, &c." Sale noticed in *Academy*, XXIII, no. 576 (19 May 1883), 355.

19.4 *The Important Collection of Pictures in Oil and Drawings in Water Colours Formed by . . . William Graham . . .* [Catalogue of the Sale]. London: Christie's, 2, 3 April 1886.

The sale continued for three more days, but most of the Pre-Raphaelite pictures — largely by Millais, Rossetti, and Burne-Jones — appear in the first two days. With 19.1 and 19.8, the sale of the Graham collection is one of the most important Pre-Raphaelite sales. For a description see Roberts, vol. II, 86–90. The following year (30 April 1887) Christie's offered the collection of John Graham of Skelmorlie Castle, Ayrshire, a relation of William Graham and also a Pre-Raphaelite patron, though on a much smaller scale.

19.5 *The Valuable Collection of Water Colour Drawings of L. R. Valpy . . .* [Catalogue of the Sale]. London: Christie's, 26 May 1888.

Many Pre-Raphaelite pictures included in the sale: five by Burne-Jones and seven by Rossetti, including *La Pia* (crayon), *Pandora*, and *Beata Beatrix*. In the same year (28 April 1888) Christie's offered the interesting collection of W. A. Turner, which contained an impressive number of water colors and oils by Madox Brown, Rossetti, and Burne-Jones, as well as representative works by Calderon, Prinsep, and Spencer Stanhope.

19.6 *The Property of Charles A. Howell* [Catalogue of the Sale]. London: Christie's, 13–15 November 1890.

For a detailed discussion of this sensational sale, at which a large number of Pre-Raphaelite items turned up, see the chapter, "Post-Obit Sale," in H. R. Angeli's *Pre-Raphaelite Twilight* (77.66), pp. 15–22. Another sale of *Books and Manuscripts . . . Including Volumes of Letters and Sketches by D. G. Rossetti,* at Sotheby's, 26 November 1890, included four lots of literary notebooks, artistic sketchbooks, and scrapbooks. From the descriptions in the catalogue, these items are of major importance, but they seem, subsequent to the sale, to have dropped from sight.

19.7 *The Valuable Collection of Modern Pictures and Water Colour Drawings of James Anderson Rose* [Catalogue of the Sale]. London: Christie's, 5 May 1891.

This collection, the property of Rossetti's solicitor, included an interesting group of drawings in pen and ink by Sandys, Madox Brown's *Romeo and Juliet,* one Thomas Seddon picture, and five Rossetti water colors. Of particular interest in the collection were eight illustrations by Rossetti for Christina's poetry.

19.8 *Ancient and Modern Pictures of Frederick Richards Leyland . . .* [Catalogue of the Sale]. London: Christie's, 28 May 1892.

Frederick Leyland's Pre-Raphaelite collection at 49 Prince's Gate (see 6.2) was one of the most impressive collections ever formed. Included in his sale were 25 drawings by Rossetti, two by Sandys, and four by Elizabeth Siddal. More important, however, were the paintings: thirteen by Rossetti, including *The Loving Cup, Found, Lady Lilith,* and *The Blessed Damozel;* four by Madox Brown; one by Sandys; one by Millais (*The Eve of St. Agnes*); *Burd Helen, Too Late,* and one other by Windus; Watts' portrait of Rossetti; and a vast number of works by Burne-Jones.

19.9 *Engravings and Drawings, the Property of the Late William Bell Scott . . .* [Catalogue of the Sale]. London: Sotheby's, 14 July 1892.

As an associate of the Pre-Raphaelites, Scott possessed many items of considerable interest: the unique (according to Scott) impression of Millais' etching for Rossetti's "St. Agnes of Intercession" (see 90.1), intended for the fifth number of *The Germ;* Rossetti's *The Laboratory,* Deverell's *Twelfth Night,* and three oils by Alice Boyd. Scott also had

a number of miscellaneous drawings and other works by Millais, Barbara Bodichon, Simeon Solomon, and Elizabeth Siddal. Many of Scott's personal possessions, including furniture, oil and water color paintings, autographs, etc. were sold at Newcastle by Mr. Muras in 1864. His collection of engravings and etchings was sold at Sotheby's, 20 to 24 April 1885. His household furnishings from No. 92 Cheyne Walk, Chelsea, were auctioned by Williamson's, 5 December 1889; a portion of his library was sold by Sotheby's, 7 to 8 March 1890. For other Scott material recently sold see 19.38. See also 4.4 for Scott items still at Penkill Castle.

19.10 *The Valuable Contents of the Residence of Ford Madox Brown . . .* [Catalogue of the Sale]. London: T. G. Wharton, Martin and Co., 29–31 May 1894.

A most valuable catalogue, including pictures, cartoons, furniture, books (presentation copies), photographs, and miscellaneous items. A number of studies by Oliver Madox Brown were also included in the sale.

19.11 *The Choice Collection of Modern Pictures and Water-Colour Drawings Formed by Frederick Craven . . .* [Catalogue of the Sale]. London: Christie's, 18 May 1895.

Works by Rossetti, Burne-Jones, and Madox Brown were included in the sale.

19.12 *The Remaining Works and the Collection of Ancient and Modern Pictures and Water-Colour Drawings of . . . G. P. Boyce . . .* [Catalogue of the Sale]. London: Christie's, 1–3 July 1897.

An important sale, including besides Boyce's own works 21 by Rossetti, three by Burne-Jones, two by Millais, and one each by Wallis and Hughes.

19.13 *Ancient and Modern Pictures and Remaining Works of Sir John Everett Millais . . .* [Catalogue of the Sale]. London: Christie's, 1 May 1897.

Seven of Millais' pictures, all late ones, were included in this sale. In another remaining works sale held at Christie's in the following year (2 July 1898), six additional pictures and five drawings by Millais were sold, together with miscellaneous works by other artists, including one work by Rossetti.

19.14 *Modern Artist's Proof Engravings, After his Own Works: The Property of Sir J. E. Millais . . .* [Catalogue of the Sale]. London: Christie's, 21 March 1898.

A similar sale of proof engravings of Millais' works was offered by Christie's on 17 May 1897.

19.15 *The Highly Important Collection of Ancient and Modern Pictures and Water-Colour Drawings of Joseph Ruston . . .* [Catalogue of the Sale]. London: Christie's, 21 May 1898.

Containing a small but select number of works by Rossetti and Burne-Jones.

19.16 *Remaining Works of . . . Sir Edward Burne-Jones . . .* [Catalogue of the Sale]. London: Christie's, 16, 18 July 1898.

A large sale including 206 drawings, pastels, water colors, chalks, and oils. See also the later remaining works sale (19.22).

19.17 *The Collection of Ancient and Modern Pictures and Water-Colour Drawings of John Bibby . . .* [Catalogue of the Sale]. London: Christie's, 3 June 1899.

This sale included seven Rossetti drawings, two water colors by Madox Brown, and three works by Arthur Hughes. Among the paintings offered were five by Windus, one by Henry Wallis, Hughes' *Ophelia* (the large version now in the City Art Gallery, Manchester), Rossetti's *La Pia* (from the Leyland collection), and a head listed simply "Pre-Raphaelite School."

19.18 *The Collection of Drawings and Pictures of H. Virtue Tebbs . . .* [Catalogue of the Sale]. London: Christie's, 10 March 1900.

A number of drawings by Boyce, Millais, Bell Scott, and Rossetti made up this sale, together with three pictures by Ford Madox Brown: *Windermere, Carrying Corn,* and a study of a pony.

19.19 *The Collection of Important Modern Pictures and Water-Colour Drawings of Walter Dunlop . . .* [Catalogue of the Sale]. London: Christie's, 12 March 1904.

Works by Hughes, Rossetti, and Millais were included in the sale.

19.20 *The Library of Algernon Charles Swinburne* [Catalogue of the Sale]. London: Sotheby's, 19–21 June 1916.

19.21 *Art Objects Belonging to Murray Marks* [Catalogue of the Sale]. London: Christie's, 2 July 1916.

For other sales of materials belonging to Murray Marks, who owned many Pre-Raphaelite objects, see 86.14, p. 200.

19.22 *The Remaining Works of the Late Sir Edward Burne-Jones . . . Consisting of Pictures, Drawings, Pastels, and Studies, Together with Many Unfinished Paintings* [Catalogue of the Sale]. London: Christie's, 5 June 1919.

Eighty-five of the original drawings for the Kelmscott *Chaucer* were sold at Sotheby's on 8 July 1919. See 2.4.

19.23 *Valuable Manuscripts and Printed Books, the Property of Charles Fairfax Murray* [Catalogue of the Sale]. London: Sotheby's, 7 July 1919.

Sale included an almost complete presentation set of Kelmscott Press books (William Morris to Edward Burne-Jones), the property of Philip Burne-Jones. See also the catalogue, *A Further Portion of the Valuable Library Collected by the Late Charles Fairfax Murray* (London: Sotheby's, 17 July 1922).

19.24 *The Library of the Late H. Buxton Forman* [Catalogue of the Sales]. New York: Anderson Galleries, no. 1480, 15–17 March 1920; no. 1493, 26–28 April 1920.

Over 1000 lots, including many manuscripts and association items of the Pre-Raphaelites, especially Rossetti, Morris, and Swinburne.

19.25 *Valuable Books, Chiefly by Celebrated English Writers of the Nineteenth and Twentieth Centuries, Including . . . the Property of Mrs. Helen Rossetti Angeli* [Catalogue of the Sale]. London: Sotheby's, 4–6 April 1921.

Books and autograph letters from the library of William Michael Rossetti.

19.26 *The Library of John Quinn* [Catalogue of the Sales]. New York: Anderson Galleries, no. 1768, 12–14 November 1923; no. 1783, 10–12 December 1923; no. 1794, 14–16 January 1924; no. 1806, 11–13 February 1924; no. 1820, 17–20 March 1924.

This magnificent collection of 19th-century printed books and manuscripts contained hundreds of items of Pre-Raphaelite interest. A useful check list of works by and about the Pre-Raphaelites.

19.27 *Drawings and Pictures of the English School Including the Property of the Late Sir Philip Burne-Jones* . . . [Catalogue of the Sale]. London: Sotheby's, 10 November 1926.

Thirty-one items of Pre-Raphaelite interest, including works by Rossetti, Simeon Solomon, Burne-Jones, Boyce, and others.

19.28 *Tower House, 9 Melbury Road, Kensington: The Contents of the Residence [of Col. T. H. Minshall] Including Some Unique Examples of Furniture Decorated by the Pre-Raphaelite Artists* . . . [Catalogue of the Sale]. London: Chesterton and Sons, 16 October 1933.

The former residence of William Burges, the architect. The furniture, most of it painted, is of considerable interest. Illustrated.

19.29 *The Celebrated Collection of Paintings and Drawings by Old Masters and by the English and French Masters of the XIXth Century, formed by . . . Lord Faringdon* . . . [Catalogue of the Sale]. London: Sotheby's, 13 June 1934.

Included in the sale were Madox Brown's "The Entombment" (design for the illustration, see 91.1), Burne-Jones's *The Six Angels of Creation*, Millais' *Esther*, Henry Wallis' *Elaine*, and five works by G. F. Watts.

19.30 *Artistic & Literary Property Connected with Rossetti, Swinburne, Ford Madox Brown, etc. Removed from "The Pines," 11 Putney Hill* . . . [Catalogue of the Sale]. London: Sotheby's, 22 March 1939.

Including books, autograph letters and documents, signed and presentation photographs, paintings and drawings by Rossetti and his circle, and a few pieces of Pre-Raphaelite furniture. A large number of Rossetti letters to H. T. Dunn, Dunn's manuscript of the *Recollections* (33.5), and a substantial number of pictures by Dunn, who was Rossetti's studio assistant, add to the interest of this sale. Of Rossetti's own works, *Reverie, Pandora, The Spirit of the Rainbow*, and a panel version of *The Loving Cup* were the most significant. The remaining contents of the house were sold by A. W. Taylor at "The Pines" on 20 March 1939. This sale was occasioned by the death of Clara Watts-Dunton. Watts-Dunton's library was sold at Sotheby's 13–16 March 1917.

19.31 *A Large Portion of the Furnishings and Effects removed from Kelmscott Manor, the Home of William Morris* [Catalogue of the Sale]. Kelmscott: Hobbs and Chambers, 19–20 July 1939.

19.32 *Valuable Printed Books, Autograph Letters . . . Etc . . . The Property of Miss E. Morse* [Catalogue of the Sale]. London: Sotheby's, 11 March 1952.

Miss Morse was a god-daughter of Holman Hunt, and her parents were neighbors of William Bell Scott. A very important sale consisting of 116 letters from Rossetti to William Bell Scott, many holograph manuscripts of Rossetti's poems, and a trial book, with manuscript alterations and corrections, of *Poems*, 1870. In addition there were numerous letters from Ruskin, Swinburne, William Michael Rossetti, and others, together with two lots of correspondence from Scott's literary and artistic friends, numbering nearly 600 letters. Many of Scott's own manuscripts were also included in the sale. Another section of the catalogue labeled simply "Other Properties" contains holograph material of related interest.

19.33 *Studies by Sir Edward Burne-Jones, the Property of his Daughter, the Late Mrs. Margaret Mackail* . . . [Catalogue of the Sale]. London: Christie's, 3 December 1954.

19.34 *The Kelmscott Press and William Morris, with Ashendene, Doves and Other Private Press Books: The Property of Sir Sydney Cockerell* . . . [Catalogue of the Sale]. London: Sotheby's, 10 December 1956.

Preface by Stanley Morrison. The sale included Morris manuscripts, books, and proofs, together with a few Burne-Jones drawings and a sketchbook, and studies for the drawings of the Kelmscott *Chaucer*.

19.35 *Eighteenth and Nineteenth Century Drawings and Paintings . . . Works by Burne-Jones, Arthur Hughes and Rossetti, the Property of Mrs. Ernestine Mills . . .* [Catalogue of the Sale]. London: Sotheby's, 19 March 1958.

19.36 *Modern Pictures and Drawings, Mainly of the British School of the Nineteenth Century, the Property of the Trustees of the Lady Lever Art Gallery, Port Sunlight . . .* [Catalogue of the Sale]. London: Christie's, 6 June 1958.

Many of the pictures and drawings in this unusual sale from a gallery were by the Pre-Raphaelites.

19.37 *Nineteenth-Century and Modern First Editions, Presentation Copies, Autograph Letters, and Literary Manuscripts Comprising the Property of . . .* [*Signora Olivia Rossetti Agresti*] . . . [*and*] . . . *A. R. Murray, Esq. from the Collection of his Father, Charles Fairfax Murray* [Catalogue of the Sale]. London: Sotheby's, 29, 30 May 1961.

Of particular interest in this excellent sale were the 464 autograph letters to Charles Augustus Howell. A large number of the Pre-Raphaelite items which appeared in this sale went to the Humanities Research Center of the University of Texas (see 3.8). The sale was noticed in *Times Literary Supplement*, no. 3096 (30 June 1961), p. 401; no. 3097 (7 July 1961), p. 424.

19.38 *Nineteenth-Century & Modern First Editions, Presentation Copies, Autograph Letters & Literary Manuscripts Comprising the Property of . . . Miss E. M. Courtney-Boyd . . .* [Catalogue of the Sale]. London: Sotheby's, 3, 4 December 1962.

Included among the Pre-Raphaelite material removed from Penkill Castle in this sale were two states of Rossetti's privately printed edition of *Poems* (1869), thirty letters from Rossetti to Alice Boyd, and other letters and manuscripts of Christina Rossetti, Dante Rossetti, and William Bell Scott. For a notice of this sale see Victoria Gaul, "Treasures from Ayrshire," *Glasgow Herald*, 3 December 1962, p. 5. For descriptions of Penkill see 4.4 and 7.12.

19.39 *Fine Eighteenth and Nineteenth-Century Drawings and Paintings, Including . . . a Group of Victorian and Pre-Raphaelite Works by Madox Brown, Frith, Holman Hunt, Hughes, Burne-Jones, Millais, and Rossetti, the Property of William Alwyn . . .* [Catalogue of the Sale]. London: Sotheby's, 14 November 1962.

In the same sale were a number of Pre-Raphaelite works from the collection of Sir Sydney Cockerell and others, including a number of Burne-Jones's and Ruskin's works, and others by Simeon Solomon, Millais, Rossetti and Sandys.

The collection of Pre-Raphaelite pictures formed by William Alwyn, dispersed in this sale, was an extremely interesting one which deserves to be recorded. A collector for only about a dozen years, Mr. Alwyn managed to bring together a collection which, while not totally representative of the whole movement, did contain many fine and distinctive works by both the major and minor artists. Ford Madox Brown's *Sardanapalus*, Hughes' *Springtide*, and Holman Hunt's *Sorrow* deserve special mention. The nucleus of the collection was made up of pictures and studies by Burne-Jones and Rossetti; no less than ten works by each artist were disposed of in this sale, including by Burne-Jones a tempera angel with cymbals, an unfinished oil on panel of a mermaid with merbabies, and a gouache panel study of *The Masque of Cupid*, and by Rossetti, the "Music" panel from *King René's Honeymoon*, a water color version of *Launcelot and Guenevere at the Tomb of Arthur*, and several interesting drawings. The Alwyn collection was impressive both in size and quality, and even lacking the scope of the collections in larger galleries, it presented a fine array of Pre-Raphaelite works seldom seen in the exhibitions of recent years.

BOOKSELLERS' CATALOGUES

20.1 *Pre-Raphaelite Brotherhood. List of Books. Being Relics of the Rossetti Family. Catalogue Nos. 341, 341A.* London: J. & M. L. Tregaskis, 1895, 1896.

All the items included were "purchased from the executor of the late Christina G. Rossetti," that is, William Michael Rossetti.

20.2 *A Catalogue of Books from the Library of . . . Gleeson White . . .* London: A. Lionel Isaacs, 1899.

With an Introduction by E. York Powell. An extremely interesting catalogue of part of the collection of the famous editor, collector, and writer. The last section is a list of the collection of illustrated books of the 1860's which Gleeson White formed while writing his work on the subject (88.3).

20.3 *Rare Books in English Literature, Including Sections Devoted to the Pre-Raphaelites & Their Circle . . . Catalogue No. 39.* London: Elkin Mathews, 1931.

Part III (pp. 48–65) consists of first editions of the works of Allingham, Crane, Dixon, Hake, Oliver Madox Brown, Morris, Patmore, Christina, Dante Gabriel, Maria F. and William Michael Rossetti, Ruskin, Scott, Swinburne, and Thomas Woolner. A few presentation copies.

20.4 *Books from the Library of the Late George Stuart Gordon . . . with a Selection of Recent Acquisitions, including two Collections of books by and about the Pre-Raphaelites [and] the Brownings. Catalogue No. 490.* Oxford: Blackwell's, 1942.

An important collection of both primary and secondary Pre-Raphaelite material, with a number of presentation and association copies and a few autograph letters and manuscripts. Two boxes of pamphlets were not catalogued. In all, 250 volumes — most of the standard sources were included in this valuable catalogue. Sold as a collection.

20.5 "The Pre-Raphaelite Brotherhood," *Catalogue No. 73.* Cheltenham: Alan Hancox, 1959.

Items 547–695 relate to the Pre-Raphaelites. Especially strong on William Morris.

20.6 *William Morris's Typographical Adventure. A Complete Collection of the Publications of the Kelmscott Press. Catalogue No. 139.* New York: Philip C. Duschnes, 1959.

Notices

SELECTED NOTICES OF EXHIBITIONS AND SALES

21.1 [Patmore, Coventry]. "A Pre-Raphaelite Exhibition," *Saturday Review*, IV, no. 88 (4 July 1857), 11–12.

Notice of the Russell Place exhibition (16.1).

21.2 Mérimée, Prosper. "Les Beaux-Arts en Angleterre," *Revue des Deux Mondes*, XI (October 1857), 866–880.

Notice of the Manchester Art Treasures exhibition (18.3). With a long section on the Pre-Raphaelites, especially Millais and Hunt.

21.3 "Mr. F. Madox Brown's Pictures," *Art Journal*, XXVII (March 1865), 94; (April 1865), 126; (May 1865), 156.

Notices of the Brown exhibition (8.1). "By that sect of painters calling themselves Pre-Raffaelite, Mr. Brown is claimed as a brother, and he has by certain of his works acknowledged himself as of 'the order.'"

21.4 Rossetti, William Michael. "Mr. Madox Brown's Exhibition, and Its Place in Our School of Painting," *Fraser's Magazine*, LXXI (May 1865), 598-607.

A notice of 8.1. Reprinted in 38.2. See that item for complete annotation.

21.5 Palgrave, Francis Turner. "Exhibition of F. Madox Brown," *Essays on Art*. London: Macmillan, 1866.

A notice of 8.1. See also 36.14 for a notice of Hunt, included in the same volume.

21.6 Lang, Andrew. *Notes on a Collection of Pictures by Mr. John Everett Millais, R.A., Exhibited at the Fine Art Society's Rooms*. London: Fine Art Society, 1881.

Notes to accompany the exhibition (12.3).

21.7 Hueffer, Francis. "Exhibitions of Rossetti's Pictures," *Italian and Other Studies*. London: Stock, 1883.

Notices of the Rossetti exhibitions at the Royal Academy (14.1) and at the Burlington Fine Arts Club (14.3). Reprinted from *The Times*, no. 30,704 (30 December 1882), p. 6; no. 30,716 (13 January 1883), p. 4; no. 30,717 (15 January 1883), p. 8.

21.8 Carr, J. Comyns. "The Rossetti Exhibitions," *Art and Letters: An Illustrated Monthly Magazine*, II (January 1883), 151.

Notices of Rossetti exhibitions (14.1 to 14.3).

21.9 Monkhouse, Cosmo. "Rossetti's Pictures at the Royal Academy," *Academy*, XXIII, no. 557 (6 January 1883), 14-15.

A notice of 14.1.

21.10 —— "Rossetti at Burlington House," *Spectator*, LVI, no. 2845 (6 January 1883), 14-15.

A notice of 14.1.

21.11 —— "Rossetti at the Burlington Club," *Academy*, XXIII, no. 559 (20 January 1883), 50-51.

A notice of 14.3.

21.12 "Rossetti's Pictures at the Royal Academy and the Burlington Fine Arts Club," *Art Journal*, XLV (February 1883), 61-62.

Notices of 14.1 and 14.3.

21.13 "The Linnell and Rossetti Pictures at Burlington House," *London Society*, XLIII (February 1883), 217-221.

21.14 Hannay, David. "The Paintings of Mr. Rossetti," *National Review*, I (March 1883), 126-134.

A notice of 14.1.

21.15 Atkinson, J. Beavington. "Contemporary Art — Poetic and Positive: Dante Gabriel Rossetti and Alma-Tadema — Linnell and Lawson," *Blackwood's Magazine*, CXXXIII (March 1883), 392-411.

The section on Rossetti (pp. 392-401) also contains a general discussion of the Pre-Raphaelites, but the section treats primarily the three posthumous exhibitions of Rossetti's works (14.1 to 14.3).

21.16 Duret, Théodore. "Les Expositions de Londres; Dante Gabriel Rossetti," *Gazette des Beaux-Arts*, Période 2, XXVIII (July 1883), 49-58.

A notice of 14.1.

21.17 Crawford, A. Gordon [= Alexander G. Wise], ed. *Notes on the Pictures of Mr. Holman Hunt, Exhibited at the Rooms of the Fine Art Society, 1886: With Criticisms by John Ruskin*. London: Reeves, 1886.

Notes to accompany the exhibition (11.4). Reprints 75.10 under the title, "Art, Nature, and the Pre-Raphaelite Principle," and brief sections from "The Three Colours of Pre-Raphaelitism" (75.11) as "Hunt and Rossetti." Also contains a postscript letter from William Holman Hunt.

21.18 —— ed. *Notes on Some of the Principal Pictures of Sir John Everett Millais, Exhibited at the Grosvenor Gallery, 1886: With a Preface and Original and Selected Criticisms, by John Ruskin*. London: Reeves, 1886.

Notes to accompany the exhibition (12.4). With a note on "Millais and Turner," reprinted from 66.1, and a section entitled

"The Pre-Raphaelite Brotherhood," reprinted from 75.2.

21.19 "Pre-Raphaelitism," *Spectator*, LIX, no. 3015 (10 April 1886), 484–485.

Comments on the basically English and 19th-century character of Pre-Raphaelite art. A favorable article praising the Pre-Raphaelites for striking the blow against commercialism, conventionalism, and cheap sentiment. Stimulated by the Millais exhibition at the Grosvenor Gallery (12.4), the Holman Hunt exhibition at the Fine Art Society (11.4), and the William Graham sale (19.4).

21.20 Shields, Frederic. "Some Notes on Dante Gabriel Rossetti," *Century Guild Hobby Horse*, n.s. I (October 1886), 140–154.

A notice of 14.1 and a general discussion of Rossetti. The article also contains a first draft of the sonnet on Blake, given to Shields by Rossetti (see pp. 144–145).

21.21 Henley, William Ernest. *A Century of Artists* . . . Glasgow: Maclehose, 1889.

Shown in the exhibition (18.7) and discussed by Henley are the works of Burne-Jones, Rossetti, Paton, and Millais.

21.22 Gray, J. M. "The Pre-Raphaelite Loan Collection at Birmingham," *Academy*, XL, no. 1014 (10 October 1891), 316–317.

A notice of 16.2.

21.23 "Pre-Raphaelites at the Century Club," *Critic*, XXII (January 1893), 24–25.

A notice of the Philadelphia exhibition (16.3) which was also shown at the Century Club (see 16.3).

21.24 "Some Pre-Raphaelite Pictures," *Saturday Review*, LXXXII, no. 2125 (18 July 1896), 59–60.

A notice of the Goupil Gallery exhibition of James Leathart's Pre-Raphaelite collection (16.4).

21.25 Baldry, A. Lys. "The Drawings of Sir Edward Burne-Jones," *Magazine of Art*, XIX (1896), 343–345.

A notice of the exhibition at the Fine Art Society (9.7).

21.26 Spielmann, Marion H. *Millais and His Works: With Special Reference to the Exhibition at the Royal Academy, 1898* . . . London: Blackwood, 1898.

Notes on the exhibition (12.6). For annotation see 37.46.

21.27 [Pennell, Elizabeth R.]. "Rossetti and Millais," *Nation*, LXVI (27 January 1898), 65–66; (3 February 1898), 86–87.

Notices of the Millais exhibition at the Royal Academy (12.6) and the Rossetti exhibition at the New Gallery (14.5).

21.28 Hueffer, Ford Madox. "The Millais and Rossetti Exhibitions," *Fortnightly Review*, LXIX, n.s. LXIII (February 1898), 189–196.

Notice of 12.6 and 14.5.

21.29 Phillips, C. "Millais's Works at Burlington House," *Nineteenth Century*, XLIII (March 1898), 376–388.

A notice of 12.6.

21.30 Beale, S. "Sir John Millais at Burlington House," *American Architect*, LIX (March 1898), 83–84.

A notice of 12.6.

21.31 Riddoch, D. S. "The Pre-Raphaelite Painters and Their Pictures at the Glasgow International Exhibition," *St. George* (The Journal of the Ruskin Society of Birmingham), V (January 1902), 18–26.

See annotation 18.7.

21.32 Ross, Robert. "Mr. Holman Hunt at the Leicester Galleries (An Inspection)." *Masques and Phases*. London: Humphreys, 1909.

A notice of 11.11.

21.33 Ricketts, Charles. *A Century of Art, 1810–1910*. London: Carfax, 1911.

A notice of the Grafton Gallery exhibition (18.10). A sensitive analysis of the Pre-Raphaelite pictures in the exhibition.

21.34 "Pre-Raphaelites at the Tate Gallery," *Athenaeum*, no. 4391 (23 December 1911), p. 804.

A notice of the Tate loan exhibition, 1911–1912 (16.8).

21.35 "Pre-Raphaelites and Post-Impressionists in London," *Nation*, XCIV (28 March 1912), 322–323.
A notice of 16.8.

21.36 Carr, J. Comyns. "The English School of Painting at the Roman Exhibition," *Coasting Bohemia*. London: Macmillan, 1914.
A notice of 18.11. Originally published in the *Fortnightly Review*, XCVI, n.s. XC (July 1911), 95–125. Contains about six pages on the Pre-Raphaelites. For complete annotation see 25.45.

21.37 Alton, John. "Pre-Raphaelites at Millbank," *New Statesman*, XXI (12 May 1923), 141–142.
A notice of the two Tate Gallery exhibitions of 1923 (18.12, 18.13), both of which were heavily slanted toward the Pre-Raphaelites. ". . . in the growth of art, the pre-Raphaelite brotherhood was hardly a branch even, but rather the mistletoe on the bough — beautiful in itself and a fascinating phenomenon, but a parasitical growth for all that." (p. 141)

21.38 Carter, A. C. R. "An Auction Causerie: Rossetti Recalled," *Studio*, XCVI (July 1928), 76.
Reminiscences of the Graham sale (19.4) and a consideration of the values of Rossetti's works. "Sometimes I wonder whether the great interest now taken by collectors in early Italian art is not due mainly to the absorption shown by the later Victorians in the works of Rossetti."

21.39 Blunt, Anthony. "The Pre-Raphaelites and Life," *Spectator*, CLII, no. 5483 (28 July 1933), 124.
A notice of the Burne-Jones centenary exhibition at the Tate (9.15).

21.40 "Burne-Jones," *National Review*, CI (August 1933), 220–224.
The exhibition at the Tate (9.15) is obviously the work of those who know nothing about the Pre-Raphaelites.

21.41 Bliss, Douglas P. "The Pre-Raphaelites," *Spectator*, CLII, no. 5508 (19 January 1934), 84.
A notice of the Royal Academy exhibition (18.15).

21.42 "Pre-Raphaelite Paintings; Bancroft Collection, Wilmington," *Art Digest*, VIII (15 May 1934), 9.
A notice of the Wilmington Society of the Fine Arts exhibition (16.12).

21.43 Rosenberg, Isaac. "The Pre-Raphaelite Exhibition," *The Collected Poems of Isaac Rosenberg*. Edited by Gordon Bottomley and D. W. Harding, with a Foreword by S. Sassoon. London: Chatto and Windus, 1937.
Notes for an article on the Tate exhibition (16.9).

21.44 "Victorian Surrealists," *Time*, XLVII (29 April 1946), 54 (p. 29 Atlantic Edition).
A notice of the Fogg Museum Pre-Raphaelite exhibition (16.13).

21.45 "Pre-Raphaelite Tragedians," *Art News*, XLV (May 1946), 22–23, 67–68.
A notice of 16.13.

21.46 Gray, Nicolette. "The Pre-Raphaelite Exhibition at Birmingham," *Burlington Magazine*, LXXXIX (July 1947), 193–194.
A notice of 16.14.

21.47 "The Pre-Raphaelites. A 15-year Survey," *Times*, no. 50,801 (1 July 1947), p. 6.
A notice of 16.14.

21.48 Mayne, Jonathan. "The Pre-Raphaelites at Birmingham," *Listener*, XXXVIII (3 July 1947), 26–27.
A notice of 16.14.

21.49 Sutton, Denys. "London Queries and Classics; Exhibition at Birmingham Gallery; Pre-Raphaelites, Poussin, Abstractions," *Art News*, XLVI (August 1947), 28–29, 36.
A notice of 16.14. "The Pre-Raphaelite tragedy has become a drawing room comedy" (p. 36).

21.50 [Pre-Raphaelite Drawings at Roland,

Browse and Delbanco], *Studio*, CXXXIV (December 1947), 177.
A notice of 16.15.

21.51 "Exposition à la Tate Gallery: Le Centenaire de la confrérie des Pré-Raphaélites," *Arts Plastiques*, nos. 9–10 (1948), pp. 415–416.
A notice of the centenary exhibition (16.16).

21.52 Lewis, Wyndham. "The [Pre-Raphaelite] Brotherhood," *Listener*, XXXIX (22 April 1948), 672.
Occasioned by the Whitechapel Pre-Raphaelite exhibition (16.19). ". . . the Pre-Raphaelite Movement proved, in the end, a rebellious, picturesque, but shallow interlude in Victorian Philistinism." For follow-up correspondence see "The P.R.B.," *Listener*, XXXIX (29 April 1948), 705, a letter by R. L. Mégroz to which Lewis replied in the issue of May 6 (p. 743).

21.53 "Current Shows and Comment," *Apollo*, XLVII (May 1948), 97–98.
A notice of the Whitechapel Pre-Raphaelite exhibition (16.19). "The time may be ripe for the rise of the Pre-Impressionists." (p. 98)

21.54 Fell, H. G. "Pre-Raphaelitism at

Whitechapel," *Connoisseur*, CXXI (June 1948), 120.
A notice of 16.19.

21.55 "The Pre-Raphaelites," *Times*, no. 51, 190 (30 September 1948), pp. 5–6.
A notice of the Tate centenary exhibition (16.16).

21.56 Gere, John. "Pre-Raphaelites at the Tate," *Burlington Magazine*, XC (November 1948), 325–326.
A notice of 16.16. Primarily a discussion of the paintings and drawings by Rossetti from Mrs. Angeli's collection which were included in the exhibition.

21.57 James, Henry. "Lord Leighton and Ford Madox Brown," *The Painter's Eye: Essays on the Pictorial Arts*. Edited with Notes by John L. Sweeney. London: Hart-Davis, 1956.
Originally published in *Harper's Weekly* (26 June 1897) and reprinted in part in *Notes on Novelists* (1914). On the Madox Brown exhibition at the Grafton Gallery (8.4).

21.58 "Return of the Pre-Raphaelites? Exhibition at the University of Kansas Museum of Art," *Connoisseur* (American Edition), CXLIII (April 1959), 132.
A notice of 16.23.

II. BIBLIOGRAPHY OF
INDIVIDUAL FIGURES

Part II is devoted entirely to bibliographies of the individual Pre-Raphaelites, their associates and affiliates. The first thirteen sections comprise a bibliography of Dante Gabriel Rossetti, who is the only figure for whom items have been organized by subject into separate sections. For all other figures in this part, items relating to primary works are listed first, followed by secondary writings. While the attempt in the Rossetti sections has been to compile a comprehensive bibliography of significant materials, the bibliographies of most of the other figures are intentionally selective. To offer full coverage for such writers as Christina Rossetti, Ruskin, Patmore, Morris, and Swinburne would require a separate volume for each.

If the Rossetti sections seem disproportionately long, it is because of his singular importance in the history of Pre-Raphaelitism. The strictures of certain critics — particularly Holman Hunt and Millais — notwithstanding, Rossetti was, for all practical purposes, the leader of the Pre-Raphaelite Movement; and it is merely quibbling to deny him that role. Ironically, while Rossetti himself is largely responsible for the complications that arise over definition, in later years, growing impatient with the controversies aroused by the movement, he seems to have tried to disassociate himself from the Brotherhood. "As for all the prattle about Pre-Raphaelitism," he is reported to have said to Hall Caine in 1880, "I confess to you I am weary of it, and long have been. Why should we go on talking about the visionary vanities of half-a-dozen boys? We've all grown out of them, I hope, by now." (25.1, p. 221) And William Sharp has preserved Rossetti's reply to a solicitous lady who at Dr. Westland Marston's one evening asked him if he were the "Pre-Raphaelite Rossetti": "Madam, I am not an 'ite' of any kind; I am only a painter." (25.3, p. 71) Commenting on these two denials, William Michael Rossetti says: "These statements I accept; but it is not the less true that in 1848 and for some years afterwards he meant a good deal by calling himself Praeraphaelite, and meant it very heartily." (24.5, I, 135–136)

The places of Ford Madox Brown, Edward Burne-Jones, William Morris, Christina Rossetti, and John Ruskin are secure in the annals of Pre-Raphaelitism. Each was closely allied with Rossetti and with other members of the group, and each made a distinct contribution to the movement and to the Pre-Raphaelite *milieu*. The twenty writers and artists catalogued in sections 46 to 65 were all associated with the movement or with the individual Pre-Raphaelites. In some instances the association was slight or ephemeral, perhaps even only personal, but in each case the influence of Pre-

Raphaelitism is demonstrable in at least a portion of the literary and artistic works of the figures included. It should be noted that the sections treating the minor Pre-Raphaelites, such as Hake, Marston, O'Shaughnessy, and Bell Scott, are the most complete — often the only — bibliographies available.

Brief introductions are provided for every writer and artist included in part II (but not for every section devoted to Rossetti). So many men and women moved on the periphery of the Pre-Raphaelite circle that only the most representative could be considered. A few entries for figures even more minor than those included among the "Minor Pre-Raphaelites, Associates, and Affiliates" will be found in sections 85 to 87. Taken as a whole, however, part II offers a reasonably thorough survey of the artists and writers whose combined efforts constituted the Pre-Raphaelite Movement.

The Pre-Raphaelite Brotherhood

DANTE GABRIEL ROSSETTI
1828–1882

[CBEL: III, 271–273, S593–594; DNB: XVII, 284–289
(Richard Garnett); EB: XXIII, 747–751 (Theodore
Watts-Dunton)]

Section 22

BIBLIOGRAPHY

A full-dress bibliography of Rossetti has not yet been undertaken. The most complete bibliographical study of Rossetti is unpublished (22.6). Of published works, the most thorough catalogue of Rossetti's writings is that by William Michael Rossetti (22.1); the most extensive list of critical and biographical works on Rossetti is that in Ehrsam's *Twelve Victorian Authors* (22.8). Minor bibliographical sections appended to individual studies of Rossetti are indicated in the annotations and are not separately listed in this section.

*   *   *

22.1 Rossetti, William Michael. *Bibliography of the Works of Dante Gabriel Rossetti*. London: Ellis, 1905.

First published in the *Bibliographer*, I (December 1902), 420–430; II (January 1903), 34–44. W. F. Prideaux submitted "Additions to the Bibliography of the Works of Dante Gabriel Rossetti," *Bibliographer*, II (April 1903), 243–247. Another list by Prideaux entitled "Rossetti Bibliography" appeared in *N&Q*, 10th ser., II (10 December 1904), 464–465. This item (22.1) incorporates Prideaux's additions and is a revision of the original *Bibliographer* articles.

22.2 ———. *Dante Gabriel Rossetti: Classified Lists of His Writings with the Dates*. London: Privately printed, 1906.

One-hundred copies printed. The two lists are of works published in the *Collected Works* (23.13), and of works published but not included in the *Collected Works*. This second list should be collated with that in the standard edition of the *Works*, 1911 (23.27).

The volume also contains an alphabetical and chronological listing of Rossetti's writings, with which compare 32.6.

22.3 Smith, Harry B. "Dante Gabriel Rossetti," *A Sentimental Library* [London]: Privately printed, 1914.

Smith owned many rare Rossetti items including the manuscript of "William and Mary," Rossetti's juvenile ballad. The volume contains descriptions of other items by authors associated with the Pre-Raphaelites, including Christina Rossetti. For other private collections with catalogues of bibliographical importance see Arnold (24.15), Quinn (19.26), and Wise (1.6).

22.4 Vaughan, Charles E. *Bibliographies of Swinburne, Morris, and Rossetti* (The English Association, Pamphlet no. 29). [Oxford: Clarendon Press], 1914.

22.5 Ghose, S. N. *Dante Gabriel Rossetti and Contemporary Criticism (1849–1882)*. Dijon: Imprimerie Darantiere, 1929 (diss. Strasbourg, 1929).

For annotation see 1.2.

22.6 Gregory, John Bonar. "A Bibliographical and Reference Guide to the Life and Works of Dante Gabriel Rossetti with a Study of the Pre-Raphaelite Movement," unpub. diss., University of London, 1931.

The most complete bibliographical study of Rossetti, but not generally accessible. The work is divided into four sections: Life, Artistic Work, Literary Work, and Literary Criticism. The actual "Bibliography and Reference Guide" is preceded by a seventy-page introduction analyzing Rossetti's role in the Pre-Raphaelite Movement, and followed by a thirty-five-page chronology of Rossetti's work.

22.7 Carter, John, and Graham Pollard. "Dante Gabriel Rossetti," *An Enquiry Into the Nature of Certain Nineteenth Century Pamphlets*. London: Constable, 1934.

For complete annotation see 1.3.

22.8 Ehrsam, Theodore G., Robert H. Deily, and Robert M. Smith. "Dante Gabriel Rossetti," *Bibliographies of Twelve Victorian Authors*. New York: Wilson, 1936.

For complete annotation see 1.5.

22.9 Todd, William B. "D. G. Rossetti's Early Italian Poets" ("Bibliographical Notes & Queries," note 142), *Book Collector*, IX (Autumn 1960), 329–331.

Identification and collation of a variant of Rossetti's first volume in the Wrenn Collection of the Humanities Research Center, University of Texas. Answered by William E. Fredeman, *Book Collector*, X (Summer 1961), 193–198, an attempt to account for the Wrenn variant, of which at least four copies are known to survive. W. B. Todd replied, *Book Collector*, X (Winter 1961), 447.

Section 23

WORKS

Rossetti's works have appeared in so many editions that to catalogue them all would be both impracticable and superfluous. Besides, many are merely reprintings rather than editions in the strict sense, and no attempt has been made to list such reprintings unless for some reason they are of particular interest. The items in this section are arranged chronologically, and no division is made between separate and collected editions. There is no definitive edition of Rossetti's complete writings, but the 1911 edition of the *Works* (23.27) is the most dependable as well as the most complete. Not included in this list of Rossetti's writings are the poems published in the 1849 catalogue of the Free Exhibition (18.1) and in the *Notes on the Royal Academy Exhibition, 1868* (62.5), Rossetti's two reviews of Thomas G. Hake's poems (48.5,

48.6), his contributions to Gilchrist's *Life of Blake* (see 86.1), and miscellaneous uncollected writings in periodicals and other publications.

* * *

23.1 *Sir Hugh the Heron: A Legendary Tale in Four Parts.* By Gabriel Rossetti, Junior. London: Printed for private circulation only by G. Polidori's Private Press, 1843.

Of this work, which has never been reprinted, Rossetti wrote: ". . . there is no knowing what fool may some day foist the absurd trash into print as a production of mine."

23.2 *Sister Helen: A Ballad.* Oxford: Printed for private circulation, 1857.

William M. Rossetti (in 22.1, no. 7) attributes this item to William Fulford, the editor of *The Oxford and Cambridge Magazine.* For evidence that it is probably a forgery see 22.7. For the history of the publication of the poem and the collation of the various texts see 23.33.

23.3 *The Early Italian Poets from Ciullo d'Alcamo to Dante Alighieri (1100–1200–1300) in the Original Metres Together with Dante's Vita Nuova Translated by D. G. Rossetti. Part I. Poets Chiefly before Dante. Part II. Dante and His Circle.* London: Smith, Elder, 1861.

A prepublication state of this volume has no publisher's imprint; for details see 22.9. The second edition, *Dante and His Circle* (London: Ellis, 1874), is essentially the same as the 1861 volume except for the organization of the material.

23.4 "Of Life, Love, and Death: Sixteen Sonnets," *Fortnightly Review,* XI, n.s. V (March 1869), 266–273.

Rossetti's major contribution to any periodical. All the sonnets were subsequently published in *Poems,* 1870 (23.8), and it is not improbable that this selection was designed to sound out opinion prior to the appearance of the forthcoming volume.

23.5 *Poems (Privately Printed).* London, 1869.

Includes fewer poems than either 23.7 or 23.8, and contains "Hand and Soul," which was dropped from 23.8. The first appearance of "Sonnets and Songs, towards a work to be called 'The House of Life'" (32 sonnets, fourteen songs).

23.6 *Hand and Soul.* [London: Privately printed, 1869].

Signed "Dante Gabriel Rossetti, 1850." Excluded from 23.8, this work originally appeared in the first number of *The Germ.* Reprinted in *Fortnightly Review,* XIV, n.s. VIII (December 1870), 692–702.

23.7 *Poems (Privately Printed).* London, 1870.

Included in this private printing were eight poems not incorporated in 23.5. "Troy Town" and "Eden Bower" were written after 23.5; the remaining six poems, W. M. Rossetti deduces, must have been recovered from Mrs. Rossetti's coffin, exhumed in October 1869. For the details of this volume and 23.5 — both "Trial Books" — see 27.89.

23.8 *Poems.* London: Ellis, 1870. "The Stream's Secret," written after 23.7, is new to this volume. Included in the earlier editions and excluded here are "Hand and Soul," "Dennis Shand," and one sonnet. The volume went through several editions (six by 1874), and there was both an American (Boston: Roberts, 1870) and a Tauchnitz (no. 1380, Leipzig, 1870) edition, the latter with a Memoir by Francis Hueffer. The sonnet "Nuptial Sleep" was dropped from *The House of Life* in 1881.

23.9 "The Stealthy School of Criticism," *Athenaeum,* no. 2303 (16 December 1871), pp. 792–794.

Rossetti's reply to Buchanan's initial attack in the *Contemporary Review* (29.16). Buchanan answered Rossetti's letter in *Athenaeum,* no. 2305 (23 December 1871), p. 887. For general discussion of the entire controversy see Survey, pp. 17–19.

23.10 *Verses.* London: Privately printed, 1881.

Unremarked by W. M. Rossetti in 22.1.

For evidence that the volume is probably a forgery see 22.7.

23.11 *Poems. A New Edition.* London: Ellis, 1881.

Contains four poems not in 23.8 and omits all the sonnets belonging to *The House of Life*, as well as three additional sonnets. The poem "One Girl" is renamed "Beauty (Sappho)" in this edition.

23.12 *Ballads and Sonnets.* London: Ellis, 1881.

For a detailed account of the complicated history of this volume see 22.1 (pp. 24–26). There were at least four English editions as well as an American (Boston: Roberts, 1881) and a Tauchnitz (no. 2098, Leipzig, 1882) edition, the latter with a Memoir of Rossetti by Francis Hueffer.

23.13 *The Collected Works of Dante Gabriel Rossetti.* Edited with Preface and Notes by William M. Rossetti. In Two Volumes. Volume I. Poems, Prose — Tales and Literary Papers. Vol. II. Translations, Prose — Notices of Fine Art. London: Ellis, 1886.

Although not an edition of Rossetti's complete works, these volumes contain many poems and translations previously unpublished. Reprinted 1887 and after.

23.14 *The Poetical Works of Dante Gabriel Rossetti. A New Edition in One Volume.* Edited with Preface by William Michael Rossetti. London: Ellis, 1891.

Identical with the first volume of 23.13 ("printed from the same stereo-plates") except that the prose has been dropped and the preface is "slightly condensed."

23.15 *Ballads and Narrative Poems.* Hammersmith: Kelmscott Press, 1893.
Published by Ellis and Elvey.

23.16 *Sonnets and Lyrical Poems.* Hammersmith: Kelmscott Press, 1894.
Published by Ellis and Elvey.

23.17 *Hand and Soul.* Hammersmith: Kelmscott Press, 1895.
Reprinted from *The Germ* for Messrs. Way & Williams of Chicago.

23.18 *The White Ship: A Little Book of Poems Selected from the Works of Dante Gabriel Rossetti.* Boston: Colesworthy, 1896.

23.19 Rossetti, William M. "Some Scraps of Verse and Prose by Dante Gabriel Rossetti," *Pall Mall Magazine*, XVI (December 1898), 480–496.

Also separately published (New York: Scott, 1898). With two exceptions all these "Scraps" were included in the 1911 edition of the *Works* (23.27). On p. 496 appears an interesting list of "stunning" words for poetry.

23.20 *Jenny.* Wausau, Wisconsin: The Philosopher Press, 1899.

23.21 *The Siddal Edition* [of the Works of Dante Gabriel Rossetti]. 7 vols. London: Ellis, 1899–1901.

Each volume contains a Prefatory Note by William M. Rossetti. This edition contains essentially the same poems as volume I of 23.13, together with the Dante translations from volume II.

23.22 *Lenore by Gottfried August Bürger.* Translated from the German by Dante Gabriel Rossetti. London: Ellis, 1900.

With a Prefatory Note by William M. Rossetti.

23.23 *Poems.* Portland, Maine: Mosher, 1902.

Essentially the 1870 text (23.8) with additional poems from the *Collected Works* (23.13). The volume contains a Preface by Mosher, a reprint of Swinburne's 1870 essay on Rossetti (27.3), and notes on the poems.

23.24 *Ballads and Sonnets.* Portland, Maine: Mosher, 1903.

The text followed is that of 1881 (23.12), but a number of poems have been added and some changes, especially in the order of *The House of Life* have been made. This edition contains a Preface and notes together with Pater's essay on Rossetti (27.7). Mosher also issued separately *Hand and Soul* (1899), *The House of Life* (1898), *The Blessed Damozel* (1895), and *The Blessed Damozel:*

A Book of Lyrics Chosen from the Works of Dante Gabriel Rossetti (1895).

23.25 *The Poems of Dante Gabriel Rossetti with Illustrations from His Own Pictures and Designs.* Edited with an Introduction and Notes, by William M. Rossetti. 2 vols. London: Ellis, 1904.

"Nuptial Sleep" is here restored to its place in *The House of Life.* In addition, many poems are included which are unavailable in previous editions. Among these are "Dennis Shand" and many of the translations. The introductory material is essentially the same as in the earlier volumes, but the notes are considerably expanded. This was the first edition of Rossetti's poems illustrated with his own pictures, and it has the distinction of being the most handsome of all the editions.

23.26 *Hartmann von Aue. Henry the Leper (Der Arme Heinrich).* Paraphrased by Dante Gabriel Rossetti. With an Introduction by William P. Trent. 2 vols. Boston: The Bibliophile Society, 1905.

Volume 1 is a facsimile of the manuscript.

23.27 *The Works of Dante Gabriel Rossetti.* Edited with Preface and Notes by William M. Rossetti. Revised and Enlarged Edition. London: Ellis, 1911.

The best edition of Rossetti's works. Many poems — especially versicles and fragments and juvenilia — and some prose are here printed for the first time. The Table of Contents is especially useful as it provides a chronological outline of Rossetti's writings, giving both the date of composition and the date of initial publication of each of his poems and prose works. Not included in the 1911 edition are "Sir Hugh the Heron," "Jan Van Hunks," and a few sonnets which were, at the time of publication, the property of Theodore Watts-Dunton. The preface is merely a reworking of those appended to earlier editions, but the notes are clear and pertinent, and more extensive than in any previous edition. A most interesting manuscript volume, formerly in the collection of Sir Sydney Cockerell, belongs to Mrs. Virginia Surtees: "Notes by William Michael Rossetti Prepared in 1911 to Accompany the Complete Works of His Brother Dante Gabriel Rossetti."

23.28 *The House of Life: A Sonnet-Sequence by Dante Gabriel Rossetti.* With an Introduction and Notes by Paull Franklin Baum. Cambridge, Mass.: Harvard University Press, 1928.

The best edition, with extensive notes on each of the sonnets and a detailed introduction to the sequence. Of the many other editions of *The House of Life* only that published by Copeland and Day of Boston in 1894 — "Being now for the first time given in its full text" — deserves particular notice.

23.29 *Dante Gabriel Rossetti: An Analytical List of Manuscripts in the Duke University Library, with Hitherto Unpublished Verse and Prose.* Edited by Paull Franklin Baum. Durham, N. C.: Duke University Press, 1931.

A detailed catalogue and examination of Rossetti manuscripts acquired by the Duke University Library in 1930. See also 27.86.

23.30 *Dante Gabriel Rossetti: An Anthology (Poets in Brief).* With an Introduction by F. L. Lucas. Cambridge University Press, 1933.

This volume contains selections from Rossetti's translations as well as original poems. The Introduction is essentially the same as 27.92.

23.31 *Dante Gabriel Rossetti: Poems, Ballads and Sonnets. Selections from the Posthumous Poems and from His Translations. Hand and Soul.* Edited by Paull Franklin Baum. New York: Doubleday Doran, 1937.

The best of all anthologies, with a valuable critical Introduction.

23.32 *Dante Gabriel Rossetti: The Blessed Damozel. The Unpublished Manuscript, Texts and Collation.* With an Introduction by Paull Franklin Baum. Chapel Hill, N. C.: University of North Carolina Press, 1937.

The standard, and only really useful, edition of the poem.

23.33 *Rossetti's Sister Helen.* Edited by Janet Camp Troxell. New Haven: Yale University Press, 1939.

The standard edition of the poem, with collations of the different versions, including the unpublished Fitzwilliam manuscript, and an Introduction by the editor.

23.34 *Poems by Dante Gabriel Rossetti.* Chosen by Lillian Irene Howarth. London: Angus and Robertson, [1950].

With a ten-page Introduction.

23.35 *Dante Gabriel Rossetti: Jan Van Hunks* (*Arents Tobacco Collection Publications. No. 3*). Edited from the Original Manuscripts by John Robert Wahl. New York: New York Public Library, 1952.

The most recent and the only scholarly edition of Rossetti's ballad, with a long Introduction. There are two earlier editions of the poem, which was first published in the *English Review*, I (January 1909), 193–200: the edition "Printed for T. Watts-Dunton" in 1912; and the edition prepared by Mackenzie Bell (London: Harrap, 1929). Watts-Dunton sold the manuscript to T. J. Wise in 1909, and despite the colophon quoted above, Wise seems to have been responsible for the first separate publication of the poem. For evidence of his connection with the volume see "A Rossetti Ballad," Wise's letter to the *TLS*, no. 1454 (12 December 1929), p. 1058, written after the appearance of Bell's edition, in the Introduction to which Bell claimed that the poem had never before been separately printed. For a detailed examination of this issue see William E. Fredeman, "D. G. Rossetti and T. J. Wise," *TLS*, no. 3090 (19 May 1961), p. 309.

23.36 *The Kelmscott Love Sonnets of Dante Gabriel Rossetti.* Edited with an Introductory Essay by John Robert Wahl. Capetown: A. H. Balkema, 1954.

A carelessly edited volume, containing an interesting discussion of the dating of certain sonnets in *The House of Life.*

23.37 *Dante Gabriel Rossetti: Poems.* Edited with an Introduction and Notes by Oswald Doughty. London: Dent, 1957.

The most recent edition of the poems.

Section 24

LETTERS

The extent of Rossetti's correspondence is only partially reflected in his published letters, as the many references to unpublished letters in the sections dealing with collections of Pre-Raphaelite materials (see sections 2 to 4) indicate. Many of his letters have been printed in the various memoirs and in books dealing with other Pre-Raphaelites. Significant groups of letters included in other volumes — such as those to Shields (58.7), to Barbara Bodichon (86.23), to Oliver Madox Brown (47.3), to James Smetham (60.1), and the letters to Swinburne included in Lang's recent edition of *The Swinburne Letters* (62.12) — are cited in annotations. A collected edition of Rossetti's letters, by Professors Oswald Doughty and John Robert Wahl, has been announced by the Clarendon Press and is listed in the 1957 *Supplement* to the *CBEL*. For a brief discussion of the published editions of Rossetti's letters see the Survey, pp. 28–29.

* * *

24.1 Prideaux, W. F. "D. G. Rossetti," *Notes & Queries*, 6th ser., VIII (10 November 1883), 364.

Refers to a letter in the *Athenaeum*, no. 1295 (21 August 1852), pp. 901–902, signed "D. G. R." and as yet unnoticed by biographers. Another note to the *Athenaeum*, no. 1304 (23 October 1852), p. 1147, referring to "The Card Dealer" and signed "H. H. H." (Rossetti's *nom de plume*) is also cited. For further discussion by Prideaux of Rossetti's revisions of "The Card Dealer" between 1852 and 1870 see *N&Q*, 7th ser., IV (17 December 1887), 481–482. It should be noted that Rossetti contributed many uncollected letters to journals, especially to the *Athenaeum*. "A Warning" concerning forgeries of his works appeared, for example, in the *Athenaeum*, no. 2647 (20 July 1878), p. 89.

24.2 [Horne, Herbert P.]. "Rossetti: Some Extracts from His Letters to Mr. Frederic Shields," *Century Guild Hobby Horse*, n.s. IV (April 1889), 82–96.

Over fifty letters from Rossetti are included in *The Life and Letters of Frederic Shields* (58.7).

24.3 Clabburn, H. T. "Some Relics of Rossetti," *Pall Mall Budget*, no. 1165 (22 January 1891), p. 14.

Extracts from Rossetti's letters to Clabburn's father pertaining to *Mary Magdalene*.

24.4 Prinsep, Valentine C. "A Collector's Correspondence," *Art Journal*, LIV (August 1892), 249–252.

Rossetti's letters to Frederick Leyland.

24.5 Rossetti, William M., ed. *Dante Gabriel Rossetti: His Family Letters, with a Memoir*. 2 vols. London: Ellis, 1895.

The letters (vol. II), all to various members of the family, serve largely to corroborate and clarify the biographical material in the *Memoir* (vol. I). In all 317 letters from Rossetti are included — 143 to William Michael Rossetti, 107 to Rossetti's mother, and 67 to other relatives, including Christina — all annotated by William Michael. The *Memoir* contains an important section on the Pre-Raphaelite Brotherhood. For a long discussion of Rossetti's family correspondence, in part a review of W. M. Rossetti's edition, see Ford Madox Hueffer, "Dante Gabriel Rossetti and His Family Letters," *Longman's Magazine*, XXVII (March 1896), 465–474 (same in *Living Age*, CCIX, 6th ser., X, no. 2700 [4 April 1896], 53–59).

24.6 Hill, George Birkbeck, ed. *Letters of Dante Gabriel Rossetti to William Allingham, 1854–1870*. London: Unwin, 1897.

Reprinted from *Atlantic Monthly*, LXXVII (May 1896), 577–595; (June 1896), 744–754; LXXVIII (July 1896), 45–57; (August 1896), 242–245. A well edited, though slightly expurgated compilation of letters now in the Pierpont Morgan Library (see 3.6 for description). For materials included in Rossetti's letters to Allingham not published by Hill see Merill L. Howe, "A Dramatic Skit by Dante Gabriel Rossetti," *MLN*, XLIX (January 1934), 39–44; also "Dante Gabriel Rossetti's Comments on 'Maud,' " *MLN*, XLIX (May 1934), 290–293. For a long review-article on the letters see Teodor de Wyzewa, "La Correspondance d'un Préraphaélite anglais," *Revue des Deux Mondes*, CXLV (February 1898), 936–946.

24.7 Rossetti, William Michael, ed. *Ruskin: Rossetti: Pre-Raphaelitism. Papers 1854 to 1862*. London: Allen, 1899.

For a long review-article on this volume see Teodor de Wyzewa, "La Correspondance de Ruskin et de Rossetti," *Revue des Deux Mondes*, CLVII (February 1900), 935–946. For additional annotation on this volume see 72.6.

24.8 ——— ed. "Some Early Correspondence of Dante Gabriel Rossetti, 1835–54," *Præraphaelite Diaries and Letters*. London: Hurst and Blackett, 1900.

Twenty-four letters to various correspondents, principally to his father and Ford Madox Brown. For complete annotation on this volume see 72.7.

24.9 ——— ed. *Rossetti Papers, 1862–1870*. London: Sands, 1903.

Contains nearly 300 letters to and from Dante Gabriel and William Michael Rossetti and various other correspondents. The volume also contains selections from William Michael's diary.

24.10 *Letters Addressed to Algernon Charles Swinburne, by John Ruskin, William Morris, Sir Edward Burne-Jones and Dante Gabriel Rossetti*. London: Printed for private circulation for Thomas J. Wise, 1919.

24.11 Rossetti, Dante Gabriel. *John Keats: Criticism and Comment*. London: Printed for private circulation only for Thomas J. Wise, 1919.

Five letters from Rossetti to H. Buxton Forman.

24.12 Swinburne, Algernon Charles, and Dante Gabriel Rossetti. *A Romance of Literature*. London: Printed for private circulation only for Thomas J. Wise, 1919.

Two letters, one from each poet, relating to the exhumation of Rossetti's poems. With a preface by T. J. Wise.

24.13 [Compton-Rickett, Arthur]. "Rossetti and Swinburne," *Times Literary Supplement*, no. 926 (16 October 1919), pp. 565–566.

Nine letters from Rossetti to Swinburne pertaining to the 1870 *Poems*. Reprinted by Compton-Rickett in *Portraits and Personalities* (London: Selwyn and Blount, 1937). For Swinburne's letters to Rossetti, and three from Rossetti to Swinburne, see 62.12. See also 62.9.

24.14 *Letters from Dante Gabriel Rossetti to Algernon Charles Swinburne Regarding the Attacks Made upon the Latter by Mortimer Collins and upon Both by Robert Buchanan*. London: Printed for private circulation only for Thomas J. Wise, 1921.

Three letters written in 1871, occasioned by the publication of Collins' novel *Two Plunges for a Pearl*.

24.15 Arnold, William Harris. "Some Victorian Books and Letters," *Ventures in Book Collecting*. New York: Scribner's, 1923.

Containing Rossetti's famous letter to Leigh Hunt, a letter from Browning to Rossetti, and various presentation copies of Rossetti's works.

24.16 Doughty, Oswald, ed. *The Letters of Dante Gabriel Rossetti to His Publisher, F. S. Ellis*. London: Scholartis Press, 1928.

Includes 92 letters from Rossetti — 59 written in 1870 and relating to the publication of *Poems*; eight concerning the *Fleshly* controversy; and the remainder pertaining to the two volumes of 1881 — from manuscripts in the British Museum. With an interesting introductory biographical essay by the editor.

24.17 Purves, John, ed. "Letters of Dante Gabriel Rossetti to Miss Alice Boyd," *Fortnightly Review*, CXXIX, n.s. CXXIII (May 1928), 577–594.

Fifteen letters from Rossetti covering both of his visits to Penkill Castle. The letters contain many interesting references to Miss Losh (see 24.18).

24.18 Troxell, Janet Camp, ed. *Three Rossettis: Unpublished Letters to and from Dante Gabriel, Christina, William*. Cambridge, Mass.: Harvard University Press, 1937.

Of particular interest in this volume are the letters to Rossetti from Holman Hunt, Bell Scott, Ruskin, and C. A. Howell. The volume also contains important groups of letters from Rossetti to his mother and to Miss Losh. Most of the letters included are in the collection of Mrs. Troxell (see 4.5). The chapter on Howell first appeared (in part) as "Charles Augustus Howell and the Exhumation of Rossetti's Poems," *Colophon*, XV (1933), [no pagination]. A full commentary is provided by the editor for each group of letters.

24.19 Baum, Paull Franklin, ed. *Dante Gabriel Rossetti's Letters to Fanny Cornforth*. Baltimore: Johns Hopkins Press, 1940.

These letters were obtained from Fanny Cornforth by Samuel Bancroft, Jr., and are now in the Pre-Raphaelite Collection at Wilmington, Delaware (see 3.1).

24.20 Troxell, Janet Camp. "A Rossetti Letter," *Times Literary Supplement*, no. 2498 (16 December 1949), p. 825.

On a letter from Rossetti to Swinburne [?] in the Ashley Library. See follow-up letter by Helen Rossetti Angeli, *TLS*, no. 2499 (23 December 1949), p. 841.

24.21 Meyerstein, E. H. W. "Rossetti on Patmore's Odes (1868)," *Times Literary Supplement*, no. 2517 (28 April 1950), p. 268.

An unpublished letter from Rossetti to Patmore.

24.22 Troxell, Janet Camp. "A Burne-Jones Murray," *Times Literary Supplement*, no. 2733 (18 June 1954), p. 393.

A letter to William Bell Scott from Rossetti regarding a forgery of Burne-Jones by

Baronet Murray Howell Murray, a friend of C. A. Howell.

24.23 Grandsen, K. W. "English Literary Autographs, XVI: Dante Gabriel Rossetti, 1828–1882; Christina Georgina Rossetti, 1830–1894," *Book Collector*, IV (Winter 1955), 309.

Illustrated.

24.24 Adrian, Arthur A. "The Browning-Rossetti Friendship: Some Unpublished Letters," *Publications of the Modern Language Association*, LXXIII (December 1958), 538–544.

Manuscript letters (in the Huntington Library) from Rossetti to Browning dealing primarily with the arrangements for sending William Page's portrait of Browning to the Royal Academy exhibition of 1856, and with Rossetti's sketch of Browning.

24.25 B[aum], P[aull] F[ranklin]. "Rossetti to George Eliot," *Duke University Library Notes*, no. 34 (1959), pp. 18–19.

A manuscript letter in the Duke University Library.

24.26 Sambrook, A. J. "D. G. Rossetti and R. W. Dixon," *Étude Anglaises*, XIV (October-December 1961), 331–338.

A pair of letters exchanged between Rossetti and Dixon (owned by Miss M. C. Barnard) in 1875 indicates Rossetti's belated recognition of Dixon's poetic abilities as revealed in his two volumes of poems (see 85.2 and 85.3). The letters are printed here for the first time. Rossetti's association with Dixon is fully described. In the second half of the article, those portions of Dixon's poems which Rossetti praised are reproduced and examined in the light of his criticism.

24.27 Packer, Lona Mosk, ed. *The Rossetti-Macmillan Letters: Some 133 Unpublished Letters Written to Alexander Macmillan, F. S. Ellis, and Others, by Dante Gabriel, Christina, and William Michael Rossetti, 1861–1889.* Berkeley: University of California Press, 1963.

With twenty-seven letters by Rossetti.

24.28 Grylls, R. Glynn [= (Lady) Rosalie Mander]. "The Reserved Rossetti Letters," *Times Literary Supplement*, no. 3231 (30 January 1964), p. 96.

The first report on the 117 letters from Rossetti to Jane Morris in the British Museum, with brief extracts. Long-awaited, the letters answer few questions: ". . . they are inconclusive, providing no evidence to support the conjectures of contemporaries and . . . survivors of the period . . . Only the fact that Janey kept them points to the preciousness of the memories that they enshrined for her."

24.29 Briggs, R. C. H. "Letters to Janey," *Journal of the William Morris Society*, I, no. 4 (Summer 1964), 2–22.

A thorough account of Rossetti's letters to Jane Morris in the British Museum, which were opened to public inspection on 27 January 1964, after fifty years of restriction. With liberal quotations from the letters and two illustrations. "The nature of Janey's stimulus for Rossetti is a mystery which these letters do nothing to solve, but that the stimulus was real and essential for him they establish beyond doubt." (p. 22)

Section 25

BIOGRAPHIES AND STUDIES PRINCIPALLY
BIOGRAPHICAL, INCLUDING CENTENARY
AND OTHER GENERAL STUDIES

25.1 Caine, T. Hall. *Recollections of Dante Gabriel Rossetti.* London: Stock, 1882.

The earliest biography of Rossetti by his last close friend. The volume contains a number of letters from Rossetti to Caine bearing on Rossetti's critical attitudes. Caine revised his *Recollections* and included them as part II of his autobiography, *My Story* (New York: Appleton, 1908). In 1928, for the Rossetti centenary, he republished with further revisions much of the material in the later volume as *Recollections of Rossetti* (London: Cassell). See 25.79.

25.2 Placci, Carlo. *Dante Gabriele Rossetti.* Firenze: Ufizio della Rassegna Nazionale, 1882.

Reprinted from *La Rassegna Nazionale,* IX (May 1882), 427–446.

25.3 Sharp, William. *Dante Gabriel Rossetti: A Record and a Study.* London: Macmillan, 1882.

With an "Artistic Record" listing in chronological order Rossetti's paintings and drawings, giving dates, medium, and owners of the 395 works listed.

25.4 Caine, T. Hall. "Obituary: Dante Gabriel Rossetti," *Academy,* XXI, no. 519 (15 April 1882), 266–268.

Lists various writers praised by Rossetti. To Caine's list Alice Meynell adds the name of Dr. T. G. Hake in "Dante Gabriel Rossetti and Contemporary Poets," *Academy,* XXI, no. 520 (22 April 1882), 286.

25.5 Watts [-Dunton], Theodore, and F. G. Stephens. "Mr. Dante Gabriel Rossetti," *Athenaeum,* no. 2842 (15 April 1882), pp. 480–482.

An obituary account of Rossetti's life. Same in *Living Age,* CLIII, 5th ser., XXXVIII, no. 1979 (27 May 1882), 504–506. Reprinted in *Old Familiar Faces* (64.2), pp. 69–76.

25.6 Hancock, Thomas. "Dante G. Rossetti," *Academy,* XXI, no. 522 (6 May 1882), 323.

Reminiscences written by a cousin of the sculptor, John Hancock.

25.7 Gosse, Edmund W. "Dante Gabriel Rossetti," *Century Magazine,* XXIV, n.s. II (September 1882), 718–725.

Highly eulogistic obituary review of Rossetti's life and work. Contains the first printing of the second of the "Church Porches" sonnets.

25.8 Robinson, Mary. "Dante Gabriel Rossetti," *Harper's Magazine,* LXV (October 1882), 691–701.

25.9 Watts [-Dunton], Theodore. "The Truth about Rossetti," *Nineteenth Century,* XIII (March 1883), 404–423.

Personal recollections; a review of Rossetti's life and of his artistic and poetic career.

25.10 "Memorials of Rossetti," *Atlantic Monthly,* LI (April 1883), 549–555.

A review-article on the biographies of Caine (25.1) and Sharp (25.3).

25.11 Knight, Joseph. *Life of Dante Gabriel Rossetti.* London: Scott, 1887.

Appended is a bibliography by J. P. Anderson, with a "Chronological List of Rossetti's Paintings and Drawings." Anderson's list is reprinted in Destrée (75.18).

25.12 Weigand, Wilhelm. "Dante Gabriel Rossetti," *Die Gegenwart,* XXXV (January 1889), 38–40.

25.13 Hardinge, William M. "A Reminiscence of Rossetti," *Universal Review,* VI (March 1890), 398–411.

25.14 Hunt, William Holman. "Memories of Rossetti," *Musical World,* LXX (July 1890), 526–528.

For annotation see 36.4.

25.15 Hinkson, K. "Dante Gabriel Rossetti — A Strayed Catholic," *Ave Maria,* n.s. XXXVII (September 1893), 281–286.

25.16 [Skelton, John]. "Mainly about Rossetti," *The Table Talk of Shirley: Reminiscences of and Letters from Froude, Thackeray, Disraeli, Browning, Rossetti, Kingsley, . . . and Others.* London: Blackwood, 1894.

Primarily a defense of Rossetti against the attacks of William Bell Scott (see 56.10). Contains ten letters from Rossetti to Skelton and many interesting reminiscences. Originally appeared in shorter form as 56.18.

25.17 Caine, Lily Hall. "A Child's Recollection of Rossetti," *New Review,* XI (September 1894), 246–255.

Reminiscences by Hall Caine's sister, who last saw Rossetti shortly before his death at Birchington. Same in *Living Age,* CCIII, 6th ser., IV, no. 2623 (13 October 1894), 102–108.

25.18 Noble, James Ashcroft. "At the Grave of Rossetti," *Bookman* (New York), I (April 1895), 170–173.
Same in *Bookman* (London), VIII (April 1895), 14–15.

25.19 Watts [-Dunton]. "The Life of D. G. Rossetti," *Spectator*, LXXVI, no. 3539 (25 April 1896), 596–597.
A letter on his friendship with Rossetti and an assertion that he has not abandoned his intention to write the poet-artist's life.

25.20 Stillman, William James. "Rossetti and Chloral," *Academy*, LIII, no. 1350 (19 March 1898), 333.
Denying responsibility for Rossetti's chloral addiction.

25.21 Barbiera, R. "La Strana Vita di Dante Gabriele Rossetti," *Immortali e dimenticati*. Milano: Cogliati, 1901.

25.22 Stillman, William James. "Rossetti and His Friends," *The Autobiography of a Journalist*. vol. II. Boston: Houghton, Mifflin, 1901.
Personal reminiscences of Rossetti. Stillman's wife, the former Marie Spartali, a minor painter and student of Ford Madox Brown, was one of Rossetti's loveliest models.

25.23 "Buchanan and Rossetti," *Bookman* (New York), XIII (August 1901), 524–526.
Contrasts the violence of Buchanan's attacks on his contemporaries, particularly Rossetti, with the kindly notices engendered by his death.

25.24 Gilchrist, Herbert H. "Recollections of Rossetti," *Lippincott's Magazine*, LXVIII (November 1901), 571–576.
"Rossetti was one of the few real democrats I have known . . . and [he] was possessed of the fulness of manhood that we associate with the genius of Samuel Johnson, and, I may add, with Walt Whitman." (p. 576)

25.25 Rossetti, William Michael. "Dante Gabriel Rossetti and Elizabeth Siddal," *Burlington Magazine*, I (May 1903), 273–295.
"With facsimiles of five unpublished drawings by Dante Rossetti in the collection of Mr. Harold Hartley." See also the identically entitled chapter in 38.8. For additional annotation see 59.1.

25.26 Benson, Arthur C. *Rossetti* (English Men of Letters). London: Macmillan, 1904.

25.27 Prinsep, Valentine C. "Dante Gabriel Rossetti: A Chapter from a Painter's Reminiscences," *Magazine of Art*, XXVII, n.s. II (1904), 281–286.
See also 30.37.

25.28 Rutledge, Guy. "Some Notes on the Life and Work of Dante Gabriel Rossetti," *Liverpool Philomathic Society Proceedings*, L (1904–1905), cxi–cxxxix.

25.29 Noguchi, Yone. "With Rossetti in London," *National Magazine*, XXIII (November 1905), 157–160.

25.30 Hubbard, Elbert. *Little Journeys to the Homes of Famous Lovers: Dante Gabriel Rossetti and Elizabeth Siddal*. East Aurora, N.Y.: The Roycrofters, 1906.

25.31 Singer, Hans Wolfgang. *Dante Gabriel Rossetti* (The Langham Series: An Illustrated Collection of Art Monographs, edited by Selwyn Brinton, vol. XIV). London: Siegle, 1906.
Originally published in German (Berlin: Bard, Marquardt, 1905) as no. 41 in the *Die Kunst* series, edited by Richard Muther.

25.32 Jiriczek, Otto L. "Dante Gabriel Rossetti," *Hochland*, IV (November 1906), 183–195.
Reprinted in *Viktorianische Dichtung* (Heidelberg: Winter, 1907).

25.33 Krapp, Lorenz. "Dante Gabriel Rossetti," *Die Kultur*, VIII (1907), 89–98.

25.34 Ranftl, Johann. "Dante Gabriel Rossetti," *Historisch-politische Blätter für das katholische Deutschland*, CXXXIX (1907), 477–500, 575–597.

25.35 Rose, G. B. "Rossetti," *Pathfinder*, II (March 1908), 2–5.

25.36 Carr, J. Comyns. "Dante Gabriel Rossetti," *Some Eminent Victorians: Personal Recollections in the World of Art and Letters*. London: Duckworth, 1908.

For complete annotation see 37.73.

25.37 Terry, Ellen. "Rossetti, Bernhardt, Irving, 1865–1867," *The Story of My Life*. London: Hutchinson, 1909.

25.38 Watts-Dunton, Theodore. "Rossettiana: A Glimpse of Rossetti and Morris at Kelmscott," *English Review*, I (January 1909), 323–332.

See also George Meredith's brief "Note on Cheyne Walk" (a letter to the editor) immediately following Watts-Dunton's article (p. 333).

25.39 Bensusan, Samuel Levy. *The Charm of Rossetti*. London: Jack [1910].

25.40 Sharp, Elizabeth Amy, ed. "The Death of Rossetti," *William Sharp (Fiona Macleod): A Memoir Compiled by His Wife*. New York: Duffield, 1910.

25.41 Swinburne, Algernon Charles. *A Record of a Friendship*. London: Printed for private circulation only for Thomas J. Wise, 1910.

A manuscript fragment by Swinburne in the Ashley Library describing his friendship with Rossetti and Elizabeth Siddal, written on Rossetti's death in 1882.

25.42 Byron, Mary C. *A Day with Dante Gabriel Rossetti*. London: Hodder and Stoughton, 1911.

25.43 Le Gallienne, Richard. "Dante Gabriel Rossetti and Elizabeth Siddal," *The Loves of the Poets*. New York: Baker, 1911.

Reprinted in *Old Love Stories Retold* (London: John Lane, 1924).

25.44 Hueffer, Ford Madox. "D. G. R.," *Bookman* (London), XL (June 1911), 113–120.

An examination of the treatment Rossetti has received at the hands of his biographers.

25.45 Carr, J. Comyns. "With Rossetti in Cheyne Walk," *Coasting Bohemia*. London: Macmillan, 1914.

In the same volume see also the chapters, "Some Memories of Millais" (37.54), "Edward Burne-Jones" (9.9), and "The English School of Painting at the Roman Exhibition" (21.36).

25.46 Taglialatela, Eduardo. *Dante Gabriel Rossetti: Rosa Maria — La Nave Bianca — La Tragedia del Re — Dante a Verona. Studio e Versione*. Roma: Vallardi, 1914.

25.47 Grasé, J. C. G. "Dante Gabriel Rossetti," *Onze Eeuw*, XIV (October 1914), 75–112.

25.48 Symons, Arthur. "A Note on Rossetti," *North American Review*, CCIV (July 1916), 128–134.

Highly impressionistic. "There was in him, as in many artists, the dust of the eyes."

25.49 Schücking, Levin Ludwig. "Rossettis Persönlichkeit," *Englische Studien*, LI (October 1917), 189–225.

Reprinted in *Essays* (Wiesbaden, 1948).

25.50 Smith, Maurice. "Dante Gabriel Rossetti" (Sohier Prize, Harvard University, 1919). Typescript in the Harvard University Library.

25.51 Miller, Joaquin [= Cincinnatus Hiner Miller]. "Recollections of the Rossetti Dinner," *Overland Monthly*, LXXV (February 1920), 138–141.

A selection from Miller's journal.

25.52 Colvin, Sidney. "Dante Gabriel Rossetti," *Memories and Notes of Persons and Places, 1852–1912*. London: Arnold, 1921.

See also the chapters on Burne-Jones (42.95) and Ruskin (45.20). The sections on Rossetti and Burne-Jones originally appeared in *Scribner's Magazine*, LXVII (January 1920), 69–82.

25.53 Dupré, Henri. *Un Italien d'Angle-*

terre, le poète-peintre, Dante Gabriel Rossetti. Paris: Dent, 1921.

25.54 Davies, Charles. *Dante Gabriel Rossetti.* London: Merton Press, 1925.
With a good working bibliography.

* * *

25.55 Arrieta, R. A. "Dante Gabriel Rossetti," *Dickens, Sarmiento: otros estudios.* Buenos Aires: El Ateneo, 1928.

25.56 Lucas, E. V. "Edward Burne-Jones and D. G. Rossetti — 1867 and on," *The Colvins and Their Friends.* London: Methuen, 1928.

25.57 Proix, J. *Un Mysticisme esthétique . . . pour le centenaire de la naissance de Dante Gabriel Rossetti.* Paris: L'Artisan du Livre, 1928.

25.58 Mégroz, R. L. *Dante Gabriel Rossetti, Painter Poet of Heaven in Earth.* London: Faber, 1928.
Divided into a biographical and a critical section. Section I contains a contrasting pair of chapters on "Lizzie Siddal" and "Lizzie Rossetti."

25.59 Waugh, Evelyn. *Rossetti: His Life and Works.* London: Duckworth, 1928.
For discussion see Survey, p. 31. For an interesting review of Waugh's study see 32.17; and *TLS,* no. 1371 (10 May 1928), pp. 341–342.

25.60 Ardagh, J. "Dante Gabriel Rossetti," *Notes & Queries,* 13th ser., CLIV (21 April 1928), 280; (16 June 1928), 431.
Lists various memorials to Rossetti in London, Birchington, and Hastings.

25.61 Hunziker, Marguerite. "A Century of Rossetti," *Mentor,* XVI (May 1928), 37–40.

25.62 Shanks, Edward. "Dante Gabriel Rossetti," *London Mercury,* XVIII (May 1928), 67–78.

25.63 Smith, Garnet. "Dante Gabriel Rossetti," *Contemporary Review,* CXXXIII (May 1928), 624–631.

25.64 Waugh, Evelyn. "D. G. Rossetti: A Centenary Criticism," *Fortnightly Review,* CXXIX, n.s. CXXIII (May 1928), 595–604.

25.65 West, Geoffrey. "Revaluations: Dante Gabriel Rossetti," *Outlook* [*New Review*], LXI (May 1928), 596–597.

25.66 Gosse, Edmund. "Rossetti," *Sunday Times,* no. 5482 (6 May 1928), p. 8.
Same in *Living Age,* CCCXXXIV, 8th ser., XLVIII, no. 4331 (July 1928), 1077–1080.

25.67 B., F. "Dante Gabriel Rossetti, 1828–1882," *Boekenschouw,* XXII (June 1928), 65–70.

25.68 Manson, J. B. "Dante Gabriel Rossetti," *Apollo,* VII (June 1928), 257–258.
With a reproduction of the *Passover in the Holy Family* in the Tate Gallery. An insignificant article.

25.69 Wolff, Lucien. "Le Centenaire de Dante Gabriel Rossetti — Rossetti et le Moyen-Age," *Revue Anglo-Américaine,* VI (June 1928), 452–458.

25.70 Hall, S. Elizabeth. "Dante Gabriel Rossetti," *Quest,* XIX (July 1928), 367–384.

25.71 Hodgson, Geraldine. "Dante Gabriel Rossetti," *Church Quarterly Review,* CVI (July 1928), 353–362.
"Rossetti's worship of beauty was temperamental, not an affectation or literary loan." The Symboliste "rêve" and Rossetti's "ectasy" are phases of Platonic "madness." Rossetti stands in the direct line of "divinely mad" poets.

25.72 Mégroz, R. L. "Dante Gabriel Rossetti (1828–1928)," *Dublin Magazine,* n.s. III (July-September 1928), 39–49.
"As a creative artist [Rossetti] is perhaps most surely and conveniently characterized as the recorder of radiant moments." (p. 48)

25.73 Monroe, Harriet. "Rossetti," *Poetry,* XXXII (August 1928), 270–277.
A centenary editorial.

25.74 De Bruyn, Jeanne. "Dante Gabriel

Rossetti Herdacht, 12 Mei 1828–9 April 1882," *Dietsche Warande*, XXVIII (December 1928), 957–971.

25.75 Smith, Harry B. "Dante Gabriel Rossetti, 1828–1928," *Century Magazine*, CXVII (December 1928), 245–253.

25.76 Lemmermayer, Fritz. "Dante Gabriel Rossetti, der Romantiker zur hundersten Wiederkehr seines Geburtsjahres," *Das Goetheanum*, VII (December 1928), 404–406.

* * *

25.77 Formichi, Carlo. "Dante Gabriel Rossetti," *University of California Chronicle*, XXXI (July 1929), 267–280.
A belated centenary review of Rossetti's life and works.

25.78 Borchardt, Rudolf. "Dante Gabriel Rossetti," *Die Horen*, VI (January 1930), 53–62; (February 1930), 133–152.

25.79 MacCarthy, Desmond. "Rossetti and Hall Caine," *Portraits*. New York: Putnam, 1931.
Reprinted (London: Oxford, 1954). A notice of 25.1.

25.80 Robertson, W. Graham. "The Spell of Rossetti," *Time Was: Reminiscences*. With a Foreword by Sir Johnston Forbes-Robertson. London: Hamish Hamilton, 1931.
Published in America (New York: Harper, 1931) as *Life Was Worth Living*. See also the letters of Graham Robertson (86.25).

25.81 Purves, John. "Dante Gabriel Rossetti and His Godfather, Charles Lyell of Kinnordy," *University of Edinburgh Journal*, IV (Summer 1931), 110–118.
Concerned primarily with Gabriele Rossetti's association with Lyell and with the circumstances surrounding Dante Gabriel's baptism. The article contains one letter from Dante Gabriel Rossetti to Lyell (in the Kinnordy collection) dated 14 November 1848, relating to Rossetti's portrait of his father and to *The Girlhood of Mary Virgin*. A long and important Rossetti letter.

25.82 Nothwang, Irene. *Die Frau, die Liebe*

und der Tod bei Dante Gabriel Rossetti. Stuttgart: Felbach, 1932 (diss. Tübingen, 1932).

25.83 Cammell, Charles Richard. *Dante Gabriel Rossetti and the Philosophy of Love*. London: Poseidon Press, 1933.
Reprinted from *Scotsman*, 6 June 1933. Conclusion: "Always tragic! One of the great lovers! Such, fitly, was the Prophet, in our tongue, of the Philosophy of Love." (p. 21) ". . . no painter of the North knew the secret [of love] till Rossetti, an Italian under an alien sky, taught his Pre-Raphaelite friends to paint the souls of women, and to portray each his own soul in the pensive countenance of his beloved." (pp. 18–19)

25.84 Larg, David. *Trial by Virgins: Fragment of a Biography*. London: Davies, 1933.
A sensational and unreliable account of Rossetti's life.

25.85 Chesson, W. H. "Rossetti's Marriage," *Quarterly Review*, CCLX (January 1933), 84–93.
A review-article on Violet Hunt's *The Wife of Rossetti* (59.7), whose assertions he supports. Chesson considers Rossetti's act of burying the poems a hypocrisy and the exhumation a sacrilege. Conclusion: ". . . if Rossetti, alive in Chelsea, had read such a book as Miss Hunt's, it would have killed him." (p. 85)

25.86 Las Vergnas, R. "Le Britannisme de Rossetti," *Revue Anglo-Américaine*, XI (December 1933), 129–135.

25.87 Wolff, L[ucien]. *Dante Gabriel Rossetti*. Paris: Didier, 1934.

25.88 Bragman, Louis J. "The Case of Dante Gabriel Rossetti: A Psychological Study of a Chloral Addict," *American Journal of Psychiatry*, XCII (March 1936), 1111–1122.
"The life of Dante Gabriel Rossetti, the greatest poet *and* painter since Michelangelo, was a darkening pilgrimage." (p. 1111) Rossetti's symptoms as a drug addict are recounted from unreliable (medically speaking) contemporary accounts, and the article puts more emphasis on the details of Rossetti's life

than on his actual drug addiction. See also 25.90.

25.89 Moore, Dom Thomas Verner. "Dante Gabriel Rossetti," *Dublin Review*, CC (April 1937), 345–360.

A vague article, hinting at Rossetti's ambiguity in philosophical thought: "Judging Rossetti's philosophy of life by its results, it was most unfortunate. Self-expression alone is an inadequate guide because of its ambiguity." (p. 360) For a reply to this article see Helen Rossetti Angeli, "Dante Gabriel Rossetti," *Dublin Review*, CCI (October 1937), 364–367.

25.90 Macht, David I., and Nellie L. Gessford. "The Unfortunate Drug Experiences of Dante Gabriel Rossetti," *Bulletin of the Institute of the History of Medicine*, VI (1938), 34–61.

See Jeannette Marks, "Drugs and Genius," *Genius and Disaster* (New York: Adelphi, 1925). See also 25.88.

25.91 Angeli, Helen Rossetti. *Dante Gabriel Rossetti: His Friends and Enemies*. London: Hamish Hamilton, 1949.

Separate chapters on Brown, Woolner, Hunt, Millais, Ruskin, Swinburne, Morris, Burne-Jones, Meredith, Whistler, Howell, Bell Scott, Browning, Elizabeth Siddal, Jane Morris, and the Rossetti family.

25.92 Doughty, Oswald. *A Victorian Romantic: Dante Gabriel Rossetti*. London: Muller, 1949.

Second edition (London: Oxford University Press, 1960). For discussion of this important biography see Survey, pp. 31–32.

25.93 Altick, Richard D. [Dante Gabriel Rossetti] in "Post-Mortems," *The Scholar Adventurers*. New York: Macmillan, 1950.

An examination of the importance of Rossetti's addiction to chloral as an almost unique, because so fully documented, medical case history.

25.94 Doughty, Oswald. "Rossetti and Mrs. Morris," *Times Literary Supplement*, no. 2575 (8 June 1951), p. 357.

This subject, of vital importance in dating some of the sonnets in *The House of Life*, was first discussed by P. F. Baum in the introduction to his edition of Rossetti's *Poems* (23.31). This article contains two interesting letters from Rossetti to Dr. Hake (28 April 1870 and 12 September 1872) which Doughty sees as further evidence of the relationship. Sir Sydney Cockerell replied, denying the romantic attachment and publishing an innocuous letter from Rossetti to Mrs. Morris (now in the Victoria and Albert Museum) in *TLS*, no. 2579 (6 July 1951), p. 421. Three further letters in the *TLS* — by Doughty, Cockerell, and Philip Henderson — concluded the controversy: no. 2585 (17 August 1951), p. 517; no. 2586 (24 August 1951), p. 533; no. 2588 (7 September 1951), p. 565. For additional comment on the relationship between Rossetti and Jane Morris see J. R. Wahl's *The Kelmscott Love Sonnets* (23.36), Doughty's life of Rossetti (25.92), and Henderson's article, "La Belle Iseult" (43.152). For Rossetti's letters to Jane Morris in the British Museum see 2.2; for Jane Morris' letters to Rossetti in the collection of Mrs. J. C. Troxell see 4.5.

25.95 Shute, Nerina. *Victorian Love Story; a Study of the Victorian Romantics Based on the Life of Dante Gabriel Rossetti: A Novel*. London: Jarrolds, 1954.

25.96 Williamson, Hugh Ross. "The Lost Letter," *Time & Tide*, XL (14 March 1959), 305–307.

A highly speculative article based on a letter from Hall Caine to Cuming Walters of the *Manchester City News* detailing intimate revelations made by Rossetti to Caine on the train from Penrith to Euston. Alice Boyd is named as Rossetti's secret love. The article generated considerable response, the consensus of which was summarized by W. D. Paden: "Several kinds of considerations oppose the identification he suggests; and until at least one piece of evidence has been supplied in its support, Mr. Williamson can scarcely expect it to be seriously considered." (4 April 1959, p. 389)

25.97 Rosenbaum, Robert A. "Dante Gabriel Rossetti, 1828–1882," *Earnest Victorians: Six Great Victorians as Portrayed in Their*

Own Words and Those of Their Contemporaries. New York: Hawthorn, 1961.

A paper-and-paste pastiche of quotations from fourteen standard sources with brief interlinking paragraphs, this chapter offers nothing new on either Rossetti or the Pre-Raphaelites.

25.98 Savarit, Jacques. *Tendances mystiques et ésotériques chez Dante-Gabriel Rossetti.* With a "lettre-frontispice" by André Maurois and a Preface by François Fosca. (*Études*

Anglaises, no. 8). Paris: Didier, 1961 (diss. Genève, 1960).

A psychological biography which examines Rossetti's literary works against the background of the romantic tradition of mysticism, his Italianate heritage and temperament, his family life in his formative years, the succession of women on whom he depended (Elizabeth Siddal, Jane Burden, Fanny Cornforth), and his final reclusion, illness, and addiction to chloral. With an extensive working bibliography.

Section 26

THE ROSSETTI FAMILY

Half the items in this section are works discussing two or more of the Rossettis as creative artists; the remainder pertain specifically to the Rossetti family or to Gabriele Rossetti. The familial bond in the Rossetti household was exceedingly strong, assuming an unusually prominent role in the lives of all the children. Most biographies of Dante Gabriel Rossetti treat his early years in detail and emphasize the importance of his Italian background and his unorthodox home environment on his later development as a writer and artist.

* * *

26.1 "The Rossettis," *London Quarterly Review*, LXXXVII, 2nd. ser., XXVII (October 1896), 1–16.

A critical review and evaluation of Dante Gabriel and Christina Rossetti.

26.2 Gregg, Frederick James. "Reminiscences of the Rossettis," *Book Buyer*, n.s. XVI (May 1898), 315–318.

26.3 Cary, Elizabeth Luther. *The Rossettis: Dante Gabriel and Christina.* New York: Putnam, 1900.

Largely devoted to the life and work of Dante Gabriel but with two chapters on Christina Rossetti.

26.4 Rowley, Charles, "The Rossettis," *Fifty Years of Work Without Wages.* London: Hodder and Stoughton, [1911].

On Dante Gabriel and William Michael Rossetti. Additional chapters on Ford Madox Brown (41.26), Shields (58.6), Morris (43.73), and Holman Hunt (36.57).

26.5 Mather, Frank Jewett. "The Rossettis," *Bookman* (New York), XLIX (April 1919), 139–147.

26.6 Symons, Arthur. "The Rossettis," *Dramatis Personae.* Indianapolis: Bobbs-Merrill, 1923.

* * *

26.7 Sharp, William. "The Rossettis," *Fortnightly Review*, XLV, n.s. XXXIX (March 1886), 414–429.

Same in *Eclectic Magazine*, n.s. XLIII (May 1886), 590–600; *Living Age*, CLXIX, 5th ser., LIV, no. 2182 (April 1886), 161–170. Treats all members of the Rossetti family, including Gabriele, Maria, and William Michael.

26.8 Festing, Gabrielle. "Literary Friendships: Gabriele Rossetti," *John Hookham Frere and His Friends.* London: Nisbet, 1899.

Contains material on Gabriele Rossetti,

with many references to the Rossetti family in general.

26.9 Giartosio de Courten, Maria L. *I. Rossetti, Storia di una famiglia.* Milano: Alpes, 1928.

26.10 Waller, R. D. *The Rossetti Family, 1824–1854.* Manchester University Press, 1932.
A scholarly study with full bibliography. The chapter "The Young Rossettis" contains sections on Dante Gabriel, Maria Francesca, William Michael (38.17), and Christina Rossetti (44.70).

26.11 Vincent, Eric Reginald. *Gabriele Rossetti in England.* Oxford: Clarendon Press, 1936.
For William Michael Rossetti's translation of Gabriele Rossetti's verse autobiography see 38.6.

26.12 Praz, Mario. "La Famiglia Rossetti," *Studi e svaghi inglesi.* Firenze: Sansoni, 1937.

26.13 Giannantonio, Pompeo. *Bibliografia di Gabriele Rossetti, 1806–1958 (Biblioteca Bibliografica Italica.* no. 16) Roma: Sansoni, 1959.
With a Biographical Note.

Section 27

STUDIES EMPHASIZING ROSSETTI'S LITERARY WORK AND INFLUENCE

27.1 [Forman, Harry Buxton]. "Criticisms on Contemporaries: No. VI. The Rossettis. Part II. [Dante Gabriel Rossetti]," *Tinsley's Magazine,* V (September 1869), 142–151.
Undoubtedly inspired by the publication of Rossetti's sixteen sonnets in the *Fortnightly Review* (23.4). This article and Forman's review of *Poems* in *Tinsley's Magazine* in March 1871 (29.15) were combined in the chapter on Rossetti in *Our Living Poets* (74.1). In *Three Rossettis* (24.18, p. 103), Mrs. J. C. Troxell suggests that a reference to a "pamphlet" by Forman in Rossetti's letter to Miss Losh of 28 February 1871, refers to a separate printing of these two articles (see *Rossetti's Sister Helen,* 23.33, p. 15). However, Rossetti's letter makes perfectly clear that the "pamphlet" refers only to an off-print of the 1871 review.

27.2 [———] "The 'Fleshly School' Controversy," *Tinsley's Magazine,* X (February 1872), 89–102.
Forman's famous attack on Buchanan and defense of Rossetti; a detailed answer to Buchanan's article (29.16). For an unsigned reply to Forman's article and a fresh attack on Rossetti see "Coterie Glory," *Saturday Review,* XXXIII, no. 852 (24 February 1872), 239–240. Buchanan himself may have been responsible for this article. He reprinted a

long excerpt from it in the Notes to the *Fleshly School* pamphlet (82.6, pp. 94–95). For full discussion of the *Fleshly* controversy see Cassidy (76.11) and the Survey, pp. 17–19.

27.3 Swinburne, Algernon Charles. "The Poems of Dante Gabriel Rossetti," *Essays and Studies.* London: Chatto and Windus, 1875.
The first important critical examination of Rossetti's poetry. A review-article on *Poems,* 1870, originally published in the *Fortnightly Review,* XIII, n.s. VII (May 1870), 551–579. Reprinted, among other places, in 23.23 and 62.6. Translated into German and printed in *Wiener Rundschau,* V (1 January 1901), 1–6; (15 January 1901), 28–31.

27.4 Bayne, Thomas. "Our Modern Poets. No. 11: Dante Gabriel Rossetti," *St. James's Magazine,* 4th ser., XXXII (October 1877), 415–430.

27.5 Caine, T. Hall. "The Poetry of Dante Rossetti," *New Monthly Magazine,* 4th ser., I (July 1879), 800–812.
Eulogistic rather than critical.

27.6 Robinson, Mary. "Dante Gabriel Rossetti," *Unsere Zeit,* n.s. I (1879), 767–778.

The earliest notice of Rossetti in a German periodical.

27.7 Pater, Walter Horatio. "Dante Gabriel Rossetti," in *The English Poets: Selections with Critical Introductions by Various Writers*. Edited by T. H. Ward. vol. IV. London: Macmillan, 1880.

Reprinted in *Appreciations* (London: Macmillan, 1889); in *Bibelot*, V (October 1899), 321–338; in 23.24; and in *Victorians on Literature and Art*, edited by R. L. Peters (New York: Appleton-Century-Crofts, 1961). For complete annotation on *The English Poets* see 84.3.

27.8 Hamilton, Walter. "Dante Gabriel Rossetti," *The Æsthetic Movement in England*. London: Reeves and Turner, 1882.

For complete annotation see 78.2.

27.9 Shairp, J. C. "Aesthetic Poetry: Dante Gabriel Rossetti," *Contemporary Review*, XLII (July 1882), 17–32.

Conclusion: "If future poets wish to win the ear of their countrymen, and to merit the honour accorded to the highest poetry, they would be wise to cultivate manlier thought and nobler sentiment, expressed in purer and fresher diction, and to make their appeal, not to the perfumed tastes of over-educated coteries, but to the broader and healthier sympathies of universal man." (p. 32) Same in *Eclectic Magazine*, n.s. XXXVI (September 1882), 341–351; and in *Living Age*, CLIV, 5th ser., XXXIX, no. 1988 (29 July 1882), 228–238.

27.10 Sharp, William. "Dante Gabriel Rossetti and Pictorialism in Verse," *Portfolio*, XIII (October 1882), 176–180.

"Suggestiveness is the soul of verbal pictorialism, as reduplication, modified by individual impression, and verified by individual insight, is the essential aim of pictorialism on canvas." (p. 176)

27.11 Milner, George. "On Some Marginalia Made by Dante Gabriel Rossetti in a Copy of Keats' Poems," *Manchester Quarterly*, II (January 1883), 1–10.

Reprinted in 33.23. A slight note made by Rossetti in the 1868 Moxon edition of Keats

— a presentation copy from William Michael Rossetti, sold in 1882 to W. A. Turner.

27.12 Waddington, Samuel. "The Sonnets of Rossetti," *Academy*, XXV, no. 630 (31 May 1884), 385.

On Rossetti's choice of sonnets for inclusion in Waddington's *English Sonnets by Living Authors* (1881).

27.13 Sarrazin, Gabriel. "Dante Gabriel Rossetti," *Poètes modernes de l'Angleterre*. Paris: Ollendorff, 1885.

Originally appeared in *Revue Indépendante* (1884).

27.14 Horne, Herbert P. "Thoughts Towards a Criticism of the Works of Dante Gabriel Rossetti," *Century Guild Hobby Horse*, n.s. II (July 1886), 91–102.

Discusses the materialistic nature of Rossetti's religion in relation to love, with an interesting comparison of "The Blessed Damozel" and Herrick's "Comfort to a Youth that has Lost his Love." The second half of the article is a review of the *Collected Works* (23.13).

27.15 Buchanan, Robert W. "A Note on Dante Rossetti," *A Look Round Literature*. London: Ward, 1887.

27.16 Fox-Bourne, H. R. "Dante Gabriel Rossetti," *Gentleman's Magazine*, CCLXII (June 1887), 596–610.

A favorable article on Rossetti's life and writings occasioned by the publication of the *Collected Works* (23.13).

27.17 Patmore, Coventry. "Rossetti as a Poet," *Principle in Art: Essays Reprinted from the St. James Gazette*. London: Bell, 1889.

In part a review of the *Collected Works* (23.13).

27.18 Bates, Herbert. "A Study of Rossetti's Verse," *Harvard Monthly*, VII (January 1889), 130–137.

27.19 Dawson, W. J. "Dante Gabriel Rossetti," *Makers of Modern English*. London: Hodder and Stoughton, 1890.

Same in *The Makers of English Poetry* (New York: Revell, 1906). Dawson sees Rossetti as "the living embodiment of the unhappy hero of Poe's poem 'The Raven'." (p. 345)

27.20 Caine, T. Hall. "Dante Gabriel Rossetti," in *The Poets and the Poetry of the Century*, edited by A. H. Miles, vol. [VIII]. London: Hutchinson, [1891–1897].
For complete annotation see 84.5.

27.21 Mabie, Hamilton Wright. "The Poetry of Dante Gabriel Rossetti," *Essays in Literary Interpretation*. New York: Dodd, Mead, 1893.
Same in *Andover Review*, XI (April 1889), 387–394. See also John Walker, "The Poetry of Dante Gabriel Rossetti," *Manchester Quarterly*, X (January 1891), 71–92, an impressionistic essay.

27.22 Worsfold, W. Basil. "The Poetry of D. G. Rossetti," *Nineteenth Century*, XXXIV (August 1893), 284–290.
Including Rossetti's "poetic" paintings. Same in *Eclectic Magazine*, n.s. LVIII (December 1893), 851–854.

27.23 Kernahan, Coulson. "A Note on Rossetti," *Sorrow and Song*. Philadelphia: Lippincott, 1894.
Essentially the same as "Rossetti and the Moralists," *Fortnightly Review*, LV, n.s. XLIX (March 1891), 406–412. An essay on Philip Bourke Marston appears in the same volume (see 50.10).

27.24 "The Poetry of Dante Gabriel Rossetti," *London Quarterly Review*, LXXXII, 2nd ser., XXII (April 1894), 104–112.
Discusses the medieval spirit, the metrical skill, the mystical incense, the sustained narration, and ("Alas!") the sensuous eroticism of Rossetti's poetry.

27.25 Jacottet, Henri. "Poètes modernes de l'Angleterre: Dante Gabriel Rossetti," *Bibliothèque Universelle et Revue Suisse*, LXII (June 1894), 503–524; LXIII (July 1894), 95–114.

27.26 Watts [-Dunton], Theodore. "Rossetti's Unpublished Poems," *Athenaeum*, no. 3578 (23 May 1896), p. 683.
A response to a statement made by William M. Rossetti that much of Rossetti's original poetry was in Watts-Dunton's possession. A declaration of intention to publish "Jan Van Hunks" and the "Sphinx" sonnets, which, with the projected "Michael Scott's Wooing" (23.27, p. 616) and "Poem for a Drawing" (p. 214), were to have been Rossetti's contributions to a joint volume of poems with Watts-Dunton. Reprinted in *Old Familiar Faces* (64.2), pp. 98–102.

27.27 Guthrie, William Norman. "Dante Gabriel Rossetti," *Modern Poet Prophets*. Cincinnati: Clarke, 1897.

27.28 Hume, James Cleland. "Rossetti, the Poet, and the Pre-Raphaelite Brothers," *Midland Monthly*, VII (January 1897), 42–52.

27.29 Morse, Charles A. L. "Rossetti's Poetry," *Catholic World*, LXV (August 1897), 633–640.

27.30 Walker, Elizabeth B. "The Ballads of Dante Gabriel Rossetti," *Citizen* (Philadelphia), IV (June 1898), 76–77.

27.31 Livingston, L. S. "First Books of Some English Authors. III. Dante Gabriel and Christina Rossetti," *Bookman* (New York), X (November 1899), 245–247.

27.32 Kenyon, James B. "Rossetti and His Sister Christina," *Loiterings in Old Fields: Literary Sketches*. New York: Eaton, 1901.
Reprinted from *Methodist Review*, LXXVIII (September 1896), 743–753. Also contains a chapter on Morris (43.50) and Christina Rossetti (44.41).

27.33 Moulton, Charles Wells, ed. "Gabriel Charles Dante Rossetti," *The Library of Literary Criticism of English and American Authors*, vol. II. Buffalo, New York: Moulton, 1901.
Volume VII contains brief sections on Marston, Allingham, and O'Shaughnessy; volume VIII on Morris, Patmore, and Christina Rossetti.

27.34 Robinson, Mary. *Grands Écrivains d'outre-manche: Les Brontë, Thackeray, Les Browning, Rossetti*. Paris: Levy, 1901.

Rossetti section reprinted from *Revue de Paris*, no. 3 (1 June 1896), 550–582.

27.35 Spens, J. "The Ethical Significance of Rossetti's Poetry," *International Journal of Ethics*, XII (January 1902), 216–225.

A serious article treating Rossetti as a "theological poet" (having certain affinities with Browning), who is always testing the question — "at what point the purely sensuous passes into the intellectual." Rossetti's poetry "deals not with the subjects of thought, but with the processes of the mind."

27.36 Galletti, Alfredo. "Dante Gabriele Rossetti e la poesia preraffaellita," *Studi di letterature straniere*. Verona: Fratelli Drucker, 1903.

27.37 Kuhns, Oscar. "Matthew Arnold and Rossetti," *Dante and the English Poets from Chaucer to Tennyson*. New York: Holt, 1904.

Not a comparative study.

27.38 Henry, Albert S. "Rossetti," *Book News Monthly*, XXII (May 1904), 1032–1033.

27.39 Hellings, Emma L. "Rossetti's Treatment of Love," *Poet Lore*, XVI (March 1905), 76–79.

27.40 Payne, William Morton. "Dante Gabriel Rossetti," *The Greater English Poets of the Nineteenth Century*. London: Bell, 1907.

27.41 Smith, Arnold. "Neo-Romanticism: Dante Gabriel Rossetti," *The Main Tendencies of Victorian Poetry*. London: Simpkin, 1907.

27.42 Brooke, Stopford A. *A Study of Clough, Arnold, Rossetti, and Morris, with an Introduction on the Course of Poetry from 1822–1852*. London: Pitman, 1908.

Also entitled *Four Poets: Clough, Arnold, Rossetti, and Morris*.

27.43 Fontainas, André. "Dante Gabriel Rossetti, le poète," *Mercure de France*, LXXIII (May 1908), 193–211.

With translations of "The Blessed Damozel," three sonnets from *The House of Life*, and one other sonnet.

27.44 Horn, Kurt. *Zur Entstehungsgeschichte von Dante Gabriel Rossettis Dichtungen*. Bernau: Grüner, 1909 (diss. Königsberg, 1909).

See also Horn's *Studien zum dichterischen Entwicklungsgange Dante Gabriel Rossettis* (*Normannia, Germanisch-romanische Bücherei*, vol. V). Berlin: Felber, 1909.

27.45 Guthrie, William Norman. "Great Translator" [Rossetti] in "Translation: A Method for the Vital Study of Literature," *Sewanee Review*, XVII (October 1909), 392–405.

See immediately following this article, William Michael Rossetti, "Dante Gabriel Rossetti as Translator — Two Letters" (pp. 405–408).

27.46 Foster, N. K. "A Word for Rossetti," *Poet Lore*, XXI (July 1910), 322–329.

27.47 Armstrong, C. B. "Dante Gabriel Rossetti" (An essay before the University Philosophical Society; awarded the President's Gold Medal), in University Philosophical Society, Trinity College [*Publications*]. Dublin: Printed by John Falconer, 1910.

A pastiche undergraduate essay of little importance. See also "Some Poets of the Victorian Era. XI. Dante Gabriel Rossetti," *Academy*, LXXIX, no. 2004 (1 October 1910), 317–318; no. 2005 (8 October 1910), 341–342.

27.48 Ulmer, Hermann. *Dante Gabriel Rossettis Verstechnik*. Bayreuth: Ellwanger, 1911 (diss. München, 1911).

27.49 Saintsbury, George E. "The Poetry of Dante Gabriel Rossetti," *Bookman* (London), XL (June 1911), 120–127.

27.50 Sharp, William. "Rossetti in Prose and Verse," *Papers Critical and Reminiscent*.

Selected and Arranged by Mrs. William Sharp. New York: Duffield, 1912.

Reprinted from *National Review*, IX (March 1887), 111–124. Same in *Eclectic Magazine*, n.s. XLV (March 1887), 702–710. The volume also contains reprinted articles on Christina Rossetti (44.31), Burne-Jones (42.38), and Philip Bourke Marston (50.4).

27.51 Willoughby, Leonard Ashley. *Dante Gabriel Rossetti and German Literature: A Public Lecture Delivered in Hilary Term, 1912, at the Taylor Institution, Oxford*. London: Frowde, 1912.

Same in *Oxford Lectures on Literature* (London: Oxford University Press, 1924).

27.52 Des Garets, Marie-L. "Dante Gabriel Rossetti, 1828–1882," *La Revue Hebdomadaire*, IV (April 1912), 212–221.

Three-page introduction followed by translations of six of Rossetti's poems.

27.53 Olivero, Federico. "Il Ritornello nella poesia di Dante Gabriele Rossetti," *Saggi di letteratura inglese*. Bari: Laterza, 1913.

Same in *Archiv für das Studium der neueren Sprachen und Literaturen*, CXXV (1910), 93–101. Also contains article on Christina Rossetti (44.47).

27.54 Boas, Mrs. F. S. *Rossetti and His Poetry* (Poetry and Life Series, edited by W. H. Hudson). London: Harrap [1914].

27.55 Clark, John Scott. "Gabriel Charles Dante Rossetti," *A Study of English and American Writers*. New York: Scribner's, 1916.

27.56 Symons, Arthur. "Dante Gabriel Rossetti," *Figures of Several Centuries*. London: Constable, 1916.

"Only Coleridge among English poets has anything like the same definite grasp upon whatever is essential in poetry" (p. 201).

27.57 Urech-Daysh, C. *Dante Gabriel Rossetti*. Basel: Hirzen [1916] (diss. Lausanne, 1915–1916).

27.58 Malmstedt, A. "Rossetti och 'The Aesthetic Movement,'" *Studier i modern Sprak-vetenskap utgivna av Nyfilologiska Sällskapet i Stockholm*, VI (1917), 193–229.

27.59 Olivero, Federico. "Sul Simbolismo di D. G. Rossetti," *Nuovi Saggi di letteratura inglese*. Torino: Libreria Editrice Internazionale, 1918.

27.60 Browning, Robert. *Critical Comments on Algernon Charles Swinburne and D. G. Rossetti, with an Anecdote Relating to W. M. Thackeray*. London: Printed for private circulation only for Thomas J. Wise, 1919.

Three letters, the second of which (to Isa Blagden) contains Browning's famous statement on Rossetti and the Pre-Raphaelites beginning, "You know how I hate the effeminacy of his school . . ."

27.61 Trombly, Albert Edmund. *Rossetti the Poet, an Appreciation* (University of Texas Bulletin, no. 2060). Austin, Texas: University of Texas Press, [1920].

Originally appeared as "Rossetti Studies," *South Atlantic Quarterly*, XVIII (July 1919), 211–221; (October 1919), 341–349; XIX (January 1920), 67–80; XX (January 1921), 33–40.

27.62 Woodberry, George Edward. "A Literary Portrait of Rossetti," *Studies of a Litterateur*. London: Selwyn and Blount, 1921.

27.63 Williams, Stanley Thomas. "Rossetti's Damozels: Blessed and Otherwise," *Texas Review* [*Southwest Review*], VI (April 1921), 247–253.

Suggests that certain excessive elements in Rossetti's poetry prevent him from capturing a modern audience.

27.64 Hearn, Lafcadio. "Studies in Rossetti," *Pre-Raphaelite and Other Poets: Lectures*. Selected and edited with an Introduction by John Erskine. New York: Dodd, Mead, 1922.

See also the "Note upon Rossetti's Prose." For complete annotation see 74.5

27.65 Pundt, Herbert. "Dante Gabriel Rossettis Einfluss auf die Gedichte des jungen William Morris," unpub. diss. Breslau, 1922.

Anhang: "Die Gedichte der Miss Siddal" (59.5).

27.66 Geisler, Friedrich. "Dante Gabriel Rossetti: das Romantische in Persönlichkeit und Dichtung," unpub. diss. Marburg, 1923.

27.67 Hearn, Lafcadio. "Definitive Rossetti," *Essays in European and Oriental Literature*. Edited by Albert Mordell. New York: Dodd, Mead, 1923.
See also the chapter on Rossetti entitled "Some Human Frailty."

27.68 MacIntyre, Carlyle F. "Der Gebrauch der Farbe in Rossettis Dichtung," unpub. diss. Marburg, 1923.
An identically entitled M.A. thesis (in English) was accepted from this writer by the University of Southern California in 1920 (Ehrsam, 1.5, p. 213).

27.69 Symons, Arthur. "Rossetti on the Cornish Coast," *Bookman* (New York), LVII (August 1923), 604–609.
Wholly subjective discussion of some of Rossetti's poems. Title refers to the fact that Symons was visiting the Cornish coast when he had these reflections on Rossetti. "Haunted and obsessed and possessed by I know not what unimaginable visions, he [Rossetti] creates a world no poet ever before created."

27.70 Fehr, Bernhard. "Dante Gabriel Rossetti," *Die Englische Literatur des 19. und 20. Jahrhunderts mit Einführung in die englische Frühromantik*. Berlin: Akademische Verlags-gesellschaft, 1923–1925.

27.71 Zenker, Augustin. "Dante Gabriel Rossetti: sein Stil im weitesten Sinne," unpub. diss. University of Vienna, 1925.

27.72 Holthausen, Ferdinand. "D. G. Rossetti und die Bibel," *Germanisch-Romanische Monatsschrift*, XIII (July-August 1925), 310–312; XIV (January-February 1926), 73–76.

27.73 Littell, Philip. "Poetry of Rossetti," in *Modern Writers at Work*, edited by J. K. Piercy. New York: Harcourt Brace, 1926.

27.74 Jones, H. Foster. "Dante Gabriel Rossetti, Medievalist and Poet," *Quarterly Journal of the University of North Dakota*, XVI (May 1926), 309–323.
"Rossetti's art ideals may be summed up in the phrase 'Art for Art's sake.' This creed he professed frankly and mercilessly." (p. 313)

27.75 Turner, A. M. "Rossetti's Reading and His Critical Opinions," *Publications of the Modern Language Association*, XLII (June 1927), 465–491.

27.76 Tietz, Eva. "Das Malerische in Rossettis Dichtung," *Anglia*, LI (1927), 278–306 (diss. Königsberg, 1925).

27.77 Mégroz, Rodolphe Louis. "Dante Gabriel Rossetti: The Man and His Poetry," *Bookman* (London), LXXIV (April 1928), 4–10.
Illustrated centenary review of Rossetti's poetry.

27.78 Hamilton, George. "Dante Gabriel Rossetti, a Review of His Poetry," *Criterion*, VII (June 1928), 91–103.
Rossetti's poetic personality falls short of his unique personality as a man.

27.79 "Stet" [= Thomas Earle Welby]. "Rossetti and His Publisher," *Back Numbers*. London: Constable, 1929.

27.80 Welby, T. Earle. *The Victorian Romantics, 1850–1870: The Early Work of Dante Gabriel Rossetti, William Morris, Burne-Jones, Swinburne, Simeon Solomon and Their Associates*. London: Howe, 1929.
For discussion see Survey, pp. 30–31.

27.81 Wallerstein, Ruth C. "The Bancroft Manuscripts of Rossetti's Sonnets, with the Text of Two Hitherto Unpublished Sonnets," *Modern Language Notes*, XLIV (May 1929), 279–284.
Manuscripts of fifteen of Rossetti's sonnets in the Bancroft Pre-Raphaelite Collection (see 3.1), together with two unpublished sonnets. See also 27.91.

27.82 Brocklehurst, J. H. "Dante Gabriel Rossetti," *Manchester Literary Club Papers*, LV (1929), 94–115.

Centenary paper on Rossetti's poetry, read 10 December 1928.

27.83 Cecil, Lord David. "Gabriel Charles Dante Rossetti," in *The Great Victorians*, edited by H. J. and Hugh Massingham. London: Nicolson and Watson, 1932.

27.84 Klenk, Hans. *Nachwirkungen Dante Gabriel Rossettis: Untersuchungen an Werken von Christina Rossetti, Coventry Patmore, Philip Bourke Marston, Theodore Watts-Dunton, Arthur W. E. O'Shaughnessy, Ernest Dowson, John Davidson*. Berlin: Bachmann, 1932 (diss. Erlangen, 1932).

27.85 Evans, B. Ifor. "Dante Gabriel Rossetti," *English Poetry in the Later Nineteenth Century*. London: Methuen, 1933.
   For complete annotation see 74.7.

27.86 Winwar, Frances [= Frances (Vinciguerra) Grebanier]. "Dante Gabriel's or William Michael's? An Attempt to Establish the Authorship of Some of Rossetti's Sonnets Published by the Duke University Press," *Publications of the Modern Language Association*, XLVIII (March 1933), 312–315.
   Offers evidence that of twelve "hitherto unpublished" sonnets in Baum's *Analytical List* (23.29), at least two had already appeared in print (see 23.19) and nine (numbers 14, 18, 20, 22, 24, 34, 36, 40, 44) are by William Michael Rossetti, from the *bouts-rimés* series of Dante Gabriel and William Michael (see *Some Reminiscences*, 38.8, pp. 79–80), in which the odd-numbered sonnets were by Dante Gabriel and the even-numbered by William Michael.

27.87 Weygandt, Cornelius. "Dante Gabriel Rossetti," *The Time of Tennyson: English Victorian Poetry as it Affected America*. New York: Appleton-Century, 1936.
   For complete annotation see 69.15.

27.88 Sanford, John Albert. "Dante: Rossetti: Pre-Raphaelitism: A Study in the Early Poetry of Dante Gabriel Rossetti," unpub. diss. Cornell University, 1937.
   Abstracted in *Cornell University Abstracts of Theses* (1937).

27.89 Troxell, Janet Camp. "The 'Trial Books' of D. G. Rossetti," *Colophon*, n.s. III (Spring 1938), 243-258.

27.90 Koziol, H. "D. G. Rossettis Reime," *Archiv für das Studium der neueren Sprachen und Literaturen*, n.s. LXXVII (July 1940), 98–99.

27.91 Baum, Paull Franklin. "The Bancroft Manuscripts of Dante Gabriel Rossetti," *Modern Philology*, XXXIX (August 1941), 47–68.
   Manuscripts in the Wilmington Society of the Fine Arts (see 3.1). All the manuscripts, with the exceptions of "Jenny" and "Wellington's Funeral," were composed after 1870. The collection contains interesting variants of some of Rossetti's poems: eighteen sonnets from *The House of Life*, nine other sonnets, and a group of fragments and miscellaneous writings. For a discussion of the Bancroft manuscript sonnets see 27.81.

27.92 Lucas, F. L. "Rossetti," *Ten Victorian Poets*. Cambridge University Press, 1942.
   Originally published as *Eight Victorian Poets* (1930). The chapter on Rossetti is a shorter version of the Introduction to Lucas' edition of Rossetti's poems (23.30). The volume also contains chapters on Morris (43.120), Christina Rossetti (44.77), Swinburne (62.35), and Patmore (52.12).

27.93 Culler, Helen S. "Studies in Rossetti's Reading," unpub. diss. Yale University, 1944.

27.94 Masefield, John. *Thanks Before Going: Notes on Some of the Original Poems of Dante Gabriel Rossetti*. London: Heinemann, 1946.
   Including a discussion of Rossetti's "Principal" and "Miscellaneous" poems and an exegetical analysis of *The House of Life*.

27.95 Cecchi, E. "Dante Gabriele Rossetti," *Scrittori inglesi e americani*. Milano: Mondadori, 1947.

27.96 Cooper, Robert Maxwell. "Dante Gabriel Rossetti: Lost on Both Sides; a Study of His Background, Criticism, and Poetry," unpub. diss. Princeton University, 1947.

Dissertation Abstracts, XV (1955), no. 10857, 415.

27.97 Simonini, R. C., Jr. "Rossetti's Poems in Italian," *Italica*, XXV (June 1948), 131–137.

27.98 Doughty, Oswald. "Rossetti as a Translator," *Theoria*, no. 5 (1953), pp. 102–112.

27.99 Le Roy, G. C. "Dante Gabriel Rossetti," *Perplexed Prophets*. Philadelphia: University of Pennsylvania Press, for Temple University Publications, 1953.

27.100 Groom, Bernard. "Rossetti, Morris, and Swinburne," *The Diction of Poetry from Spenser to Bridges*. University of Toronto Press, 1955.

27.101 Doughty, Oswald. *Dante Gabriel Rossetti* (Writers and Their Work, no. 85). London: Longmans, 1957.
Contains a good working bibliography of Rossetti.

27.102 Fairchild, Hoxie Neale. "Dante Gabriel Rossetti," *Religious Trends in English Poetry. Vol. IV. 1830–1880. Christianity and Romanticism in the Victorian Era*. New York: Columbia University Press, 1957.
Tends to overemphasize the importance of religion in Rossetti's life and art.

27.103 Lo Schiavo, Renato. *La Poesia di Dante Gabriele Rossetti* (*Letture di pensiero e d'arte*). Roma: Edizioni di Storia e Letteratura, 1957.

27.104 Ray, S. N. "The First Literary Friendship of D. G. Rossetti," *Notes & Queries*, CCII, n.s. IV (October 1957), 435–454.
Major Robert Calder Campbell, retired

officer and minor poet, was Rossetti's first literary mentor. He introduced Rossetti to Ebenezer Jones, and he was also responsible for the cult of Keats among the Pre-Raphaelites.

27.105 Henderson, Stephen E. "A Study of Visualized Detail in the Poetry of Tennyson, Rossetti, and Morris," unpub. diss. University of Wisconsin. *Dissertation Abstracts*, XX (1959), 1015.

27.106 Holberg, Stanley M. "Image and Symbol in the Poetry of Dante Gabriel Rossetti," unpub. diss. University of Maryland, 1958. *Dissertation Abstracts*, XX (1959), 1016–1017.

27.107 Kühnelt, H. H. "Die Bedeutung der italienischen Malerei für den Dichter Dante Gabriel Rossetti," *Anglia*, LXXII (1955), 438–454.

27.108 Weatherby, David. "Problems of Form and Content in the Poetry of Dante Gabriel Rossetti," *Victorian Poetry*, II (Winter 1964), 11–19.
". . . Rossetti was capable both of variety and intensity, genuinely a poet, capable of rendering feeling as language. It is too often, though, exactly that and no more — just good *poetry*; he wrote only a few good *poems*. For despite his conscious efforts at the creation of poetic forms, his content, which in the final analysis is the only thing that can validate form, often failed him. Or he failed it." (p. 19) Rossetti's lack of faith in the reality of his material . . . is responsible for many of our current objections to his work. His surfaces seem overwrought, not because they are . . . exceedingly ornate but because there is often no solid fabric beneath them; and his love poetry seems unhealthily sensuous because the physical fact is not always redeemed by the idea." (p. 15)

Section 28

STUDIES OF INDIVIDUAL POEMS OR PROSE WORKS

28.1 Buchanan, Robert. "'The House of Life,' &c., Re-examined," *The Fleshly School of Poetry and Other Phenomena of the Day*. London: Strahan, 1872.

Although the entire pamphlet relates generally to Rossetti, this chapter, together with the previous one, "Mr. D. G. Rossetti," provides Buchanan with most of his examples of the "nastiness" of the Fleshly School. For complete annotation see 82.6. See also 29.16.

28.2 Wilkins, W. "Dante Rossetti's 'Hand and Soul,' " *Academy*, XXI, no. 522 (6 May 1882), 323.

In the "Correspondence" section. Contains an interesting reference to the projected organization of a Dante Gabriel Rossetti Society in Dublin. For the answer to this letter see G. Barnett Smith, "Rossetti's 'Hand and Soul,' " *Academy*, XXI, no. 523 (13 May 1882), 341.

28.3 St. Johnston, Alfred. "Rossetti's 'Sudden Light,' " *Academy*, XXV, no. 624 (19 April 1884), 279.

In the "Correspondence" section. Discusses textual differences in Rossetti's poem as it appeared in 1863 (see 84.1), 1870 and 1881. Variants provided.

28.4 Hardinge, William M. "A Note on the Louvre Sonnets of Rossetti," *Temple Bar*, XCI (March 1891), 433–443.

With notes and paraphrases by William Michael Rossetti.

28.5 Kingsland, William G. "Rossetti's 'Jenny': With Extracts from an Hitherto Unpublished Version of the Poem," *Poet Lore*, VII (January 1895), 1–6.

From a manuscript in the Ashley Library.

28.6 Bourget, Paul. "Etudes anglaises," *Etudes et portraits*. Paris: Lemerre, 1899.

Part V, "Croquis Londoniens," chapter 8, "Oxford en été," contains two sections on Rossetti, one dealing with the Oxford murals, the other with "Jenny." Reprinted from "Lettres de Londres," *Le Journal de Debats* (1884).

28.7 Laughlin, Clara Elizabeth. "Dante Gabriel Rossetti and 'The House of Life,' " *Stories of Authors' Loves*. Vol. I. Philadelphia: Lippincott, 1902.

Same in *Book Lover*, II (January-February 1902), 512–516; and in *Delineator*, LVIII (July 1901), 93–96.

28.8 Pàntini, Romualdo. "La 'Casa di Vita'

di Dante Gabriele Rossetti," *L'Italia Moderna*, II (August 1904), 527–538.

28.9 Tyrrell, R. L. "A Literary Causerie: The Growth of a Poem," *Academy*, LXX, no. 1771 (14 April 1906), 356–358.

Rossetti's revisions of "The Blessed Damozel." See also the brief article in *Academy*, LXXII, no. 1823 (13 April 1907), 365–366, referring to "that benign pirate" T. B. Mosher's edition of the poem with variant readings. For a complete collation of the variants of the poem see Baum's edition (23.32).

28.10 Prideaux, W. F. "Palgrave's 'Golden Treasury,' " *Notes & Queries*, 10th ser., VIII (16 November 1907), 393.

Concerning the publication history of "The Blessed Damozel" in answer to an earlier query by "W. B.," (2 November 1907), pp. 351–352. Other correspondence appears in same issue as Prideaux' note. Another short note by Prideaux on the same subject appeared in the issue of 7 December 1907 (p. 454).

28.11 Jiriczek, Otto L. "Zum Erstdruck von D. G. Rossettis 'Sister Helen,' " *Germanisch-Romanische Monatsschrift*, III (April 1911), 247.

A note correcting certain information in William Michael Rossetti's *Bibliography* (22.1) pertaining to the *Dusseldorf Artists' Album* (1854), with a note on the contents of the *Album*. See also 23.33, in which facsimiles of "Sister Helen" from the *Album* are reproduced.

28.12 Suddard, Mary. "The House of Life," *Keats, Shelley, and Shakespeare: Studies and Essays in English Literature*. Cambridge University Press, 1912.

Considers *The House of Life* as the work of a coterie (the PRB), "a later blossoming of the Renaissance."

28.13 Wagschal, Friedrich. "E. B. Brownings *Sonnets from the Portuguese* und D. G. Rossettis *House of Life*," *Zeitschrift für französischen und englischen Unterricht*, XIII (1914), 207–217.

28.14 Tisdel, Frederick M. "Rossetti's

'House of Life,'" *Modern Philology*, XV (September 1917), 257–276.

28.15 McKillop, Alan D. *"Festus* and *The Blessed Damozel,"* *Modern Language Notes*, XXXIV (February 1919), 93–97.

Philip James Bailey's poem, introduced to Rossetti by the American, Charles Ware, in 1845, was more influential on Rossetti's poem than Poe's "Raven." Parallel passages cited.

28.16 Zakrzewska, Maja. "Untersuchungen zur Konstruktion und Komposition von D. G. Rossettis Sonettenzyklus *The House of Life*," unpub. diss. Freiburg, 1922.

28.17 Williams, Stanley T. "Two Poems by Rossetti," *Studies in Victorian Literature*. London: Allen and Unwin, 1924.

Discusses "The Blessed Damozel" and "Jenny."

28.18 Trombly, Albert Edmund. "A Translation of Rossetti's," *Modern Language Notes*, XXXVIII (February 1923), 116–118.

"The Leaf." See Baum (28.32). Though Rossetti's poem purports to be a translation from Leopardi, it is actually from Arnault's "La Feuille."

28.19 Wallerstein, Ruth C. "Personal Experience in Rossetti's 'House of Life,'" *Publications of the Modern Language Association*, XLII (June 1927), 492–504.

28.20 Horn, Kurt. *"The Staff and Scrip* von D. G. Rossetti. Uebertragung und Erläuterung," *Zeitschrift für französischen und englischen Unterricht*, XXVI (1927), 575–591.

28.21 Förster, M. "Die älteste Fassung von D. G. Rossettis Ballade 'Sister Helen,'" in *Die Leipziger Neunundneunzig: Festschrift des Leipziger Bibliophilen-Abends* [25th memorial volume of the Leipzig Bibliophile Society]. Leipzig: [Privately printed], 1929.

28.22 Morse, B. J. "A Note on the Autobiographical Elements in Rossetti's 'Hand and Soul,'" *Anglia*, LIV, (1930), 331–337.

28.23 Waller, R. D. "'The Blessed Dam-

ozel,'" *Modern Language Review*, XXVI (April 1931), 129–141.

The influence of Dante and the Italian poets on Rossetti's poem.

28.24 Johnson, G. C. Ashton. "'The House of Life,'" *Poetry Review*, XXII (September-October 1931), 343–359.

A comparison of *The House of Life* with Shakespeare's sonnets.

28.25 DeVane, W. C. "The Harlot and the Thoughtful Young Man: A Study of the Relation between Rossetti's 'Jenny' and Browning's 'Fifine at the Fair,'" *Studies in Philology*, XXIX (January 1932), 463–484.

DeVane sees "Fifine" as Rossetti himself saw it, as an attack upon "Jenny." DeVane makes a good case for Browning's sympathy with Buchanan and for "Fifine" being his answer to the psychological situation in Rossetti's "Jenny," a technique Browning often employed in his poetry.

28.26 Symons, Arthur. "Notes on Two Manuscripts," *English Review*, LIV (May 1932), 514–520.

A Swinburne manuscript and the original manuscript of Rossetti's "Eden Bower" (pp. 518–520), the latter formerly in Symons' possession. A superficial but interesting description.

28.27 Knickerbocker, K. L. "Rossetti's 'The Blessed Damozel,'" *Studies in Philology*, XXIX (July 1932), 485–504.

A comparison of the several versions of "The Blessed Damozel" and a reading of the poem which endeavors to demonstrate biographical implications in Rossetti's successive revisions of the poem. The article contains the first reference to the curious Morgan manuscript of the poem. An interesting speculation about Rossetti's attempt to create the idea of precocity regarding the composition of "The Blessed Damozel." See also 28.30.

28.28 Howe, Merill L. "Some Unpublished Stanzas by Dante Gabriel Rossetti," *Modern Language Notes*, XLVIII (March 1933), 176–179.

With poem "Border Song." See also S. N.

Ray, "Rossetti's 'Border Song,'" *MLN*, LVIII (March 1943), 246, a note in reply to Howe's article, tracing the discovery of the ballad through *Notes & Queries*. For original identification see W. F. Prideaux, "Dante G. Rossetti: George Meredith," *N&Q*, 8th ser., VI (13 October 1894), 286–287, speculation that "A Border Song," signed "D.G.R." in *Once a Week* (II, p. 66) is by Rossetti, though it was not included in the *Collected Works* edited by W. M. Rossetti in 1886. This article was answered by E. Walford, the subeditor of *Once a Week*, confirming Rossetti's authorship and indicating that Rossetti contributed several other pieces as well, in *N&Q*, 8th ser., VI (20 October 1894), 318–319. Two further notes by Prideaux appeared, completing the discussion: VI (22 December 1894), pp. 496–497; VII (23 March 1895), 233.

28.29 Howarth, R. G. "On Rossetti's 'Jenny,'" *Notes & Queries*, 15th ser., CLXXIII (10 July 1937), 20–21.

Suggests that the absence of juvenile amours in Rossetti's youth and the early composition of the poem may point to a literary source in *The Memoirs of Harriette Wilson* (1825). Cites incident, quoted in Angela Thirkell's biography of Harriette Wilson, of Lord Ponsonby coming to the room when Harriette was asleep.

28.30 Sanford, J. A. "The Morgan Manuscript of Rossetti's 'The Blessed Damozel,'" *Studies in Philology*, XXXV (July 1938), 471–486.

The Morgan manuscript of "The Blessed Damozel" appears to be "a deliberate attempt on Rossetti's part to substantiate the legend of his precocity." (p. 471) Sanford considers the manuscript "worthless for scholarly purposes" despite Baum's acceptance of it (23.32). "The manuscript, which purports to be a copy of the original draft of the poem is clearly a spurious version." (p. 483) See also 28.27.

28.31 Ray, S. N. *Rossettiana — First Series*. Dacca (India): Privately printed, 1941.

Two sections: "Browning and the Rossetti Circle," and "Towards the Identification of the New Beloved of *The House of Life*."

28.32 Baum, Paull Franklin. "Rossetti's 'The Leaf,'" *Modern Language Quarterly*, II (June 1941), 187–189.

Concerned generally and specifically with Rossetti's translation. See also Trombly (28.18) and Guthrie (27.45) to whom reference is made.

28.33 Jackson, Elizabeth. "Notes on the Stanza of Rossetti's 'The Blessed Damozel,'" *Publications of the Modern Language Association*, LVIII (December 1943), 1050–1056.

Attempts to trace the origins of Rossetti's stanza form, perhaps to Longfellow or Holmes. Suggests that its real importance is that it throws some light on the development of the poet's feelings for the verse, and that it demonstrates the limitations of our prosodic terminology.

28.34 Culler, Dwight and Helen. "Sources of 'The King's Tragedy,'" *Studies in Philology*, XLI (July 1944), 427–441.

Cites the principal source as "The Dethe of the Kynge of Scotis," a prose chronicle translated about 1440 from an unknown Latin original. This work, *The Life and Death of King James*, edited by Joseph Stephenson, was published for the Maitland Club in 1837, and a copy appeared in the Rossetti Sale (19.2, lot 512). An interesting article despite excessive biographical speculation.

28.35 Baum, Paull Franklin. "Rossetti, 'The White Ship,'" *Duke University Library Notes*, no. 20 (July 1948), pp. 2–6.

28.36 Bowra, C. M. "The House of Life," *The Romantic Imagination*. Cambridge, Mass.: Harvard University Press, 1949.

A lecture given during 1948–1949 when Bowra was Charles Eliot Norton Professor of Poetry at Harvard University. Reprinted in *Victorian Literature: Modern Essays in Criticism*, edited by Austin Wright (New York: Oxford University Press, 1961). Rossetti's *House of Life* is not strictly speaking a sonnet sequence. The sonnets "reflect not a crisis but a lifetime, and through them he tells what his most enthralling discoveries have been." (p. 203) Bowra also comments extensively on Pre-Raphaelitism as an aspect of Romanticism. For the essay on Christina Rossetti in the same volume see 44.80.

28.37 Lang, Cecil Y. "The French Originals of Rossetti's 'John of Tours' and 'My Father's Close,'" *Publications of the Modern Language Association,* LXIV (December 1949), 1219–1222.

Compares Rossetti's two "Old French" translations with their probable originals in Gérard de Nerval's "Les Vieilles ballades françaises," *La Sylphide,* 9 July 1842.

28.38 Bellinger, Rossiter. "Rossetti's Two Translations from Old French," *Modern Language Notes,* LXV (April 1950), 217–223.

"John of Tours" and "My Father's Close." See 28.37.

28.39 Metzdorf, Robert F. "The Full Text of Rossetti's Sonnet on *Sordello,*" *Harvard Library Bulletin,* VII (1953), 239–243.

"Recovery in full of an autograph sonnet by D. G. Rossetti. This underlines the favor that *Sordello* found with D. G. R. and emphasizes the fact that R. B.'s early poems were favorites with the Pre-Raphaelites." (Austin Wright in "Victorian Bibliography for 1953," *MP,* 1954)

28.40 Boyd, Evelyn Mae. "Dante Gabriel Rossetti's 'The House of Life': A Study of Its Italian Background," unpub. diss. Columbia University. *Dissertation Abstracts,* XIV (1954), no. 8614, 1217–1218.

28.41 Shen, Yao. "Accident or Universality," *Western Humanities Review,* X (Winter 1955–1956), 77–79.

Notes similarity in theme between Pai Chü Yi's "Song of a Guitar" and Rossetti's "The Blessed Damozel."

28.42 Lauter, Paul. "The Narrator of 'The Blessed Damozel,'" *Modern Language Notes,* LXXIII (May 1958), 344–348.

The poem represents the lover's vision of his lady and his fancies as to what he hopes she is thinking. The author draws a close parallel with Poe's "Raven."

28.43 Johnston, Robert DeSales. "Imagery in Rossetti's *House of Life,*" unpub. diss. University of Missouri, 1959. *Dissertation Abstracts,* XX (1960), 2783–2784.

28.44 Lindberg, John. "Rossetti's Cumaean Oracle," *Victorian Newsletter,* no. 22 (Fall 1962), pp. 20–21.

On Sonnet CI, "The One Hope," in *The House of Life.* Suggests that this last sonnet "implies that Rossetti's theme is inexhaustible, not to terminate in a round century of rimes. The sequence might continue in recurring cycles as an aesthetic extension of personality."

28.45 Robillard, Douglas J. "Rossetti's 'Willowwood' Sonnets and the Structure of *The House of Life,*" *Victorian Newsletter,* no. 22 (Fall 1962), pp. 5–9.

Sees evidence in *The House of Life* of "a carefully planned construction that brings all of the sonnets into a working arrangement with one another and should give us an aesthetically satisfying whole."

28.46 Kodama, Sanechika. "D. G. Rossetti's 'One Dream Alone,'" *Dōshisha Daigaku Jimbungaku* [Studies in the Humanities, of Dōshisha University], no. 35 (1958), 1–15.

Article in Japanese.

28.47 Hyder, Clyde K. "Rossetti's *Rose Mary:* A Study in the Occult," *Victorian Poetry,* I (August 1963), 197–207.

28.48 Vogel, Joseph F. "'White Rose' or 'White Robe' in 'The Blessed Damozel,'" *English Language Notes,* I (December 1963), 121–123.

On a textual variant in the Morgan Library manuscript of Rossetti's poem.

28.49 Vogel, Joseph F. *"The House of Life,* LXXXVII," *Explicator,* XXI, no. 8 (April 1963), item 64.

28.50 Bracker, Jon. "Notes on the Texts of Two Poems by Dante Gabriel Rossetti," *Library Chronicle of the University of Texas,* VII (Summer 1963), 14–16.

Textual emendations of Rossetti's "The Carillon" (later "Antwerp and Bruges") and "The Orchard Pit" based on readings in Doughty (23.37). See also in the same issue

Carl J. Weber, "The 'Discovery' of Fitz-Gerald's Rubáiyát: Three Scholars Discuss a Swinburne Autograph in the Wrenn Collection." (pp. 3–13)

Section 29

SELECTED REVIEWS OF ROSSETTI'S POEMS

THE EARLY ITALIAN POETS

29.1 [Skelton, John]. "The *Vita Nuova* of Dante," *Fraser's Magazine*, LXV (May 1862), 580–594.

Compares Rossetti's with other translations.

29.2 "The Growth of the Early Italian Poetry and Mr. Dante Gabriel Rossetti's Translation," *National Review*, XV (July 1862), 60–95.

29.3 "Poems by Mr. and Miss Rossetti," *Ecclesiastic and Theologian*, XXIV (September 1862), 419–429.

Exceedingly high praise for Rossetti's translations. For comments on Christina Rossetti's *Goblin Market* see 44.17.

*   *   *

POEMS, 1870

29.4 [Skelton, John]. "The Poems of Dante Gabriel Rossetti," *Fraser's Magazine*, n.s. I (May 1870), 609–622.

Same in *Living Age*, CV, 4th ser., XVII, no. 1358 (11 June 1870), 686–697; also in *Eclectic Magazine*, n.s. XII (August 1870), 143–154.

29.5 Morris, William. "Poems by Dante Gabriel Rossetti," *Academy*, I, no. 8 (14 May 1870), 199–200.

For Swinburne's long review-article see 27.3.

29.6 Hake, Thomas Gordon. "Poems by Dante Gabriel Rossetti," *New Monthly Magazine*, CXLVI (June 1870), 681–700.

For Rossetti's two reviews of Hake's poems see 48.5 and 48.6.

29.7 [Hutton, R. H.]. "Mr. Rossetti's Poems," *Spectator*, XLIII, no. 2189 (11 June 1870), 724–725.

This attribution was made by R. H. Tener.

29.8 [Marston, Westland]. "Poems. By Dante Gabriel Rossetti," *Athenaeum*, no. 2218 (30 April 1870), pp. 573–574.

The following minor reviews should also be mentioned: the two by Joseph Knight in the *Globe*, no. 22,375 (20 April 1870), pp. 1–2, and *Sunday Times*, no. 2455 (1 May 1870), p. 7; Alfred Austin's in the *Standard*, 26 May 1870, p. 3; Amédée Pichot's in *Revue Britannique*, CCLXVII (June 1870), 560–561; and short, unsigned notices in the *North British Review*, XIII (July 1870), 598–599; *Saturday Review*, XXIX (14 May 1870), 651–652; and *Broadway*, 3rd ser., I (October 1870), 286–288.

29.9 [Howells, W. D.]. "Poems by Dante Gabriel Rossetti," *Atlantic Monthly*, XXVI (July 1870), 115–118.

Among other American reviews the following may be noted: *Old and New*, II (July 1870), 92–94; *Harper's Magazine*, XLI (August 1870), 463; *New Englander*, XXIX (October 1870), 717; *Lippincott's Magazine*, VI (September 1870), 340–342; and *Western Lakeside Monthly*, IV (November 1870), 320–323. See also 29.11 and 29.13.

29.10 "Reviews of Poems. By Dante Gabriel Rossetti," *New Eclectic Magazine*, VII (July 1870), 110–117.

29.11 [Lowell, James Russell]. "Poems by D. G. Rossetti," *Nation*, XI (14 July 1870), 29–30.

"I suspect the '*Nation*' is by Poetaster Lowell," Rossetti wrote to Ellis (24.16, p. 82).

29.12 "Poems by Dante Gabriel Rossetti," *Blackwood's Magazine*, CVIII (August 1870), 178–183.

"What do you think," Rossetti wrote to F. S. Ellis on 9 September 1870 (24.16, p. 85), "of the *Blackwood* article being written by an intimate of mine? Perhaps Morris told you. It isn't certified yet, but looks suspicious. I've written to ask him if he did it." Conceivably this may be an unrecorded example of William Bell Scott's perfidy, anticipating the attack in *Autobiographical Notes* (56.10).

29.13 Dennett, J. R. "Dante Gabriel Rossetti's *Poems*," *North American Review*, CXI (October 1870), 471–480.

Confuses Dante Gabriel and William Michael Rossetti. An attack on Rossetti and on the affectation of the Pre-Raphaelites. Buchanan, in both his article (29.16) and pamphlet (82.6) uses Dennett's review to support his own response to Rossetti's poems.

29.14 [Colvin, Sidney]. "The Poetical Writings of Mr. Dante Gabriel Rossetti," *Westminster Review*, XCV (January 1871), 55–92.

Also discusses *Early Italian Poets*. The *Westminster* had an earlier review in XCIV (July 1870), 226–227. Colvin reviewed the volume previously in *Pall Mall Gazette*, 21 April 1870, p. 7.

29.15 [Forman, H. Buxton]. "Dante Gabriel Rossetti, Poet," *Tinsley's Magazine*, VIII (March 1871), 150–160.

Revised and combined with Forman's 1869 article on Rossetti (27.1), this review was reprinted in *Our Living Poets* (74.1).

29.16 Maitland, Thomas [= Robert Buchanan]. "The Fleshly School of Poetry: Mr. D. G. Rossetti," *Contemporary Review*, XVIII (October 1871), 334–350.

In 1872, Buchanan expanded this article into his notorious pamphlet (82.6). For Rossetti's answer see 23.9. For a discussion of the whole *Fleshly* controversy see Survey, pp. 17–19. Buchanan's article is reprinted in Albert Mordell, *Notorious Literary Attacks* (New York: Boni and Liveright, 1926); and in Walter E. Houghton and G. Robert Stange, *Victorian Poetry and Poetics* (Boston: Houghton Mifflin, 1959). Buchanan was probably responsible for the earlier review in the *Contemporary*, XIV (June 1870), 480–481.

29.17 [Courthope, W. J.]. "The Latest Development of Literary Poetry: Swinburne,

Rossetti, Morris," *Quarterly Review*, CXXXII (January 1872), 59–84.

Same in *Eclectic Magazine*, n.s. XV (April 1872), 385–399. The section on Rossetti's *Poems* occupies pp. 69–75. Buchanan in the Notes to the *Fleshly* pamphlet includes a two-page excerpt from this article treating Rossetti's "Jenny" (82.6, pp. 92–93).

29.18 Wedmore, Frederick. "The Poetry of Mr. Rossetti," *St. James's Magazine*, n.s. IX (April 1872), 31–40.

29.19 [Earle, J. C.]. "Rossetti's Poems," *Catholic World*, XIX (May 1874), 263–272.

* * *

DANTE AND HIS CIRCLE

29.20 "Rossetti's Translations from the Early Italian Poets," *Nation*, XVIII (5 March 1874), 159–160.

29.21 "Rossetti's *Dante and His Circle*," *London Quarterly Review*, XLII (July 1874), 299–313.

* * *

POEMS and BALLADS AND SONNETS, 1881

29.22 [Watts-Dunton, Theodore]. "Dante Gabriel Rossetti's New Poems," *Athenaeum*, no. 2815 (8 October 1881), 457–460.

Same in *Eclectic Magazine*, n.s. XXXIV (December 1881), 851–858.

29.23 [Lowell, James Russell]. "New Poetry of the Rossettis and Others," *Atlantic Monthly*, XLIX (January 1882), 119–126.

A review of Rossetti's *Ballads and Sonnets*, Christina Rossetti's *A Pageant*, Oscar Wilde's *Poems*, and other volumes.

29.24 Symonds, J. A. "Notes on Mr. D. G. Rossetti's New Poems," *Macmillan's Magazine*, XLV (February 1882), 318–328.

29.25 Bayne, Thomas. "The Poetry of Dante Gabriel Rossetti," *Fraser's Magazine*, n.s. XXV (March 1882), 376–384.

Same in *Living Age*, CLII, 5th ser., XXXVII, no. 1971 (31 March 1882), 817–822.

29.26 "Rossetti's Poems," *Edinburgh Review*, CLV (April 1882), 322–337.

Reviews both volumes most unfavorably. The Pre-Raphaelites, including Rossetti, are treated as "aesthetic separatists." Same in *Living Age*, CLIII, 5th ser., XXXVIII, no. 1978 (20 May 1882), 436–444.

29.27 "The Poetry of Rossetti," *British Quarterly Review*, LXXVI (July 1882), 109–127.

An unfavorable review of Rossetti's poetry.

Section 30

STUDIES EMPHASIZING ROSSETTI'S ARTISTIC WORK AND INFLUENCE

30.1 Tirebuck, W. E. *Dante Gabriel Rossetti, His Work and Influence: Including a Brief Survey of Present Art Tendencies*. London: Stock, 1882.

30.2 Smith, G. Barnett. "Dante Gabriel Rossetti," *Time* (London), VII (May 1882), 163–173.

An account of Rossetti and his works, which are characterized by a "loftiness — frequently absolute sublimity — of imagination." (p. 165)

30.3 Ruskin, John. "Realistic Schools of Painting: D. G. Rossetti and W. Holman Hunt," *The Art of England: Lectures Given in Oxford*. Orpington: Allen, 1883.

For complete annotation see 45.2.

30.4 Tirebuck, W. E. "Dante Gabriel Rossetti," *Art Journal*, XLV (January 1883), 27–28.

30.5 Stephens, Frederic George. "Earlier Works of Dante Gabriel Rossetti," *Portfolio*, XIV (May 1883), 87–91; (June 1883), 114–119.

30.6 Barrington, Emilie Isabel. "The Painted Poetry of Watts and Rossetti," *Nineteenth Century*, XIII (June 1883), 950–970.

30.7 Benton, Joel. "Dante Gabriel Rossetti, the Apostle of Beauty," *Manhattan*, II (September 1883), 249–253.

30.8 Colvin, Sidney. "Rossetti as a Painter," *Magazine of Art*, VI (1883), 177–183.

30.9 Rossetti, William Michael. "Notes on Rossetti and His Works," *Art Journal*, XLVI

(May 1884), 148–152; (June 1884), 165–168; (July 1884), 204–208.

A chronological survey of Rossetti's art works, anticipating 32.6. For a brief correction by G. P. Boyce see p. 255 of the July number.

30.10 Carr, J. Comyns. "Rossetti's Influence on Art," *Papers on Art*. London: Macmillan, 1885.

Originally appeared in *English Illustrated Magazine*, I (1883), 28–40.

30.11 Swinburne, Louis Judson. *Rossetti and the Pre-Raphaelites*. New Haven, Connecticut, 1885.

For annotation see 77.20.

30.12 Gurney, Alfred. "Dante Gabriel Rossetti: A Painter's Day-Dream, and the Vision that Ensued," *Monthly Packet*, 3rd ser., IX (February 1885), 185–193.

On *Hand and Soul*, as an artistic *Confessio fidei* — a parabolic plot summary of Rossetti's prose story.

30.13 Wood, Charles James. "Dante Gabriel Rossetti," *Andover Review*, VIII (December 1887), 573–592.

Rossetti's mode of expression ultimately "burst the bonds of Preraphaelite conventionalism, and expanded in the large room of Romanticism . . ."

30.14 Rossetti, William Michael. "The Portraits of Dante Gabriel Rossetti," *Magazine of Art*, XII (1889), 21–26, 57–61, 138–140.

Includes both self-portraits and likenesses by other artists. Profusely illustrated.

30.15 Shields, Frederic. "A Note Upon Rossetti's Method of Drawing in Crayons," *Century Guild Hobby Horse*, n.s. V (April 1890), 70–73.

See also 30.73.

30.16 Layard, George Somes. "Rossetti," *Tennyson and His Pre-Raphaelite Illustrators: A Book about a Book*. London: Stock, 1894.

For complete annotation see 88.1.

30.17 Stephens, Frederic George. *Dante Gabriel Rossetti* (Portfolio Artistic Monographs, no. 5). London: Seeley, 1894; 2nd ed., 1908.

Also issued in the series of Miniature Portfolio Monographs, 1908.

30.18 Wood, Esther. *Dante Gabriel Rossetti and the Pre-Raphaelite Movement*. London: Sampson, Low, Marston, 1894.

For discussion see Survey, pp. 25–26.

30.19 Chesneau, Ernest. "Peintres anglais contemporains: Dante Gabriel Rossetti," *L'Art*, LIX, 20ᵉ année, tome IV (1894), 207–226.

30.20 Sartorio, G. A. "Nota su Dante Gabriele Rossetti pittore," *Il Convito*, II (February 1895), 121–150; IV (April 1895), 261–286.

30.21 Hueffer, Ford Madox. *Rossetti: A Critical Essay on His Art*. London: Longmans, 1896.

For a brief discussion see Survey, p. 24.

30.22 Ortensi, Ulisse. "Artisti contemporanei: Dante Gabriele Rossetti," *Emporium*, IV (July 1896), 3–14; (August 1896), 83–95.

30.23 Bell, Mrs. Arthur (N. D'Anvers). "Dante Gabriel Rossetti," *Representative Painters of the XIXth Century*. London: Sampson, Low, Marston, 1899.

Other artists included in this volume are Hunt (36.37), Millais (37.51), and Burne-Jones (42.43).

30.24 Marillier, Henry Currie. *Dante Gabriel Rossetti: An Illustrated Memorial of His Art and Life*. London: Bell, 1899.

Abridged and revised edition, 1904; further abridged for "Bell's Miniature Series of Painters," 1906. Marillier's work is still the standard study of Rossetti's art. The volume contains a list of paintings, drawings, and more important studies by Rossetti, based in part on W. M. Rossetti (32.6) and William Sharp (25.3), but "revised and considerably amplified." This is the standard catalogue of Rossetti's works; reprinted in part, without the descriptions in Cary (26.3). For an interesting review of Marillier see William M. Rossetti, "Mr. Marillier's Record of Dante Rossetti," *Magazine of Art*, XXIII (1900), 217–223. For a brief discussion see Survey, p. 24.

30.25 Cary, Elizabeth Luther. "Rossetti and the Pre-Raphaelites," *Critic*, XXXVII (October 1900), 320–326.

From advance sheets of 26.3.

30.26 Forsyth, Peter Taylor. *Religion in Recent Art: Expository Lectures on Rossetti, Burne-Jones, Watts, Holman Hunt, and Wagner*. London: Hodder and Stoughton, 1901.

30.27 Bancroft, Samuel, Jr. "Rossetti and the Pre-Raphaelite Brotherhood and Their Influence on Late English Art." Typescript of a speech delivered 6 February 1901, in the Wilmington Society of the Fine Arts.

For annotation see 78.10.

30.28 "The Pre-Raphaelite Brotherhood [Second Article]: Dante Gabriel Rossetti," *Werner's Magazine*, XXVII (May 1901), 193–202.

For complete annotation see 67.21.

30.29 Muthesius, H[ermann]. "Dante Gabriel Rossetti," *Kunst und Kunsthandwerk*, IV (1901), 373–389.

30.30 Henley, William Ernest. "Rossetti," *View and Reviews. Essays in Appreciation: Art*. London: Nutt, 1902.

30.31 Rossetti, Helen M. M. (Angeli). *The Life and Work of Dante Gabriel Rossetti*

(Easter Number of the *Art Journal*). London: Virtue, 1902.

An early study of Rossetti's art, profusely illustrated. Collected in 75.22.

30.32 Muther, Richard. "Rossetti, Burne-Jones, und Watts," *Neue Deutsche Rundschau*, XIII (August 1902), 859–881.

30.33 Aronstein, P. "Dante Gabriel Rossetti und der Präraphaelismus," *Verhandlungen des 10. allgemeinen deutschen Neuphilologentages vom 20. bis 23. V. 1902 zu Breslau*. Hannover: Meyer, 1903.

30.34 *Rossetti* (Masters in Art: A Series of Illustrated Monographs, vol. IV, pt. 48). Boston: Bates, 1903.

Life and works, with plates and a brief bibliography.

30.35 Wiley, Edwin. "Dante Gabriel Rossetti and the Pre-Raphaelites," *The Old and the New Renaissance: A Group of Studies in Art and Letters*. Nashville, Tennessee: Publishing House of the M. E. Church, South, Bigham and Sons, Agents, 1903.

30.36 Cary, Elizabeth Luther. "Rossetti as an Illustrator," *Lamp [Bookbuyer]*, XXVII (November 1903), 321–328.

30.37 Prinsep, Valentine C. "The Oxford Circle: Rossetti, Burne-Jones, and William Morris. A Chapter from a Painter's Reminiscence[s]," *Magazine of Art*, XXVII, n.s. II (1904), 167–172.

For further reminiscences by Prinsep see 25.27.

30.38 Jessen, Jarno [= Anna Michaelson]. *Rossetti* (Künstler-Monographien, no. LXXVII). Bielefeld und Leipzig: Velhagen und Klasing, 1905.

30.39 Vitale, Zaira. "Le Modelle di D. G. Rossetti," *Revista d'Italia*, anno VIII, vol. 2 (September 1905), 448–459.

Discusses among other of Rossetti's models: Jane Burden (Morris), Christina Rossetti, Elizabeth Siddal, Ruth Herbert, Annie Miller, Marie Stillman, Alexa Wilding, Aggie Monetti, Miss Mackenzie, Elene Smith.

30.40 Dupouey, Charles M. *Notes sur l'art et la vie de D. G. Rossetti*. Paris: Chapelot, 1906.

30.41 Lawrence, Frederic. "The Romanticists around Dante Gabriel Rossetti," *London Quarterly Review*, CVIII, 4th ser., VI (October 1907), 269–282.

A brief survey of the PRB with emphasis on Rossetti, whose vision was greater than the rest. Millais and Holman Hunt saw external nature; Rossetti saw the symbolic truth underlying nature.

30.42 Pissarro, Lucien. *Rossetti* (Masterpieces in Colour, edited by T. Lemon Hare). New York: Stokes, [1908].

Collected in 75.25.

30.43 Cary, Elizabeth Luther. "Rossetti's Water Colours," *Scrip. Notes on Art*, III (March 1908), 173–178.

30.44 Ross, Robert. "Art in America. Rossetti: An Observation," *Burlington Magazine*, XIII (May 1908), 116–123.

A defense of Rossetti, "who I think it no exaggeration to say was, with the exception of Turner, the greatest personality in the English school of the nineteenth century."

30.45 Knight, William Angus. "The Pre-Raphaelites, Especially Dante Gabriel Rossetti, with Reminiscences," *Six Lectures on Some Nineteenth Century Artists, English and French*. Chicago: The Art Institute, 1909.

For annotation see 75.26.

30.46 Mourey, Gabriel. *Dante Gabriel Rossetti et les Préraphaélites anglais* (Les Grands Artistes). Paris: Laurens, [1909].

For annotation see 77.28.

30.47 Symons, Arthur. *Dante Gabriel Rossetti* (International Art Series). London: Unwin, [1909].

Identical editions published in France and Germany in the same year. Profusely illustrated.

30.48 Fryer, Alfred C. "The Religious Art of a Painter Poet," *The Religious Thoughts*

Plate I. "Pre-Raffaelleite Chorus,"

BY JOHN BURLEY WARING (82.5)

, we live in wretched days, there are few whom we can
praise,
e the happy band of brothers, who "Pre-Raffaelleite"
re called;
the rest will come to grief, with no hope of relief,
d by our prophet, Buskin, will be regularly mauled.

l no more will we say, of the painters of to-day,
o, if they only join our ranks, may yet perhaps be
aved;
: for Raffaelle and his crew, we will pink them through
nd through,
d Buskin's name in blood upon their souls shall be
ngraved.

t Raffaelle was a fool, like all others of his school,
hout sentiment or soul, — a sensual heathen brute;
although he has a name, yet Buskin soon his fame
ll scratch and tear to tatters, and trample under foot.

for wretched Buonarotti, so contorted, coarse, and dotty,
h a humbug diabolical has never yet been known;
emissary from Hades, from whom gentlemen and ladies
uld turn in proper horror, and entirely disown!

re's that satyr, J. Romano; that immoral Tiziano;
rgione, Tintoretto, Guido, — demons one and all,
om we loathe, abhor, detest; and we swear to take no
est
, we dance upon their monuments, both great and small.

Rembrandt's simply bosh; and Ruben's actual slosh;
l those who dare say otherwise are fools, and dogs, and
aves.
dyke, Ostade, and Snyders, with the squad of Dutch
utsiders,
re a set of heartless, pagan, drunken, muddle-headed
naves.

As for poor old Claude Lorraine, Buskin makes it very
plain
That a muff more unartistic we couldn't well conceive;
Whilst dull Salvator Rosa is a "maladetta cosa,"
And they and all who follow them are doomed without
reprieve.

The Poussins and Le Brun, we will show you very soon,
Were nothing more than pagans of the deepest, blackest
dye,
In fact, throughout the century, to take an oath we venture,
ye
Will find no Christian sentiment, or anything that's high.

And every single Spaniard is ridiculously mannered;
Velasques and Murillo, with Zurbaran as well;
Old Cano and El Greco, would a pretty party make, oh!
In a place that mayn't be mentioned, as I need not tell.

In that *place* they all have got, let us hope, a fiery lot,
For the dark artistic crimes which they committed here on
earth,
Whilst we shout with might and main, till the heavens
vibrate again,
That High Art in Great Britain has at last been brought
to birth.

And Buskin swears that now, if your knee you do not bow,
And humbly, to the Genius of this Infant so divine,
He will give you such a slashing, — such a mashing,
crashing, thrashing,
As befits a set of donkeys, or a herd of filthy swine.

So, you see, we must be right; and, having put you in a
fright,
Go, burn your stupid ancient daubs, and come to us to
school;
Then perhaps you may, some day, find out the proper way
To look on Art and Nature, and cease to be a fool.

Plate II. Illustrated Title Pages

By John Nettleship (51.1)

By Edward Burne-Jones (92.1)

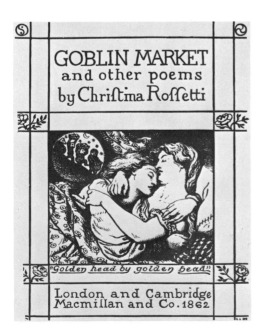

By Dante Gabriel Rossetti (44.3)

By William Bell Scott (56.5)

of Some of Our Poets. London: Mowbray, 1911.

30.49 Chester, Austin. "The Art of Dante Gabriel Rossetti," *Windsor Magazine,* XXXV (April 1912), 571–586.

30.50 Binyon, Laurence. "Zeichnungen Dante Gabriel Rossettis," *Die graphischen Künste,* XXXV (1912), 15–20.

30.51 Schoepe, Max. *Der Vergleich bei Rossetti: Teil I: Bilder aus der Natur.* Berlin: Märkische, 1913 (diss. Kiel, 1913).

30.52 —— *Der Vergleich bei Dante Gabriel Rossetti. Eine stilistische Untersuchung* (*Normannia. Germanisch-romanische Bücherei,* vol. XIII). Berlin: Felber, 1914.
Except for the additional section, "Zusammenfassende Charakteristik der Vergleiche," essentially the same as 30.51.

30.53 Galletti, Alfredo. "Dante Gabriele Rossetti e il romanticismo preraffaellita," *Saggi e Studi.* Bologna: Zanichelli, 1915.
For annotation see 77.30.

30.54 Cary, Elizabeth Luther. "Dante Gabriel Rossetti, Illustrator," *Print Collector's Quarterly,* V (1915), 317–339.

30.55 Fry, Roger. "Rossetti's Water Colours of 1857," *Burlington Magazine,* XXIX (June 1916), 100–109.
Rossetti "fails to assimilate into the form all the material of his imagination." His form is "clear, definite and truly expressive almost exactly in proportion as he [is] concerned with the accessories of his drama . . . When he [is] most occupied with the central core of his theme, with the passion, his form [falls] to pieces, he [becomes] a mere illustrator and not a very good one." (p. 100) Five of Rossetti's water colors in the Tate Gallery are reproduced.

30.56 Wood, T. Martin. "The True Rossetti," *Studio,* LXIX (October 1916), 3–15.
Eleven illustrations, four in color. Reproductions from the Rae Collection of Rossetti water colors (see 6.6). Title refers to Rossetti as a water-colorist.

30.57 Lynd, Robert. "Rossetti and Ritual," *Old and New Masters.* London: Unwin, 1919.

30.58 Williamson, G. C. "Dante Gabriel Rossetti," *Murray Marks and His Friends: A Tribute of Regard.* London: John Lane, 1919.
For complete annotation see 86.14.

30.59 Phelps, Mrs. J. Q. "The Mysticism of Rossetti," *Fine Arts Journal,* XXXVII (September 1919), 37–40.

30.60 Sapori, Francesco. *Dante Gabriele Rossetti: I maestri dell'arte* (*Monographie d'artisti Italia moderna,* no. 27). Torino: Celanza, 1921.

30.61 McQuilland, Louis J. "Dante Gabriel Rossetti and the Pre-Raphaelites," *Bookman's Journal,* XI (November 1924), 60–62.

30.62 Schäfer, Josy. "Rossettis Ansichten über Kunst und Künstler," unpub. diss. Erlangen, 1925.

30.63 Gerwig, Henrietta. "Dante Gabriel Rossetti," *Fifty Famous Painters.* New York: Crowell, 1926.

30.64 Bateman, Arthur B. "Rossetti, the Pre-Raphaelites, and a Moral," *London Quarterly Review,* CXLIX, 5th ser., XXV (April 1928), 223–233.
For annotation see 77.33.

30.65 Meldrum, David S. "Rossetti as a Painter," *Bookman* (London), LXXIV (April 1928), 10–14.

30.66 Rigillo, M. "Dante Gabriel Rossetti e il Preraffaellismo," *Rassegna Nazionale,* anno L, vol. III (July-August 1928) 3–7.

30.67 Cortissoz, Royal. "Dante Gabriel Rossetti," *Scribner's Magazine,* LXXXIV (November 1928), 617–625.
An interesting, illustrated article pointing out the conflict between ideas and execution in Pre-Raphaelite art. In monochrome, Cortissoz says, only the ideas are apparent. The Pre-Raphaelites "were fertile, interesting designers and capable draughtsmen. None of

them was an absolute master of the art of painting . . . They . . . knew all about the pleasures of the imagination." (p. 617) Same in *The Painter's Craft* (New York: Scribner's, 1930).

30.68 Binyon, Laurence. "Rossetti and the Pre-Raphaelites," *English Water-Colours.* London: Black, 1933.
For brief annotation see 77.36.

30.69 Seiler, Magdalene. *D. G. Rossettis künstlerische Entwicklung.* Greifswald: Mitau, 1933 (diss. Greifswald, 1933).

30.70 Hamill, Alfred E. "Dante Gabriel Rossetti in America," *Notes & Queries,* 14th ser., CLXV (18 November 1933), 358–359.
Locates Rossetti's works in America. Supplementary additions: 9 December 1933, p. 408.

30.71 Davies, Randall. "Rossetti's Earliest Drawings," *Burlington Magazine,* LXXVI (January 1940), 22 and 26.
A Faust illustration signed with monogram and dated 1846, two other drawings with the same monogram, and another unsigned Faust subject. Illustrated.

30.72 Minondo, Venancio. *Dante Gabriel Rossetti en el Prerrafaelismo.* Buenos Aires: Editorial Ideas, 1947.

30.73 Mills, Ernestine. "Rossetti's Method of Oil Painting," *Apollo,* XLIX (February 1949), 49.
Descriptions of Rossetti's technique from Shields's notebook. See also 30.15.

30.74 Flemming, Hanns Theodor. "Die stilistische Entwicklung der Malerei von Dante Gabriel Rossetti," unpub. diss. Berlin Freie Universität, 1954.

30.75 Schmutzler, Robert. "The English Origins of Art Nouveau," *Architectural Review,* CXVII (February 1955), 109–116.
See also the continuation of this article: "Blake and Art Nouveau," *Architectural Review,* CXVIII (August 1955), 91–97. The most important sources of *Art Nouveau* are Blake, Rossetti, and Japan. Rossetti is important not only because of his designs (many in imitation of Blake) but because "without him Swinburne could not have written his brilliant essay . . . and without this essay Blake would not have become the ideal of a whole group of poets and writers."

30.76 Ferriday, Peter. "Peacock Room," *Architectural Review,* CXXV (June 1959), 407–414.
Brief section on the influence of Rossetti in the Aesthetic Movement.

30.77 Sewter, A. C. "D. G. Rossetti's Designs for Stained Glass," *Journal British Society of Master Glass-Painters,* XIII (1960–1961), 419–424.

30.78 Mander, Rosalie. "Rossetti's Models," *Apollo,* LXXVIII (July 1963), 18–22.
"It was through women's beauty that Rossetti expressed his genius." (p. 22) Profusely illustrated, including color reproductions of *La Bocca Baciata* and *La Pia.*

Section 31

STUDIES AND NOTICES OF INDIVIDUAL PICTURES

31.1 [Lushington, Vernon]. "Two Pictures," *Oxford and Cambridge Magazine,* I (August 1856), 479–488.
Rossetti's *Dante's Dream* and Ford Madox Brown's *The Last of England.*

31.2 [Stephens, Frederic George]. "Mr. Rossetti's New Pictures," *Athenaeum,* no. 1982 (21 October 1865), pp. 545–546.
Blue Bower, Venus Verticordia, The Beloved.

31.3 "Two Drawings by Rossetti," *Nation,* III (20 December 1866), 501–502.

Exhibited in the Artist's Fund Loan Collection: no. 227, "Before the Battle"; no. 251, "Dante Meeting Beatrice."

31.4 [Stephens, Frederic George]. "Mr. Rossetti's New Picture," *Athenaeum*, no. 2300 (25 November 1871), p. 694.
Dante's Dream.

31.5 [——] "Pictures by Mr. Rossetti," *Athenaeum*, no. 2494 (14 August 1875), pp. 219–221.
Proserpina, La Bella Mano, La Ghirlandata, Venus Astarte, The Question.

31.6 [——] "Mr. Rossetti's New Pictures," *Athenaeum*, no. 2581 (14 April 1877), pp. 486–487.
Venus Astarte. Including two sonnets, "Astarte Syriaca" and "A Sea Spell"; also discusses *A Sea Spell* and *The Blessed Damozel.*

31.7 [——] "A New Picture by Mr. Rossetti," *Athenaeum*, no. 2633 (13 April 1878), p. 481.
The Blessed Damozel, the new version with predella.

31.8 [——] "Mr. Rossetti's New Picture," *Athenaeum*, no. 2658 (5 October 1878), pp. 439–440.
A Vision of Fiammetta.

31.9 [——] "Mr. Rossetti's New Pictures," *Athenaeum*, no. 2714 (1 November 1879), pp. 566–567.
Lady at the Window, Dante's Dream, The Blessed Damozel.

31.10 Caine, T. Hall. *A Disquisition on Dante Gabriel Rossetti's Painting in Oil Entitled "Dante's Dream."* Liverpool: Printed at the "Daily Post" and "Echo" Offices, 1881.
A lecture given by Caine at the Walker Art Gallery.

31.11 [Stephens, Frederic George]. "Mr. Rossetti's New Pictures," *Athenaeum*, no. 2783 (26 February 1881), p. 304.
Day Dream, La Pia.

31.12 G[urney], A[lfred]. *A Dream of*

Fair Women: A Study of Some Pictures by Dante Gabriel Rossetti. London: Kegan Paul, 1883.
Inspired by the Royal Academy exhibition of Rossetti's works (14.1), the Reverend Gurney takes his readers on a conducted tour through the "beauty haunted chambers of the Palace of Art."

31.13 Monkhouse, William Cosmo. "*Rosa Triplex,*" *Magazine of Art,* VI (1883), 271–272.

31.14 "*Ecce Ancilla Domini* by Dante Gabriel Charles Rossetti," *Portfolio,* XIX (July 1888), 125–127.

31.15 [Stephens, Frederic George]. "*Beata Beatrix* by Dante Gabriel Rossetti," *Portfolio,* XXII (May 1891), 45–47.
Reprinted in *Modern Paintings,* ed. Esther Singleton. New York: Dodd, Mead, 1911. See 36.55.

31.16 [——] "*Rosa Triplex* by Dante Gabriel Rossetti," *Portfolio,* XXIII (October 1892), 197–199.

31.17 Monkhouse, Cosmo. "A Sketch of Tennyson by Rossetti . . ." *Scribner's Magazine,* XXI (January 1897), 125–126.
Reproduction (p. 120) and discussion of one version of Rossetti's sketch of Tennyson, then in Monkhouse's possession, now in City Museum and Art Gallery, Birmingham. See also 31.35.

31.18 White, Gleeson. "'A Sea Spell.' An Appreciation," *The Dome,* II (1898), 91–94.

31.19 Marillier, Henry Currie. "The Salutations of Beatrice: as Treated Pictorially by D. G. Rossetti," *Art Journal,* LXI (December 1899), 353–357.

31.20 Sawvel, Franklin B. "*Dante's Dream* and *Captive Andromache,*" *Education, A Monthly Magazine,* XXI (September 1900), 32–36.

31.21 Whiting, Mary Bradford. "*Beata Beatrix,*" *Temple Bar,* CXXVI (September 1902), 270–282.

Traces the influence of Dante on Rossetti and gives a short list of pictures by Rossetti for which Beatrice is the subject (p. 278). Also discusses the relationship between Elizabeth Siddal and Rossetti, for which the latter found the parallel in Dante.

31.22 Cary, Elizabeth Luther. "A Rossetti Model," *Scrip. Notes on Art*, I (June 1906), 286–288.

Wilfred Hawtrey, son of the Rev. H. C. Hawtrey, whom Rossetti saw while staying at Broadlands, the home of Lord (William Francis Cowper) and Lady (Georgiana) Mount Temple, in 1876, became the model for one of the angel-children in the version of *The Blessed Damozel* commissioned by William Graham. See Marillier (30.24), p. 189.

31.23 Stevens, W. Bertrand. "*Ecce Ancilla Domini* (Behold the Handmaiden of the Lord)," *Chautauquan*, XLVI (March 1907), 103–104.

31.24 Burns, J. "*Mary Magdalene at the House of Simon* by D. G. Rossetti," *Sermons in Art by the Great Masters*. London: Duckworth, 1908.

Also contains chapters on pictures by Holman Hunt (36.46) and Burne-Jones (42.77).

31.25 Cary, Elizabeth Luther. "New Rossetti Water Color in the Metropolitan Museum, *Lady Lilith*," *International Studio*, XXXV (October 1908), Supp. 125–130.

31.26 Linton, John. "Dante Gabriel Rossetti," *The Cross in Modern Art: Descriptive Studies of Some Pre-Raphaelite Paintings*. London: Duckworth, 1916.

Discussions of *The Girlhood of Mary Virgin*, *Ecce Ancilla Domini*, and *Beata Beatrix*. Illustrated. For complete annotation see 75.27.

31.27 Forbes-Robertson, Sir Johnston. "D. G. Rossetti, 1828–1928. The Tribute of a Friend," *Times*, no. 44,890 (11 May 1928), pp. 17–18.

Recounting his experience in sitting for the head of Love in Rossetti's *Dante's Dream* in 1871.

31.28 Williamson, G. C. "The Cases of an Art Expert. II. The Rossetti Miniature," *Country Life*, LXXX (11 July 1936), 35–36. Illustrated.

31.29 Murray, E. Croft. "An Early Drawing by Rossetti," *British Museum Quarterly*, XI (March 1937), 95–96.

Rossetti's drawing illustrating some lines from Poe's "The Sleeper."

31.30 "D. G. Rossetti (1828–1882)," *Russell-Cotes Bulletin*, XVIII (December 1939), 45–48.

A discussion of *Arthur's Tomb* (1854) and *How They Met Themselves* (1864). Illustrated.

31.31 "D. G. Rossetti's *King René's Honeymoon*," *Apollo*, XXXIV (December 1941), 153.

A more elaborate version, in oil on canvas, of the panel painted for the cabinet, in the collection of Mrs. Virginia Surtees. Reproduced in color on cover. See 79.14

31.32 Gaunt, William. "Two Portrait Drawings by Dante Gabriel Rossetti," *Connoisseur*, CX (December 1942), 140–141, 158.

Portraits of Dr. Thomas Gordon Hake and his son, George.

31.33 "*Venus Verticordia*," *Russell-Cotes Bulletin*, September 1946, pp. 1–3.

Recently acquired by the Russell-Cotes Art Gallery, Bournemouth. An interesting, brief discussion of nudity in nineteenth-century art.

31.34 Paden, W. D. "*La Pia de' Tolomei* by Dante Gabriel Rossetti," *Register of the Museum of Art* (University of Kansas), II (November 1958), *passim*.

"A special issue devoted to the Museum's painting . . ." A provocative study of the background of the painting — its various versions, its significance as Rossetti's last major work, and its symbolic meaning in terms of Rossetti's life and art, especially as regards his increasing physical and psychological disorders, stemming from his emotional entanglement with Jane Morris. The monograph is divided into two parts: the first an investigation of the biographical relevance of

La Pia (which Rossetti began in 1868 and did not complete until 1881); the second, "Notes on *La Pia*, Its Chronology and Its Variants." The notes to the first part (pp. 20–32) are of special interest. A double-page color reproduction of the painting is also included in the monograph.

31.35 Fredeman, William E. "Rossetti's Impromptu Portraits of Tennyson Reading *Maud*," *Burlington Magazine*, CV (March 1963), 117–118.

With illustrations of the three extant versions of Rossetti's portrait. See also letter of correction *Burlington Magazine*, CV (September 1963), 413.

31.36 Rogers, Millard F., Jr. "The Salutation of Beatrice: By Dante Gabriel Rossetti," *Connoisseur*, CLIII, no. 617 (July 1963), 180–181.

Illustrated by Dante Gabriel Rossetti's canvas in the Toledo Museum of Art.

31.37 Adrian, Arthur A. "The Genesis of Rossetti's 'Found,'" *Texas Studies in Literature and Language*, V (1963), 79–82.

Section 32

STUDIES OF ROSSETTI'S WORK AND INFLUENCE IN BOTH LITERATURE AND ART

32.1 Stillman, William James. "Rossetti, the Painter and Poet." *Putnam's Monthly Magazine*, XVI, n.s. VI (July 1870), 95–101.

A general discussion of Rossetti's pictures and poems, but not a review of *Poems*, 1870. Stillman praises Rossetti's imaginative faculty, completeness, and coherence. "Even in his portraits Rossetti fails, unless the subject inclines more or less to the type which he reflects." (p. 99) "This demands more than external beauty, be it ever so exquisite, and is only absolutely content with a certain gravity and intensity of character, deep, inscrutable, sphinx-like, or still more when these characteristics go with the expression of intense and restrained passion." (p. 99) The article is introduced by a brief survey of the Pre-Raphaelite Movement.

32.2 Myers, Frederic William Henry. "Rossetti and the Religion of Beauty," *Essays: Modern*. London: Macmillan, 1883.

Same in *Cornhill Magazine*, XLVII (February 1883), 213–224. Reprinted in *Bibelot*, VIII (October 1902), 337–367.

32.3 Quilter, Harry. "The Art of Rossetti," *Contemporary Review*, XLIII (February 1883), 190–203.

Same in *Eclectic Magazine*, n.s. XXXVII (April 1883), 448–457. Reprinted in *Preferences* (68.4) as "The Painting and the Poetry of Dante Gabriel Rossetti." In part a defense of Rossetti against the charge of sensualism.

32.4 Ward, Julius H. "Rossetti in Poetry and Art," *American Church Review*, XLI (April 1883), 371–379.

32.5 Nicholson, P. W. *Dante Gabriel Rossetti, Poet and Painter* (The Round Table Series, edited by H. B. Baildon, vol. VI). Edinburgh: Brown, 1887.

32.6 Rossetti, William Michael. *Dante Gabriel Rossetti as Designer and Writer*. London: Cassell, 1889.

A chronological survey of Rossetti's artistic works and of his writings, together with a prose paraphrase of the sonnets in *The House of Life*.

32.7 [Warre, F. Cornish]. "Dante Gabriel Rossetti," *Quarterly Review*, CLXXXIV (July 1896), 185–214.

Pre-Raphaelitism was not a revolution. "The spirit of Pre-Raphaelism was already in the air. The beginnings of it were in the 'Lakers,' the 'Cockney School,' the Mediaevalists of Düsseldorf and Munich, the Romanticists of Germany and France. Tennyson's 'Mariana,' 'Lady of Shalott,' and 'Palace of Art' were waiting ten years for the artists

whose kindred genius illustrated them in
1856. But the spiritual father of the new
Romanticists in England . . . was Robert
Browning." (p. 195)

32.8 Harper, Janet. "Dante Gabriel Ros-
setti: Artist and Poet," *Westminster Review*,
CXLVI (August 1896), 312–321.
Superficial and sentimental.

32.9 Agresti, Antonio. *Poesie di Dante G.
Rossetti tradotte con uno studio su la pittura
inglese e su l'opera pittorica e la vita del-
l'autore.* Firenze: Barbèra, 1899.

32.10 Wilmersdoerffer, A. "Dante Gabriel
Rossetti und sein Einfluss," *Westermanns
Illustrierte Deutsche Monatshefte*, LXXXV
(February 1899), 592–610.

32.11 Kassner, Rudolf. "Dante Gabriel Ros-
setti," *Die Mystik, die Künstler, und das
Leben: über englische Dichter und Maler im
19. Jahrhunderts.* Leipzig: Diederichs, 1900.
Reissued 1920 (Leipzig: Insel) with title
Englische Dichter.

32.12 Waldschmidt, Wolfram. *Dante Gab-
riel Rossetti, der Maler und der Dichter: Die
Anfänge der präraphaelitischen Bewegung in
England.* Jena und Leipzig: Diederichs, 1905.

32.13 Galletti, Alfredo. "Un Poeta-pittore
dell'amore e della morte: Dante Gabriele Rossetti," *La Lettura*, VI (April 1906), 322–329.

32.14 Rutter, Frank. *Dante Gabriel Rossetti,
Painter and Man of Letters.* London: Richards, 1908.

32.15 Venkatesan, N. K. *Dante Gabriel
Rossetti: The Pre-Raphaelite Painter-Poet.*
Madras: Srinivasa Varadachari, 1918.
For annotation see 77.31.

32.16 Block, Lotte. "Dante Gabriel Rossetti,
der Malerdichter, eine Untersuchung seines
künstlerischen Schaffens," *Giessener Beiträge
zur Erforschung der Sprache und Kultur
Englands und Nordamerikas.* Giessen: English Seminar, 1925 (diss. Giessen, 1925).

32.17 Taylor, Rachel Annand. "A King in

Exile," *Spectator*, CXL, no. 5211 (Literary
Supplement) (12 May 1928), 719–721.
A sympathetic article on Rossetti's art and
poetry, and a review of Waugh's life of Rossetti (25.59). Of some critics of the Pre-
Raphaelites, Miss Taylor comments that it
is easier to market the frailties than the vic-
tories of genius. Her title, of course, is based
on Whistler's comment: "You must not say
anything against Rossetti. Rossetti was a
king."

32.18 Bergum, Edwin B. "Rossetti and the
Ivory Tower," *Sewanee Review*, XXXVII
(October 1929), 431–446.
". . . Pre-Raphaelitism was at bottom only
the evidence of a religious movement . . ."
(p. 431)

32.19 Bachschmidt, Friedrich Wilhelm. *Das
Italienische Element in Dante Gabriel Rossetti.* Breslau: Walter, 1930 (diss. Münster,
1930).

32.20 Christoffel, Ulrich. "D. G. Rossetti,"
*Malerei und Poesie: die symbolische Kunst
des 19. Jahrhunderts.* Vienna: Gallus-Verlag,
1948.

32.21 Hough, Graham. "Rossetti and the
P.R.B.," *The Last Romantics.* London: Duck-
worth, 1949.
For discussion see Survey, pp. 34–35.

32.22 Doughty, Oswald. "Rossetti's Conception of the 'Poetic' in Poetry and Painting," *Essays by Divers Hands (Transactions
of the Royal Society of Literature.* n.s.
XXVI). London: Oxford University Press,
1953.

32.23 De Pilato, Sergio. *Dante Gabriele
Rossetti, poeta e pittore.* Roma: Edizioni
Conchiglia, 1954.

32.24 Peterson, Carl Adrian. "The Poetry
and Painting of Dante Gabriel Rossetti," unpub. diss. University of Wisconsin, 1961.
Dissertation Abstracts, XXI (1961), 3460.

32.25 Bristol, Frank Milton. "The Poet-
Painter," *The Ministry of Art.* Cincinnati:
Curts and Jennings, 1897.

STUDIES COMPARING ROSSETTI WITH OTHER ARTISTS, INCLUDING STUDIES OF ROSSETTI AND HIS CIRCLE

33.1 Armes, William D. "De Quincey and Rossetti," *Critic*, XVIII (December 1890), 328.

A letter to the editor comparing a note in De Quincey on the experience of opium with Rossetti's "Monochord."

33.2 [Taylor, Una A]. "William Morris and Dante Gabriel Rossetti," *Edinburgh Review*, CXCI (April 1900), 356–379.

For annotation see 43.48.

33.3 Agresti, Antonio. "La Vita Nuova di Dante e i quadri di D. G. Rossetti," *La Vita Nuova di Dante con le illustrazioni di D. G. Rossetti*. Roma-Torino: Rouxeviarengo, 1902.

33.4 Wyzewa, Teodor de. "Deux peintres préraphaélites," *Peintres de jadis et d'aujourd'hui*. Paris: Perrin, 1903.

Rossetti and Edouard Steinle.

33.5 Dunn, Henry Treffry. *Recollections of Dante Gabriel Rossetti and His Circle (Cheyne Walk Life)*. Edited and annotated by Gale Pedrick, with a Prefatory Note by William Michael Rossetti. London: Elkin Mathews, 1904.

33.6 Fuller, Edward. "Arnold, Newman, and Rossetti," *Critic*, XLV (September 1904), 273–276.

Applying St. Paul's category of the three-fold nature of man, Arnold represents the soul, Newman the spirit, Rossetti the body. A general discussion and three reviews. For Rossetti, of Benson's biography (25.26).

33.7 Dalby, W. Burkitt. "Rossetti and His Circle," *London Quarterly Review*, CIV, 4th ser., II (July 1905), 21–39.

33.8 Shaw, Wilfred B. "Rossetti and Botticelli: A Comparison of Ideals and Art," *Craftsman*, IX (December 1905), 341–356.

Their works are both "visionary," and "only as an art lover is a lover of poetry, can he concede high qualities of art to Botticelli or the Pre-Raphaelites." (p. 356) For an excellent study of the influence of Botticelli see Michael Levey, "Botticelli and Nineteenth Century England," *Journal of the Warburg and Courtauld Institutes*, XXIII (July–December 1960), 291–306.

33.9 Compton-Rickett, Arthur. "Keats and Rossetti," *Personal Forces in Modern Literature*. London: Dent, 1906.

33.10 Weygandt, Cornelius. "Two Pre-Raphaelite Poets: William Morris and Dante Gabriel Rossetti," *Book News Monthly*, XXIV (June 1906), 687–690.

For other articles in the same issue of this journal see 67.26.

33.11 Watts-Dunton, Theodore. "Rossetti and Charles Wells: A Reminiscence of Kelmscott Manor." in *Joseph and His Brethren: A Dramatic Poem by Charles Wells*. With an Introduction by A. C. Swinburne (The World's Classics). London: Oxford University Press, 1908.

33.12 Routh, James. "Parallels in Coleridge, Keats, and Rossetti," *Modern Language Notes*, XXV (February 1910), 33–37.

For contrasting point of view see 33.23.

33.13 Bassalik-de Vries, Johanna. *William Blake in His Relation to Dante Gabriel Rossetti*. Basel: Brin, 1911 (diss. Zurich, 1910–1911).

33.14 Butterworth, Walter. *Dante Gabriel Rossetti in Relation to Dante Alighieri*. London: Sheratt and Hughes, 1912.

Reprinted from *Manchester Quarterly*, XXXI (April 1912), 117–131.

33.15 Toynbee, Paget. *Chronological List*,

with Notes, of Paintings and Drawings from Dante by Dante Gabriel Rossetti. Torino: Fratelli Bocca, 1912.

Reprinted from *Scritti varii de erudizione, e di critica in onore di Rodolfo Renier* (Torino, 1912).

33.16 Kitchen, Paul C. "The Influence of Dante on Rossetti," unpub. diss. University of Pennsylvania, 1913.

33.17 Villard, Léonie. *The Influence of Keats on Tennyson and Rossetti.* Saint-Étienne: Mulcey, 1914 (diss. Paris, 1914).

33.18 Van Roosbroeck, Gustave L. "Rossetti and Maeterlinck," *Modern Language Notes,* XXXIV (November 1919), 439–441.

In the "Correspondence" section. Discusses the influence of Rossetti's "An Old Song Ended" on Maeterlinck's "Et s'il revenait un jour."

33.19 Galimberti, Alice. "Gli esuli: Il Culto di Dante in casa Rossetti," *Dante nel pensiero inglese.* Firenze: Le Mourier, 1921.

33.20 Beerbohm, Max. *Rossetti and His Circle.* London: Heinemann, 1922.

For annotation see 82.9.

33.21 Broers, Bernarda C. "Dante and Rossetti," *Mysticism in the Neo-Romanticists.* Amsterdam: Paris, 1923 (diss. Amsterdam, 1923).

For complete annotation see 73.8.

33.22 Buchan, John. "Morris and Rossetti," *Homilies and Recreations.* London: Nelson, 1926.

33.23 Shine, Wesley Hill. "The Influence of Keats upon Rossetti," *Englische Studien,* LXI (May 1927), 183–219.

Includes a reprint of Milner's article (27.11); challenges opinion of Routh (33.12).

33.24 Symons, Arthur. "Dante Gabriel Rossetti," *Studies in Strange Souls.* London: Sawyer, 1929.

With a parallel section on Swinburne (see 62.29).

33.25 Whiting, Mary Bradford. "Dante and Rossetti," *Congregational Quarterly,* VII (April 1929), 207–214.

Sees Dante as the dominating influence on Rossetti. "It is in Rossetti's attitude towards love that the impress of Dante's spirit is most vividly seen." (p. 207) With a list of Rossetti's works from Dante, with the dates. See also Toynbee (33.15). For Dantesque influences on a single painting of Rossetti's see 31.21.

33.26 Olivero, Federico. *Il Petrarca e Dante Gabriele Rossetti.* Firenze: Tipocalcografia Classica, 1933.

Reprinted from *Annali della cattedra petrarchesca,* IV, 1932.

33.27 Farmer, Albert J. "Le Mouvement préraphaélite: Rossetti et Morris," *Le Mouvement esthétique et "décadent" en Angleterre (1873–1900)* (*Bibliothèque de la Revue de Littérature Comparée,* tome 75). Paris: Champion, 1931 (diss. Paris, 1931).

33.28 Morse, B. J. "Dante Gabriel Rossetti and William Blake," *Englische Studien,* LXVI (March 1932), 364–372.

33.29 Klinnert, Adelheid. *Dante Gabriel Rossetti und Stefan George.* Würzburg: Mayr, 1933 (diss. Bonn, 1933).

33.30 Morse, B. J. "Dante Gabriel Rossetti and Dante Alighieri," *Englische Studien,* LXVIII (September 1933), 227–248.

33.31 Farrell, Ralph. "Rossetti," *Stefan Georges Beziehungen zur englischen Dichtung* (*Germanische Studien,* no. 192). Berlin: Ebering, 1937.

33.32 Bowman, Estella. "Rossetti and His Circle," *Northwest Missouri State Teachers College Studies,* II (1938), 43–66.

33.33 Ford, George H. "Rossetti," *Keats and the Victorians: A Study of His Influence and Rise to Fame, 1821–1895* (Yale Studies in English, vol. 101). New Haven: Yale University Press, 1944.

Part III, on Rossetti, consists of three separate chapters: "Conflicts in Victorian

Taste after 1850," "Rossetti's Standards of Poetry and Prophecy," and "Keats' Influence on Rossetti." The middle chapter is concerned partially with the influence of Keats on the Pre-Raphaelites (see 77.9). Part IV contains separate chapters on Morris (43.121) and Swinburne (62.36). An excellent study. Georges Lafourcade's "Essay on Swinburne and Keats," in his edition of Swinburne's *Hyperion and Other Poems* (London: Faber, 1927), contains a brief section on "Keats and the Pre-Raphaelites."

33.34 Preston, Kerrison. *Blake and Rossetti.* London: Moring, 1944.

With a chapter on "Rossetti and Art" that consists principally of a reprinting of "Hand and Soul," and a chapter on Mrs. Rossetti. A superficial examination of an important aspect of Rossetti studies.

33.35 Gray, Nicolette. *Rossetti, Dante, and Ourselves.* London: Faber, 1947.

Suggests that Rossetti's treatment of Dante in his art and poetry may present a false picture of Dante and the Middle Ages.

33.36 Kühnelt, Harro Heinz. "Edgar Allan Poe and D. G. Rossetti," unpub. diss. Innsbruck, 1948.

Printed in *Bedeutung von Edgar Allan Poe für die englische Literatur* (Innsbruck, 1949).

33.37 West, T. Wilson. "D. G. Rossetti and Ezra Pound," *Review of English Studies,* n.s. IV (January 1953), 63–67.

Cites a few parallel passages and notes general similarities in diction, particularly in Pound's early poems.

33.38 Wahl, John Robert. "Two Pre-Raphaelite Poets: Studies in the Poetry and Poetic Theory of William Morris and D. G. Rossetti," unpub. diss. Oxford University, 1954.

33.39 [Runden, John P.] "Rossetti and a Poe Image," *Notes & Queries,* CCIII, n.s. V (June 1958), 257–258.

A comparison of Poe's two "Helen" poems with Rossetti's two "Portraits." See also "Echoes of Poe in Rossetti's 'Beryl Song,'" *N&Q,* 14th ser., CLXVIII (2 February 1935), 77.

33.40 Mellown, Elgin W. "Hopkins, Hall Caine, and D. G. Rossetti," *Notes & Queries,* CCIV, n.s. VI (March 1959), 109–111.

In March 1881, R. W. Dixon persuaded Hopkins to contribute three sonnets to Hall Caine's *Sonnets of Three Centuries* (84.4). Caine, on the advice of a "critic of utmost eminence," later revealed by Caine to be Rossetti, rejected them. "If, in time," Mellown says, "Hopkins comes to be considered as having affinities with the pre-Raphaelites, this judgment by the leader of the Brotherhood should be remembered." For an excellent discussion of Hopkins' affinities with the Pre-Raphaelites see 78.22.

33.41 Paolucci, Anne. "Ezra Pound and D. G. Rossetti as Translators of Guido Cavalcanti," *Romanic Review,* LI (Winter 1960), 256–267.

33.42 Ryals, Clyde de L. "The 'Inner Experience': The Aesthetic of Rossetti and Isak Dinesen" [Baroness Karen Blixen], *Revue des Langues Vivantes,* XXVI (1960), 368–374.

A comparison of Rossetti's *Hand and Soul* with Dinesen's "The Young Man with the Carnation." Both works proclaim that "art is a religious activity" (p. 373), but "whereas Rossetti saw art as a religious activity, he none the less saw art as a manifestation of God which exists for its own sake; for Baroness Blixen art as religious activity is but the fulfillment of the commands of God, the lot of one who has been chosen by God to follow a certain destiny in the world in order to explain the ways of God to man. For her, art is similar to love . . ." (p. 374)

33.43 Laver, James. "Rossetti and the Influence of Japan," *Whistler.* New York: Cosmopolitan Book Corp., 1930.

Section 34

COLLECTIONS OF REPRODUCTIONS
OF ROSSETTI'S WORKS

34.1 Carrington, FitzRoy, *Pictures and Poems by Dante Gabriel Rossetti*. New York: Russell, 1899.

An attempt to demonstrate the close relationship that existed between Rossetti's poetry and painting. The method is to juxtapose poems and paintings on subjects which Rossetti treated in both media. Numerous illustrations and an Introduction by the editor.

34.2 Rossetti, William Michael. *Permanent Photographs after the Works of Dante Gabriel Rossetti: With Explanatory Text*. London: Mansell, 1900.

An illustrated advertisement-catalogue.

34.3 *Dante Gabriel Rossetti* (Newnes' Art Library). London: Newnes, [1905].

With a long Introduction on Rossetti by Ernest Radford and reproductions of 56 of his finished works.

34.4 Angeli, Helen Rossetti. *Dante Gabriele Rossetti (Collezione di monografie illustrate: Artisti moderni, no. I)*. Bergamo: Instituto Italiano d'Arti Grafiche, 1906.

With a long introduction in Italian (translated from 30.31) and 107 illustrations.

34.5 *Masterpieces of Dante Gabriel Rossetti (1828–1882): Sixty Reproductions from the Original Oil Paintings*. London: Gowans and Gray, 1912.

Illustrations without text. Reprinted in France, Belgium, and Germany.

34.6 Drawings of Rossetti (Newnes' modern Master Draughtsmen). London: Newnes, n.d.

With an Introduction by T. Martin Wood and 48 plates.

OTHER PRE-RAPHAELITE BROTHERS

Section 35

JAMES COLLINSON
1825?–1881

[DNB: IV, 837–838 (Lionel Cust)]

The reputation of James Collinson has been the most short-lived of all the original Pre-Raphaelites. Today, he is sometimes remembered as the painter of a few insignificant, but extremely pretty, pictures; more often he is dismissed as the rather unstable lover of Christina Rossetti. Almost no work has been done on Collinson, but references to his relationship with Christina Rossetti and to his association with the Pre-Raphaelites will be found in biographies and studies of the poetess and in works treating the origin and history of the PRB.

*   *   *

35.1 Bodkin, Thomas. "James Collinson," *Apollo*, XXXI (May 1940), 128–133.

A discussion of Collinson's life and work and of his association with the PRB. The only major account of Collinson available.

Six of Collinson's works are reproduced: *St Elizabeth of Hungary* (Johannesburg Municipal Gallery of Art), *For Sale* and *To Let* (formerly in Professor Bodkin's possession and recently sold at Sotheby's — two similar works are in Sheffield), *The New Bonnet,* *The Emigration Scene,* and *Good For a Cold,* the last of which was engraved by W. H. Simmons for Lloyd Brothers & Co. in 1857

Section 36

WILLIAM HOLMAN HUNT
1827–1910

[DNB: S, I, 323–328 (Walter Armstrong); EB: XIII, 937–938 (Cosmo Monkhouse)]

For Holman Hunt, Pre-Raphaelitism always remained untainted by the contributions of Rossetti and his followers. Rossetti's *Found,* Hunt conceded as Rossetti's only Pre-Raphaelite picture. In his monumental history of the movement, Hunt stuck to the letter of Pre-Raphaelitism as, in retrospect, he interpreted what he and Millais had been about in 1848 and 1849. The controversy spawned by Hunt in his *Pre-Raphaelitism and the Pre-Raphaelite Brotherhood,* debunking the later tendency to ascribe to Rossetti the role of founder and leader of the Brotherhood, has been thoroughly surveyed by Mrs. Helen Rossetti Angeli, in her *Dante Gabriel Rossetti: His Friends and Enemies* (25.91, pp. 58–73), who clearly shows, first, that Rossetti never made claims about his role in the movement (to the contrary, on two separate occasions he de-emphasized his position, insisting on the primacy of Hunt and Millais); and, second, that Hunt's crusade against Rossetti in his history of the movement was inconsistent with earlier pronouncements which he made about his old friend and Pre-Raphaelite brother.

Though the controversy may now be academic, it is clear that Rossetti and Hunt represent two sides — extremes might be more accurate — of the Pre-Raphaelite impulse. Hunt was essentially what Rossetti never was — a literalist who viewed art as a didactic instrument for furthering moral and religious values. The differences between Rossetti and Hunt are grounded on temperamental distinctions which are reflected in their works. But Holman Hunt's view of Pre-Raphaelitism is too restrictive and self-centered, and it fails to account for the impact of the movement on nineteenth-century aesthetics precisely because it insists on a single, exclusive application of the term to a kind of plein-air naturalism from which Hunt never deviated. More importantly, by denying Rossetti and the later Pre-Raphaelites a place in the movement, Hunt's definition makes no allowance for its literary side.

Hunt may well have been the most consistent of the Pre-Raphaelite painters, but his art is static, and as a painter he never developed beyond the bare principles of simplicity and truth which marked the Brotherhood during its incipience. Hunt is a more unattractive personality and a less colorful artist than some of the other Pre-Raphaelites, and he lacked the dynamism of Rossetti and Morris, but his type of Pre-Raphaelitism is thoroughly representative of the major emphasis on detail which characterized the early movement — an emphasis not without its influence on the development of later art, particularly on the theories concerning the observation of reality expressed by the Surrealists (see Salvador Dali, 76.8).

*　　*　　*

36.1   Hunt, William Holman. "Materials in use by Artist Painters," *Architect*, XXIII (24 April 1880), 281–283; (1 May 1880), 300–303; (8 May 1880), 327–329; (15 May 1880), 336–337.

See also "Methods of the Pre-Raphaelite Brotherhood: Holman Hunt," in *Papers of the Society of Mural Decorators & Painters in Tempera: Second Volume, 1907–1924*, ed. John D. Batten (Brighton: Printed for the Society, 1925). The article consists of notes on "A Meeting at Holman Hunt's Studio" (5 November 1907) by Batten, with a long letter from Hunt on the technical aspects of Pre-Raphaelite painting.

36.2   ——— "The Pre-Raphaelite Brotherhood: A Fight for Art," *Contemporary Review*, XLIX (April 1886), 471–488; (May 1886), 737–750; (June 1886), 820–833.

For annotation see 75.13.

36.3   ——— "Painting the Scapegoat," *Contemporary Review*, LII (July 1887), 21–38; (August 1887), 206–220.

36.4   ——— "Memories of Rossetti," *Musical World*, LXX (July 1890), 526–528.

A lecture at Queen's House, Chelsea, repeating that given at the unveiling ceremonies of the Rossetti memorial fountain. Personal recollections, largely anecdotal.

36.5   ——— *The Obligations of the Universities towards Art. The Romanes Lecture, 1895: Delivered in the Sheldonian Theatre, May 30, 1895*. London: Frowde, 1895.

36.6   ——— "Religion and Art," *Contemporary Review*, LXXI (January 1897), 41–52.

A paper read before the Church Congress stating that the formation of the Clergy and Artists' Association calls for reforms in church art. Frequent references to his own works. Same in *Living Age*, CCXII, 6th ser., XIII, no. 2745 (13 February 1897), 440–448.

36.7   ——— *Pre-Raphaelitism and the Pre-Raphaelite Brotherhood*. 2 vols. London: Macmillan, 1905–1906.

For annotation see 75.23.

36.8   ——— *Oxford Union Society: The Story of the Painting of the Pictures on the Walls and the Decorations on the Ceiling of the Old Debating Hall (Now the Library) in the Years 1857–8–9*. Oxford University Press, 1906.

For annotation see 79.3.

* * *

36.9   Gautier, Théophile. "MM. Millais — W. Hunt," *Les Beaux-Arts en Europe. 1855. Première Série*. Paris: Lévy, 1855.

With two other brief sections on Noel Paton and C. A. Collins.

36.10   [Stephens, Frederic George]. *William Holman Hunt and His Works: A Memoir of the Artist's Life, with Descriptions of His Pictures*. London: Nisbet, 1860.

Published anonymously. A pamphlet written by Stephens at the request of Gambart, the dealer, and sold on the occasion of the exhibition of *The Finding of Christ in the Temple*. The last third of the pamphlet (pp. 85–120) consists of press notices giving opinions of the picture, together with a few others relating to *The Light of the World*.

36.11   " 'The Finding of the Saviour in the Temple.' Notes on Mr. Holman Hunt's Picture," *Once a Week*, III (July 1860), 64–66.

Discusses idealization and realization in Pre-Raphaelite paintings. For other contemporary notices of this picture see 36.10.

36.12   Glover, Richard. *"The Light of the World"; or, Holman Hunt's Great Allegorical Picture Translated into Words*. London: Wertheim, 1862; 2nd ed., 1863; 3rd ed., London: Sampson, Low, and Marston, 1871.

36.13   "Pre-Raphaelite Art. Holman Hunt's Picture, 'The Finding of the Saviour in the Temple,' " *Clack! A Journal of Literary, Scientifick, and Artistick Talk for One and All in Ye Counties of Devon and Cornwall*, I (1865), 67–69.

The magazine of the Clack Club, Plymouth.

36.14   Palgrave, Francis Turner. "Recent Works by Holman Hunt," *Essays on Art*. London: Macmillan, 1866.

Written, June 1864. Also contains a notice of Ford Madox Brown's exhibition (8.1). See 21.5.

36.15 Rossetti, William Michael. "Holman Hunt," *Fine Art, Chiefly Contemporary: Notices Reprinted, with Revisions.* London: Macmillan, 1867.
Individual notices of eight of Hunt's paintings, reprinted from various journals. For complete annotation see 38.2.

36.16 Cracroft, Bernard. "Mr. Holman Hunt's Isabel," *Fortnightly Review*, IX, n.s. III (June 1868), 648–657.
Reprinted separately in London the same year.

36.17 Stephens, Frederic George. "English Artists of the Present Day. XXI. William Holman Hunt," *Portfolio*, II (March 1871), 33–39.
Reprinted in 75.9.

36.18 Hamerton, Philip Gilbert. "The Frame of Mr. Holman Hunt's Temple Picture," *Portfolio*, III (January 1872), 16.

36.19 "Mr. Holman Hunt's Picture (Shadow of Death)," *Athenaeum*, no. 2358 (4 January 1873), p. 23.
See also "'The Shadow of Death,'" *Athenaeum*, no. 2405 (29 November 1873), pp. 702–703.

36.20 "Holman Hunt and his *Shadow of Death*," *Appleton's Journal*, XI (May 1874), 656–658.

36.21 Hamerton, Philip Gilbert. "Technical Notes," *Portfolio*, VI (March 1875), 45–48.
Notes on Holman Hunt's technique in painting.

36.22 "William Holman Hunt," *The National Portrait Gallery*. Second Series. London: Cassell, [1876].

36.23 Fenn, W. W. "Our Living Artists: William Holman Hunt," *Magazine of Art*, III (1880), 384–387.

36.24 Ruskin, John. "Realistic Schools of Painting: D. G. Rossetti and W. Holman Hunt," *The Art of England: Lectures Given in Oxford*. Orpington: Allen, 1883.
For complete annotation see 45.2.

36.25 Stephens, Frederic George. "'The Triumph of the Innocents,'" *Portfolio*, XVI (April 1885), 80–83.

36.26 Atkinson, J. B. "Mr. Holman Hunt: His Work and Career," *Blackwood's Magazine*, CXXXIX (April 1886), 540–558.

36.27 Machar, Agnes M. "Holman Hunt and the Pre-Raphaelites," *Andover Review*, XII (December 1889), 579–596.
For annotation see 77.3.

36.28 *"Christ Among the Doctors:* An Exposition of the Design for the Mosaic in Clifton College Chapel," *Contemporary Review*, LVIII (August 1890), 181–192.

36.29 Story, Alfred T. "William Holman Hunt," *Tinsley's Magazine*, XLV (September 1890), 305–316.

36.30 Sturgis, Russell. "Hunt's *Light of the World*," *Scribner's Magazine*, XL (December 1906), 768.

36.31 M[acColl], D. S. "Mr. Holman Hunt's New Picture," *Spectator*, LXVI, no. 3282 (23 May 1891), 724–725.
On *May Day, Magdalen Tower*.

36.32 Farrar, Frederic William. "Mr. Holman Hunt's 'May Day, Magdalen Tower,'" *Contemporary Review*, LIX (June 1891), 814–818.

36.33 ——— *William Holman Hunt: His Life and Work* (Special Number of the *Art Journal*). London: Virtue, 1893.
Part III, "The Artist's Home and Studio," is by Mrs. Alice Meynell. The biographical sketch is also by her. The discussion of the pictures is by Farrar. Collected in 75.22.

36.34 Layard, George Somes. "Holman Hunt," *Tennyson and His Pre-Raphaelite Illustrators: A Book about a Book*. London: Stock, 1894.
For complete annotation see 88.1.

36.35 Tugman, E. A. *Concentrated Lives: Lessons from Mr. Holman Hunt's "The Triumph of the Innocents."* London: SPCK, 1894.

36.36 Chesneau, Ernest. "Peintres anglais contemporains: W. Holman Hunt," *L'Art,* LIX, 20ᵉ année, tome IV (1894), 280–299.

36.37 Bell, Mrs. Arthur (N. D'Anvers). "William Holman Hunt," *Representative Painters of the XIXth Century.* London: Sampson, Low, Marston, 1899.

For complete annotation see 30.23.

36.38 Forsyth, Peter Taylor. *Religion in Recent Art: Expository Lectures on Rossetti, Burne-Jones, Watts, Holman Hunt, and Wagner.* London: Hodder and Stoughton, 1901.

36.39 Bayliss, Sir Wyke. *Five Great Painters of the Victorian Era: Leighton, Millais, Burne-Jones, Watts, Holman Hunt.* London: Sampson, Low, Marston, 1902.

The articles originally appeared in *Good Words* in 1899.

36.40 Williamson, George C. *Holman Hunt* (Bell's Miniature Series of Painters). London: Bell, 1902.

The *verso* of the title page announces that a longer work on Hunt by the same author is in preparation, but this longer work never seems to have appeared. Contains a brief list of Hunt's chief works in public and private collections, and a brief catalogue of Hunt's "missing pictures."

36.41 Bénédite, Léonce, *et al. The Gospels in Art: The Life of Christ by Great Painters from Fra Angelico to Holman Hunt.* London: Hodder and Stoughton, 1904.

36.42 Stephens, F. G. [Holman Hunt's *Pre-Raphaelitism and the Pre-Raphaelite Brotherhood*]. [London: Privately printed, 1906].

A reply to charges made by Holman Hunt against Stephens. For annotation see 77.4.

36.43 Sturgis, Russell. "Artists with Theories, Convictions, and Principles,"

Scribner's Magazine, XL (July 1906), 125–128.

For annotation see 67.27.

36.44 Schleinitz, Otto Julius Wilhelm von. *William H. Hunt* (Künstler-Monographien, no. LXXXVIII). Bielefeld und Leipzig: Velhagen und Klasing, 1907.

36.45 Stevens, W. Bertrand. "Representative English Paintings: *The Light of the World,*" *Chautauquan,* XLV (February 1907), 365–366.

36.46 Burns, J. *"The Light of the World* by W. Holman Hunt," *Sermons in Art by the Great Masters.* London: Duckworth, 1908.

Also contains a chapter on *The Scape-Goat.* For complete annotation see 31.24.

36.47 Coleridge, Mary E. *Holman Hunt* (Masterpieces in Colour, edited by T. Lemon Hare). New York: Stokes, [1908].

Collected in 75.25.

36.48 Bardoux, Jacques. "Le Peintre Holman Hunt," *Silhouettes d'outre-manche.* Paris: Hachette, 1909.

36.49 Staley, J. Edgcumbe. *The Charm of Holman Hunt.* London: Jack, [1910].

36.50 Masson, Flora. "Holman Hunt and the Story of a Butterfly," *Cornhill Magazine,* CII, n.s. XXIX (November 1910), 641–647.

An obituary remembrance. Reprinted as "Holman Hunt and Sir Atalanta" in *Victorians All* (London: Chambers, 1931).

36.51 Hueffer, Ford Madox. "William Holman Hunt," *Fortnightly Review,* XCIV, n.s. LXXXVIII (October 1910), 657–665.

An obituary study. Same in *Living Age,* CCLXVII, 7th ser., XLIX, no. 3462 (12 November 1910), 387–393.

36.52 Rossetti, William Michael. "Reminiscences of Holman Hunt," *Contemporary Review,* XCVIII (October 1910), 385–395.

An interesting account of Hunt's life and a gentle protest against certain remarks in Hunt's *Pre-Raphaelitism and the Pre-Raphaelite Brotherhood* (36.7). Same in *Living*

Age, CCLXVII, 7th ser., XLIX, no. 3462 (12 November 1910), 393–401.

36.53 Agresti-Rossetti, Olivia. "William Holman Hunt," *Rassegna Contemporanea*, III (November 1910), 487–498.

36.54 Adolph, R. E. "Hunt's Painting *The Light of the World*," *Ladies' Home Journal*, XXVII (December 1910), 10–11.

36.55 Farrar, Frederic William. "The Shadow of Death," in *Modern Paintings*, edited by Esther Singleton. New York: Dodd, Mead, 1911.
Also includes discussions of paintings by Burne-Jones (42.87), Millais (37.80), and Rossetti (31.15).

36.56 Clodd, Edward. "William Holman Hunt (1827–1910)," *Memories*. London: Chapman and Hall, 1916.
Originally appeared in *Fortnightly Review*, CVI, n.s. C (August 1916), 325–331.

36.57 Rowley, Charles. "Holman Hunt," *Fifty Years of Work Without Wages*. London: Hodder and Stoughton, [1911].
For complete annotation see 26.4.

36.58 Linton, John. "William Holman Hunt," *The Cross in Modern Art: Descriptive Studies of Some Pre-Raphaelite Paintings*. London: Duckworth, 1916.
Discussion of *The Shadow of Death*, *The Scapegoat*, and *The Light of the World*. Illustrated. For complete annotation see 75.27.

36.59 Shrewsbury, H. W. *Brothers in Art: Studies in William Holman Hunt . . . and John Everett Millais. . . . With Verse Interpretations*. London: Epworth, 1920.

36.60 Pace, Charles Nelson. "The Light of the World," *Pictures that Preach*. New York: Abingdon, 1924.

36.61 Slade, William. *A Centenary Appreciation of Holman Hunt*. Hastings: Privately printed, 1927.
Dedicated to Mrs. Holman Hunt, "as a small tribute to the memory of the great artist, who gave the best years of his manhood to the interpretation of the Bible and the life of Christ."

36.62 Banner, Delmar Harmood. "Holman Hunt and Pre-Raphaelitism," *Nineteenth Century*, CII (October 1927), 546–557.
A centenary review of Hunt's life, art, and ideas.

36.63 Briggs, O. M. "Holman Hunt's *The Light of the World*," *Mentor*, XV (December 1927), 14–15.

36.64 Dearmer, Percy. "Holman Hunt and the Pre-Raphaelite Movement," *Contemporary Review*, CXXXIV (July 1928), 74–81.
For annotation see 77.7.

36.65 Vaughan, Herbert M. "Sir John Everett Millais (1829–1896) and William Holman Hunt (1827–1910) — The Pre-Raphaelite Brotherhood," *From Anne to Victoria: Fourteen Biographical Studies between 1702 and 1901*. London: Methuen, 1931.

36.66 Gissing, A. C. *William Holman Hunt: A Biography*. London: Duckworth, 1936.
A spirited attack on Rossetti who "never understood the real spirit of Pre-Raphaelitism." Gissing attributes Rossetti's success to the perseverance of the true founder of the Pre-Raphaelite Brotherhood. With a very incomplete list of Hunt's major works hung in public galleries.

36.67 "William Holman Hunt, O. M. Contemporary Notices of His Exhibits in Water-Colour," *The Old Water-Colour Society's Club. Thirteenth Annual Volume*, edited by Randall Davies. London: OW-CS, issued only to members, 1936.
With twelve illustrations and a list of Hunt's water colors exhibited at the Society's gallery between 1869 and 1903.

36.68 Bodkin, Thomas. "Two English Drawings," *Miscellanea Leo van Puyvelde*. Bruxelles: Editions de la Connaissance, 1949.
Comparing two drawings by Holman Hunt and Mulready, of Emily Chester, a young

model in the Kensington Life Academy. Illustrated.

36.69 Davidson, Angus. "Holman Hunt and the Tennysons," *Edward Lear, Landscape Painter and Nonsense Poet, 1812–1888.* Harmondsworth: Penguin Books, 1950.

Originally published in 1938. Examines the influence of Hunt and the Pre-Raphaelites on the development of Lear as a painter.

36.70 Kirby, H. T. "May Morning on Magdalen Tower," *Country Life*, CIX, no. 2832 (27 April 1951), 1284–1286.

A reproduction of Hunt's version in Birmingham, with a partial key to the figures in the large version in the Lady Lever Gallery.

36.71 Holman-Hunt, Diana. *My Grandmothers and I.* London: Hamilton, 1960.

An exciting and satirical account of her girlhood by Hillary Holman Hunt's daughter, with particularly interesting jibes at the remnants of Pre-Raphaelitism that lived in the memory and house of Holman Hunt's second wife. Reviewed by Evelyn Waugh, "The Only Pre-Raphaelite," *Spectator*, CCV, no. 6903 (14 October 1960), 567.

36.72 Roskill, Mark. "Holman Hunt's Differing Versions of the 'Light of the World,'" *Victorian Studies*, VI (March 1963), 229–244.

An historical analysis of the composition of the three versions, at Keble College, Manchester, and St. Paul's together with an examination of the technical and aesthetic characteristics of each. The author extends his conclusions about Hunt to the Pre-Raphaelite Movement as a whole: "The insights into Holman Hunt's artistic character . . . are aimed at contributing afresh towards the understanding of pre-Raphaelite art as a Victorian phenomenon. To comprehend more fully and clearly the relationship between external gestures (made with voice or pen or brush) and internal promptings in the personalities of the Brotherhood can help us to grasp what kind of 'breakdown' it was in the interaction between the different planes of human experience that made pre-Raphaelite art into so much of an ultimate dead-end, devoid of aesthetic (as opposed to social or psychological) significance." (p. 244) With five plates of the several versions and a frontispiece portrait of Hunt.

Section 37

JOHN EVERETT MILLAIS
1829–1896

[DNB: XXII, S, 1039–1046 (Cosmo Monkhouse);
EB: XVIII, 459–460 (Cosmo Monkhouse)]

Pre-Raphaelitism was no more than an interlude in the artistic development of the boy-genius who capped his career by accepting in the last year of his life the presidency of the Royal Academy. By joining the ranks of the opposition in 1854, Millais not only abandoned the Pre-Raphaelite Brotherhood, of which he was a charter member; he also threw over the greatest promise of any artist of the century. A country-squire artist who decades before had renounced the revolutionary affiliations of his youth, Millais, at the time of his death, was the most popular and the most highly remunerated painter in England. Philistia was indeed glad of him, by his design, for he gave it what it wanted: a succession of sermon-paintings (from *Her First Sermon* on) that confirmed the sentimental and saccharine values of the middle classes. In return, the Philistines paid and adored — and washed. After all, could any greater testimony to the truth of the adage that "Cleanliness is next to Godliness" be found than the sweet and charming curly-head who looked out from Pears' soap ads? By Philistia's

Plate III. The Pre-Raphaelite Brotherhood

JAMES COLLINSON, WHO WAS ALSO A MEMBER,
IS NOT SHOWN AS NO PORTRAIT HAS BEEN FOUND.

William Holman Hunt,
by W. B. Richmond

William M. Rossetti,
by W. Rothenstein

John Everett Millais,
by C. R. Leslie

Dante Gabriel Rossetti,
by W. H. Hunt

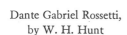

Frederick George Stephens,
by J. E. Millais

Thomas Woolner,
by D. G. Rossetti

Plate IV and Plate V.   Minor Pre-Raphaelite

William Allingham
George Price Boyce
Oliver Madox Brown
Charles Allston Collins
Walter Howell Deverell
Thomas Gordon Hake

John Payne
Frederick Sandys
William Bell Scott
Thomas Seddon
Frederic Shields
Elizabeth Siddal

Arthur Hughes
Philip Bourke Marston
Alexander Munro
Arthur O'Shaughnessy
Coventry Patmore
Joseph Noel Paton

James Smetham
Simeon Solomon
Algernon Charles Swinburne
George Frederick Watts
Theodore Watts-Dunton
William Lindsay Windus

Plate VI. Associates and Later Pre-Raphaelites

William Morris, by G. F. Watts

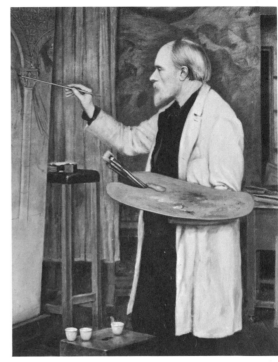

Edward Burne-Jones, by P. Burne-Jones

Christina Rossetti, by D. G. Rossetti

John Ruskin, by G. Richmond

Ford Maddox Brown,
by D. G. Rossetti

standards his rewards were great; the tragedy is that they were in no way commensurate with his talents.

Millais never lost the brilliance of technique which set him apart from the other Pre-Raphaelites. Where they were, at least in the beginning, amateurs, Millais was an accomplished and skillful artist who thoroughly understood his medium. His first pictures which so incited his contemporaries are now seen to be remarkable productions from the brush of a young man still in his teens. The criticism of *Lorenzo and Isabella* and *Christ in the House of His Parents* was severe, and Millais (perhaps with some coaxing and intimidation from his parents) decided that the PRB could only hinder what was obviously destined to be a magnificent and lucrative career. Conformity seemed little enough to pay for riches and fame, and it need not be assumed that Millais lost anything very dear to him when he sacrificed his principles and his integrity for the most lucrative art career of the century.

Arthur Symons' brilliant "Sic Transit" on Millais is the best and most succinct statement of Millais' giant failure (see 37.43). Symons lamented Millais' inability to make the "great refusal," his lack of conviction, and "the mastery of a hand which worked without emotion, without imagination, without intellectual passion." He abhorred the obituary tributes to Millais as the great Englishman, the great salmon fisherman, and the most respectable artist of the century:

> My thoughts have turned, as I read these commendations of the good citizen, so English, so sporting, whose private virtues were so undeniably British, to a painter, also a man of genius, whose virtues were all given up to his art, and who is now living in a destitute and unhonoured obscurity. It has seemed to me that there, in that immaculate devotion to art, I find the true morality of the artist; while in the respectability of Millais I see nothing to honour, for its observance of the letter I take to have been a desecration of the spirit. (37.43, Peters, p. 323)

* * *

37.1 Gautier, Théophile. "MM. Millais — W. Hunt," *Les Beaux-Arts en Europe. 1855. Première Série.* Paris: Lévy, 1855.
For annotation see 36.9.

37.2 "Men of Mark — No. XXIX: John Everett Millais," *London Review*, XVIII (22 February 1862), 183–184.

37.3 "Millais' 'Parables,'" *New Path*, I (March 1864), 145–152.

37.4 *The Cornhill Gallery.* London: Smith, Elder, 1865.
For annotation see 90.7.

37.5 Payne, J. Bertrand. *The Lineage and Pedigree of the Family of Millais, Recording Its History from 1331 to 1865.* London: Privately printed, 1865.

37.6 *Millais's Illustrations: A Collection of Drawings on Wood by John Everett Millais.* [Cover title: *Millais's Collected Illustrations*]. London: Strahan, 1866.
For annotation see 95.52.

37.7 Tyrwhitt, R. St. J. "Millais and Doré," *Contemporary Review*, II (August 1866), 482–487.
In part a review of 37.6, with a brief comparison of the two artists.

37.8 Rossetti, William Michael. "Millais," *Fine Art, Chiefly Contemporary: Notices Reprinted, with Revisions.* London: Macmillan, 1867.
Individual notices of 26 Millais' paintings, reprinted from various journals. For complete annotation see 38.2.

37.9 *Twenty Nine Illustrations by J. E.*

Millais, Designed for "The Cornhill Maga-zine," with Extracts Descriptive of Each Pic-ture. London: Smith, Elder, 1867.

Reprinted from *The Cornhill Gallery* (37.4).

37.10 Davis, Bliss. *A Short and Popular Guide to the Fine Painting of John Everett Millais, . . . ; of "Moses," and How It Should be Viewed.* London: Gravatt, 1871.

37.11 Colvin, Sidney. "English Artists of the Present Day. XVIII. John Everett Mil-lais, R. A.," *Portfolio*, II (January 1871), 1–6.

Reprinted in 75.9.

37.12 " 'The Head of Hur,' by J. E. Millais, R. A.," *Portfolio*, II (January 1871), 24–25.

37.13 "John Everett Millais," *Once a Week*, XXVI (June 1872), 563–564.

An insignificant note accompanied by a clever caricature entitled "Nature before Art," in which Millais, astride a palette, holds the reins attached to three paint brushes (the PRB), and rides toward a bright star labeled "Ruskin."

37.14 Champlin, J. D., Jr. "John Everett Mil-lais," *Appleton's Journal*, XII (October 1874), 513–515.

37.15 "John Everett Millais, R.A.," *The National Portrait Gallery*. Second Series. Lon-don: Cassell, [1876].

37.16 Brainard, Erastus. *The Millais Gal-lery: A Series of the Most Renowned Works of Millais . . . with a Sketch of the Life and Works of the Artist.* Boston: Osgood, 1878.

37.17 Hunt, William Morris. *Talks on Art, with a Letter from John Everett Millais.* London: Macmillan, 1878.

37.18 Wilson, H. Schütz. "Our Living Artists: John Everett Millais, R.A." *Maga-zine of Art*, II (1879), 33–38.

37.19 Oldcastle, John. "Mr. Millais's House at Palace Gate," *Magazine of Art*, IV (1881), 290–295.

In a series of articles entitled "The Homes of Our Artists."

37.20 Duranty, E. *John Everett Millais, R.A.* (Modern Artists: A Series of Illus-trated Monographs, edited by F. G. Dumas). London: Virtue, [1882].

37.21 Sheldon, George William. "John Everett Millais," *Hours with Art and Artists*. New York: Appleton, 1882.

37.22 Barrington, Emilie Isabel. "Why is Mr. Millais Our Popular Painter?" *Fort-nightly Review*, XXXVIII, n.s. XXXII (July 1882), 60–77.

37.23 Stephens, Frederic George. "John Everett Millais," *Artists at Home*. Photo-graphed by J. P. Mayall . . . with Biographi-cal Notices and Descriptions by Frederic George Stephens. London: Sampson, Low, Marston, 1884.

37.24 Zimmern, Helen. "John Everett Mil-lais," *Grands peintres français et étrangers: Ouvrages d'art*. Paris: Launette, 1884–1886.

37.25 ——— *John Everett Millais*. Paris, 1886.

37.26 Armstrong, Walter. *Sir John Millais, Royal Academician: His Life and Work* (Christmas Number of the *Art Journal*). London: Virtue, 1885.

Reissued with slightly different title in 1896, and in *Presidents of the Royal Acad-emy: Lord Leighton, Sir J. E. Millais, Sir E. J. Poynter* (London: Virtue, 1906).

37.27 [*A Series of Woodcuts After J. E. Millais, R.A. Cut by Swain & Dalziel.* Lon-don: n.p., n.d.].

For annotation see 95.77.

37.28 Van Rensselaer, M. G. "Notes from England. III. Modern Painters," *American Architecture*, XVIII (November 1885), 258–259; (December 1885), 292.

37.29 Armstrong, Walter. "Millais," *Na-tional Review*, VI (February 1886), 784–795.

Occasioned by the Grosvenor Gallery exhibition (12.4). Same in *Eclectic Magazine*, n.s. XLIII (April 1886), 449–456.

37.30 Zimmern, Helen. "Sir John Millais," *Die Kunst unserer Zeit*. Munich, 1891.

37.31 Layard, George Somes. "Millais and *Once a Week*," *Good Words*, XXXIV (August 1893), 552–558.
For annotation see 89.2.

37.32 Spielmann, Marion H. " 'The Blind Girl' by Sir J. E. Millais, Bart., R.A." *Magazine of Art*, XVI (1893), 374.
An account of Millais' incorrect handling of the rainbow in the first painting of the picture.

37.33 Layard, George Somes. "Millais," *Tennyson and His Pre-Raphaelite Illustrators: A Book about a Book*. London: Stock, 1894.
For complete annotation see 88.1.

37.34 Chesneau, Ernest. "Peintres anglais contemporains: John Everett Millais," *L'Art*, LIX, 20° année, tome IV (1894), 227–242.

37.35 Gower, Lord Ronald. "Work in Paris — Millais — The Empress Eugénie," *My Reminiscences*. London: Kegan Paul, 1895.

37.36 Underhill, John. "Character Sketch: Sir John Everett Millais, Bart., R.A.," *Review of Reviews*, XI (March 1895), 319–327.

37.37 Beale, S. "Sir John Millais," *American Architect*, LIII (March 1896), 84–86.
Written on the occasion of Millais' election as president of the Royal Academy.

37.38 Low, Francis H. "Some Early Recollections of Sir John Everett Millais . . . ," *Strand*, XI (June 1896), 603–611.

37.39 "Artisti contemporanei: Sir John Everett Millais, P.R.A.," *Emporium*, IV (September 1896), 163–183.

37.40 Pennell, Joseph, and Elizabeth R. "John Everett Millais, Painter and Illus-

trator," *Fortnightly Review*, LXVI, n.s. LX (September 1896), 443–450.

37.41 Spielmann, Marion H. "In Memoriam: Sir John Everett Millais, P.R.A.," *Magazine of Art*, XIX (September 1896), i–xvi (suppl.).
With an engraving of Millais' *A Reverie*.

37.42 Macleod, Donald. "Sir John Everett Millais, P.R.A.," *Good Words*, XXXVII (October 1896), 693–698.

37.43 Symons, Arthur. "The Lesson of Millais," *Savoy*, no. 6 (October 1896), pp. 57–58.
Reprinted in *Studies in Modern Painters* (New York: Rudge, 1925), and in *Victorians on Literature and Art*, edited by R. L. Peters (New York: Appleton-Century-Crofts, 1961). A penetrating obituary notice. For a more devastating attack on Millais' failure, published during his lifetime, see [Gleeson White], "Sir John Everett Millais," *Letters to Living Artists* (London: Elkin Mathews, 1891).

37.44 Darmesteter, Mary (Robinson). "John Everett Millais," *Gazette des Beaux-Arts*, période 3, XVIII (August 1897), 89–104.

37.45 Richmond, Sir William Blake. *Leighton, Millais and William Morris: A Lecture Delivered to the Students of the Royal Academy*. London: Macmillan, 1898.
Reprinted in *Leighton House* (n.d.), a gallery publication.

37.46 Spielmann, Marion H. *Millais and His Works: With Special Reference to the Exhibition at the Royal Academy, 1898. With a Chapter, "Thoughts on Our Art of Today," by Sir John Everett Millais, Bart., P.R.A.* London: Blackwood, 1898.
In addition to notes on the Royal Academy exhibition (12.6), and other notes on works not exhibited, the volume contains a chronological list of all of Millais' works, providing essentially the same details as 37.52. A bare chronology, reprinted from Spielmann, appears in Baldry (37.50). Millais' chapter first appeared in *Magazine of Art*, XI (1888), 289–292.

37.47 Stevenson, R. A. M. "John Everett Millais, R.A.," *Art Journal*, LX (January 1898), 1–5.

37.48 Spielmann, Marion H. "John Everett Millais," *Revue de l'Art Ancien et Moderne*, XIII (January 1898), 33–48; (February 1898), 95–102.

37.49 Beale, S. "The Religious Art of Millais," *American Architect*, LIX (March 1898), 75–76.

37.50 Baldry, Alfred Lys. *Sir John Everett Millais: His Art and Influence*. London: Bell, 1899.
Condensed for "Bell's Miniature Series of Painters" (London, 1901).

37.51 Bell, Mrs. Arthur (N. D'Anvers). "Sir John Everett Millais," *Representative Painters of the XIXth Century*. London: Sampson, Low, Marston, 1899.
For complete annotation see 30.23.

37.52 Millais, John Guille. *The Life and Letters of Sir John Everett Millais*. 2 vols. London: Methuen, 1899.
The authorized biography. Five chapters on the Pre-Raphaelites. Millais' son took much of his information on the Pre-Raphaelites from Holman Hunt. Volume II contains a chronological list of Millais' works in oil, water color, and black and white. See also the abridged version (London: Methuen, 1905). A portfolio of thirty photogravure reproductions of Millais' works was issued as part of the set, but it is rarely found with the volumes.

37.53 Monkhouse, Cosmo. "John Everett Millais," *British Contemporary Artists*. London: Scribner's, 1899.
Brief review of the life and art of Millais, whose portrait work is stressed. Numerous illustrations. Reprinted from *Scribner's Magazine*, XX (December 1896), 659–680.

37.54 Carr, J. Comyns. "Some Memories of Millais," *Speaker*, n.s. I (November 1899), 197–198.
Same in *Living Age*, CCXXIV, 7th ser.,

VI, no. 2898 (20 January 1900), 197–200. Reprinted in 25.45.

37.55 G., J. L. "Sir John E. Millais' Life and Work," *Critic*, XXV (December 1899), 1101–1108.
An article based on the *Life and Letters* (37.52), with numerous illustrations.

37.56 Weisbach, Werner. "John Everett Millais," *Zeitschrift für Bildende Kunst*, X (1899), 179–183, 214–219, 246–254.

37.57 Keary, C. F. "John Everett Millais," *Edinburgh Review*, CXCI (January 1900), 182–206.
Reviews both 37.50 and 37.52.

37.58 "Sir John Everett Millais, P.R.A.," *Magazine of Art*, XXIII (1900), 313–316.
In part a review of 37.52.

37.59 Thomas, Ralph. *Serjeant Thomas and Sir J. E. Millais, Bart., P.R.A.* London: Printed for the author, 1901.
A reply to 37.52. Included in the volume is a section, "Recollections of Johnny Millais," by Florence E. Williams (née Thomas) which the author sent from Sydney for publication shortly after the death of Millais.

37.60 "The Pre-Raphaelite Brotherhood [First Article]: Sir John Everett Millais," *Werner's Magazine*, XXVII (April 1901), 96–107.
For complete annotation see 67.21.

37.61 Fenn, W. W. "Memories of Millais," *Chambers's Journal*, 6th ser., IV (November 1901), 833–837.

37.62 Bayliss, Sir Wyke. *Five Great Painters of the Victorian Era: Leighton, Millais, Burne-Jones, Watts, Holman Hunt*. London: Sampson, Low, Marston, 1902.

37.63 *Twenty India Paper Proofs of the Drawings by Sir John Everett Millais . . . to the Parables of Our Lord, Engraved on Wood by the Brothers Dalziel: With 20 Facsimile Letters . . . from Millais to the Dalziels during the Progress of the Work*. London: Issued privately from the Camden Press by Charles Dalziel, 1902.

37.64 Fenn, W. W. "Millais and Music: Some More Memories," *Chambers's Journal*, 6th ser., V (November 1902), 822–825.

37.65 Douglas, Langston. *A Little Gallery of Millais*. London: Methuen, 1904.
With a thirty-two page introduction and twenty illustrations.

37.66 Holme, Charles J. *The Royal Academy from Reynolds to Millais*. London: Studio Special Publication, 1904.
Cover title: *The Record of a Century*. Contains few references to Millais and only three reproductions from his works.

37.67 Cox, Kenyon. "Millais," *Old Masters and New*. New York: Fox, Duffield, 1905.
For complete annotation see 77.53.

37.68 Fenn, W. W. "Ruskin and Millais in Scotland: A Memory of Ruskin," *Chambers's Journal*, 6th scr., VIII (September 1905), 645–647.

37.69 Dolman, Frederick. "The Story of a Picture, Sir John Everett Millais' *The Huguenot*," *Canadian Magazine*, XXVII (June 1906), 99–108.

37.70 "A Great Artist at Work," *Chambers's Journal*, 6th ser., IX (September 1906), 653–656.

37.71 Stevens, W. Bertrand. "The Huguenot," *Chautauquan*, XLVI (April 1907), 226–228.

37.72 Baldry, Alfred Lys. *Millais* (Masterpieces in Colour, edited by T. Lemon Hare). New York: Stokes [1909].
Collected in 75.25.

37.73 Carr, J. Comyns. "Millais and Leighton," *Some Eminent Victorians: Personal Recollections in the World of Art and Letters*. London: Duckworth, 1908.
With additional chapters on Rossetti (25.36) and Burne-Jones (42.78).

37.74 [Hardie, Martin]. *Catalogue of Prints. Wood engravings after Sir John Everett Millais . . . in the Victoria and Albert Museum*. London: H. M. Stationery Office, 1908.
For annotation see 89.5.

37.75 Lehmann, R. C., ed. *Memories of Half a Century: A Record of Friendships*. London: Smith, Elder, 1908.
Reminiscences of Frederick and Nina Lehmann. Contains references to many of the Pre-Raphaelites and a few brief letters from Millais.

37.76 *Millais* (Masters in Art: A Series of Illustrated Monographs, vol. IX, pt. 107). Boston: Bates, 1908.
Life and works, with plates and a brief bibliography.

37.77 MacColl, D. S. "Millais's Portrait of Tennyson," *Burlington Magazine*, XIII (June 1908), 127–128.

37.78 Reid, J. Eadie. *Sir J. E. Millais, P.R.A.* (Makers of British Art). London: Scott, 1909.
With 29 illustrations and four appendixes, including a bibliography, a list of pictures exhibited at the Royal Academy (1846–1896), later prices commanded by Millais' works, and a list of Millais' pictures in public galleries.

37.79 Harlow, James. *The Charm of Millais*. London: Jack, [1910].

37.80 Millais, John Guille. "The Huguenot," in *Modern Paintings*, edited by Esther Singleton. New York: Dodd, Mead, 1911.
For complete annotation see 36.55.

37.81 Phythian, J. E. *Millais*. London: Allen, 1911.

37.82 Chester, Austin. "The Art of John Everett Millais," *Windsor Magazine*, XXXVIII (August 1913), 247–262.

37.83 Linton, John. "John Everard [*sic*] Millais," *The Cross in Modern Art: Descriptive Studies of Some Pre-Raphaelite Paintings*. London: Duckworth, 1916.
Discussion of *The Carpenter's Shop*. Illustrated. For complete annotation see 75.27.

37.84 Hutchinson, H. G. "Watts, Millais, and Burne-Jones," *Portraits of the Eighties.* London: Unwin, 1920.

37.85 Shrewsbury, H. W. *Brothers in Art: Studies in William Holman Hunt . . . and John Everett Millais . . . With Verse Interpretations.* London: Epworth, 1920.

37.86 Sullivan, Edmund J. "Millais and the Illustration of Verse," *The Art of Illustration.* London: Chapman and Hall, 1921.

37.87 Fish, Arthur. *John Everett Millais.* New York: Funk and Wagnalls, 1923.
With four chapters on Millais' Pre-Raphaelitism. Profusely illustrated, many in color. The text is essentially biographical.

37.88 "Painter of Best Sellers: Sir John Millais," *Mentor*, XIV (June 1926), 40–43.

37.89 Rutter, Frank. "John Everett Millais," *Bookman* (London), LXXVI (April 1929), 1–5.
An illustrated centenary article.

37.90 Sickert, Richard. "John Everett Millais," *Fortnightly Review*, CXXXI, n.s. CXXV (June 1929), 753–762.
Centenary study.

37.91 Vaughan, Herbert M. "Sir John Everett Millais (1829–1896) and William Holman Hunt (1827–1910) — The Pre-Raphaelite Brotherhood," *From Anne to Victoria: Fourteen Biographical Studies between 1702 and 1901.* London: Methuen, 1931.

37.92 "Sir John Everett Millais," *Picture Post*, II (14 January 1939), 38–43.
Great British Masters, no. 16.

37.93 "Cover Plate," *Apollo*, XXXIII (June 1941), 152–154.
Millais' *The Bridesmaid* is reproduced in color on the cover.

37.94 West, Anthony. "Success Story," *New Statesman and Nation*, XXII (30 August 1941), 202–203.
The ironic inevitability of Millais' rise to success was a reaction against Pre-Raphaelitism and especially against Rossetti.

37.95 McPharlin, Paul. "The Dalziel Parables 1864," *Publisher's Weekly*, CXLIII (2 January 1943), 41–46.

37.96 MacColl, D. S. "A Picture that Shocked the 1850's," *Listener*, XXXIV (20 December 1945), 729–730.
On Millais' *Christ in the House of His Parents.*

37.97 James, Sir William Milburne, ed. *John Ruskin and Effie Gray: The Story of John Ruskin, Effie Gray, and John Everett Millais, Told for the First Time in Their Unpublished Letters.* New York: Scribner's, 1947.
For annotation see 45.32.

37.98 Evans, Joan. "Millais' Drawings of 1853," *Burlington Magazine*, XCII (July 1950), 198 and 201.
Argues (see also John Gere, 83.8, Plates 61 and 62) that many of Millais' early drawings record in near diary-like fashion Millais' love affair with Euphemia Chalmers Gray Ruskin. Discussed here is Millais' drawing of a wedding scene (between Ruskin and Effie?) in the Victoria and Albert Museum. Illustrated.

37.99 Jones, L. E. "Sir John Millais While Painting 'Ophelia,' " *À la Carte.* London: Secker and Warburg, 1951.
An extremely amusing imaginary page from Millais' diary.

37.100 "Does History Repeat Itself?" *Scottish Art Review*, IV (Summer 1952), 27.
Published extracts from contemporary criticisms of Millais' *Christ in the House of His Parents.*

Section 38

WILLIAM MICHAEL ROSSETTI

1829–1919

[CBEL: III, 724, S673; DNB: S,II, 479–480 (Frederick Page)]

As both official amanuensis of the PRB and self-appointed recorder of all matters Pre-Raphaelite and familial, William Michael Rossetti played a major role in the history of the Pre-Raphaelite Movement. It might be said that from its incipience William Michael was the publicity agent of the Brotherhood. A nonartistic member of the group, he made no (or only very slight) overtures in the direction of painting, though he did on occasion write the odd poem, not the least "odd" of which is the cover-sonnet for *The Germ* that William Bell Scott said would "almost need a Browning Society's united intellects" to decipher. But William Michael Rossetti, a scrupulously honest man, had no illusions about his poetic powers:

> I never found much difficulty in writing in verse. On the other hand, I never discovered it to be my natural form of expression . . . My verse-writing, as I advanced a little in years, was not, I think, exactly commonplace; but it had neither the impulse which abolishes stiffness of phrase nor the fluidity which ensures verbal music . . . To be a quasi-poet, a pleasing poetaster, was never my ambition; I felt that in the long run I should prefer to stay outside the arena of verse altogether. And so, after making some few experiments, I did. (38.8, I, pp. 77–78)

A civil servant in the Inland Revenue Board from 1845 to 1894, William Michael was the most stable member of the Rossetti family, and for much of his life he was its primary support. Criticism was his life-long avocation, beginning with the editorship of *The Germ* in 1850. In the same year he became the unpaid picture reviewer for the *Critic*, later transferring to the *Spectator*. Throughout his long life he contributed to the leading journals. During 1855–1856 he contributed a monthly article, "Art News from London," to the American journal, the *Crayon*. His first published volume was *Swinburne's Poems and Ballads* (62.13), in which he defended Swinburne against the ravages of contemporary reviewers, including one Robert Buchanan. In 1867 he brought together his articles on art and notices of exhibitions, a large proportion of which was devoted to Ford Madox Brown, Millais, and Holman Hunt (see 38.2). Except for a few articles, William Michael began his long series of publications on Rossetti and the Pre-Raphaelites with the edition of Rossetti's *Collected Works* in 1886; and from that date until his death in 1919, he published nearly twenty-five separate articles, editions, biographies, and bibliographies. In addition to his work on the Pre-Raphaelites, he prepared editions of Shelley, Blake, and Whitman; he edited the Moxon Popular Poets series, for which he provided the introductions (collected in 38.5); he wrote numerous articles on art and other subjects; and he wrote a life of Keats.

As a critic William Michael is not always reliable, but he is always conscientious. In his *Reminiscences* (38.8, I, p. 95), looking back over a long career as a critic, he remarked,

If all my old critiques were to be reprinted . . . , and if I were to reread them, I do not believe that I should in a single instance be compelled to confess to myself, "There I said what I knew to be neither true nor fair; a bad personal motive was at the bottom of it."

If he withholds family information, if he is too thoroughly committed to maintaining the family honor, if he is sometimes too coy or simply naïve, he had cause, considering the literary vultures with whom he had to contend; he did not always tell the *whole* truth about Rossetti, but he made it his business to refute the lies, and to restore the perspective when fanciful inference twisted fact to its own devices. In all, William Michael Rossetti performed a useful service in the role which he took upon himself. Without his massive efforts, scholarship would be hard put to come by the materials which he made available.

William Michael's prolific writings are not complete within this section, the present list consisting primarily of items not relegated to other sections. A complete listing will be found in the Index. Very little research has been done on William Michael, though such recent studies as Lawrence Chewning's dissertation (38.21) and Jerome Thale's article on "The Third Rossetti" (38.22) have done something to restore critical interest in this last survivor of the original PRB.

* * *

38.1 Rossetti, William Michael. "Art News from London," *Crayon*, I (25 April 1855), 263–265.

William Michael contributed this section monthly for the two years (1855 and 1856) that William J. Stillman served as coeditor of the *Crayon*. The series contains much incidental material of importance on the Pre-Raphaelites. "Let there be no mistake about what Pre-Raphaelitism means. It has nothing to do with the technical deficiencies, or technical practice, or choice of subjects, of painters who lived before Raphael, but with the condition of mind which actuated them to represent whatever was in hand — whether typically or naturally — with a resolute adherence to truth of feeling and truth of fact, and a resolute disregard of all mere grace and all mere dexterity which would interfere with the first or affect the second. Pre-Raphaelitism, at its lowest, is reverent faith in Nature, whether seen with the poet's eye or with the catalogue-compiler's, whether rendered with the artist's hand or with the transcriber's. At its highest — and the young men who founded the school understood it at its highest — this faith in Nature takes a far wider range; involving that sincerity of thought which shall always invent something specific and something new in conception —

something truly natural in idea, as well as express this through a medium of visible nature studied with that love of observance which cannot but catch, out of her infinity, beauties ever fresh and individual." (p. 263)

38.2 ―――― *Fine Art, Chiefly Contemporary: Notices Reprinted, with Revisions.* London: Macmillan, 1867.

Containing William Michael's 1851 *Spectator* article on "Præraphaelitism" (75.8); his 1865 *Fraser's* article on Ford Madox Brown (21.4); and two sections on Millais (37.8) and Holman Hunt (36.15), consisting of discussions of individual pictures, reprinted from various journals.

38.3 ―――― *Notes on the Royal Academy Exhibition, 1868.* Part I by Wm. Michael Rossetti. Part II by Algernon C. Swinburne. London: Hotten, 1868.

Some material by both authors on Rossetti and the Pre-Raphaelites. For further annotation see 62.5.

38.4 ―――― "Mrs. Holmes Grey," *Broadway Annual*, I (February 1868), 449–459.

William Michael's blank verse narrative was enthusiastically praised by D. G. Rossetti and Swinburne. The poem, written much earlier (probably in 1849), William Michael Rossetti intended to exemplify Pre-Raphaelite realism.

38.5 ———— *Lives of Famous Poets.* London: Ward, 1878.
Revised reprints of the Prefaces to the Moxon Popular Poets series.

38.6 ———— ed. *Gabriele Rossetti: A Versified Autobiography.* London: Sands, 1901.
A translation with an introduction and supplementary material.

38.7 ———— ed. *Rossetti Papers, 1862 to 1870.* London: Sands, 1903.
For complete annotation see 24.9.

38.8 ———— *Some Reminiscences.* 2 vols. New York: Scribner's Sons, 1906.

38.9 ———— *Democratic Sonnets* (The Contemporary Poets Series). 2 vols. London: Rivers, 1907.

* * *

38.10 Garnett, R. S., ed. *Letters about Shelley Interchanged by Three Friends — Edward Dowden, Richard Garnett, and William Michael Rossetti.* New York: Hodder and Stoughton, 1917.

38.11 Ghodes, Clarence, and Paull Franklin Baum, eds. *Letters of William Michael Rossetti Concerning Whitman, Blake, and Shelley to Anne Gilchrist and her Son, Herbert Gilchrist; with Appendices Containing a Letter to President Cleveland and an Uncollected Whitman Circular.* Durham: Duke University Press, 1934.

38.12 Troxell, Janet Camp, ed. *Three Rossettis: Unpublished Letters to and from Dante Gabriel, Christina, William.* Cambridge, Mass.: Harvard University Press, 1937.
For annotation see 24.18.

* * *

38.13 [Forman, Harry Buxton]. "Criticisms on Contemporaries: No. VI. The Rossettis. Part III. [William Michael Rossetti]," *Tinsley's Magazine,* V (October 1869), 276–281.

Although included in the same series as the parallel articles on Dante Gabriel (27.1) and Christina Rossetti (44.20), this article was not reprinted in *Our Living Poets* (74.1).

38.14 Hamilton, Walter. "William Michael Rossetti," *The Æsthetic Movement in England.* London: Reeves and Turner, 1882.
For complete annotation see 78.2.

38.15 Eagle, Solomon [= John Collings Squire]. "W. M. Rossetti," *Books in General.* 3rd series. London: Hodder and Stoughton, [1921].
Essay reprinted from the *New Statesman.* An obituary notice and a review of Rossetti's life and work.

38.16 Horn, Kurt. "William Michael Rossetti," *Zeitschrift für französischen und englischen Unterricht,* XXIII (1924), 32–51, 128–146, 319–338.

38.17 Waller, R. D. "The Young Rossettis: William Michael," *The Rossetti Family, 1824–1854.* University of Manchester Press, 1932.
For complete annotation see 26.10.

38.18 Blodgett, Harold. "William Michael Rossetti," *Walt Whitman in England* (Cornell Studies in English, XXIV). Ithaca: Cornell University Press, 1934.

38.19 Justus, Wilhelm. *William Michael Rossetti im Kreise der Präraphaeliten.* Bochum-Langendreer: Pöppinghaus, 1934 (diss. Münster, 1934).

38.20 Lang, Cecil Y. "ALS: Swinburne to William Michael Rossetti," *Journal Rutgers University Library,* XIV (December 1950), 1–8.
For annotation see 7.8.

38.21 Chewning, Lawrence H., Jr. "William Michael Rossetti as Critic and Man of Letters," unpub. diss. University of Virginia, 1951.

38.22 Thale, Jerome. "The Third Rossetti," *Western Humanities Review,* X (Summer 1956), 277–284.

38.23 Packer, Lona Mosk, ed. *The Rossetti-Macmillan Letters: Some 133 Unpublished Letters Written to Alexander Macmillan, F. S. Ellis, and Others, by Dante Gabriel, Christina, and William Michael Rossetti, 1861–1889.* Berkeley: University of California Press, 1963.

38.24 Packer, Lona Mosk. "William Michael Rossetti and the Quilter Controversy: 'The Gospel of Intensity,'" *Victorian Studies*, VII (December 1963), 170–183.

On W. M. Rossetti's response to Quilter's article in *Macmillan's Magazine* in 1880 (see 71.9). Containing previously unpublished correspondence.

38.25 Peattie, Roger W. "William Michael Rossetti," *Times Literary Supplement*, no. 3257 (30 July 1964), p. 665.
An hitherto unprinted letter from A. H. Clough to Dr. Adolph Heimann pertaining to W. M. Rossetti's review of the *Bothie* in the first number of *The Germ*.

Section 39

FREDERIC GEORGE STEPHENS

1828–1907

[CBEL: III, 726, S677; DNB: S, I, 405–406 (Robert Steele)]

One of the two nonartistic members of the Pre-Raphaelite Brotherhood, Frederic George Stephens made a few furtive attempts at painting, between 1848–1850 — most of his works are now in the Tate Gallery — but he quickly turned to art criticism, in which occupation he spent practically his entire life. His first effort in that direction was the essay he contributed as "John Seward" to *The Germ*, entitled "The Purpose and Tendency of Early Italian Art." During a career of forty years as Art Editor of the *Athenaeum*, Stephens ground out literally hundreds of articles and notes and contributed regularly to the leading art periodicals. In addition, he wrote a great many monographs and compiled catalogues on a number of artists, such as Reynolds, Cruikshank, William Mulready, Bewick, Alma-Tadema, Gainsborough, Edwin Landseer, Palmer, Van Dyke, and others.

Very little has been written on Stephens, though he is discussed in most works dealing with the individual Pre-Raphaelites and in the various histories of the movement. His own writings that are included in the several sections of the Bibliography — too extensive for duplication in this section — can be located easily through the Index. For a description of the Stephens Papers in the Bodleian see 2.8.

*   *   *

39.1 Stephens, F. G. [Holman Hunt's *Pre-Raphaelitism and the Pre-Raphaelite Brotherhood*]. [London: Privately printed, 1906].
A reply to charges made by Holman Hunt against Stephens. For annotation see 77.4.

39.2 Manson, J. B., ed. *Frederick George Stephens and the Pre-Raphaelite Brothers, with Reproductions of Twenty-Four Pictures from His Collection, and Notes.* London:

Privately published by Donald Macbeth, 1920.
Stephens' collection (reproduced in part) includes four paintings by himself; five portraits of Stephens, by Millais, Hunt, Madox Brown, Fisk, and Legros. The volume also contains illustrated studies and finished works by Millais, Brown, Rossetti (an oil painting of Miss Siddal), Hunt, and Burne-Jones; one pencil drawing by James Collin-

son, a water color by G. P. Boyce, and the original study for Millais' *Christ in the House of His Parents.*

39.3 Taylor, Basil. "F. G. Stephens and the P.R.B.," *Architectural Review,* CIV (October 1948), 171–178.

A selection from some recently (1948) discovered letters to Stephens in the possession of Mr. I. A. Iggulden, now in the Bodleian (2.8).

39.4 Grylls, R. Glynn. [= (Lady) Rosalie Mander]. "The Correspondence of F. G.

Stephens," [2 parts], *Times Literary Supplement,* no. 2875 (5 April 1957), p. 216; no. 2876 (12 April 1957), p. 232.

A description of the correspondence in the possession of Mr. J. C. Iggulden from the collection of Colonel H. F. Stephens (Stephens' son who died unmarried in 1932), now in the Bodleian Library, Oxford (see 2.8).

39.5 "One of the Pre-Raphaelites — When F. G. Stephens Taught Drawing at University College School," *Times,* no. 54,395 (26 February 1959), p. 12.

Section 40

THOMAS WOOLNER

1825–1892

[CBEL: III, 313, S596; DNB: XXI, 905–907 (Richard Garnett); EB: XXVIII, 817–818]

Among the poetical "Light Brigade" who orbited in the Pre-Raphaelite galaxy was Thomas Woolner, the sculptor-poet and member of the PRB. Woolner's verse contributed to *The Germ,* especially "My Beautiful Lady," has a freshness and spontaneity, a starkness and simplicity totally absent in his published volumes. Woolner seems to have sensed instinctively his ineptness as a poet, and he is reported to have confessed to William Bell Scott, ". . . poetry is not my proper work in this world . . . I must sculpture it, not write it." (56.10, I, p. 271) And, indeed, much of the verse in his five volumes is "sculptured," almost as if he had set unshaped stones to do the work of words. As a sculptor, Woolner attained a popularity and a reasonable prosperity, but he left behind few works that have proved of great permanence as indispensable things of beauty from the past. Today, he is remembered primarily as a member of the Brotherhood, and he is dutifully given his place in the Pre-Raphaelite roll call in the volumes detailing the history of the movement. Woolner may well have been the most minor of all the Pre-Raphaelites, both as a poet and an artist, but he does reveal the Pre-Raphaelite concern with universal artistry, and the tendency to fuse (or confuse) the plastic and the verbal arts.

* * *

40.1 Woolner, Thomas. *My Beautiful Lady.* London: Macmillan, 1863; 2nd edition, 1864; 3rd edition, 1866.

The 3rd edition has a title page vignette by Arthur Hughes (see 93.6). Selected Reviews: *Macmillan's Magazine,* IX (January 1864), 255–260 [same in *Living Age,* LXXX, 3rd ser., XXIV, no. 1027 (6 February 1863), 243–247]; *Fraser's Magazine,*

LXVIII (December 1863), 801–806; *Chambers's Journal,* 4th ser., I (March 1864), pp. 204–206.

40.2 ———— *Pygmalion.* London: Macmillan, 1881.

40.3 ———— *Silenus.* London: Macmillan, 1884.

40.4 ——— *Tiresias.* London: Bell, 1886.

40.5 ——— *Poems. Nelly Dale. Children.* London: Bell, 1887.

40.6 ——— *My Beautiful Lady. Nelly Dale* (Cassell's National Library). London: Cassell, 1893.
With an Introduction by H[enry] M[ackenzie].

* * *

40.7 [Forman, H. Buxton]. "Criticisms on Contemporaries. No. X. Mr. Coventry Patmore and Mr. Woolner," *Tinsley's Magazine,* VI (April 1870), 257–266.
Praises *My Beautiful Lady* over *The Angel in the House.* Reprinted in *Our Living Poets* (74.1).

40.8 Tupper, John L. "English Artists of the Present Day. No. XIX. Thomas Woolner," *Portfolio,* II (July 1871), 97–101.
Reprinted in 75.9.

40.9 Hamilton, Walter. "Thomas Woolner," *The Æsthetic Movement in England.* London: Reeves and Turner, 1882.
For complete annotation see 78.2.

40.10 Meynell, Alice. "The Brush, the Chisel, and the Pen," *Art Journal,* XLIV (March 1882), 85–87.
A comparative review of Rossetti's *Ballads and Sonnets* and Woolner's *Pygmalion,* together with a general discussion of Pre-Raphaelite poetry. "The reform or revolution in modern English art which bears that name [Pre-Raphaelitism] was rather a literary than a pictorial movement."

40.11 Le Gallienne, Richard. "Thomas Woolner," in *The Poets and the Poetry of the Century,* edited by A. H. Miles, vol. [V]. London: Hutchinson, [1891–1897].
For complete annotation see 84.5.

40.12 "Thomas Woolner," *Athenaeum,* no. 3390 (15 October 1892), 522–523.

40.13 Stephens, Frederic George. "Thomas Woolner, R.A.," *Art Journal,* LVI (March 1894), 80–86.

40.14 Woolner, Amy. *Thomas Woolner, R. A., Sculptor and Poet: His Life in Letters.* London: Chapman and Hall, 1917.
The only full-length account of Woolner's life and art. The volume contains six letters from Rossetti to Woolner (1848–1857), a chronological list of Woolner's sculptures, and a list of his published writings.

40.15 Evans, B. Ifor. "Minor Pre-Raphaelite Poets: William Bell Scott; William Allingham; Thomas Woolner; Arthur O'Shaughnessy; John Payne; Philip Bourke Marston; William Sharp (Fiona Macleod)," *English Poetry in the Later Nineteenth Century.* London: Methuen, 1933.
For complete annotation see 74.7.

40.16 "Thomas Woolner: My Beautiful Lady," *Bodleian Library Record,* III (1950), 108–110.
A brief account of the recently acquired manuscript of the printer's copy of Woolner's poems published in 1863. The title poem had first been published in *The Germ* in 1850: variants between the manuscript and the published version of this and other poems are noted.

Associates and Later Pre-Raphaelites

Section 41

FORD MADOX BROWN
1821–1893

[DNB: XXII, S, 296–299 (F. G. Stephens); EB: IV,
657–658 (William M. Rossetti)]

A sufficient amount has been written on Ford Madox Brown to obviate the necessity of here reviewing his position in relation to the Pre-Raphaelites. Born in Calais, Brown received his early training on the Continent, and he is the only member or associate of the movement who had any contact at all with the German Nazareners, who by some critics have been taken to be the progenitors of the English Pre-Raphaelites.

Brown's natural antipathy for fetish, affectation, or coteries probably forestalled his accepting membership in the Pre-Raphaelite Brotherhood, but of all the nonmembers he was the closest to the movement.

Brown's reputation was very insecure in his own lifetime, and he has not found an audience in the modern world, though two pictures, *The Last of England* and *Work* always generate considerable interest, the latter as a kind of *tour de force*, the former as almost the Pre-Raphaelite picture *par excellence*. An able draftsman, though a weak colorist, Brown, representing the conservative side of Pre-Raphaelitism, was a plodding, competent painter who, perhaps because he lacked that flamboyant air of self-importance associated with some of the other members of the group, has suffered a neglect incommensurate with his abilities and his position in the history of nineteenth-century art.

* * *

41.1 B[rown], F[ord] M[adox]. *The Slade Professorship: Address to the Very Rev. the Vice-Chancellor of the University of Cambridge.* London: [Privately printed for Ford Madox Brown, 37 Fitzroy Sq. W.], December 20, 1872. See also J. P. Seddon "Mr. Ford Madox Brown and the Slade Professorship at Cambridge," *Architect*, VII (11 January 1873), 19–20.

41.2 —— "The Gambier Parry Process," *Royal Institute of British Architects: Sessional Papers*, XXXI (1880–1881), 273–276.

An interesting paper (read 12 May 1881) describing Brown's adaptation of the Gambier Parry "Spirit Fresco" process for the mural decorations in the Manchester Town Hall.

41.3 —— *Manchester Town Hall — Mural Paintings in the Great Town Hall: 12 Panels with Descriptions.* Manchester: no publisher, n.d.

The descriptions are the same as those in 16.7. For a general description of Brown's murals see 41.11.

41.4 —— "Of Mural Painting," *Arts and Crafts Essays by Members of the Arts and Crafts Society.* With a Preface by William Morris. London: Longmans, 1903.

This volume contains essays on the other arts and crafts by Morris, Emery Walker, J. H. Pollen, T. J. Cobden-Sanderson, May Morris, and Walter Crane.

* * *

41.5 *The Cartoons of Ford Madox Brown.* London: Privately printed, 1895.

Twenty plates — scenes from the Old and New Testament and from the "English Worthies" — in portfolio. The originals were secured at the sale of the artist's effects (19.10) by Harold S. Rathbone, a former pupil of Brown's, who had the set of 23 drawings reproduced. The cartoons were prepared for Morris and Company in the early days when Brown was a partner in the firm.

41.6 Rossetti, William Michael, ed. "Madox Brown — Some Letters, Followed by a Diary," *Præraphaelite Diaries and Letters.* London: Hurst and Blackett, 1900.

Six letters plus selections from Brown's diary for the years 1847 to 1856 (pp. 61–202). For other contents of the volume see 72.7. A brief selection from Brown's diary for 1854 is included in 24.7. See also 41.30.

* * *

41.7 [Lushington, Vernon]. "Two Pictures," *Oxford and Cambridge Magazine*, I (August 1856), 479–488.

Rossetti's *Dante's Dream* and Ford Madox Brown's *The Last of England.*

41.8 Colvin, Sidney. "English Painters of the Present Day. VIII. Ford Madox Brown," *Portfolio*, I (June 1870), 81–86.

Reprinted in 75.9.

41.9 Dafforne, James. "The Works of Ford Madox Brown," *Art Journal*, XXXV (April 1873), 105–108.

41.10 Shields, Frederic J. "The Works of Ford Madox Brown," *Transactions of the Manchester Literary Club*, I (1874–1875), 40–47.

A paper read before the club on 11 January 1875. Another brief paper read at the *conversazione* of 23 November 1874, entitled "On two pictures by Mr. Madox Brown," appears in the same volume of the Club's *Transactions* (pp. 48–50), with a Commentary by Walter Tomlinson. The two pictures discussed are *Cromwell on His Farm* and the portrait of Professor H. Fawcett and his wife.

41.11 Rossetti, William Michael. "Mr. Madox Brown's Frescoes in Manchester," *Art Journal*, XLIII (September 1881), 262–263.

41.12 Chesneau, Ernest. "Peintres anglais contemporains: Ford Madox Brown," *L'Art*, XXXI, 8ᵉ année, tome IV (1882), 81–87, 101–105, 161–166.

41.13 Rossetti, William Michael. "Ford Madox Brown: Characteristics," *Century Guild Hobby Horse*, n.s. I (April 1886), 48–54.

41.14 [Horne, Herbert P.]. "A Note Upon the Drawing of 'King René's Honeymoon,' by Ford Madox Brown," *Century Guild Hobby Horse*, n.s. III (October 1888), 158–160.

41.15 Image, Selwyn. "St. Michael and St. Uriel; Designs by Mr. Ford Madox Brown for Painted-Glass: with Notes on Other Drawings of his for Glass; and Some Incidental Remarks on the Art of Glass Painting," *Century Guild Hobby Horse*, n.s. V (July 1890), 112–119.

41.16 Rossetti, Lucy Madox. "Ford Madox Brown," *Magazine of Art*, XIII (1890), 289–296.

A study by the artist's daughter, Mrs. William Michael Rossetti.

41.17 Stephens, Frederic George. "Ford Madox Brown, His Early Studies and Motives," *Portfolio*, XXIV (April 1893), 62–66; (May 1893), 69–73.

41.18 Hueffer, Ford Madox. *Ford Madox Brown: A Record of His Life and Work.* London: Longmans, 1896.

The only full-length biographical and critical study of Brown's life and art. Illustrated with Brown's own works. The volume includes six letters from Rossetti to Brown. In two appendices are provided a list of Madox Brown's most important works with the date and place of execution or exhibition and the then owners, and a catalogue of some of Brown's designs for stained glass.

41.19 "A Note on the Cartoons of Ford

Madox Brown," *Magazine of Art*, XIX (1896), 29–30.

A review, in part, of Rathbone's printed collection (41.5) and an obituary account of the artist's life and letters, with reference to his sale (19.10).

41.20 Wilson, H. "Ford Madox Brown," *Artist*, XIX (January 1897), 1–6.

In part a review of 41.18.

41.21 Comer-Brett, John. "Ford Madox Brown," *Moring's Quarterly*, I (February 1897), 13–15.

A brief appreciative note written at the time of the Grafton Gallery exhibition (8.4), with one illustration, a cartoon for the Mother of St. John the Baptist.

41.22 Zimmern, Helen. "Artisti contemporanei: Ford Madox Brown," *Emporium*, VI (November 1897), 323–329.

41.23 "Madox Brown's Designs for Furniture," *Artist*, XXII (May 1898), 44–50.

With designs for tiles and stained glass and reproductions of furniture executed by Brown for Morris and Company.

41.24 Rossetti, Helen M. Madox (Angeli). *Ford Madox Brown*. London: Whitechapel Art Gallery, 1902.

A brief discussion of Brown's life and works, including his association with the Pre-Raphaelites, by his granddaughter. Printed by Thomas Moring at the De La More Press.

41.25 Cox, Kenyon. "Ford Madox Brown and Preraphaelitism," *Old Masters and New*. New York: Fox, Duffield, 1905.

For complete annotation see 77.53.

41.26 Rowley, Charles. "Ford Madox Brown," *Fifty Years of Work Without Wages*, London: Hodder and Stoughton, [1911].

For complete annotation see 26.4.

41.27 Chester, Austin. "The Art of Ford Madox Brown," *Windsor Magazine*, XXXVIII (September 1913), 367–382.

41.28 Linton, John. "Ford Madox Brown," *The Cross in Modern Art: Descriptive Studies of Some Pre-Raphaelite Paintings*. London: Duckworth, 1916.

Discussions of *Christ Washing Peter's Feet* and *Work*. Illustrated. For complete annotation see 75.27.

41.29 Soskice, Juliet M. *Chapters from Childhood: Reminiscences of an Artist's Granddaughter*, with a Foreword by A. G. Gardiner. London: Selwyn and Blount, 1921.

41.30 Aitken, James, ed. "Ford Madox Brown (1821–1893)," *English Diaries of the XIX Century*. Harmondsworth: Penguin Books, 1944.

Selections reprinted from *Præraphaelite Diaries and Letters* (41.6).

41.31 Klingender, Francis D. *Art and the Industrial Revolution*. London: Carrington, 1947.

Contains a very brief section on Ford Madox Brown.

41.32 McCarthy, Justin. "A Fitzroy Square Bohemia," *Reminiscences*. Vol. I. London: Chatto and Windus, 1899.

On the social activities of Ford Madox Brown and the Pre-Raphaelites.

41.33 Friswell, Laura Hain. "Madox Brown — The Pre-Raphaelite Young Ladies — 'A Great Distinction' — The Pre-Raphaelite Young Ladies on William Morris . . . ," *In the Sixties and Seventies: Impressions of Literary People and Others*. Boston: Turner, 1906.

Section 42

EDWARD BURNE-JONES
1833–1898

[DNB: XXII, S, 340–344 (T. Humphrey Ward);
EB: IV, 848–850 (Laurence Binyon)]

Rossetti and Burne-Jones are most often taken as the Pre-Raphaelites *par excellence*. Their pictures seem to capture in their vague symbolism, in their languid otherworldliness, and in their subdued sensuality the essence of Pre-Raphaelitism. This is not to suggest that their pictures offer any clarification of Pre-Raphaelite principles. On the contrary, the very vagueness and nebulousness of their work is symptomatic of the haze which enfolds Pre-Raphaelitism, of the aesthetic fog which never quite seems to lift.

That Burne-Jones should have been closely identified with Rossetti was almost inescapable. When he and Morris went up to Oxford, neither had any intention of becoming an artist. Until they encountered the work of the Pre-Raphaelites, and later came under the personal spell of Rossetti, both looked toward orders and a life dedicated to the church. Rossetti, like some great spiritual alchemist led them down the steps of the temple, not into the world of the present but into a magical world of the past, into a world whose only reality existed in the imagination. He was the sorcerer whose most singular gift was his conviction that the human imagination was a living force capable of transforming the dull stirrings of the human heart and psyche into the gold of art. His unstinting generosity and praise, his constant encouragement in the face of failure, and, most of all, his own unbounded enthusiasm for art and poetry — these were the sources of his leadership and they explain the devotion which he inspired in his followers.

As was to be expected, the early work of Burne-Jones, like that of Morris, shows most clearly the influence of Rossetti. But Rossetti's influence was never completely absent from Burne-Jones's art, for there is in everything he did a hint of the poetic, which, after Keats, Rossetti had stressed, could only be expressed in paint: ". . . if, as I hold, the noblest picture is a painted poem," Rossetti said, "then I say that in the whole history of art there has never been a painter more greatly gifted than Burne-Jones with the highest qualities of poetic invention." (quoted in Baldwin, 42.119, pp. 141–142)

The most salient characteristic of Burne-Jones's art is its idealism. The world he records is removed from the realms of ordinary experience, and his people move in tableaux, subjects of a tapestried kingdom which has no counterpart in the world of reality. A fair proportion of the inhabitants of his world are angels — mild protests against the world of factories and smokestacks, those eyesores of industry against which the Pre-Raphaelites had initially rebelled. His giant androgynous figures stand like frozen memories in a garden of yesterday, staring out, almost with disbelief, at the world before them. They were but the trappings of a vision of life and experience which Burne-Jones pursued to the end, not without disillusionment. The loneliness of the Palace of Art is unique, and like other of the Pre-Raphaelites he learned too late

Plate VII. Decorated Book Covers

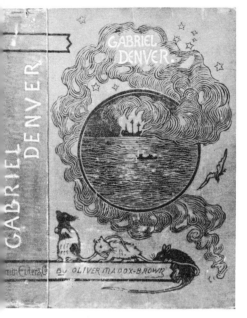

By Ford Madox Brown (47.1)

By Joseph Noel Paton (53.1)

By Simeon Solomon (61.2)

By Dante Gabriel Rossetti (48.6)

Plate VIII. Other Pre-Raphaelite Illustrations

The Choice of Paris: An Idyll, by Florence Claxton (82.3)

The Three Maids of Elfinmere, illustrating
William Allingham's poem (46.4 and 90.2)

Drawing by J. E. Millais for
Tennyson's "Locksley Hall" (90.3)

the terrible frustration of dealing with a world that has no wish to be converted: " 'Rossetti could not set it right,' " he lamented, " 'and Morris could not set it right — and who the devil am I?' . . . But he ended: 'What does that matter even then? I have learned to know Beauty when I see it, and that's the best thing.' 'And to shew it to us,' answered a friend's quiet voice." (42.63, II, 318)

T. Earle Welby's final note on Burne-Jones is an effective summary of the limitations of Burne-Jones's art:

> He had an angel as some have had a devil; an angel, somewhat ineffectual as the robust may think, without any urgent or indeed very specific message; and his true success was but to make us aware of that gracious presence, a presence, not a power, at pause, and so pure as to be almost devoid of character. (42.102, p. 61)

* * *

42.1 [Burne-Jones, Edward]. "Essay on the Newcomes," *Oxford and Cambridge Magazine*, I (January 1856), 50–61.

Contains a brief section on *The Germ* (pp. 60–61) and another on Rossetti's illustration for Allingham's *The Music Master* (see 46.4 and 90.2). For Burne-Jones's other contributions to *The Oxford and Cambridge Magazine* see the list of author attributions in H. B. Forman's *Books of William Morris* (43.1). The "Essay on the Newcomes" is reprinted in *Bibelot*, IV (October 1898), 321–359.

42.2 —— "Letters to a Child," *Strand*, XVII (April 1899), 375–380.

See 42.6.

42.3 —— *Pictures of Romance and Wonder.* New York: Russell, 1902.

42.4 —— *The Beginning of the World: Being Twenty-Five Pictures Illustrative of a Portion of the Book of Genesis.* London: Longmans, 1902; 2nd ed., 1903.

Published in America as *In the Dawn of the World* (Boston: Goodspeed, 1903).

42.5 —— *The Flower Book: Reproductions of Thirty Eight Water-Colour Designs.* London: Fine Art Society, 1905.

"The pictures in this book are not of flowers themselves, but of subjects suggested by their names." Burne-Jones began this series in 1882 "as a rest from more laborious work." The original drawings are in the British Museum.

42.6 —— *Letters to Katie.* With an Intro-

ductory Note by W. Graham Robertson. London: Macmillan, 1925.

Burne-Jones's letters to Katherine Lewis, the youngest daughter of a close friend. These amusing letters with their comic illustrations reveal an attractive side of Burne-Jones, suppressed in his art.

* * *

42.7 Colvin, Sidney. "English Painters of the Present Day. III. Edward Burne-Jones," *Portfolio*, I (February 1870), 17–22.

Reprinted in 75.9.

42.8 Wedmore, Frederick. "Some Tendencies in Recent Painting," *Temple Bar*, LIII (July 1878), 334–348.

On Burne-Jones and Albert Moore.

42.9 "Contemporary Portraits: Edward Burne-Jones," *Dublin University Magazine*, XCIV, n.s. IV (July 1879), 40–50.

Reprinted in part as "Mr. E. Burne-Jones," in *American Architecture*, VI (13 September 1879), 87.

42.10 Wedmore, Frederick. "Burne-Jones," *Studies in English Art. Second Series.* London: Bentley, 1880.

42.11 Ruskin, John. "Mythic Schools of Painting: E. Burne-Jones and G. F. Watts," *The Art of England: Lectures Given in Oxford.* Orpington: Allen, 1883.

For complete annotation see 45.2.

42.12 Stephens, Frederic George. "Edward Burne-Jones, A.R.A.," *Portfolio*, XVI

(November 1885), 220–225; (December 1885), 227–232.

42.13 Philips, Claude. "Edward Burne Jones," *Magazine of Art*, VIII (1885), 286–294.

The founders of the Pre-Raphaelite school "were inspired with the love of nature, and earnestly sought to render it with something of the untiring care and minuteness of the early Flemings and of the school of Dürer[;] the second school, or later development, of which Mr. Burne Jones is now the undisputed chief, has in externals approached more closely to the manner of the early Italian Renaissance . . . With the so-called Pre-Raphaelites of the first school . . . Mr. Burne Jones has little or nothing in common." (pp. 286–287)

42.14 Stephens, Frederic George. "Mr. Edward Burne-Jones, A.R.A., as a Decorative Artist," *Portfolio*, XX (November 1889), 214–219.

See also by Stephens "Mr. Edward Burne-Jones's Mosaics at Rome," *Portfolio*, XXI (May 1890), 101–108.

42.15 [White, Gleeson]. "Edward Burne Jones, Esq., A.R.A.," *Letters to Living Artists*. London: Elkin Mathews, 1891.

42.16 Bell, Malcolm. *Edward Burne-Jones: A Record and Review*. London: Bell, 1892.

1st and 2nd editions in small folio; 3rd and 4th editions, revised, in octavo (1894, 1898). The work was also condensed for "Bell's Miniature Series of Painters" (1901), and translated into German, appearing as no. 3 in the *Die Kunst* series (1902), by Rudolf Klein. The standard work on Burne-Jones's art. Contains both a chronological catalogue of Burne-Jones's finished pictures and a list of cartoons for stained glass. The catalogue is reprinted in Destrée (75.18). For an illustrated review-article on this volume see 42.23.

42.17 Leprieur, Paul. "Burne Jones, décorateur et ornemaniste," *Gazette des Beaux-Arts*, période 3, VIII (November 1892), 381–399.
Illustrated.

42.18 Moore, George. "Mr. Burne-Jones and the Academy," *Modern Painting*. London: Scott, 1893.

Letter to the editor of *The Speaker* on Burne-Jones's relationship with the Royal Academy.

42.19 Cartwright, Julia. "Edward Burne-Jones, A.R.A.," *Art Journal*, LV (January 1893), 1–9.

42.20 MacColl, D. S. "Mr. Burne-Jones," *Spectator*, LXX, no. 3368 (14 January 1893), 46–47.

42.21 Bryce, Mary R. L. "Edward Burne-Jones: His Art and Influence," *Blackwood's Magazine*, CLIII (June 1893), 861–864.

42.22 Leprieur, Paul. "La Légende de Persée par M. Burne Jones," *Gazette des Beaux-Arts*, période 3, X (December 1893), 462–477.
Illustrated.

42.23 "Edward Burne-Jones, A.R.A.," *Magazine of Art*, XVI (1893), 102–105.
An illustrated review-article on 42.16.

42.24 Cartwright, Julia. *Sir Edward Burne-Jones, Bart.: His Life and Work* (The Art Annual, Christmas Number of the *Art Journal*). London: Virtue, 1894.
Collected in 75.22.

42.25 Lahor, Jean. "Sir Edward Burne-Jones," *La Revue de Paris*, no. 5 (1 September 1894), 102–122.

42.26 Rawnsley, H. D. "The Great Tapestry in Exeter College Chapel, Oxford," *Magazine of Art*, XVII (1894), 284–286.
The Adoration of the Magi.

42.27 Meade, L. T. "Sir Edward Burne-Jones, Bart.," *Strand*, X (July 1895), 16–26.

42.28 B., G. "Artisti contemporanei: Sir Edward Burne-Jones," *Emporium*, II (December 1895), 445–465; III (January 1896), 36–56.

42.29 "Mosaics by Sir Edward Burne-Jones

at Rome," *Magazine of Art*, XVIII (1895), 256–260.
Burne-Jones's mosaics in the apse of the American Church in Rome. Ilustrated.

42.30 "Studies by Sir Edward Burne-Jones," *Studio*, X (May 1896), 199–208.
Preliminary drawings and studies for large pictures exhibited at the Fine Art Society, 1896 (see 9.7). With eight illustrations.

42.31 Wilson, H. "The Work of Sir Edward Burne-Jones, More Especially in Decoration and Design," *Architectural Review*, I (March 1897), 171–181; (April 1897), 225–233; (May 1897), 273–281.

42.32 Weis, Irene. *Burne-Jones* (Great Artists). Boston: Perry Picture Co. [1898].

42.33 La Sizeranne, Robert de. "The Late Sir Edward Burne-Jones, Bart., D.C.L.," *Artist*, XXII (June 1898), suppl. 1–6.

42.34 "Some Studies by Sir Edward Burne-Jones," *Studio*, XIV (June 1898), 38–50.
A collection of photographic studies of Burne-Jones's works made by F. Hollyer and exhibited in Pembroke Square. Eight illustrations. See 9.8.

42.35 Rinder, E. Wingate. "Sir Edward Burne-Jones: The Man," *Independent*, L (July 1898), 110–113.

42.36 Cartwright, Julia. "In Memoriam — Edward Burne-Jones," *Art Journal*, LX (August 1898), 247–248.

42.37 Hueffer, Ford Madox. "Sir Edward Burne-Jones," *Contemporary Review*, LXXIV (August 1898), 181–195.
Burne-Jones was a Celtic voice in an Anglo-Saxon age.

42.38 Sharp, William. "Edward Burne-Jones," *Fortnightly Review*, LXX, n.s. LXIV (August 1898), 289–306.
Reprinted in 27.50.

42.39 ——— "Sir Edward Burne-Jones," *Atlantic Monthly*, LXXXII (September 1898), 375–383.

42.40 Cartwright, Julia. "Review" [Edward Burne-Jones], *Quarterly Review*, CLXXXVIII (October 1898), 338–359.
A long review-discussion of Bell (42.16), Cartwright (42.24), and La Sizeranne (70.8).

42.41 "The Cupid and Psyche Frieze by Sir Edward Burne-Jones, at No. 1, Palace Green," *Studio*, XV (October 1898), 3–13.
History of the frieze in the Earl of Carlisle's town house. Illustrated.

42.42 "In Memoriam: Sir Edward Burne-Jones, Bart.," *Magazine of Art*, XXI (1898), 513–528.
Three parts: "A Tribute from France" by Robert de la Sizeranne; "A Tribute from Belgium" by Fernand Khnopff; and a brief tribute by M. H. Spielmann.

42.43 Bell, Mrs. Arthur (N. D'Anvers). "Sir Edward Burne-Jones," *Representative Painters of the XIXth Century*. London: Sampson, Low, Marston, 1899.
For complete annotation see 30.23.

42.44 Monkhouse, Cosmo. "Burne-Jones," *British Contemporary Artists*. London: Scribner's, 1899.
Reprinted from *Scribner's Magazine*, XV (February 1894), 135–153.

42.45 Caffin, Charles H. "Mosaics in the American Church at Rome," *Harper's Weekly*, XLIII, no. 2194 (7 January 1899), [9]–10.
Illustrations, p. 9.

42.46 Jacobs, Joseph. "Some Recollections of Sir Edward Burne-Jones," *Nineteenth Century*, XLV (January 1899), 126–131.
Notes, amid other trivia, Burne-Jones's strong attraction to Roman Catholicism.

42.47 [Taylor, Una]. "Burne-Jones: His Ethics and Art," *Edinburgh Review*, CLXXXIX (January 1899), 24–47.

42.48 Bell, Malcolm. "Some Features of the Art of Sir Edward Burne-Jones," *Studio*, XVI (April 1899), 175–183.

42.49 Bénédite, Léonce. "Deux idéalistes:

Burne-Jones et Gustave Moreau," *Revue de l'Art Ancien et Moderne*, V (April 1899), 265–290, (May 1899), 357–378; VI (July 1899), 57–70.

42.50 Slayter, John A. "An Ethical Retrospect of the Traditions and Aims of Sir Edward Burne-Jones," *Architectural Review*, VI (September 1899), 70–75.

Burne-Jones, "the great star that has risen in modern mystical art."

42.51 "The Christina Rossetti Memorial. Sir Edward Burne-Jones's Last Work," *Magazine of Art*, XXII (1899), 88–90.

For annotation see 44.39.

42.52 Kassner, Rudolf. "Edward Burne-Jones," *Die Mystik, die Künstler, und das Leben: über englische Dichter und Maler im 19. Jahrhundert.* Leipzig: Diederichs, 1900.

Reissued 1920 (Leipzig: Insel) with title *Englische Dichter*.

42.53 Vallance, Aymer. *The Decorative Art of Sir Edward Burne-Jones, Baronet* (Easter Number of the *Art Journal*). London: Virtue, 1900.

42.54 Cartwright, Julia. "Burne-Jones," *Gazette des Beaux-Arts*, période 3, XXIV (July 1900), 25–38; (September 1900), 237–252.

42.55 Burne-Jones, Philip. "Notes on Some Unfinished Works of Sir Edward Burne-Jones, Bart.," *Magazine of Art*, XXIII (1900), 159–167.

42.56 Roberts, W. "The British Museum: The Burne-Jones Drawings," *Magazine of Art*, XXIII (1900), 453–456.

Concerning drawings left to the Museum by the artist.

42.57 *Burne-Jones* (Masters in Art: A Series of Illustrated Monographs, vol. II, pt. 19). Boston: Bates, 1901.

Text, illustrations, and brief bibliography.

42.58 Forsyth, Peter Taylor. *Religion in Recent Art: Expository Lectures on Rossetti,* Burne-Jones, Watts, Holman Hunt, and Wagner. London: Hodder and Stoughton, 1901.

42.59 Schleinitz, Otto Julius Wilhelm von. *Burne-Jones (Künstler-Monographien.* LV). Bielefeld und Leipzig: Velhagen und Klassing, 1901.

42.60 *The Work of Edward Burne-Jones: Ninety-one Photogravures Directly Reproduced from the Original Paintings.* London: Berlin Photographic Co. [1901].

200 copies signed by Sir Philip Burne-Jones. An elephant folio volume.

42.61 Bayliss, Sir Wyke. *Five Great Painters of the Victorian Era: Leighton, Millais, Burne-Jones, Watts, Holman Hunt.* London: Sampson, Low, Marston, 1902.

42.62 Muther, Richard. "Rossetti, Burne-Jones, und Watts," *Neue Deutsche Rundschau*, XIII (August 1902), 859–881.

42.63 B[urne]-J[ones], G[eorgiana]. *Memorials of Edward Burne-Jones.* 2 vols. London: Macmillan, 1904.

An intimate and detailed account of Burne-Jones's life and friendships.

42.64 De Lisle, Fortunée. *Burne-Jones* (Little Books on Art). London: Methuen, 1904.

Containing a list of Burne-Jones's works, a list of the principal sales, and a useful bibliography.

42.65 Melani, Alfredo. "Edoardo Burne-Jones," *Nell'Arte e nella vita.* Milano: Hoepli, 1904.

42.66 "Studies by Sir Edward Burne-Jones," *Studio*, XXXI (May 1904), 312–320.

Six illustrations.

42.67 Prinsep, Valentine C. "The Oxford Circle: Rossetti, Burne-Jones, and William Morris. A Chapter from a Painter's Reminiscence[s]," *Magazine of Art*, XXVII, n.s. II (1904), 167–172.

For further reminiscences by Prinsep see 25.27.

42.68 Cox, Kenyon. "Burne-Jones," *Old Masters and New*. New York: Fox, Duffield, 1905.
For complete annotation see 77.53.

42.69 "Burne-Jones," *Edinburgh Review*, CCI (January 1905), 237–254.

42.70 Cartwright, Julia. "Edward Burne-Jones," *Monthly Review*, XVIII (March 1905), 17–36.
A review-article on 42.63. Same in *Living Age*, CCXLV, 7th ser., XXVII, no. 3176 (20 May 1905), 461–472.

42.71 Knight, William Angus. "Edward Burne-Jones," *Fortnightly Review*, LXXXVI, n.s. LXXX (October 1906), 671–684.
Essentially the same as Knight's lecture included in 75.26.

42.72 *Sir Edward Burne-Jones*. [First Series]. (Newnes' Art Library). London: Newnes, [1907].
With a long Introduction on Burne-Jones by Malcolm Bell and reproductions of 56 of his finished works.

42.73 *Sir Edward Burne-Jones*. Second Series. (Newnes' Art Library). London: Newnes, [1907].
With a long Introduction on Burne-Jones by Arsene Alexandre and reproductions of 48 of his finished works.

42.74 *Drawings of Sir Edward Burne-Jones* (Newnes' Drawings of the Great Masters). London: Newnes, [1907].
With a long Introduction by T. Martin Wood and 46 plates.

42.75 Cortissoz, Royal. "Edward Burne-Jones," *Munsey's Magazine*, XXXVI (February 1907), 573–587.
Subtitled: "The English Pre-Raphaelite painter and his dreams — a maker of poetic and romantic pictures who never grasped some of the elements of good art, yet created in his work a compelling special glamour."
". . . You do not find in Burne-Jones quite the dark, unwholesome hothouse languor that you find in Rossetti. His morbidity is rather that of the temperament which is happy enough and healthy enough in its own world, but takes on a certain effeminate and slightly feverish tone from lack of occasional contact with the world at large." (p. 582)

42.76 Lavell, Cecil Fairfield. "Burne-Jones and the Pre-Raphaelites," *Chautauquan*, XLVI (March 1907), 69–78.
For annotation see 77.54.

42.77 Burns, J. *"The Star of Bethlehem*, by Sir Ed. Burne-Jones," *Sermons in Art by the Great Masters*. London: Duckworth, 1908.
For complete annotation see 31.24.

42.78 Carr, J. Comyns. "Edward Burne-Jones," *Some Eminent Victorians: Personal Recollections in the World of Art and Letters*. London: Duckworth, 1908.
For complete annotation see 37.73.

42.79 *The Golden Stairs by Sir Edward Burne-Jones* (Masterpieces, no. 1). London: Fairbairns, 1908.
Color reproduction of the painting with a brief text. No more published in this series.

42.80 Phythian, J. E. *Burne-Jones*. London: Richards, 1908.

42.81 "King Cophetua and the Beggar Maid," *Art Journal*, LXX (August 1908), 230–231.

42.82 Vallance, Aymer. "Some Examples of Tapestry Designed by Burne-Jones and J. H. Dearle," *Studio*, XLV (October 1908), 13–24.
Ten illustrations.

42.83 Baldry, Alfred Lys. *Burne-Jones* (Masterpieces in Colour, edited by T. Lemon Hare). New York: Stokes, [1909].

42.84 Smith, R. Catterson. "Sir Edward Burne-Jones," in *Nine Famous Birmingham Men: Lectures Delivered in the University*, edited by J. W. Muirhead. Birmingham: Cornish, 1909.

42.85 Bensusan, Samuel Levy. *The Charm of Burne-Jones*. London: Jack, [c. 1910].

42.86 Vallance, Aymer. "Sir Edward Burne-Jones's Designs for Painted Glass," *Studio*, LI (November 1910), 91–103.

Sixteen illustrations, two in color.

42.87 Bell, Malcolm. "The Mirror of Venus," in *Modern Paintings*, edited by Esther Singleton. New York: Dodd, Mead, 1911.

For complete annotation see 36.55.

42.88 Oeser, Hermann. "Edward Burne-Jones, ein Naturalist des Schönen," *Von Menschen, von Bildern und Büchern*. Heilbraun: Salzer, 1913.

42.89 *Burne-Jones: Huit reproductions fac-similés en couleurs*. Paris: Lafitte, 1914.

42.90 Pelo, F. B. "An Artist at Play, as Shown in Six Hitherto Unpublished Drawings by Sir Edward Burne-Jones," *Bellman*, XXII (February 1917), 123–125.

Reproductions of six small pencil drawings by Burne-Jones (from 1865–1866) depicting the artist, caricatured as an old man, and his son Philip as a child.

42.91 *Letters Addressed to Algernon Charles Swinburne, by John Ruskin, William Morris, Sir Edward Burne-Jones and Dante Gabriel Rossetti*. London: Printed for private circulation for Thomas J. Wise, 1919.

42.92 Williamson, G. C. "Sir Edward Burne-Jones," *Murray Marks and His Friends: A Tribute of Regard*. London: John Lane, 1919.

For complete annotation see 86.14.

42.93 Hutchinson, H. G. "Watts, Millais, and Burne-Jones," *Portraits of the Eighties*. London: Unwin, 1920.

Personal reminiscences.

42.94 Hellman, G. S. "From a Burne-Jones Sketchbook," *Harper's Magazine*, CXLI (November 1920), 769–774.

Discusses a Burne-Jones sketchbook in the Art Institute of Chicago, with special reference to studies for *The Mirror of Venus* and *The Romaunt of the Rose*. Thirty-nine drawings in all.

42.95 Colvin, Sidney. "Edward Burne-Jones," *Memories and Notes of Persons and Places, 1852–1912*. London: Arnold, 1921.

For complete annotation see 25.52.

42.96 Bénédite, Léonce. "Moreau et Burne-Jones," *Notre Art, nos maitres*. Paris: Flammarion, 1922.

42.97 Villers, Sirieyx de. "Burne-Jones; Le Mysticisme celtique — Ses principaux tableaux," *Les Grands Mystiques de la peinture*. Lyon: Les Éditions du Fleuve, 1924.

42.98 "Burne-Jones in a Puckish Mood," *Literary Digest*, LXXXVIII (9 January 1926), 24–25.

42.99 "Story Paintings of Perseus. Sir Edward Burne-Jones," *Mentor*, XIV (October 1926), 11–13.

42.100 Lucas, E. V. "Edward Burne-Jones and D. G. Rossetti — 1867 and on," *The Colvins and Their Friends*. London: Methuen, 1928.

42.101 Swinnerton, Frank. "Morris, Burne-Jones, Birmingham," *A London Bookman*. London: Secker, 1928.

On the house at No. 1, Palace Green, built for George Howard, later Earl of Carlisle, designed by Philip Webb and decorated by Morris and Burne-Jones, the proposed destruction of which resulted in a letter of protest to the *Times*.

42.102 Welby, T. Earle. *The Victorian Romantics, 1850–1870: The Early Work of Dante Gabriel Rossetti, William Morris, Burne-Jones, Swinburne, Simeon Solomon and Their Associates*. London: Howe, 1929.

For discussion see Survey, pp. 30–31.

42.103 B[eddington], B. *A Few Notes Written by My Sister Maud Beddington about Sir Edward Burne-Jones and of his Kindness and Help in her Art*. Rye: [Privately printed] by Adams and Sons, n.d.

There is an illustrated version of this pamphlet entitled *Notes by Maud Beddington about Sir Edward Burne-Jones and his Art*, which includes reproductions of works by Maud Beddington, very much in the tradition of Burne-Jones. See Plate VIII.

42.104 Thirkell, Angela. *Three Houses.* London: Oxford University Press, 1931.
Largely reminiscences of early childhood by Burne-Jones' granddaughter.

42.105 Armstrong, Martin. "Edward Burne-Jones," in *The Great Victorians*, edited by H. J. and Hugh Massingham. London: Nicolson and Watson, 1932.

42.106 Stevenson, C. Bernard. "Sir Edward Burne-Jones," *The Old Water-Colour Society's Club. Ninth Annual Volume*, edited by Randall Davies. London: OW-CS, issued only to members, 1932.
With a list of Burne-Jones's works exhibited in the Society's gallery.

42.107 Baker, C. H. Collins. "The Pre-Raphaelite Movement and Burne-Jones," *British Painting*, with a Chapter on Primitive Painting by Montague R. James. London: Medici Society, 1933.

42.108 Horner, Lady Frances. "Sir Edward Burne-Jones," *Times Remembered*. London: Heinemann, 1933.
Memories of Burne-Jones, Rossetti, Tennyson, Browning, and Ruskin.

42.109 Bateman, Arthur B. "Edward Burne-Jones (1833–1898)," *London Quarterly Review*, CLVIII, 6th ser., II (October 1933), 447–452.
A centenary study. "Into . . . a world of shoddy ideas Burne-Jones was born . . . , finding his pilgrimage shared by Rossetti, Madox Brown, Alfred Stevens, Millais, and William Morris, men whose chivalrous battles for England's green and pleasant land were more real if less sanguinary than those of the knights they painted. It was due to their genius that a magic gleam of romance fell upon the age of Commerce . . . " (pp. 447–448)

42.110 Baldwin, Stanley. "Burne-Jones," *The Torch of Freedom: Speeches and Addresses*. London: Hodder and Stoughton, 1937.

A lecture delivered at the Burne-Jones centenary exhibition at the Tate Gallery (9.15), 16 June 1933.

42.111 "Sir Edward Burne-Jones," *Picture Post*, II (21 January 1939), 39–42.
Great British Masters, no. 17, illustrated.

42.112 Ironside, Robin. "Burne-Jones and Gustave Moreau," *Horizon*, I (June 1940), 406–424.

42.113 Constable, W. G. "'Hope' by Edward Burne-Jones," *Boston Museum Bulletin*, XXXIX (February 1941), 12–14.
Correction and addition in the April number (p. 19). On the acquisition of this picture by the Boston Museum of the Fine Arts — a history of the picture's origin and an analysis of its symbolism. Contains an interesting letter from Burne-Jones about hanging his pictures under glass to give them an "ætherial varnish."

42.114 Tunstall, Edward A., and Antony Kerr. "Painted Rooms at the Queen's College, Oxford," *Burlington Magazine*, LXXXII (February 1943), 42, 46–47.
Decorations in what may have been digs for Burne-Jones and Morris during early Oxford days. The designs — obviously influenced by Rossetti — may be (though no certainty is possible) "the earliest substantive work of Morris and Burne-Jones," and thus mark the arrival of the second and so different Pre-Raphaelite generation.

42.115 Green, Roger Lancelyn. "Burne-Jones and 'The Fairy Family,'" *Times Literary Supplement*, no. 2221 (26 August 1944), p. 420.
For annotation see 89.16.

42.116 Harris, M. P. *"Perseus and Andromeda," National Gallery of South Australia Bulletin*, VIII (January 1947), [6–7].

42.117 Christoffel, Ulrich. "Edward Burne-Jones," *Malerei und Poesie: die symbolische Kunst des 19. Jahrhunderts*. Vienna: Gallus-Verlag, 1948.

42.118 Hanford, F. E., and G. A. C. Evans. "The Grange and Sir Edward Burne-Jones," *The Story of the Grange, North End Crescent, Fulham.* London: Fulham History Society Publications, 1953.

The text of two lectures, the second on Burne-Jones by Evans, delivered on Valentine's Day, 1947, in the Fulham Library.

42.119 Baldwin, A. W. "The Burne-Joneses, 1860–1920," *The Macdonald Sisters.* London: Davies, 1960.

Section 43

WILLIAM MORRIS
1834–1896

[CBEL: III, 314–317, S596–597; DNB: XXII, S, 1069–1075 (J. W. Mackail); EB: XVIII, 871–873 (Arthur Waugh)]

Morris' *The Defence of Guenevere* is in many respects the most Pre-Raphaelite volume of poetry which the movement produced, and it was the first publication of any kind — apart from *The Germ* and *The Oxford and Cambridge Magazine* — that bore the Pre-Raphaelite stamp. In everything that Morris did during his early years (from about 1856 until the middle of the 1860's) the animating force of Rossetti is palpably evident; and despite the breach (for whatever causes) that sundered the relationship between the two in later years, the course of Morris' entire life was altered by his early encounter with Rossetti. The spell of Rossetti impels *The Defence of Guenevere, La Belle Iseult,* the Oxford Union ceiling, and other of Morris' works; even when his influence is not obviously apparent in design and form, the very atmosphere betrays his presence. In a sense, *The Defence of Guenevere* was a crystallization of all that was best in the energies generated by the first wave of Pre-Raphaelitism, tempered by the new attitudes and concerns brought to the second by Morris and Burne-Jones.

By the time of *The Earthly Paradise*, Morris had begun to strike out on his own, though he had not yet left wholly behind the trappings of his Pre-Raphaelite period. His excursions into Icelandic literature and lore, his increasing interest in translation, his involvement in all phases of the Arts and Crafts Movement (fostered to so great a degree by his activities in Morris and Company, in which both Rossetti and Ford Madox Brown had a definite role), and his concern with socialism and the political implications of art — all these activities lured Morris away from poetry, away from Pre-Raphaelitism, away from his youthful inspiration. In all that he later accomplished Morris never quite equaled his achievement in *The Defence of Guenevere*. He carried with him into unchartered fields the legacy of his Pre-Raphaelite apprenticeship, and his contributions in a dozen fields are indisputable; but the magic of that crowded world of Camelot, limned when his visions and illusions were at their greenest, he never again recaptured.

What Morris took with him from his early association with the Pre-Raphaelites was their strong sense of rebellion against an ugly age, their belief in decoration for its own sake, and their belief in universal artistry — it was, after all, Rossetti's commitment to this principle that had lured Morris into the arts in the first instance. This last concept Morris modified and extended, giving it a social significance beyond Rossetti's intention. Every man might not be an artist (as Rossetti said), but every man was capable of responding to the beautiful and entitled to the right of response. Thus, Morris blended early the aesthetic with the social (and moral); the political corollaries were inherent, though he did not seize them at the outset. Morris' principal task, from the founding of Morris and Company on, was to reintroduce into everyday life the beautiful things which the rise of industry and the corresponding decline of craftsmanship had destroyed. His ultimate turning to politics was almost inevitable, and it may be explained simply by his desire to restore to the England of the nineteenth century not the life of the Middle Ages but what he understood to be the animating spirit of art that flourished at that time. Morris thus gave to Pre-Raphaelitism a new dimension — the dimension of romantic medievalism, which differed from Rossetti's by its emphasis on the practical rather than the ideal. Morris retreated from the empty days about which he had idly sung, and it was a costly retreat, made at the expense of his poetic instincts, which henceforth had to be sublimated in wallpapers, tapestries, chintzes, carpets, furniture, and books. Perhaps the essential difference between Rossetti and Morris, as exponents of an early and later Pre-Raphaelitism, is to be found in the contrasting temperaments of the two men. Rossetti was a visionary, an idealistic romantic, an idle dreamer; Morris, as a man of action, found only partial satisfaction in possessing dreams and ideals; his mission became that of translating abstract ideals into the furniture of reality.

In *English Poetry in the Later Nineteenth Century*, B. Ifor Evans begins his discussion of Morris with the statement that "Rossetti never influenced a man more unlike himself than William Morris." (43.102, p. 81) In many respects this is only a half truth, for the two men are rather complementary than direct opposites. Rossetti was introspective, lethargic, and self-centered (but not self-sufficient); Morris was energetic, expressive, and socially aware (he may have disliked introspective poetry, but he had a private side to his nature, as Rossetti seems not to have had). Both men are enigmatic, with elements which simultaneously attract and repel. Rossetti and Morris represent two sides of the same whole: introspection versus action, pure versus applied (or practical) idealism, youth versus maturity. Rossetti wanted a clean, well-lighted place for himself and his friends; Morris sought to make it of the world.

The absence of a thorough bibliography of Morris' writings and secondary sources treating Morris and his activities remains a serious barrier to research. His major writings have been twice catalogued (see Forman and Temple Scott, 43.1 and 43.2), but neither work is fully satisfactory, and a large body of lectures, articles, reviews, and notes by Morris have never been hunted out and described. For secondary sources, Ehrsam's section on Morris (43.7) is still the most complete listing, but Howard Mumford Jones' chapter on the Pre-Raphaelites (1.11), which includes Morris, makes valuable additions and appraisals of materials between 1936 and 1956. The present section is necessarily highly selective, since a large portion of the material available on Morris — especially that dealing with his later career, particularly with his socialism — is in the main extraneous to a consideration of his role within the Pre-Raphaelite Movement, though his sociopolitical aesthetic was certainly conditioned by his early association with the Pre-Raphaelites and with the ideas of Ruskin. Also excluded from the present list are the many source studies of Morris' strongly derivative poetry, and criticism dealing with his translations. Some attempt has been made to include the most important of those works demonstrating the close link between Pre-Raphaelitism and the Arts and Crafts Movement, but that subject is too broad and too complicated to be fully examined in this section.

The most recent development in the history of Morris studies is the formation of the William Morris Society, an organization founded in 1955, whose purpose is "to deepen understanding and stimulate a wider appreciation of Morris, his friends, and their work." With a membership of approximately five hundred, the Society is concerned with all aspects of Morris' life and career in the several arts. The Society has published a number of lectures and pamphlets on Morris, and it has sponsored two major exhibitions, the *Typographical Adventure* exhibition in 1957 (13.9) and the recent centenary exhibition of Morris and Company (13.12). A number of the Society's publications are included in this section. In 1961, the Society issued the first number of the *Journal* (43.171), which promises to prove an important organ in the development of Morris studies. The William Morris Society performs a necessary function, and it is to be hoped that as it grows and expands it will widen somewhat its focus (there has been, perhaps inadvertently, a noticeable preoccupation with Morris' activities in the Arts and Crafts, especially in printing) to take in not only Morris, but also those friends without whom Morris' talents might have remained undiscovered.

* * *

43.1 Forman, H. Buxton. *The Books of William Morris Described, with Some Account of His Doings in Literature and in the Allied Crafts*. London: Hollings, 1897.

Especially valuable for bibliographical information on *The Oxford and Cambridge Magazine* and for the identification of contributors to that journal, taken from Morris' own list.

43.2 Scott, Temple. *A Bibliography of the Works of William Morris*. London: Bell, 1897.

Includes both Morris' own works and secondary sources.

43.3 *A Note by William Morris on His Aims in Founding the Kelmscott Press: Together with a Short Description of the Press by S. C. Cockerell, & an Annotated List of the Books Printed Thereat*. Hammersmith: Kelmscott Press, 1898.

The last book printed at the Kelmscott Press, with a full bibliography of the press,

giving all the particulars (including types, paper, illustrations) of each publication. Reprinted in Sparling (43.89).

43.4 Vaughan, Charles E. *Bibliographies of Swinburne, Morris, and Rossetti* (The English Association, Pamphlet no. 29). [Oxford: Clarendon Press], 1914.

43.5 Carter, John, and Graham Pollard. "William Morris," *An Enquiry Into the Nature of Certain Nineteenth Century Pamphlets*. London: Constable, 1934.

For annotation see 1.3.

43.6 Ohtski, Kenji. *List of New Contributions, Home and Foreign, to the W. Morris Bibliography in His Year*. Tokyo, 1934.

Reprinted from *Tokio-do-Geppo* ("The Reader's Friend"), December 1934, pp. 1–5. See 13.5.

43.7 Ehrsam, Theodore G., Robert H. Deily, and Robert M. Smith. "William Morris,"

Bibliographies of Twelve Victorian Authors. New York: Wilson, 1936.
For complete annotation see 1.5.

43.8 Flower, R. "The William Morris Manuscripts," *British Museum Quarterly,* XIV (1939–1940), 8–12.
For a description of the Morris manuscripts in the British Museum see 2.2.

43.9 Briggs, R. C. H. *A Handlist of the Public Addresses of William Morris to be Found in Generally Accessible Publications.* London: William Morris Society, 1961.

* * *

43.10 *The Oxford and Cambridge Magazine for 1856: Conducted by Members of the Two Universities,* edited by William Fulford. Oxford: Numbers 1 to 12, January to December 1856.
For annotation see 72.4.

43.11 Morris, William. *The Defence of Guenevere and Other Poems.* London: Bell and Daldy, 1858; 2nd edition, 1875.
Published in a limited number of copies and hardly noticed by the critical press. For an interesting account of the *Defence* as a book of "Pre-Raphaelite Minstrelsy" see *Athenaeum,* no. 1588 (3 April 1858), pp. 427–428.

43.12 —— *The Life and Death of Jason: A Poem.* London: Bell and Daldy, 1867.

43.13 —— *The Earthly Paradise: A Poem.* 3 vols. London: Ellis, 1868–1870.
G. D. H. Cole notes that "much of Morris's writing is really picture. His prose romances are mostly woven tapestries of words. *The Earthly Paradise* has much the character of a series of Pre-Raphaelite paintings." (43.23, p. xi)

43.14 —— *Love is Enough, or the Freeing of Pharamond: A Morality.* London: Ellis, 1873.

43.15 —— *The Story of Sigurd the Volsung, and the Fall of the Niblungs.* London: Ellis, 1877.

43.16 —— *Hopes and Fears for Art: Five Lectures Delivered in Birmingham, London, and Nottingham, 1878–1881.* London: Ellis, 1882.
Morris' first lecture, "The Decorative Arts" (1878) appears here as "The Lesser Arts."

43.17 —— *News from Nowhere, or An Epoch of Rest, Being Some Chapters from a Utopian Romance.* London: Reeves and Turner, 1891.
A so-called, piratical, "Author's Edition" was published by Roberts Brothers, Boston, in 1890.

43.18 —— *Poems by the Way.* Hammersmith: Kelmscott Press, 1891.
The popular edition was published by Reeves and Turner in the same year.

43.19 —— *Address on the Collection of Paintings of the English Pre-Raphaelite School, Delivered in the [Birmingham] Museum and Art Gallery, October 2, 1891.* Birmingham: [Printed for the Corporation], [1891].
For annotation see 75.14.

43.20 —— *Pre-Raphaelite Ballads.* Illustrated by H. M. O'Kane. New York: Wessels, 1900.
The title of this volume, which includes four of Morris' ballads, was not chosen by Morris.

43.21 Morris, May, ed. *The Collected Works of William Morris.* 24 vols. London: Longmans, 1910–1915.
The standard edition, with invaluable introductions by May Morris.

43.22 *Guenevere. Two Poems by William Morris. The Defence of Guenevere and King Arthur's Tomb.* With Eight Decorations by Dante Gabriel Rossetti, and a Foreword by Gordon Bottomley. London: Fanfrolico Press, 1930.

43.23 Cole, G. D. H., ed. *William Morris. Stories in Prose, Stories in Verse, Shorter Poems, Lectures, and Essays.* Centenary Edition. London: Nonesuch Press, 1934.
The best one-volume edition of Morris'

works, with a perceptive Introduction by Professor Cole.

43.24 Morris, May. (ed.). *William Morris: Artist, Writer, Socialist.* [*Vol. I*]: *The Art of William Morris. William Morris as a Writer.* [*Vol. II*]: *Morris as a Socialist. With an Account of "William Morris as I Knew Him,"* by *George Bernard Shaw.* Oxford: Blackwell's 1936.

These two volumes, in which much of Morris' work is printed for the first time, are supplementary volumes to the *Collected Works* (43.21).

* * *

43.25 Henderson, Philip, ed. *The Letters of William Morris to His Family and Friends.* London: Longmans, 1950.

With a long Introduction. The volume also contains the prospectus of Morris, Marshall, Faulkner, and Co.

43.26 Arnot, R. Page, ed. *Unpublished Letters of William Morris* (Labour Monthly Pamphlets, 1951 series, no. 6). London: Trinity Trust, 1951.

* * *

43.27 Austin, Alfred. "Mr. Matthew Arnold. Mr. Morris," *The Poetry of the Period.* London: Bentley, 1870.

43.28 Forman, H. Buxton. "William Morris," *Our Living Poets: An Essay in Criticism.* London: Tinsley, 1871.

For complete annotation see 74.1.

43.29 [Courthope, W. J.]. "The Latest Development of Literary Poetry: Swinburne, Rossetti, Morris," *Quarterly Review*, CXXXII (January 1872), 59–84.

For annotation see 29.17.

43.30 Mackail, J. W. "William Morris," in *The English Poets: Selections with Critical Introductions by Various Writers*, edited by T. H. Ward, vol. V. London: Macmillan, 1880.

For complete annotation see 84.3.

43.31 Hamilton, Walter. "William Morris," *The Æsthetic Movement in England.* London: Reeves and Turner, 1882.

For complete annotation see 78.2.

43.32 [Prinsep, Valentine C.]. "Morris: A Prophet Among the Painters," *Nation*, XXXIX (18 September 1884), 240–241; (25 September 1884), 261–262.

An early note on Morris' socialistic concepts.

43.33 Pater, Walter H. "Aesthetic Poetry," *Appreciations.* London: Macmillan, 1889.

Primarily on Morris. Dropped from the 1890 and later editions. Reprinted in *Bibelot*, V (October 1899), 303–319; and in Richard Aldington, ed., *Walter Pater: Selected Works* (London: Heinemann, 1948).

43.34 Forman, H. Buxton. "William Morris," in *The Poets and the Poetry of the Century*, edited by A. H. Miles, vol. [VI]. London: Hutchinson, [1891–1897].

For complete annotation see 84.5.

43.35 Crane, Walter. "William Morris: Poet, Artist and Craftsman, and Social Reconstructor," *Progressive Review*, I (November 1896), 148–152.

Obituary article. Morris "united Pre-Raphaelite vividness with a dream-like wistful sweetness and flowing narrative, woven in a kind of rich medieval tapestry of verse . . . "

43.36 Sharp, William. "William Morris: The Man and His Work," *Atlantic Monthly*, LXXVIII (December 1896), 768–781.

43.37 Symons, Arthur. "William Morris," *Studies in Two Literatures.* London: Smithers, 1897.

Contains other chapters on Christina Rossetti (44.35) and Thomas Gordon Hake (48.18). Reprinted in *Collected Works*, vol. VII (London: Wells, 1924).

43.38 Vallance, Aymer. *The Art of William Morris.* London: Bell, 1897.

A deluxe edition with forty color plates and a bibliographical appendix by Temple Scott, essentially the same as 43.2. In August 1897, Vallance brought out the less elaborate but greatly enlarged *William Morris, His Art, His Writings, and His Public Life: A Record*, with seven new chapters and revisions of earlier ones. The latter volume also included a "Chronological Survey of Morris's Printed Works," by Temple Scott.

43.39 Crane, Walter. "William Morris," *Scribner's Magazine*, XXII (July 1897), 88–99.
Relating Morris' art to his socialistic ideal.

43.40 Frantz, Henri. "Un Rénovateur de l'art industriel, William Morris," *Gazette des Beaux-Arts*, période 3, XVIII (December 1897), 503–509.

43.41 Crane, Walter. "Note on the Work and Life of William Morris," *Magazine of Art*, XX (1897), 89–91.

43.42 Richmond, Sir William Blake. *Leighton, Millais and William Morris: A Lecture Delivered to the Students of the Royal Academy*. London: Macmillan, 1898.
For annotation see 37.45.

43.43 Ricketts, Charles, and Lucien Pissarro. *De la typographie et de' l'harmonie de la page imprimée: William Morris et son influence sur les arts et métiers*. London: Vale Press, 1898.
Translated by Richard K. Kellenberger, "William Morris and His Influence on the Arts and Crafts," *Colby Library Quarterly*, III (1952), 69–75.

43.44 Day, Lewis Forman. *William Morris and His Art* (Easter Number of the *Art Journal*). London: Virtue, 1899.

43.45 Mackail, J. W. *The Life of William Morris*. 2 vols. London: Longmans, 1899.
Despite factual slips and obscurantism, particularly regarding Morris' socialistic activities with which Mackail was not in sympathy, still the standard biography.

43.46 Streeter, A. "William Morris and Pre-Raphaelitism," *Month*, XCIV (December 1899), 595–608.
For annotation see 77.14.

43.47 Kassner, Rudolf. "William Morris," *Die Mystik, die Künstler, und das Leben: über englische Dichter und Maler im 19. Jahrhundert*. Leipzig: Diederichs, 1900.
Reissued 1920 (Leipzig: Insel) with title *Englische Dichter*.

43.48 [Taylor, Una A.]. "William Morris and Dante Gabriel Rossetti," *Edinburgh Review*, CXCI (April 1900), 356–379.
A review-article on Rossetti's *Family Letters* (24.5), Mackail's *Life* (43.45), Vallance (43.38), and Bate's *Pre-Raphaelite Painters* (75.21). With a comparison of Morris and Rossetti.

43.49 Ashbee, C. R. *An Endeavour Towards the Teaching of John Ruskin and William Morris: Being a Brief Account of the Work, the Aims, and the Principles of the Guild of Handicraft in East London*. London: Arnold, 1901.

43.50 Kenyon, James B. "William Morris — Poet, Socialist, and Master of Many Crafts," *Loiterings in Old Fields: Literary Sketches*. New York: Eaton, 1901.
For complete annotation see 27.32.

43.51 Mackail, J. W. *William Morris: An Address*. London: Doves Press, 1901.
Reprinted *Bibelot*, VIII (September 1902), 297–333.

43.52 Sargent, Irene. [William Morris], *Craftsman*, I (October 1901), *passim*.
The entire issue, written solely by Irene Sargent, is devoted to Morris. Contains chapters on Morris' friendship with Burne-Jones, on Morris and Company, and on the opera *Patience* and the Aesthetic Movement. Volume II, by the same author, was devoted to Ruskin.

43.53 "The Kelmscott Press," *Connoisseur*, I (December 1901), 255–267.
This article contains (pp. 266–267) a complete list of Kelmscott books, with size, type, number issued, original price, and auction values.

43.54 Cary, Elizabeth Luther. *William Morris: Poet, Craftsman, Socialist*. New York: Putnam, 1902.

43.55 Chesterton, G. K. "William Morris and His School," *Twelve Types*. London: Humphreys, 1902.

Reprinted in America as *Varied Types* (New York: Dodd, Mead, 1903); also reprinted in *Simplicity and Tolstoy* (London: Humphreys, 1912).

43.56 Yeats, William Butler. "The Happiest of the Poets," *Ideas of Good and Evil*. London: Bullen, 1903.

Reprinted from *Fortnightly Review*, LXXIX, n.s. LXXIII (March 1903), 535–541. Reprinted *Bibelot*, XVIII (April 1912), 112–128.

43.57 Day, Lewis Forman. "William Morris and His Decorative Art," *Contemporary Review*, LXXXIII (June 1903), 787–796.

Same in *Living Age*, CCXXXVIII, 7th ser., XX, no. 3079 (11 July 1903), 102–109.

43.58 Prinsep, Valentine C. "The Oxford Circle: Rossetti, Burne-Jones, and William Morris. A chapter from a Painter's Reminiscence[s]," *Magazine of Art*, XXVII, n.s. II (1904), 167–172.

For further reminiscences by Prinsep see 25.27.

43.59 Weygandt, Cornelius. "Two Pre-Raphaelite Poets: William Morris and Dante Gabriel Rossetti," *Book News Monthly*, XXIV (June 1906), 687–690.

For other articles in the same issue of this journal see 67.26.

43.60 Dickinson, Thomas. "William Morris and Aesthetic Socialism," *Arena*, XXXVI (December 1906), 613–617.

Morris' social-aesthetic ideas were misinterpreted or simply not understood in his own day, even by the Social Democratic Federation and the Socialist League. Dickinson comments on the inconsistency of Morris' ideal of the utmost democracy and extreme individualism. "Not to make . . . art common but to make universal its impulse was the dream of his aesthetic socialism," not "Art for Art's Sake," but "Art for Man's Sake."

43.61 Mackail, J. W. *William Morris and His Circle.* Oxford: Clarendon Press, 1907.

Discusses, in a lecture on the Oxford Brotherhood, the influence of Rossetti and the secularization and socialization of Morris' mind during the Oxford days. Morris and Company he sees as an extension of the Oxford Brotherhood.

43.62 Schleinitz, Otto Julius Wilhelm von. "William Morris, sein Leben und Wirken," *Zeitschrift für Bücherfreunde*, XI (April 1907), 27–44; (May 1907), 59–78; (June 1907), 107–124; (July 1907), 146–165.

43.63 Brooke, Stopford A. *A Study of Clough, Arnold, Rossetti, and Morris, with an Introduction on the Course of Poetry from 1822–1852.* London: Pitman, 1908.

Also entitled *Four Poets: Clough, Arnold, Rossetti, and Morris.*

43.64 Jackson, Holbrook. *William Morris, Craftsman-Socialist.* London: Cape, 1908.

Revised, with four new chapters, 1926.

43.65 Noyes, Alfred. *William Morris* (English Men of Letters). London: Macmillan, [1908].

43.66 Durrant, William Scott. "The Influence of William Morris," *Westminster Review*, CLXIX (May 1908), 542–549.

43.67 Kellner, Leon. "William Morris," *Die englische Literatur im Zeitalter der Königin Viktoria*. Leipzig: Tauchnitz, 1909.

For annotation see 69.5.

43.68 Vallance, Aymer. *The Merton Abbey Arras Tapestries.* London: Morris and Company, 1909.

Reprinted from 42.82.

43.69 Watts-Dunton, Theodore. "Rossettiana: A Glimpse of Rossetti and Morris at Kelmscott," *English Review*, I (January 1909), 323–332.

43.70 Dodds, T. L. "William Morris: Handicraftsman, Socialist, Poet, and Novelist," *Liverpool Philomathic Society Proceedings*, LV (1909–1910), li–lxxx.

43.71 Crane, Walter. *William Morris to Whistler: Papers and Addresses on Arts and Crafts and the Commonweal.* London: Bell, 1911.

43.72 [Marillier, Henry Currie]. *A Brief Sketch of the Morris Movement and of the Firm Founded by William Morris to Carry Out His Designs and the Industries Revived or Started by Him: Written to Commemorate the Firm's Fiftieth Anniversary in June 1911.* London: Privately printed for Morris and Company, Decorators, Ltd., 1911.

43.73 Rowley, Charles. "William Morris," *Fifty Years of Work Without Wages.* London: Hodder and Stoughton, [1911]
For complete annotation see 26.4.

43.74 Jackson, Holbrook. "The Ideas of William Morris," *Bookman* (London), XXXIX (February 1911), 226–229.
There is no separation between the ideas and the art of William Morris. Numerous illustrations, including portraits.

43.75 Drinkwater, John. *William Morris: A Critical Study.* London: Secker, 1912.

43.76 Compton-Rickett, Arthur. *William Morris: A Study in Personality,* with an Introduction by R. B. Cunninghame Graham. London: Jenkins, 1913.
With an "Analytical Biography," that is, a comparative chronology.

43.77 [Marillier, Henry Currie]. *A Note on the Morris Stained Glass Work.* London: Privately printed for Morris & Company, Ltd., 1913.

43.78 *Stained Glass Windows.* London: Morris & Company Art Works, Ltd., n.d.
A list of Morris windows with a brief introduction.

43.79 Clutton-Brock, Arthur. *William Morris: His Work and Influence* (Home University Library of Modern Knowledge). London: Williams, 1914.

43.80 Dyce, Alan. "William Morris," *Sewanee Review,* XXII (July 1914), 257–275.

43.81 Watts-Dunton, Theodore. "William Morris," *Old Familiar Faces.* London: Jenkins, 1916.
Includes the obituary originally published in *Athenaeum,* no. 3598 (10 October 1896), pp. 486–488; and a review of Morris' poetry and prose from *Athenaeum,* no. 3191 (22 December 1888), pp. 843–846. For complete annotation see 64.2.

43.82 *Letters Addressed to Algernon Charles Swinburne, by John Ruskin, William Morris, Sir Edward Burne Jones and Dante Gabriel Rossetti.* London: Printed for private circulation for Thomas J. Wise, 1919.

43.83 Elton, Oliver. "William Morris," *A Survey of English Literature, 1830–1880.* Vol. II. London: Arnold, 1920.
For annotation see 69.11.

43.84 Vidalenc, G[eorge]. *William Morris (Art et esthétique).* Paris: Félix Alcan, 1920.

43.85 Glasier, John Bruce. *William Morris and the Early Days of the Socialist Movement: Being Reminiscences of Morris' Work as a Propagandist, and Observations on His Character and Genius, with Some Account of the Persons and Circumstances of the Early Socialist Agitation; Together with a Series of Letters Addressed by Morris to the Author.* With a Preface by May Morris. London: Longmans, 1921.

43.86 Hearn, Lafcadio. "William Morris," *Pre-Raphaelite and Other Poets: Lectures.* Selected and edited with an Introduction by John Erskine. New York: Dodd, Mead, 1922.
For complete annotation see 74.5.

43.87 Pundt, Herbert. "Dante Gabriel Rossettis Einfluss auf die Gedichte des jungen William Morris," unpub. diss. Breslau, 1922.

43.88 Broers, Bernarda C. "William Morris," *Mysticism in the Neo-Romanticists.* Amsterdam: Paris, 1923 (diss. Amsterdam, 1923).
For complete annotation see 73.8.

43.89 Sparling, Henry Halliday. *The Kelmscott Press and William Morris, Master-Craftsman.* London: Macmillan, 1924.

One of the most authoritative accounts of the Kelmscott Press. Reprints 43.3.

43.90 Wolff, Lucien. "Le Sentiment médiéval en Angleterre au XIXᵉ siècle et la première poésie de William Morris," *Revue Anglo-Américaine*, I (August 1924), 491–504; II (October 1924), 29–38.

43.91 Evans, B. Ifor. *William Morris and His Poetry* (Poetry and Life Series, edited by W. H. Hudson). London: Harrap, 1925.

43.92 Marillier, Henry Currie. "The Merton Abbey. William Morris' Great Revival," *Landmark*, VII (1925), 255–258.

43.93 Buchan, John. "Morris and Rossetti," *Homilies and Recreations*. London: Nelson, 1926.

43.94 Marillier, Henry Currie. *History of the Merton Abbey Tapestry Works Founded by William Morris*. London: Constable, 1927.
    With a section of illustrations. Many color reproductions of the tapestries.

43.95 Helmholtz-Phelan, Anna Augusta von. *The Social Philosophy of William Morris*. Durham, N.C.: Duke University Press, 1927.

43.96 Swinnerton, Frank. "Morris, Burne-Jones, Birmingham," *A London Bookman*. London: Secker, 1928.
    For annotation see 42.101.

43.97 Welby, T. Earle. *The Victorian Romantics, 1850–1870: The Early Work of Dante Gabriel Rossetti, William Morris, Burne-Jones, Swinburne, Simeon Solomon and Their Associates*. London: Howe, 1929.
    For discussion see Survey, pp. 30–31.

43.98 Farmer, Albert J. "Le Mouvement préraphaélite: Rossetti et Morris," *Le Mouvement esthétique et "décadent" en Angleterre (1873–1900)* (*Bibliothèque de la Revue de Littérature Comparée*, tome 75). Paris: Champion, 1931 (diss. Paris, 1931).

43.99 Marillier, Henry Currie. *The Morris Movement: A Lecture*. London: Privately printed by the Chiswick Press for Morris and Company, 1931.
    A lecture delivered at the Victoria and Albert Museum, 5 November 1931.

43.100 Murray, J. Middleton. "William Morris," in *The Great Victorians*, edited by H. J. and Hugh Massingham. London: Nicolson and Watson, 1932.

43.101 Davies, Frank. "William Morris's *Sir Peter Harpdon's End*," *Philological Quarterly*, XI (July 1932), 314–317.

43.102 Evans, B. Ifor. "William Morris," *English Poetry in the Later Nineteenth Century*. London: Methuen, 1933.
    For complete annotation see 74.7.

43.103 *Addresses Commemorating the One-Hundredth Anniversary of the Birth of William Morris: Delivered before the Yale Library Associates in the Sterling Memorial Library*. New Haven: Overbrook Press, 1934.
    Two lectures: "William Morris as Poet" by Chauncey Brewster Tinker (reprinted in 68.16); and "The Ordeal of William Morris" by Carl P. Rollins.

43.104 Bloomfield, Paul. *Life and Work of William Morris*. London: Barker, 1934.

43.105 —— *The Life of William Morris: Two Lectures Given Before the Royal Society of Arts*. London: Royal Society of Arts, 1934.
    Same in *Royal Society of Arts Journal*, LXXXII (21 September 1934), 1103–1116; (28 September 1934), 1119–1132.

43.106 Brinton, Mrs. Anna (Cox). *A Pre-Raphaelite Aeneid of Virgil in the Collection of Mrs. Edward Laurence Doheny of Los Angeles, being an Essay in Honor of the William Morris Centenary, 1934*. Los Angeles, California: Printed by Ward Ritchie, 1934.

43.107 Crow, Gerald H. *William Morris, Designer* (special Winter number of the *Studio*). New York: Studio Publications, 1934.
    Richly illustrated. Suggesting the broad scope of Morris' activities, associations, and influence.

43.108 *Some Appreciations of William Morris.* Walthamstow: Walthamstow Antiquarian Society, 1934.

Appreciations by Shaw, May Morris, J. W. Mackail, G. K. Chesterton, Herbert Read, H. C. Marillier, G. D. H. Cole, and others.

43.109 *Speeches in Commemoration of William Morris: Delivered at a Town's Meeting Held in the Bath's Hall, Walthamstow, on . . . March 24th 1934, by John Drinkwater, Holbrook Jackson, and Professor H. J. Laski.* London: Walthamstow Borough Council, 1934.

The three speeches included are "The Literary Influence of William Morris" (John Drinkwater), "William Morris and the Arts and Crafts Movement" (Holbrook Jackson), and "The Social Philosophy of William Morris" (H. J. Laski).

43.110 Weekly, Montague. *William Morris.* London: Duckworth, 1934.

43.111 Wiles, H. V. *William Morris of Walthamstow.* London: Walthamstow Press, 1934.

43.112 Calthrop, Herbert. "Topsy-Turvy," *Architect's Journal*, LXXIX (March 1934), 455–458.

On Morris, Jane Morris, and Rossetti.

43.113 Evans, B. Ifor. "William Morris, His Influence and Reputation," *Contemporary Review*, CXLV (March 1934), 315–323.

43.114 "In Memoriam: William Morris," *Philobiblon*, VII (1934), *passim.*

The Morris centenary number. Seven articles, two by May Morris (one a reworking of a B.B.C. broadcast). The entire issue stresses the importance of Morris as a maker of books. A number of Morris' letters to Joseph Batchelor (a paper maker) are included. The issue also contains a reprinting of Morris' "Note" and Cockerell's "Short Description" of the Kelmscott Press (43.3).

43.115 Weygandt, Cornelius. "William Morris," *The Time of Tennyson: English Victorian Poetry as it Affected America.* New York: Appleton-Century, 1936.

For complete annotation see 69.15.

43.116 Baldwin, Stanley. "William Morris," *The Torch of Freedom: Speeches and Addresses.* London: Hodder and Stoughton, 1937.

A lecture delivered at the William Morris Centenary exhibition at the Victoria and Albert Museum (13.7), 9 February 1934.

43.117 Lewis, C. S. "William Morris," *Rehabilitations and Other Essays.* London: Oxford University Press, 1939.

An interesting and incisive account and reappraisal of Morris as a poet and artist. More than other writers of the age, "Morris faced the facts . . . There are many writers greater than Morris. You can go on from him to all sorts of subtleties, delicacies, and sublimities which he lacks. But you can hardly go behind him." (p. 55)

43.118 Eshleman, Lloyd W. *A Victorian Rebel: The Life of William Morris.* New York: Scribner's, 1940.

Reissued as *William Morris, Prophet of England's New Order*, by L. E. Grey (London: Cassell, 1949).

43.119 Maurer, Oscar, Jr. "William Morris and the Poetry of Escape," in *Nineteenth Century Studies*, edited by Herbert Davies, William C. DeVane, and R. C. Bald. Ithaca, New York: Cornell University Press, 1940.

43.120 Lucas, F. L. "William Morris," *Ten Victorian Poets.* Cambridge University Press, 1942.

For complete annotation see 27.92.

43.121 Ford, George H. "Morris, Swinburne, and Some Others," *Keats and the Victorians: A Study of His Influence and Rise to Fame, 1821–1895.* New Haven: Yale University Press, 1944.

For complete annotation see 33.33.

43.122 Short, Clarice. "William Morris and Keats," *Publications of the Modern Language Association*, LIX (June 1944), 513–523.

Revised from an unpublished Master's thesis, Cornell University, 1941. "Stimulated by Rossetti to enthusiasm for Keats, Morris appears to have shared the Pre-Raphaelite penchant for drawing scenes from Keats' poems . . . When Morris' imagery was most concrete, it often resembled Keats' description of art objects, painting, sculpture, and architecture; when concise, Keats' images from nature; and when passionate, Keats' crucial scenes." (p. 514) Produces many close parallel passages from the poetry of Keats and Morris.

43.123 Grennan, Margaret R. *William Morris, Medievalist and Revolutionary*. New York: King's Crown Press, 1945.

43.124 Litzenberg, Karl. "William Morris and the 'Literary' Tradition," *Michigan Alumnus*, LIII (1946), 48–55.

43.125 Briggs, Martin S. "John Ruskin and William Morris," *Men of Taste*. London: Batsford, 1947.

43.126 De Carlo, Giancarlo. *William Morris*. Roma: Il Balcone, 1947.

43.127 Godwin, Edward and Stephani. *Warrior Bard: The Life of William Morris*. London: Harrap, 1947.
   A sentimental and romantic, superficial treatment of Morris and his Circle.

43.128 Masefield, John. "William Morris," *Thanks Before Going with Other Gratitude for Old Delight, Including A Macbeth Production and Various Papers Not before Printed*. London: Heinemann, 1947.

43.129 Meynell, Esther. *Portrait of William Morris*. London: Chapman and Hall, 1947.

43.130 Mitchell, Charles. "William Morris at St. James's Palace," *Architectural Review*, CI (January 1947), 2, 37–38.
   Reprinted (London: William Morris Society, 1960).

43.131 Jackson, Holbrook, "William Morris," *Dreamers of Dreams: The Rise and Fall of 19th Century Idealism*. London: Faber, 1948.

43.132 Thompson, Francis. "Pre-Raphaelite Morris," *Literary Criticisms*. Newly Discov-

ered and Collected by the Rev. Terence L. Connolly, S.J. New York: Dutton, 1948.
   For annotation see 77.16.

43.133 Young, George Malcolm. "Topsy," *Daylight and Champaign: Essays*. London: Hart-Davis, 1948.
   Reprinted in G. M. Young, *Victorian Essays*, Chosen and Introduced by W. D. Handcock (London: Oxford University Press, 1962). A review-article on 43.24.

43.134 Hough, Graham. "William Morris," *The Last Romantics*. London: Duckworth, 1949.
   For discussion see Survey, pp. 34–35.

43.135 Pevsner, Nikolaus. *Pioneers of Modern Design: From William Morris to Walter Gropius*. New York: Museum of Modern Art, 1949.
   First appeared as *Pioneers of the Modern Movement* (London: Faber, 1936). Reprinted (London: Penguin Books, 1960).

43.136 Prouting, Norman. "Morris and the Victorian Revival," *Apollo*, LIV (July 1951), 17–22; (August 1951), 51–56.
   Profusely illustrated.

43.137 Henderson, Philip. *William Morris* (Writers and Their Work, Pamphlet no. 85). London: Longmans, 1952.
   With a good working bibliography.

43.138 Wahl, John Robert. "Two Pre-Raphaelite Poets: Studies in the Poetry and Poetic Theory of William Morris and D. G. Rossetti," unpub. diss. Oxford University, 1954.

43.139 Dahl, Curtis. "Morris's 'The Chapel in Lyoness': An Interpretation," *Studies in Philology*, LI (July 1954), 482–491.

43.140 Floud, Peter. "William Morris as an Artist: A New View," *Listener*, LII (7 October 1954), 562–564.
   A B.B.C. Third Programme broadcast, 19 September 1954. An unorthodox view of Morris, emphasizing discrepancies between his artistic theories, in his writings, and his practices, as a designer of wallpapers and carpets. Morris is seen not as a revolutionary

innovator but as a Victorian classical designer.

43.141 —— "The Inconsistencies of William Morris," *Listener*, LII (14 October 1954), 615–617.

A B.B.C. Third Programme broadcast, 25 September 1954. Further evidence of contradictions between Morris' theories about art and his own practices. The paradox of Morris lay in his determined opposition to machine production, when, in fact, his own designs were best suited to machine multiplication, and they were in reality "serial handproduction[s] on a factory basis" rather than examples of individual craftwork.

43.142 Groom, Bernard. "Rossetti, Morris, and Swinburne," *The Diction of Poetry from Spenser to Bridges*. Toronto University Press, 1955.

43.143 Thompson, E. P. *William Morris, Romantic to Revolutionary*. London: Lawrence and Wishart, 1955. 2nd edition, 1961.

See Jessie Kocmanová, "Some Remarks on E. P. Thompson's Opinion of the Poetry of William Morris," *Philologica Pragensia*, no. 3. University of Prague, 1960.

43.144 Pevsner, Nikolaus. "William Morris, C. R. Ashbee and the Twentieth Century," *Manchester Review*, VII (Winter 1956), 437–458.

Originally appeared (in German) in *Deutsche Vierteljahrsschrift für Literaturwissenschaft und Geistesgeschichte* (1936). Translated by Evelyn Heaton.

43.145 Macleod, Robert Duncan. *William Morris as Seen by His Contemporaries*. London: Holmes, 1957.

43.146 Pevsner, Nikolaus. "Architecture and William Morris," *Journal of the Royal Institute of British Architects*, 3rd ser., LXIV (March 1957), 172–177.

43.147 *The Works of Geoffrey Chaucer: A Facsimile of the William Morris Kelmscott Chaucer, with the Original 87 Illustrations by Sir Edward Burne-Jones*, edited by John

T. Winterich. Cleveland: World Publishing Company, 1958.

With an Introduction and a Glossary.

43.148 Arnot, R. Page. *George Bernard Shaw and William Morris*. London: William Morris Society, 1958.

A lecture given at the general meeting with the Shaw Society on the occasion of the Shaw centenary, 11 May 1956.

43.149 McLean, Ruari. *Modern Book Design from William Morris to the Present Day*. London: Faber, 1958.

43.150 Ritchie, Ward. *William Morris and His Praise of Wine*. Los Angeles: Ward Ritchie Press, 1958.

Although Morris' poem has been previously printed (see 43.24), this pamphlet includes an unpublished rough draft of a sonnet by Morris which is scribbled on the reverse of one page of the "Praise of Wine" manuscript, owned by Mr. Ritchie.

43.151 *William Morris* (Victoria and Albert Museum Small Picture Book, no. 43). London: H. M. Stationery Office, 1958.

With a brief Introduction by Peter Floud.

43.152 Henderson, Philip. "La Belle Iseult," *The Saturday Book*, no. 18, edited by John Hadfield. London: Hutchinson, 1958.

On the Rossetti-Jane Morris affair. Jane is seen as a "mournful Pre-Raphaelite pin-up, created out of the fervid romantic imaginations of Morris and Rossetti to torment them both."

43.153 Henderson, Stephen E. "A Study of Visualized Detail in the Poetry of Tennyson, Rossetti, and Morris," unpub. diss. University of Wisconsin. *Dissertation Abstracts*, XX (1959), 1015.

43.154 Ehrsites, T. H. "William Morris and the Kelmscott Press," *American Book Collector*, X (March 1959), 1925.

43.155 Floud, Peter. "Dating Morris Patterns," *Architectural Review*, CXXVI (July 1959), 14–20.

Based on Patent Office registers (1832–1910) discovered by Floud. Illustrated.

43.156 Briggs, R. C. H. "A Note on the Monumental Brasses in the Church of St. Giles, Great Coxwell," *William Morris Society: Fourth Annual Report and Notes.* London: William Morris Society, 1959.
Illustrated.

43.157 Wahl, John Robert. "The Mood of Energy and the Mood of Idleness: A Note on *The Earthly Paradise*," *English Studies in Africa*, II (March 1959), 90–97.

43.158 Caflish, Max. *William Morris: Der Erneurer der Buchkunst.* Bern: Monotype Corporation, 1960.
A lecture given on 14 November 1958 at the Swiss National Library in Bern on the occasion of the *Typographical Adventure* exhibition (13.9).

43.159 Cole, G. D. H. *William Morris as a Socialist.* London: William Morris Society, 1960.
A lecture given to the William Morris Society at the Art Worker's Guild, 16 January 1957. With a "Memoir of Professor G. D. H. Cole" by H. D. Hughes.

43.160 Gordon, Walter Kelly. "A Critical Selected Edition of William Morris's *Oxford and Cambridge Magazine* (1856)," unpub. diss., University of Pennsylvania, 1960. *Dissertation Abstracts*, XXI (1961), 3781–3782.
Emphasizes the Pre-Raphaelite qualities of the magazine.

43.161 Jordon, R. Furneaux. *The Medieval Vision of William Morris.* London: William Morris Society, 1960.
A lecture given at the Victoria and Albert Museum, 14 November 1957.

43.162 Macdonald, Jean. *A Guide to Red House.* London: William Morris Society, 1960.
Issued on the occasion of the Society's garden party at Red House, May 1960. Further descriptions of this famous house are by Mark Girouard, "Red House, Bexley Heath, Kent," *Country Life*, CXXVII, no. 3302 (16

June 1960), 1382–1385; and Elizabet Stavenow, "Red House," *Arkitektur* (Stockholm), I (December 1959), 261–264.

43.163 Faulkner, Peter. "W. B. Yeats and William Morris," *Threshold*, IV (January 1960), 18–27.
See also Faulkner's Peter Floud Memorial essay, *William Morris and W. B. Yeats* (Dublin: Dolmen Press, 1962), and his article "Morris and Yeats," *Journal of the William Morris Society*, I, no. 3 (Summer 1963), 19–23.

43.164 Stedman, Jane W. "A Victorian in Iceland," *Opera News*, XXIV (20 February 1960), 8–9, 23.
A comparison of Morris' "Hill of Venus" with Wagner's *Tannhäuser*. For *Sigurd*, Morris drew principally on the Volsung Saga rather than on the Nibelungenlied, which was Wagner's primary source.

43.165 Sewter, A. C. "William Morris' Designs for Stained Glass," *Architectural Review*, CXXVII (March 1960), 196–200. Illustrated.

43.166 Perrine, Laurence. "Morris's Guenevere: An Interpretation," *Philological Quarterly*, XXXIX (April 1960), 234–241.
Morris does not condone Guenevere's conduct. "The poem is not Morris's defence of Guenevere, but Guenevere's defence of herself. Morris has merely taken one of Malory's characters in a moment of stress and brought her intensely alive. His task had been not to excuse or to blame, but to vivify." (p. 241)

43.167 Lowe, W. F. "Restoration of Morris Windows at the Victoria and Albert Museum," *Museum Journal*, LX (August 1960), 121–122.

43.168 Floud, Peter. "The Wallpaper Designs of William Morris," *Penrose Annual*, LIV (1960), 41–45 + 8 pp. illustrations.

43.169 Kocmanová, Jessie. "Two Uses of the Dream Form as a Means of Confronting the Present with the National Past," *Brno*

Studies in English. Vol. II. Prague: University of Brno, 1960.

On Morris' utopian allegories.

43.170 Stingle, Richard. "William Morris," *Association of Canadian University Teachers of English Report*, 1960, pp. 4–10.

". . . to read Morris aright, it seems to me, is to read him in terms of symbolic image and not in terms of allegory." (p. 5)

43.171 *The Journal of the William Morris Society.* Vol. I, Number 1, Winter 1961.

Scheduled to appear biannually, the *Journal* contains articles on Morris and his circle and a periodic survey of Morris scholarship. The second number was a memorial issue to the late Sir Sydney Cockerell, containing a bibliography of "The Published Writings of Sir Sydney Cockerell" and a check list of his letters to the public press. Numbers 3 and 4 appeared in the Summer 1963 and the Summer, 1964, respectively.

43.172 Lindsay, Jack. *William Morris, Writer.* London: William Morris Society, 1961.

A lecture given at Caxton Hall, 14 November 1958.

43.173 Lilienthal, Theodore. *A William Morris Press Goes West.* Berkley: Tamalpais Press, 1961.

This article, describing the purchase of Morris' Albion Proof Press No. 2331, now in the Huntington Library, first appeared in *Hoja Volante*, the quarterly publication of the Zamorano Club of Los Angeles.

43.174 Gray, Donald. "Arthur, Roland, Empedocles, Sigurd, and the Despair of Heroes in Victorian Poetry," *Boston University Studies in English*, V (Spring 1961), 1–17.

A study of four Victorian heroes who are unable to realize their ambitions to reshape the world.

43.175 Morris, Barbara. "William Morris. A Twentieth Century View of His Woven Textiles," *Handweaver & Craftsman*, XII (Spring 1961), 6–11, 54–55.

Illustrated with eight of Morris' original designs. See also Mrs. Morris' companion article, "William Morris, His Designs for Carpets and Tapestries," *Handweaver & Craftsman*, XII (Fall 1961), 18–21 +; illustrated.

43.176 Fairbank, Alfred. "William Morris and Calligraphy," *Journal of the William Morris Society*, I (Winter 1961), 5–6.

43.177 Sewter, A. C. "Notes on Morris & Co.'s Domestic Stained Glass," *Journal of the William Morris Society*, I (Winter 1961), 22–28.

43.178 Le Mire, Eugene D. "The Unpublished Lectures of William Morris: A Critical Edition, Including an Introductory Survey and a Calendar and Bibliography of Morris's Public Speeches," unpub. diss., Wayne State University, 1962. *Dissertation Abstracts*, XXIV (February 1964), 3325.

43.179 ———— "Morris' Reply to Whistler," *Journal of the William Morris Society*, I, no. 3 (Summer 1963), 3–10.

On Morris' lecture, *Of the Origins of Ornamental Art* (1886), which the author sees as an answer to Whistler's *Ten O'Clock* lecture and the clearest statement Morris made of his approach to Pre-Raphaelite principles.

43.180 Fredeman, William E. "William Morris & His Circle: A Selective Bibliography of Publications, 1960–1962," *Journal of the William Morris Society*, I, no. 4 (Summer 1964), 23–33.

Section 44

CHRISTINA GEORGINA ROSSETTI

1830–1894

[CBEL: III, 273–275, S594; DNB: XVII, 283–284
(Richard Garnett); EB: XXIII, 746–747 (Edmund
Gosse)]

Christina Rossetti's role in the Pre-Raphaelite Movement is not at all clear. She moved
in Pre-Raphaelite circles, and even modeled for Rossetti; but in most respects Christina
occupied a sphere completely her own. Certainly she was never, as one writer called her,
the Pre-Raphaelite Queen. Christina's poetry, at least the secular part of her canon, bears
traces of the Pre-Raphaelite influence, notably that of Dante Gabriel Rossetti, but on the
whole her poetry is clearer and more precise, though more restricted, than that generally
associated with the movement.

Goblin Market (1862) was the first volume of poems published by the Pre-Raphaelites
or their associates to receive general recognition, Morris' *Defence of Guenevere* having
fallen on critically deaf ears, and the poetry of *The Germ* (to the first three issues of
which Christina contributed as Ellen Alleyn) and *The Oxford and Cambridge Magazine*
having a limited, ephemeral vogue. The title poem of this volume has long been accepted as the most Pre-Raphaelite poem that Christina wrote, but in the most recent
exegesis of the poem, Lona Mosk Packer says that "Once *Goblin Market* is read as the
complex, rich, and meaningful work it actually is, the prevalent critical view that the
poem has the bright, clear, obvious pigmentation and the lightly woven surface texture
of a Pre-Raphaelite painting will no longer be tenable." (44.86, p. 375) Professor
Packer's reading of the poem in terms of the complexities of its "emotional relevance"
hardly disposes of its obvious Pre-Raphaelite characteristics, the principal one of which
is the accumulation of decorative detail, explicitly described. That it is employed for
symbolic (though private) effect is perfectly consistent with the uses to which ornamen-
tation is frequently put in both the painting and poetry of the Pre-Raphaelites. In addition, of course, "Goblin Market" echoes the ballad forms revived by the Pre-Raphaelites
(as B. Ifor Evans has pointed out, the poem raises problems not unlike those in "The
Ancient Mariner").

In the recurring melancholy and iteration of the death wish in Christina Rossetti's
poetry there is also the strong note of sadness that always lies just beneath the surface of
the beautiful in Pre-Raphaelite art. Frequently, too, the highly exotic quality of her
verse suggests a not un-Pre-Raphaelite application. But even in the 1862 volume, the
other side of Christina Rossetti impresses itself in the "Devotional Pieces" which occupy
an entire section of the volume. Her second work, *The Prince's Progress*, also shows
evidence of Pre-Raphaelite influence, and her later concern with the sonnet in her two
sequences draws its examples from Dante Gabriel Rossetti.

In her devotional poems, Pre-Raphaelitism has manifestly no part. The secular and
spiritual conflict with which Christina wrestled is dramatically demonstrated in the two
extremes of her poetry, and her struggle may in her mind have been associated with the

freedom of Gabriel, which, from her opposite nature, Christina might envy but never emulate.

* * *

44.1 Ehrsam, Theodore G., Robert H. Deily, and Robert M. Smith. "Christina Georgina Rossetti," *Bibliographies of Twelve Victorian Authors*. New York: Wilson, 1936.
For complete annotation see 1.5.

* * *

44.2 Rossetti, Christina Georgina. *Verses.* Dedicated to her Mother. London: Privately printed at G. Polidori's, 1847.
Reprinted by the Eragny Press, 1906, edited by J. D. Symon.

44.3 ———— *Goblin Market and Other Poems.* With Two Designs by D. G. Rossetti. London: Macmillan, 1862. 2nd edition, 1865. See Plate II.

44.4 ———— *The Prince's Progress and Other Poems*. With Two Designs by D. G. Rossetti. London: Macmillan, 1866.

44.5 ———— *Commonplace and Other Short Stories.* London: Ellis, 1870.

44.6 ———— *Sing-Song: A Nursery Rhyme Book.* With 120 Illustrations by Arthur Hughes, Engraved by the Brothers Dalziel. London: Routledge, 1872. 2nd edition, Macmillan, 1893.

44.7 ———— *Speaking Likenesses*. With Pictures Thereof by Arthur Hughes. London: Macmillan, 1874.

44.8 *Goblin Market, The Prince's Progress, and Other Poems*. New Edition. With Four Designs by D. G. Rossetti. London: Macmillan, 1875.

44.9 ———— *A Pageant and Other Poems.* London: Macmillan, 1881.

44.10 ———— *Poems: New and Enlarged Edition*. With Four Designs by D. G. Rossetti. London: Macmillan, 1890.

44.11 ———— *Verses.* London: SPCK, 1893.
Reprinted from *Called to be Saints* (1881),

Time Flies (1885), and *The Face of the Deep* (1892), devotional works by Christina Rossetti, all SPCK publications.

44.12 ———— *New Poems, Hitherto Unpublished or Uncollected*, edited by William M. Rossetti. London: Macmillan, 1896.

44.13 ———— *Maude: A Story for Girls.* With an Introduction by William M. Rossetti. London: James Bowden, 1897.

44.14 ———— *The Poetical Works.* With Memoir and Notes by William M. Rossetti. London: Macmillan, 1904.
The standard edition of Christina Rossetti's poetry. The Introduction by W. M. Rossetti contains a check list of portraits of Christina Rossetti.

* * *

44.15 Rossetti, William Michael, ed. *The Family Letters of Christina Georgina Rossetti, with Some Supplementary Letters and Appendices.* London: Brown, Langham, 1908.
Contains, besides the many letters to and from Christina Rossetti and various members of the family, selections from William Michael Rossetti's diary (1871–1895) pertaining to Christina Rossetti, and extracts from a diary kept by Christina Rossetti and her mother (1881–1886).

44.16 Troxell, Janet Camp, ed. *Three Rossetti: Unpublished Letters to and from Dante Gabriel, Christina, William.* Cambridge, Mass.: Harvard University Press, 1937.
For annotation see 24.18.

* * *

44.17 "Poems by Mr. and Miss Rossetti," *Ecclesiastic and Theologian*, XXIV (September 1862), 419–429.
Review of *The Early Italian Poets* and *Goblin Market*. Of Christina Rossetti's book, "illustrated with two rather grotesque woodcuts exceedingly Prae-Raphaelesque in character": ". . . its author [may] yet give to the reading public something better than

anything in the book before us." (p. 429) See 29.3.

44.18 Norton, Mrs. Charles Eliot. " 'The Angel in the House' and 'The Goblin Market,' " *Macmillan's Magazine*, VIII (September 1863), 398–404.
A review with numerous quotations. Same in *Living Age*, LXXIX, 3rd ser., XXIII, no. 1011 (17 October 1863), 124–129.

44.19 [Rudd, F. A.] "Christina Rossetti," *Catholic World*, IV (March 1867), 839–846.

44.20 [Forman, H. Buxton]. "Criticisms on Contemporaries: No. VI. The Rossettis. Part I. [Christina Rossetti]," *Tinsley's Magazine*, V (August 1869), 59–67.
Reprinted in *Our Living Poets* (74.1).

44.21 Lubbock, Percy. "Christina Rossetti," in *The English Poets: Selections with Critical Introductions by Various Writers*, edited by T. H. Ward. Vol. V. London: Macmillan, 1880.
For complete annotation see 84.3.

44.22 [Symons, Arthur]. "Miss Rossetti's Poetry," *London Quarterly Review*, LXVIII, 2nd ser., VII (July 1887), 338–350.

44.23 ——— "Christina G. Rossetti," *The Poets and the Poetry of the Century*, edited by A. H. Miles. Vol. [VII]. London: Hutchinson, [1891–1897].
For complete annotation see 84.5.

44.24 Nash, Joseph J. Glendinning. *A Memorial Sermon Preached at Christ Church, Woburn Square . . . , for the Late Christina G. Rossetti*. London: Skeffington, 1895.

44.25 Noble, James Ashcroft. "The Burden of Christina Rossetti," *Impressions and Memories*. London: Dent, 1895.

44.26 Proctor, Ellen A. *A Brief Memoir of Christina G. Rossetti*. London: SPCK, 1895.
With a brief Preface by William M. Rossetti.

44.27 Watts [-Dunton], Theodore. "Reminiscences of Christina Rossetti," *Nineteenth Century*, XXXVII (February 1895), 355–366.

44.28 Coleridge, Christobel R. "The Poetry of Christina Rossetti," *Monthly Packet*, LXXXIX (March 1895), 276–282.

44.29 Meynell, Alice. "Christina Rossetti," *New Review*, XII (February 1895), 201–206.
Same in *Living Age*, CCIV, 6th ser., V, no. 2643 (2 March 1895), 569–572.

44.30 Law, Alice. "The Poetry of Christina G. Rossetti," *Westminster Review*, CXLIII (April 1895), 444–453.
Stresses Pre-Raphaelite tendencies — aestheticism, mysticism, melancholy, medieval coloring — in Christina Rossetti's poetry.

44.31 Sharp, William. "Some Reminiscences of Christina Rossetti," *Atlantic Monthly*, LXXV (June 1895), 736–749.
Reprinted in 27.50.

44.32 Johnson, M. "Christina Rossetti," *Primitive Methodist Quarterly Review*, XXXVII, n.s. XVII (July 1895), 469–481.

44.33 Benson, Arthur C. "Christina Rossetti," *Essays*. New York: Macmillan, 1896.
Same in *National Review*, XXIV (February 1895), 753–763; and in *Living Age*, CCIV, 6th ser., V, no. 2644 (9 March 1895), 620–626.

44.34 Gosse, Edmund. "Christina Rossetti," *Critical Kit-Kats*. London: Heinemann, 1896.
Reprinted from *Century Magazine*, XLVI, n.s. XXIV (June 1893), 211–217. Reprinted in *Selected Essays: First Series* (London: Heinemann, 1928). "As a religious poet of our time she has no rival but Cardinal Newman." Praises Christina Rossetti's sonnets above even those of Dante Gabriel. "To find her exact parallel . . . we must go back to the middle of the seventeenth century. She is the sister of George Herbert; she is of the family of Crashaw, of Vaughan, of Wither." (p. 156) The essay as it appears in *Critical Kit-Kats* contains an obituary account, not, of course, part of the version as originally published.

44.35 Symons, Arthur. "Christina Rossetti," *Studies in Two Literatures*. London: Smithers, 1897.

For complete annotation see 43.37.

44.36 Bell, Mackenzie. *Christina Rossetti: A Biographical and Critical Study*. London: Thomas Burleigh, 1898.

Despite its age, still one of the basic works on Christina Rossetti. The volume contains a detailed bibliography of the poetess by J. P. Anderson and a chronological list of portraits and photographs.

44.37 Westcott, Brooke Foss. *An Appreciation of the Late Christina Georgina Rossetti*. London: SPCK, 1899.

44.38 Livingston, L. S. "First Books of Some English Authors. III. Dante Gabriel and Christina Rossetti," *Bookman* (New York), X (November 1899), 245–247.

44.39 "The Christina Rossetti Memorial. Sir Edward Burne-Jones's Last Work," *Magazine of Art*, XXII (1899), 88–90.

A description, with illustrations, of Burne-Jones's decorations for Christina Rossetti's memorial in Christ Church, Woburn Square, where she attended church for nearly twenty years.

44.40 Cary, Elizabeth Luther. *The Rossettis: Dante Gabriel and Christina*. New York: Putnam, 1900.

44.41 Kenyon, J. B. "Rossetti and His Sister Christina," *Loiterings in Old Fields: Literary Sketches*. New York: Eaton, 1901.

For complete annotation see 27.32.

44.42 More, Paul Elmer. "Christina Rossetti," *Shelburne Essays: Third Series*. New York: Putnam, 1905.

44.43 Agresti-Rossetti, Olivia. "Cristina-Giorgina Rossetti," *Nuova Antologia*, CCVII, 5th ser., CXXIII (May 1906), 37–52.

44.44 Breme, Mary Ignatia. *Christina Rossetti und der Einfluss der Bibel auf ihre Dichtung: Eine literarisch-stilistische Untersuchung* (*Münstersche Beiträge zur englischen Literaturgeschichte*, no. 4). Münster: Schöningh, 1907.

44.45 Hueffer, Ford Madox. "Christina Rossetti and Pre-Raphaelite Love," *Memories and Impressions: A Study in Atmospheres*. New York: Harper, 1911.

For annotation see 77.55.

44.46 ———. "Christina Rossetti," *Fortnightly Review*, XCV, n.s. LXXXIX (March 1911), 422–429.

44.47 Olivero, Federico. "Poeti mistici, Christina Rossetti," *Saggi di letteratura inglese*. Bari: Laterza, 1913.

44.48 Lowther, George. "Christina Rossetti," *Contemporary Review*, CIV (November 1913), 681–689.

44.49 Venkatesan, N. K. *Christina Georgina Rossetti: An Essay*. Madras: Srinivasa Varadachari, 1914.

Reprinted from *Educational Review* (Madras), XIX (May 1913), 269–276; XX (April 1914), 221–230; (August 1914), 477–484; (September 1914), 539–549.

44.50 Mason, Eugene. "Two Christian Poets, Christina G. Rossetti and Paul Verlaine," *A Book of Preferences in Literature*. London: Wilson, 1915.

44.51 Watts-Dunton, Theodore. "Christina Georgina Rossetti," *Old Familiar Faces*. London: Jenkins, 1916.

Includes the obituary originally published in the *Athenaeum*, no. 3506 (5 January 1895), pp. 16–18; and a review of *New Poems* from the *Athenaeum*, no. 3564 (15 February 1896), pp. 207–209. For complete annotation see 64.2.

44.52 Parker, Elizabeth. "The Love Affairs of Christina Rossetti," *University Magazine* [McGill, Toronto, Dalhousie] XVIII (April 1919), 246–255.

On James Collinson and Charles Cayley.

44.53 Wilde, Justine Frederike de. *Christina Rossetti, Poet and Woman*. Nijkerk: Callenbach, 1923 (diss. Amsterdam, 1923).

44.54 De la Mare, Walter. "Christina Rossetti," *Essays by Divers Hands* (Transactions of the Royal Society of Literature. n.s. VI). London: Oxford University Press, 1926.

44.55 Birkhead, Edith. *Christina Rossetti and Her Poetry.* London: Harrap, 1930.

44.56 Sanders, Mary Frances. *The Life of Christina Rossetti.* London: Hutchinson, [1930].

44.57 Stuart, Dorothy. *Christina Rossetti* (English Men of Letters). London: Macmillan, 1930.

44.58 Rossetti, Geoffrey W. "Christina Rossetti," *Criterion*, X (October 1930), 95–117.

A perceptive article by Christina Rossetti's nephew. With quotations from a few of the poet's letters. See 44.89.

44.59 Green, Kathleen Conygham. "Christina Georgina Rossetti: a Study and Some Comparisons," *Cornhill Magazine*, n.s. LXIX (December 1930), 662–670.

There is an artlessness in Christina Rossetti that transcends all but the greatest art. A centenary study.

44.60 Kent, Muriel. "Christina Rossetti: A Reconsideration," *Contemporary Review*, CXXXVIII (December 1930), 759–767.

A centenary study.

44.61 Waugh, Arthur. "Christina Rossetti, December 5, 1830; December 5, 1930," *Nineteenth Century*, CVIII (December 1930), 787–798.

Pre-Raphaelitism is seen as an interlude in Christina Rossetti's career, when "engulfed in the turbulent waters" of the movement she produced in *Goblin Market* and *The Prince's Progress* two uncharacteristic books which are "deliberate exercises in poetic expression" and "uncongenial to her native genius." A short note on Christina Rossetti by Waugh appeared in *Reticence in Literature* (London: Wilson, 1915).

44.62 Woolf, Virginia. "I am Christina Rossetti," *Nation and Athenaeum*, XLVIII (6 December 1930), 322–324.

Reprinted in *Second Common Reader* (New York: Harcourt, Brace, 1932). A centenary study and a review of Sanders' *Life* (44.56).

44.63 Shove, Fredegond. *Christina Rossetti: A Study.* Cambridge University Press, 1931.

44.64 Stuart, Dorothy. *Christina Rossetti* (English Association Pamphlet, no. 78). London: Oxford University Press, 1931.

44.65 Thomas, Eleanor Walter. *Christina Georgina Rossetti.* New York: Columbia University Press, 1931 (diss. Columbia, 1931).

With a good working bibliography.

44.66 Zabel, Morton D. "Christina Rossetti and Emily Dickinson," *Poetry*, XXXVII (January 1931), 213–216.

A centenary comparison: "They lived in different worlds but each found in isolation the fulfilment of high lyric impulse."

44.67 Morse, B. J. "Some Notes on Christina Rossetti and Italy," *Anglia*, LV, n.s. XLIII (1931), 101–105.

Denying the insularity generally ascribed to Christina Rossetti, this author notes that she never wrote a single impassioned poem on England.

44.68 Klenk, Hans. *Nachwirkungen Dante Gabriel Rossettis: Untersuchungen an Werken von Christina Rossetti, Coventry Patmore, Philip Bourke Marston, Theodore Watts-Dunton, Arthur W. E. O'Shaughnessy, Ernest Dowson, John Davidson.* Berlin: Bachmann, 1932 (diss. Erlangen, 1932).

44.69 Teasdale, Sara. *Christina Rossetti.* New York: Macmillan, 1932.

44.70 Waller, R. D. "The Young Rossettis: Christina," *The Rossetti Family, 1824–1854.* Manchester University Press, 1932.

For complete annotation see 26.10.

44.71 Dubslaff, Friedrich. *Die Sprachform der Lyrik Christina Rossettis* (Studien zur englischen Philologie, no. 77). Halle: Niemeyer, 1933 (diss. Göttingen, 1933).

44.72 Evans, B. Ifor. "Christina Georgina Rossetti," *English Poetry in the Later Nineteenth Century*. London: Methuen, 1933.
For complete annotation see 74.7.

44.73 Morse-Boycott, Desmond L. "Christina Rossetti, 1830–1894," *Lead Kindly Light: Studies of the Saints and Heroes of the Oxford Movement*. New York: Macmillan, 1933.

44.74 Evans, B. Ifor. "The Sources of Christina Rossetti's 'Goblin Market,'" *Modern Language Review*, XXVIII (April 1933), 156–165.
In *Goblin Market* the poetry of the Pre-Raphaelites and their associates first gained attention. An attempt to trace the sources of *Goblin Market* to Thomas Keightley's *The Fairy Mythology*, to William Allingham's "The Fairies," to the *Arabian Nights*, and to various books by William Hone. See also 44.86.

44.75 Shipton, Irene M. "Christina Rossetti: The Poetess of the Oxford Movement," *Church Quarterly Review*, CXVI (July 1933), 219–229.
Miss Shipton fails to provide a convincing argument to substantiate her title. Save for noting Christina Rossetti's ascetic tendencies and observing that "the motive-power of Christina's life was religious" (p. 222), she does not substantiate it at all.

44.76 Green, Zaidee Eudora. "Saint by Chance," *English Review*, LXII (March 1936), 330–337.
A silly article, arguing that Christina Rossetti consciously assumed the role of saint (restraining an intensely passionate nature and playing the martyr in her two love affairs) after her accidental canonization by the PRB. That is, that she began "to play the role of the virgin to measure up to her brother's famous painting." (p. 333)

44.77 Lucas, F. L. "Christina Rossetti," *Ten Victorian Poets*. Cambridge University Press, 1942.
For complete annotation see 27.92.

44.78 Belloc, Elizabeth. "Christina Rossetti," *Catholic World*, CLV (September 1942), 674–678.
For comparison see 44.19.

44.79 Robb, Nesca Adeline. "Christina Rossetti," *Four in Exile*. London: Hutchinson, [1948].

44.80 Bowra, C. M. "Christina Rossetti," *The Romantic Imagination*. Cambridge, Mass.: Harvard University Press, 1949.
A lecture given during 1948–1949, when Bowra was Charles Eliot Norton Professor of Poetry at Harvard University. "Christina Rossetti presents in a remarkable manner the case of a poet whose naturally romantic tendencies were turned into a different channel by the intensity of her religious faith." (p. 269) See also 28.36.

44.81 Zaturenska, Marya. *Christina Rossetti: A Portrait with a Background*. New York: Macmillan, 1949.

44.82 Sawtell, Margaret. *Christina Rossetti, Her Life and Religion*. London: Mowbray, 1955.

44.83 Garlitz, Barbara. "Christina Rossetti's 'Sing Song' and Nineteenth Century Children's Poetry," *Publications of the Modern Language Association*, LXX (June 1955), 539–543.

44.84 Fairchild, Hoxie Neale. "Christina Georgina Rossetti," *Religious Trends in English Poetry. Vol. IV: 1830–1880. Christianity and Romanticism in the Victorian Era*. New York: Columbia University Press, 1957.

44.85 Packer, Lona Mosk. "Beauty for Ashes: A Biographical Study of Christina Rossetti's Poetry," unpub. diss., University of California, 1957.

44.86 ———— "Symbol and Reality in Christina Rossetti's *Goblin Market*," *Publications of the Modern Language Association*, LXXIII (September 1958), 375–385.
Goblin Market is not just a "Pre-Raphaelite masterpiece which combines a realistic use of detail with the vague symbolism and re-

ligiosity of a Blessed Damozel." (p. 375) Rather it should be seen as a symbolic, yet realistically treated, manifestation of Christina Rossetti's own frustrations in her love for William Bell Scott. The article provides a detailed explication of the poem together with comparisons from Christina Rossetti's other works. Speculative but highly provocative.

44.87 ——— "Christina Rossetti and Alice Boyd of Penkill Castle," *Times Literary Supplement*, no. 2991 (26 June 1959), p. 389.
Unpublished letters from Christina Rossetti to Alice Boyd.

44.88 ——— "The Protestant Existentialism of Christina Rossetti," *Notes & Queries*, CCIV, n.s. VI (June 1959), 213–215.

44.89 ——— "Christina Rossetti's Correspondence with Her Nephew: Some Unpublished Letters," *Notes & Queries*, CCIV, n.s. VI (December 1959), 425–432.

44.90 Swann, Thomas Burnett. *Wonder and Whimsey: The Fantastic World of Christina Rossetti*. Francestown, New Hampshire: Marshall Jones, 1960.

44.91 Putt, S. Gorley. "Christina Rossetti, Alms-giver," *English*, XIII (Autumn 1961), 222–223.
A brief record of nine letters, now in the Yale University Library, from Christina Rossetti to William Bryant of Clerkenwell, "an expert (so it would seem) in the art of begging letters." Only one letter is quoted in full.

44.92 Packer, Lona Mosk. "Christina Rossetti's 'Songs in a Cornfield': A Misprint Uncorrected," *Notes & Queries*, CCVII, n.s. IX (March 1962), 97–100.
An interesting piece of textual criticism, with information concerning Rossetti's participation in the publication of *The Prince's Progress*. The article includes two previously unpublished letters from Rossetti to Macmillan, and another from Christina Rossetti to

her publisher dealing with Rossetti's designs for the volume.

44.93 ——— "F. S. Ellis and the Rossettis: A Publishing Venture and Misadventure, 1870," *Western Humanities Review*, XVI (Summer 1962), 243–253.
On Christina Rossetti's change of publishers, from Macmillan to Ellis, in 1870. Her decision was influenced primarily by D. G. Rossetti's attempt to "gather together under one publishing banner . . . 'a little knot of congenial writers,' that is, a literary coterie of producing poets," including Morris, the Rossettis, Swinburne, and W. B. Scott. The article, a chapter from the author's biography of Christina Rossetti (44.94), draws on unpublished letters in the British Museum.

44.94 ——— *Christina Rossetti*. Berkeley: University of California Press, 1963.
A biographical examination of Christina Rossetti focusing on her poetry. Drawing on a variety of previously unused and unpublished manuscript sources, including the notebooks in the British Museum and the Bodleian, Professor Packer arrives at a reading of Christina Rossetti's life and poetry that is psychologically of major importance. She identifies William Bell Scott, the minor Pre-Raphaelite poet and intimate associate of her two brothers, as the innominate lover in Christina Rossetti's life. A controversial volume, this biography depends too exclusively on unsupportable conjecture in pressing the case for Scott as the inspirational source of Christina's poetry. See also 44.85 and 44.86 and the Introduction to Christina Rossetti (section 44).

44.95 ———, ed. *The Rossetti-Macmillan Letters: Some 133 Unpublished Letters Written to Alexander Macmillan, F. S. Ellis, and Others, by Dante Gabriel, Christina, and William Michael Rossetti, 1861–1889*. Berkeley: University of California Press, 1963.
Sixty-eight letters from Christina Rossetti.

44.96 ——— "Swinburne and Christina Rossetti: Atheist and Anglican," *University of Toronto Quarterly* XXXIII (October 1963), 30–42.

Section 45

JOHN RUSKIN

1819–1900

[CBEL: III, 691–707, S669–671; DNB: XXII, S,
1177–1199 (E. T. Cook); EB: XXIII, 858–861
(Frederic Harrison)]

Enough has been said about John Ruskin in the Survey (pp. 9–13) to make extensive discussion of him at this point unnecessary. A detailed bibliography of Ruskin is not really pertinent to the present study. His influence on the Brotherhood is indisputable, and his role in the subsequent reception and critical appraisal of Pre-Raphaelitism must be understood if the movement is to be seen in its proper perspective. The works on Ruskin which are included in this section have, in general, some relation to his connection with the Pre-Raphaelites, but the standard biographies, most of which discuss this connection, have also been included, together with a few works which treat the aesthetic principles that governed his criticism of the arts. Of Ruskin's works, only the massive and magnificent Cook and Wedderburn edition and two separate works are cited. His specific writings on the Pre-Raphaelites can be located through the Index. Anyone interested in a more detailed bibliography should consult the standard bibliography (vol. XXXVIII of the *Works*, 45.3). For Ruskin's own writings, the *Bibliography* edited by Thomas J. Wise (London, 1889–1893) may prove more convenient and almost as useful.

* * *

45.1 Ruskin, John. *Notes on Some of the Principal Pictures Exhibited in the Rooms of the Royal Academy* . . . . Vols. I–V. London: Smith, Elder, 1855–1859.
Commonly referred to as *Academy Notes*.

45.2 ——— *The Art of England: Lectures Given in Oxford.* Orpington: Allen, 1883.
The first two lectures are of primary importance: I. "Realistic Schools of Painting: D. G. Rossetti and W. Holman Hunt" (30.3, 36.24). II. "Mythic Schools of Painting: E. Burne-Jones and G. F. Watts" (42.11, 63.1). The occasion of the lectures was Ruskin's reappointment as Slade Professor of Art at Oxford.

45.3 Cook, E. T., and A. D. O. Wedderburn, eds. *The Works of John Ruskin: Library Edition.* 39 vols. London: Allen, 1902–1912.

* * *

45.4 Rossetti, William Michael. "Ruskin as a Writer on Art," *Broadway*, n.s. II (March 1869), 48–59.

45.5 B[edford], H. "Mr. Ruskin as an Art Critic," *Month*, XV (July–August 1871), 26–47.
Concentrates primarily on *Modern Painters*.

45.6 Hamilton, Walter. "John Ruskin," *The Æsthetic Movement in England.* London: Reeves and Turner, 1882.
For complete annotation see 78.2.

45.7 Collingwood, W. G. *The Life and Works of John Ruskin.* 2 vols. London: Methuen, 1893.
Abridged edition, 1900.

45.8 Chesneau, Ernest. "Peintres anglais contemporains: L'Esthétique préraphaélite. Le 'Germ.' John Ruskin," *L'Art*, LIX, 20ᵉ année, tome IV (1894), 564–587.

45.9 La Sizeranne, Robert de. *Ruskin et la religion de la beauté*. Paris: Hachette, 1897. Translated into English by the Countess of Galloway (London: Allen, 1899).

45.10 Rossetti, William Michael, ed. *Ruskin: Rossetti: Pre-Raphaelitism. Papers 1854 to 1862*. London: Allen, 1899.
For annotation see 72.6.

45.11 Meynell, Alice. *John Ruskin*. Edinburgh: Blackwood, 1900.

45.12 Parkes, Kineton. "Ruskin and Pre-Raphaelitism," *New Century Review*, VII (February 1900), 133–143.
For annotation see 77.40.

45.13 Ashbee, C. R. *An Endeavour Towards the Teaching of John Ruskin and William Morris: Being a Brief Account of the Work, the Aims, and the Principles of the Guild of Handicraft in East London*. London: Arnold, 1901.

45.14 McCarthy, Justin. "Ruskin and the Pre-Raphaelites," *Portraits of the Sixties*. London: Unwin, 1903.
For annotation see 77.41.

45.15 Fenn, W. W. "Ruskin and Millais in Scotland: A Memory of Ruskin," *Chambers's Journal*, 6th ser., VIII (September 1905), 645–647.

45.16 Milsand, J. *L'Esthétique anglaise: Étude sur Mr. John Ruskin*. 2nd ed. Lausanne: Frankfurter, 1906.
The first edition was published in Paris by Baillère in 1864.

45.17 Earland, Ada. *Ruskin and His Circle*. New York: Putnam's, 1910.
Discusses Ruskin's role in the acceptance of Pre-Raphaelitism and his relationship with several of the Pre-Raphaelites, including Rossetti, Burne-Jones, and Morris.

45.18 Cook, E. T. *Life of John Ruskin*. 2 vols. London: Allen, 1911.

45.19 *Letters Addressed to Algernon Charles Swinburne, by John Ruskin, William Morris, Sir Edward Burne-Jones and Dante Gabriel Rossetti*. London: Printed for private circulation for Thomas J. Wise, 1919.

45.20 Colvin, Sidney. "John Ruskin," *Memories and Notes of Persons and Places, 1852–1912*. London: Arnold, 1921.
For complete annotation see 25.52.

45.21 Shuster, George N. "Ruskin, Pater, and the Pre-Raphaelites," *The Catholic Spirit in Modern English Literature*. London: Macmillan, 1922.

45.22 Wilenski, R. H. "Technique of the Pre-Raphaelites: The Daguerreotype and Ruskin," *The Modern Movement in Art*. London: Faber, 1927. Revised edition, 1935. See 76.4.

45.23 Williams-Ellis, Amabel. *The Tragedy of John Ruskin*. London: Cape, 1928.

45.24 Rosenblatt, Louise. "La Défense du beau: Ruskin et les Préraphaélites," *L'Idée de l'art pour l'art dans la littérature anglaise pendant la période victorienne* (*Bibliothèque de la Revue de Littérature Comparée*, tome 70). Paris: Champion, 1931 (diss. Paris, 1931).

45.25 Ladd, H. A. *The Victorian Morality of Art: An Analysis of Ruskin's Aesthetic*. New York: Long and Smith, 1932.
The best work available on Ruskin's aesthetic theories.

45.26 Wilenski, R. H. "John Ruskin," in *The Great Victorians*, edited by H. J. and H. Massingham. London: Nicolson and Watson, 1932.

45.27 Wilenski, R. H. *John Ruskin: An Introduction to the Further Study of His Life and Works*. London: Faber, 1933.

45.28 Curtin, Frank Daniel. "Aesthetics in English Social Reform: Ruskin and His Followers," in *Nineteenth Century Studies*, edited by Herbert Davies, William C. DeVane, and R. C. Bald. Ithaca, New York: Cornell University Press, 1940.

45.29 Ironside, Robin. "Pre-Raphaelite

Paintings at Wallington: A note on William Bell Scott and Ruskin," *Architectural Review*, XCII (December 1942), 147–149.

For annotation see 79.20.

45.30 ——— "The Art Criticism of Ruskin," *Horizon*, VIII (July 1943), 8–20.

"The defenceless and . . . voracious sensibility by which Ruskin was continually either oppressed or exalted, must be considered not only as explaining but also as excusing, the laughable, sometimes touching, puerilities of phrase and thought which weaken, at too many points, usually at the least opportune, the great but ill-sustained beauty of his judgements." (p. 8)

45.31 Briggs, Martin S. "John Ruskin and William Morris," *Men of Taste*. London: Batsford, 1947.

45.32 James, Sir William Milburne, ed. *John Ruskin and Effie Gray: The Story of John Ruskin, Effie Gray, and John Everett Millais, Told for the First Time in Their Unpublished Letters*. New York: Scribner's, 1947.

Appeared in England as *The Order of Release* (London: Murray, 1948). A selection from 633 letters, edited with an Introduction and running commentary. Appeared in part as "Ruskin and Effie Gray; Extracts from an Unpublished Correspondence," *Cornhill Magazine*, CLXII (Winter 1946), 163–178; (Spring 1947), 258–274. See also 45.34. For Whitehouse's reply to James' indictment see 45.39.

45.33 Roudolphi, Marthe A. P. "Ruskin et le Préraphaélisme." Unpublished dissertation (Doctorat ès Lettres), University of Paris, 1947.

45.34 Quennell, Peter, ed. "Ruskin and the Women," *Atlantic Monthly*, CLXXIX (February 1947), 37–45.

Letters relating to the Ruskin, Effie Gray, Millais triangle. See 45.32.

45.35 Jackson, Holbrook. "Ruskin," *Dreamers of Dreams: The Rise and Fall of 19th Century Idealism*. London: Faber 1948.

45.36 Jump. J. D. "Ruskin's Reputation in the Eighteen-Fifties: The Evidence of the Three Principal Weeklies," *Publications of the Modern Language Association*, LXIII (June 1948), 678–685.

45.37 Hough, Graham. "Ruskin," *The Last Romantics*. London: Duckworth, 1949.

For discussion see Survey, pp. 34–35.

45.38 Leon, Derrick. *Ruskin, the Great Victorian*. London: Routledge, 1949.

The best and most thorough modern account of Ruskin, his art and influence.

45.39 Whitehouse, J. Howard. *Vindication of Ruskin*. London: Allen and Unwin, 1950.

An unconvincing reply to James (45.32). Ruskin's deposition, answering the charges made in the annulment suit, is included in the volume.

45.40 Evans, Joan. *John Ruskin*. London: Cape, 1954.

With a useful bibliography of secondary materials. The Ruskin *Diaries* have also been edited by Miss Evans, but they contain little of relevance to the Pre-Raphaelites.

45.41 Quennell, Peter. *John Ruskin* (Writers and Their Work, Pamphlet no. 76). London: Longmans, 1956.

45.42 Edwards, R. "Ruskin on English Contemporary Artists," *Connoisseur* (American edition), CXLIV (November 1959), 91–95.

45.43 Dearden, James S. "Some Portraits of John Ruskin," *Apollo*, LXXIII (December 1960), 190–195; "Further Portraits of John Ruskin," *Apollo*, LXXIV (June 1961), 171–178.

Twenty-three illustrations of Ruskin portraits in the Ruskin Galleries, Bembridge School, Isle of Wight, and Brantwood, Coniston.

45.44 Rosenberg, John D. *The Darkening Glass: A Portrait of John Ruskin*. New York: Columbia University Press, 1960.

Minor Pre-Raphaelites, Associates, and Affiliates

Section 46

WILLIAM ALLINGHAM

1 8 2 4 – 1 8 8 9

[CBEL: III, 276–277, S594; DNB: XXII, S, 38–40
(Richard Garnett); EB: I, 696]

William Allingham is probably the best of the minor poets who moved on the outer ring of the Pre-Raphaelite circle — and probably the least Pre-Raphaelite. His connection with the group began in 1849, when, on a visit to London, he met Coventry Patmore who introduced him to Woolner, through whom he made contact with the Brotherhood. Never able to extricate himself from the menial task of making a living (as a civil servant in the Customs Service), Allingham could devote only part of his energies to literature, although he did spend most of 1854 doing journalistic hackwork in London. His most important encounter with the Pre-Raphaelites came with their illustration of his *Music Master* in 1855 (see 46.4 and 90.2). Allingham was acquainted with most of the Pre-Raphaelites, but he was on intimate terms only with Rossetti and Woolner and, for a time, with Arthur Hughes. Rossetti's letters to Allingham reveal a correspondent with whom he shared both personal and literary confidences; and, while Allingham's replies can only be surmised, it is fairly evident that the two poets received mutual benefit from their friendship. The cause of their break is not revealed — Rossetti broke eventually with almost all his early acquaintances — but there is no reference in Allingham's *Diary* to Rossetti later than 1867.

Though his connection with the Pre-Raphaelites was primarily a personal one, Allingham does have some poetical affinities with them. His most obvious Pre-Raphaelite quality is the melancholy mood which pervades his poetry, the sense of transiency and urgency that impels it. Allingham's first volume of poems was published after his acquaintance with the Brotherhood, but it would be erroneous to press too closely the case for Allingham as a Pre-Raphaelite. In the first instance, many of the tendencies which he shares with them are essentially romantic, and others, such as his melancholy and use of mood-music, are characteristic of the celtic traditions on which he drew. (On this subject, it is interesting to note that Allingham's verse is never concerned with the political themes that occupy other nineteenth-century Irish poets.) As to purely decorative effects, often found in Pre-Raphaelite poetry, Allingham admired them, but he rejected them in his own writing. He shared with the Pre-Raphaelites their "real love of nature and delicate truth of touch," such as he saw in Woolner's *Germ* version of "My Beautiful Lady," but he consciously spurned other qualities, one of which he called the "quaint guildmark . . . of the P.R.B." "I can't bear to be verbally quaint myself," he wrote in his *Diary*, "yet often I like it in another." (46.22, p. 91)

"Pre-Raphaelite interest," B. Ifor Evans says, "though it enters into some of [Allingham's] lyrics, does not explain him fully as a poet." (46.32, pp. 109–110) Touched by

Pre-Raphaelitism, Allingham did not succumb to the point that he lost what in his best poetry is individually his own.

* * *

46.1 O'Hegarty, P. S. *A Bibliography of William Allingham.* Dublin: Privately printed, 1945.
Reprinted from the *Dublin Magazine* (April 1945) in 35 copies only.

* * *

46.2 Allingham, William. *Poems.* London: Chapman and Hall, 1850.

46.3 ——— *Day and Night Songs.* London: Routledge, 1854.

46.4 ——— *The Music Master, A Love Story, and Two Series of Day and Night Songs.* London: Routledge, 1855.
With nine illustrations by the Pre-Raphaelites. The volume contains one design by Millais, seven by Hughes, and Rossetti's "The Maids of Elfen-Mere." The 1855 volume was reprinted by Bell and Daldy in 1860 with the title *Day and Night Songs; and The Music Master. A Love Poem. Day and Night Songs* was reissued by Philip and Sons in 1884 in a cover designed by Rossetti. See 90.2.

46.5 ——— *Poems.* Boston: Tichnor and Fields, 1861.
First American edition, important because it contained everything in the 1855 volume plus twenty other poems not published in England until 1865.

46.6 ——— *Laurence Bloomfield in Ireland: A Modern Poem.* London: Macmillan, 1864.

46.7 ——— *Fifty Modern Poems.* London: Bell and Daldy, 1865.

46.8 ——— *Songs, Ballads and Stories: Including Many now First Collected, the Rest Revised and Rearranged.* London, Bell, 1877.

46.9 *Evil May-Day.* London: Stott, [1882].

46.10 ——— *Ashby Manor: A Play in Two Acts.* London: Stott, [1883].

46.11 ——— *The Fairies.* London: Thomas de la Rue, [1883].

46.12 ——— *Blackberries. Picked off Many Bushes by D. Pollex and Others. Put in a Basket by William Allingham.* London: Philip, 1884.

46.13 ——— *Irish Songs and Poems.* London: Reeves and Turner, 1887.

46.14 ——— *Flower Pieces and Other Poems.* London: Reeves and Turner, 1888.
With a frontispiece and another illustration by Rossetti (see 96.6).

46.15 ——— *Life and Phantasy.* London: Reeves and Turner, 1889.
With a frontispiece by Millais and a design by Arthur Hughes, both reprinted from 46.4.

46.16 ——— *Thought and Word, and Ashby Manor: A Play in Two Acts.* London: Reeves and Turner, 1890.

46.17 ——— *Varieties in Prose: Rambles by Patricius Walker.* 3 vols. London: Longmans, 1893.

46.18 ——— [Uniform edition of Allingham's works]. 6 vols. London: Reeves and Turner, 1884–1890.
Blackberries (1884), *Irish Songs and Poems* (1887), *Flower Pieces* (1888), *Laurence Bloomfield* (1888), *Life and Phantasy* (1889), *Thought and Word and Ashby Manor* (1890).

46.19 Allingham, William. *Sixteen Poems.* Selected by William Butler Yeats. Dundram: Dun Emer Press, 1905.

46.20 ——— *Poems* Selected and Arranged by Helen Allingham (Golden Treasury Series). London: Macmillan, 1912.

46.21 ——— *By the Way: Verses, Frag-*

ments, and Notes. Arranged by Helen Allingham. London: Longmans, 1912.

* * *

46.22 Allingham, Helen, and D. Radford, eds. *William Allingham, A Diary.* London: Macmillan, 1907.

With detailed references to the Pre-Raphaelites, especially Rossetti. With a bibliography of Allingham's writings.

46.23 Hill, George Birkbeck, ed. *Letters of Dante Gabriel Rossetti to William Allingham, 1854–1870.* London: Unwin, 1897.

For annotation see 24.6.

46.24 Allingham, Helen, and E. B. Williams, eds. *Letters to William Allingham.* London: Longmans, 1911.

Contains letters from nearly all the Pre-Raphaelites: Madox Brown (4), Arthur Hughes (8 plus six from Allingham to Hughes), Burne-Jones (16), Lady Burne-Jones (3), Holman Hunt (3), Millais (5), Morris (3), Stephens (2), Woolner (8), and Rossetti (1). For Rossetti's letters to Allingham see 46.23.

46.25 [Allingham, Helen, ed.]. [*Letters from William Allingham to Mr. and Mrs. Browning*]. [1913].

No title, imprint, or date. The letters, seven in all, acquired from the Browning sale in 1913, were presumably published as an addendum to the *Letters to William Allingham* (46.24).

* * *

46.26 Yeats, William Butler. "William Allingham," in *The Poets and the Poetry of the Century*, Edited by A. H. Miles. Vol. [V]. London: Hutchinson, [1891–1897].

For complete annotation see 84.5.

46.27 Johnson, Lionel. "Allingham," in *A Treasury of Irish Poetry*, edited by S. A. Brooke and T. W. Ralleston. London: Murray, 1900.

46.28 Macdonald, F. W. "A Literary Diary: William Allingham," *Recreations of a Book Lover.* London: Hodder and Stoughton, 1911.

In part a review of 46.22. See also the chapter "Carlyle and Allingham."

46.29 Graves, Alfred Perceval. "William Allingham," *Transactions of the Royal Society of Literature*, 2nd ser., XXXII (1913), 147–184.

A lecture delivered 28 May 1913. Reprinted, in revised form, in *Irish Literary and Musical Studies* (London: Mathews, 1913).

46.30 Boyd, Ernest A. "The Transition. William Allingham. The Crystallization of the New Spirit: The Irish Literary Societies," *Ireland's Literary Renaissance.* New York: Knopf, 1922.

46.31 Kropf, Hans. *William Allingham und seine Dichtung im Lichte der irischen Freiheitsbewegung.* Biel: Andres, 1928 (diss. Bern, 1928).

Includes a list of articles on and references to Allingham.

46.32 Evans, B. Ifor. "Minor Pre-Raphaelite Poets: William Bell Scott; William Allingham; Thomas Woolner; Arthur O'Shaughnessy; John Payne; Philip Bourke Marston; William Sharp (Fiona Macleod)," *English Poetry in the Later Nineteenth Century.* London: Methuen, 1933.

For complete annotation see 74.7.

46.33 Howe, M. L. "Notes on the Allingham Canon," *Philological Quarterly*, XII (July 1933), 290–297.

46.34 Farren, Robert. "William Allingham," *The Course of Irish Verse.* London: Sheed and Ward, 1948.

46.35 Taylor, Geoffrey, ed. "William Allingham," *Irish Poets of the Nineteenth Century* (The Muses' Library). London: Routledge and Kegan Paul, 1951.

With an introduction and over fifty pages of selections.

46.36 Browne, J. N. "Ulster Poetry," *The Arts in Ulster: A Symposium*, edited by S. H. Bell. London: Harrap, 1951.

Includes Samuel Ferguson and William Allingham.

46.37 Macdonogh, W. I. P. "William Allingham," unpub. diss., Trinity College, Dublin, 1952.

46.38 Burto, William C. "William Allingham: 1824–1889," unpub. diss., Harvard University, 1954.

46.39 White, H. O. "An Allingham Pamphlet," *Times Literary Supplement*, no. 2842 (17 August 1956), p. 487.
Reference to a thirty-two page privately printed (?) pamphlet of Allingham's poems entitled *Flower Pieces* recently located in Trinity College, Dublin Library.

46.40 Freeman, Ronald E. "William Allingham: the Irish Years, 1824–1863," unpub. diss., University of Illinois, 1957. *Dissertation Abstracts*, XVIII (1957), 587.

46.41 O'Reilly, A. M. P. "A Critical Study of William Allingham with Special Reference to Laurence Bloomfield in Ireland," unpub. diss., Bedford College, University of London, 1957–58.

46.42 ———— "Laurence Bloomfield — an Historical Document," *Donegal Annual*, 1959, pp. 102–110.

Section 47

OLIVER MADOX BROWN

1855–1874

[CBEL: III, 539; DNB: III, 22–23 (Westland Marston)]

Of *Gabriel Denver*, Dante Gabriel Rossetti wrote to its author, "I really believe it must be the most robust literary effort of any imaginative kind that anyone has produced at the age at which you wrote it . . ." (47.3, p. 83) Precociousness was the most singular characteristic of Oliver Madox Brown, and if Rossetti was overextravagant in his praise (as he often was), *Gabriel Denver* is a remarkable book, which, despite the attacks of contemporary reviewers, showed considerable promise and a high degree of merit.

When he died at the age of nineteen, Oliver Madox Brown had published one novel and nearly completed two others; he had composed a little poetry (most of which he destroyed) and written a few short stories. He had also painted a good many pictures. His talent was universally acclaimed by the Pre-Raphaelites, and had he lived he might have proved the novelist of the group. *The Black Swan*, the earliest and far superior version of *Gabriel Denver*, though immature, draws heavily on the gothic romanticisms of Poe and Rossetti, and in thematic conception — in part the novel is concerned with diabolical possession and the story depends heavily on symbolism — it bears a close resemblance to the works of Hawthorne.

Oliver Madox Brown ("Nolly" to his friends and intimate biographers) was a close friend of Philip Bourke Marston, the blind poet, and through him, of O'Shaughnessy. The Fitzroy Square evenings and Ford Madox Brown's association with the Pre-Raphaelites brought him into contact with many immediate and fringe members of the group. Most of the writings on him have been, like Rossetti's praise, hyperbolic and, owing perhaps to the tragic effect that his death had on his father, reverential. Oliver Madox Brown may not have been the genius that by consensus he was acknowledged as among the Pre-Raphaelites, but he would repay serious study, and *Gabriel Denver* (and *The Black Swan*) might with great profit be revived.

*　　*　　*

47.1 Brown, Oliver Madox. *Gabriel Denver*. London: Smith, Elder, 1873; 2nd ed., 1875.

Bound in boards decorated by Ford Madox Brown. See Plate VII.

47.2 Rossetti, William M., and F. Hueffer, eds. *The Dwale Bluth, Hebditch's Legacy, and Other Literary Remains of Oliver Madox-Brown . . . with a Memoir and Two Portraits*. 2 vols. London: Tinsley, 1876.

Besides the works indicated in the title, the volumes also contain *The Black Swan* and thirteen lyrics, one short story and another prose fragment. Philip Bourke Marston's "Lament," which first appeared in *All in All* in 1874, is also included. See Watts-Dunton's review, "Oliver Madox Brown's Literary Remains," *Examiner*, 29 January 1876, pp. 127–129.

47.3 Ingram, John H. *Oliver Madox Brown: A Biographical Sketch, 1855–1874*. London: Stock, 1883.

The only full-length study of Oliver Madox Brown. Contains details of his friendships and writings, with many of his letters to his publishers, to Philip Marston, and to Rossetti. Five letters from Rossetti to Brown are printed in the volume.

47.4 McCarthy, Justin. "Oliver Madox Brown," *Gentleman's Magazine*, XVI (February 1876), 161–165.

47.5 Marston, Philip Bourke. "Oliver Madox Brown," *Scribner's Monthly*, XII (July 1876), 425–428.

47.6 Ingram, John H. "Oliver Madox Brown," in *The Poets and the Poetry of the Century*, edited by A. H. Miles. Vol. [VIII]. London: Hutchinson, [1891–1897].

For complete annotation see 84.5.

47.7 Hueffer, Ford Madox. "The Younger Madox Browns: Lucy, Catherine, Oliver," *Artist*, XIX (February 1897), 49–56.

With reproductions of three paintings each by Oliver and Lucy Madox Brown and two portraits by Catherine.

47.8 Darmesteter, James. "Oliver Madox-Brown," *English Studies*. Translated by Mary Darmesteter (A. Mary Robinson). London: Unwin, 1896.

"In the limbo of the paradise of poets, the souls of children, floating in the mists of dawn, are frail, uncertain visions with little individual feature. Their aureole is made of the vague glimmer of the future. They have done little and dreamed much; and in their dreams it is difficult to see how much is all their own. Mostly they shine by a reflected light. Oliver Madox-Brown is assuredly one of the most vivid, one of the most personal, of these touching phantoms. Chatterton was a prodigy, but rather of assimilation than invention, an echo rather than a voice. Oliver was a voice, a voice still young, broken, uncertain. But he spoke true in his death agony. Had he lived he would have ranked among the great. His qualities were those which cannot be imitated: intensity of vision, dramatic force, power of emotion." (pp. 168–169)

Section 48

THOMAS GORDON HAKE

1809–1895

[CBEL: III, 288–289; DNB: XXII, S, 799–801
(Richard Garnett); EB: XII, 827]

To call Dr. Thomas Gordon Hake a Pre-Raphaelite poet would be a mistake, though he was undoubtedly influenced by the poetry and by the general aesthetic temper of the movement. In poetry, Hake went to school with Rossetti, who paid him the singular (and for Rossetti the unique) compliment of reviewing on two separate occasions volumes of his poetry. Rossetti's interest in Hake began many years prior to their actual meeting, before Hake turned, at the age of fifty, to the writing of poetry. What little recognition Hake's serious, often obscure poetry of ideas received was in part Rossetti's doing. It was perhaps the very serious, intellectualized quality that first attracted Rossetti to Hake's verse, but in his reviews Rossetti finds that poetry most praiseworthy in which Hake maintains a simple, almost expository style.

The lyrical muse was no mistress to Dr. Hake, and his verse is more often than not monotonous and commonplace, when it is not unintelligible. Occasionally as in the volume *Parables and Tales* (1872 — illustrated by Hughes with a cover designed by Rossetti; reviewed by Rossetti), he manages to clothe an old saw in a new garment, but these poems are heavily didactic and excessively sentimental. One of the most interesting poems in the volume is "The Blind Boy," a pitiful little narrative inspired by Philip Bourke Marston.

What is finally the attraction of Hake (apart from his apparent warmth of personality, as evidenced by his befriending of Rossetti in later years) is the fact that although he came to a literary career relatively late, his abilities began to mature and develop as he grew older. *New Symbols* (1876) and *Maiden Ecstasy* (1880) are generally regarded as his best volumes, but few books written by an octogenarian have the merit and promise of Hake's book of sonnets, *The New Day* (1892), written in his eightieth year. Hake's poetry is too intellectual, and too abstract; one critic (Arthur Symons) has called him the most exotic of English poets. His *Memoirs of Eighty Years*, which he himself superintended, is a matter-of-fact autobiography, but it contains vitally relevant material on Rossetti and frequent references to the other Pre-Raphaelites with whom Hake, through Rossetti, was acquainted. A distinctly minor poet, Hake is nevertheless interesting, and his poetry does to some degree demonstrate the impact of Pre-Raphaelite ideas and tendencies.

* * *

48.1   Hake, Thomas Gordon. *Poetic Lucubrations: Containing the Misanthrope and Other Effusions.* London: Hunt, 1828.

48.2 ——— *The Piromides: A Tragedy.* London: Daunders, 1839.

48.3 ——— *Vates: or the Philosophy of Madness; Being an Account of the Life, Actions, Passions, and Principles of a Tragic Writer. Parts I–IV.* London: Southgate, 1840.
Illustrated by Landseer. Later republished in *Ainsworth's Magazine* under title *Valdarno: or, The Ordeal of Art Worship.*

48.4   *The World's Epitaph.* London: Printed for private circulation, 1866.
Contains a brief preface.

48.5 ——— *Madeline, with Other Poems and Parables.* London: Chapman and Hall, 1871.
Reviewed by Rossetti in *Academy*, II, no. 17 (1 February 1871), 105–107; reprinted in 23.27 (pp. 621–627).

48.6 ——— *Parables and Tales.* London: Chapman and Hall, 1872.
Illustrated by Arthur Hughes (93.33). A very few copies were issued with a cover designed by Rossetti. Reprinted with Hughes' illustrations and a preface by Hake's son, Thomas, by Elkin Mathews in 1917. Reviewed by Dante Gabriel Rossetti in *Fortnightly Review*, XIX, n.s. XIII (April 1873), 537–542. Rossetti's review is reprinted in 23.27 (pp. 631–635). See Plate VII.

48.7 ——— *New Symbols.* London: Chatto and Windus, 1876.

48.8 ——— *Legends of the Morrow*. London: Chatto and Windus, 1879.

48.9 ——— *Maiden Ecstasy*. London: Chatto and Windus, 1880.

48.10 ——— *The Serpent Play. A Divine Pastoral*. London: Chatto and Windus, 1883.

48.11 Hodgson, W. Earl, ed. *The New Day: Sonnets by Thomas Gordon Hake*. London: Remington, 1890.
     With a preface by Hodgson and a portrait by Rossetti.

48.12 Hake, Thomas Gordon. *Memoirs of Eighty Years*. London: Bentley, 1892.
     Chapters LIV and LV are of special interest for matters relating to Rossetti and the Pre-Raphaelites.

48.13 Meynell, Alice, ed. *The Poems of Thomas Gordon Hake*. London: Elkin Mathews, 1894.
     With a brief prefatory note by Alice Meynell and Rossetti's portrait of Hake.

* * *

48.14 Ward, T. H. "Thomas Gordon Hake," in *The English Poets: Selections with Critical Introductions by Various Writers*, edited by T. H. Ward. Vol. 5. London: Macmillan, 1880.
     For complete annotation see 84.3.

48.15 Henley, William Ernest. "Gordon Hake," *View and Reviews. Essays in Appreciation: Literature*. London: Nutt, 1890.

48.16 Bayne, Thomas. "Thomas Gordon Hake," in *The Poets and the Poetry of the Century*, edited by A. H. Miles. Vol. [IV]. London: Hutchinson, [1891–1897].
     For complete annotation see 84.5.

48.17 Watts-Dunton, Theodore. "Dr. Gordon Hake," *Athenaeum*, no. 3508 (19 January 1895), 84–86; no. 3509 (26 January 1895), 118.
     Reprinted in *Old Familiar Faces* (64.2).

48.18 Symons, Arthur. "Thomas Gordon Hake," *Studies in Two Literatures*. London: Smithers, 1897.
     For complete annotation see 43.37.

Section 49

ARTHUR HUGHES

1832–1915

[DNB: S, II, 275–276 (Malcolm Bell)]

John Gere in his Notes on Arthur Hughes in *Pre-Raphaelite Painters* (83.8, p. 42), comments that Arthur Hughes, though relatively unknown, is one of the most important Pre-Raphaelite painters. Anyone familiar with Hughes' painting and illustration will readily concur in this opinion. Unfortunately, Hughes is hardly better known today than he was when Percy Bate lamented his anonymity in 1898; and the paucity of material available on Hughes makes it almost impossible to discover relevant facts relating to his life and art. Apart from the few works listed, the brief section in the *DNB*, and the section in Forrest Reid's book on illustrations (88.9, 83–95), there has been very little done on this most interesting minor Pre-Raphaelite.

Hughes' association with Pre-Raphaelitism dates from the period of *The Germ*, and the exhibition of *Ophelia* in the Royal Academy exhibition of 1852. Although he lived well into the present century, the period of his real greatness antedates 1870. A delicate and sensitive artist with a subtle sense of color and shading, Hughes often walks the knife-edge between sentiment and sentimentality in his choice and handling of subject. *The Long Engagement* (Birmingham), *Ophelia* (Manchester), *Home from Sea* (Ashmolean), *The Eve of St. Agnes*, *The Tryst*, and *April Love* (Tate Gallery; a smaller version of *April Love* belongs to John Gere), *As You Like It* (Walker Art Gallery), and *Prospero* (in the collection of Charles A. and Mrs. J. A. R. Munro — see 4.3) — these are Hughes' best and most Pre-Raphaelite works.

A quiet, retiring man (Ford Madox Brown noted Hughes' presence at a meeting in his diary: "young, handsome, silent"), Hughes was on the warmest terms with Hunt, Rossetti, Millais, Brown, and the other Pre-Raphaelites, especially Alexander Munro with whom for some years he shared a studio during the 1850's. Hughes began his artistic career with the illustrations for Allingham's *Music Master* (see 46.4 and 90.2; for Arthur Hughes' excellent and prolific work in the field of book illustration see section 93); he participated in the painting of the Oxford Union frescoes; and he was a "Non-Resident (Artistic)" member of the Hogarth Club (see 72.5). In *Some Reminiscences* William Michael Rossetti made the following observations on Hughes:

> As a painter, he was one of those who most sympathized with the ideas which guided the Præraphaelite Brotherhood, and his style conformed pretty faithfully (not servilely) to theirs; if the organization had been kept up a little longer, and if new members had ever been admitted . . . Mr. Hughes would doubtless have been invited to join. He has produced many charming pictures — of a kind which, without being didactic, appeals intimately to the feelings; yet as they had (like himself) no "pushing" quality either in subject or in execution, they never brought him into a position of great prominence, and he has reached the twilight of life without receiving the full measure of his due. (38.8, I, 147–148)

* * *

49.1 Rossetti, William M. "English Painters of the Present Day. X. Arthur Hughes," *Portfolio*, I (August 1870), 113–119.

Within the same section (and pagination) are the following other brief sketches: "XI. W. L. Windus, XII. Miss Spartali, XIII. The Younger Madox Browns." Reprinted in 75.9.

49.2 Housman, Laurence. "The Illustrations of Arthur Hughes," *Bibliophile*, I (July 1908), 231–237.

For annotation see 89.15.

49.3 "'Home from Work' by Arthur Hughes," *Russell-Cotes Bulletin*, XI (March 1932), 4–5.

49.4 Mander, Rosalie. "'The Tryst' Unravelled," *Apollo*, LXXIX (March 1964), 221–223.

Identifying the source of Hughes' picture, commissioned by Miss Ellen Heaton, as Mrs. Browning's *Aurora Leigh*. The article draws on several letters from Hughes to Miss Heaton (now in the possession of Miss K. O. Heaton), in which the artist pleads poetic license in his visual translation of the poem. With three illustrations: Hughes' self-portrait in the National Portrait Gallery, *The Tryst* and *That was a Piedmontese*, both in the Tate Gallery, the latter picture, taken from Mrs. Browning's *Poems Before Congress*, also commissioned by Miss Heaton.

Section 50

PHILIP BOURKE MARSTON

1850–1887

[CBEL: III, 347–348; DNB: XII, 1145–1146 (Richard
Garnett); EB: XVII, 777 (Thomas Seccombe)]

"Think of a child born with a beautiful gift of poetry, and a most affectionate nature, and the most beautiful face I ever saw in a man . . . ," Swinburne wrote to Lady Henrietta Swinburne, expressing his grief and shock over the death of Philip Bourke Marston (62.12, V, 181) — ". . . what a pleasure it was to me to have him here and talk to him and read to him and see his poor blind eyes become so expressive of pleasure and emotion that nothing but the vague direction of their look reminded one that they could see nothing."

Philip Marston's career followed a pattern of disaster and tragedy unparalleled in the history of English letters. Blind from the age of three, Marston, in the decade between 1870 and 1880, experienced the deaths of all those family and friends whom he loved and on whom his blindness forced him to depend. His mother, who more than anyone else was responsible for his literary education, died in 1870. In 1871, his fiancée, Mary Nesbit, died in the year of their engagement. These two losses were followed by the deaths of his two sisters, Cecily and Eleanor, the latter the wife of Arthur O'Shaughnessy — both of whom had served as Philip's amanuenses. In 1874, Oliver Madox Brown's death added to what B. Ifor Evans has called the "melancholy roll-call"; and as fate would have it, Marston was to outlive both O'Shaughnessy and Rossetti by nearly five years, the last few of which were spent in reduced and unfortunate straits.

These sad events are the necessary facts of Marston's life, and though they tend to forestall criticism, predisposing the reader to a sympathetic response to Marston the man, they are nevertheless essential to an understanding of his poetry; for as sadness plagued his life, so it became the dominant theme expressed in his successive volumes. Love and death are his persistently reiterated themes, understandably coupled with overtones of introspective self-pity.

Marston's poetic vein was not wide and his range was limited both by the events of his unhappy life and by his physical disability. That he was, as Swinburne called him, "a poet of real genius," puts the case too strongly, but considering that he never had even the opportunity to learn to read, his achievement in an art distinctly verbal is remarkable. As B. Ifor Evans has accurately observed, Marston's poetry poses problems that are psychological as well as literary:

> What images from the world of experience can penetrate to a mind that saw dimly for a few years and then not at all? For Marston, sounds and depths and odours are more impressive than shapes and colours; the images of the sea and tides, and clouds, and, in kindlier moments, the qualities of flowers are the resources of his poetry. Above all, the varied qualities of sound suggest to his mind the imagery which normal men gain from visual sensation. (50.15, p. 122)

This last point is crucial in Marston's poetry, for it imposes on the reader an almost synaesthetic responsibility of translating visual images into the more abstract (because less easily articulated) impressions of the other senses.

In tone and mood there is a monotonous sameness in Marston's poetry, a melancholy and despair, a heaviness which shackles the lyric impulse. Under the influence of Rossetti, Marston made the sonnet his special verse form, but while many of his sonnets are interesting, the nature of the form restricted further those limitations which inhibited Marston's poetic sensibilities. Most marked in all his poetry is its strong sensualistic quality. William Sharp noted that his

> poetic insight is subtle in only one direction: it is love — sexual love, in the broadest sense — that is the magnet of his poetic energy. He nowhere in his poems, or in his prose tales, manifests any depth of vision into the life of nature or of man, save in the direction indicated. (50.6, pp. lxxi–lxxii)

During his lifetime, Marston had a greater vogue in America than in England, and it was in America that he published most of his short stories (see 50.4). But Philip Bourke Marston was never a popular poet; and the severe physical and psychic handicaps under which he wrote, and which inescapably precondition the reader's reaction, are probably sufficient to preclude his ever attaining a wide and lasting audience.

* * *

50.1 Marston, Philip Bourke. *Song-Tide, and Other Poems*. London: Ellis, 1871.
2nd edition (London: Chatto and Windus, 1874). Published in America by Roberts Brothers, Boston.

50.2 —— *All in All: Poems and Sonnets*. London: Chatto and Windus, 1874.

50.3 —— *Wind-Voices (Poems)*. London: Stock, 1883. Published in America by Roberts Brothers, Boston.

50.4 —— *For a Song's Sake and Other Stories*. With a Memoir by William Sharp. London: Scott, [1887].

50.5 —— *Garden Secrets*. Edited with a Biographical Sketch by Louise Chandler Moulton. Boston: Roberts, 1887.

50.6 —— *Song-Tide: Poems and Lyrics of Love's Joy and Sorrow*. Edited with an Introductory Memoir by William Sharp (The Canterbury Poets). London: Scott, 1888.
The Memoir is essentially the same as that included in 50.4. It was also reprinted in 27.50. This edition contains selections from the three volumes of verse published during Marston's lifetime.

50.7 —— *A Last Harvest: Lyrics and Sonnets from the Book of Love*. Edited with a Biographical Sketch by Louise Chandler Moulton. London: Elkin Mathews, 1891.
Containing poems previously unpublished.

50.8 —— *The Collected Poems: Comprising "Song-Tide," "All in All," "Wind-Voices," "A Last Harvest," and "Aftermath."* Edited with a Biographical Sketch by Louise Chandler Moulton. London: Ward, 1892.
The Biographical Sketch is essentially the same as that in 50.7.

* * *

50.9 Drinkwater, John. "Philip Bourke Marston," in *The English Poets: Selections with Critical Introductions by Various Writers*, edited by T. H. Ward. Vol. V. London: Macmillan, 1880.
For complete annotation see 84.3.

50.10 Kernahan, Coulson. "Philip Bourke Marston," in *The Poets and the Poetry of the Century*, edited by A. H. Miles. Vol. [VIII]. London: Hutchinson, [1891–1897].
For complete annotation see 84.5. This essay was slightly expanded for inclusion in *Sorrow and Song* (27.23).

50.11 Le Gallienne, Richard. "Philip Bourke Marston: Last Harvest," *Retrospective Reviews*. Vol. I. London: John Lane, 1896.

A review of 50.7, with critical comment on the poet.

50.12 Osborne, Charles Churchill. *Philip Bourke Marston*. London: Privately printed (The Times Book Club), 1926.

50.13 Gosse, Edmund. "A Blind Poet," *Leaves and Fruit*. London: Heinemann, 1927.

An examination of Marston's life and work. A long review-article on 50.12.

50.14 Klenk, Hans. *Nachwirkungen Dante Gabriel Rossettis: Untersuchungen an Werken von Christina Rossetti, Coventry Patmore, Philip Bourke Marston, Theodore Watts-Dunton, Arthur W. E. O'Shaughnessy, Ernest Dowson, John Davidson*. Berlin: Bachmann, 1932 (diss. Erlangen, 1932).

50.15 Evans, B. Ifor. "Minor Pre-Raphaelite Poets: William Bell Scott; William Allingham; Thomas Woolner; Arthur O'Shaughnessy; John Payne; Philip Bourke Marston; William Sharp (Fiona Macleod)," *English Poetry in the Later Nineteenth Century*. London: Methuen, 1933.

For complete annotation see 74.7.

Section 51

ARTHUR WILLIAM EDGAR O'SHAUGHNESSY
1844–1881

[CBEL: III, 1055, S699; DNB: XIV, 1202–1203
(Richard Garnett); EB: XX, 349]

Remembered, when at all, for his lines, "We are the music makers, / And we are the dreamers of dreams," ("Ode," *Music and Moonlight*), O'Shaughnessy is now seldom anthologized (but see George B. Woods' *Poetry of the Victorian Period*, revised edition in collaboration with Jerome H. Buckley, 1955). Besides the single issue of the *Bibelot* devoted to O'Shaughnessy's poems (XVI [April 1905], 117–150), the only recent reprinting is Percy's edition (51.6), below.

A devoted student of French literature, O'Shaughnessy made numerous translations; one-half of his last volume, *Songs of A Worker*, consisted of "Translations from Contemporary French Poets," including Coppée, Verlaine, D'Hervilly, Prudhomme, Mendès, and others. His second volume, *Lays of France*, comprises five free adaptations of the lays of Marie de France. O'Shaughnessy was greatly influenced by both Swinburne and Baudelaire, from whom, no doubt, he inherited what Edmund Gosse in *Silhouettes* (p. 178) called his "flute-music, not strong in quality nor wide in range, but of a piercing tenderness." His first work, *An Epic of Women*, is generally regarded as his best, especially the poem "Bisclavaret"; but Sarrazine's song to her dead lover in "Chaitivel" (*Lays of France*) is often cited as his most sustained and effective lyric.

O'Shaughnessy was the brother-in-law of the blind poet, Philip Bourke Marston (see section 50), and he was an intimate of the Pre-Raphaelite circle, sharing many of their general poetic tendencies. Unable to devote his whole energies to his poetry, he was, in his nonpoetic life, a herpetologist and ichthyologist in the zoological department of the British Museum. A distinctly minor poet, O'Shaughnessy has been aptly described by W. A. Percy (51.6, pp. 2–3) as

. . . a poet who had no range, no profundity or originality of thought, no interest, so far as his art reveals, in everyday life, or simple joys and sorrows, or heroic deeds, no ability to construct or invent a tale because facts in themselves meant nothing to him. Yet here is a poet, authentically of the sacred band, blessed with the divine gusto. This he is because of the gift of music and the gift of ecstasy . . . He is a singer or nothing.

* * *

51.1 O'Shaughnessy, Arthur W. E. *An Epic of Women and Other Poems.* London: Hotten, 1870.

Dedicated to John Payne, whose first volume, *The Masque of Shadows* (54.1), also 1870, was dedicated to O'Shaughnessy. 2nd edition 1871. This volume is of special interest for the Blake-like illustrations of John Nettleship (title page reproduced in John Hayward, *English Poetry: An Illustrated Catalogue* [Cambridge University Press, 1950], plate 282). See Plate II.

51.2 ———— *Lays of France (Founded on the Lays of Marie).* London: Ellis, 1872.

2nd edition, Chatto and Windus, 1874.

51.3 ———— *Music and Moonlight: Poems and Songs.* London: Chatto and Windus, 1874.

51.4 ———— and Eleanor O'Shaughnessy. *Toyland.* London: Daldy, 1875.

With an engraved frontispiece by Dalziel after a design by Arthur Boyd-Houghton, which originally appeared in *Good Words* (1863, p. 636). The original painting from which the engraving was made is in the Ashmolean Museum, Oxford.

51.5 ———— *Songs of A Worker.* London: Chatto and Windus, 1881.

A posthumous volume, edited with a brief Introduction by O'Shaughnessy's cousin, the Rev. A. W. Newport Deacon.

51.6 ———— *Poems.* Selected and Edited by William Alexander Percy. New Haven: Yale University Press, 1923.

Selections from all four of O'Shaughnessy's volumes of poems are included in this non-critical edition. Besides the separately listed reviews below, the following should be noted: A. Porter, "Arthur O'Shaughnessy's Poems," *Spectator*, CXXXI, no. 4963 (11 August 1923), 196–197; G. H. Clarke [Arthur O'Shaughnessy's Poetry], *Sewanee Re-*

view, XXXI (October–December 1923), 486–489; "Arthur O'Shaughnessy's Poems," *Contemporary Review*, CXXVI (July 1924), 125–128. See also 51.15 and 51.16.

* * *

51.7 Forman, H. Buxton. "John Payne and Arthur W. E. O'Shaughnessy," *Our Living Poets: An Essay in Criticism.* London: Tinsley, 1871.

For complete annotation see 74.1.

51.8 Gosse, Edmund. "Arthur O'Shaughnessy," in *The English Poets: Selections with Critical Introductions by Various Writers,* edited by T. H. Ward. Vol. IV. London: Macmillan, 1880.

For complete annotation see 84.3.

51.9 Hamilton, Walter. "Arthur W. E. O'Shaughnessy," *The Æsthetic Movement in England.* London: Reeves and Turner, 1882.

For complete annotation see 78.2.

51.10 Garnett, Richard. "Arthur O'Shaughnessy," in *The Poets and the Poetry of the Century,* edited by A. H. Miles. Vol. [VIII]. London: Hutchinson, [1891–1897].

For complete annotation see 84.5.

51.11 Moulton, Louise Chandler. *Arthur O'Shaughnessy: His Life and His Work, with Selections from His Poems.* London: Elkin Mathews, 1894.

The first long study of O'Shaughnessy's life and work. The author was personally acquainted with the poet, and her treatment is fulsome rather than critical.

51.12 Le Gallienne, Richard. "Arthur O'Shaughnessy," *Retrospective Reviews.* Vol. II. London: John Lane, 1896.

A review of 51.11, with critical comment on the poet.

51.13 *A Pathetic Love Episode in a Poet's Life. Being Letters to Arthur W. E.*

O'Shaughnessy. Also a Letter from Him Containing a Dissertation on Love. [London: Privately printed for distribution by Clement Shorter, 1916].

Letters from Helen Snee to O'Shaughnessy. With an Introduction by Clement Shorter. 25 copies only.

51.14 Broers, Bernarda C. "O'Shaughnessy," *Mysticism in the Neo-Romanticists.* Amsterdam: Paris, 1923 (diss. Amsterdam, 1923).

For complete annotation see 73.8.

51.15 Gosse, Edmund. "Arthur O'Shaughnessy," *Silhouettes.* London: Heinemann, 1925.

A review of 51.6.

51.16 Lucas, F. L. "A Painted Lily," *Authors Dead and Living.* New York: Macmillan, 1926.

A review of 51.6, first published in *New Statesman*, XXI (September 1923), 596–598. ". . . there is a time for all things and all moods, and not least for this last rose of pre-Raphaelitism — or, perhaps rather, this arum lily, a little festered, from its grave." (p. 130)

51.17 Klenk, Hans. *Nachwirkungen Dante Gabriel Rossettis: Untersuchungen an Werken von Christina Rossetti, Coventry Patmore, Philip Bourke Marston, Theodore Watts-Dunton, Arthur W. E. O'Shaughnessy, Ernest Dowson, John Davidson.* Berlin: Bachmann, 1932 (diss. Erlangen, 1932).

51.18 Brönner, Oskar. *Das Leben Arthur O'Shaughnessys* (*Würzburg Beiträge zur englischen Literaturgeschichte*, no. 6). Hei-

delberg: Winters, 1933 (diss. Würzburg, 1933).

51.19 Evans, B. Ifor. "Minor Pre-Raphaelite Poets: William Bell Scott; William Allingham; Thomas Woolner; Arthur O'Shaughnessy; John Payne; Philip Bourke Marston; William Sharp (Fiona Macleod)," *English Poetry in the Later Nineteenth Century.* London: Methuen, 1933.

For complete annotation see 74.7.

51.20 Hearn, Lafcadio. "Three Silences: Arthur O'Shaughnessy," *Complete Lectures on Art, Literature and Philosophy.* Vol. III. Tokyo: Hokuseido Press, 1932.

Vol. II also contains a short "Note on Arthur O'Shaughnessy."

51.21 Anderson, George K. "Marie de France and Arthur O'Shaughnessy: A Study in Victorian Adaptation," *Studies in Philology*, XXXVI (July 1939), 529–549.

51.22 Fairchild, Hoxie Neale. "Rima's Mother," *Publications of the Modern Language Association*, LXVIII (June 1953), 357–370.

Identifies O'Shaughnessy's poem "Colibri" (1881) as a primary source for W. H. Hudson's *Green Mansions.*

51.23 Goldstein, Sanford M. "The Poetry of Arthur O'Shaughnessy," unpub. diss., University of Wisconsin, 1953. *Dissertation Abstracts*, XIV (1954), 480–481.

51.24 Paden, W. D. "Arthur O'Shaughnessy: The Ancestry of a Victorian Poet," *Bulletin of the John Rylands Library*, XLVI (March 1964), 429–477.

Section 52

COVENTRY PATMORE

1823–1896

[CBEL: III, 270–271, S593; DNB: XXII, S, 1121–1124 (Richard Garnett); EB: XX, 928 (Arthur Waugh)

When the members of the Cyclographic Club, the immediate forerunner of the PRB, drew up their "List of Immortals," in 1848, Coventry Kersey Dighton Patmore, a junior assistant at the British Museum and the author of a thin volume of *Poems* (1844), was not only included but given one star along with Tennyson, Mrs. Browning, and Boccaccio. (Four were possible, but only Christ had that distinction. Shakespeare and the Author of Job had three; and Homer, Dante, Leonardo, Chaucer, and Browning had two.) When *The Germ* was inaugurated in 1850, Patmore was asked to contribute. Two poems and an article on Macbeth appeared in the first three numbers of the magazine. A particular friend of Woolner, and for Rossetti a poetic "stunner," Patmore became intimate with the group in the early days of the Brotherhood, and it was he who first suggested to Ruskin the defense of the Pre-Raphaelites against the unreasonable attacks of the press. J. C. Reid, Patmore's capable biographer, has expressed puzzlement that the PRB should have taken Patmore's early derivative verse to heart, since, save in the presentation of detail, it had so little in common with Pre-Raphaelite principles. In part, the Pre-Raphaelite Brothers were attracted to Patmore because of their genuine unbounded enthusiasm for all poets and artists. But it is equally obvious from the frequency of references to Patmore in "The P.R.B. Journal" that he was also for them a liaison, a "friend of friends," and in the memoirs there is frequent mention of Patmore's willingness to introduce the Pre-Raphaelites to the great and to the potentially great.

> We all saw a good deal of Mr. Patmore, and we all looked up to him for his performances in poetry, his general intellectual insight and maturity, and his knowledge of important persons whom we came to know through him — Tennyson in especial. (Quoted in 52.11, p. 73)

Patmore's affiliation with the Pre-Raphaelites lasted throughout the 1850's, but their ways then parted. Patmore, who became the herald of domesticity in poetry, remained intimate throughout his life with Woolner and Stephens, but his period of influence on the Pre-Raphaelites, in most instances personal, really touches only the Brotherhood stage of the movement.

*   *   *

52.1 Page, Frederick, ed. *The Poems of Coventry Patmore, with an Introduction*. London: Oxford University Press, 1949.

The standard edition of the poems. An earlier but still good edition is that edited by Basil Champneys (London: Bell, 1906).

52.2 Champneys, Basil. *Memoirs and Correspondence of Coventry Patmore*. 2 vols. London: George Bell and Sons, 1900.

With four letters from Rossetti to Patmore plus extracts from other letters. For another Rossetti letter to Patmore see 24.21.

52.3 Forman, H. Buxton. "Coventry Patmore," *Our Living Poets: An Essay in Criticism*. London: Tinsley, 1871.

For complete annotation see 74.1.

52.4 Garnett, Richard. "Coventry Patmore," in *The Poets and the Poetry of the Century*, edited by A. H. Miles. Vol. [V]. London: Hutchinson, [1891–1897].

For complete annotation see 84.5.

52.5 Gosse, Edmund. *Coventry Patmore*. London: Hodder and Stoughton, 1905.

52.6 Burdett, Osbert. *The Idea of Coventry Patmore*. London: Oxford University Press, 1921.

52.7 Baum, Paull Franklin. "Coventry Patmore's Literary Criticism," *University of California Chronicle*, XXV (1923), 244–260.

52.8 Broers, Bernarda C. "Coventry Pat-

more," *Mysticism in the Neo-Romanticists.* Amsterdam: Paris, 1923 (diss. Amsterdam, 1923).
For complete annotation see 73.8.

52.9 Klenk, Hans. *Nachwirkungen Dante Gabriel Rossettis: Untersuchungen an Werken von Christina Rossetti, Coventry Patmore, Philip Bourke Marston, Theodore Watts-Dunton, Arthur W. E. O'Shaughnessy, Ernest Dowson, John Davidson.* Berlin: Bachmann, 1932 (diss. Erlangen, 1932).

52.10 Page, Frederick. *Patmore, A Study in Poetry.* Oxford University Press, 1933.

52.11 Patmore, Derek. *Portrait of My Family.* London: Cassell, 1935.
Revised as *The Life and Times of Coventry Patmore* (London: Constable, 1949). Both volumes contain a chapter on Patmore's relationship with the Pre-Raphaelites.

52.12 Lucas, F. L. "Coventry Patmore," *Ten Victorian Poets.* Cambridge University Press, 1942.
For complete annotation see 27.92.

52.13 Reid, J. C. *The Mind and Art of Coventry Patmore.* London: Routledge, 1957.
A scholarly study with a thorough bibliography.

Section 53

JOSEPH NOEL PATON

1821–1901

[CBEL: III, 303; DNB: S, I, 78–80 (J. L. Caw); EB: XX, 930]

Percy Bate in his *English Pre-Raphaelite Painters* (75.21) includes Noel Paton (together with Hughes and other artists) among those painters on whom Pre-Raphaelitism had a permanent influence, but he does not specify to any real extent the nature of that influence. Paton's style shares with the Pre-Raphaelites the cluttered-canvas effects of overelaborated detail (see especially his picture *Dawn: Luther at Erfurt*, reproduced in Bate); but he is also capable of the artistic poeticizing and the dramatic intensity found in so many Pre-Raphaelite works. A sculptor and illustrator as well as a painter, Paton was also a poet, and his two volumes of verse, particularly *Poems by a Painter*, evince the concern with the reciprocal effects of poetry and art that is to so marked a degree a characteristic of Pre-Raphaelitism.

*   *   *

53.1 Paton, Joseph Noel. *Poems by a Painter.* Edinburgh: Blackwood, 1861.
This title, William Bell Scott says of his own 1854 volume (56.5) "was afterwards appropriated by Sir J. Noel Paton, a painter of sufficient power and invention to exonerate him from intentional transfer." (56.7, p. vii) See Plate VII.

53.2 ——— *Spindrift.* Edinburgh: Blackwood, 1867.

*   *   *

53.3 Halkett, George R. "Our Living Artists: Sir Joseph Noel Paton," *Magazine of Art*, III (1880), 1–6.

53.4 Miles, Alfred H. "Sir Joseph Noel Paton," in *The Poets and the Poetry of the Century*, edited by A. H. Miles. Vol. [V]. London: Hutchinson, [1891–1897].
For complete annotation see 84.5.

53.5 Story, Alfred T. "Sir Noel Paton: His Life and Work," *Art Journal*, LVII (April 1895), 97–128.
Five parts, profusely illustrated. ". . . not withstanding any temporary influence of the

Pre-Raphaelites, the final impression left on Sir Noel's art was slight, and *moral* rather than technical." (p. 104)

53.6 Pinnington, Edward. "Sir Noel Paton, R.S.A.," *Art Journal*, LXIV (February 1902), 70–72.

Section 54
JOHN PAYNE
1842–1916
[CBEL: III, 352–353, S612]

Not every poet has a society devoted to the commemoration of his life and works, but of all those poets who have stimulated such adulation, it is doubtful whether any has more quickly been forgotten than John Payne. The formation of the John Payne Society in 1905 (largely the work of Payne's principal disciple, Thomas Wright of Olney) was but the *reductio ad absurdum* of a long period of overrated devotion and loyal praise. This is not to deny Payne the talent that he obviously possessed, only to disparage the vanity that led him, when he did not win public favor, to create a cult of devotees who supported his view that he was the great, unsung poet of the century. "It is the younger generation," Payne wrote in his *Autobiography* (54.13), "men of my own standing, who are jealous of me and who, having obtained . . . control of the Press, contrive to keep my name and work not only from receiving its due recognition, but even from coming to the knowledge of the public." (p. 18) Thomas Wright echoes Payne's view in the eulogium of what must surely be the most embarrassingly naïve biography ever written.

> The obituaries of the greatest man of letters of the century will be looked back upon as among the curiosities of literature. When Tennyson died (and the amount of him that is imperishable is quite trivial) there were notices by the acre — many of them illustrated. One would have thought the crack of doom had come . . . When Payne died *The Times* gave him exactly four and a half inches of feeble comment, and even for that his patient ghost had to wait thirteen days . . . Other leading papers wasted even less upon him. Most of them, even to this very day, are in blissful ignorance that the greatest writer of recent years has passed away. (54.11, p. 267)

Payne's overestimation of his own abilities pervades the whole of Wright's book and his every expression of vainglory and his constant tendency to bolster his own ego by denigrating his fellow poets is dutifully and almost reverentially recorded by his indiscriminating Boswell.

The irony is that Payne showed relative promise in his first publications, which were highly praised by Rossetti and Swinburne. As a close friend of O'Shaughnessy, Payne had gained entrée to Pre-Raphaelite circles, and his first volume *The Masque of Shadows* contained a number of romances and ballads, and a dream-like atmosphere which echoed the Pre-Raphaelites, especially Morris. *Intaglios*, his book of sonnets written before but published after *The Masque of Shadows*, bore clearly the marks of Rossetti's influence. Between 1870 and 1880, Payne published five volumes of original verse. He then entered that stage of his literary career which was to win him his principal recognition — translation. His work in this area was prodigious, revealing a versatile and intelligent and gifted man. Twenty-three years after his last volume, Payne once again returned to original poetry, and his *Carol and Cadence* (1908) is of some interest, not only for the inspiration of Helen Snee, that sad beauty who wandered through the lives of O'Shaughnessy, Nettleship, and Payne (see 51.13), but because in this volume Payne abandoned the sonnet and returned to the ballads and romances wherein had lain the promise of his first volume. Like most of the minor Pre-Raphaelite poets, Payne is derivative in form and theme and imitative in subject matter.

Like so many of them he had only a veneer of poetry. His first two volumes are of considerable interest in examining the Pre-Raphaelite milieu, but he was unable to sustain even the narrow thread of originality that they contained. His chief frustration lay in his refusal to recognize his poetic limitations, and this refusal produced a bitterness and disillusionment that runs through much of his later verse. Payne never forgave Victorian society for its awareness of his limited talents (just as he never forgave Richard Burton his superior translation of *The Arabian Nights*), and he went to oblivion leaving only the cult whom he had somehow convinced of his greatness to mourn his passing.

* * *

54.1 Payne, John. *The Masque of Shadows and Other Poems.* London: Pickering, 1870.
Dedicated to Arthur O'Shaughnessy, whose first volume, *An Epic of Women* (51.1), also 1870, was dedicated to Payne.

54.2 ——— *Intaglios: Sonnets.* London: Pickering, 1871. Payne's first-written volume, but second-published.

54.3 ——— *Songs of Life and Death.* London: King, 1872.

54.4 ——— *Lautrec: A Poem.* London: Pickering, 1878.

54.5 ——— *New Poems.* London: Pickering, 1880.

54.6 *Poetical Works: Definitive Edition.* 2 Vols. London: Villon Society, 1902.

54.7 Robinson, Tracy and Lucy. *Selections from the Poetry of John Payne.* With an Introduction by Lucy Robinson. New York: John Lane, The Bodley Head, 1906.
See 54.13.

54.8 Payne, John. *Carol and Cadence: New Poems, 1902–1907.* London: Villon Society for private subscription, 1908.
A selection from this volume was issued as *Nature and Her Lover, and Other Poems*

from "Carol and Cadence," with an Introduction by Thomas Wright (London: John Payne Society, 1922).

* * *

54.9 Forman, H. Buxton. "John Payne and Arthur W. E. O'Shaughnessy," *Our Living Poets: An Essay in Criticism.* London: Tinsley, 1871.
For complete annotation see 74.1.

54.10 Garnett, Richard. "John Payne," in *The Poets and the Poetry of the Century,* edited by A. H. Miles. Vol. [VIII]. London: Hutchinson, [1891–1897].
For complete annotation see 84.5.

54.11 Wright, Thomas. *The Life of John Payne.* London: Unwin, 1919.
Includes three letters from Rossetti to Payne. With a bibliographical appendix. The volume contains much interesting information about Payne's and O'Shaughnessy's relationship with Helen Snee.

54.12 Broers, Bernarda C. "John Payne," *Mysticism in the Neo-Romanticists.* Amsterdam: Paris, 1923 (diss. Amsterdam, 1923).
For complete annotation see 73.8.

54.13 Wright, Thomas, ed. *The Autobiography of John Payne . . .* With Preface and

Annotations, . . . [and] Ten Drawings by Cecil W. Paul Jones and Seven Photographs. Olney: Thomas Wright, 1926.

Payne's fragment autobiography written as notes in connection with 54.7.

54.14 Evans, B. Ifor. "Minor Pre-Raphael-ite Poets: William Bell Scott; William Allingham; Thomas Woolner; Arthur O'Shaughnessy; John Payne; Philip Bourke Marston; William Sharp (Fiona Macleod)," *English Poetry in the Later Nineteenth Century.* London: Methuen, 1933.

For complete annotation see 74.7.

Section 55

FREDERICK SANDYS

1829–1904

[DNB: S, I, 263–265 (Robert Ross); EB: XXIV, 144]

Frederick Sandys' first contact with the Pre-Raphaelites came with his introduction to Rossetti after the appearance of *The Nightmare* (82.2), his magnificent caricature of the Pre-Raphaelite heresy via Millais' *Sir Isumbras at the Ford*. Once established, his friendship with the group was permanent — until he broke with Rossetti, who accused him of plagiarizing his ideas, in 1869 — and in the wood-engraving revival of the 1860's and 1870's Sandys found a medium compatible with the Pre-Raphaelitism of his earlier Academy work. (see Introduction to section 97) Esther Wood has given perhaps the best summary of Sandys' relationship with the Pre-Raphaelites:

> . . . A pre-Raphaelite in every essential quality — absolute fidelity to nature, earnestness of spirit, and singleness of artistic purpose — he was in no way associated with the conscious beginnings of the movement . . . A classicist by nature and temperament, yet steeped in the same romantic mysticism that inspired the pre-Raphaelite Brotherhood, he is stronger than any of them in the presentment of a dramatic crisis, though he has little of the brooding sensuous warmth that breathes from nearly all their paintings. He deals less than they with the subtle intimacies of passion, and more with its typical effects and expressions. It may be said . . . that the personal note so dominant in Holman Hunt and Rossetti is subordinated . . . We miss in him the cry of plaintive regret, the burden of mystery which we hear and feel in *The Scapegoat* and *The Blessed Damozel*; yet there is in all his work a certain solemnity and largeness of outlook, pertaining to a mind in which the more poignant phases of imaginative genius have been outgrown early and in secret, leaving the faculties at once fresh and mature. (55.4, pp. 9–10)

The question of influence is always risky, but in Sandys' case it was solely through the Pre-Raphaelites that he was introduced to the possibilities of illustration, and in that revival which the Pre-Raphaelites inaugurated he made his greatest and most lasting — and it may be said, his most genuinely Pre-Raphaelite — contribution to nineteenth-century art.

* * *

55.1 [Gray, J. M.]. "Frederick Sandys," *Art Journal*, XLVI (March 1884), 73–78.

55.2 [———] "Frederick Sandys and the Woodcut Designers of Thirty Years Ago," *Century Guild Hobby Horse*, n.s. III (October 1888), 147–157.

With a list of wood-engraving designs by Sandys.

55.3 Pennell, Joseph. "An English Illustrator," *Quarto*, I (1896), 33–37.
For annotation see 89.11.

55.4 Wood, Esther. *A Consideration of the Art of Frederick Sandys* (special Winter number of *The Artist*). London: Constable, 1896.

Principally concerned with Sandys as a painter. With 30 illustrations of Sandys' works, a list of pictures exhibited at the Royal Academy, and a list of Sandys' illustrations for periodicals.

55.5 White, Gleeson. "A Great Illustrator (Frederick Sandys)," *Pall Mall Magazine*, XVI (November 1898), 328–338.

A general treatment of Sandys as an illustrator, with an unreliable list of his published drawings.

55.6 Bate, Percy. "The Late Frederick Sandys: A Retrospect," *Studio*, XXXIII (October 1904), 3–17.

Twelve illustrations.

55.7 Baldry, Alfred Lys. "Drawings by Frederick Sandys," *Art Journal*, LXXI (May 1909), 149–151.

55.8 S[andys], M[ary] F., ed. *Reproduc-*

tions of Woodcuts by F. Sandys, 1860–1866. London: Published for Mrs. Sandys, [1910].

With an Introduction by Borough Johnson. Twenty-five woodcuts are included.

55.9 Williamson, G. C. "Anthony Frederick Sandys," *Murray Marks and his Friends: A Tribute of Regard*. London: John Lane, 1919.

For annotation see 86.14.

55.10 Sullivan, Edmund J. "Sandys and Boyd Houghton," *The Art of Illustration*. London: Chapman and Hall, 1921.

55.11 Chamberlain, Arthur B. "Works by Frederick Sandys in the Birmingham Art Gallery," *Apollo*, II (November 1925), 258–263.

Medea, Morgan-le-Fay, and a portrait of Mrs. C. A. Howell, all acquired in 1925.

55.12 "A Fine Pre-Raphaelite Draughtsman," *Times*, No. 55,535 (30 October 1962), p. 16.

Section 56

WILLIAM BELL SCOTT

1811–1890

[CBEL: III, 305; DNB: XVII, 1051–1053 (Ronald Bayne); EB: XXIV, 475]

In a fit of pique, Swinburne wrote in "The New Terror" of William Bell Scott, "here . . . is a man whose name would never have been heard, whose verse would never have been read, whose daubs would never have been seen, outside some æsthetic Lilliput of the North, but for his casual and parasitical association with the Trevelyans, the Rossettis, and myself." (62.6, vol. XVI, 14; see also 56.10)

Swinburne's diatribe against Scott (after the posthumous publication of his *Autobiographical Notes*) is patently unjust, but he was obviously as puzzled as William Michael Rossetti and the remainder of surviving Pre-Raphaelites at the perfidy of this friend of long standing, who, Swinburne was perfectly right in saying, owed so great a debt to his Pre-Raphaelite companions. By 1847, when Rossetti wrote to Scott, expressing his admiration of *The Year of the World*, Scott had found little recognition of either his literary or his artistic efforts. His reaction is interesting in the light of later attacks on Rossetti in his same diary: "This appreciative criticism from an unknown but evidently poetry-loving correspondent pleased me much . . . I was, it seemed, not destined to be wholly unknown at a sufficient distance." (56.10, I, p. 244) Shortly afterwards, Rossetti sent Scott a sheaf of his poems under the title, "Songs of the Art Catholic," which included some of his finest earlier pieces. With characteristic patronizing, Scott found the poems "admirable" but he was disturbed lest the title betray an undermining of this "wonderfully gifted boy" by the "Oxford tractarianism just then distracting weak intellects." (I, p. 246) The meeting of Scott and Rossetti over Christmas 1847 led ultimately to Scott's being included among the contributors to *The Germ* and to his being accepted by the Pre-Raphaelites, though his employment at the Government School of Design in Newcastle (which position he maintained until 1864) prevented his playing a decisively active role in the Brotherhood phase of the movement.

Although Scott's earliest poetry had been printed in *The Edinburgh University Souvenir* (1835), his association with the Pre-Raphaelites provided him with a new and fresh inspiration, which he acknowledged in the "Dedicatio Postica" of his 1875 *Poems*, paying tribute to the assistance of Rossetti, Morris, and Swinburne (in that order). The octave of the sonnet is revealing:

> Now many years ago in life's midday,
>   I laid the pen aside and rested still,
>   Like one bare-footed on a shingly hill:
> Three poets then came past, each young as May,
> Year after year, upon their upward way,
>   And each one reached his hand out as he passed,
>   And over me his friendship's mantle cast,
> And went on singing, everyone his lay.

Under their impetus, Scott's *Poems by a Painter* appeared in 1854, and it was probably this volume more than any other which inclined H. Buxton Forman to include Scott among the "Pre-Raphaelite Group" in his *Our Living Poets*, 1870 (56.12). It was primarily "the deep correlation between the two arts" that ranked Scott with the Pre-Raphaelites, apart from general resemblances, and similarities in verse forms, such as the ballad.

Neither Scott's poetry nor his painting matched that of the major Pre-Raphaelites. Scott was pedantic and self-inflated, incapable of the spontaneity that marks Morris' *Defence of Guenevere*, the sheer lyrical effervescence of Swinburne's *Poems and Ballads* or the magic and mystery of Rossetti's early poems and ballads. A whole bevy of second-rate verse writers was caught in the Pre-Raphaelite maelstrom; Scott was better than some and no worse than others, but he failed to win either in his lifetime or afterwards the recognition that he felt was his due. After the publication of his *Autobiographical Notes*, Scott was accused of being ungenerous, unappreciative, jealous, malicious, and disloyal.

One of Max Beerbohm's most trenchant cartoons in *Rossetti and His Circle* (82.9) is that showing the back garden at Cheyne Walk. Leaning against a tree in the center of a circle of admirers is Dante Rossetti. Around him are Burne-Jones, Brown, Pater, Morris, Swinburne (on his knees with hands devoutly clasped) and an indefinite young man whose identification is uncertain. In the foreground, eyed suspiciously by a frightened wombat, stands Scott, dour and doubtful, "wondering what it is those fellows seem to see in Gabriel." However, manuscript material recently discovered (see 3.10) may alter appreciably the view of Scott epitomized in this caricature.

* * *

56.1 *The Edinburgh University Souvenir.* Edinburgh: Dunlop, 1835.

An anthology of poetry and prose containing some of Scott's earliest poetry. For a discussion of this volume see 56.10.

56.2 Scott, William Bell. *Hades; or, The Transit: And The Progress of Mind. Two Poems.* Edinburgh, Last, 1838.

Another edition, published in London by Henry Renshaw, also appeared in 1838. With two etchings by Scott.

56.3 ———— *The Year of the World: A Philosophical Poem on "Redemption from the Fall."* Edinburgh: Tait, 1846.

Also published in London by Simpkin and Marshall, 1846.

56.4 ———— ed. *Memoir of David Scott, R.S.A. Containing His Journals in Italy; Notes on Art, and Other Papers.* Edinburgh: Black, 1850.

With seven illustrations by William Bell Scott. The influence of David Scott should not be overlooked in considering the works of Scott.

56.5 ———— *Poems.* London: Smith, Elder, 1854.

Entitled, on the frontispiece and on the spine, *Poems by a Painter.* With three illustrations by Scott. See Plate II.

56.6 ———— *Mural Paintings. Chevy Chase at Sir W. C. Trevelyan, Bart.'s, Wallington, Northumberland. The King's Quair at Penkill Castle, Ayrshire. Two Papers, Read at the Meetings of the Institute of British Architects, . . . December 2, 1867; January 6, 1868.*

Offprint from the *Sessional Papers of the Royal Institute of British Architects,* XVIII (1867–1868), 31–46, 85–93.

The first lecture was separately printed as *William Bell Scott's Pictures in the Hall at Wallington, Illustrative of the English Border,* and contained synopses of the eight pictures. Both reprints contain the eighteen spandrels in which Chevy Chase is depicted.

56.7 ———— *Poems: Ballads, Studies from Nature, Sonnets, Etc.* London: Longmans, 1875.

Illustrated with seventeen etchings by Scott and Laurence Alma-Tadema.

56.8 ———— *A Poet's Harvest Home: Being One Hundred Short Poems.* London: Stock, 1882.

56.9 ———— *Illustrations to The King's Quair of King James I of Scotland. Painted on the Staircase of Penkill Castle, Ayrshire, by William Bell Scott. June 1865 to August 1868. Etched by Him in 1885.* Edinburgh: Privately printed for T. & A. Constable, 1887.

With an Introduction by Scott containing important details on Rossetti during 1869 and 1870.

56.10 ———— *Autobiographical Notes . . . and Notices of His Artistic and Poetic Circle of Friends, 1830–1882,* edited by W. Minto. 2 vols. London: Osgood, 1892.

Containing, as Ford Madox Hueffer commented, a "quantom of Mephistophelean passages anent Rossetti." (24.5, p. 466) The two volumes contain extracts from nine letters of Rossetti (1847–1865) and ten complete letters written from Kelmscott (all except one written in 1871). Swinburne reviewed this work in "The New Terror," *Fortnightly Review,* LVIII, n.s. LII (December 1892), 830–833; reprinted Bonchurch, 62.6, XVI, 11–17. See also Swinburne's letter to the editor of the *Academy* (24 December 1892, pp. 590–591), reprinted in *The Swinburne Letters,* 62.12, VI, 47–51, entitled in the British Museum manuscript "The Poison of a Parasite."

56.11 ———— *A Poet's Harvest Home: Being One Hundred Short Poems. With an Aftermath of Twenty Short Poems.* London: Elkin Mathews, 1893.

Illustrated by Scott.

* * *

56.12 [Forman, H. Buxton]. "Criticisms on Contemporaries: No. XII. Mr. William Bell

Scott," *Tinsley's Magazine*, VIII (May 1871), 387–394.
Reprinted in *Our Living Poets* (74.1).

56.13 "William Bell Scott, Poet and Painter," *London Quarterly Review*, XLV (October 1875), 149–167.

56.14 Rossetti, William Michael. "William Bell Scott and Modern British Poetry," *Macmillan's Magazine*, XXXIII (March 1876), 418–429.
In part a review of 56.7. A study of various Pre-Raphaelite and Spasmodic poets.

56.15 "Mr. William Bell Scott," *Athenaeum*, no. 3292 (29 November 1890), 745.
An obituary notice.

56.16 Horne, Herbert P. "William Bell Scott, Poet, Painter, and Critic: Born 12 September, 1811; Died 22 November, 1890," *Century Guild Hobby Horse*, n.s. VI (January 1891), 16–27.
Also separately reprinted (1891).

56.17 Knight, Joseph. "William Bell Scott," in *The Poets and the Poetry of the Century*, edited by A. H. Miles. Vol. [IV]. London: Hutchinson, [1891–1897].
For complete annotation see 84.5.

56.18 [Skelton, John]. "Dante Rossetti and Mr. William Bell Scott," *Blackwood's Magazine*, CLIII (February 1893), 229–235.
Reprinted in revised form in 25.16.

56.19 Chester, Austin. "The Art of William Bell Scott," *Windsor Magazine*, XL (September 1914), 413–428.

56.20 Broers, Bernarda C. "William Bell Scott," *Mysticism in the Neo-Romanticists*. Amsterdam: Paris, 1923 (diss. Amsterdam, 1923).
For complete annotation see 73.8.

56.21 Evans, B. Ifor. "Minor Pre-Raphaelite Poets: William Bell Scott; William Allingham; Thomas Woolner; Arthur O'Shaughnessy; John Payne; Philip Bourke Marston; William Sharp (Fiona Macleod)," *English Poetry in the Later Nineteenth Century*. London: Methuen, 1933.
For complete annotation see 74.7.

56.22 Ironside, Robin. "Pre-Raphaelite Paintings at Wallington: A Note on William Bell Scott and Ruskin," *Architectural Review*, XCII (December 1942), 147–149.

56.23 Smith, K. H. "A Biographical and Critical Study of William Bell Scott," unpub. diss., University of Durham, 1952.

Section 57

THOMAS SEDDON

1821–1856

[DNB: XVII, 1116–1117 (R. E. Graves); EB: XXIV, 577]

The son of a prominent cabinetmaker and the brother of the architect, J. P. Seddon, Thomas Seddon moved freely in Pre-Raphaelite circles, though he was not a member of the Brotherhood. Seddon accompanied Holman Hunt on his first trip to the Holy Land in 1853, and under the tutelage of Hunt he acquired the meticulous devotion to detail and the fidelity to external fact that characterized one group (and one period) within the Pre-Raphaelite Movement. Seddon might, in fact, be called the "arch Pre-Raphaelite", so devoted was he to this one aspect of Pre-Raphaelite painting. In 1856, Seddon returned to the east but he died at Cairo, where he is buried. Ruskin, in his address (57.1) at the Seddon Exhibition at the Society of Arts (17.1), identified Seddon with the more important of the two classes of Pre-Raphaelites — what he called the "prosaic" Pre-Raphaelites (as opposed to the "poetic"): "The spirit of the present age," Ruskin said, "was strictly scientific, and all that they could do more than was done in the earlier ages must be on the side of truth, and could not be on the side of imagination." (*CW*, 45.3, XIV, p. 468) Numerous examples of Seddon's emphasis on the accuracy of detail are presented in the *Memoir* by his brother. And if Holman-Huntistic standards were sufficient to entitle their bearer to artistic distinction, Seddon would have to be ranked the most absolutely pure of all the minor, nonmembers of the Pre-Raphaelite entourage.

* * *

57.1 Ruskin, John. "Speech on Thomas Seddon," *Journal of the Society of Arts*, V (May 1857), 360–362.

A résumé of Ruskin's address on Seddon as a Pre-Raphaelite artist delivered at the Seddon Exhibition, May 6, 1857 (17.1). The résumé is reprinted in *CW* (45.3, XIV, 464–470). The exhibition, under the superintendence of the Seddon Subscription Fund headed by William Michael Rossetti, continued throughout May. A brief biographical note on Seddon appears on p. 419 of the same volume of the *Journal*.

57.2 [Seddon, John P.] *Memoir and Letters of the Late Thomas Seddon, Artist. By His Brother*. London: Nisbet, 1858.

Section 58

FREDERIC JAMES SHIELDS

1833–1911

[DNB: S, I, 306–307 (P. G. Konody)]

A Manchester artist, Shields had no contact with the Pre-Raphaelites until the Manchester Art Treasures Exhibition in 1857 (see 18.3). Of the Pre-Raphaelite pictures which he saw there by Millais, Hunt, Hughes, and Madox Brown, Shields recorded that they were a "marvellous unparalleled gathering." It was not until seven years later that he was introduced to Rossetti, but from 1865 on he was an especially intimate friend of both Rossetti and Ford Madox Brown. Shields' major work was religious in theme, and he does not seem to have been much swayed by Rossetti's particular brand of romantic mysticism. His own style echoed the realistic side of Pre-Raphaelitism, but his pietistic view of art was more nearly akin to Holman Hunt's than to that of most of the other Pre-Raphaelites. Shield's finest, and most thoroughly Pre-Raphaelite work, consists of his designs for book illustrations, and though these designs are few in number they have a strength and grandeur hardly surpassed by any of the other illustrators of the period. For Shields' illustrations see section 99.

* * *

58.1 Scudder, Horace E. "An English Interpreter," *Atlantic Monthly*, L (October 1882), 464–475.

An early discussion of Shields' life and art, valuable for details of Shields' stained glass windows at Eaton Hall Chapel (the seat of the Grosvenor family) illustrating *Te Deum* *Laudamus*. Reference is also made to the *Pilgrim's Progress*. Selections from Shields' Dickensian autobiography are also included in the article (pp. 472–474).

58.2 Stephens, Frederic George. "Frederic J. Shields and His Works: A Narrative Partly

His Own," *Portfolio*, XV (July 1884), 134–137.
Supplementary to 58.1.

58.3 Ewart, Henry C., ed. "Frederic Shields. An Autobiography," *Toilers in Art*. London: Isbister, 1891.

58.4 Langridge, I. "The Chapel of the Ascension and Mr. Frederic Shields," *Art Journal*, LXIV (November 1902), pp. 337–343.

58.5 Shields, Frederic J. *The Chapel of the Ascension: Its Story and Scheme*. 5th ed. London: Stock, 1904.
A revised edition was prepared in 1911. This chapel in the Bayswater Road, for which Shields did the murals and decorations, was destroyed by bombs in the Second World War. In addition to this volume, Shields also wrote a small pamphlet entitled *Panels in the Chapel of the Ascension* (no publication facts

available) which was illustrated. The Autotype Fine Art Company issued a set of 28 reproductions from the series of the "Prophets and Apostles" with a descriptive handbook accompanying the portfolio. A second set of four autotypes was also issued. For details of Shields' work on the Chapel of the Ascension see 58.7.

58.6 Rowley, Charles. "Frederic Shields," *Fifty Years of Work Without Wages*. London: Hodder and Stoughton, [1911].
For annotation see 26.4.

58.7 Mills, Ernestine. *The Life and Letters of Frederic Shields*. London: Longmans, 1912.
An extremely dull but indispensable volume, with references to most of the Pre-Raphaelites and many letters to Shields from Ford Madox Brown, Rossetti, Christina Rossetti, and others. Over fifty letters from Rossetti to Shields are included. The volume also contains extracts from Shields' diary.

Section 59

ELIZABETH ELEANOR SIDDAL (ROSSETTI)

1834–1862

From Ford Madox Brown's Diary, October 6th. [1854]:

> Called on Dante Rossetti. Saw Miss Siddal, looking thinner and more deathlike and more beautiful and more ragged than ever; a real artist, a woman without parallel for many a long year. Gabriel as usual diffuse and inconsequent in his work. Drawing wonderful and lovely Guggums one after another, each one a fresh charm, each one stamped with immortality . . . (24.7, p. 19)

Brown ridiculed as the "incarnation of exaggeration" Ruskin's pronouncement that the drawings of Elizabeth Siddal were better even than Rossetti's, but he hastened to add, "However, he is right to admire them. She is a stunner and no mistake." (p. 33) And that seems to have been the consensus of all the early Pre-Raphaelites: Elizabeth Siddal was indeed a stunner. Only Christina Rossetti, who somehow never seemed to take to her, has left just the slightest censorious comment on her influence on Rossetti, in her poem, "In an Artist's Studio" (1856). Until the displacement of Elizabeth Siddal by the dark-eyed, somber beauty of Jane Morris, her face was, however, about the only one that looked out from all Gabriel's canvases; and Christina wasn't far wrong in her interpretation of the restricting effect of Elizabeth Siddal on her brother's art: "every canvas means/The same one meaning, neither more nor less." Rossetti said to Brown once that "when he first saw her, he felt his destiny was defined" (p. 33), and certainly she assumes the central position in Rossetti's life and art. Theirs was a totally compulsive relationship, and when she was no longer present as a physical reality, the ghost of her memory lived on to torture and torment the man who had loved her, almost to the point of his own destruction, both as man and artist.

Elizabeth Eleanor Rossetti (née Siddal — also known as The Sid, Gug, Guggums, Lizzie, and Ida) was discovered, according to tradition, by Deverell in a milliner's establishment, and she was quickly drafted as the model for which Pre-Raphaelitism had been founded. Her years with Rossetti need not be reviewed. For a while she masqueraded as his student, and she did produce a number of water colors and drawings. *We Are Seven, Pippa Passes, Clerk Saunders, The Haunted Tree,* and a few others have been reproduced. Ruskin became her patron and agreed to buy everything she did; but the largest body of her art work, which Rossetti had the foresight to have photographed, has been seen only by a handful of persons. Her poetry is even more scant, and none was published in her lifetime. William Michael Rossetti printed from time to time a total of fifteen of her poems. All are sad and derivative like her drawings, pale echoes of Rossetti.

It is tempting to say that Elizabeth Siddal was, after all, the only Pre-Raphaelite. In a grim way, she stood for what it all meant; and she combined in her fragile beauty and in her tragic life the legendary aspect that inspires the movement's art and poetry. Rossetti's gesture of burying his poems with her is perhaps the most magnificently sophomoric event in the entire Pre-Raphaelite Movement. As a symbolic act it had for him, no doubt, a cathartic, perhaps even a punitive significance; the subsequent exhumation and publication of the poems, unfortunately, opened a door through which a succession of literary ghouls have insidiously stolen. But perhaps the burying of the poems was as much a defining of Rossetti's destiny as was the meeting with her in the first place.

Few letters of hers have survived, and if she actually spoke, her words have nowhere been recorded. We have Swinburne's testimony about her intelligence and ability: "Except Lady Trevelyan," he wrote to William Rossetti, "I never knew so brilliant and appreciative a woman — so quick to see and so keen to enjoy that rare and delightful fusion of wit, humour, character-painting, and dramatic poetry — poetry subdued to dramatic effect — which is only less wonderful and delightful than the very highest works of genius." (62.12, VI, p. 93)

"Love born to an early death" (a line from one of her poems) aptly epitomizes this sad beauty.

* * *

59.1 Rossetti, William Michael. "Dante Gabriel Rossetti and Elizabeth Siddal," *Burlington Magazine*, I (May 1903), 273–295.

One poem of Elizabeth Siddal's, "A Silent Wood," is printed for the first time in this article. For other of her poems see *Family Letters* (24.5, one poem); *Ruskin: Rossetti: Pre-Raphaelitism* (24.7, eight poems); *Some Reminiscences* (38.8, five new poems and a reprinting of "A Silent Wood"). For additional annotation see 25.25.

59.2 Vitale, Zaira. "Eleonora Siddal Rossetti," *Emporium*, XIX (June 1904), 430–447.

Profusely illustrated, reprinting many of the illustrations in 59.1.

59.3 Hubbard, Elbert. *Little Journeys to the Homes of Famous Lovers: Dante Gabriel Rossetti and Elizabeth Siddal.* East Aurora, N.Y.: The Roycrofters, 1906.

59.4 Le Gallienne, Richard. "Dante Gabri-

el Rossetti and Elizabeth Siddal," *The Loves of the Poets*. New York: Baker, 1911.
For annotation see 25.43.

59.5 Pundt, Herbert. "Anhang: Die Gedichte der Miss Siddal," in "Dante Gabriel Rossettis Einfluss auf die Gedichte des jungen William Morris," unpub. diss., Breslau, 1922.

59.6 Wiegler, Paul. "Guggum," *Genius in Love and Death*. Translated by C. Raushenbush. London: Boni and Liveright, 1929.

59.7 Hunt, Violet. *The Wife of Rossetti, Her Life and Death*. London: John Lane, 1932.
A sensational and unreliable account of the life, and more especially the death, of Rossetti's wife. For a general discussion of this book and others of the same genre see Survey, pp. 36–37. See also "Rossetti's Marriage" (25.85).

59.8 Nothwang, Irene. *Die Frau, die Liebe und der Tod bei Dante Gabriel Rossetti*. Stuttgart: Felbach, 1932 (diss. Tübingen, 1932).

59.9 Ferguson, John, and N. C. Hunter. "The Merciless Lady. A Play in a Prologue and Four Acts." Unpublished play, presented at the Birmingham Repertory Theater, Saturday, 6 October 1934.

59.10 Sitwell, Sacheverell. "Dumb Tones and Shuddering Semitones of Death," *Dance of the Quick and the Dead*. London: Faber, 1936.
An impressionistic reconstruction of the last day of Miss Siddal's life and of the incidents leading to her tragic death. Reprinted in *The Selected Works of Sacheverell Sitwell* (New York: Bobbs-Merrill, 1953).

59.11 Procter, Ida. "Elizabeth Siddal: The Ghost of an Idea," *Cornhill Magazine*, no. 990 (Winter 1951–1952), pp. 368–386.
Miss Procter suggests that the ghost of Pre-Raphaelitism, the memory of Elizabeth Siddal, lived on after the Pre-Raphaelite idea was long dead. "She was not to be thought of as altogether lost to the Pre-Raphaelite view: it was only the semblance of a trance. She who had not been wholly real in life was not to be thought of as really dead. She had become the ghost of the Pre-Raphaelite idea." (p. 372)

59.12 Batchelor, Paula. *Angel with Bright Hair*. London: Methuen, 1957.
A novel based on the life of Elizabeth Siddal.

59.13 Coley, Curtis G. "Miss Siddal by Sir John Everett Millais," *Bulletin of the Art Association of Indianapolis*, LI (March 1964), 2–3.

Section 60

JAMES SMETHAM

1821–1889

[CBEL: III, 306; DNB: XVIII, 403 (Richard Garnett)]

"Photography, Pre-Raphaelitism, and Ruskinism" — these, according to Smetham's biographer, William H. Davies (60.1, p. 45), were the adverse influences on James Smetham. But Smetham's problem was more deeply rooted, and it led ultimately to his insanity and to twelve years of incarceration prior to his death in 1889.

Apart from his friendship with Ruskin, Rossetti, and Shields, Smetham's principal Pre-Raphaelite tendency was his attempt, albeit unsuccessful, to function in both painting and poetry. From 1863 until about 1868, Smetham was frequently in the company of Rossetti, and he received encouragement and help from both Rossetti and Ruskin. But his life was a continuous and unremitting series of frustrations, which, coupled with what seems from the outset to have been megalomaniacal delusions and an increasing religious monomania, led ultimately to his complete mental and physical collapse in 1877. Perhaps Smetham's most lasting contribution, apart from his few pictures and poems, is his essay on Blake reprinted in part as an addendum to Gilchrist's *Life of Blake* (86.1). In a little poem entitled "The Painter and the Poet" in the *Literary Works* (60.2), written after the rejection of his pictures by the Royal Academy, Smetham saw the motivation of the creative artist as "love of beauty, not applause." Rossetti once caught Smetham's weakness with acute precision:

> I am afraid you will think no better of me for pronouncing the commonplace verdict that what you lack is simply ambition, i.e. the feeling of pure rage and self-hatred when any one else does better than you do. This in an ambitious mind leads not to envy in the least, but to self-scrutiny on all sides, and that to something if anything can. You comfort yourself with other things, whereas art must be its own comforter or else comfortless. (60.1, p. 162)

Smetham wanted desperately the applause that he renounced, but for all that he is remembered, he stamped "beauty and eternity/On nought or next to nothing."

* * *

60.1 Smetham, Sara, and William Davies, eds. *Letters of James Smetham, with an Introductory Memoir*. London: Macmillan, 1891.

With five letters from Rossetti to Smetham. The volume also contains a selection from Smetham's poetry. The Memoir is by William Davies. For a long review see *Portfolio*, XXIV (May 1893), 107–110.

60.2 Davies, William, ed. *The Literary Works of James Smetham*. London: Macmillan, 1893.

Including essays and poems. The essay on Blake was printed in part in Gilchrist's *Life of Blake* (86.1)

60.3 [Horne, Herbert P.]. "Potentia Silentii: Being a Selection of Passages from the Letters and Papers of James Smetham," *Century Guild Hobby Horse*, n.s. II (October 1887), 123–130; n.s. III (January 1888), 8–12.

60.4 "James Smetham and C. Allston Collins," *Art Journal*, LXVI (September 1904), 281–284.

With two reproductions of Smetham's works and four of Collins'.

60.5 Beardmore, William G. *James Smetham: Painter, Poet, and Essayist*. London: Kelly, [1906].

60.6 Davies, Trevor H. " 'The Letters of James Smetham.' The Use of Imagination in Religion," *Spiritual Voices in Modern Literature*. New York: Doran, 1919.

A sermon.

60.7 Grigson, Geoffrey. "James Smetham," *Cornhill Magazine*, no. 976 (Autumn 1948), pp. 332–346.

Section 61

SIMEON SOLOMON

1840?–1905

[DNB: S, I, 354–355 (E. M. Lloyd)]

When Helen Rossetti Angeli published her important volume on Rossetti's friends and enemies in 1949 (see 25.91), Simeon Solomon, the most shadowy and, in many respects, the most fascinating figure who moved in the Pre-Raphaelite sphere, received not even so much as a casual reference. In omitting him, Mrs. Angeli was doing no more than following conventional practice; for after the disgrace of his legal conviction for pederasty in 1873, Simeon Solomon was sent to Coventry by the Pre-Raphaelites, who henceforth agreed to pretend that this "greatest artist of us all" (as Burne-Jones is reported to have called him) had simply never existed. Swinburne, at whose doorstep the degradation of Solomon has frequently been laid, made a complete volte-face, fearing contagion in the public mind by association, and he later referred to Solomon as "a thing unmentionable alike by men and women, as equally abhorrent to either — nay, to the very beasts . . ." (62.12, IV, 107)

Solomon's promise at the outset of his career is unquestionable. He was a student in the Royal Academy Schools at fifteen, and he entered his first picture for exhibition at eighteen. A precocious artist, Solomon drew heavily in his early pictures on the Hebraic tradition in which he was so thoroughly grounded. From the outset his work was sensitive and mystical, though he gradually turned to the epicene quality which is now recognized as the Solomon type. An early friend of Henry Holiday, Marcus Stone, and Albert Moore, with whom he was associated in the Sketching Club (see 86.13), Solomon was praised by such critics as Thackeray, Pater, and Swinburne.

That his meeting with Swinburne was the turning point in his life is made clear by the letters from Solomon which have survived and which are printed in Lang's edition of *The Swinburne Letters* (62.12, vol. II). Swinburne's dissipation in the decade before his incarceration at The Pines was an unhappy model for the impressionable and tractable Solomon, who followed his leader into a quagmire of corruption from which, unfortunately, there was no Watts-Dunton to retrieve him. His later years were spent in poverty, desolation, and disgrace, an outcast from his family and friends — at one time a shoelace vendor in the Mile End Road, at another a sidewalk artist in Bayswater — a mendicant artist unable or unwilling to help himself. A hopeless dipsomaniac, Solomon was reduced even to disposing of Swinburne's (indiscreet? — they have not survived) letters for pelf. His later pictures, despite Alfred Werner's recent obtuse and unaesthetic evaluations of them (see 61.16), are merely vapid and repetitive stencils of incomplete mystical visions, the fuzzy residue of his former genius. Many of them painted to secure the price of another binge, these pictures are often no more than sketches that hardly betray the confident power of *The Finding of Moses* (which Thackeray lauded in *The Roundabout Papers* in 1860), *Bacchus* (which Pater praised so highly), and *Habet* — his three deservedly best known works. The reproductions in Julia Ford's book (61.10), most of them from Solomon's later work, offer a convenient source for studying this impaired and lame stage of Solomon's creativity.

In 1871, Solomon published his *Vision of Love Revealed in Sleep*, an allegorical fragment perhaps suggested by Rossetti's *Hand and Soul*. Interesting as an essay in poetic rhapsodizing, the *Vision* is ultimately a failure, lacking as Swinburne said, "even that much coherence which is requisite to keep symbolic or allegoric art from absolute dissolution and collapse; that unity of outline and connection of purpose, that gradation of correlative parts and significance of corresponsive details, without which the whole aerial and tremulous fabric of symbolism must decompose into mere confusion of formless and fruitless chaos." (*Bibelot*, XIV, 61.6, p. 295)

In the best, and almost the only, analysis of Solomon's life and work, Bernard Falk (61.14) says that Solomon had little in common with the Pre-Raphaelites. But that he was more than personally associated with them is evident from even a cursory examination of his paintings and drawings. His strongest artistic affinities are with Rossetti and Burne-Jones, and these are more apparent in his later and most unsuccessful works. Had Simeon Solomon remained true to his initial vision and had he fulfilled the expectations of his artistic promise of 1858–1860, he might well have surpassed all the Pre-Raphaelites and have become a greater artist than any of them. As it happened, his style degenerated into what can only be called a grotesque parody of the worst characteristics of Pre-Raphaelitism.

In a facetious moment, Solomon prepared a kind of autobiographical epitaph, which effectually and pathetically epitomizes the "psychic portrait-painter of Death, Night, and Sleep":

A HISTORY OF SIMEON SOLOMON
From his cradle to his grave

As an infant he was very fractious. He developed a tendency toward designing. He had a horrid temper. He was hampered. He illustrated the Bible before he was sixteen.

He was hated by all of his family before he was eighteen. He was eighteen at the time he was sent to Paris. His behavior there was so disgraceful that his family — the Nathans, Solomons, Moses, Cohens, etc., et hoc genus homo — would have nothing to do with him. He returned to London to pursue his disgraceful course of Art, wherein he displayed such marvelously exquisite effects of coleography that the world wondered. He then turned his headlong course into another channel — that of illustrating books for youths. His "Vision of Love Revealed in Sleep" is too well known. After the publication of this his family repudiated him forever.

His appearance is as follows:

Very slender, dark, a scar on one or two eyebrows, a slouching way with him, a certain nose, one under lip.

That is
S.S. (61.10, pp. 24–25)

*   *   *

61.1 Solomon, Simeon. *A Mystery of Love in Sleep.* [London]: no imprint, 1871.

There are two copies of this version of 61.2 in the British Museum, one in the Ashley Library. According to Thomas J. Wise, this is the "First" edition. Another copy is in the collection of John Bryson of Balliol College, Oxford (see 4.2), with a letter of authentication from Wise. A copy of this version was listed in Bertram Dobell's *Catalogue of Privately Published Works* (1906), and the Bryson copy was listed in Deighton and Bell's (Cambridge) Catalogue no. 63, May 1942. It is also mentioned in the *DNB* article on Solomon.

61.2 ——— *A Vision of Love Revealed in Sleep.* London: Printed for the author, to be had of F. S. Ellis, 1871.

Reprinted in entirety in *Bibelot*, XV (January, February 1909), 5–55; and issued separately by the Mosher Press in the same year. For a review of the *Vision* other than Swinburne's (61.6) see John A. Symonds in *Academy*, II, no. 21 (1 April 1871), 189–190; reprinted in *Bibelot*, XV (February 1909), 57–64. See also *Athenaeum*, no. 2265 (25 March 1871), p. 368. See Plate VII.

61.3 [———] *Cleopatra's Needle; or, The Labours of Cupid: A Farce in One Act.* London: Speaight, 1877.

Attributed to Solomon by Thomas J. Wise, in the *Ashley Catalogue*, but no further confirmation of this ascription has been found.

* * *

61.4 *Sketches Invented and Drawn by Simeon Solomon for his Friend E. J. Poynter: 20 Photographs.* London: [Issued by Frederick Hollyer], 1865.

61.5 Colvin, Sidney. "English Painters of the Present Day. IV. Simeon Solomon," *Portfolio*, I (March 1870), 33–35.
Reprinted in 75.9.

61.6 Swinburne, Algernon Charles. "Simeon Solomon: Notes on His 'Vision of Love' and Other Studies," *Dark Blue*, I (July 1871), 568–577.
Never reprinted by Swinburne, but often reprinted: in the Bonchurch edition of Swinburne's *Works* (62.6); in *Bibelot*, XIV (September 1908), 291–316; in *A Pilgrimage of Pleasure: Essays and Studies.* Bibliography by E. J. O'Brien (Boston, 1913); and privately in *Les Fleurs du Mal and Other Studies* (1913).

61.7 "Inquest," *Times*, no. 37,789 (18 August 1905), p. 9.
A short account of Solomon's life and of the circumstances surrounding his death.

61.8 Ross, Robert. "A Note on Simeon Solomon," *Westminster Gazette*, 24 August 1905, 1–2.
An obituary account.

61.9 Symons, Arthur. [Simeon Solomon] in "The Painting of the Nineteenth Century," *Studies in Seven Arts.* London: Constable, 1906. 2nd edition, 1925.
Reprinted in *Bibelot*, XVII (April 1911), 152–158; in *From Toulouse-Lautrec to Rodin* (London: John Lane, 1929); and in *Studies on Modern Painters* (New York: Rudge, 1925).

61.10 Ford, Julia Ellsworth. *Simeon Solomon, An Appreciation.* New York: Sherman, 1908.
With an Introduction; selections from *A Vision of Love Revealed in Sleep*; 23 reproductions from Solomon's late works; a partial listing of his paintings, drawings, and sketches; and a list of photographic reproductions from his works. See also *King Solomon and the Fair Shulamite from "The Song of Songs."* With Illustrations after Drawings by Simeon Solomon ("A Poetic Idyl Arranged in Sequence by Julia Ellsworth Ford," New York: Sherman, 1908); seven early drawings are reproduced.

61.11 Ross, Robert. "Simeon Solomon," *Masques and Phases.* London: Humphreys, 1909.
Originally appeared in *Academy*, LXIX, no. 1755 (23 December 1905), 1336–1337. Reprinted as "Simeon Solomon. A Biography" in *Bibelot*, XVII (April 1911), 139–151. One letter from Simeon Solomon is printed in *Robert Ross. Friend of Friends* (86.24).

61.12 Williamson, G. C. "Simeon Solomon," *Murray Marks and His Friends: A Tribute of Regard.* London: John Lane, 1919.
For complete annotation see 86.14.

61.13 Welby, T. Earle. *The Victorian Romantics, 1850–1870: The Early Work of Dante Gabriel Rossetti, William Morris, Burne-Jones, Swinburne, Simeon Solomon and Their Associates.* London: Howe, 1929.
For discussion see Survey, pp. 30–31.

61.14 Falk, Bernard. "Tragedy of Simeon Solomon: Fall from Glory," *Five Years Dead — A Postscript to "He Laughed in Fleet Street."* With Chapters on Simeon Solomon, the Artist, and the Stolen Gainsborough Portrait. London: Hutchinson, 1937.
The most detailed account of Solomon's life and art available.

61.15 Gaunt, William. *The Aesthetic Adventure.* New York: Harcourt Brace, 1945.
A sequel to Gaunt's history of the Pre-Raphaelite Movement (66.24). Of special interest is the brief section treating Simeon Solomon, pp. 49–54.

61.16 Werner, Alfred. "The Sad Ballad of Simeon Solomon," *Kenyon Review*, XXII (Summer 1960), 392–407.
A superficial biographical examination of the artist. Illustrated.

Section 62
ALGERNON CHARLES SWINBURNE
1 8 3 7 – 1 9 0 9
[CBEL: III, 317–323, S597–599; DNB: S, I, 456–465
(Edmund Gosse); EB: XXVI, 234–235 (Edmund
Gosse)]

None of the associates of the Pre-Raphaelites has left a more specific appraisal of his role in the movement than Swinburne. In the postscript to a letter to John Nichol (2 April 1876), Swinburne took issue with Nichol's reference to his (Swinburne's) Pre-Raphaelite tendencies, saying that the term was in "no sense applicable to anything I have written since I was an undergraduate." (62.12, III, p. 168) The poet then proceeded to an examination of Pre-Raphaelitism as a critical term:

> Before 1861 my early work had no doubt a savour of the same influences as the earlier work of Morris and Rossetti, — but from the date of 'Chastelard' and 'Atalanta' onwards I cannot trace in any part of my work, classical, modern, or historic, a trace of any quality that could correctly or even plausibly be labelled 'Preraphaelite' either for praise or blame. Knowing how warmly and fully I admire and enjoy the work of the two poets with whom it is or was the fashion to class me, you will not attribute it to want of sympathy, much less I hope to any assumption of superiority, when I confess that I cannot imagine what critical code or what principle of classification can possibly bring together as members of the same school the authors respectively of 'The Earthly Paradise' and of 'Songs before Sunrise,' of 'The House of Life' and of 'Bothwell.'
>
> I do not see one point in common, as to choice of subject, turn of mind, tone of thought, trick of speech, aim or method, object or style, except that each, I hope I may say, is a good workman who chooses and uses his tools — 'his speculative and official instrument of language' — to the best of his ability. I really see no bond of community or even connexion between us beyond the private and casual tie of personal intimacy at one time of life. The always (I think) rather foolish and now long since obsolete word Preraphaelite was never applicable to any but the work of my earliest youth written at college, and has so long ceased to be applicable (at least in the original sense) to the poetic work of my two elders that I think for the sake of common accuracy it should now be disused. (62.12, III, 168–169)

Swinburne's strictures are, of course, too sweeping, but they do emphasize the problem of articulating in precise and specific terms what Pre-Raphaelitism means in reference to poetry. On a denotative level, it applies to certain commonly recognized devices and techniques which recur in the poetry of Rossetti, Morris, Swinburne, and the minor poets. It may also refer to the choice of verse forms, such as the ballad, with which all three poets experimented and which in the early period was their dominant verse medium; or it may apply to similarities in the choice or handling of subjects, particularly those from Arthurian literature which characterize the Oxford (and poetic) period of Pre-Raphaelitism. The connotative applications of the term are equally, and perhaps more vitally important, however, in labeling poetry Pre-Raphaelite. What emerges is a mood, a tone, a treatment — an attitude toward life that has any of a variety of extraliterary implications, sometimes in terms of social or political reform (a constant tendency in Romantic poetry), but more often in terms of aesthetic reform. Set against the background of an idealized vision of the past, this poetry takes, generally, two directions — a nostalgic longing for a nobler age of human dignity, or disillusionment stemming from the degeneration of human values, which may lead to a morbid preoccupation with the forms of that degeneration.

Swinburne is undoubtedly right in protesting at the unrestricted application of the term Pre-Raphaelite to his own works after the Oxford period, but a marked Pre-Raphaelite influence is certainly apparent in both *Poems and Ballads* (1866) and *Songs before Sunrise* (1871). After 1879, Swinburne published over twenty volumes, but it is the poetry of the years between 1860 and 1879 upon which his poetic reputation rests. It is difficult to assess clearly the tremendous importance of *Poems and Ballads*. More than any other single volume it pointed toward the poetry of the future, and for that reason it is probably the pivotal collection of poetry in the nineteenth century. It was also the first volume from a poet identified with the Pre-Raphaelite school to attract much attention, and the storm of protest which the volume aroused was more salutary to the Pre-Raphaelite cause than the oblivion to which Morris' *Defence of Guenevere*, for instance, had been immediately consigned. So closely was *Poems and Ballads* associated with the Pre-Raphaelites that the publication of Rossetti's *Poems* in 1870 seemed (to Buchanan and others) but the culmination of tendencies which had been inaugurated by Swinburne four years before.

Swinburne's intimacy with the Pre-Raphaelite group at Oxford had a permanent influence on his poetry. During the period of his friendship with Rossetti, especially during his tenancy at Cheyne Walk, the two poets exerted reciprocal influences on one another. While in the final analysis Swinburne may not be a Pre-Raphaelite poet, Pre-Raphaelitism must be regarded as a transitional stage through which he moved. The direction of his later writings was distinctly away from Pre-Raphaelitism, but it is significant that Swinburne seldom attained, except in isolated lyrics, the imaginative power of that early poetry written under the stimulus of the Pre-Raphaelite impulse.

* * *

62.1 Vaughan, Charles E. *Bibliographies of Swinburne, Morris, and Rossetti* (The English Association, Pamphlet no. 29). [Oxford: Clarendon Press], 1914.

62.2 Carter, John, and Graham Pollard. "Algernon Charles Swinburne," *An Enquiry Into the Nature of Certain Nineteenth Century Pamphlets*. London: Constable, 1934.
   For complete annotation see 1.3.

62.3 Ehrsam, Theodore G., Robert H. Deily, and Robert M. Smith. "Algernon Charles Swinburne," *Bibliographies of Twelve Victorian Authors*. New York: Wilson, 1936.
   For complete annotation see 1.5.

62.4 Hyder, Clyde K. "Algernon Charles Swinburne," in *The Victorian Poets: A Guide to Research*, edited by Frederic E. Faverty. Cambridge, Mass.: Harvard University Press, 1956.
   See also 1.11.

* * *

62.5 Swinburne, Algernon Charles. *Notes on the Royal Academy Exhibition, 1868*. Part I. by Wm. Michael Rossetti. Part II. by Algernon C. Swinburne. London: Hotten, 1868.

Of particular interest in Swinburne's section are the notes on Millais, Sandys, and Rossetti. Three sonnets by Rossetti — "Lady

Lilith," "Sibylla Palmifera," and "Venus Verticordia" — were first printed in Part II.

62.6 Swinburne, Algernon Charles. *The Complete Works* (The Bonchurch Edition), edited by Sir Edmund Gosse and Thomas J. Wise. 20 vols. London: Heinemann, 1927.

While incomplete and inaccurate in many respects, the Bonchurch edition remains the most useful collection of Swinburne's works. Besides the actual works, the edition consists of letters, Gosse's *Life*, and a revised version of Wise's two-volume bibliography (1919–1920). For the texts of poems and tragedies published by Swinburne, the eleven-volume edition published by Chatto and Windus (1904–1906) is much more authoritative. It should be noted that T. J. Wise, in both *A Swinburne Library* (1925) and the *Catalogue* of the Ashley Library (1.6), prints some of Swinburne's Pre-Raphaelite poems unavailable elsewhere, as does volume I of the Bonchurch edition.

62.7 Hughes, Randolph, ed. *Lesbia Brandon. Together with an Historical and Critical Commentary. Being Largely a Study (and Elevation) of Swinburne as a Novelist.* London: Falcon Press, 1952.

Contains frequent references to Rossetti and the Pre-Raphaelites, especially as they were associated with Swinburne. Hughes' rabid and messianic diatribes unfortunately divert attention from much original criticism. Reviewed by C. Y. Lang in a letter to the *Times Literary Supplement*, no. 2648 (31 October 1952), p. 716.

* * *

62.8 Gosse, Sir Edmund, and Thomas J. Wise, eds. *The Letters of Algernon Charles Swinburne*. 2 vols. London: Heinemann, 1918.

Reprinted in the Bonchurch edition (62.6), which includes 33 additional letters, eighteen of them to William Michael Rossetti.

62.9 Hake, Thomas, and Arthur Compton-Rickett, eds. *The Letters of Algernon Charles Swinburne, with Some Personal Recollections.* London: Murray, 1918.

See especially the sections dealing with Swinburne's letters to Rossetti.

62.10 Swinburne, Algernon Charles, and Dante Gabriel Rossetti. *A Romance of Literature.* London: Printed for private circulation only for Thomas J. Wise, 1919.

For annotation see 24.12.

62.11 Lang, Cecil Y. "Some Swinburne Manuscripts," *Journal Rutgers University Library*, XVIII (December 1954), 1–11.

Calls attention (pp. 2–3) to a considerable body of manuscripts of Swinburne's Pre-Raphaelite verse.

62.12 ——— (ed.) *The Swinburne Letters.* 6 vols. New Haven: Yale University Press, 1959–1962.

The definitive edition of Swinburne's letters and a major contribution to nineteenth-century scholarship. An invaluable source book for students of the Pre-Raphaelite Movement. See the review-article by Edmund Wilson, 62.38.

* * *

62.13 Rossetti, William Michael. *Swinburne's Poems and Ballads: A Criticism.* London: Hotten, 1866.

A defense in a more polemical vein than Swinburne's own apology in *Notes on Poems and Reviews* (London: Hotten, 1866).

62.14 Austin, Alfred. "Mr. Swinburne," *The Poetry of the Period.* London: Bentley, 1870.

62.15 Forman, H. Buxton. "Swinburne," *Our Living Poets: An Essay in Criticism.* London: Tinsley, 1871.

For complete annotation see 74.1.

62.16 [Courthope, W. J.] "The Latest Development of Literary Poetry: Swinburne, Rossetti, Morris," *Quarterly Review*, CXXXII (January 1872), 59–84.

For annotation see 29.17.

62.17 Gosse, Edmund. "Algernon Swinburne," in *The English Poets: Selections with Critical Introductions by Various Writers,* edited by T. H. Ward. Vol. V. London: Macmillan, 1880.

For complete annotation see 84.3.

62.18 Hamilton, Walter. "Algernon Charles

Swinburne," *The Æsthetic Movement in England*. London: Reeves and Turner, 1882.
For complete annotation see 78.2.

62.19 Sarrazin, Gabriel. "Algernon Charles Swinburne," *Poètes modernes de l'Angleterre*. Paris: Ollendorff, 1885.

62.20 Symons, Arthur. "Algernon Charles Swinburne," in *The Poets and the Poetry of the Century*, edited by A. H. Miles. Vol. [VI]. London: Hutchinson, [1891–1897].
For complete annotation see 84.5.

62.21 *Letters Addressed to Algernon Charles Swinburne, by John Ruskin, William Morris, Sir Edward Burne-Jones, and Dante Gabriel Rossetti*. London: Printed for private circulation for Thomas J. Wise, 1919.

62.22 Browning, Robert. *Critical Comments on Algernon Charles Swinburne and D. G. Rossetti, with an Anecdote Relating to W. M. Thackeray*. London: Printed for private circulation only for Thomas J. Wise, 1919.
For annotation see 27.60.

62.23 [Compton-Rickett, Arthur]. "Rossetti and Swinburne," *Times Literary Supplement*, no. 926 (16 October 1919), pp. 565–566.
For annotation see 24.13.

62.24 *Letters from Dante Gabriel Rossetti to Algernon Charles Swinburne Regarding the Attacks Made upon the Latter by Mortimer Collins and upon Both by Robert Buchanan*. London: Printed for private circulation only for Thomas J. Wise, 1921.
For annotation see 24.14.

62.25 Hearn, Lafcadio. "Studies in Swinburne," *Pre-Raphaelite and Other Poets: Lectures*. Selected and edited with an Introduction by John Erskine. New York: Dodd, Mead, 1922.
For complete annotation see 74.5.

62.26 Broers, Bernarda C. "Swinburne," *Mysticism in the Neo-Romanticists*. Amsterdam: Paris, 1923 (diss. Amsterdam, 1923).
For complete annotation see 73.8.

62.27 Nicolson, Harold. *Swinburne*. London: Macmillan, 1926.

62.28 Lafourcade, Georges. *La Jeunesse de Swinburne (1837–1867) (Publications de la Faculté des Lettres de l'Université de Strasbourg)*. 2 vols. London: Oxford University Press, 1928.
Both volumes contain sections treating the Pre-Raphaelite influence on Swinburne.

62.29 Symons, Arthur. "Algernon Charles Swinburne," *Studies in Strange Souls*. London: Sawyer, 1929.
With a parallel section on Rossetti (see 33.24).

62.30 Welby, T. Earle. *The Victorian Romantics, 1850–1870: The Early Work of Dante Gabriel Rossetti, William Morris, Burne-Jones, Swinburne, Simeon Solomon and Their Associates*. London: Howe, 1929.
For discussion see Survey, pp. 30–31.

62.31 Lafourcade, Georges. *Swinburne: A Literary Biography*. London: Bell, 1932.

62.32 Turner, W. J. "Algernon Charles Swinburne," in *The Great Victorians*, edited by H. J. and Hugh Massingham. London: Nicholson and Watson, 1932.

62.33 Evans, B. Ifor. "Algernon Charles Swinburne," *English Poetry in the Later Nineteenth Century*. London: Methuen, 1933.
For complete annotation see 74.7.

62.34 Weygandt, Cornelius. "Algernon Charles Swinburne," *The Time of Tennyson: English Victorian Poetry as it Affected America*. New York: Appleton-Century, 1936.
For complete annotation see 69.15.

62.35 Lucas, F. L. "Swinburne," *Ten Victorian Poets*. Cambridge University Press, 1942.
For complete annotation see 27.92.

62.36 Ford, George H. "Morris, Swinburne, and Some Others," *Keats and the Victorians: A Study of His Influence and Rise to Fame, 1821–1895*. New Haven: Yale University Press, 1944.
For complete annotation see 33.33.

62.37 Groom, Bernard. "Rossetti, Morris,

and Swinburne," *The Diction of Poetry from Spenser to Bridges*. University of Toronto Press, 1955.

62.38 Swinburne, Algernon Charles. *The Novels: Love's Cross Currents. Lesbia Brandon*. With an Introduction by Edmund Wilson. New York: Farrar, Straus and Cudahy, 1962.

The Introduction, "Swinburne of Caphaeton and Eton," in part a review of C. Y. Lang's edition of the *Letters* (62.12), also appeared in the *New Yorker*, 6 October 1962, pp. 165–200.

62.39 Peters, Robert L. "Algernon Charles Swinburne and the Use of Integral Detail," *Victorian Studies*, V (June 1962), 289–302.

An important examination of one aspect of Swinburne's aesthetic. Swinburne's interest in intense literalism was totally aesthetic, with none of the religious or moral overtones associated with early Pre-Raphaelite or other Victorian art. Swinburne criticized "the unbridled pursuit of the ornate," and attacked "rampant detail and purely ornamental surface richness," but, recognizing the service which detail can render the imagination, he anticipated in his criticism, particularly of Rossetti and Keats, the moderns' emphasis on organic imagery and structure.

Section 63
GEORGE FREDERICK WATTS
1817–1904

[DNB: S, I, 610–619 (Sidney Colvin); EB: XXVIII, 420–422 (Malcolm Bell)]

The connection of G. F. Watts with the Pre-Raphaelites is almost solely a personal one, although some of his more romantic paintings contain just enough of Burne-Jones and the late tone of Pre-Raphaelitism to be deceptive at first glance. Watts and the Little Holland House coterie saw a good deal of the Pre-Raphaelites about the time of the Oxford Union venture, and Watts may have been briefly tempted by the contagion of the Pre-Raphaelite spirit, but only very briefly. He does seem to have been responsible for, as he put it, plunging Val Prinsep into the "Pre-Raphaelite Styx."

Ronald Chapman, Watts' most recent (and best) biographer, has aptly identified the contrast between Watts' and the Pre-Raphaelite style, and succinctly made the case for their influence on the older painter:

> The aims of the Brotherhood were definitely opposed to the Grand Manner in art. Rossetti's ideas of mural decoration were distinctly mediaeval and not at all in line with Watts' views on the subject, as the Union paintings clearly show . . . In almost all matters connected with art Watts and the Pre-Raphaelites were starting from opposite poles. To them realism was a main tenet of faith, to Watts, as to all Grand Mannerists, realism was a low form of art. Nevertheless, the Pre-Raphaelite movement was more a freemasonry of friends than a dogmatic institution. And Watts' connection with so many of the later brotherhood undoubtedly helped to bring him much more before the public than he had been. Gradually, as the Pre-Raphaelites gained control of the organs of art criticism, his pictures received more consideration. (63.13, pp. 79–80)

It might be pointed out that there are more similarities than differences between Watts and the Pre-Raphaelites in the choice of subjects. Where he differed primarily was in treatment and, to a lesser degree, in technique. Watts made his most permanent contribution to English art as a portrait painter, and among the finest examples of this side of his art are the likenesses he left of several of the Pre-Raphaelites — Millais, Rossetti, Morris, and Swinburne, now all in the National Portrait Gallery.

* * *

63.1 Ruskin, John. "Mythic Schools of Painting: E. Burne-Jones and G. F. Watts," *The Art of England: Lectures Given in Oxford*. Orpington: Allen, 1883.

For complete annotation see 45.2.

63.2 Barrington, Emilie Isabel. "The Painted Poetry of Watts and Rossetti." *Nine⁺ enth Century*, XIII (June 1883), 950–970.

63.3 Spielmann, Marion H. *The Works of Mr. G. F. Watts, R. A., with a Complete Catalogue of his Pictures* (Extra number of the *Pall Mall Gazette*, no. 22). London: "Pall Mall Gazette" Office, 1886.

63.4 Forsyth, Peter Taylor. *Religion in Recent Art: Expository Lectures on Rossetti, Burne-Jones, Watts, Holman Hunt, and Wagner*. London: Hodder and Stoughton, 1901.

63.5 Bayliss, Sir Wyke. *Five Great Painters of the Victorian Era: Leighton, Millais, Burne-Jones, Watts, Holman Hunt*. London: Sampson, Low, Marston, 1902.

From articles originally appearing in *Good Words*.

63.6 Muther, Richard. "Rossetti, Burne-Jones, und Watts," *Neue Deutsche Rundschau*, XIII (August 1902), 859–881.

63.7 Barrington, Mrs. Russell. *G. F. Watts: Reminiscences*. New York: Macmillan, 1905.

63.8 Watts, M. S. *George Frederic Watts*. 3 vols. London: Macmillan, 1912.

Vols. 1 and 2 are subtitled *The Annals of an Artist's Life*; vol. 3, *His Writings*. Many references to the Pre-Raphaelites.

63.9 Linton, John. "George Frederick Watts," *The Cross in Modern Art: Descriptive Studies of Some Pre-Raphaelite Paintings*. London: Duckworth, 1916.

Discussions of *Mammon, Great Possessions*, and *Love and Death*. Illustrated. For complete annotation see 75.27.

63.10 Hutchinson, H. G. "Watts, Millais, and Burne-Jones," *Portraits of the Eighties*. London: Unwin, 1920.

Personal reminiscences.

63.11 Alston, Rowland Wright. *The Mind and Works of G. F. Watts . . . with . . . Special Reference to the Watts Gallery, Compton, Guildford*. London: Methuen, 1929.

63.12 Newton, Eric. "Watts and the Pre-Raphaelites," *English Painting*. London: Longmans, 1945; rev. ed., 1948.

63.13 Chapman, Ronald. "Friends, Pre-Raphaelites, Critics," *The Laurel and the Thorn: A Study of G. F. Watts*. London: Faber, 1945.

Section 64

THEODORE WATTS-DUNTON

1832–1914

[CBEL: III, 756, S677; DNB: S, II, 558–559 (V. H. Rendall); EB: XXVIII, 422–423]

It almost seems that Watts-Dunton was destined to become the Emmeline Grangerford of the Pre-Raphaelite Movement in its final desuetude and ultimate collapse, as one by one its adherents went the way of all Fleshly Poets. His "Tributes" — both reviews and obituaries — punctuate the *Athenaeum* from 1876, when he joined the staff of that journal; and the roll-call of Pre-Raphaelites whom he celebrated reads like the reminiscent muster with which Mr. Chips took his leave of this world.

It was as a solicitor that Watts-Dunton first encountered Rossetti and Swinburne in the early seventies. A faithful and devoted friend, and a competent, though "sympathetic," critic ("Criticism was to him an act of sympathy" comment the editors of his *Life and Letters* [64.7 p. 243]), he began his affiliation with the *Athenaeum* three years before Swinburne began what was to be his thirty-year sojourn at The Pines. To this journal he contributed countless reviews, notices, obituaries, and articles. In addition, he wrote for numerous other journals, and he published some poetry and two or three novels, the most successful of which, curiously, was *Aylwin*, that thinly veiled gypsy saga which employed a barely disguised Rossetti as one of its principal characters.

A minor man of letters, Watts-Dunton was no Pre-Raphaelite. He is included among the ranks of the affiliates only because chance so inextricably linked his life with two of the major and many of the minor figures of the movement. In Cecil Lang's edition of *The Swinburne Letters* (62.12), more than 250 are addressed to Watts-Dunton, and there survive more than 300 letters from Rossetti to this "hero of friendship." Watts-Dunton is probably no better remembered as a literary figure and critic (reviewer rather) than he deserves to be, but he is too frequently slandered as a kind of Putney jailor at whose doorstep is laid the unproductivity of Swinburne after 1880. In fairness, Watts-Dunton was not responsible for nipping the bud of Swinburne's poetic rose; Swinburne was a dying genius when Watts-Dunton found him. He quite literally saved his life, and whatever survives of poetic greatness in the later Swinburne is owing to the care and devotion of his stodgy old friend "who passionately wanted [Swinburne] to assume in the domain of contemporary letters the rank that genius put within reach." (Lang, 62.12, I, xliii)

* * *

64.1 Watts-Dunton, Theodore. *Aylwin: A Novel.* London: Hurst and Blackett, 1898.

This *roman à clef* has a number of disguised Pre-Raphaelite characters, including Rossetti. A key to the novel by Thomas St. E. Hake appeared in *N & Q*, 9th ser., IX (7 June 1902), 450–452; X (2 August 1902), 89–91; reprinted in the World's Classics edition of the novel (1904). See also W. Robertson Nicoll, "The Significance of *Aylwin*," *Contemporary Review*, LXXIV (December 1898), 798–809, which also reviews other of Watts-Dunton's publications. *Aylwin* was adapted for the motion picture in 1920. Produced by Henry Edwards and issued by Hepworth and Company, the leading roles were played by Edwards and Miss Christie White.

64.2 ———— *Old Familiar Faces.* London: Jenkins, 1916.

Articles, mostly obituaries, reprinted from the *Athenaeum*. Essays included are those on Christina Rossetti (44.51), D. G. Rossetti (25.5, 27.26), William Morris (43.81), and Thomas Gordon Hake (48.17).

64.3 ———— *Poetry and the Renascence of Wonder: With a Preface by Thomas Hake.* London: Herbert-Jenkins, 1916.

Contains many references to Rossetti and the Pre-Raphaelites. Originally published in the *Encyclopaedia Britannica*, 9th edition.

* * *

64.4 Bell, Mackenzie. "Theodore Watts [-Dunton]," in *The Poets and the Poetry of the Century*, edited by A. H. Miles. Vol. [VI]. London: Hutchinson, [1891–1897]. For complete annotation see 84.5.

64.5 Kernahan, Coulson. "A Nature Poet," *Wise Men and a Fool.* London: Ward, Lock, 1901.

64.6 Douglas, James. *Theodore Watts-Dunton: Poet, Critic, Novelist.* New York: John Lane, 1904.

With separate sections on Rossetti and Morris and many references throughout to the Pre-Raphaelites.

64.7 Hake, Thomas, and Arthur Compton-Rickett. *Life and Letters of Theodore Watts-Dunton: Including Some Personal Reminiscences by Clara Watts-Dunton.* 2 vols. London: Jack, 1916.

With separate sections on Rossetti, Christina Rossetti, and Burne-Jones.

64.8 Ellis, S. M. "Theodore Watts-Dunton," *Mainly Victorian.* London: Hutchinson [1924].

64.9 Klenk, Hans. *Nachwirkungen Dante Gabriel Rossettis: Untersuchungen an Werken von Christina Rossetti, Coventry Patmore, Philip Bourke Marston, Theodore Watts-Dunton, Arthur W. E. O'Shaughnessy, Ernest Dowson, John Davidson.* Berlin: Bachmann, 1932 (diss. Erlangen, 1932).

64.10 Truss, Tom James. "Theodore Watts-Dunton as Critic," unpub. diss., University of Wisconsin, 1958. *Dissertation Abstracts,* XVIII (1958), 1049–1050.

Attempts to define in precise terms the characteristics of Watts-Dunton's criticism, with particular reference to the aims of the art of Tennyson, Browning, Rossetti, Morris, and Swinburne.

64.11 ———— "Theodore Watts-Dunton: A Primary Bibliography," *Bulletin of Bibliography,* XXIII (May–August 1961), 114–117.

Contains two sections: A) "Works in periodicals signed by Theodore Watts-Dunton or variously attributed to him, chronologically arranged"; B) "Contributions to units other than periodicals, all signed unless otherwise noted."

Section 65

WILLIAM LINDSAY WINDUS
1822–1907

[DNB: S, I, 694–695 (Frank W. Gibson)]

When William Windus went to London in 1850 and saw Millais' *Christ in the House of His Parents* at the Royal Academy, he was converted to the Pre-Raphaelite cause. It was through his (and other Liverpool artists') conversion that the Liverpool Academy solicited contributions from the Pre-Raphaelites, who received in Liverpool the first real recognition of their work. Pre-Raphaelite artists took the annual prize at the Liverpool exhibitions in 1851, in 1852 and 1853, in 1857, and again in 1858, Millais winning it twice.

The first picture that Windus entered at the Royal Academy (in 1856) was *Burd Helen*, one of the most distinctively characteristic Pre-Raphaelite pictures (of a type) that was ever produced. His next major work, *Too Late* (Tate Gallery), was exhibited at the Royal Academy in 1858, and was also Pre-Raphaelite in its techniques. These two paintings are Windus' best known and most Pre-Raphaelite works, but all of his paintings after 1850 demonstrate a high degree of finish and other Pre-Raphaelite techniques. As Mary Bennett has rightly indicated, Windus' works "help to reveal the effects on an ordinary provincial artist of the ideas of the new lively minded Brotherhood of self-styled Pre-Raphaelites." (65.4, p. 21)

* * *

65.1 Dibden, E. Rimbault. "William Lindsay Windus," *Magazine of Art*, XXIII (1900), 49–56.

65.2 Marillier, Henry Currie. "W. L. Windus," *The Liverpool School of Painters: An Account of the Liverpool Academy from 1810 to 1867, with Memoirs of the Principal Artists*. London: Murray, 1904.

65.3 [Smith, James]. *Two Liverpool Artists. In Memoriam: D. A. Williamson; W. L. Windus (1823–1907)*. [Liverpool]: no imprint, 1907.

65.4 Bennett, Mary. "William Windus and the Pre-Raphaelite Brotherhood in Liverpool," *Liverpool Bulletin* (Libraries, Museums & Arts Committee. Walker Art Gallery Number), VII, no. 3 (1958–1959), 19–31.

For annotation see 77.68.

III. BIBLIOGRAPHY OF THE PRE-RAPHAELITE MOVEMENT

This part of the Bibliography, devoted to the movement as a whole, provides a comprehensive survey of works relating directly to the varied activities of the Pre-Raphaelites in all three stages of the movement.

The range of criticism on the Pre-Raphaelite Movement is partially governed by the nature of the subject itself. Many of the items in the several sections of this part are ephemeral, yet frequently these seemingly slight publications contain the single piece of information or the necessary clue for bringing some aspect of Pre-Raphaelitism into focus. The first six sections of this part are limited to more or less general studies, many of which are merely undistinguished factual accounts of the history of the movement that tend to be repetitive and of little value. This is particularly true of the art histories itemized in section 70. But the classification of a work in one of these six general sections should not be construed as implying that a given item is without merit. The general histories of the movement catalogued in section 66, for example, are indispensable for anyone wishing to examine Pre-Raphaelitism either critically or historically, and these are in fact, with very few exceptions, about the only entire books which have been devoted to the subject.

The twin concern of the Pre-Raphaelites with literature and art has occasioned the obvious pairing of sections, as in sections 69 and 70 (literary and art histories), 74 and 75 (studies emphasizing literary and artistic aspects of Pre-Raphaelitism), and the combination of the two in section 76. It is perhaps significant that so few writers have widened their sights to include the literary side of the movement, but even fewer have concentrated on the relationship between Pre-Raphaelite painting and poetry. Interestingly enough, the reverse is nearly the case with Rossetti alone, as the dominant figure of the movement (compare for example sections 27 and 28 [literary studies] with 30 and 31 [artistic studies]); but the difficulties encountered as soon as any attempt is made to transfer generalizations about Rossetti (or any other single Pre-Raphaelite) to the movement as a whole are sufficient to forestall any but the most temerarious critics. Numerous studies have been made comparing all sorts of likely and unlikely artists and writers with the Pre-Raphaelites. These comparative studies, many of them duplicates from sections in part II, appear in section 77, where they are classified by figures when more than one such study exists.

A few items perversely refused to be categorized, but to avoid duplication within the sections of a single part it has been necessary to relegate an overlapping item to the section most compatible with its content, nature, and purpose. Sections 80 to 85 are slight but essential categories, which, while they perhaps accommodate few items, catalogue material inappropriate to other sections in the bibliography.

In a sense, part III carries the burden of the Bibliography as a whole — and this is the principal reason for placing it after, rather than before, the Bibliography of Individual Figures. Made up of individual writers and artists, by whose accomplishments ultimately the movement must eventually be evaluated, Pre-Raphaelitism nevertheless became a thing in itself, with recognizable features and identifiable scars. This section is intended to demonstrate not only by the breadth and scope of the writings on the movement but through the variety of those writings the complexity of Pre-Raphaelitism itself.

General Discussions of Pre-Raphaelitism

Section 66

SEPARATE WORKS ON PRE-RAPHAELITISM: GENERAL

66.1 [Ruskin, John]. *Pre-Raphaelitism: By the Author of "Modern Painters."* London: Smith, Elder, 1851.

Not until the second edition (1862) did Ruskin's name appear on the title page. For discussion of Ruskin's role in the Pre-Raphaelite Movement see Survey, pp. 9–13. Among reviews of Ruskin's pamphlet the following may be mentioned: *Leader*, II, no. 74 (23 August 1851), 803–804; *Economist*, IX, no. 417 (23 August 1851), 933–934 ("The pamphlet is only a defense of Pre-Raphaelitism if Mr. Turner be a Pre-Raphaelite."); *Builder*, X, no. 449 (13 September 1851), 571–572; *Daily News*, no. 1629 (17 August 1851), p. 3; *Athenaeum*, no. 1243 (23 August 1851), pp. 908–909; *Tait's Edinburgh Magazine*, XVIII (October 1851), 626–629; *Art Journal*, XIII (November 1851), 285–286. See also 67.4. *Pre-Raphaelitism* has been reprinted many times — in *CW* (45.3, XII, 337–393); in the Everyman's Library (no. 218), edited by Laurence Binyon (London: Dent, 1907); and, most recently (in part) in *Victorians on Literature and Art*, edited by Robert L. Peters (New York: Appleton-Century-Crofts, 1961). David Wooster's edition of *Selections from the Literary and Artistic Remains of Paulina*

Jermyn Trevelyan (London: Longmans, 1879) contains a review of Ruskin's *Pre-Raphaelitism* reprinted from the *Scotsman*, 3 January 1852.

66.2 Rippingille, Edward Villiers. *Obsoletism in Art: A Reply to the Author of Modern Painters in His Defence of "Pre-Raphaelitism."* London: Bentley, 1852.

The Pre-Raphaelites are treated as pure copyists who fail because they imitate only nature and do not temper nature with art. "We have the consolation of knowing that the mischief produced [by Pre-Raphaelitism], whatever it may be, cannot extend very far, or lead to any very ruinous consequences; since revolutions in the arts of peace, those happy pursuits, to which men bring the best qualities of their hearts and minds, are in comparison harmless." (p. 54) A selection from Rippingille's *Reply* appeared prior to publication in *Bentley's Miscellany*, XXXI (June 1852), 598–609.

66.3 Hopley, Edward. *A Letter on Pre- and Post-Raffaelism.* London, 1853.

Reviewed in *Athenaeum*, no. 1345 (6 August 1853), p. 943. No copy of this publication or further verification of its existence has been located.

66.4 Ballantyne, John. *What is Pre-Raphaelitism?*. Edinburgh: Blackwood, 1856.

For discussion see Survey, pp. 10–11. Reviewed in *Art Journal*, XVIII (April 1856), 127; *Athenaeum*, no. 1485 (12 April 1856), p. 463.

66.5 Young, Edward. *Pre-Raffaellitism: Or, A Popular Enquiry into Some Newly-Asserted Principles Connected with the Philosophy, Poetry, Religion, and Revolution of Art*. London: Longmans, 1857.

For discussion see Survey, p. 11. Reviewed in *Art Journal*, XIX (April 1857), 131; *Athenaeum*, no. 1531 (28 February 1857), pp. 282–283.

66.6 Massey, Gerald. *Lectures on Pre-Raphaelitism*. [London, 1858].

Referred to in Esther Wood, *Dante Gabriel Rossetti and the Pre-Raphaelite Movement* (77.21), but no copy of this publication or verification of its existence has been located. Writing to Mrs. Tennyson on 11 February 1858, Thomas Woolner records: "From Liverpool I went to Newcastle and stayed a few days with my friend W. B. Scott: while there I went to hear Gerald Massey deliver a lecture on Pre-Raphaelitism; it was very good and stated the truth of the movement in a popular and attractive manner." (40.14, p. 141) Massey's second lecture, delivered at Edinburgh on 17 March 1858, is referred to by William Sharp in his biography of Rossetti (25.3, p. 71).

66.7 Thomas, William Cave. *Pre-Raphaelitism Tested by the Principles of Christianity: An Introduction to Christian Idealism*. London: Wertheim, MacIntosh, and Hunt, 1860.

The "tendency of the modern Pre-Raphaelite or individualistic doctrine, is to reduce the illustration of the sacred writings, which has always been the highest ambition of artists, to the level of the art of 'familiar subjects'?" (p. 19) "It was important that the new school of art should be tested by Christian principles since its advocates have attributed to it an exalted religious fervour,

an extraordinary reverent spirit; but a careful comparison of its opinions with the letter and spirit of Christianity, shows it to be false and unholy in its tendencies. In insisting on the faithful and minute imitation of nature as it *is*, with all its imperfections on it, it offends against the letter of the law. In not striving toward the reformation, the restoration, the renewal of nature to rectitude, to Christ, it offends against the spirit of Christianity. Christian idealism does not question the talent of the advocates, or of the professors of the individualistic school of Art, but enters its protest against talent misapplied." (pp. 29–30) For brief discussion of this volume see Survey, p. 101. Reviewed in *Art Journal*, XXIII (April 1861), 100.

66.8 Chuĭko, Vladimir Viktorovich. *Dorafaelisty i ikh posliedovateli v Anglii*. St. Petersburg, 1886.

Reprinted from *Vestnik iziashchnykh iskustv*, IV, 1886.

66.9 Parkes, Kineton. *The Pre-Raphaelite Movement*. London: Reeves and Turner, 1889.

Originally appeared in *Ruskin Reading Guild Journal*, I (1889), 108–113, 145–149, 172–174, 197–200. For a brief discussion and a quotation see Survey, p. 25.

66.10 Fred, W. *Die Prae-Raphaeliten: Eine Episode englischer Kunst (Ueber Kunst der Neuzeit*, no. 4). Strassburg: Heitz, 1900.

66.11 Jessen, Jarno [= Anna Michaelson]. *Prärafaelismus (Die Kunst*, no. 45, ed. Richard Muther). Berlin: Marquardt, [1906].

Reprinted as *Prerafaelismo . . . con aggiunte originali sul Prerafaelismo in Italia del Dr. Enrico Thovez* (Torino: Clausen, 1907).

66.12 *A Brief Account of the English Pre-Raphaelites*. New York: Dodd, Mead, [1906].

With a list of books on the Pre-Raphaelite Brotherhood and on the Italian Pre-Raphaelites.

66.13 Hueffer, Ford Madox. *The Pre-*

Raphaelite Brotherhood: A Critical Mono-graph. London: Duckworth, 1907.
For discussion see Survey, pp. 26–27.

66.14 Agresti, A[ntonio]. *I Prerafaellisti; contributo alla storia dell'arte.* Torino: Società Tipografico-Editrice Nazionale, 1908.
Antonio Agresti also published an article entitled "I Prerafaellisti" in *Rassegna Contemporanea*, ser. II, vol. VI, 1913.

66.15 Braschi, A. *I Preraffaelliti.* Milano: Vallardi 1910.

66.16 Singer, Hans Wolfgang. *Der Prae-Raphaelitismus in England* (*Die Kultur des modernen England*, ed. Ernst Sieper). München: Oldenbourg, 1912.

66.17 Woods, Mrs. Matthew. *Some Women of the Pre-Raphaelite Movement.* Philadelphia: Browning Press, 1914.
"The season of 1913–1914 of the Philadelphia Society of Arts and Letters was devoted to a consideration of the Pre-Raphaelite Brotherhood. The following paper was read at the closing meeting on the evening of April 8, 1914, and is published by request."

66.18 Vinciguerra, Mario. *Il Preraffaellismo inglese.* Bologna: Zanichelli, 1925.

66.19 Waugh, Evelyn. *P.R.B.: An Essay on the Pre-Raphaelite Brotherhood, 1847–1854* [Stratford-on-Avon]: [Privately printed by] Alastair Graham, 1926.

66.20 Luxardo, Lelio. *Preraffaelliti e Preraffaellismo in Inghilterra, note critiche.* Bologna: Zanichelli, 1929.
With 30 illustrations.

66.21 Welby, T. Earle. *The Victorian Romantics, 1850–1870: The Early Work of Dante Gabriel Rossetti, William Morris,* *Burne-Jones, Swinburne, Simeon Solomon and Their Associates.* London: Howe, 1929.
Listed separately under each of the figures in the title. For discussion see Survey, pp. 30–31.

66.22 Bickley, Francis Lawrence. *The Pre-Raphaelite Comedy.* London: Constable, 1932.
A popular account of the PRB, focusing principally on Rossetti.

66.23 Winwar, Frances [= Frances (Vinciguerra) Grebanier]. *Poor Splendid Wings: The Rossettis and Their Circle.* Boston: Little, Brown, 1933.
Published in England as *The Rossettis and Their Circle* (London: Hurst and Blackett, 1934). A semifictional account of the Pre-Raphaelite Movement. Although extensive research obviously went into the volume — a long bibliography is appended — the re-creations of conversations are unbelievable and the general tone is far too intimate.

66.24 Gaunt, William. *The Pre-Raphaelite Tragedy.* London: Cape. 1942.
Reissued as *The Pre-Raphaelite Dream* (London: Reprint Society, 1943). A journalistic and popular, highly entertaining account of the Pre-Raphaelite Movement. For the sequel to this volume see *The Aesthetic Adventure* (61.15).

66.25 Eulenberg, Herbert. *Die Prä-Raphaeliten.* Düsseldorf: Kaiserwerth, 1946.

66.26 Alden, J. E. *The Pre-Raphaelites and Oxford: A Descriptive Handbook.* Oxford: Alden, 1948.
A short description of what Oxford has to show of Pre-Raphaelite art and a guide to its location. A superficial analysis by a nonspecialist, but useful as a summary. For discussion of Pre-Raphaelite materials at Oxford see 2.8.

Section 67

ARTICLES ON PRE-RAPHAELITISM: GENERAL

67.1 Dickens, Charles. "Old Lamps for New Ones," *Household Words*, I (15 June 1850), 265–267.

Dickens' famous attack on the Pre-Raphaelites, with especially vitriolic emphasis on Millais' *Christ in the House of His Parents.*

The condemnation of the picture and the movement is based on moral rather than aesthetic criteria, and the essay is interesting as revealing Dickens' frequent lapses in aesthetic judgment. Quoted in part and discussed in the Survey, p. 9.

67.2 B[allantyne], J[ohn]. "The Pre-Raffaellites," *Art Journal*, XIII (July 1851), 185–186.

One of the earliest critical reviews of the movement. See also 66.4.

67.3 "The Pre-Raphaelites," *Tait's Edinburgh Magazine*, XVIII (August 1851), 512–513.

A bitter denunciation of Pre-Raphaelite paintings in the Royal Academy exhibition, especially of Millais' *Christ in the House of His Parents* and *The Return of the Dove to the Ark*. "It is difficult to say, where an artist's taste leads him to select models as nearly approaching to deformity as possible . . . how many of the defects of drawing, anatomy, and proportion, are due to nature, how many to the artist; they are, however, sufficiently numerous to satisfy the claims of both." (p. 513)

67.4 "Pre-Raphaelitism," *Irish Quarterly Review*, I (December 1851), 740–762.

In part a review of Ruskin's pamphlet (66.1). "Whether those gentlemen will realize the high hopes and expectations Mr. Ruskin indulges in — and 'found a new and noble school in England,' remains to be seen, but that they possess the essential qualities likely to lead them to greatness — industry, perseverance, and earnestness, is undeniable."

67.5 "Minor Topics of the Month: Pre-Raphaelitism," *Art Journal*, XVI (August 1854), 250.

Depreciating Pre-Raphaelite style as "unadapted to the age." An account of Dr. G. F. Waagen's letter to the *Times*, no. 21,792 (13 July 1854), p. 7.

67.6 "Pre-Raphaelitism," *Ecclesiastic and Theologian*, XVII (January 1855), 1–5.

Laudatory but uninformative, even of serious contemporary opinion. A severe criticism of 71.3.

67.7 [Stillman, William J.]. "Pre-Raphaelitism," *Crayon*, I (4 April 1855), 219–220.

67.8 [———] "Pre-Raphaelitism and Its Lessons," *Crayon*, I (18 April 1855), 241–242.

67.9 "The English Pre-Raphaelites," *Eclectic Review*, 5th ser., XI (January 1856), 1–20.

A companion article to "The Italian Pre-Raphaelites," *Eclectic Review*, 5th ser., X (December 1855), 641–658. An examination of the Pre-Raphaelite heresy by way of reviews of *The Germ*, Ruskin's *Lectures on Architecture and Painting*, and C. R. Leslie's *A Handbook for Young Painters*. The article is presented as a trial in which the Pre-Raphaelites, as plaintiffs, are seeking to overthrow three centuries of art tradition. Ruskin and Leslie are the respective counsels. The Pre-Raphaelites are "Englishmen who, decrying their own times and nation, put on the mask and disguise of a foreign land and medieval period." (p. 6) The principal charge brought against the Pre-Raphaelites is that their forms are "ugly," "vulgar," "grotesque," "odd, quaint, and repulsive." Specific charges: first, that the Pre-Raphaelites merely imitate the Nazareners; second, that Pre-Raphaelite art is circumscribed within the pale of the Roman Catholic Church; and, finally, that the Pre-Raphaelites disregard the glories of the present age. More than most, this article is motivated by the smug complacency so often attributed to the Victorians. For a review of this article see *Crayon*, III (March 1856), 96.

67.10 Y., A. — R.S. "Pre-Raphaelitism from Different Points of View," *Fraser's Magazine*, LIII (June 1856), 686–693.

The points of view are those of Ruskin (66.1), Ballantyne (66.4), and Gautier (37.1).

67.11 [Durand, John B.]. "Pre-Raphaelitism," *Crayon*, V (March 1858), 84–85.

67.12 "Modern Pre-Raphaelitism," *Dublin University Magazine*, LVII (June 1861), 687–695.

A scathing, but amusing, account of Pre-Raphaelitism, especially unfair to Millais and

Holman Hunt. Rossetti is not mentioned, and the article is more particularly an attack on Ruskin and on the last volume of *Modern Painters*. "Endless word spinning, rash dogmatism, and affected phraseology form Mr. Ruskin's chief pretensions to the rank of a deep original thinker." (p. 690)

67.13 Sturgis, Russell. "Pre-Raphaelitism," *Nation*, I (31 August 1865), 273–274.

For brief discussion and quotation see Survey, pp. 20–21.

67.14 "Concerning Præ-Raphaelitism: Its Art, Literature, and Professors," *London and County Review*, I (March 1868), 51–60.

Same in *Every Saturday*, V (4 April 1868), 443–446. An amusing attack on Pre-Raphaelitism through a discussion of 75.8. The author is especially hard on Ruskin, in whose writings are united the "most unmitigated nonsense with the most refined diction . . ." The author explains Pre-Raphaelite principles by creating and analyzing an imaginary Pre-Raphaelite painting — "Cupid Lost in a Forest." William Michael Rossetti is compared with Ruskin, and the two become the "flaming links of fine-art literature."

67.15 McCarthy, Justin. "The Pre-Raphaelites in England," *Galaxy*, XXI (June 1876), 725–732.

One of the most interesting and entertaining articles on the Pre-Raphaelites. Written by an Englishman for an American audience, the article treats primarily the later, decorative side of the Movement. The average Pre-Raphaelite, McCarthy says, "is quite a distinct figure . . . in the literary history of our time; and take him for all in all, with his narrow-gauge ideas, his pedantry, his whimsicality, and his nonsense, one must admit that he is a picturesque as well as a new figure, and that he has claims and merits much beyond that of almost any of the types of artistic affectation which we knew before his day." (p. 732) On the more facetious side, McCarthy asks, "Who is Pre-Raphael?" and notes that it is impossible in Pre-Raphaelite art to distinguish between the hero and heroine. After commenting that there is a good deal of kissing in Pre-Raphaelite poetry — generally kissing under rather "lugubrious

circumstances" — he asserts that to appreciate Pre-Raphaelite poems properly one should be able to enjoy an opium revel in a graveyard. Finally, he imagines the typical volume of Pre-Raphaelite poetry, entitled "Songs of Love and Death," illustrated with Burne-Jones's *Love Among the Ruins* as the frontispiece.

67.16 Rossetti, William Michael. "Præraphaelitism: Its Starting Point and Its Sequel," *Art Monthly Review*, I, no. 10 (August 1876), 102–105.

A précis of the movement with an introductory note that Whistler (as much as Burne-Jones) belongs to the "Præraphaelite idea."

67.17 ———— "The Pre-Raphaelite Brotherhood," *Magazine of Art*, IV (1881), 434–437.

A general review of the history of the movement.

67.18 Wilde, Oscar. "The English Renaissance," *New York Daily Tribune*, 10 January 1882, p. 2.

Wilde's first lecture delivered in America on the occasion of his visit in 1882. The lecture dealt in large part with the contribution of the Pre-Raphaelites to the English Renaissance. Printed on the same day in the *Sun* (New York, p. 1). The lecture also appeared in separate form on 19 January (New York: The Seaside Library, LVIII, no. 1183, 1882). Reprinted in numerous other places, including the *Bibelot*, XI (July 1905), 205–237.

67.19 Kennedy, H. A. "The Pre-Raphaelite Movement," *Artist*, XXI (January 1898), 25–40.

67.20 "The English Pre-Raphaelites," *Magazine of Art*, XXIII (1900), 125–128.

In part a review of Bate's *English Pre-Raphaelite Painters* (75.21).

67.21 "The Pre-Raphaelite Brotherhood," *Werner's Magazine*, XXVII (April 1901), 96–107; (May 1901), 193–202; (June 1901), 261–265.

A three-part article. Parts one and two are on Millais (37.60) and Rossetti (30.28); Part III is subtitled, "William Holman Hunt —

D. Maclise — Albert Moore — Edward Burne-Jones — George Frederick Watts — Ford Madox Brown — and Others."

67.22 Housman, Laurence. "The Spirit of Pre-Raphaelitism," *Magazine of Fine Arts*, I (April 1906), 406–415.

Occasioned by the publication of Holman Hunt's history of the movement (75.23). "He does not seem to see, either in his own work or that of others, the force which for a time gave Pre-Raphaelitism so singular a distinction over contemporary art." (p. 406)

67.23 "The Pre-Raphaelite Brotherhood," *Quarterly Review*, CCIV (April 1906), 352–374.

"Pre-Raphaelitism was a revolt in the midst of a revolt, a Gironde, a 'mountain' in a very French Revolution of the arts. As a producing agency, it gave the world ten or a dozen pictures, five or six poems, a few statues; and it has caused an inordinate number of memoirs." (pp. 352–353) Many of the memoirs are reviewed in the article.

67.24 "Pre-Raphaelitism," *Church Quarterly Review*, LXII (April 1906), 21–43.

A long review-article stimulated by Hunt's history (75.23), retracing the history of the movement and discussing the controversial points and issues in Hunt's two volumes.

67.25 Bright, Norma K. "Social Intercourse Among the Pre-Raphaelites," *Book News Monthly*, XXIV (June 1906), 691–695.

67.26 "Pre-Raphaelitism in Outline," *Book News Monthly*, XXIV (June 1906), 696–698.

Brief sections on Holman Hunt ("The Founder of the [Movement]"), Rossetti ("The Acknowledged Leader of the Group"), Millais ("The Most English of the Pre-Raphaelites"), Morris ("The Mechanical Genius of the Movement"), Ruskin ("The Defender of Pre-Raphaelitism"), Swinburne ("Poetic Sympathizer with the Movement"), and Watts-Dunton ("A Pre-Raphaelite Admirer"). The June 1906 issue of the *Book News Monthly* was devoted principally to Pre-Raphaelitism, though it was not a special issue. For other articles in the same issue see 33.10 (43.59), 67.25, 74.3, 79.17.

67.27 Sturgis, Russell. "Artists with Theories, Convictions, and Principles," *Scribner's Magazine*, XL (July 1906), 125–128.

A long review-article of Hunt's *Pre-Raphaelitism and the P.R.B.* (75.23). Considers Hunt's two volumes as the first "official" or "trustworthy" account of the Pre-Raphaelite Movement, that of 1847–1848. With a general discussion of the Movement.

67.28 Hueffer, Ford Madox. "An Old Circle," *Harper's Magazine*, CXX (February 1910), 364–372.

Personal reflections on the Pre-Raphaelites, most of which were later incorporated into 77.55.

67.29 ———— "Some Pre-Raphaelite Reminiscences," *Harper's Magazine*, CXX (April 1910), 762–768.

A preliminary study for 77.55, with slight extracts from Ford Madox Brown's diary. See also by Hueffer, "Group of Pre-Raphaelite Poets," *Harper's Magazine*, CXXI (October 1910), 778–785.

67.30 Pennell, Elizabeth Robins. "My Glimpse of the Pre-Raphaelites," *American Magazine of Art*, XI (November 1919), 3–6.

67.31 Hunt, Violet. "Stunners," *Artwork*, VI (Summer 1930), 77–87.

An illustrated account of the women of the Pre-Raphaelite Movement.

67.32 ———— "Beginning of the Pre-Raphaelites," *Saturday Review*, CLII, no. 3953 (1 August 1931), 144; no. 3954 (8 August 1931), 177–178; no. 3955 (15 August 1931), 208–209; no. 3956 (22 August 1931), 232–233; no. 3957 (29 August 1931), 261.

67.33 "Pre-Raphaelites and Peacocks," *Bookman* (New York), LXXV (November 1932), 691–693.

Comments on and quotations from Ellen Terry's *Memoirs*. Reference to Rossetti's animals and to the model, Miss Herbert. With a reproduction of Holman Hunt's portrait of Rossetti.

67.34 Hueffer, Ford Madox. "Pre-Raphaelite Epitaph," *Saturday Review of Literature*, X (20 January 1934), 417–419.

Winwar's (66.23) and Bickley's (66.22) books show very well where the Pre-Raphaelites stand today. "Esthetically they have disappeared. In the memory of the flesh they have brilliantly survived."

67.35 Burroughs, Bryson. "1935 Views the Pre-Raphaelites," *American Magazine of Art*, XXVIII (January 1935), 6–13.
Reprinted as "Modern View of the Pre-Raphaelites," *Metropolitan Museum of Art Bulletin*, n.s. V (May 1947), 229–233.

67.36 Rey, R. "Les Préraphaélites," *La Renaissance*, XXI (April 1938), 15–24, 47; (November 1938), 13–21, 48.
The first article is on the PRB, the second on the later period of the Movement. English summaries are provided in both articles.

67.37 Patmore, Derek. "Le Centenaire des Préraphaélites," *Arts*, no. 182 (1 October 1948), p. 3.
Includes a reproduction of an unpublished drawing of Tennyson Patmore by Holman Hunt.

67.38 ——— "The Pre-Raphaelites," *Spectator*, CLXXXI, no. 6275 (1 October 1948), 427.
Centenary article. For other illustrated centenary articles see Geoffrey Grigson, "The Pre-Raphaelite Rebellion," *Picture Post*, XL (11 September 1948), 15–18; and Olive Cook, "The Pre-Raphaelites," *The Saturday Book*, no. 8, ed. Leonard Russell. London: Hutchinson, 1948.

67.39 Bliss, Douglas Percy. "Pre-Raphaelite Centenary," *Scottish Art Review*, II (1948), 2–6.

67.40 Giartosio de Courten, Maria L. "La 'fratellanza preraffaellita' cent'anni dopo," *Nuova Antologia*, CCCCXLVII, no. 1788 (December 1949), 380–395.

67.41 Davis, Arthur Kyle. "Passionate Pre-Raphaelites, Victorian Romantics," *Virginia Quarterly Review*, XXVII (Winter 1951), 154–160.
A review-article discussing among other works Doughty's *Rossetti* (25.92) and Zaturenska's *Christina Rossetti* (44.81).

67.42 Greenwood, Julia. "Young and Angry, Then as Now," *Listener*, LX (3 July 1958), 13–14.
On the Pre-Raphaelites. For resulting correspondence see the issues for 10 July (p. 57) and 17 July (p. 94).

67.43 D'Agostino, Nemi. "I Preraffaeliti," *Belfagor*, XIV (1959), 404–414.

67.44 Gállego, Julian. "P.R.B. (Los Prerafaelistas)," *Revista de ideas estéticos*, XVII (1959), 309–327.

67.45 MacInnes, Colin. "A Pre-Raphaelite Memory," *Spectator*, no. 7059 (11 October 1963), 453–455.
Reminiscences of the J. W. Mackails and their Kensington house by Burne-Jones's great-grandson.

Section 68

GENERAL DISCUSSIONS OF PRE-RAPHAELITISM
IN CRITICAL STUDIES, COLLECTIONS OF
ESSAYS, MEMOIRS, AND OTHER WORKS

68.1 Timbs, John. "What is Pre-Raphaelitism?," *Things Not Generally Known, Familiarly Explained: A Book for Old and Young*. London: David Bogue, 1856.
Cited as an example of the variety of references available on Pre-Raphaelitism. Reprinted in the appendix to *Painting Popularly Explained* (London: Crosby, Lockwood, 1889).

68.2 Rod, Edouard. "Les Préraphaélites anglais," *Etudes sur le dix-neuvième siècle*. Paris: Perrin, 1888.
Originally appeared in *Gazette des Beaux-*

Arts, période 2, XXXVI (September 1887), 177–195; (November 1887), 399–416. Translated and reprinted in *Connoisseur*, II (March 1888), 109–123; (June 1888), 175–187.

68.3 Howitt, Mary. "The Pre-Raphaelites," *An Autobiography*, edited by her daughter, Margaret. 2 vols. London: Isbister, 1889.

A very brief subsection, but the volumes also contain numerous personal reminiscences of various Pre-Raphaelites.

68.4 Quilter, Harry. "A Chapter in the History of Pre-Raphaelitism," *Preferences in Art, Life, and Literature*. London: Swan Sonnenschein, 1892.

Separate sections within the chapter on Madox Brown, Rossetti, Hunt, Ruskin, and Millais. The Rossetti section is reprinted from 32.3.

68.5 Weigand, Wilhelm. "Die Präraphaeliten," *Essays* (*Zur Psychologie des 19. Jahrhunderts*, no. 5). München: Merhoff, 1892.

68.6 Nordau, Max. "The Pre-Raphaelites," *Degeneration*. New York: Appleton, 1895.

Translated from *Entartung* (Berlin: Duncker, 1893). "In the world of art . . . the religious enthusiasm of degenerate and hysterical Englishmen sought its expression in Pre-Raphaelitism. An accurate definition of the connotation of this word is an impossibility, in that it was invented by mystics, and is as vague and equivocal as are all word-creations of the feeble and deranged mind." (p. 77) With an amusing attack on "The Blessed Damozel" (pp. 87–91). See also Ettore Ciccotti, *La Fanciulla beata di Dante Gabriel Rossetti e un giudizio di Max Nordau* (Milano: Kantorowicz, 1893).

68.7 Bazalgette, Léon. "La Banquerante du Préraphaélitisme," *L'Esprit nouveau dans la vie artistique, sociale et religieuse*. Paris: Société d'éditions scientifiques, 1898.

68.8 Laurent, Raymond. "Le Préraphaélisme en Angleterre; introduction à l'étude du Préraphaélisme anglais," *Études anglaises*. Paris: Grasset, 1910.

Same in *Nouvelle Revue*, n.s. XL (15 May 1906), 170–186.

68.9 Pollen, Anne. "Hampstead and the Pre-Raphaelites (1858–1860); The Critics of Contemporary Art," *John Hungerford Pollen, 1820–1902*. London: Murray, 1912.

68.10 Pennell, E. R. and Joseph. "The First Idea of the Journal. The Pre-Raphaelites and Others. The Years 1885–1897," *The Whistler Journal*. Philadelphia: Lippincott, 1921.

Not an actual journal kept by Whistler, but reminiscences of Whistler by the Pennells, with long verbatim reports of the artist's conversations and detailed descriptions of his activities. See also the chapter "Charles Augustus Howell, His Friends and Enemies."

68.11 Stirling, A. M. W. "Tales of the Pre-Raphaelites and Others," *Life's Little Day: Some Tales and Other Reminiscences*. London: Butterworth, 1924.

Anecdotes about the Pre-Raphaelites, especially Burne-Jones, Rossetti, and the De Morgans.

68.12 Beza, Marcu. "Pre-Raphaelites," in *From Confucius to Mencken*, edited by Francis Henry Pritchard. New York: Harper, 1929.

Reprinted in *World's Best Essays* (New York: Harper, 1929), and in England as *Great Essays of All Nations* (London: Harrap, 1929).

68.13 Vaughan, Herbert M. "Sir John Everett Millais (1829–1896) and William Holman Hunt (1827–1910) — The Pre-Raphaelite Brotherhood," *From Anne to Victoria: Fourteen Biographical Studies between 1702 and 1901*. London: Methuen, 1931.

68.14 Osgood, Charles G. "The Pre-Raphaelites," *The Voice of England*. New York: Harper, 1935. 2nd edition, 1952.

68.15 Grigson, Geoffrey. "The Preraphaelite Myth," *The Harp of Aeolus and Other Essays on Art, Literature, & Nature*. London: Routledge, 1947.

Same in *Architectural Review*, XCII (August 1942), 27–30. Motto: "They did not find, they sought: and therefore they faked." For discussion see Survey, pp. 36–37.

68.16 Tinker, Chauncey B. "The Amusing Pre-Raphaelites," *Essays in Retrospect: Collected Articles and Addresses*. New Haven: Yale University Press, 1948.
Same in *Literary Review*, III (3 February 1923), 429–430. The volume also contains an essay on "William Morris as Poet," reprinted from 43.103.

68.17 Willis, Cloudesley S. "The Pre-Raphaelites," *A Short History of Ewell and Nonsuch*. 2nd ed. Epsom: Pullinger's 1948; 1st ed., 1931.
Recollections of Millais and Holman Hunt during the painting of the initial studies for *Ophelia* and *The Hireling Shepherd*. "The Pre-Raphaelite Brotherhood was the name chosen for themselves by the group of young men who, in 1848, opened a window, and let in Nature to refresh British art." (p. 80)

68.18 Newton, Eric. "Pre-Raphaelite," *In My View*. London: Longmans, 1950.
"What characterizes [Pre-Raphaelitism] is not its meticulous detail but the passion behind the detail, not the sentiment but the urgency behind the sentiment, not the little gaucheries and archaisms but the enthusiasm that made it necessary to invent them, not the bright and often inharmonious colour but the wild protest against drabness, the Gothic optimism that turned heraldic colour into a religion. (p. 242) "How easy it is to forget that it is no longer necessary to defend them from the outmoded charge of being 'literary.' Of course they were literary. So was Wagner. So was Giotto. So is most art." (p. 243) This article was occasioned by the various centenary exhibitions.

68.19 Woodring, Carl Ray. "Pre-Raphaelites and Feminists," *Victorian Samplers: William and Mary Howitt*. Bloomington: Indiana University Press, 1952.

68.20 Young, Vernon. "From Pre-Raphaelitism to Bloomsbury," *The Turn of the Century* (Arts Yearbook, no. 1). New York: Art Digest, 1957.
For discussion see Survey, pp. 37–38.

68.21 Hudson, Derek. "The Pre-Raphaelites," *The Forgotten King and Other Essays*. London: Constable, 1960.
Reprinted from *Times Literary Supplement*, no. 2437 (16 October 1948), p. 582, entitled "A Glorious Failure." A centenary essay on the Pre-Raphaelites and a review of Ironside's *Pre-Raphaelite Painters* (83.8).

68.22 Robsjohn-Gibbings, Terence Harold. "Art into Magic," *Mona Lisa's Mustache: A Dissection of Modern Art*. New York: Knopf, 1947.
An amusing, greatly oversimplified account of the Pre-Raphaelite Movement as a "mystic fandango," an essentially occult movement presided over by "'that sly Italian'" Rossetti, "the Svengali of the Pre-Raphaelites," who, through developing the legends of Arthur and Dante, sought to transform Victorian life through a kind of mystical aesthetic occultism, uniting the arts and "eventually form[ing] a whole population of painters." Millais and Hunt, "babes in the woods when it came to occultism," are presented as "two unwilling Trilbys who, try as they would, could not quite escape an influence they had never fully understood." "Pre-Raphaelitism and Ruskin were made for each other." Rossetti, who "behind the façade of art and aesthetics was a power-seeker," later encountered at Oxford Ned and Top, the two Exeter undergraduates who took literally the "reactionary phantasmagoria" about medieval art which survived at Oxford, "the sleeping-place of a belated yet still living medievalism," the "training-ground for the perpetuation of feudalism," the "five-hundred-year-old cocoon of medieval stonework," whose inhabitants "dreamed of a butterfly existence in a world made 'Gothic' again . . ." Ned and Top became apprentices to the "sorcerer" Rossetti, but neither had the gift for "magic." "In Ned the occult teachings of the master produced only an unmysterious and languishing aestheticism" (of the sort described in *Patience*). Morris, "like a bearded lady of Shalott, . . . worked feverishly night and day at his loom while his overheated imagination mirrored the phantasmagoria of a medieval heaven on earth. Then one day the mirror cracked. His dream was over." Rossetti "remained to the end the occult Svengali of

Victorian aesthetics . . . , [a kind of] al-chemist, attempting to distill the old medieval magic and sorcery and infuse it into poetry

and painting with which to spellbind and destroy the hated middle classes." (pp. 25–39)

Section 69

GENERAL DISCUSSIONS OF PRE-RAPHAELITISM IN LITERARY HISTORIES

69.1 Stedman, Edmund Clarence. "Latter-Day Singers: Robert Buchanan. — Dante Gabriel Rossetti. — William Morris," *The Victorian Poets*. Boston: Houghton, Mifflin, 1876.

A fourth "latter-day singer" treated in the ensuing chapter is Swinburne. One can only speculate on the reaction of the Pre-Raphaelites on finding themselves allied with the arch-enemy, Buchanan. This volume, one of the most popular studies of the Victorian poets, went through many editions before finally going out of print around the turn of the century. The section including the Pre-Raphaelites originally appeared in *Scribner's Monthly*, IX (February 1875), 426–438; 485–496.

69.2 Hodgkins, Louise Manning. *A Guide to the Study of Nineteenth Century Authors*. Boston: Heath, 1890.

With brief sections on Rossetti, Morris, and Swinburne. One of the first of the literary handbooks.

69.3 Sharp, Amy. "Dante Gabriel Rossetti, William Morris, and Algernon Charles Swinburne," *Victorian Poets*. London: Methuen, 1891.

69.4 Saintsbury, George. *A History of Nineteenth Century Literature (1780–1900)*. London: Macmillan, 1896.

Chapter VI, "The Second Poetical Period," contains a brief section on the Pre-Raphaelites, including Rossetti, Christina Rossetti, Morris, Swinburne, O'Shaughnessy, Hake, Marston, and Woolner.

69.5 Kellner, Leon. "Dante Gabriel Rossetti und die Präraffaeliten," *Die Englische Literatur im Zeitalter der Königin Viktoria*. Leipzig: Tauchnitz, 1909.

Reprinted in *Die Englische Literatur der neuesten Zeit* (Leipzig: Tauchnitz, 1921).

69.6 Magnus, Laurie. "Pre-Raphaelitism," *English Literature in the Nineteenth Century*. London: Melrose, 1909.

69.7 Saintsbury, George. "The Præ-Raphaelite School," *A History of English Prosody from the Twelfth Century to the Present Day*. Vol. III. London: Macmillan, 1910.

A discussion of the poetry of Dante Gabriel and Christina Rossetti, Swinburne, Canon Dixon, James Thomson, and O'Shaughnessy.

69.8 Walker, Hugh. "The Pre-Raphaelites," *The Literature of the Victorian Era*. Cambridge University Press, 1910; rev. ed., 1921.

See also the section "The Later Pre-Raphaelites" in Walker's *Outlines of Victorian Literature* (Cambridge University Press, 1913).

69.9 Bell, A. F. "Rossetti, Morris, and Swinburne," *Leaders in English Literature*. London: Bell, 1915.

69.10 Thompson, A. H. "The Rossettis, William Morris, Swinburne, and Others," in *The Cambridge History of English Literature*, edited by A. W. Ward and A. R. Waller. Vol. XIII. Cambridge University Press, 1916.

Bibliography (vol. XIII, pp. 490–497) by G. A. Brown.

69.11 Elton, Oliver. *A Survey of English Literature, 1830–1880*. Vol. II. London: Arnold, 1920.

With chapters on the Rossettis, Morris, Swinburne, and "Other Poets," the last including O'Shaughnessy, Allingham, and the other minor Pre-Raphaelites — Hake, Dixon, Marston, and Sebastian Evans.

69.12 Hearn, Lafcadio. "The Minor Singers," *A History of English Literature, in a*

Series of Lectures. Vol. II. Tokyo: Hokuseido Press, 1927.

Including Christina Rossetti, Morris, and O'Shaughnessy.

69.13 Grierson, Herbert J. C. "Arnold and the Pre-Raphaelite Group," *Lyrical Poetry from Blake to Hardy* (Hogarth Lectures in Literature, no. 5). London: Published by Virginia and Leonard Woolf at the Hogarth Press, 1928.

Published in America as *Lyrical Poetry of the Nineteenth Century* (New York: Harcourt Brace, 1929).

69.14 Cunliffe, John W. "Mid-Victorian Poets," *Leaders in the Victorian Revolution.* New York: Appleton-Century, 1934.

Includes brief sections on the Rossettis, Patmore, Swinburne, Morris, and others.

69.15 Weygandt, Cornelius. "The Victorian Minors," *The Time of Tennyson: English Victorian Poetry as it Affected America.* New York: Appleton-Century, 1936.

Contains brief sections on the minor Pre-Raphaelite poets, including Hake, Bell Scott, Allingham, O'Shaughnessy, Marston, and Watts-Dunton. The volume also contains separate chapters on Rossetti (27.87), Morris (43.115), and Swinburne (62.34).

69.16 Grierson, Herbert J. C., and J. C. Smith. "Mid-Victorian Poetry, ii. The Pre-Raphaelite Group," *A Critical History of English Poetry.* London: Chatto and Windus, 1944.

69.17 Chew, Samuel C. "Rossetti and His Circle," in *A Literary History of England,* edited by Albert C. Baugh. New York: Appleton-Century-Crofts, 1948.

With a good working bibliography.

69.18 Cooke, John D., and Lionel Stevenson. *English Literature of the Victorian Period.* New York: Appleton-Century-Crofts, 1949.

Brief bio-bibliographical sections on the Rossettis, Morris, Swinburne, Ruskin, and Patmore. Allingham, Dixon, Marston, and O'Shaughnessy are treated briefly in the section on "Minor Poets." The Pre-Raphaelites

are discussed in the introductory chapter, "Fine Arts" (pp. 76–81).

69.19 Batho, Edith C., and Bonamy Dobrée. *The Victorians and After, 1830–1914* (Introductions to English Literature, vol. IV), rev. ed. London: Cresset Press, 1950.

The "Poetry" section of the "Bibliography" contains notes on Allingham, the Rossettis, Morris, Swinburne, Dixon, Marston, Bell Scott, and Woolner.

69.20 Vines, Sherard. "The Pre-Raphaelites and After," *One Hundred Years of English Literature.* London: Duckworth, 1950.

69.21 Westland, Peter. "Pre-Raphaelites and Others," *The Victorian Age* (The Teach Yourself History of English Literature, vol. V). London: English Universities Press, 1950.

69.22 Churchill, R. C. "The Oxford Movement and the Pre-Raphaelites," *English Literature of the Nineteenth Century.* London: University Tutorial Press, 1951.

Brief discussions of Patmore, Dixon, Christina Rossetti, the PRB, and the influence of Ruskin, Rossetti, Morris, and Swinburne. No attempt to compare the Pre-Raphaelite with the Oxford Movement.

69.23 Parrott, Marc, and Robert Bernard Martin. *A Companion to Victorian Literature.* New York: Scribner's, 1955.

Sections on Rossetti, Morris, and Swinburne.

69.24 Robson, W. W. "Pre-Raphaelite Poetry," in *From Dickens to Hardy: The Pelican Guide to English Literature.* VI, edited by Boris Ford. London: Penguin Books, 1958.

Limited to a discussion of the poetry of Dante Gabriel and Christina Rossetti and Morris. All three the author regards as "might have beens." Christina Rossetti's poetry is "deprived, depressed, montonous" ("a common feature of Victorian Romantic Poetry"); Morris is essentially a "day-dream" poet, whom it is difficult to give a "high place purely as a writer"; Rossetti is allowed "to pass the final judgement on his own work": "Look in my face: my name is Might-have-been; / I am also called No-More, Too-late, Farewell."

69.25 Kunitz, Stanley J., and Howard Haycraft, eds. *British Authors of the Nineteenth Century*. New York: Wilson, 1936.
Containing brief bio-bibliographical and critical articles, this volume is especially useful for general information on the minor Pre-Raphaelite poets: Allingham, Oliver Madox Brown, Sebastian Evans, Thomas Gordon Hake, Marston, and O'Shaughnessy. Portraits are provided for many of the writers included.

Section 70

GENERAL DISCUSSIONS OF PRE-RAPHAELITISM IN ART HISTORIES

70.1 Humphreys, Henry Noel. "The Pre-Raphaelites," *Ten Centuries of Art. Its Progress in Europe from the IXth to the XIXth Century* . . . London: Grant, 1852.

70.2 Burger, W. [=Théophile Etienne Joseph Thoré]. "Ecole anglaise . . . les Pré-Raphaélites . . . ," *Trésors d'art en Angleterre*. Bruxelles: Claassen, 1860.

70.3 Chesneau, Ernest. "Le Préraphaélitisme — Conclusion," *L'Art et les artistes modernes en France et en Angleterre*. Paris: Didier, 1864.
Also contains a brief chapter on Hunt, Millais, and Dyce.

70.4 Shepherd, George H. "Pre-Raphaelitism," *A Short History of the British School of Painting*. London: Sampson, Low, 1881.
Brief discussion of Millais, Hunt, Rossetti, and Brown.

70.5 Chesneau, Ernest. "Les Préraphaélites," *La Peinture anglaise* (*Bibliothèque de l'enseignement des Beaux-Arts*). Paris: Quantin, 1882.
Translated into English by Lucy N. Etherington as *The English School of Painting*, with a Preface by Professor Ruskin (London: Cassell, 1884). See also the chapter "Pre-Raphaelite Landscape." For discussion see Survey, pp. 21–22.

70.6 Redgrave, Richard and Samuel. "The Pre-Raphaelites," *A Century of Painters of the English School*. 2nd ed. London: Sampson, Low, 1890.
The section on the Pre-Raphaelites did not appear in the first edition of 1865.

70.7 Michel, André. "Le Préraphaélisme," *Histoire de l'art*. Vol. VIII. Paris: Collin, [1890].

70.8 La Sizeranne, Robert de. "Les Origines préraphaélites," *La Peinture anglaise contemporaine*. Paris: Hachette, 1895.
Translated into English by H. M. Poynter (London: Constable, 1898). The volume was first published in part in *Revue des Deux Mondes*, CXXV (October 1894), 562–596; CXXVI (November 1894), 326–357; CXXVII (January 1895), 372–412. Two chapters were translated by Poynter and published in the *Artist*: "Germs of English Art in 1841," XXII (August 1898), 211–216; "The Battle of the P.R.B.," XXIV (February 1899), 90–96; (April 1899), 181–186. Besides the general section on the Pre-Raphaelites, there are separate chapters on the major artists. For discussion see Survey, pp. 22–24.

70.9 Muther, Richard. *The History of Modern Painting*. 3 vols. New York: Macmillan, 1896.
Revised and enlarged to four volumes, 1907. For particular matter treating the Pre-Raphaelites see vol. II, 560–608; vol. III, 572–597. Also contains brief bibliographical sections on the individual artists.

70.10 Temple, Sir Alfred George. *The Art of Painting in the Queen's Reign: Being a Glance at Some of the Painters and Paintings of the British School During the Last Sixty Years*. London: Chapman and Hall, 1897.
Chapter IV treats Millais, Madox Brown, Holman Hunt, Rossetti, and Burne-Jones; chapter XIV, Arthur Hughes, Sandys, Strud-

wick, and Simeon Solomon, among other minor artists.

70.11 Hoppin, James Mason. "English Pre-Raphaelites," *Great Epochs in Art History*. New York: Houghton, Mifflin, 1901.
Additional chapters on Burne-Jones and Rossetti.

70.12 MacColl, Douglas S. "English Art, Grand, Philistine, and 'Decadent,'" *Nineteenth Century Art, with a Chapter on Early Art Objects* . . . Glasgow: MacLehose, 1902.
This section on the Pre-Raphaelites includes brief chapters on Rossetti, Hunt, Millais, Brown, and Burne-Jones.

70.13 Sharp, William. "The Pre-Raphaelite Movement . . . ," *Progress of Art in the Century* (The Nineteenth Century Series, vol. XXII). London: Linscott, 1902.
With additional chapters on Rossetti, Burne-Jones, and Morris and the later Pre-Raphaelites.

70.14 Muther, Richard. "Die Praerafaeliten: Die Epigonen des Praerafaelitentums," *Geschichte der englischen Malerei*. Berlin: Fischer, 1903.

70.15 Dayot, Armand. "Préraphaélisme," *La Peinture anglaise de ses origines à nos jours*. Paris: Laveur, 1908.

70.16 Meier-Graefe, Julius. "English Reaction," *Modern Art, Being a Contribution to a New System of Aesthetics*. Translated by F. Simmonds and G. W. Chrystal. London: Heinemann, 1908.
The general section on "English Painting" contains an interesting, antagonistic discussion of the Pre-Raphaelites, especially of Burne-Jones. "Rossetti had an actual experience of life out of which he made pictures." Rossetti had a spiritual harmony even when outward harmony was lacking. "Pre-Raphaelitism was not a tendency. So utterly did it absorb all the artistic interest of the country, that we must perforce recognize it as representative, unless we are to deny the existence of an English art since Constable." (p. 198) Whistler, the author sees as "fundamentally an unfrocked Pre-Raphaelite." (p.

199) In this chapter see also the section, "Morris and His Circle."

70.17 Phythian, J. E. "The Pre-Raphaelite Brotherhood," *Fifty Years of Modern Painting, Corot to Sargent*. New York: Dutton, 1908.
With another long chapter on "The Course of Pre-Raphaelitism."

70.18 Rambosson, Yvanhoé. "Les Préraphaélites et quelques peintres récents," *Histoire de la peinture: La Peinture anglaise* (Collection d'Art). Paris: Nilsson, [1908].

70.19 Armstrong, Sir Walter. "Painting — From the Pre-Raphaelite Revolt to the Present Day," *Art in Great Britain and Ireland* (Ars Una). London: Heinemann, 1909.
Published simultaneously in Germany, France, Spain, and England.

70.20 MacFall, Haldane. "Realism and Pre-Raphaelite Academism, 1850," *A History of Painting*, with a Preface by Frank Brangwyn. Vol. III. *The Modern Genius*. London: Jack, 1911.
Chapters XI to XV are pertinent. See especially chapter XIII: "Wherein the British Painters take the Figure into the open air, and Realism passes into the Glamour of the Sunlight."

70.21 Maguinness, Irene. "Revolt from Convention: The Pre-Raphaelite Brotherhood and Its Influence," *British Painting*. London: Sidgwick, 1920.

70.22 Charpentier, John. *La Peinture anglaise. Les Origines et le portrait. La Peinture de genre. Le Paysage. Les Précurseurs des Préraphaélites. Le Préraphaélisme* (Bibliothèque internationale de critique, no. 42). Paris: La Renaissance du Livre, 1921.

70.23 Hind, C. Lewis. "The Pre-Raphaelite Brotherhood," *The Great Painters in Art and Life* (John O'London's Little Books, no. 8). London: Newnes, [c. 1925].

70.24 Bell, Clive. "The Pre-Raphaelites," *Landmarks in Nineteenth-Century Painting*. London: Chatto and Windus, 1927.

Essentially the same as Bell's articles in *New Republic*, XLIV, no. 569 (28 October 1925), 251–253; and in *Nation and Athenaeum*, XXXVIII (19 December 1925), 433–435. An adverse and biased, but amusing, article. Bell regards the Pre-Raphaelites as "didactic pamphleteers, minor poets, or little historians." They were not painters. See also 71.13.

70.25 Waldmann, Emil. "Die Schule der Prärafaeliten," *Englische Malerei*. Breslau: Hirt, 1927.

70.26 Lambotti, Paul. "Les Préraphaélites," *La Peinture anglaise*. Paris-Bruges: Brouwer, [1929].

70.27 Johnson, Charles. "Pre-Raphaelites: Rossetti and His Influence," *English Painting from the Seventh Century to the Present Day*. London: Bell, 1932.
Other chapters on Hunt, Millais, and Madox Brown. See also the chapter "The Pre-Raphaelites" in Johnson's *A Short Account of British Painting* (London: Bell, 1934).

70.28 Baker, C. H. Collins. "The Pre-Raphaelite Movement and Burne-Jones," *British Painting*, with a Chapter on Primitive Painting by Montague R. James. London: Medici Society, 1933.

70.29 De Montmorency, Miles F. "The Pre-Raphaelite Movement," *Short History of Painting in England*. London: Dent, 1933.

70.30 Rothenstein, John. "The Pre-Raphaelites," *An Introduction to English Painting*. London: Cassell, 1933. Reprinted 1947.

70.31 Underwood, Eric. "Pre-Raphaelitism — the Movement," *A Short History of English Painting*. London: Faber, 1933.
With a parallel chapter on "Pre-Raphaelitism — the Men."

70.32 Wilenski, R. H. "The Pre-Raphaelite Movement," *English Painting*. London: Faber, 1933.

70.33 —— *An Outline of English Painting from the Middle Ages to the Period of the Pre-Raphaelites*. London: Faber, 1933.
Only a short treatment of the Pre-Raphaelites (pp. 61–70). Wilenski's *Outline of English Painting* (New York: Philosophical Library, 1948) also contains a brief section on the Pre-Raphaelites (pp. 98–113).

70.34 Fry, Roger. "Pre-Raphaelites," *Reflections on English Painting*. London: Faber, 1934.
Devastatingly abusive.

70.35 Smith, Solomon Charles Kaines. "The Pre-Raphaelites," *Painters of England*. London: Medici Society, 1934.

70.36 Leroy, Alfred. "L'Ecole des Préraphaélites (1848–1900)," *Histoire de la peinture anglaise (800–1938): Son évolution et ses maîtres*. Paris: Michel, [1939].
With a Preface by André Maurois. Translated into German in 1944.

70.37 Armfield, Maxwell. "Tempera and the Pre-Raphaelites," *Tempera Painting Today*. London: Pentagon Press, 1946.

70.38 Bertram, Anthony. "The Pre-Raphaelites and Their Companions," *A Century of British Painting, 1851–1951*. New York: Studio Publications, 1951.
The chapter "The Medieval Revival and the Æsthetic Movement" contains considerable material on Burne-Jones and Morris.

70.39 Short, Ernest. "The Pre-Raphaelites (1848–1898): Origin of the P.R.B. — Millais, Holman-Hunt, Rossetti, Burne-Jones," *A History of British Painting*. London: Eyre and Spottiswoode, 1953.

70.40 Shipp, Horace. "The Pre-Raphaelite Revolt. Madox Brown, Rossetti, Holman Hunt, Millais, Burne-Jones," *The English Masters*. London: Newnes, 1955.
Revised from *The British Masters* (1933).

70.41 Digeon, Aurélien. "Les Préraphaël-ites," *L'École anglaise de peinture.* Paris: Tisné, [1956].
English edition (New York: Universe Books, 1959).

70.42 Orpen, William. "The Pre-Raphael-ites: The Art of Ford Madox Brown, Rossetti, Holman Hunt, Millais, and Burne-Jones," *The Outline of Art.* Revised by Horace Shipp. London: Newnes, 1957.

70.43 Boase, T. S. R. "The Pre-Raphaelites," *English Art, 1800–1870* (Oxford History of English Art). Oxford: Clarendon Press, 1959.

70.44 Canaday, John. "The Pre-Raphaelite Ideal; Rossetti; William Morris and the Arts and Crafts. Rossetti's Followers. Hunt, Millais, Ruskin," in the chapter "Outside France, 1850–1900," *Main Streams of Modern Art.* New York: Holt, 1959.

Section 71

ARTICLES AND SEPARATE PUBLICATIONS
PARTIALLY DEVOTED TO PRE-RAPHAELITISM

71.1 R[each], A[ngus] B. "Town Talk and Table Talk," *Illustrated London News,* XVI (4 May 1850), 306.
The first public notice of the Brotherhood, revealing the [in]significance of the letters "P.R.B."

71.2 "The Pictures of the Season," *Blackwood's Magazine,* LXVIII (July 1850), 82.
A reference to the aberrations of Pre-Raphaelitism. Of Millais' *Christ in the House of His Parents*: "Such a collection of splay feet, puffed joints, and misshapen limbs was assuredly never before made within so small a compass." Rossetti, who did not exhibit at the Royal Academy, is acknowledged as the "high priest of the retrograde school." See also *Blackwood's Magazine,* LXXIX (February 1856), 218–220, in which Pre-Raphaelitism, equated with Realism, is castigated for its pernicious influence on the drama: ". . . the Pre-Raphaelitism of the picture galleries is but one of the forms in which the tendency to realism is manifested." (p. 220) For other contemporary notices of the Pre-Raphaelite pictures (mainly by Hunt and Millais) exhibited at the Royal Academy, 1850–1851 see: *Times,* no. 20,484 (9 May 1850), p. 5; *Spectator,* XXIII, no. 1140 (5 May 1850), 427; *Athenaeum,* no. 1179 (1 June 1850), pp. 590–591; no. 1232 (9 June 1851), p. 609; *Builder,* VIII, no. 382 (1 June 1850), 256; *Guardian,* no. 230 (1 June 1850), p. 396. For notices of Rossetti's works exhibited at the Free Gallery in 1849 and 1850 see 18.1.

71.3 Young, Edward. *Art, Its Constitution and Capacities; Popularly Considered, Being the First of Two Lectures on the Uses and Abuses of Art. Delivered at Bristol, January 19, 1854, and Published by Request.* Bristol: Chilcott, 1854.
An attack on the Pre-Raphaelites preliminary to 66.5 is included in this lecture. The second lecture seems not to have been published.

71.4 "Art," *Westminster Review,* LXIII (January 1855), 292–302.
On the German and English Pre-Raphaelites.

71.5 "Ruskin Versus Raphael," *Art Journal,* XXI (August 1859), 229–232; (September 1859), 261–264.
An attack on Ruskin and incidentally on the Pre-Raphaelites anent a recent Academy exhibition. Contains a long note at the conclusion of part I on the Pre-Raphaelites.

71.6 Bayne, Peter. "Glimpses of Recent British Painting," *Essays, Biographical, Critical, and Miscellaneous.* Edinburgh: Hogg, 1859.
Pre-Raphaelitism is the principal matter treated, pp. 381–400. See also the chapter "Mr. Ruskin's System of Art-Criticism."

71.7 Colvin, Sidney. "English Painters and Painting in 1867," *Fortnightly Review*, VIII, n.s. II (October 1867), 464–476.

Material on the Pre-Raphaelites, pp. 470–476.

71.8 Payne, John Burnell. "English Art," *Macmillan's Magazine*, XX (June 1869), 156–162.

Partially devoted to the Pre-Raphaelites.

71.9 Quilter, Harry. *Sententiae Artis: First Principles of Art for Painters and Picture Lovers*. London: Isbister, 1886.

Contains brief paragraph-sections on "Rossetti's 'Found,' " "Rossetti's Sense of Beauty," and "Blake's Pre-Raphaelitism." There are also sections on Millais, John Brett, G. P. Boyce, Burne-Jones, and Hunt. See also Quilter's article, "The New Renaissance; or the Gospel of Intensity," *Macmillan's Magazine*, XLII (September 1880), 391–400 — an attack on the "art for art's sake" tendencies of the aesthetic poets and painters, who inherited these tendencies from the Pre-Raphaelites. See 38.24.

71.10 Plowman, Thomas F. "The Aesthetes, the Story of a Nineteenth Century Cult," *Pall Mall Magazine*, V (January 1895), 27–44.

With a significant discussion of Rossetti and the Pre-Raphaelites. "The keynote of the aestheticism of the future was struck when the Brotherhood insisted upon the intimate relationship of one art with another, and sought to unite under one banner the poet, the painter, and the critic . . ." (p. 29)

71.11 Sulman, Thomas. "A Memorable Art Class," *Good Words*, XXXVIII (August 1897), 547–551.

Same in *Living Age*, CCXIV, 6th ser., XV, no. 2777 (18 September 1897), 889–893. Reminiscences of Ruskin and Rossetti in the Working Men's College.

71.12 "English Art in the Victorian Age," *Quarterly Review*, CLXXXVII (January 1898), 209–233.

Contains about ten pages on the Pre-Raphaelites.

71.13 Bell, Clive. "Alid ex Alio," *Art*. London: Stokes, 1914.

". . . the Pre-Raffaelites were not artists, but archaeologists who tried to make intelligent curiosity do the work of impassioned contemplation. As artists they do not differ essentially from the ruck of Victorian painters." (p. 18) See also 70.24.

71.14 Burdett, Osbert. *The Beardsley Period: An Essay in Perspective*. New York: Boni and Liveright, 1925.

An enlightened consideration of the Pre-Raphaelites as aesthetic precursors of the 1890's.

71.15 Plomer, William. "Art Nouveau: A Hint for Connoisseurs," *New Statesman and Nation*, II (28 November 1931), 672.

Decries taste in Victorian artifacts: "It is quite evident that the pre-Raphaelites were responsible for these later whimsies of craftsmanship . . ." See also Robert Schmutzler, on the influence of Rossetti on *Art Nouveau* (30.75).

71.16 Furst, Herbert. "Art and Temperament — VI," *Apollo*, XXXIII (June 1941), 152–154.

On the Pre-Raphaelites: "One must . . . look for the expression of the religious temperament outside the Renaissance tradition . . ." The Pre-Raphaelites, especially Millais and Holman Hunt, possessed it.

71.17 House, Humphry. "Man and Nature: Some Artists' Views," *Listener*, XXXIX (15 April 1948), 614–617.

Includes material on the Pre-Raphaelites. Reprinted in *All in Due Time* (see 74.13).

71.18 Munby, A. N. L. "Letters of British Artists of the XVIIIth and XIXth Centuries — Part VI," *Connoisseur*, CXXII (December 1948), 99–103.

Letters of Pre-Raphaelite interest in Munby's collection: one of exceptional length and interest from Woolner to Browning (now in Trinity College, Cambridge); three others — one each from Maclise, Landseer, and Holman Hunt, the first two containing pertinent references to Pre-Raphaelitism, the last dealing with Hunt's 1886 exhibition at the Fine Art Society (see 11.4).

71.19 Buckley, Jerome H. "The Fear of Art," *The Victorian Temper: A Study in Literary Culture*. Cambridge, Mass.: Harvard University Press, 1951.
An invaluable background study of Victorian aesthetics, with special reference in the chapter cited to Rossetti and the Pre-Raphaelites.

71.20 Hubbard, Hesketh. "The 1850's," *A Hundred Years of British Painting, 1851–1951*. London: Longmans, 1951.
With an eight-page section on the Pre-Raphaelites.

71.21 Praz, Mario. *The Romantic Agony*. Oxford University Press, 1951
With a general discussion of Pre-Raphaelitism as a manifestation of Romanticism.

71.22 Decker, Clarence R. " 'The Fleshly School' — Baudelaire in England," *The Victorian Conscience*. New York: Twayne, 1952.
"The Fleshly School of Poetry" is "a memorable current in the moving stream of English literature, while 'The Stealthy School of Criticism' is only vaguely recalled as a muddy episode in literary-moral history." (p. 77)

71.23 Reynolds, Graham. *Painters of the Victorian Scene*. London: Batsford, 1953.
Material on the Pre-Raphaelites, pp. 15–21.

71.24 Dutton, Ralph. *The Victorian Home: Some Aspects of Nineteenth-Century Taste and Manners*. London: Batsford, 1954.
Treats briefly the influence of Pre-Raphaelitism, especially of William Morris, on nineteenth-century interior decoration.

71.25 Woodward, John. "Painting and Sculpture," in *The Early Victorian Period, 1830–1860* (Connoisseur Guides). London: The Connoisseur, 1958.
With a brief section on the Pre-Raphaelites.

Primary Works and Studies of Specific Aspects of Pre-Raphaelitism

Section 72

DOCUMENTS OF THE PRE-RAPHAELITE MOVEMENT

Two of the items in this brief section are reprints of *The Germ*, but they have been included separately rather than as annotations owing to the importance of this journal and to the genuine scarcity of a complete run of the original four numbers. Actually, there are all too few primary documents available for the study of Pre-Raphaelitism, but the few which do exist cover roughly the periods of the first and second Brotherhoods. Except for Boyce's *Diaries*, none of the documents is later than the late 1850's, but by that time the formal organization of the movement had dissolved, a sign perhaps that Pre-Raphaelitism had matured and that it had become recognized as a serious force in contemporary English art.

* * *

72.1 *The Germ: Thoughts towards Nature in Poetry, Literature, and Art*. Numbers 1 and 2, January and February 1850. Continued as *Art and Poetry, Being Thoughts towards Nature, Conducted Principally by Artists*. Numbers 3 and 4, March and April [dated May] 1850.
The literary organ of the Pre-Raphaelite

Brotherhood. For discussion see Survey, pp. 7–81. The following reviews of *The Germ* may be noted: *Spectator*, XXIII, no. 1124 (12 January 1850), 43; *Literary Gazette*, no. 1722 (19 January 1850), p. 47; *Builder*, VIII, no. 363 (19 January 1850), 34; S. C. Hall in *Art Journal*, XII (March 1850), 96; *Weekly Dispatch*, no. 2515 (20 January 1850), p. 38; *John Bull*, XXX, no. 1522 (11 February 1850), 91; *Guardian*, no. 244 (8 August 1850), p. 623; *Bell's Weekly Messenger*, no. 2784 (20 April 1850), p. 7; *Critic*, IX (15 February 1850), 94–95; (1 June 1850), 278. William Michael Rossetti (*Some Reminiscences*, 38.8, vol. I, 93) ascribes both reviews in the *Critic* to Edward William (later Serjeant) Cox.

72.2 *The Germ: Thoughts towards Nature in Poetry, Literature, and Art. MDCCCL.* Portland, Maine: Mosher, 1898.

The first reprint of *The Germ*. Published as an Introduction to this edition is James Ashcroft Noble's article, "A Pre-Raphaelite Magazine" (73.5).

72.3 Rossetti, William Michael, ed. *The Germ . . . Being A Facsimile Reprint of the Literary Organ of the Pre-Raphaelite Brotherhood, Published in 1850: With an Introduction.* London: Stock, 1901.

The four parts in facsimile, with a separately bound Preface by W. M. Rossetti detailing the history and contents of the original publication. See W. E. Henley, "The Pre-Raphaelite Brethren," *Pall Mall Magazine*, XXV (1901), 257–263, a pejorative review, critical of both W. M. Rossetti's Preface and of Rossetti and the PRB: "In conclusion: Dante Rossetti imagined *The Germ*, made *The Germ* possible, floated *The Germ*, and in the long run died of *The Germ*." (p. 263) Rossetti is seen as a complete amateur.

72.4 *The Oxford and Cambridge Magazine for 1856: Conducted by Members of the Two Universities*, edited by William Fulford. Oxford: Numbers 1–12, January to December 1856.

The literary journal of the second "Brotherhood," with many contributions by William Morris (who financed the journal) and Burne-Jones, and three poems by Dante Rossetti.

For full bibliographical details on this journal see H. B. Forman, *The Books of William Morris* (43.1), pp. 22–33; for a critical selected edition see 73.11. Morris' writings of the journal are reprinted in *The Hollow Land and Other Contributions to the Oxford and Cambridge Magazine* (London: Longmans, 1903). A contemptuous review of the magazine appeared in the *Saturday Review*, III, no. 70 (28 February 1857), 196–197. See also the chapter on "*The Oxford and Cambridge Magazine*," in *In a Nook with a Book* (Cincinnati: Jennings, n.d.), by Frederic William Macdonald, the brother of Georgiana Burne-Jones.

72.5 *Rules of the Hogarth Club, and List of Membership.* London: [Privately Printed], 1860.

The club's rooms were at 6, Waterloo Place, S.W. Membership was divided into three classes: Artistic, Nonartistic, and Honorary. Members were classified as resident (London) and nonresident. Meetings were held each Friday at 8:00 P.M. except between 15 September and 15 October, when the club's rooms were closed. Annual exhibitions were held from 1 February to 31 May, and the exhibitions were private. The club was founded in 1858 and continued to function until 1862. Originally organized as a competitor of the Royal Academy, the Hogarth Club included among its membership nearly all the major and minor Pre-Raphaelites. Millais and Collinson were the only members of the PRB who were never associated with the club. Its officers were Ford Madox Brown, Rossetti, Morris, and F. G. Stephens. For a list of the membership see 72.6 (pp. 216–217). For a contemporary discussion of the Hogarth Club see "The Modern Pre-Raffaelite Painters," *Art Journal*, XX (December 1858), 374. A notice of one of the Hogarth Club exhibitions appeared in the *Art Journal*, XXII (May 1860), 159.

72.6 Rossetti, William Michael, ed. *Ruskin: Rossetti: Pre-Raphaelitism. Papers 1854 to 1862.* London: Allen, 1899.

This volume consists primarily of letters exchanged among the Pre-Raphaelites and their friends: forty letters from Rossetti to

William Rossetti, Madox Brown, Elizabeth Siddal, and others; seventy letters from Ruskin to Rossetti, plus letters from Browning, Bell Scott, Brown, and others. Also included are selections from Brown's diary (1854–1855), notes and letters on the two 1857 exhibitions (see 16.1 and 18.4), the "Prospectus of Morris, Marshall, Faulkner & Co." (pp. 268–271), and a list of the members of the Hogarth Club. See also 24.7.

72.7 Rossetti, William Michael, ed. "The P.R.B. Journal," *Præraphaelite Diaries and Letters*. London: Hurst and Blackett, 1900.

For a discussion of the "Journal" see Survey, p. 9, n. 4. Besides the "Journal" the volume also contains some early correspondence of D. G. Rossetti (24.8) and selections from Ford Madox Brown's diary (41.6).

72.8 Street, Arthur E. "George Price Boyce with Extracts from G. P. Boyce's Diaries, 1851–1875," *The Old Water-Colour Society's Club: Nineteenth Annual Volume*, edited by Randall Davies. London: OW-CS. Issued only to members, 1941.

Almost the entire volume is given over to Boyce's diary, a valuable source of contemporary, on-the-spot, uncensored gossip about the Pre-Raphaelites and their circle. The unpublished portions of Boyce's witty and fascinating personal account of the period are unfortunately unrecoverable, the diary having been destroyed during the war. The volume also contains a list of Boyce's works in the winter exhibition of the Society, 1898–1899 (see 17.5), eight reproductions from Boyce's own works, and other reproductions from the works of Rossetti, Sandys, Simeon Solomon, and others. Street's article is reprinted with slight abridgments from the *Architectural Review*, V (February 1899), 151–160.

Section 73

STUDIES OF *THE GERM* AND
THE OXFORD AND CAMBRIDGE MAGAZINE

73.1 [Burne-Jones, Edward]. "Essay on the Newcomes," *Oxford and Cambridge Magazine*, I (January 1856), 50–61.

A brief but important discussion of *The Germ* (pp. 60–61). See 42.1 for annotation.

73.2 [Payne, John Burnell]. "A Pre-Raphaelite Magazine. 'The Germ,'" *Every Saturday*, V (16 May 1868), 618–622.

A reprint of one part of a longer article. For annotation see 76.2.

73.3 Keary, C. F. "The Germ," *Macmillan's Magazine*, XXXIV (September 1876), 439–447.

Reviews two phases of Pre-Raphaelitism: "If . . . the external life of the nineteenth century is so ugly, we cannot hope to mend it much by make-believe of the Pre-Raphaelite character." (p. 447)

73.4 Hamilton, Walter. "The Germ," *The Æsthetic Movement in England*. London: Reeves and Turner, 1882.

For complete annotation see 78.2.

73.5 Noble, James Ashcroft. "A Pre-Raphaelite Magazine," *The Sonnet in England and Other Essays*. London: John Lane, 1896.

Originally appeared in *Fraser's Magazine*, n.s. XXV (May 1882), 568–580. Reprinted in the Mosher edition of *The Germ* (72.2).

73.6 Radford, Ernest. "The Life and Death of *The Germ*," *Idler*, XIII (March 1898), 227–233.

A summary of the contents plus some critical comment. Illustrated with reproductions from pictures by Rossetti at the New Gallery exhibition (14.5).

73.7 Rossetti, William Michael. "Preface," *The Germ . . . Being A Facsimile Reprint of the Literary Organ of the Pre-Raphaelite Brotherhood, Published in 1850: With an Introduction*. London: Stock, 1901.

The most detailed and authoritative account of *The Germ*. See also 72.3.

73.8 Broers, Bernarda C. "The Pre-Raphaelites. *The Germ,*" *Mysticism in the Neo-Romanticists*. Amsterdam: Paris, 1923 (diss. Amsterdam, 1923).

With separate chapters on Rossetti (33.21), Morris (43.88), O'Shaughnessy (51.14), Patmore (52.8), Payne (54.12), Bell Scott (56.20), and Swinburne (62.26).

73.9 Jervis, H. "Carlyle and *The Germ,*" *Times Literary Supplement*, no. 1907 (20 August 1938), p. 544.

Describing a manuscript letter of Carlyle, dated 31 March 1850, in praise of *The Germ,* in the County Seely Library, Newport.

73.10 Hough, Graham. "Books in General," *New Statesman and Nation*, XXXVI (7 August 1948), 117.

The Germ, the first of the little reviews devoted wholly to the arts. Written on the occasion of the Pre-Raphaelite centenary.

73.11 Gordon, Walter Kelly. "A Critical Selected Edition of William Morris's *Oxford and Cambridge Magazine* (1856)," unpub. diss., University of Pennsylvania, 1960. *Dissertation Abstracts*, XXI (1961), 3781–3782.

Emphasizes the Pre-Raphaelite qualities of *The Oxford and Cambridge Magazine*.

Section 74

STUDIES EMPHASIZING LITERARY ASPECTS OF PRE-RAPHAELITISM

74.1 Forman, H. Buxton. "The Pre-Raphaelite Group," *Our Living Poets: An Essay in Criticism*. London: Tinsley, 1871.

Poets included in this group are D. G. Rossetti (27.1), Christina Rossetti (44.20), Patmore (52.3), W. B. Scott (56.12), and Woolner (40.7). The volume also contains chapters on Morris (43.28) and Swinburne (62.15), and an appendix on "John Payne and Arthur W. E. O'Shaughnessy" (54.9, 51.7). Most of the articles are reprinted from *Tinsley's Magazine*, but an article on William Michael Rossetti which appeared in that journal (38.13) is not reprinted in this volume.

74.2 Galletti, Alfredo. "Dante Gabriele Rossetti e la poesia preraffaellita," *Studi di letterature straniere*. Verona: Fratelli Drucker, 1903.

74.3 Earle, Anne M. "Pre-Raphaelite Ideals. As Expressed in the Printing and the Poetry of the Brotherhood," *Book News Monthly*, XXIV (June 1906), 681–686.

In the same issue of *Book News Monthly* (pp. 687–690), see the article by Cornelius Weygandt, "Two Pre-Raphaelite Poets: William Morris and Dante Gabriel Rossetti." (33.10 and 43.59) For full details of this issue of *Book News Monthly*, devoted primarily to the Pre-Raphaelites, see 67.26.

74.4 Brawley, Benjamin. "Pre-Raphaelitism and Its Literary Relations," *South Atlantic Quarterly*, XV (January 1916), 68–81.

". . . Pre-Raphaelitism was only an esoteric revival of the Romantic spirit"; "Back to Nature" only a shibboleth. The revolutionary spirit in Pre-Raphaelite poetry is "positively blasphemous." "Pre-Raphaelitism was simply Romanticism decadent." "The Pre-Raphaelites and their disciples were over-rated in 1870 and are still over-rated; and time is very likely to prove that the 'Renascence of Wonder' was by no means a rebirth, but rather the last flicker of the light of old romance." (p. 81)

74.5 Hearn, Lafcadio. *Pre-Raphaelite and Other Poets: Lectures*. Selected and edited with an Introduction by John Erskine. New York, Dodd, Mead, 1922.

Two chapters on Rossetti (27.64), and one each on Morris (43.86), Swinburne (62.25), and Robert Buchanan.

74.6 Axmann, M. *Die Präraffaelitische Dichtung im Urteile Ihrer Zeit*. Hildesheim: Borgmeyer, 1930 (diss. Breslau, 1930).

74.7 Evans, B. Ifor. "Minor Pre-Raphaelite Poets: William Bell Scott; William Allingham; Thomas Woolner; Arthur O'Shaughnessy; John Payne; Philip Bourke Marston;

William Sharp (Fiona Macleod)," *English Poetry in the Later Nineteenth Century.* London: Methuen, 1933.

One of the few studies of the minor Pre-Raphaelite poets, this volume is listed separately under each of the poets in the title, except William Sharp. The volume also contains chapters on Rossetti (27.85), Morris (43.102), Swinburne (62.33), and Christina Rossetti (44.72).

74.8 Mégroz, R. L. "Pre-Raphaelite Poetry," *Modern English Poetry, 1882–1932.* London: Nicholson, 1933.

Pre-Raphaelite poetry is considered as the immediate ancestor of modern poetry.

74.9 De Armond, Anna Janney. "What is Pre-Raphaelitism in Poetry?," *Delaware Notes,* 19th series (1946), pp. 67–88.

". . . to define Pre-Raphaelitism in poetry, one must explain . . . not a single, static movement, but an actual development in poetic theory and poetic practice." (p. 86)

74.10 "Pre-Raphaelite Poetry," *Times Lit-*

erary *Supplement,* no. 2426 (31 July 1948), pp. 421–423.

A front article prompted by the centenary of *The Germ.*

74.11 Lang, Cecil Y. "Studies in Pre-Raphaelitism," unpub. diss., Harvard University, 1949.

Studies of the influence of Keats, Tennyson, and Ruskin on the Pre-Raphaelites, with a final chapter on "The Personal and Literary Relations of Rossetti and Swinburne, with a Discussion of Swinburne's Pre-Raphaelitism."

74.12 Hübner, Walter. "Die Präraffaeliten," *Die Stimmen der Meister: eine Einführung in Meisterwerke des englischen Dichtens und Denkens.* Berlin: Gruyter, 1950.

Discusses Rossetti, Morris, and Swinburne.

74.13 House, Humphry. "Pre-Raphaelite Poetry," *All in Due Time.* London: Hart-Davis, 1955.

The collected essays and broadcasts of House. For discussion see Survey, p. 34. See also 71.17.

Section 75

STUDIES EMPHASIZING ARTISTIC ASPECTS OF PRE-RAPHAELITISM

75.1 Ruskin, John. "The Pre-Raphaelites," *Times,* no. 20,800 (13 May 1851), pp. 8–9.

Ruskin's first letter to the *Times* in defense of the PRB, written in answer to a letter in the same publication for 7 May 1851. Ruskin's second letter, "The Pre-Raphaelite Artists," appeared on 30 May 1851 (no. 20,815, pp. 8–9), followed by a brief rejoinder by the *Times* critic. Both letters were reprinted in *Arrows of the Chace* (75.12), and both appear in *CW* (45.3, XII, 318–323). The letters have most recently been reprinted, together with reproductions of four of the pictures concerned, by Joan Evans (ed.), "The Pre-Raphaelites," *The Lamp of Beauty: Writings on Art by John Ruskin* (London: Phaidon, 1959). See "Punch Among the Pictures," *Punch,* XX (21 May 1851), 219: "The pictures of the P.R.B. *are* true and that's the worst of them."

75.2 ———— "Pre-Raphaelitism," *Lectures on Architecture and Painting.* London: Smith, Elder, 1854.

One of a series of lectures on architecture and painting delivered at Edinburgh in 1853. Reprinted *CW* (45.3, XII, 134–164).

75.3 Perrier, Charles. "Ecole anglaise. Les Préraphaélites — les aquarellistes," *L'Artiste,* ser. V, tome XVI (September 1855), 29–32.

75.4 [Stephens, Frederic George]. "The Two Pre-Raphaelitisms," *Crayon,* III (August 1856), 225–228; (October 1856), 289–292; (November 1856), 321–324; (December 1856), 353–356.

Although these articles have been attributed to W. J. Stillman (see Dickason, 80.8), it is clear from correspondence and accounts of William Michael Rossetti in the Stephens

Papers (see 2.8, Bodleian, Add. MSS. Don. e 76) that the articles were in fact written by Stephens. Another series of articles, similarly entitled, appear in the following year (1857) in volume IV: (September 1857), 261–265; (October 1857), 298–302; (November 1857), 325–328; (December 1857), 361–363. Whether Stephens was responsible for this later series it is not possible to say. From the evidence in the correspondence of W. M. Rossetti, it would appear that Stephens did not deal directly with Stillman, but acted entirely through Rossetti, who contributed a regular column (see 38.1) to the *Crayon* until Stillman ceased to be editor, after the December number, 1856.

75.5 Ruskin, John. "Pre-Raphaelitism in Liverpool," *Liverpool Albion*, 11 January 1858.
Reprinted in *Arrows of the Chace* (75.12); *CW* (45.3, XIV, 327–328).

75.6 ——— "Generalization and the Scotch Pre-Raphaelites," *Witness* (Edinburgh), 27 March 1858.
Reprinted in *Arrows of the Chace* (75.12); *CW* (45.3, XIV, 329–331).

75.7 Delaborde, Henri. "Les Préraphaélites à propos d'un tableau de Raphaël," *Revue des Deux Mondes*, XVI (July 1858), 241–260.

75.8 Rossetti, William Michael. "Præraphaelitism," *Fine Art, Chiefly Contemporary: Notices Reprinted, with Revisions*. London: Macmillan, 1867.
Originally appeared in *Spectator*, XXIV, no. 1214 (4 October 1851), 955–957. For complete annotation see 38.2.

75.9 *English Painters of the Present Day*. Essays by J. Beavington Atkinson, Sidney Colvin, P. G. Hamerton, W. M. Rossetti, and Tom Taylor. With Twelve Photographs after the Originals. London: Seeley, 1871.
Relevant essays included in this volume (all reprinted from the *Portfolio*) are those on Ford Madox Brown (41.8), Burne-Jones (42.7), Simeon Solomon (61.5), Arthur Hughes, W. L. Windus, Marie Spartali, and the younger Madox Browns (49.1). A second

volume, *English Artists of the Present Day* (London: Seeley, 1872), contained reprinted essays on Millais (37.11), Hunt (36.17), and Woolner (40.8).

75.10 Ruskin, John. *Letters to "The Times" on the Principal Pre-Raphaelite Pictures in the Exhibition of 1854. From the Author of "Modern Painters,"* edited by Ernest Willett. London: Reprinted for private circulation only, 1876.
An authorized reprint. Includes Ruskin's letters on "The Light of the World," *Times*, no. 21,733 (5 May 1854), p. 9; and "The Awakening Conscience," *Times*, no. 21,750 (25 May 1854), p. 7. These, together with the two letters of 1851 (75.1) were reprinted in *Arrows of the Chace* (75.12). The 1854 letters were also reprinted in Ruskin's *Notes* for the exhibition of Hunt's works at the Fine Art Society (21.17); the first letter appeared in abridged form in 11.8. Both letters reprinted in *CW* (45.3, XII, 328–335).

75.11 ——— "The Three Colours of Pre-Raphaelitism," *Nineteenth Century*, IV (November 1878), 925–931; (December 1878), 1072–1082.
Reprinted in *CW* (45.3, XXXIV, 147–174).

75.12 ——— "Pre-Raphaelitism," *Arrows of the Chace, Being a Collection of Scattered Letters Published Chiefly in the Daily Newspapers*. 2 vols. London: Allen, 1880.
Contains the 1851 letters to the *Times* (75.1), the 1854 letters (75.10), "Pre-Raphaelitism in Liverpool" (75.5), and "Generalization and the Scotch Pre-Raphaelites" (75.6).

75.13 Hunt, William Holman. "The Pre-Raphaelite Brotherhood: A Fight for Art," *Contemporary Review*, XLIX (April 1886), 471–488; (May 1886), 737–750; (June 1886), 820–833.
Reprinted in the *Contemporary Review*, XCVIII (November 1910), 592–609; (December 1910), 702–725. The history of this series of articles is recounted in the introductory section of 68.4, in which Harry Quilter admits to having ghost-written the series,

Hunt's prepared version having proved unsatisfactory. See also 75.23.

75.14 Morris, William. *Address on the Collection of Paintings of the English Pre-Raphaelite School, Delivered in the* [*Birmingham*] *Museum and Art Gallery: October 2, 1891.* Birmingham: [Printed for the Corporation], [1891].

For the exhibition see 16.2. The lecture is reprinted in 43.24 (vol. I, 296–310), and in Walter E. Houghton and G. Robert Stange (eds.), *Victorian Poetry and Poetics* (Boston: Houghton, Mifflin, 1959), pp. 600–605.

75.15 Gurlitt, Cornelius. "Die Präraphaeliten, eine britische Malerschule," *Westermanns Illustrierte Deutsche Monatshefte*, LXXII (April 1892), 106–136; (May 1892), 253–282; (June 1892), 327–345; (July 1892), 480–496.

Profusely illustrated. See also the excerpt from this article, "Pre-Raphaelitism," in *Public Opinion*, XIII (April 1892), 95–96.

75.16 Chesneau, Ernest. "Peintres anglais contemporains: les alliés du Préraphaélisme et son évolution," *L'Art*, LIX, 20ᵉ année, tome IV (1894), 385–407.

75.17 Baldwin, Elbert F. "The Nativity as Interpreted by the English Pre-Raphaelites," *Outlook*, L (15 December 1894), 1042–1045.

75.18 Destrée, Olivier Georges. *Les Préraphaélites: Notes sur l'art décoratif et la peinture en Angleterre.* Bruxelles: Dietrich, 1894.

With catalogues of the works of Rossetti by J. P. Anderson (25.11), and of Burne-Jones by Malcolm Bell (42.16).

75.19 Mourey, Gabriel. "L'Art: les préraphaélites," *Passé le Détroit: la vie et l'art à Londres.* Paris: Ollendorff, 1895.

Brief sections on Rossetti, Burne-Jones, Brown, Millais, Hunt, Hughes; other sections on Morris, Walter Crane, Watts, Swinburne, Whistler, and the decorative arts. Translated into English by Georgina Latimer as *Across the Channel: Life and Art in London* (London: Allen, 1896).

75.20 Low, Will H. "A Century of Painting, Notes Descriptive and Critical. — The Pre-Raphaelite Brotherhood — Dante Gabriel Rossetti, Holman Hunt, and John Everett Millais. Dyce a Precursor, Madox Brown an Ally, — Burne-Jones and His Influence on the Group," *McClure's Magazine*, VII (June 1896), 65–72.

75.21 Bate, Percy H. *The English Pre-Raphaelite Painters: Their Associates and Successors.* London: Bell, 1899.

Revised edition, 1901. With separate chapters on all the major and most of the minor Pre-Raphaelites, including many figures on the extreme fringe of the Movement. Profusely illustrated with seven photogravure plates and 82 half-tone reproductions. For discussion of this volume see Survey, p. 26.

75.22 *Pre-Raphaelite Painters.* London: Virtue, 1902.

A collective reprint of the special numbers of the *Art Journal* for Rossetti (30.31), Hunt (36.33), Millais (37.26), and Burne-Jones (42.24).

75.23 Hunt, William Holman. *Pre-Raphaelitism and the Pre-Raphaelite Brotherhood.* 2 vols. London: Macmillan, 1905–1906.

Second edition, revised from the author's notes by M. E. Holman Hunt, was published by Chapman and Hall in 1913. For Hunt's earlier articles on the history of the movement see 75.13. One of the most useful accounts of the origin and history of the PRB, despite its bias. Among the reviews of Hunt's work — many of them controversial — the following may be noted: "William Holman Hunt. The First and Last of the Pre-Raphaelites," *Living Age*, CCXLVIII, 7th ser., XXX, no. 3210 (13 January 1906), 117–121; "Who was the Real Leader of the Pre-Raphaelites?," *Current Literature*, XL (March 1906), 274–277; "W. H. Hunt, Father of Pre-Raphaelitism," *Independent*, LX (March 1906), 572–574; E. L. Cary, "Holman Hunt's Pre-Raphaelitism," *Critic*, XLVIII (June 1906), 529–531; "The Pre-Raphaelites," *Outlook*, LXXXIII (August 1906), 810–812. Selections from Hunt's volumes appeared as "Pre-Raphaelite Aims and Methods," in

Artists on Art, from the XIV to the XX Century, edited by Robert J. Goldwater and Marco Treves (New York: Pantheon, 1947).

75.24 T., A. "The Pre-Raphaelites and the Royal Academy," *Burlington Magazine*, VIII (February 1906), 344–346.

In part a review of 75.23.

75.25 *The Leaders of the English Pre-Raphaelites: Holman Hunt, Rossetti, and Millais.* New York: Stokes, [1908].

A collective reprint of three volumes in the series "Masterpieces in Colour," edited by T. Lemon Hare: *Rossetti* (30.42), *Hunt* (36.47), *Millais* (37.72). There is no title page; title is stamped on front cover.

75.26 Knight, William Angus. "The Pre-Raphaelites, Especially Dante Gabriel Rossetti, with Reminiscences," *Six Lectures on Some Nineteenth Century Artists, English and French*. Chicago: The Art Institute, 1909.

Same in *Nineteenth Century Artists, English and French* (Edinburgh: Schulze, 1910). These Scammon Lectures were given by Professor Knight at the Art Institute of Chicago in 1907. "[The PRB] was not only an artistic but a literary revolt, and a poetical renaissance. It was a new way of looking at, of appraising and reproducing both Man and Nature, which found a simultaneous expression in all the departments . . . of the Beautiful . . ." (p. 96) The lecture on Burne-Jones, also printed in the volume, is essentially the same as 42.71.

75.27 Linton, John. *The Cross in Modern Art: Descriptive Studies of Some Pre-Raphaelite Paintings*. London: Duckworth, 1916.

Emphasizes religious qualities of Pre-Raphaelite art through discussions of particular pictures of Ford Madox Brown (41.28), Rossetti (31.26), Millais (37.83), Holman Hunt (36.58), and G. F. Watts (63.9). ". . . in this significant group of painters there exists, beneath all their differences, a real unity of spirit and aim and outlook, for which the word 'Pre-Raphaelitism,' in default of a better, may be used. Their influence . . . lay less in the creation of a new school of Art, than in the noble and enduring expression they gave to the moral and spiritual forces of their generation. This was their true bequest to the future; by this their claim to greatness is established . . . Their Art reflects, not only the austere intellectual analysis before which the separating walls everywhere crumbled, but the incomparably splendid synthesis which their genius achieved. This synthesis was essentially religious." (pp. 3–4) The fulsome tone of this book is nowhere better indicated than in the response of an anonymous reviewer in an unidentified newspaper: "We know of few books that better deserve to be placed in the hands of a youth or maiden who desires to love the highest in art and to learn the lessons taught by painters inspired by the resolution to bring home to the mind great truths expressed in artistic form."

75.28 Galimberti, Alice. *Il Medioevo Italiano nell'arte preraffaellita*. Rome: Direzione della Nuova Antologia, 1922.

Reprinted from *Nuova Antologia*, CCCIV, 6th series, CCXX (October 1922), 246–255.

75.29 Reid, Forrest. "The Pre-Raphaelite Group," *Illustrators of the Sixties*. London: Faber, 1928.

For annotation see 88.9.

75.30 Neumeyer, Alfred. "Die präraffaelitische Malerei im Rahmen der Kunstgeschichte des 19. Jahrhunderts," *Deutsche Vierteljahrsschrift für Literaturwissenschaft und Geistesgeschichte*, XI (1933), 67–77.

75.31 Oppé, A. P. "The Pre-Raphaelites," in *Early Victorian England, 1830–1865*, edited by G. M. Young. 2 vols. London: Oxford University Press, 1934.

A sensitive and perceptive account of the Pre-Raphaelites. In the chapter "Art," vol. II, 159–176.

75.32 Rosenberg, Isaac. "The Pre-Raphaelites and Imagination in Paint," *The Collected Poems of Isaac Rosenberg*. Edited by Gordon Bottomley and D. W. Harding, with a Foreword by S. Sassoon. London: Chatto and Windus, 1937.

75.33 Mourey, Gabriel. "Les Préraphaélites et les peintres anglais du XIXe siècle," *Visages du Monde*, no. 54 (1938), pp. 89–92.

75.34 Reitlinger, Henry. "The Pre-Raphaelites," *From Hogarth to Keene: With 87 Reproductions of Black and White Drawings by English Story-Telling Artists and Illustrators.* London: Methuen, 1938.

The chapter on "The Sixties" also contains much information on the Pre-Raphaelites.

75.35 Allen, Josephine L. "A Pre-Raphaelite Drawing," *Metropolitan Museum of Art Bulletin*, n.s. I (January 1943), n.p. [inside back cover].

A drawing in the Burne-Jones tradition acquired by the museum.

75.36 Pickford, R. W. "The Pre-Raphaelite Painters," *The Psychology of Cultural Change* (*British Journal of Psychology*, Monograph Supplement no. XXVI). Cambridge University Press, 1943.

75.37 Gere, John. "Pre-Raphaelite Drawings," *Alphabet and Image*, no. 6 (January 1948), pp. 18–32.

Mainly on Rossetti and Millais. Illustrated.

75.38 Carter, Charles. "The Pre-Raphaelites as Religious Painters," *Quarterly Review*, CCLXXXVI (April 1948), 248–261.

". . . whatever posterity may decide about the merits of the Pre-Raphaelite painters, the fact is undoubted that during the course of a few years they produced a number of religious pictures some of which must be regarded as among the most significant to be painted in this country since the Reformation." (p. 250) They were not, however,

great religious painters; their emphasis on literal truth denies the universality of religious truth, and their didacticism vitiates the spiritual influence of genuine religious expression.

75.39 Gaunt, William. "The Lesser Known Pre-Raphaelite Painters," *Apollo*, 1948 Annual, pp. 5–9.

Brief references to Calderon, Brett, Windus, W. S. Burton, Martineau, Hughes, Smetham, and Elizabeth Siddal. "These artists," says Gaunt, "represent the realist strain in Pre-Raphaelitism . . . they are incomplete Pre-Raphaelites . . ."

75.40 Thomas, Daniel. "Some Pre-Raphaelite Paintings," *Art Gallery of New South Wales Quarterly*, IV (October 1962), 119–125.

A discussion of pictures by "members of the circle though not of the Pre-Raphaelite Brotherhood itself." With nine illustrations by Brown, J. M. Strudwick, J. Spencer Stanhope, Burne-Jones, and Millais.

75.41 Bennett, Mary. "A Check List of Pre-Raphaelite Pictures Exhibited At Liverpool, 1846–67, and Some of Their Northern Collectors," *Burlington Magazine*, CV (November 1963), 486–495.

An extremely useful article for its discussion of Pre-Raphaelite pictures exhibited at the Liverpool Academy, the listing of the important, early patrons of Pre-Raphaelite art, and the present location of many of the pictures exhibited between 1846 and 1867. Nine illustrations.

Section 76

STUDIES EMPHASIZING BOTH THE LITERARY AND ARTISTIC ASPECTS OF PRE-RAPHAELITISM; STUDIES OF THE PRE-RAPHAELITE AESTHETIC, OR OF PRE-RAPHAELITE TECHNIQUES, AIMS, OR METHODS

76.1 "Pre-Raphaelitism in Art and Literature," *British Quarterly Review*, XVI (August 1852), 197–220.

In part a review of *The Germ*, Ruskin's

pamphlet (66.1), and the Royal Academy exhibition of 1852.

76.2 Payne, John Burnell. "Pre-Raphaelite

Poetry and Painting," *London Student*, I, no. 1 (April 1868), 17–29; no. 2 (May 1868), 87–96; no. 4 (July 1868), 214–224.

A three-part article: I. " 'The Germ' "; II. "The Theory"; III. "The Results." This is the article to which W. M. Rossetti vaguely alludes in the "Preface" to his edition of *The Germ* (73.7) as having appeared in "some magazine." Part I of the article was reprinted anonymously in *Every Saturday* (see 73.2). See also 71.8.

76.3 Chesneau, Ernest. "Peintres anglais contemporains: L'Esthétique préraphaélite. Le 'Germ.' John Ruskin," *L'Art*, LIX, 20ᵉ année, tome IV (1894), 564–587.

76.4 Wilenski, R. H. "Technique of the Pre-Raphaelites: The Daguerreotype and Ruskin," *The Modern Movement in Art*. London: Faber, 1927; revised edition, 1935.

76.5 Housman, Laurence. "Pre-Raphaelitism in Art and Poetry," *Essays by Divers Hands (Transactions of the Royal Society of Literature*, n.s. XII). London: Oxford University Press, 1933.

For discussion see Survey, pp. 24–30.

76.6 Zabel, Morton D. "The Romantic Idealism of Art, 1800–1848. Aspects of English Esthetics in the Nineteenth Century before Ruskin and the Pre-Raphaelites," unpub. diss., University of Chicago, 1934.

76.7 Laurie, A. P. "The Technique of Rembrandt, Turner, the Pre-Raphaelites, and the French Impressionists," *New Light on Old Masters*. London: Sheldon Press, 1935.

76.8 Dali, Salvador. "Le Surréalisme spectral de l'éternel féminin préraphaélite," *Minotaure*, no. 8 (1936), 46–49.

Discusses "surrealistic" techniques in the details of Pre-Raphaelite art, such as the background of Holman Hunt's *The Scapegoat*, with illustrations. An important and perceptive article treating the influence of the Pre-Raphaelites on Dali and other surrealistic painters.

76.9 Spender, Stephen. "The Pre-Raphaelite Literary Painters," *New Writing and Daylight*, VI (1945), 123–131.

One of the most stimulating articles ever written on the Pre-Raphaelites, with wide and penetrating insights into both aspects of their art. ". . . the attempt to paint poetry according to the Pre-Raphaelite formula of truth makes the mistake of *copying* poetry in painting." (p. 127) "Poetic truth and photography are at war in . . . so many Pre-Raphaelite paintings." Rossetti, however, a "truly literary painter," "understood something of the spirit of fourteenth-century poetry in his painting." (p. 128) "Romantic poetry then was and is the 'ineducible mystery' of Pre-Raphaelitism. . . . The æsthetic aims of the movement were too unpainterly to produce anything but amateurs." (p. 129) "The Pre-Raphaelites represented the cult of a misconceived mediævalism, an attempted refusal to be contaminated by the modern world which was, in fact, a refusal to recognize that the basic condition of the life of every contemporary is that he is involved in the guilt of the whole society in which he lives. Thus the Pre-Raphaelite poetry maintained the balance of a precarious innocence which was a refusal to recognize facts, an innocence which only Holman Hunt, who never grew up, entirely accepted, which, with Rossetti, toppled over into morbidity, with Ruskin into madness, and which collapsed into the success story of Millais." (p. 130)

76.10 Buck, Richard D. "A Note on the Methods and Materials of the Pre-Raphaelite Painters," in *Paintings and Drawings of the Pre-Raphaelites and Their Circle* [Cambridge, Massachusetts]: Fogg Museum of Art, Harvard University, 1946.

The most detailed technical analysis of Pre-Raphaelite paintings available. An introductory section in the catalogue of the 1946 Fogg Museum Pre-Raphaelite exhibition (see 16.13). "It is not intended in this technical note to make aesthetic evaluations of Pre-Raphaelite painting. But aesthetic expression can not be entirely divorced from the materials and methods used, and it should not be so separated. Pre-Raphaelite painting — in fact, the bulk of nineteenth-century painting — suffers because, purposely or accidentally, painters lost touch with the traditional craftsmanship which had previously distinguished the work of even the minor artists. Many nineteenth-century artists experimented to regain control of their materials — the Pre-Raphaelites made such experiments — but it was experimentation in a curious void unaided by the empirical knowledge of materials that had been built up in the past, or by the exact data from controlled experimentation which will be available to the artist of the future." (pp. 17–18)

76.11 Cassidy, John A. "Robert Buchanan and the Fleshly Controversy," *Publications of the Modern Language Association*, LXVII (March 1952), 65–93.
For discussion of this important article see Survey, pp. 17–19. See also G. G. Storey's "Robert Buchanan's Critical Principles: Reply to Cassidy's Article on Buchanan," *PMLA*, LXVIII (December 1953), 1228–1232.

76.12 Welland, D. S. R. *The Pre-Raphaelites in Literature and Art* (Life, Literature, and Thought Library). London: Harrap, 1953.
For discussion see Survey, p. 34.

76.13 Fredeman, William Evan. "The Pre-Raphaelites and Their Critics: A Tentative Approach Toward the Aesthetic of Pre-Raphaelitism," unpub. diss., University of Okla-

homa, 1956. *Dissertation Abstracts*, XVI (August 1956), 971.

76.14 ———— "Pre-Raphaelites in Caricature: 'The Choice of Paris: An Idyll' by Florence Claxton," *Burlington Magazine*, CII (December 1960), 523–529.
A study of critical strictures against the Pre-Raphaelites made through various literary and visual caricatures. See 82.3. Illustrated.

76.15 Forsyth, R. A. "The Temper of Pre-Raphaelitism and the Concern with Natural Detail," *English Studies in Africa*, IV (September 1961), 182–190.
The purposes of Pre-Raphaelitism are seen as embodied essentially in Rossetti's "Hand and Soul." "These two, which Chiaro, though never deeply concerned with purely natural detail, had united in exemplary fashion, the Victorian zealots [i.e., the Pre-Raphaelites] welded together in their ornate creations with a characteristic moral earnestness that merged their method ["Hand"] and intention ["Soul"] in the larger social context, which was the true *milieu* of their revolt." (p. 189)

76.16 Hough, Graham. "The Aesthetic of Pre-Raphaelitism," in "Rossetti and the P.R.B.," *The Last Romantics*. London: Duckworth, 1949.

Section 77

STUDIES EMPHASIZING THE RELATIONSHIP OF INDIVIDUAL ARTISTS AND WRITERS WITH THE PRE-RAPHAELITES

Two or more items relating to a single figure who is in any way compared with the Pre-Raphaelites are grouped for convenience. Some of the items in this section emphasize relationships of the most tenuous sort and might have been classified in other sections. However, if the intention of an article or book seemed to lay *primary* stress on Pre-Raphaelite connections, the item has been included in this section.

*   *   *

ROBERT BROWNING

77.1 Watkin, Ralph Granger. *Robert Browning and the English Pre-Raphaelites*. Breslau: Fleischmann, 1905 (diss. Breslau, 1905).

Traces the influence of the Pre-Raphaelites in furthering Browning's reputation.

77.2 Cramer, Maurice Browning. "What Browning's Literary Reputation Owed to the Pre-Raphaelites, 1847–1856," *ELH*, VIII (December 1941), 305–321.

Stresses the admiration of the Pre-Raphaelites for Browning and the importance of their patronage in the development of his career. See also Cramer's article "Browning's Reputation at Oxford, 1855–1859," *PMLA*, LVII (March 1942) 232–240, in which he traces the influence of Rossetti in stimulating interest in Browning's poetry among the Oxford undergraduates after the publication of *Men and Women* in 1855.

WILLIAM HOLMAN HUNT

77.3 Machar, Agnes M. "Holman Hunt and the Pre-Raphaelites," *Andover Review*, XII (December 1889), 579–596.

Ruskin and the Pre-Raphaelites did for painting what Burns did for poetry — "sent it back to the fresh, pure well-spring of nature . . ."

77.4 Stephens, F. G. [Holman Hunt's *Pre-Raphaelitism and the Pre-Raphaelite Brotherhood*] [London: Privately printed, 1906].

A four-page pamphlet answering Holman Hunt's statements about Pre-Raphaelitism and his rejection of Stephens and William Michael Rossetti as PRB's of the original strain. A shorter version of this pamphlet appeared in a letter to the *Times*, 16 February 1906. This pamphlet, which Hunt never saw, is discussed in 75.23, 2nd edition (1913), II, 385–392.

77.5 "Holman Hunt and the Pre-Raphaelite Movement," *Chautauquan*, LI (December 1910), 12–13.

An obituary notice of England's Christian artist *par excellence*.

77.6 Banner, Delmar Harmood. "Holman Hunt and Pre-Raphaelitism," *Nineteenth Century*, CII (October 1927), 546–557.

A centenary review of Hunt's life, art, and ideas.

77.7 Dearmer, Percy. "Holman Hunt and the Pre-Raphaelite Movement," *Contemporary Review*, CXXXIV (July 1928), 74–81.

On the centenary of the Pre-Raphaelite triumvirate: Hunt (1927), Rossetti (1928), Millais (1929).

JOHN KEATS

77.8 Mengin, Urbain. "John Keats et les origines du préraphaélisme anglais," *L'Italie des romantiques*. Paris: Plon-Nourit, 1902.

77.9 Ford, George H. *Keats and the Victorians: A Study of His Influence and Rise to Fame, 1821–1895*. New Haven: Yale University Press, 1944.

Chapter VIII in part Three, on Rossetti, is a discussion of Keats and the Pre-Raphaelites. For complete annotation see 33.33.

77.10 Unwin, Rayner. "Keats and Pre-Raphaelitism," *English*, IX (Summer 1951), 229–235.

An interest in medievalism (archaism), a general concern with beauty, a brilliance and purity of color, a realistic treatment of nature tempered by imagination, and a similar subject matter are the principal similarities between Keats and the Pre-Raphaelites. See also 74.11, in which nearly identical conclusions are drawn.

ROBERT BRAITHWAITE MARTINEAU

77.11 Martineau, Helen. "A Pre-Raphaelite Painter," *Studio*, LXXXVII (April 1924), 207–208.

Illustrated.

77.12 ——— "Robert Braithwaite Martineau; a Follower of the Pre-Raphaelites," *Connoisseur*, CX (December 1942), 97–101.

Illustrated.

77.13 ——— "Echo of a Pre-Raphaelite Painter, R. B. Martineau," *Studio*, CXXXIV (September 1947), 78–79.

Three of Martineau's works are reproduced: *The Knight's Guerdon*, *The Princess with the Golden Ball*, and *The Last Day in the Old Home*.

WILLIAM MORRIS

77.14 Streeter, A. "William Morris and Pre-Raphaelitism," *Month*, XCIV (December 1899), 595–608.

The great change that Morris wrought in Pre-Raphaelitism lay in the element of health he brought to it, the vigor with which he endowed it. Morris' Pre-Raphaelitism was a practical, utilitarian variety.

77.15 Farmer, Albert J. "Le Mouvement préraphaélite: Rossetti et Morris," *Le Mouvement esthétique et "décadent" en Angleterre (1873–1900)* (*Bibliothèque de la Revue de Littérature Comparée*, tome 75). Paris: Champion, 1931 (diss. Paris, 1931).

77.16 Thompson, Francis. "Pre-Raphaelite Morris," *Literary Criticisms*. Newly Discovered and Collected by the Rev. Terence L. Connolly, S.J. New York: Dutton, 1948.

Originally appeared in *Academy*, LXV, no. 1630 (1 August 1903), 111–113. Discusses *The Defence of Guenevere*. Occasioned by an article on the poem.

77.17 Wahl, John Robert. "Two Pre-Raphaelite Poets: Studies in the Poetry and Poetic Theory of William Morris and D. G. Rossetti," unpub. diss. Oxford University, 1954.

CHARLES READE

77.18 Burns, Wayne. "Pre-Raphaelitism in Charles Reade's Early Fiction," *Publications of the Modern Language Association*, LX (December 1945), 1149–1164.

A discussion of what Reade, who had pretensions as an art critic, has to say about art and artists in *Christie Johnstone* (1853). The article establishes a close relationship between Reade's theories of painting and those of his contemporaries and attempts to show that Reade's study of Pre-Raphaelite doctrine influenced the development of his "matter of fact" theory of fiction.

77.19 ——— "Charles Reade's *Christie Johnstone*: A Portrait of the Artist as a Young Pre-Raphaelite," in *From Jane Austen to Joseph Conrad: Essays Collected in Memory of James T. Hillhouse*, edited by Robert C. Rathburn and Martin Steinmann, Jr. Minneapolis: University of Minnesota Press, 1958.

"*Christie Johnstone* (1853) expresses Charles Reade's own quest for personal and artistic fulfillment. It is his *David Copperfield*, his *Sons and Lovers*, his *Portrait of the Artist as a Young Man*. And while it does not measure up to any of these novels, it is a

work of considerable artistic merit, and one that is crucial to an understanding of Reade's artistic development. For in his portrait of the artist as a Pre-Raphaelite son and lover can be discerned the fear of self-recognition that caused him, in his later writing, to seek refuge from imagination in fact and social purpose." (p. 208) See also Burns's *Charles Reade: A Study in Victorian Authorship* (New York: Bookman Associates, 1961), in which he discusses (pp. 93–103) the influence of Pre-Raphaelitism on Reade's fictional technique.

DANTE GABRIEL ROSSETTI

77.20 Swinburne, Louis Judson. *Rossetti and the Pre-Raphaelites*. New Haven, Connecticut, 1885.

A thorough analysis of the origins of Pre-Raphaelitism and of the artistic and poetic career of Rossetti. Reviews many of the contemporary works on Rossetti. One of the earliest and most detailed accounts of Pre-Raphaelitism published in America. Originally appeared in the *New Englander and Yale Review*, XLIV, n.s. VIII (July 1885), 502–522; (September 1885), 635–654.

77.21 Wood, Esther. *Dante Gabriel Rossetti and the Pre-Raphaelite Movement*. London: Sampson, Low, Marston, 1894.

For discussion see Survey, pp. 25–26.

77.22 Hume, James Cleland. "Rossetti, the Poet, and the Pre-Raphaelite Brothers," *Midland Monthly*, VII (January 1897), 42–52.

77.23 Cary, Elizabeth Luther. "Rossetti and the Pre-Raphaelites," *Critic*, XXXVII (October 1900), 320–326.

"From advance sheets of *The Rossettis*" (26.3).

77.24 Aronstein, P. "Dante Gabriel Rossetti und der Präraphaelismus," *Verhandlungen des 10. allgemeinen deutschen Neuphilologentages vom 20. bis 23. V. 1902 zu Breslau*. Hannover: Meyer, 1903.

77.25 Wiley, Edwin. "Dante Gabriel Rossetti and the Pre-Raphaelites," *The Old and the New Renaissance: A Group of Studies in*

Art and Letters. Nashville, Tennessee: Publishing House of the M. E. Church, South, Bigham and Sons, Agents, 1903.

77.26 Wyzewa, Teodor de. "Deux peintres préraphaélites," *Peintres de jadis et d'aujourd'hui.* Paris: Perrin, 1903.

On Rossetti and Edouard Steinle.

77.27 Waldschmidt, Wolfram. *Dante Gabriel Rossetti, der Maler und der Dichter: Die Anfänge der präraphaelitischen Bewegung in England.* Jena und Leipzig: Diederichs, 1905.

77.28 Mourey, Gabriel. *Dante Gabriel Rossetti et les Préraphaélites anglais (Les Grands Artistes).* Paris: Laurens, [1909].

Separate chapters on the origins and doctrines of the PRB, on five of the individual painters (Hunt, Rossetti, Millais, Madox Brown, Burne-Jones, and Watts), and on the influence of the Pre-Raphaelites.

77.29 Dick, Stewart. "Rossetti and the Pre-Raphaelites," *Master Painters, being Pages from the Romance of Art.* London: Foulis, 1911.

Largely biographical. See also by Stewart Dick, *Our Favorite Painters* (London: Foulis, 1923), which contains chapters on Brown, Millais, Hunt, Rossetti, and Burne-Jones.

77.30 Galletti, Alfredo. "Dante Gabriele Rossetti e il romanticismo preraffaellita," *Saggi e Studi.* Bologna: Zanichelli, 1915.

Reprinted in *Studi di letteratura inglese* (1918).

77.31 Venkatesan, N. K. *Dante Gabriel Rossetti: The Pre-Raphaelite Painter-Poet.* Madras: Srinivasa Varadachari, 1918.

Reprinted from *Educational Review* (Madras), XXIII (October 1917), 587–594; (November 1917), 687–694; (December 1917), 785–792; XXIV (January 1918), 1–5.

77.32 McQuilland, Louis J. "Dante Gabriel Rossetti and the Pre-Raphaelites," *Bookman's Journal,* XI (November 1924), 60–62.

77.33 Bateman, Arthur B. "Rossetti, the Pre-Raphaelites, and a Moral," *London Quarterly Review,* CXLIX, 5th ser. XXV (April 1928), 223–233.

Centenary study of Rossetti. The relationship between Rossetti and the Pre-Raphaelites proved an obstacle to the artistic development of both. The result for Rossetti was the stultification of his own genius, and because the Pre-Raphaelites refused to recognize the genius of Rossetti, in whom the imaginative quality was supreme, the movement failed too, and substituted a meaningless slogan — "'The Return to Nature" — for the genuine reformation of what they saw to be degenerate tendencies in art. In reality, "the Pre-Raphaelites never returned to nature in any sense that mattered to art. For nature had little place either in the emotional content of their painting or in the significance of its ideas." Rossetti, allowed to develop without Pre-Raphaelitism, might have become an English Daumier.

77.34 Rigillo, M. "Dante Gabriele Rossetti e il Preraffaellismo," *Rassegna Nazionale,* anno L. vol. III (July–August 1928), 3–7.

77.35 Gregory, John Bonar. "A Bibliographical and Reference Guide to the Life and Works of Dante Gabriel Rossetti with a Study of the Pre-Raphaelite Movement," unpub. diss., University of London, 1931.

Primarily bibliographical, but very much concerned with Rossetti's association with the Pre-Raphaelites. For additional annotation see 22.6.

77.36 Binyon, Laurence. "Rossetti and the Pre-Raphaelites," *English Water-Colours.* London: Black, 1933.

The emphasis is on Rossetti, with brief mention of Millais, Brown, and Simeon Solomon.

77.37 Sanford, John Albert. "Dante: Rossetti: Pre-Raphaelitism: A Study in the Early Poetry of Dante Gabriel Rossetti," unpub. diss., Cornell University, 1937.

Abstracted in *Cornell University Abstracts of Theses* (1937).

77.38 Minondo, Venancio. *Dante Gabriel Rossetti en el Prerrafaelismo.* Buenos Aires: Editorial Ideas, 1947.

77.39 Hough, Graham. "Rossetti and the P.R.B.," *The Last Romantics*. London: Duckworth, 1949.

For discussion see Survey, pp. 34–35.

JOHN RUSKIN

77.40 Parkes, Kineton. "Ruskin and Pre-Raphaelitism," *New Century Review*, VII (February 1900), 133–143.

"It is no exaggeration to say that without Mr. Ruskin there would not have been a Pre-Raphaelite Movement."

77.41 McCarthy, Justin. "Ruskin and the Pre-Raphaelites," *Portraits of the Sixties*. London: Unwin, 1903.

"The peculiar influence of the Pre-Raphaelites suffused all intellectual society throughout England in those days and spread itself over continental Europe and across the Atlantic." (pp. 197–198)

77.42 Shuster, George N. "Ruskin, Pater, and the Pre-Raphaelites," *The Catholic Spirit in Modern English Literature*. London: Macmillan, 1922.

77.43 Rosenblatt, Louise. "La Défense du beau: Ruskin et les Préraphaélites," *L'Idée de l'art pour l'art dans la littérature anglaise pendant la période victorienne* (*Bibliothèque de la Revue de Littérature Comparée*, tome 70). Paris: Champion, 1931 (diss. Paris, 1931).

77.44 Roudolphi, Marthe A. P. "Ruskin et le Préraphaélisme," unpub. diss. (Doctorat ès Lettres), University of Paris, 1947.

FREDERIC GEORGE STEPHENS

77.45 Manson, J. B., ed. *Frederick George Stephens and the Pre-Raphaelite Brothers, with Reproductions of Twenty-Four Pictures from His Collection, and Notes*. London: Privately published by Donald Macbeth, 1920.

For annotation see 39.2.

77.46 Taylor, Basil. "F. G. Stephens and the P.R.B.," *Architectural Review*, CIV (October 1948), 171–178.

For annotation see 39.3.

77.47 Grylls, R. Glynn [= (Lady) Rosalie Mander]. "The Correspondence of F. G. Stephens — II. The Pre-Raphaelite Brotherhood." *Times Literary Supplement*, no. 2876 (12 April 1957), p. 232.

For annotation see 39.4.

77.48 "One of the Pre-Raphaelites — When F. G. Stephens Taught Drawing at University College School," *Times*, no. 54,395 (26 February 1959), p. 12.

OTHER FIGURES RELATED TO THE PRE-RAPHAELITES

77.49 Forgues, E. D. "Un Peintre dans les highlands; journal et opinions d'un Pré-raphaélite," *Revue des Deux Mondes*, XLIV (April 1863), 960–989.

In part a review of P. G. Hamerton's *A Painter's Camp* and *Thoughts about Art* (78.1).

77.50 Leroi, Paul. "M. Chesneau et la confrérie préraphaélite," *L'Art*, LIX, 20e année, tome IV (1894), 918–923.

A review of Chesneau's writings on the Pre-Raphaelites (see 30.19, 36.36, 37.34, 41.12, 70.3, 70.5, 75.16, 76.3).

77.51 White, Gleeson. "The Work of Charles Ricketts," *Pageant*, I (1896), 79–93.

On Ricketts as a Pre-Raphaelite.

77.52 Dafforne, J[ames]. "The First of the Pre-Raphaelites: William Dyce, R.A.," in *Fifty Years of Art, 1849–1899: Being Articles and Illustrations Selected from "The Art Journal."* London: Virtue, 1900.

Reprinted from *Art Journal*, XXII (October 1860), 293–296, but the title is different in the original article. See also 87.15.

77.53 Cox, Kenyon. "Ford Madox Brown and Preraphaelitism," *Old Masters and New*. New York: Fox, Duffield, 1905.

This chapter and the two on Millais (37.67) and Burne-Jones (42.68) reprinted from the *Nation*.

77.54 Lavell, Cecil Fairfield. "Burne-Jones and the Pre-Raphaelites," *Chautauquan*, XLVI (March 1907), 69–78.

Burne-Jones interpreted the Pre-Raphaelite ideal as it was interpreted by Rossetti.

77.55 Hueffer, Ford Madox. "Christina Rossetti and Pre-Raphaelite Love," *Memories and Impressions: A Study in Atmospheres*. New York: Harper, 1911.

Published in England as *Ancient Lights and New Reflections, Being the Memoirs of a Young Man* (London: Chapman and Hall, 1911). A rollicking, inaccurate account of some of the figures and events of the Pre-Raphaelite Movement.

77.56 Stirling, A. M. W. "A Painter of Dreams: The Life of Roddam Spencer Stanhope, Pre-Raphaelite," *A Painter of Dreams and Other Biographical Studies*. London: John Lane, 1916.

77.57 Smith, Minnie Bernhard. "Bernhard Smith and His Connection with Art; of 'The Founders of the P.R.B.'" Typescript ("Proof one of seven") in the British Museum, 1917.

"The 7 were privately banded together to work faithfully avoiding trickery or short cuts in art. Others followed their ideals (Bateman, Collins, Deverell, Stephens, Burne-Jones, etc.). But there were 7 and no more of the original P.R.B.'s." An attempt to include Smith, who was an early associate of the Rossettis and of Woolner, among the number of the original Brotherhood. Smith himself, who went to Australia with Woolner and Bateman in 1851, always claimed membership in the PRB, and a number of his works are signed with the group's letters. This unpublished manuscript contains various letters, selections from Smith's diaries and journals, and reminiscences by his daughter.

William Michael Rossetti makes the following observations regarding Smith's association with the Pre-Raphaelites: "It has sometimes been said that Bernhard Smith was a member of the P.R.B., and indeed it is a fact that Dante Rossetti, in inscribing a book to him when he was once about to leave London, added these initials to his name. This however was one of the rather arbitrary acts in which my brother indulged himself now and again; for in truth Smith never was a P.R.B.; he was not elected, nor even put up for election; and it might be added that he

had not done anything fairly entitling him to rank as a colleague of Millais and Holman Hunt." (*Reminiscences*, 38.8, vol. I, 151) For a brief discussion of Bernhard Smith in Australia see the section "Sculptors and Pre-Raphaelites" (pp. 72–77) in the chapter "Art and Gold" in Bernard Smith, *Place, Taste, and Tradition. A Study of Australian Art Since 1878* (Sidney: Ure Smith, 1945). A short note on Bernhard Smith and the PRB, by William Michael Rossetti, also appeared in *Pall Mall Gazette* (10 September 1886, p. 6).

77.58 Ellis, S. M. "George Meredith: His Association with the Pre-Raphaelites," *Bookman* (London), LXXIII (February 1928), 253–257.

Occasioned by the Meredith centenary, this article treats the history of Meredith's friendship with the Pre-Raphaelites and his brief tenure as Rossetti's house companion at Cheyne Walk. The most obvious influence of the Pre-Raphaelites on Meredith is in the pictorial quality of his descriptions: ". . . the exquisite fidelity, the beauty akin to sadness, the warm gleams of romance caught from the realms of the imagination, that belong to the conception of the Pre-Raphaelites." (p. 251) For a brief note on Meredith's leaving Cheyne Walk see 25.38.

77.59 Justus, Wilhelm. *William Michael Rossetti im Kreise der Präraphaeliten*. Bochum-Langendreer: Pöppinghaus, 1934 (diss. Münster, 1934).

77.60 "Henry Justice Ford's 'Remembering Happier Things,'" *Russell Cotes Museum Bulletin*, XIV (December 1935), 50–52.

Ford is considered as a minor Pre-Raphaelite.

77.61 Moser, Max. "Die Spätpräraphaeliten und Wagner," *Richard Wagner in der englischen Literatur des XIX Jahrhunderts* (*Schweizer Anglistische Arbeiten*, VII). Bern: Francke, 1938.

Brief discussions of Ford Madox Brown, Rossetti, Morris, Swinburne, and John Payne.

77.62 Newton, Eric. "Watts and the Pre-

Raphaelites," *English Painting*. London: Longmans, 1945. Revised ed., 1949.

77.63 Goldring, Douglas. *The Last Pre-Raphaelite: The Life of Ford Madox Ford.* London: Macdonald, 1948.
Published in America as *Trained for Genius: The Life and Writings of Ford Madox Ford* (New York: Dutton, 1949).

77.64 Grigson, Geoffrey. " 'Gordale Scar' to the Pre-Raphaelites," *Listener*, XXXIX (1 January 1948), 24–25.
Discusses James Ward's picture at the Tate Gallery; also the relation of John Linnell and William Mulready to the PRB. The article contains a long description of Ward's picture, tracing the strain in English painting out of which the moral literalness of the Pre-Raphaelites developed.

77.65 Pevsner, Nikolaus. "Colonel Gillum and the Pre-Raphaelites," *Burlington Magazine*, XCV (March 1953), 78 + 81; illustrations, 76 + 79.
Interesting biographical sketch of Gillum and his association with the Hogarth Club, the firm of Morris and Company, and the Pre-Raphaelites in general.

77.66 Angeli, Helen Rossetti. *Pre-Raphaelite Twilight: The Story of Charles Augustus Howell.* London: Richards, 1954.
The only full-length account of Howell. Of special note are Howell's letters to William Michael and Dante Gabriel Rossetti and Ford Madox Brown. Howell is one of the most interesting and puzzling figures who moved in the Pre-Raphaelite circle.

77.67 Norman, Sylva. "Pre-Raphaelites in Pursuit," *Flight of the Skylark: The Development of Shelley's Reputation*. Norman, Oklahoma: University of Oklahoma Press, 1954.

Full discussion of the influence of Shelley on the Pre-Raphaelites.

77.68 Bennett, Mary. "William Windus and the Pre-Raphaelite Brotherhood in Liverpool," *Liverpool Bulletin*. (Libraries, Museums & Arts Committee. Walker Art Gallery Number.) VII (1958–1959), 19–31.
With a descriptive catalogue of Windus' works in the Walker Art Gallery, and a list of other collections known to possess works by Windus.

77.69 Doughty, Oswald. "A Minor Pre-Raphaelite: John Lucas Tupper," *English Miscellany: A Symposium of History, Literature and the Arts*. Vol. 11. Rome: Published for the British Council by Edizioni di storia e letteratura, 1960.
A biographical account emphasizing the almost hypnotic impact of Dante Gabriel Rossetti on Tupper and other minor Pre-Raphaelites (including Collinson, Madox Brown, and Woolner) who had "no real poetic talent" but who were driven "under his own poetic enthusiasm and the urgency of the moment, into temporary poetic production." (p. 209) Many of Tupper's poems are quoted in full or in part, most of them from William Michael Rossetti's edition of 1897, published "as an act of piety stimulated by the poet's widow." For Tupper's poems see 85.6.

77.70 Colomb, Simone. "Préraphaélitisme et réaction Whistlérienne," *L'Art Anglais* (*Arts, styles et techniques*, ed. Norbert Dufourcq). Paris: Libraire Larousse, 1947.

77.71 "A Fine Pre-Raphaelite Draughtsman," *Times*, no. 55,535 (30 October 1962), p. 16.
On Frederick Sandys.

Section 78

STUDIES COMPARING PRE-RAPHAELITISM WITH OTHER LITERARY AND ARTISTIC MOVEMENTS, OR STUDIES CONCERNED WITH PRE-RAPHAELITE INFLUENCES

78.1 Hamerton, Philip G. "The Reaction from Pre-Raphaelitism," *Thoughts about Art.* London: Macmillan, 1873. Revised edition, 1882.

Originally appeared in *Fine Arts Quarterly Review*, II (May 1864), 255–262. "The father and mother of modern Pre-Raphaelitism were modern literary thought and modern scientific investigation of the facts of nature." (p. 185)

78.2 Hamilton, Walter. "The Pre-Raphaellites," *The Æsthetic Movement in England.* London: Reeves and Turner, 1882.

Additional chapters on *The Germ* (73.4), Ruskin (45.6), the *Jonas Fisher* and *Fleshly* controversies, Wilde, and the "Poets of the Æsthetic School," among whom are included Rossetti (27.8), O'Shaughnessy (51.9), Woolner (40.9), Morris (43.31), Swinburne (62.18), and William Michael Rossetti (38.14). The third edition (1882) is considerably expanded and revised. For discussion see Survey, p. 16–17.

78.3 Merriman, Helen B. "The English Pre-Raphaelite and Poetical School of Painters," *Andover Review*, I (June 1884), 594–612.

A superficial discussion of the Pre-Raphaelites, the English idealists, who are contrasted with the Impressionists, the French realists.

78.4 "Influence of the Pre-Raphaelites on Art," *Journal of Decorative Art*, VII (December 1887), 179.

A review of a lecture given by E. Baldwin Brown, Watson-Gordon Professor of Fine Art at Edinburgh on Wednesday, 26 October 1887.

78.5 Frith, William P. "Crazes in Art: Pre-Raphaelitism and Impressionism," *Magazine of Art*, XI (1888), 187–191.

An attack on the movement which Frith sees as sincere but ridiculous. Its principles,

which should have been means to an end, became an end in themselves. Impressionism, Frith regards as even more dangerous than Pre-Raphaelitism.

78.6 La Sizeranne, Robert de. "Rose + Croix, Préraphaélites et esthètes — la reconnaissance esthétique des côtés de la manche," *Le Correspondant*, CLXVI (March 1892), 1127–1140.

Discusses the relationship between Pre-Raphaelitism and the French Ordre de la Rose-Croix.

78.7 Graf, A. "Preraffaelliti, simbolisti ed esteti," *Foscolo, Manzoni e Leopardi.* Torino: Loescher, 1898.

78.8 Ruettenauer, Benno. "Die Romantik und der Präraphaelismus," *Symbolische Kunst (Ueber Kunst der Neuzeit, no. 5).* Strassburg: Heitz, 1900.

78.9 Sturgis, Russell. "The Pre-Raphaelites and Their Influence," *Independent*, LII (18 January 1900), 181–183; (25 January 1900), 246–249.

78.10 Bancroft, Samuel, Jr. "Rossetti and the Pre-Raphaelite Brotherhood and Their Influence on Late English Art." Typescript of a speech delivered 6 February 1901, in the Wilmington Society of the Fine Arts.

An earlier version of the speech was read before the "Interchange Club," 9 April 1895. Baum's *Letters to Fanny Cornforth* (24.19) contains an excerpt from this manuscript in the Foreword.

78.11 Beers, Henry Augustin. "The Pre-Raphaelites," *A History of English Romanticism in the Nineteenth Century.* New York: Holt, 1901.

Treats the Pre-Raphaelites as Romantics,

by which Beers means, in general, medieval-ists.

78.12 Mauclair, Camille. "The Influence of the Pre-Raphaelites in France," *Artist*, XXXII (December 1901), 169–180.

Pre-Raphaelitism was a "reasoned protest against the abuse of realism and against the exclusion of intellectuality from painting." Its motive was first of all a "moral and intellectual protest." The influence of Pre-Raphaelitism, especially of Rossetti, was important on a group of French "intellectual painters" (as opposed to the "Realists," principally the Impressionists) led by Delacroix, who sought to "realize perfectly an idealized art" (Chassériau, Chenavard, Puvis de Chavannes, Gustave Moreau, and a host of minors). "Of all French artists Moreau had most in common with the Pre-Raphaelites . . ." Pre-Raphaelitism, which influenced French poetry as well as art, opened the way for a close union of French and English idealistic art. See also 78.25.

78.13 Zueblin, Rho Fisk. "The Pre-Raphaelites: the Beginnings of the Arts and Crafts Movement," *Chautauquan*, XXXVI (October 1902), 57–61.

The first in a series of articles on the Arts and Crafts Movement, running from October 1902 to June 1903. Other topics included a survey of the movement in England and its influence on English letters, two papers on the economics of the movement, and separate articles on the Continental tendencies, the production of industrial art in America, the education of the producer and consumer, and the patronage of the Arts and Crafts. The Arts and Crafts Movement has two sides — an art side and a social, economic awakening; the former derives from the Pre-Raphaelites, the latter from Ruskin. "The Romantic Movement, beginning in love of wonder and mystery, ended in trying realistically to make this comport with actual life and turned into the Gothic Revival. Such is the change of Pre-Raphaelitism into the Arts and Crafts Movement." (p. 60)

78.14 Sickert, Bernard. "The Pre-Raphaelite and Impressionist Heresies," *Burlington Magazine*, VII (May 1905), 97–102.

78.15 March-Phillipps, L. "Pre-Raphaelitism and the Present," *Contemporary Review*, LXXXIX (May 1906), 704–713.

Same in *Living Age*, CCXLIX, 7th ser., XXXI, no. 3233 (23 June 1906), 738–746. The author particularly praises Morris, who more than all the others found "the living power in art."

78.16 Ranftl, Johann. "Romantik und Prärafaelismus," *Historisch-politische Blätter für das katholische Deutschland*, CXXXVIII (1906), 449–468, 493–506.

According to the *Internationale Bibliographie der Kunst Wissenschaft* (VI–VII, 1907–1908, p. 121, item 2396), another article by Ranftl entitled "Präraffaelitische Skizzen" appeared in the *Kunst-historische Studien Jahrbuch für 1906* (published at Graz in 1907), but efforts to locate this publication have failed.

78.17 Cundall, H. M. "The Influence of Pre-Raphaelitism," *A History of British Water Colour Painting*. London: Murray, 1908. Revised edition, 1929.

Contains brief discussions of the major and minor Pre-Raphaelites.

78.18 Ashbee, Charles B. "Man and the Machine, the Pre-Raphaelites and Their Influence upon Life," *House Beautiful*, XXVII (February 1910), 75–77; (March 1910), 101–104, 112.

78.19 Marriott, Charles. "Impressionism and Pre-Raphaelitism," *Modern Movements in Art*. London: Chapman and Hall, 1920.

"The kind of truth to nature attempted by the Pre-Raphaelites might seem strange to the ordinary person, but only on account of the degree to which it was attempted. There was nothing in it that he could not understand. It was essentially non-optical. This is important, because it is common to hear people talk about the 'photographic Realism of the Pre-Raphaelites.' Nothing could have been less photographic in principle. It only resembled photography in presenting a lot of detail. The detail was presented in an entirely different way. The Realism of the Impressionists, on the other hand, *was* photographic in principle, though it evaded the photographic consequence by suppressing detail. Nothing done by hand can ever be quite the same as a thing done by machinery; because, in spite of the worst efforts of the doer, the hand will have its say in the matter; but, so far as principle is concerned, photography made Impressionism a blind-alley occupation, while it left Pre-Raphaelitism absolutely unchallenged. There was no extremity of detail to which the Pre-Raphaelite painter could not go without for a moment coming into competition with photography; but the Impressionist could only evade photography by insisting upon the selective capacity of the 'artistic eye.'" (p. 90)

78.20 Hearn, Lafcadio. "Two New Schools: Spasmodic and Pre-Raphaelite," *A History of English Literature, in a Series of Lectures.* Vol. II. Tokyo: Hokuseido Press, 1927.

Hearn concentrates on Rossetti and Swinburne. See also 69.12.

78.21 Mander, Sir Geoffrey. "Pre-Raphaelite Links," *Spectator*, CLXXIV, no. 6096 (27 April 1945), 381.

Discusses links with the Pre-Raphaelite past, both people and places.

78.22 Rothenstein, Elizabeth. "The Pre-Raphaelites and Ourselves," *Month*, n.s. I (March 1949), 180–198.

Written on the occasion of the Tate Gallery centenary exhibition (16.16), this article is in part a review discussion of 33.35, 66.26, and 83.8. This article contains an illuminating discussion of G. M. Hopkins as "the one man who did realize to the full the P.R.B. ideal."

78.23 Heath-Stubbs, John. "Pre-Raphaelitism and the Aesthetic Withdrawal," *The Darkling Plain: A Study of the Later Fortunes of Romanticism in English Poetry from George Darley to W. B. Yeats.* London: Eyre and Spottiswoode, 1950.

For discussion see Survey, pp. 35–36.

78.24 Garland, Madge. "Post Pre-Raphaelites," *The Changing Face of Beauty — Four Thousand Years of Beautiful Women.* New York: Barrows, 1957.

See also the brief sections, "Revolt and Counter-revolt," "Rossetti's Models," and "The Cult of Long Hair." Illustrated.

78.25 Lethève, Jacques. "La Connaissance des peintres préraphaélites anglais en France (1855–1900)," *Gazette des Beaux-Arts*, période 6, LIII (May–June 1959), 315–327.

The influence of Pre-Raphaelitism between the Universal Exhibition of 1855 and the development of *Art Nouveau*. After 1878, the influence of the Movement came principally through the works of Burne-Jones, and, less important in painting circles than among writers and people of fashion, it created a snobbish cult of Pre-Raphaelitism (Huysmans, Barrès, Bourget, Lorrain). The taste for the Pre-Raphaelites ceased with the last years of the century. The article contains a brief English summary. The notes are of particular importance for French writings on Pre-Raphaelitism in the nineteenth century. See also 78.12.

78.26 Sypher, Wylie. "Nazarenes, Lyonnais, and Pre-Raphaelites," *Rococo to Cubism in Art and Literature.* New York: Random House, 1960.

"Pre-Raphaelitism was always an art of the intellectuals, a rather stilted or even esoteric variant of an *avant-garde* painting and poetry. Because its roots were shallow, it never attained a coherent symbolism although most of the Pre-Raphaelite painters and poets had an air of consecration and were devoted to symbolic effects and suggestions, giving their work a halo of implied meaning even if it is hard to say what these meanings are. Their affectations have an almost ritualistic tone. Everything is *posed*; and their most photographic details seem unnatural. The air of prearrangement and contrivance — one indelible mark of mannerism — hangs over their work; and they are fond of "pure" line and "pure" color — though their line is usually harsh and metallic, and their color is often insipid and liquid, or else sour." (p. 198) For a detailed account of the so-called German Pre-Raphaelites see K. Andrews, *The Nazarenes: A Brotherhood of German Painters in Rome* (Oxford: Clarendon Press, 1964).

Section 79

STUDIES OF PARTICULAR PRE-RAPHAELITE
ACTIVITIES

The items in this section are grouped under three headings: those relating to the Oxford Union murals, those concerned with the illustrations of the Moxon *Tennyson*, and those pertaining to various other activities. Not all the items in the bibliography which involve Pre-Raphaelite endeavors are included in this section. Exhibitions and illustrations, for example, occupy large blocks of sections in other parts of the bibliography; two of the most important activities — the publication of *The Germ* and the formation of the Hogarth Club — are included in section 72; and, of course, the activities of the individual Pre-Raphaelites appear in the several sections of part II. The Pre-Raphaelites were engaged in so many enterprises, both personal and artistic, that their influence is apparent in many unsuspected areas, and it is the purpose of this section to indicate briefly something of the scope and impact of that engagement.

* * *

THE OXFORD UNION MURALS

79.1 [Patmore, Coventry]. "Walls and Wall Paintings at Oxford," *Saturday Review*, IV, no. 113 (26 December 1857), 583–584.

A laudatory notice of the murals. For one reply to Patmore's article see "Oxford and Wall Paintings," *Building News*, 1 January 1858, p. 2. See also "Minor Topics of the Month: Pre-Raffaelite Art in Oxford," *Art Journal*, XX (February 1858), 62.

79.2 *The Fresco Question: Remarks Addressed to the Members of the Oxford Union Society* [Oxford: Union Society, 1871].

79.3 Hunt, William Holman. *Oxford Union Society; The Story of the Painting of the Pictures on the Walls and the Decorations on the Ceiling of the Old Debating Hall (Now the Library) in the Years 1857-8-9.* Oxford University Press, 1906.

A collection of photographs of the faded murals done by the Pre-Raphaelites in 1857. With an Introduction by C. J. Holmes and a seven-page Preface by Holman Hunt. Twelve plates, including Morris' ceiling and Munro's sculpture.

79.4 Morrah, Herbert Arthur. "Art and the Union: Dante Gabriel Rossetti, William Morris, Edward Burne-Jones and the Pre-Raphaelite Movement; A Tragic Comedy

Still Repining for Development; The Arthurian Frescoes Described and Illustrated," *The Oxford Union, 1823–1923.* London: Cassell, 1923.

79.5 "Eighty Years After," *Architectural Review*, LXXIX (May 1936), 247–250.

Occasioned by the restoration of the Pre-Raphaelite murals by Professor E. W. Tristram.

79.6 Patmore, Derek. "Pre-Raphaelites Restored: the Wall Paintings in the Oxford Union Library," *Studio*, CXI (June 1936), 324–325.

With a reproduction of Rossetti's *Sir Lancelot's Vision of the San Grael*.

79.7 *The Pre-Raphaelite Mural Paintings: Old Library.* Oxford: Union Society, 1936.

In 1936, an attempt was made by Professor E. W. Tristram and others to clean and restore the faded and damaged murals. The project unfortunately met with no permanent success, though temporarily some of the paintings were restored to a state more nearly resembling their original brilliance. This pamphlet, with two reproductions showing the state of one of the paintings before and after restoration, was issued in conjunction with the ceremonies celebrating the restoration of the murals.

79.8 Rothenstein, William. "Pre-Raphaelite Paintings at the Oxford Union," *Men and Memories. Vol. III. Recollections 1922–1938.* London: Faber, 1939.

Giving details of the background of the restoration of the murals in 1936. Mention should be made of the other two volumes of Rothenstein's *Memories,* both of which contain frequent reference to the Pre-Raphaelites.

THE MOXON TENNYSON

79.9 Layard, George Somes. *Tennyson and His Pre-Raphaelite Illustrators: A Book about a Book.* London: Stock, 1894.

For complete annotation see 88.1.

79.10 Hardie, Martin. "The Moxon Tennyson: 1857," *Book Lover,* VII (1907), 45–51.

79.11 Smyser, William Emory. "Romanticism in Tennyson and His Pre-Raphaelite Illustrators," *North American Review,* CXCII (October 1910), 504–515.

For annotation see 88.6.

79.12 Friedman, Albert B. "The Tennyson of 1857," *More Books,* XXIII (January 1948), 15–22.

See also 88.13.

OTHER ACTIVITIES

79.13 Destrée, Olivier Georges. "Some Notes on the Stained Glass Windows and Decorative Paintings of the Church of St. Martin's-on-the-Hill, Scarborough," *Savoy,* no. 6 (October 1896), 76–90.

A description of the church as a "sort of decorative museum of pre-Raphaelite art."

79.14 Seddon, John P. *King René's Honeymoon Cabinet . . . Illustrated from Photographs of the Panels Painted by D. G. Rossetti, Sir Edward Burne-Jones, Ford Madox Brown, etc.* London: Batsford, 1898.

The cabinet, designed by Seddon to house his professional drawings and decorated with the paintings of various Pre-Raphaelites, illustrates Seddon's principal artistic theory: ". . . that in the unity and fellowship of the several arts lies their power." William Morris

and the Firm were commissioned to decorate the cabinet with ten panels illustrative of the fine arts (Rossetti did "Music" and "Gardening"; Burne-Jones, "Painting" and "Sculpture"; Ford Madox Brown, "Architecture"; Val Prinsep, "Embroidery"; "Pottery," "Weaving," "Metal Work," and "Glass Blowing" were done by other, unspecified, artists), all of which are reproduced in the volume, together with a photographic frontispiece of the cabinet. The final chapter, "The Hereditary Earls of Anjou," is by George H. Birch. The cabinet is now in the William Morris Room at the Victoria and Albert Museum. See also the brief article dealing with the cabinet (exhibited at the Grafton Gallery exhibition of Ford Madox Brown [8.4]) in *Magazine of Art,* XX (1897), 323–324.

79.15 ——— "The Works of the P.R.B. in Llandaff Cathedral," *The Public Library Journal: Quarterly Magazine of the Cardiff and Penarth Free Public Libraries, and the Welsh Museum,* IV (March 1903), 28–30; (June 1903), 49–51; (September 1903), 66–70.

79.16 Thomas, T. H. "The Pre-Raphaelite Pictures at the Turner House Gallery, Penarth," *The Public Library Journal,* IV (April 1904), 99–101.

79.17 Cary, Elizabeth Luther. "The Handicraft of the Pre-Raphaelites," *Book News Monthly,* XXIV (June 1906), 699–700.

79.18 Wroot, Herbert E. "Pre-Raphaelite Windows at Bradford," *Studio,* LXXII (November 1917), 69–73.

Commissioned by Walter Dunlop and executed by Morris and Company in 1862, the windows are from designs by Hughes (1), Rossetti (2), Prinsep (1), Burne-Jones (4), Madox Brown (4), and Morris (4).

79.19 Sparke, Archibald. "Pre-Raphaelite Stained Glass," *Notes & Queries,* 12th ser., IV (December 1918), 337.

Provides a list of Pre-Raphaelite stained glass, in response to a query in the August number (p. 217). Further additions were made by other writers: V (March 1919), 74; (April 1919), 105–106. Sparke also provided a similar, though less complete, answer to a query on Pre-Raphaelite tapestries in *N&Q*, 12th ser., IV (April 1918), 110.

79.20 Ironside, Robin. "Pre-Raphaelite Paintings at Wallington: A Note on William Bell Scott and Ruskin," *Architectural Review*, XCII (December 1942), 147–149.

A record of William Bell Scott's works at Wallington (see 56.6) and of Scott's acquaintance with Lady Trevelyan. The cycle of eight scenes from Northumbrian history (*Iron and Coal in 1861* is reproduced) is "one of the earliest works of art in which industry is taken seriously and recognized as the nineteenth century's contribution to civi-lization." (p. 149) Scott worked on the pictures between 1856 and 1861, and they were exhibited in June of 1861 at the French Gallery in Pall Mall (17.2). Among the other artists who contributed to the decorative art at Wallington were Hughes, Woolner, Ruskin, and Lady Trevelyan herself.

79.21 Bennett, Mary. "The Pre-Raphaelites and the Liverpool Prize," *Apollo*, LXXVI (December 1962), 748–753.

Profusely illustrated, this article discusses the championship of the Pre-Raphaelites by the Liverpool Academy of Arts, to which the Pre-Raphaelites were frequent contributors in the 1850's. See also 65.2 and 77.68.

Section 80

STUDIES OF PRE-RAPHAELITISM IN AMERICA

The subject of the so-called American Pre-Raphaelite Movement is discussed at length in the "Survey of Pre-Raphaelite Scholarship" (pp. 11–13). The number of items in this section is not extensive, but three of the items are of primary importance in any consideration of the Pre-Raphaelites. The two journals which are listed first are important as almost the earliest art periodicals in America, and they were both instrumental in promulgating Pre-Raphaelite ideals in North America. David Dickason's history of the American Pre-Raphaelites is certain to remain the major study in the field for years to come, but one may reasonably argue that he presses too hard his case for this American counterpart of the PRB in England. That there was tremendous enthusiasm in America for Pre-Raphaelite art is evinced by the magnitude of the collections formed during the nineteenth century — especially after the Exhibition of British Art in 1857 (see 18.4) — and still extant (see especially 3.1 and 3.3). Men such as William J. Stillman, Charles Eliot Norton, and Samuel Bancroft, Jr., were highly influential in bringing Pre-Raphaelite art to America, and in insuring that the Movement would not remain for Americans merely an ephemeral and insular manifestation of a few unknown English artists.

*   *   *

80.1 *The Crayon: A Journal Devoted to the Graphic Arts, and the Literature Related to Them*, edited by William J. Stillman and John Durand. New York: January 1855 to July 1861.

The Crayon started as a weekly but became a monthly after its first year. Stillman continued as editor until the conclusion of volume III, December 1856. The journal carried "J. Durand, Editor and Proprietor" on its masthead until it folded with volume VIII half completed in July 1861. *The Crayon* is of great significance both for the sympathetic interest in Pre-Raphaelitism exemplified by its editors and for its influence on the American movement.

80.2 *The New Path*. Published by the Society for the Advancement of Truth in Art. New York: May 1863 to December 1865.

The New Path continued intermittently for twenty-four issues. With volume II (1864), the magazine became independent financially of the original sponsors, but it retained the same editorial policy. After July 1864, no issues appeared until April 1865, and the journal ceased publication with the December 1865 number. Numbers 1 to 12, May 1863 to April 1864, contain frequent references to Pre-Raphaelitism and many articles which reflect Pre-Raphaelite tendencies, such as the article entitled "The Limits of Mediaeval Guidance," I, no. 12 (April 1864), 158–160. *The New Path* is not an easy journal to locate, and extensive quotations from it can be found in Dickason's history (80.8).

80.3 Lillie, L. C. W. "Two Phases of American Art," *Harper's Magazine*, LXXX (January 1890), 206–216.

Discusses (pp. 212–216) the influence of Pre-Raphaelitism on American art and the formation of the American Pre-Raphaelites.

80.4 Rummell, John, and E. M. Berlin. "The Pre-Raphaelite Influence upon American Painters," *Aims and Ideals of Representative American Painters*. Buffalo, New York: E. M. Berlin, 1901.

As the shortest single chapter on the Pre-Raphaelites in any book, this article deserves to be quoted *in toto*: "It is precisely this matter of artistic selection that most people fail to understand. No doubt the eloquent, but oftentimes erroneous, teaching of John Ruskin in regard to the study of Nature has misled both artists and laymen. It is certain that in France it was more generally under-

stood that it is the function of the artist to interpret Nature, not, as was a long time thought in England, to make a literal copy of her. During the middle of the nineteenth century many of our American painters were strongly influenced by the Pre-Raphaelite movement in England, and, like the Pre-Raphaelites, made the least possible use of the principle of selection, and painted Nature with literal fidelity to detail, overlooking the fact that the peculiar effect of Nature resides in the whole and not in the parts." (Chap. V, p. 27)

80.5 Cary, Edward. "Some American Pre-Raphaelites: a Reminiscence," *Scrip. Notes on Art*, II (October 1906), 1–7.

80.6 P., F. Q. "Pre-Raphaelitism in Modern Massachusetts," *American Magazine of Art*, XXIX (June 1936), 384–385.

Conference at Wheaton College under the general title of "Patron and Artist in the Pre-Renaissance and Modern Worlds."

80.7 Dickason, David H. "The American Pre-Raphaelites," *Art in America*, XXX (July 1942), 157–165.

80.8 —— *The Daring Young Men: The Story of the American Pre-Raphaelites*. Bloomington: Indiana University Press, 1953.

The only full account of the subject of the American Pre-Raphaelites. Mr. Dickason's book is the main source for most of the factual details in the discussion of the American Pre-Raphaelites in the Survey (pp. 11–13).

Section 81

FICTIONAL AND DRAMATIC INTERPRETATIONS OF THE PRE-RAPHAELITES

81.1 Beaumont, Averil [= Mrs. Margaret Hunt]. *Magdalen Wynyard or, The Provocations of a Pre-Raphaelite*. 2 vols. London: Chapman and Hall, 1872.

A novel. Of Bernard Langley, the nephew of Marmaduke Wynyard: "He cultivated literature, health, and art; contributed one or two successfully scornful epigrams to some of the most exciting debates at the Union, and

fancied he furthered the liberal cause thereby; but, in the main, he gave himself to the study of Ruskin, and the question of old style *versus* Pre-Raphaelitism." (I, 28) As an example of the application of the term Pre-Raphaelite as an impressionistic appellation see also Kate Field, "A Pre-Raphaelite at Saratoga," *Lippincott's Magazine*, II (September 1868), 256–259 — a tale.

81.2 Mallock, W. H. *The New Republic, or Culture, Faith and Philosophy in an English Country House.* 2 vols. London: Chatto and Windus, 1877.

A thinly-veiled *roman à clef* involving the leading intellectual leaders of the period in a satiric symposium. Arnold, Jowett, Tyndall, Huxley, Clifford, Pater, and Ruskin are the disguised characters. Ruskin appears as Mr. Herbert, Pater as Mr. Rose the Pre-Raphaelite.

81.3 Lee, Vernon [= Violet Paget]. *Miss Brown: A Novel.* 3 vols. London: Blackwoods, 1884.

A *roman à clef* on Rossetti and the Pre-Raphaelites.

81.4 Watts-Dunton, Theodore. *Aylwin: A Novel.* London: Hurst and Blackett, 1898.

For annotation see 64.1.

81.5 Ferguson, John, and N. C. Hunter. "The Merciless Lady: A Play in a Prologue and Four Acts." Uunpublished play, presented at the Birmingham Repertory Theater, Saturday, 6 October 1934.

The subject of this drama is Miss Siddal and the Pre-Raphaelites.

81.6 Morris, Thomas Baden. "We Dig for the Stars." Unpublished play, written in 1946, produced in 1952.

Based on the lives of Rossetti and his circle. The play, suppressed in 1946, was presented semiprivately at the Irving Theater Club in Leicester Square, 1 April 1952. Reviewed in *Times*, 2 April 1952. Noticed in *"The Stage" Yearbook* (London: Carson and Comerford, 1953), p. 133, where a complete list of the cast is given. See also R[oy] W[alker], "Pre-Raphaelitis," *Theater*, VI, no. 145 (12 April 1952), p. 19.

81.7 Shute, Nerina. *Victorian Love Story; a Study of the Victorian Romantics Based on the Life of Dante Gabriel Rossetti: A Novel.* London: Jarrolds, 1954.

81.8 Batchelor, Paula. *Angel with Bright Hair.* London: Methuen, 1957.

A novel based on the life of Elizabeth Siddal.

Section 82

CARICATURES, SATIRES, PARODIES, AND ATTACKS ON THE PRE-RAPHAELITES

Caricatures and satires of the Pre-Raphaelites, like the fictional and dramatic interpretations in section 81, reflect two extremes of reaction to the Movement. The satiric impulse may be the result of good-natured indulgence and sympathy, as in the case of Max Beerbohm's *Rossetti and His Circle*, or it may indicate a vindictive desire to castigate the opposition. Certainly, Buchanan's scurrilous attack was motivated by animus, and the *Fleshly School* pamphlet is humorous only because of its excesses. Almost all satires and caricatures tend to be topical, but they do frequently represent a more serious criticism than the form itself suggests. Beerbohm's drawings are incisive, depicting the most vulnerable aspects of Pre-Raphaelitism, yet simultaneously catching the spirit and camaraderie of the Movement as no other work before or since has done. The following items are divided into two groups — visual caricatures and literary satires, parodies, and attacks, Waring's *Poems by Tennyson Longfellow Smith*, Du Maurier's *Legend of Camelot*, and Beerbohm's *Rossetti and His Circle* combining the two. For a detailed account of the Pre-Raphaelites in caricature see W. E. Fredeman's article in the *Burlington Magazine* (76.14).

*   *   *

VISUAL CARICATURES

82.1 Earl, [?]. *Nature and Art, Dedicated without Permission to the Pre-Raphaelites.* [London], 1851.

An engraving of a china dog being sniffed at by a real dog, with Millais' picture in the background. For a discussion of this engraving see 72.7 (p. 293).

82.2 Sandys, Frederick. *The Nightmare.* London, 1857.

Sandys' caricature of Millais' *Sir Isumbras at the Ford* depicts three figures — Rossetti, Millais (in armor), and Holman Hunt — astride a braying jackass branded "J. R. Oxon." From the saddle hangs a bucket of paint, stamped on the outside "P.R.B." On the opposite bank of the stream sit Titian, Raphael, and Michaelangelo, begging to be carried across with the Pre-Raphaelites.

82.3 Claxton, Florence. *The Choice of Paris: An Idyll.* 1860.

A caricature in oil. Exhibited at the Portland Gallery in 1860. One version of the picture is now in the collection of Mr. Ralph Dutton, and has recently been exhibited, for the first time since 1860 (see 18.23). An engraving after the picture appeared with an explanatory note in the *Illustrated London News*, XXXVI (2 June 1860), 541–542. See Plate VIII for version in the collection of Ralph Dutton. See also 76.14.

82.4 Solomon, Simeon. *A Pre-Raphaelite Studio Fantasy.*

Nothing is known about this picture which was exhibited at the Whitechapel Spring Exhibition, 1905. The present location is unknown.

LITERARY SATIRES, PARODIES, AND ATTACKS

82.5 [Waring, John Burley]. *Poems Inspired by Certain Pictures at the Art Treasures Exhibition, Manchester, by Tennyson Longfellow Smith, of Cripplegate Within, Edited by his Friend, the Author of "Thorns & Thistles." Illustrated by the Hon. Botibol Bareacres; and Dedicated, with Profound Admiration and Awe, to that Greatest of Modern Poets, Philosophers, Artists, Art-Critics, and Authors, the Immortal Buskin.* Manchester: Sold at the Bookstall of the Exhibition, 1857.

Poems and drawings parodying Hunt's *The Awakened Conscience, The Hireling Shepherd, The Two Gentlemen of Verona,* and *Claudio and Isabella*; Collins' *Convent Thoughts*; and Millais' *Autumn Leaves.* With a final "Pre-Raffaelleite Chorus" (accompanied by a drawing showing the Pre-Raphaelites charging into battle on the dusty plains of art) set to the air of "The One-Horse Chaise." Two of the drawings were reproduced as insets in 76.14. For the Manchester exhibition see 18.3. See Plate I.

82.6 Buchanan, Robert. *The Fleshly School of Poetry and Other Phenomena of the Day.* London: Strahan, 1872.

Expanded from Buchanan's pseudonymous attack on Rossetti in the *Contemporary Review* (29.16). The pamphlet is reprinted in part in Robert L. Peters, *Victorians on Literature and Art* (New York: Appleton-Century-Crofts, 1961). For full discussion of the *Fleshly* controversy see Cassidy (76.11) and the Survey, pp. 17–19.

82.7 [Carnegie, James, Earl of Southesk]. *Jonas Fisher: A Poem in Brown and White.* London: Trübner, 1875.

For a brief discussion of the *Jonas Fisher* controversy see Survey, p. 19, n.29. See also by Carnegie, *Britain's Art Paradise: or, Notes on Some Pictures in the Royal Academy: MDCCCLXXI* (Edinburgh: Edmonston and Douglas, 1871), which contains (*passim*) amusing strictures on the painting of Millais.

82.8 Du Maurier, George. *A Legend of Camelot, Pictures and Poems, &c.* London: Bradbury, Agnew, 1898.

Originally appeared in *Punch*, L (March 1866), 94, 97, 109, 128, 131. A series of caricatures on the Pre-Raphaelite "type," with a "metrical romance" parodying Morris and Pre-Raphaelite medieval themes. The five wood engravings are reproduced in Gleeson White's *English Illustration* (88.3).

82.9 Beerbohm, Max. *Rossetti and His Circle.* London: Heinemann, 1922.

Twenty-three caricatures of the Pre-Raphaelites, the original drawings for which are in the Tate Gallery. With text accompanying each drawing, and an Introduction by the author.

82.10 Jones, L. E. "Sir John Millais While Painting 'Ophelia,'" *À la Carte.* London: Secker and Warburg, 1951.

An extremely amusing imaginary page from Millais' diary.

Section 83

COLLECTIONS OF REPRODUCTIONS OF PRE-RAPHAELITE ART

83.1 "British Pre-Raphaelite Painters. A Scrapbook of Reproductions." In the New York Public Library, n.d.

83.2 Rossetti, William Michael, ed. *Permanent Photographs after the Works of the Pre-Raphaelite School: With an Explanatory Note.* London: Mansell, 1900.

A catalogue including Rossetti, Burne-Jones, Watts, Albert Moore, Millais, Hunt, and Solomon.

83.3 *The Pre-Raphaelite Brotherhood* (Newnes's Art Library). London: Newnes, [1905].

With a long Introduction on the Brotherhood by J. E. Phythian and reproductions of 56 Pre-Raphaelite pictures by various artists.

83.4 *A Few Masterpieces of the Pre-Raphaelite Sshool.* New York: Berlin Photographic Company, [1905].

83.5 *Twelve English Pre-Raphaelite Drawings: Reprinted from the Originals in the City of Birmingham Museum and Art Gallery.* With a Foreword by Whitworth Wallis. London: Methuen, 1925.

83.6 *A Picture Book of the Pre-Raphaelites and Their School* (Victoria and Albert Museum, Picture Book no. 16). London: H. M. Stationery Office, 1926.

Pictures and other art objects from the Victoria and Albert collection (see 2.10). Twenty reproductions.

83.7 *The Pre-Raphaelite Brotherhood* (Picture Book no. 1). Birmingham: City Museum and Art Gallery, 1948.

Twelve reproductions. See 2.1 for description of Birmingham collection.

83.8 Ironside, Robin, ed. *Pre-Raphaelite Painters.* With a Descriptive Catalogue by John Gere. London: Phaidon, 1948.

In general the best book of illustrations available, though the quality of the registration is very poor. John Gere's catalogue is excellent and authoritative. For reviews see Derek Hudson (68.21) and Sir John Squire, *Illustrated London News,* CCXIII (30 October 1948), 482; also, A. D. B. Sylvester, "The Light that Failed," *New Statesman and Nation,* XXXVI (27 November 1948), 469.

83.9 *A Picture Book of Pre-Raphaelite Paintings in the Manchester City Art Galleries.* Manchester: Art Galleries Committee of the Corporation, 1952.

Twenty pictures reproduced. See 2.6 for description of Manchester's Pre-Raphaelite collection.

Other Works Relating to Pre-Raphaelitism

Other Works Relating to Pre-Raphaelitism

Section 84

ANTHOLOGIES WITH REPRESENTATIVE
SELECTIONS BY PRE-RAPHAELITE POETS

No attempt has been made to include in this section all the numerous collections in which the Pre-Raphaelite poets — usually only the two Rossettis, Morris, and Swinburne — have been anthologized. The common older and modern anthologies of Victorian poetry are restricted to major poets and to fairly standardized selections. The anthologies listed are either out of the ordinary or, as in the cases of Miles and Ward, nineteenth-century collections of major importance. *The Poets and the Poetry of the Century* is indispensable as literally the only available collection of the minor poets, whose works, originally published in small editions and now almost unprocurable, with the single exception of O'Shaughnessy (see 51.6), have never been reprinted.

* * *

84.1 Craig, Isa, ed. *Poems: An Offering to Lancashire. Printed and Published for the Art Exhibition for the Relief of distress in the Cotton Districts.* London: Emily Faithfull, 1863.

Contains Rossetti's "Sudden Light" and other contributions by Christina Rossetti, George MacDonald, Allingham, Monckton Milnes, Frederick Locker, Isa Craig, and others. "The Art Exhibition for the Sale of Paintings, Drawings, and Other Works of Art for the Relief of the Distress in the Cotton Districts" was held at the Gallery of the Society of British Artists, Suffolk Street. To this exhibition, which commenced on 14 January 1863, Millais and Ruskin contributed works.

84.2 *A Welcome: Original Contributions in Poetry and Prose.* London: Emily Faithfull, 1863.

Contains Christina Rossetti's "Dream Love," Dante Gabriel Rossetti's "Lost Days," William Allingham's "His Town," and other selections in prose and verse by Sydney Dobell, George MacDonald, Charles Kingsley, Anthony Trollope, and others.

84.3 Ward, Thomas Humphrey, ed. *The English Poets: Selections with Critical In-troductions by Various Writers.* 5 vols. London: Macmillan, 1880.

The following pertinent introductions should be noted: Dante Gabriel Rossetti by Walter Pater (27.7); William Morris by J. W. Mackail (43.30); Christina Rossetti by Percy Lubbock (44.21); Thomas Gordon Hake by T. H. Ward (48.14); Philip Bourke Marston by John Drinkwater (50.9); Arthur O'Shaughnessy by Edmund Gosse (51.8); and Algernon Swinburne by Edmund Gosse (62.17). See also the article on R. W. Dixon by H. C. Beeching (vol. 5, 267–270).

84.4 Caine, T. Hall, ed. *Sonnets of Three Centuries: A Selection, Including Many Examples Hitherto Unpublished.* London: Stock, 1882.

Selections from Oliver Madox Brown, R. W. Dixon, Marston, O'Shaughnessy, Paton, Patmore, Christina, Dante Gabriel, and William Michael Rossetti, William Bell Scott, and Swinburne. With a sixteen-page Preface by Caine.

84.5 Miles, Alfred H., ed. *The Poets and the Poetry of the Century.* 10 vols. London: Hutchinson, [1891–1897].

Reissued in eleven volumes (London: Routledge, 1905–1907). Despite obvious dating of the critical introductions, Miles remains one of the most valuable anthologies of nineteenth-century poetry. Besides those sections separately listed (D. G. Rossetti [27.20], Thomas Woolner [40.11], Morris [43.34], Christina Rossetti [44.23], Allingham [46.26], Oliver Madox Brown [47.6], Hake [48.16], Marston [50.10], O'Shaughnessy [51.10], Patmore [52.4], Noel Paton [53.4], John Payne [54.10], William Bell Scott [56.17], Swinburne [62.20], and Watts-Dunton [64.4]), the following essays should be noted: R. W. Dixon by A. H. Miles (V, 555–557); Sebastian Evans by Joseph Knight (V, 453–457); and G. A. Simcox by A. H. Miles (VIII, 29–30).

84.6 Parkes, Kineton, ed. *The Painter-Poets* (The Canterbury Poets, edited by William Sharp). London: Walter Scott, n.d.

With an Introduction, and selections from the poetry of Ford Madox Brown, Oliver Madox Brown, James Collinson, Walter Crane, Walter H. Deverell, Arthur Hughes, William Morris, Noel Paton, John Orchard, Dante Gabriel Rossetti, John Ruskin, William Bell Scott, and Thomas Woolner.

84.7 Stedman, Edmund Clarence, ed. *A Victorian Anthology, 1837–1895: Selections Illustrating the Editor's Critical Review of British Poetry in the Reign of Victoria.* New York: Houghton, Mifflin, 1895.

Designed as a supplementary volume to Stedman's *The Victorian Poets* (69.1). Pre-Raphaelite poets included in the anthology are Allingham, Ford Madox Brown, Oliver Madox Brown, Canon Dixon, Hake, Marston, Morris, O'Shaughnessy, Paton, Payne, Christina Rossetti, D. G. Rossetti, William Bell Scott, Swinburne, Watts-[Dunton], and Woolner. With brief biographical notes by the editor.

84.8 Palgrave, Francis Turner, ed. *The Golden Treasury. Selected from the Best Songs and Lyrical Poems in the English Language and Arranged with Notes. Second Series.* London: Macmillan, 1897.

Since in his first selection (1861) the editor surveyed English poetry to 1850, the Pre-Raphaelites did not figure. Included in the second series are twelve poems by D. G. Rossetti, fifteen by Christina Rossetti, and seventeen by Arthur O'Shaughnessy.

Section 85

MINOR VERSE OF PRE-RAPHAELITE INTEREST

85.1 MacLennan, John Ferguson. *Poems on Præraphaelite Principles.* London, c. 1860.

Referred to by Ghose (1.2, p. 81), who probably picked up the title from William Michael Rossetti's *Some Reminiscences* (38.8, vol. I, 170) where the title is given as *Poems on the Præraphaelite Principle.* Efforts to locate this volume have proved unavailing; if it does exist, it must have been privately printed.

85.2 Dixon, Richard Watson. *Christ's Company and Other Poems.* London: Smith, Elder, 1861.

85.3 ———— *Historical Odes and Other Poems.* London: Smith, Elder, 1864.

85.4 Evans, Sebastian. *Brother Fabian's Manuscript: and Other Poems.* London: Macmillan, 1865.

85.5 Simcox, G. A. *Poems and Romances.* London: Strahan, 1869.

85.6 Rossetti, William Michael, ed. *Poems by the Late John Lucas Tupper.* London: Longmans, 1897.

For a detailed examination of Tupper's Pre-Raphaelite poetry see Doughty (77.69).

Section 86
VARIOUS CRITICAL STUDIES, MEMOIRS, BIOGRAPHIES, COLLECTIONS OF LETTERS, AND DIARIES CONTAINING PRE-RAPHAELITE MATERIALS

The volumes listed in this section are highly selective owing to the wide associations of the Pre-Raphaelites. Many pertinent memoirs, diaries, and the like, because they contain specific chapters or parts relating either to individual figures or to various Pre-Raphaelite activities, are classified in the appropriate sections of the bibliography. The volumes included here are of a more general nature.

*   *   *

86.1 Gilchrist, Herbert H., ed. *Anne Gilchrist: Her Life and Writings*. With a Prefatory Notice by William M. Rossetti. London: Unwin, 1887.

With seven letters from Dante Gabriel Rossetti to Alexander Gilchrist, written in 1861, and six to Mrs. Gilchrist relating to the editing of the *Life of Blake . . . with Selections from His Poems and Writings* (London: Macmillan, 1863; 2nd edition revised and enlarged, 1880), for which both William Michael and Dante Gabriel Rossetti provided extensive editorial assistance. The volume also contains reminiscences of many of the other Pre-Raphaelites, including Ford Madox Brown, together with numerous letters from W. M. Rossetti to Mrs. Gilchrist. For information concerning Blake's notebook, which sold at the Rossetti Sale in 1882 (see 19.2), see Geoffrey Keynes (ed.). *The Note-Book of William Blake, Called the Rossetti Manuscript* (London: Nonesuch, 1935); and Chapter Two of *A Bibliographical Study of William Blake's Notebook* (Tokyo: Hokuseido Press, 1953), by Bunsho Jugaku. Rossetti's contributions to Gilchrist's *Life of Blake* are reprinted in the 1911 edition of his *Works* (23.27).

86.2 Palgrave, G. Francis. *Francis Turner Palgrave: His Journals and Memories of His Life*. London: Longmans, 1898.

Contains letters to and from W. M. Rossetti and many references to Dante Rossetti and other contemporaries of the Pre-Raphaelites.

86.3 Jay, Harriett. *Robert Buchanan: Some Account of His Life, His Life's Work, and His Literary Friendships*. London: Unwin, 1903.

The only full-length biography. A sympathetic account of Buchanan's life and literary career. See especially the chapter entitled "The Fleshly School of Poetry, 1870."

86.4 Davies, J. L. *The Working Men's College, 1854–1904: Records of its History and its Work for Fifty Years, by Members of the College*. London: Macmillan, 1904.

Chapter 5, "Art Teaching in the College in its Early Days," contains memories of Ruskin, Rossetti, and others.

86.5 Barrington, Mrs. Russell. *The Life, Letters and Work of Frederic Leighton*. 2 vols. London: Allen, 1906.

86.6 Crane, Walter. *An Artist's Reminiscences*. London: Methuen, 1907.

Contains valuable material on Morris, the Arts and Crafts Movement, early socialism, and many of the minor Pre-Raphaelites.

86.7 Pennell, Elizabeth Robins and Joseph. *The Life of James McNeill Whistler*. 2 vols. Philadelphia: Lippincott, 1908.

86.8 Francis, John Collins. *Notes by the Way: With Memoirs of Joseph Knight . . . and the Rev. Joseph Woodfall Ebsworth . . .* London: Unwin, 1909.

References *inter alia* to Rossetti, P. B.

Marston, F. G. Stephens, and others of the Pre-Raphaelite group. A letter from Rossetti to Knight appears on p. xxv.

86.9 Browning, Oscar. *Memories of Sixty Years at Eaton, Cambridge, and Elsewhere.* London: John Lane, 1910.

86.10 Whiting, Lilian. *Louise Chandler Moulton: Poet and Friend.* Boston: Little, Brown, 1910.
Louise Moulton was a friend and biographer of both Philip Bourke Marston and Arthur O'Shaughnessy (see 50.7 and 51.11).

86.11 Norton, Sara, and M. A. DeWolfe Howe, eds. *Letters of Charles Eliot Norton with Biographical Comment.* 2 vols. New York: Houghton, Mifflin, 1913.
Norton corresponded with many of the Pre-Raphaelites, especially Rossetti and Ruskin, and these two volumes contain numerous references to Pre-Raphaelitism.

86.12 Francillon, R. E. "The 'Decemviri' — Algernon Charles Swinburne — James MacNeill Whistler — Joseph Knight — The Marston Circle — Dante Gabriel Rossetti — William Morris . . . Philip Bourke Marston — Oliver Madox Brown . . . Arthur O'Shaughnessy . . . ," *Mid-Victorian Memories.* London: Hodder and Stoughton, [1914].

86.13 Holiday, Henry. *Reminiscences of My Life.* London: Heinemann, 1914.
Notes on Simeon Solomon and most of the other Pre-Raphaelites.

86.14 Williamson, G. C. *Murray Marks and His Friends: A Tribute of Regard.* London: John Lane, 1919.
Separate chapters on Rossetti (30.58), Burne-Jones (42.92), Sandys (55.9), Simeon Solomon (61.12), and Charles Augustus Howell.

86.15 Stirling, A. M. W. *William De Morgan and His Wife.* London: Butterworth, 1922.

86.16 Forbes-Robertson, Johnston. *A Player Under Three Reigns.* London: Unwin, 1925.
The chapter entitled "The Theater Royal Back Drawing-Room" contains reminiscences of Brown, Sandys, Alma-Tadema, Rossetti, and Swinburne.

86.17 Ionides, Luke. *Memories.* Paris: Privately printed by Herbert Clarke, 1925.

86.18 Carr, Mrs. J. Comyns. *Reminiscences.* London: Hutchinson, [1926].
Contains interesting material on many of the figures closely associated with the Pre-Raphaelites, by the wife of the nineteenth-century art critic, editor, and playwright.

86.19 Stirling, A. M. W. *The Richmond Papers, from the Correspondence and Manuscripts of George Richmond, R.A., and His Son Sir William Richmond, R.A., K.C.B.* London: Heinemann, 1926.
Many references to the Pre-Raphaelites, particularly to Morris and Burne-Jones.

86.20 Abbott, Claude Colleer, ed. *The Correspondence of Gerard Manley Hopkins and Richard Watson Dixon.* London: Oxford University Press, 1935.
This volume and its companion, *The Letters of Gerard Manley Hopkins to Robert Bridges* (London: Oxford University Press, 1935), contain frequent and important references to Rossetti and the Pre-Raphaelites.

86.21 Lethaby, W. R. *Philip Webb and His Work.* London: Oxford University Press, 1935.
Contains a chapter on "The Morris Firm."

86.22 Child, Ruth C. *The Aesthetic of Walter Pater.* New York: Macmillan, 1940.
Interesting for the comparison between Pater's aesthetic and that of the Pre-Raphaelites, especially Rossetti.

86.23 Burton, Hester. *Barbara Bodichon, 1827–1891.* London: Murray, 1949.
Chapter IX, "Friends," contains information concerning Barbara Bodichon's friendship with Rossetti, together with three previously unpublished letters written to her during his stay at Scalands in 1870. Reference is also made to fifteen additional letters from Rossetti, written between 1870 and 1876. Barbara Bodichon was a close associate of many of the Pre-Raphaelites, including

Rossetti, Holman Hunt, and William Alling-ham.

86.24 Ross, Margery, ed. *Robert Ross. Friend of Friends. Letters to Robert Ross, Art Critic and Writer, Together with Extracts from his Published Articles.* London: Cape, 1952.
Contains interesting material on Simeon Solomon and other Pre-Raphaelites.

86.25 Preston, Kerrison, ed. *Letters from Graham Robertson.* London: Hamish Hamilton, 1953.
Contains numerous references to the Pre-Raphaelites, especially Rossetti.

86.26 Abbott, Claude Colleer, and Anthony Bertram, eds. *Poet and Painter, Being the Correspondence between Gordon Bottomley and Paul Nash, 1910–1946.* London: Oxford University Press, 1955.

Numerous references to Rossetti and the Pre-Raphaelites.

86.27 Sambrook, James. *A Poet Hidden: The Life of Richard Watson Dixon, 1833–1900.* London: Athlone Press, 1962.

86.28 Linton, W. J. *Memories.* London: Lawrence, 1885.
Chapters IX, XXI, and XXII contain material on William Bell Scott, Rossetti, Swinburne, Millais, and others.

86.29 Blunt, Wilfred. *Cockerell: The Life of Sydney Carlyle Cockerell, Friend of Ruskin and Morris, and Director of the Fitzwilliam Museum.* London: Hamish Hamilton, 1964.
A biography by Cockerell's literary executor, drawing on Cockerell's extensive diary and on many thousands of letters.

Section 87

ARTICLES AND SEPARATE PUBLICATIONS
TREATING FIGURES ON THE FRINGE OF
THE PRE-RAPHAELITE MOVEMENT

87.1 " 'The Death of Chatterton,' " *Athenaeum,* no. 1652 (25 June 1859), pp. 841–842.
An account of the trial involving copyright in connection with the engraving of Henry Wallis' picture in the *National Magazine.* The judgment is reported in the *Athenaeum,* no. 1684 (4 February 1860), p. 177.

87.2 Scott, William Bell. "Alexander Munro," *The British School of Sculpture. Illustrated by Twenty Engravings from the Finest Works of Deceased Masters of the Art, and Fifty Woodcuts. With a Preliminary Essay and Notices of the Artists.* London: Routledge, 1872.

87.3 Clayton, Ellen C. *English Female Artists.* 2 vols. London: Tinsley, 1876.
Volume II contains brief but informative sections on Alice Boyd (pp. 37–41), Rebecca Solomon (pp. 129–130), Marie Spartali (pp. 135–137), and Lucy Rossetti (pp. 116–124).

87.4 Meynell, Wilfred. "Val Prinsep, A.R.A.: Painter and Dramatist," *Magazine of Art,* VI (1883), 405–409.

87.5 Shaw, George Bernard. "J. M. Strudwick," *Art Journal,* LIII (April 1891), 97–103.
Illustrated. Strudwick was a studio assistant of Burne-Jones, whose style his most resembles.

87.6 Hardinge, William M. "A Reminiscence of Mrs. W. M. Rossetti," *Magazine of Art,* XVIII (1895), 341–346.
Includes four reproductions of paintings by Lucy Madox Rossetti: *The Duet, Après le Bal, Romeo at the Tomb of Juliet,* and *Lord Surrey and the Fair Geraldine.*

87.7 Steelcraft, Framley. "Illustrated Interviews. No. LI — Mr. Val C. Prinsep. R.A.,"

Strand Magazine, XII (December 1896), 603–615.

87.8 Day, Lewis Forman. "A Disciple of William Morris," *Art Journal*, LXVII (March 1905), 84–89.
On Henry Dearle, who made many of the designs for Merton Abbey tapestries.

87.9 Chester, Austin. "The Art of Philip H. Calderon," *Windsor Magazine*, XXXVII (February 1913), 338–348.

87.10 —— "The Art of Val C. Prinsep," *Windsor Magazine*, XXXIX (April 1914), 613–628.

87.11 Benson, A. C. "Charles Fairfax Murray," *Memories and Friends*. London: Murray, 1924.
Contains valuable information on the background to Benson's "English Men of Letters" biography of Rossetti, much of the material for which he had from Murray. See also "Charles Fairfax Murray: Drawings," *Connoisseur*, CL (July 1962), 158–162, a brief article on Murray, with reproductions of four of his drawings exhibited in the second Maas Gallery exhibition of "Pre-Raphaelites and Their Contemporaries" (16.26).

87.12 Rothenstein, John. "Walter John Knewstub," *Artwork*, VI (Summer 1930), 87.
Rossetti's studio assistant before H. T. Dunn.

87.13 Ellis, S. M. "Charles Allston Collins," *Wilkie Collins, Le Fanu and Others*. London: Constable, 1931.

87.14 Pedrick, Gale. "Dante Gabriel Rossetti's Guardian Angel," *Listener*, LXIV (27 October 1960), 738–739, 743.
On Henry Treffry Dunn.

87.15 Staley, Allen. "William Dyce and Outdoor Naturalism," *Burlington Magazine*, CV (November 1963), 470–476.
A general study of the works of Dyce (the first of any significance since 77.52) and an examination of his affinity with the Pre-Raphaelites. With reproductions of six of Dyce's paintings.

87.16 Handley-Read, C. "Notes on William Burges's Painted Furniture," *Burlington Magazine*, CV (November 1963), 496–509.
An elaborately illustrated article which traces the development of painted Victorian Gothic furniture. While the emphasis is on Burges, there are numerous references to, and comparisons with, the painted Pre-Raphaelite furniture of the same period.

87.17 Gere, John. "Alexander Munro's 'Paolo and Francesca,'" *Burlington Magazine*, CV (November 1963), 509–510.
With two reproductions of Munro's marble group (in the City Museum and Art Gallery, Birmingham) and four studies for the group. Munro's design is very close to Rossetti's water color of 1855.

IV. BIBLIOGRAPHY OF PRE-RAPHAELITE ILLUSTRATIONS

Among the many contributions of the Pre-Raphaelites to the mainstream of nine-teenth-century English art is their work in the revival of wood-engraved illustrations for the journals and books of the period. Not since Blake had the illustration of books in England laid serious claim to artistic consideration, although on the Continent Doré and Menzel had added new dimensions to the art of wood engraving.

The beginning of the revival of interest in book illustration in England is generally associated with the appearance of three magazines in 1859 and 1860: *Once a Week*, *Good Words*, and *The Cornhill Magazine*. There were, however, many antecedents of this revival, in three of the most important of which the Pre-Raphaelites took an active part. A concern with illustration may in fact be considered an integral part of the Pre-Raphaelite innovation. Looking backward to Blake, and pointing forward to the experiments in the production of beautiful books made by Morris and Burne-Jones at the Kelmscott Press, the Pre-Raphaelites made their first crude overtures in book illustration in *The Germ*, though the illustrations there were etchings rather than wood engravings. At this stage of the Movement, the illustration of books was only an experiment, but the etchings in *The Germ* underscore the early interest of the group in the practical arts, a phase of their aesthetic that was not to be fully manifested until the advent of the Oxford "Brotherhood" and the foundation of Morris and Company. Five years elapsed before the first conjoint effort was made — by Millais, Hughes, and Ros-setti — to illustrate a single volume, Allingham's *The Music Master* (1855); but it was the Moxon *Tennyson* (1857), in which the Pre-Raphaelites pre-eminently figured as the illustrators, more than any single volume, which created an awareness of the potential of the carefully executed wood engraving to enhance an already beautifully made book.

The impetus behind the Pre-Raphaelite concern with illustration was both aesthetic and narrative. Mention has already been made of their early attraction to the practical arts. On the purely aesthetic level, the purpose of the illustration is to beautify the volume in which it appears. It is also an attempt to effect a marriage of the arts. At the same time, however, illustration was a means of complementing the narrative im-pulse in Pre-Raphaelite art and poetry. This strong tendency in Pre-Raphaelitism iron-ically never led to the production of anything more than allegorical fiction, such as Rossetti's "Hand and Soul" and Simeon Solomon's *A Vision of Love Revealed in Sleep*, unless Oliver Madox Brown's *Gabriel Denver* and other works are conceded as a kind of Pre-Raphaelite fiction. But the narrative aspect is one of the most easily recognized characteristics of almost all Pre-Raphaelite painting and poetry, and it underlies most of the illustrations executed by the group.

The range of Pre-Raphaelite illustrations is extensive. Of particular interest are the designs they executed for one another's works (three in *The Germ*; Rossetti's title pages for Christina Rossetti's *Goblin Market* and *The Prince's Progress*) and illustrations from the works of the Romantic poets (Tennyson, Byron, Goethe, Keats, and Coleridge). Among the other categories of their illustrations may be included those for fairy tales (Burne-Jones' earliest illustrations for *The Fairy Family*; many of Arthur Hughes' drawings); hymns and songs (Millais' illustrations for Leslie's *Little Songs for Me to Sing*); domestic novels and stories (Millais' illustrations for the novels of Trollope and Harriet Martineau); legends and ballads, and myths (medieval, Norse, Breton, and native); classical literature (Millais' illustrations for the *Odyssey*); exotic literature (the *Arabian Nights*); English classics (Shields' designs for Bunyan and Defoe); moral anecdotes (especially the illustrations of Millais); children's literature (Hughes' illustrations for Christina Rossetti and George MacDonald); poems (based on legends and sagas, both foreign and domestic); bizarre and fanciful subjects (Sandys' illustrations "Until Her Death" and *"Amor Mundi"*); satirical drawings or caricatures (Millais' drawings for *Punch*; Sandys' *The Nightmare*); and religious subjects (Millais' *Parables*; *Dalziel's Bible Gallery*).

The Pre-Raphaelites were by no means the only, or necessarily the best artists working in the field of book illustration during the nineteenth century. Most of them did at one time or another experiment with the wood-engraved illustration. Hughes and Millais were the most industrious and probably the most consistently skillful. Ford Madox Brown, Holman Hunt, and Burne-Jones executed only a very few illustrations each. Rossetti, a capable draftsman, tended toward too complex designs and lacked the patience to work concertedly in this medium. Many of the best illustrations of the period were produced by the associates of the Pre-Raphaelites — Shields, Sandys, and Solomon. Dozens of other artists took part in the revival, the success of which depended so vitally on the collaboration of the two firms of Dalziel and Swain, which for twenty years or more were almost solely responsible for executing the designs submitted by the various artists. The present bibliography does not record the illustrations made by artists other than the Pre-Raphaelites. The significant contributions of such artists as Pinwell, Boyd-Houghton, Walker, Birkett Foster, Poynter, Gilbert, Pickersgill, Lawson, Du Maurier, Tenniel, and other of the great illustrators have been examined in the two classic works on the subject by Forrest Reid (88.9) and Gleeson White (88.3). These two pioneer researchers concentrated on the period of the 1860's, and in any study of the illustrations of the time their works must be acknowledged as the principal sources. Their treatment of the Pre-Raphaelites was not definitive, however, and this bibliography is an attempt to catalogue all the Pre-Raphaelite illustrations for books and periodicals which it has been possible to locate. Doubtless many have been overlooked, but also many inaccuracies in previous studies have been corrected and many obscurities clarified.

The listing for the ten artists included in sections 91–100 is chronological by artist.

Each section is preceded by a brief introduction in which the characteristics of the illustrations of the individual artist are discussed. The primary emphasis throughout is on wood engravings, but steel engravings and a few process illustrations are also included in order to provide a full catalogue of each artist's contribution to illustrated literature. Illustrations for the Kelmscott Press publications and those which are merely photographic or line reproductions of paintings have been purposely excluded, the former because they have been adequately treated elsewhere (see 43.3), the latter because properly speaking they are not illustrations and therefore do not come within the purview of this survey.

In almost every instance, cross references refer to reprints, which are indicated; that an illustration was eventually reprinted is not, however, noticed under the original source. Volume numbers are given for periodicals only when more than one volume was issued in a given year. Page numbers are cited for illustrations appearing in books, except when the illustrations are not enumerated, as in books containing only designs by a single artist. For periodicals, months are given in some instances rather than page numbers, especially for serialized items extending over a period of many months. Page numbers are given for separate illustrations. Page numbers, as well as publication data, are taken from volumes examined in the British Museum unless otherwise indicated. Because of peculiarities in the binding up of periodicals, page numbers may differ in other copies. When these peculiarities are obvious (without reference to other copies) mention is made of the fact. A not unusual example is when the story or poem illustrated appears in one monthly issue and the illustration in another. Titles of illustrations are placed within quotation marks only when the title is taken from the work illustrated (double) or from a line within the text (single). When the illustration has an alternate title (generally in a reprint) that title is placed in square brackets after the pagination. The type of work illustrated is indicated except when it is obvious from the title, such as *Passages from the Poems of Thomas Hood*. For both periodical and book illustrations, the sequence of the entry is the same: number of illustrations, title of illustration (except for book illustrations), page number in parentheses (where applicable), alternate title (if any) in square brackets, title and type of work illustrated, and author (for periodicals or anthology volumes only).

References

Section 88
GENERAL DISCUSSIONS OF PRE-RAPHAELITE ILLUSTRATIONS

88.1 Layard, George Somes. *Tennyson and His Pre-Raphaelite Illustrators: A Book about a Book*. London: Stock, 1894.

Separate sections on the illustrations of Hunt (36.34), Millais (37.33), and Rossetti (30.16), for the Moxon *Tennyson* (90.3). For discussion see Survey, pp. 15–16.

88.2 Pennell, Joseph. "A Golden Decade in English Art," *Savoy*, no. 1 (January 1896), 112–124.

On the illustrators of the Sixties, especially the Pre-Raphaelites.

88.3 White, Gleeson. *English Illustration:*

"*The Sixties*," *1855–1870*. Westminster: Constable, 1897.

Together with Reid (88.9), the most important study of the Pre-Raphaelites as illustrators.

88.4 [Dalziel, George and Edward]. *The Brothers Dalziel: A Record of Fifty Years' Work in Conjunction with Many of the Most Distinguished Artists of the Period, 1840–1890*. London: Methuen, 1901.

See especially chapters 3 and 4, treating Millais, Holman Hunt, Rossetti, Hughes, Burne-Jones, and others.

88.5 Hardie, Martin. "The Moxon Tennyson: 1857," *Book Lover*, VII (1907), 45–51.

Seven illustrations.

88.6 Smyser, William Emory. "Romanticism in Tennyson and His Pre-Raphaelite Illustrators," *North American Review*, CXCII (October 1910), 504–515.

Rossetti is seen as an "Ariel of Art," whose drawings [for Tennyson] are not illustrations, but "wonderful creations rather original and occult." "The romantic naturalism, the medieval sense of wonder and mystery and spiritual beauty which are the essential quality of Pre-Raphaelite art, when brought to bear upon the poetry of Tennyson, interpret, and imaginatively enrich it, both in its own naturalism, and its peculiar Romantic character." (p. 505) "The primary and essential element of the Pre-Raphaelite spirit is not romance. It is her twin sister Naturalism." (p. 508) The Pre-Raphaelites were attracted to Tennyson by the naturalistic elements in his poetry, though Tennyson was not himself a Pre-Raphaelite.

88.7 Hardie, Martin. *Catalogue of Modern Wood-Engravings*. (Victoria and Albert Museum. Department of Engraving, Illustration and Design.) London: H. M. Stationery Office, 1916.

Catalogues the holdings of illustrations, including those by the Pre-Raphaelites, in the Victoria and Albert Museum.

88.8 *Book Illustration of the Sixties* [Catalogue of the Exhibition]. London: National Gallery, Millbank (The Tate Gallery), 18 January to 31 December 1923.

Examples from all the Pre-Raphaelite illustrators.

88.9 Reid, Forrest. "The Pre-Raphaelite Group," *Illustrators of the Sixties*. London: Faber, 1928.

Included in this chapter are discussions of Rossetti, Hunt, Brown, Lawless, Sandys, Millais, Hughes, Poynter, Burne-Jones, Solomon, and H. H. Armstead. There is also a chapter on "Allingham's *Music Master* and the Moxon *Tennyson*."

88.10 Reitlinger, Henry. "The Pre-Raphaelites," *From Hogarth to Keene: With 87 Reproductions of Black and White Drawings by English Story-Telling Artists and Illustrators*. London: Methuen, 1938.

For annotation see 75.34.

88.11 James, Philip. *English Book Illustration, 1800–1900*. London: King Penguin Books, 1947.

88.12 Friedman, Albert B. "The Tennyson of 1857," *More Books*, XXIII (January 1948), 15–22.

88.13 ——— "English Illustrators of the 1860's," *More Books*, XXIII (December 1948), 372–380.

Section 89
WORKS ON THE ILLUSTRATIONS OF INDIVIDUAL PRE-RAPHAELITE ARTISTS

JOHN EVERETT MILLAIS

89.1 "Millais' 'Parables,'" *New Path*, I (March 1864), 145–152.
A critical and appreciative review of 95.37.

89.2 Layard, George Somes. "Millais and *Once a Week*," *Good Words*, XXXIV (August 1893), 552–558.
67 illustrations by Millais appeared in *Once a Week*, the last in 1868.

89.3 Pennell, Joseph and Elizabeth R. "John Everett Millais, Painter and Illustrator," *Fortnightly Review*, LXVI, n.s. LX (September 1896), 443–450.

89.4 *The Woodcut Illustration of Millais* [Catalogue of the Exhibition]. London: Hacon and Ricketts (at the Sign of the Dial, 52 Warwick Street), 16 March 1898.
For annotation see 12.5.

89.5 [Hardie, Martin.] *Catalogue of Prints: Wood Engravings after Sir John Everett Millais . . . in the Victoria and Albert Museum*. London: H. M. Stationery Office, 1908.
A valuable work on Millais' wood engravings, with lists of separate engravings, books and periodicals illustrated by Millais, and books of reference.

89.6 Sullivan, Edmund J. "Millais and the Illustration of Verse," *The Art of Illustration*. London: Chapman and Hall, 1921.

89.7 McPharlin, Paul. "The Dalziel Parables 1864," *Publisher's Weekly*, CXLIII (2 January 1943), 41–46.

DANTE GABRIEL ROSSETTI

89.8 Cary, Elizabeth Luther. "Rossetti as an Illustrator," *Lamp* [*Bookbuyer*], XXVII (November 1903), 321–328.

89.9 ——— "Dante Gabriel Rossetti, Illus-

trator," *Print Collector's Quarterly*, V (1915), 317–339.

FREDERICK SANDYS

89.10 [Gray, J. M.]. "Frederick Sandys and the Woodcut Designers of Thirty Years Ago," *Century Guild Hobby Horse*, n.s. III (October 1888), 147–157.
With a list of Sandys' designs.

89.11 Pennell, Joseph. "An English Illustrator," *Quarto*, I (1896), 33–37.
Originally appeared as "Ein englischer Illustrator: Frederick Sandys," *Pan*, I (September 1895), 205–208.

89.12 White, Gleeson. "A Great Illustrator (Frederick Sandys)," *Pall Mall Magazine*, XVI (November 1898), 328–338.

89.13 S[andys], M[ary] F., ed. *Reproductions of Woodcuts by F. Sandys, 1860–1866*. London: Published for Mrs. Sandys by Carl Hentschel, [1910].
With an Introduction by Borough Johnson; 25 illustrations are reproduced.

89.14 Sullivan, Edmund J. "Sandys and Boyd Houghton," *The Art of Illustration*. London: Chapman and Hall, 1921.

OTHER ARTISTS

89.15 Housman, Laurence. "The Illustrations of Arthur Hughes," *Bibliophile*, I (July 1908), 231–237.
Impressionistic and imprecise, with specific references to no more than one or two illustrations. Eight illustrations from Hughes' drawings.

89.16 Green, Roger Lancelyn. "Burne-Jones and 'The Fairy Family,'" *Times Literary Supplement*, no. 2221 (26 August 1944), p. 420.

A note on the first work illustrated by Burne-Jones (92.1). Two unused illustrations for *The Fairy Family* are reproduced in 42.63.

For a second article on the same volume see "Burne-Jones's Earliest Picture," *TLS*, no. 2854 (9 November 1956), p. 665.

Joint Illustrations

Section 90

BOOKS AND PERIODICALS ILLUSTRATED CONJOINTLY OR IN COLLABORATION BY PRE-RAPHAELITE ARTISTS

90.1 *The Germ*. London, 1850. See 72.1.

Four etchings. *Hunt*: "My Beautiful Lady" (no. 1, January, 1), poem by Thomas Woolner. *Collinson*: "The Child Jesus" (no. 2, February, 49), his own poem. *Brown*: "Cordelia" (no. 3, March, 97–98), poem by W. M. Rossetti. *Deverell*: "Viola and Olivia" (no. 4, April[May], 145), poem by J. L. Tupper. Another etching, illustrating Rossetti's "St. Agnes of Intercession," was prepared by Millais for the fifth number of the magazine which never appeared. A unique (?) impression of this engraving is in the collection of the City Museum and Art Gallery, Birmingham.

90.2 Allingham, William. *The Music Master, A Love Story, and Two Series of Day and Night Songs*. London: Routledge, 1855. See 46.4.

Nine illustrations, a vignette, and ornaments. *Hughes*: Crossing the Stile (frontis. ["Oh! Were My Love"]); "The Fairies" (19); "Lady Alice" (64); Milly (104); Under the Abbey-Wall (117 ["The Music Master"]); The Boy's Grave (191 ["A Boy's Burial"]); Window (221 ["On the Twilight Pond"]); Vignette (title page) and ornaments. *Millais*: "The Fireside Story" (216). *Rossetti*: "The Maids of Elfen-Mere" (202). *The Music Master* was reissued as *Day and Night Songs* in 1860, with the same illustrations, "The Fairies" appearing as the frontispiece, and again in 1884, without illustrations, in covers designed by Rossetti. In 1889, two of the illustrations were used in Allingham's *Life and Phantasy* (46.15), Millais' "The Fireside Story" appearing as the

frontispiece, and Hughes' "The Fairies" illustrating the poem "Vivant."

90.3 Tennyson, Alfred. *Poems*. London: Moxon, 1857.

Thirty illustrations by the Pre-Raphaelites and a photographic frontispiece, a relief of Tennyson after a medallion by Thomas Woolner. *Hunt*: "Recollections of the Arabian Nights" (13, 19); "The Ballad of Oriana" (51, 55); "The Lady of Shalott" (part I, 67); "Godiva" (281); "The Beggar Maid" (359). *Millais*: "Mariana" (7); "The Miller's Daughter" (86, 93); "The Sisters" (109); "A Dream of Fair Women" (Cleopatra, 149; Queen Eleanor, 161); "The Death of the Old Year" (172); "Dora" (213, 219); "The Talking Oak" (242, 255 [The Bridal Toilet]); "Locksley Hall" (267, 274 [The Letter]); "St. Agnes' Eve" (309); "The Day Dream" ('The Sleeping Palace,' part I, 317; 'The Revival,' part II, 323); "Edward Gray" (340); "The Lord of Burleigh" (353). *Rossetti*: "The Lady of Shalott" (part IV, 75); "Mariana in the South" (82); "The Palace of Art" (St. Cecilia, 113; The Weeping Queens [The Death of Arthur], 119); "Sir Galahad" (305). The Pre-Raphaelite illustrations for this volume were reprinted, together with six photogravures of the original drawings in *Some Poems by Alfred Lord Tennyson* (London: Freemantle, 1901), with a Preface by Joseph Pennell and an Introduction by William Holman Hunt. See Plate VIII.

90.4 Willmott, Robert Aris, ed. *The Poets of the Nineteenth Century*. London: Routledge, 1857.

Four illustrations. *Brown*: "The Prisoner of Chillon" (111), by Byron. *Hughes*: "The Vision of Serena" (21), by William Hayley. *Millais*: "The Dream" (123), by Byron; "Love" (137), by Coleridge.

90.5 *Passages from the Poems of Thomas Hood.* Illustrated by the Junior Etching Club. In 34 Plates. London: Gambart, 1858.

Three illustrations. *Millais*: "The Bridge of Sighs" (plate 10); "Ruth" (plate 27). *Solomon*: "The Haunted House" (plate 7).

90.6 Willmott, Robert Aris, ed. *English Sacred Poetry, of the Sixteenth, Seventeenth, Eighteenth and Nineteenth Centuries.* London: Routledge, 1862.

Three illustrations. *Hunt*: "The Lent Jewels" (frontis.), by Richard Chenevix Trench. *Sandys*: "Life's Journey" (60), by George Wither; "The Little Mourner" (321), by Dean Henry Alford.

90.7 *The Cornhill Gallery.* London: Smith, Elder, 1865.

Thirty-one illustrations by Millais and Sandys, all reprints, from the *Cornhill Magazine*. The reprints of Millais include his illustrations for *Framley Parsonage* (95.14) and *The Small House at Allington* (95.40). The same twenty-nine illustrations are reprinted in 95.55. The two Sandys reprints are "The Portent" (97.1) and "Manoli" (97.4).

90.8 Gatty, Mrs. Alfred. *Parables From Nature: With Notes on the Natural History.* 3rd and 4th Series. London: Bell and Daldy, 1865.

Three illustrations. *Burne-Jones*: "The Deliverer" (53 [The Nativity]). *Scott*: "Red Snow" (frontis.); "The Master of the Harvest" (42). Reissued in 1880, 1st to 5th series.

90.9 *Pictures of Society. Grave and Gay. From the Pencils of Celebrated Artists and the Pens of Popular Authors.* London: Sampson Low, 1866 [1865?].

Four illustrations. Reprints. *Millais*: "I Remember" (26), poem by the author of "Festus" [Philip James Bailey] — see 95.23, "The Border Witch"; "A Moment of Suspense"

(178), anonymous poem, and "A Matter of Moment" (192), anonymous story — both reprints from unidentified periodicals. *Sandys*: "Lancashire's Lesson" (207), anonymous anecdote — see 97.8, "The Hardest Time of All."

90.10 *Touches of Nature by Eminent Artists and Authors.* London: Cassell, [1866].

Nine illustrations. Reprints. *Hunt*: "Go, Work While it is Called To-Day" (6), poem by Dora Greenwell — see 94.5, "Go and Come." *Millais*: "The Parting" (4), and "Arrested" (39), anecdotes by [Dinah M. Mulock] — both reprints from unidentified sources; "A Contrast" (51), parable by Thomas Guthrie — see 95.31, "The Pharisee and the Publican"; "The Lost Piece of Money" (66), parable by Thomas Guthrie — see 95.31. *Sandys*: "Hoping Against Hope" (5), poem by Christina Rossetti — see 97.13, "If"; "Sleep" (27), poem by Dora Greenwell — see 97.9; "Until Her Death" (42), poem by [Dinah M. Mulock] — see 97.5. *Shields*: "Even As Thou Wilt" (38), poem by Isa Craig — see 99.8.

90.11 [Heaton, Mrs. Charles], ed. *Routledge's Sunday Album for Children.* London: Routledge, 1873.

Three illustrations. Reprints. *Hunt*: "The Harvest" (29), unsigned poem — see 90.10, "Go, Work While it is Called To-Day," and 94.5, "Go and Come"; "The Lent Jewels" (79), moral tale based on Trench's poem — see 90.6. *Millais*: "Parting" (97), poem — see 90.10, original source unidentified. Reissued in shorter form as *Sunday Reading for Good Children* (London: Routledge, [1873]), where all the illustrations appear with the same pagination.

90.12 *Dalziels' Bible Gallery: Illustrations from the Old Testament.* London: Camden Press, 1880.

Twelve illustrations (no pagination). *Brown*: Joseph's Coat; The Death of Eglon; Elijah and the Widow's Son. *Burne-Jones*: The Parable of the Boiling Pot. *Hunt*: Eliezer and Rebekah at the Well. *Sandys*: Jacob Hears the Voice of the Lord. *Solomon*: Melchizedek Blesses Abram; Hagar and Ishmael; Abraham and Isaac; The Infant Moses;

Naomi and the Child Obed; Hosannah! The six designs by Simeon Solomon were chosen from a total of twenty intended for this volume; the remaining fourteen were printed in *Art Pictures from the Old Testament* (100.5).

90.13 Seguin, L. G. *Rural England*. London: Strahan, [1881].

Five illustrations. Four reprints. *Hughes*: Initial letter illustration to "The Hamlet" (204). *Millais*: Going Out to Dinner (167), The Hunt-Ball (168), and Squire Talbot at Home (169), illustrations to "The Hall" — see 95.56, 95.60, 95.62–95.64, Millais' illustrations for *Phineas Finn*; Theodora (180), illustration to "Our Aristocratic Suburb" — see 95.42, "Oh! the Lark is singing."

Books and Periodicals Illustrated by Separate Artists

Section 91

FORD MADOX BROWN

[Reid (88.9), pp. 48–50]

Ford Madox Brown was not widely active as an illustrator, and even in the periodicals he appears less frequently than any Pre-Raphaelite artist, with the exception of William Bell Scott and Burne-Jones. Brown's designs are not particularly suited to the limitations imposed by the engraving. They are weakened by excessive detail and by an improper focus in the over-all composition. The areas of light and shade are poorly distributed, and the bare, bold outlines assume a starkness and harsh quality owing to the absence of the gradations of shading. Among Brown's illustrations, only "The Traveller" and his two designs for Rossetti's "Down Stream" escape these general weaknesses. Besides the nine wood engravings catalogued by White and Reid, two volumes illustrated by Brown with steel engravings have been included in the following list. Mention should also be made of Brown's cover design for Oliver Madox Brown's *Gabriel Denver* (47.1). For Brown's contributions to jointly illustrated volumes see 90.1, 90.4, 90.12.

* * *

91.1 *Lyra Germanica. The Christian Life. 2nd Series*. Translated from the German by Catherine Winworth. London: Longmans, 1868.

Three illustrations. "At the Sepulchre" (38 [The Entombment]), by Viktor Straus; The Sower (45 ["The Whole World Restored in Christ"]), Abraham and Isaac (174 ["Faith That Worketh by Love"]), by F. C. Gallent.

91.2 *Once a Week*. n.s. Vol. III, 1869.

One illustration. The Traveller (145), independent illustration.

91.3 *The Poetical Works of Lord Byron*.

Edited with a Critical Memoir by W. M. Rossetti. London: Moxon, 1870.

Eight illustrations, steel engravings (two by Oliver Madox Brown). Numerous head and tailpieces. *F. M. Brown*: "Childe Harold's Pilgrimage" (18); "The Corsair" (107); "Sardanapalus" (273); "The Two Foscari" (294); "Don Juan" (401). *O. M. Brown*: "Mazeppa" (150); "The Deformed Transformed" (309). The illustrated title page is also by F. M. Brown.

91.4 *The Dark Blue*. II, 1871–1872.

One illustration and a tailpiece. "Down Stream" (211, 212), poem by D. G. Rossetti.

91.5 Blind, Mathilde. *Dramas in Miniature.* London: Chatto and Windus, 1891.
 One illustration. "The Message" (frontis., from p. 25).

91.6 Hueffer, Ford Madox. *The Brown Owl: A Fairy Story.* London: Unwin, 1892.

Two illustrations. One a title-page vignette, the other a headpiece. Steel engravings. The American edition (Stokes) is dated 1891. A frontispiece by Ford Madox Brown also appeared in *The Feather* by Hueffer (London: Unwin, 1892).

Section 92

EDWARD BURNE-JONES

[Reid (88.9), pp. 99–100]

Burne-Jones's major contribution to illustrated literature was for the Kelmscott Press publications, which, because they have been treated elsewhere (see 43.3), are not included in the present survey. The special nature of the Kelmscott illustrations and the lateness of their appearance place them outside the mainstream of the revival of wood engraving in England. Reference should be made, however, to Burne-Jones's drawings for "The Story of Cupid and Psyche" in *The Earthly Paradise*, but never published with it. Two sets of the drawings — 44 out of a total 70 — were hand-printed from blocks cut by William Morris and his assistants. One of these sets, formerly in the possession of Fairfax Murray, is in the Department of Prints of the Metropolitan Museum of Art. An indefinite number of sets — ten or twelve according to Murray — were also printed on large paper by F. S. Ellis. Eighty-six drawings and studies for this series, also formerly belonging to Murray, are in a volume in the Birmingham City Museum and Art Gallery (see 5.5, pp. 81–87 for description). Most of the drawings in this series date from about 1865. When the grandiose scheme for the illustration of *The Earthly Paradise* — as originally conceived it was to have nearly 500 illustrations — was abandoned, Ruskin acquired the final tracings (whether he purchased them or received them as a gift from Burne-Jones is a source of controversy) which he later gave to the Ruskin School of Drawing, Oxford. Twenty-four of these woodcuts were used to illustrate an edition of Robert Bridges' poetic version of the story of Eros and Psyche, published by the Gregynog Press in 1935.

 With the exception of "Summer Snow" and the steel engravings for *The Fairy Family* most of the illustrations listed below are awkward and graceless. It is paradoxical that the artist should have willingly acknowledged such weak designs as "Sigurd" and "The Deliverer" and yet have remained ashamed of the charming designs for *The Fairy Family*, his first attempt at book illustration. Not included among the listed illustrations is the frontispiece to Ford Madox Hueffer's *The Queen Who Flew* (London: Bliss, 1894), which, though it was unavailable for examination, is probably a photographic reproduction. Also unlisted is Burne-Jones's design for "Labour" ("When Adam Delved and Eve Span") which appeared in *The Daily Chronicle*, February 11, 1895; and the pale remnant of the larger scheme — the one design, cut by Morris ("Three Women Playing on Instruments"), which appeared on the title page of all three volumes of *The Earthly Paradise* (43.13). For Burne-Jones's contributions to jointly illustrated volumes see 90.8 and 90.12.

* * *

92.1 [Maclaren, Archibald]. *The Fairy Family. A Series of Ballads & Metrical Tales. Illustrating the Fairy Mythology of Europe.* London: Longmans, 1857.

Two illustrations and a tailpiece. The frontispiece and title page are steel engravings. "Whisper, whisper" (frontis. illustrating part II of "The Elf-Folk," p. 7); title page. The tailpiece (279) is a woodcut. Burne-Jones made other designs for this volume, but they were not used. Two of these — "Little Mabel Smiling Lies" for part I of "The Elf-Folk" and "The Sun with [bright and cheerful face]" for part II of "The Pixies" — reproduced by Walter Cockerell from the original pen and ink drawings appear opposite page 120 in *Memorials*, I (42.63). For discussion of this volume see 89.16. See also Plate II.

92.2 *Good Words.* 1862.

One illustration. Sigurd the Crusader (248 ["King Sigurd, the Crusader"]), a norse saga by the author of "The Martyrdom of Kelavane."

92.3 ——— 1863.

One illustration. "The Summer Snow" (380), anonymous poem. Attributed to Christopher Jones in the Index.

92.4 [Bulwer-Lytton, Edward Robert] [= Owen Meredith]. *King Poppy: a Story without End.* London: Longmans, 1892.

Two illustrations. A half-title page illustration used also as a cover design, and a frontispiece. Steel engravings.

Section 93

ARTHUR HUGHES

[Reid (88.9), pp. 83–95]

Arthur Hughes is probably best remembered as an illustrator of children's stories and fairy tales, and, indeed, his delicate fancy seems to have found its best expression in his designs for the works of Christina Rossetti and George MacDonald. These subjects were congenial to Hughes' own imaginative temperament. When he attempted more earth-bound themes, the results were often vague and weak, out of touch with the substance of reality. The charge of banality aside, such is not the case, however, for most of his contributions to the 1871 volume of *Good Words* (93.29) and for his "Blessing in Disguise," which appeared in *The Sunday Magazine*, 1868–1869 (93.14).

Reference should be made to one untraceable item, not included below, which is mentioned casually without a source by White (88.3). That authority says that Hughes did several designs for a poem by Jean Ingelow entitled "The Shepherd's Lady," but he comments that the "artist has lost sight" of these designs. In the Dalziel Collection of the Prints Room of the British Museum, there are four unidentified drawings, two of them dealing with pastoral subjects. It is possible that the latter were intended designs for Ingelow's poem, but this is only to hazard a guess. There is no evidence that the illustrations were ever executed. The list below contains one incomplete item: for the 1870–1871 volume of *Good Words for the Young* (93.22), no months are given for the serialized items. The copy examined in the British Museum was bound without wrappers and, contrary to previous publication practice, no date, volume number, or other identifying mark appears on the pages of the journal.

Hughes was a prolific designer who continued to illustrate well beyond the period of the 1860's and the 1870's. If the illustrations for such works as *Enoch Arden* and *Tom Brown's School Days* have paled through familiarity, they are nevertheless sensitive and skillfully executed drawings by a highly imaginative and creative artist. Hughes' later illustrations suffer seriously by comparison with his early designs, but for purposes of completeness, it seemed unreasonable to omit them. For Hughes' contributions to jointly illustrated volumes see 90.2 and 90.4.

* * *

93.1 *The Queen.* 1861. Christmas Number.
Two illustrations. "Hark! the Herald Angels Sing" (297), poem by George MacDonald; "Born on Christmas Eve, and Died on Christmas Eve" (297), poem by F. Greenwood.

93.2 *The Cornhill Magazine.* Vol. III, 1863.
One illustration. At the Brook (582), "Margaret Denzil's History," anonymous serialized story.

93.3 *Good Words.* 1864.
One illustration. "At the Sepulchre" (728), poem by E. M. Murray.

93.4 *London Society.* 1865.
One illustration. "The Farewell Valentine" (181), anonymous tale.

93.5 Tennyson, Alfred. *Enoch Arden.* London: Moxon, 1866.
Twenty-five illustrations and a cover design. A few of the illustrations are full-page, but the majority are half-page drawings.

93.6 Woolner, Thomas. *My Beautiful Lady.* 3rd edition. London: Macmillan, 1866.
One illustration. A title page vignette.

93.7 MacDonald, George. *Alec Forbes of Howglen* (Standard Library). London: Hurst and Blackett, [1867].
One illustration. A steel-engraved frontispiece.

93.8 —— *Dealings with the Fairies.* London: Strahan, 1867.
Twelve illustrations. All twelve, plus one additional design, were later reprinted in Greville MacDonald's edition of his father's work, *Fairy Tales* (London: Fifield, 1904; reprinted Allen and Unwin, 1920).

93.9 —— *England's Antiphon* (The Sunday Library). London: Macmillan, 1868.
Three illustrations. The text was published in three parts, appearing in October, November, and December. In the bound copy in the British Museum, two of the illustrations appear in part I, the frontispiece having been transferred from part III.

93.10 Palgrave, Francis Turner. *The Five Days' Entertainments at Wentworth Grange.* London: Macmillan, 1868.
Seventeen illustrations.

93.11 Farrar, F. W. *Seekers after God.* London: Macmillan, 1868.
One illustration. Aurelius and his Mother (frontis.).

93.12 *Good Cheer* [Christmas Issue of *Good Words*]. 1868.
One illustration. "A Will of Her Own" (27), anonymous story.

93.13 *Good Words for the Young.* 1868–1869.
Thirty-eight illustrations. 28 to *At the Back of the North Wind*, by George MacDonald, four designs for each monthly installment, appearing November to April, June to September; 10 to *The Boy in Grey*, by Henry Kingsley, appearing March to May.

93.14 *The Sunday Magazine.* 1868–1869.
One illustration. "Blessing in Disguise" (156 ["Looking Back"]), poem by M. — see 93.39.

93.15 [Hughes, Thomas]. *Tom Brown's School Days: By an Old Boy.* 6th Edition. London: Macmillan [1868, dated] 1869.
Forty-three illustrations. 23 full-page and eleven half-page illustrations and nine initial

vignettes. *Tom Brown's School Days* was first published in 1857, but not until the 6th edition was it illustrated, by Hughes and Sidney Prior Hall, who contributed fifteen illustrations, most of them half-page and initials. The illustrated sequel to this volume, *Tom Brown at Oxford* (1870), is solely the work of Sidney Hall.

93.16 *Good Words.* 1869.
   Two illustrations. "Carmina Nuptialia" (625, 688), poem in two parts, by Gerald Massey.

93.17 *Good Words for the Young.* 1869–1870.
   Ninety illustrations. 36 to *Ranald Bannerman's Boyhood*, by George MacDonald, three designs for each monthly installment, November 1869 to October 1870; 48 to *At the Back of the North Wind*, four designs for each monthly installment, November 1869 to October 1870; four to Kingsley's *The Boy in Grey*, two designs each in the June and July installments; one each to "Touching the Moon" (37) and "The White Princess" (268), playettes in the Lilliput Revels series by Matthew Browne [= William Brighty Rands].

93.18 MacDonald, Louisa Powell. *Chamber Dramas for Children.* London: Strahan, 1870.
   One illustration. A half-title page vignette. Numerous head and tailpieces.

93.19 *Good Words.* 1870.
   Two illustrations. "Fancy" (777), "The Mariner's Cave" (865), poems by Jean Ingelow.

93.20 *London Society.* 1870.
   One illustration. "Not Mine," anonymous poem. In the British Museum copy, the poem appears in the December number, page 501; the illustration is bound in the July number, page 51.

93.21 *National Nursery Rhymes.* London: Novello, [1870–1871].
   Two illustrations. "My Lady Wind" (38); "Little Tommy Tucker" (46).

93.22 *Good Words for the Young.* 1870–1871.
   Forty-six illustrations. 30 to *The Princess and the Goblin*, by George MacDonald, four designs for each monthly installment, November to June, except for May when only two appeared; one each to "The Black Showman and the White Showman" (17), "The Whisper" (225), "Barbara Petlamb" (100), "The Pedlar's Diamond" (172), "Lock & Key" (264), "Little Keeper" (321), "Handsome is That Handsome Does" (449), and "The Nephew of Charlemagne" (641), poems and playettes in the Lilliput Revels series; four illustrations entitled Government (33), Science (72), Mercy (145), Trade (201), illustrating lectures on the above subjects in the Lilliput Lecture series by Matthew Browne; two final illustrations to "King Arthur's Great Boar Hunt. An Ancient Fairy Tale" (249, 329), by the author of "Stone Edge."

93.23 *The Sunday Magazine.* 1870–1871.
   Three illustrations. "My Heart" (10), poem by George MacDonald; "The First Sunrise" (302), poem by A.B.; "Tares & Wheat" (353), story by Hugh Macmillan.

93.24 MacDonald, George. *At the Back of the North Wind.* London: Strahan, 1871.
   Seventy-six illustrations. Reprints — see 93.13 and 93.17

93.25 *Christmas Carols.* London: Novello, 1871.
   Three illustrations. A frontispiece and two illustrations for "Sleep! Holy Babe!" and "When Christ was Born of Mary Free." Companion volume to 93.21.

93.26 Kingsley, Henry. *The Boy in Grey.* London: Strahan, 1871.
   Fourteen illustrations. Reprints — see 93.13 and 93.17.

93.27 [Browne, Matthew] *Lilliput Lectures.* London: Strahan, 1871.
   Four illustrations. Reprints — see 93.22.

93.28 MacDonald, George. *Ranald Bannerman's Boyhood.* London: Strahan, 1871.
   Thirty-six illustrations. A frontispiece and

23 illustrations on plate paper plus cuts in text. Reprints — see 93.17.

93.29 *Good Words.* 1871.

Four illustrations. Two designs for a projected illustrated edition of *The Window; or the Loves of the Wrens*, with music composed by Arthur Sullivan and lyrics written by Alfred Tennyson: "Fly, little letter, apace, apace" (frontis., from p. 33), "A Song from 'The Loves of the Wrens'"; "And I May Die But the Grass Will Grow" (113), "The Mist and the Rain." Two further illustrations: Sun Comes, Moon Comes (183), "The Dial," poem by F. W. Simmons; "The Mother and the Angel" (648), anonymous poem.

93.30 *Good Words for the Young.* 1871–1872.

Thirty-three illustrations. One to "The Wind and the Moon" (80), poem by George MacDonald; eight to *The History of Gutta Percha Willie*, by George MacDonald; 24 to "Innocent's Island," a long rhymed chronicle by [Matthew Browne]. Both Reid and White mention nine illustrations to *Gutta Percha Willie*. However, one drawing (112), ascribed to Hughes in the Index, is signed "F.A.F.," and only eight illustrations appear in the separately published volume (93.38).

93.31 *The Sunday Magazine.* 1871–1872.

Three illustrations. "Sunday Musings" (24), poem by Gerald Massey; "Daria" (473), poem by Dora Greenwell; "Night & Day" (505), poem by C.E.M.

93.32 [Browne, Matthew]. *Lilliput Legends.* London: Strahan, 1872.

Two illustrations. Reprints. "Dorothea" (frontis., from p. 81), a story — see "Innocent's Island," 93.30; "Silversail and the Carrier-Pigeon" (117), a story — see 93.14.

93.33 Hake, Thomas Gordon. *Parables and Tales.* London: Chapman and Hall, 1872.

Nine illustrations. A few copies have a cover designed by D. G. Rossetti. See 48.6.

93.34 MacDonald, George. *The Princess and the Goblin.* London: Strahan, 1872.

Thirty illustrations. Reprints — see 93.22.

93.35 Rossetti, Christina. *Sing-Song: A Nursery Rhyme Book.* London: Routledge, 1872.

One hundred and twenty illustrations. A frontispiece, a title-page vignette, and the remainder half-page illustrations.

93.36 *Good Words.* 1872.

Five illustrations. "Will o'the Wisp" (49), poem by Robert Buchanan; "The Carpenter" (97), poem by George MacDonald; "Vanity Fair" (128, 129), poem by Robert Buchanan; "The Man with Three Friends" (241), poem by Dora Greenwell, from a story in the *Gesta Romanorum*.

93.37 *Good Things for the Young of All Ages: A Picturesque Magazine for Boys and Girls.* 1872–1873.

Fifteen illustrations. Ten to "Sinbad in England," a tale by William Gilbart, one design for each monthly installment, November to April, June and July, September and October; two to "Henry and Amy. The Twin Captives of Ghuznes" (72, 73), a story by Captain Felix; three others: "A Secret about a Poor Hunchback" (17), story by Charles Camden; "The Wonderful Organ" (24), story by Marianne Beaufort; "My Daughter" (136), poem by [Matthew Browne]. White refers to this volume as containing ten illustrations for "Sinbad" and six or seven others. Reid says that there are 24 Hughes illustrations for this year, half of which appeared in the Christmas number. No Christmas number is bound with the British Museum copy for this year, nor is it traceable as a separate publication.

93.38 MacDonald, George. *The History of Gutta Percha Willie: The Working Genius.* London: King, 1873.

Eight illustrations. Reprints — see 93.30.

93.39 *Good Words.* 1873.

One illustration. A reprint. "Looking Back" (640 ["Blessing in Disguise"]), poem by May Paul — see 93.14.

93.40 Rossetti, Christina. *Speaking Likenesses.* London: Macmillan, 1874.

Twelve illustrations. The frontispiece (Maggie Meets the Fairies in the Wood) and the title-page vignette ('A chair pressed gently against flora till she sat down') are repeated on pages 79 and 22.

93.41 Thackeray, [Ann]. *Old Kensington* (Vol. I of *Works*). London: Smith, Elder, 1875.

One illustration. A vignette on the title page of the *Works*. The year 1873 appears on the second title page of the novel.

93.42 ———— *The Village on the Cliff* (Vol. II of *Works*). London: Smith, Elder, 1875.

One illustration. A vignette on the title page of the *Works*. The year 1867 appears on the second title page of the novel.

93.43 ———— *Five Old Friends and a Young Prince* (Vol. III of *Works*). London: Smith, Elder, 1875.

One illustration. A vignette on the title page of the *Works*. The year 1868 appears on the second title page of the novel. The three volumes (93.41–93.43) are from the "Uniform Edition" of *The Works of Miss Thackeray*. Each volume contains three title pages (one for the *Works* and two for the individual volume), the first two of which are tipped in. The edition, judging from the dates on the second title pages, was probably made up from remainder sheets and cased in uniform boards.

93.44 *The Graphic*. Christmas Number, 1887.

One illustration. A full-page illustration in color, a composite drawing of three different Christmas scenes (26).

93.45 *The London Home Monthly*. 1895.

Seven illustrations. Five to "Graih My Chree. A Manx Ballad" (33, 35, 37, 39, 40), by Hall Caine; two to "Good-Night" (90, 91), poem by Frederick Greenwood.

93.46 *Babies' Classics*. Chosen by Lilia Scott MacDonald. London: Green, 1904.

One full-page frontispiece illustration, 66 smaller designs, and numerous initial letters and other ornaments. An elaborately decorated volume.

93.47 MacDonald, George. *Phantastes: A Faerie Romance for Men and Women. A New Edition*. With Thirty-Three New Illustrations by Arthur Hughes. Edited by Greville MacDonald. London: Fifield, 1905.

93.48 MacDonald, Greville. *The Magic Crook or the Stolen Baby: A Fairy Story*. London: Vineyard Press, 1911.

Fifty-three illustrations, including a frontispiece and a title-page vignette.

93.49 ———— *Jack and Jill: A Fairy Story*. London: Dent, 1913. Twenty-eight illustrations, including frontispiece.

93.50 ———— *Trystie's Quest or Kit King of the Pigwidgeons*. London: Vineyard Press, [1913].

Twenty-eight illustrations, including frontispiece.

Section 94

WILLIAM HOLMAN HUNT

[Reid (88.9), pp. 46–48]

Holman Hunt's best designs for illustrations appear in those items listed in section 90. Of the Pre-Raphaelite contributions to the Moxon *Tennyson* (90.3), Hunt's designs are the most conscientiously executed in accordance with the text, and his "Lady of Shalott" is among the finest illustrations in the entire volume. "The Light of Truth" (a subject fraught with many pitfalls of the sort to which Hunt later succumbed) and "Active and Passive" in *Parables From Nature* (94.3) are both admirable drawings, the first for its grace and fineness of detail, the second for its over-all strength of composition. Some items discussed in previous surveys of Hunt's illustrations have here been omitted. The engraving of Hunt's "Eve of St. Agnes," which appeared in the Christmas Number of *The Queen* (1861), is mentioned by Reid (p. 47), but because it reproduces a painting it has been excluded from this list. Also unlisted are the fourteen reproductions of Hunt's works in Sir Edwin Arnold's *The Light of the World, or The Great Consummation* (London: Longmans, 1892). Many of the illustrations are photogravure reproductions of Hunt's paintings; others appeared in Longman's *Illustrated New Testament* (1863); a few were prepared by Hunt especially for this edition of Arnold's poem, including two engravings, reproduced photographically: "Christ Before Pilate" and "Did Some Man Find Hid Shekels in a Field." For Holman Hunt's contributions to jointly illustrated volumes see 90.1, 90.3, 90.6, 90.10 to 90.12.

* * *

94.1 *Once a Week.* Vol. II, 1860.
One illustration. "Witches and Witchcraft" (438), story by Azile L. Nostaw.

94.2 ——— Vol. III, 1860.
Two illustrations. "At Night" (102 [The Wife's Death]), anonymous poem; "Temujin" (630), poem by H. P.

94.3 Gatty, Mrs. Alfred. *Parables From Nature: With Notes on the Natural History.* [1st and 2nd Series] London: Bell and Daldy, 1861.
Two illustrations. "The Light of Truth" (44); "Active and Passive" (92). Reissued in 1880, 1st to 5th series.

94.4 Mulock, Dinah M. *Studies from Life* (Standard Library). London: Hurst and Blackett, [1862].
One illustration. A steel-engraved frontispiece. "Lost" (from p. 323).

94.5 *Good Words.* 1862.
One illustration. "Go and Come" (32), poem by D.

94.6 Watts, Isaac. *Divine and Moral songs.* London: Nisbet, [1867].
One illustration. "A Morning Song of Praise" (47). Done in the new graphotype engraving process.

94.7 *Good Words.* 1878.
One illustration. "Born at Jerusalem" (473), poem by Dinah M. Mulock. A drawing of a sleeping baby, Gladys Mulock Holman Hunt.

94.8 Bunyan, John. *The Pilgrim's Progress* (Golden Treasury Series). London: Macmillan, 1886.
One illustration. Title-page vignette, steel-engraved by C. H. Jeens.

94.9 *Pearl: An English Poem of the Fourteenth Century.* Edited with a Modern Rendering by Israel Gollancz. London: Nutt, 1891.
One illustration. A frontispiece.

Section 95

JOHN EVERETT MILLAIS

[Reid (88.9), pp. 64–83]

The canon of Millais' illustrations is more complicated than that of any other artist treated in this part of the bibliography. A prolific illustrator, Millais made designs for a dozen separate periodicals and for nearly three-dozen books, counting reprints. It is precisely because his work in illustrations is so extensive that no listing of his designs can safely claim definitiveness.

Millais' drawings for the popular domestic novel of the day are overwhelmingly numerous. Although often undistinctive, they are important, for they parallel the sentimental and banal themes and subjects with which the artist occupied himself in his paintings after his defection to the populace. If many of his designs lack inspiration, however, they are seldom deficient in the technical sense, as are many of the illustrations executed by other Pre-Raphaelite artists.

One item mentioned by J. G. Millais in his life of his father (37.52) — a drawing for *Maggie Band* (London: Sampson Low, 1862) — has been excluded because attempts at verification proved fruitless. Neither the British Museum nor the Victoria and Albert Museum has an edition illustrated by Millais. J. G. Millais also refers to two designs made by Millais for the Golden Treasury edition of *Robinson Crusoe*, but only one, a title-page vignette appears in that edition (95.50). A few items, unavailable for examination, but for which adequate publication details were obtainable, have been included, contrary to general practice throughout this part. These are Trollope's *Rachel Ray* (95.38) and *Kept in the Dark* (95.75), Thackeray's *Barry Lyndon* (95.72), and Wilkie Collins' *No Name* (95.35). Though not listed below, attention should be called to the two unidentified reprints in *Pictures of Society* (90.9). No source has been found for "A Moment of Matter"; "A Moment of Suspense" is probably the same as "The Christmas Wreaths of Rockton," which appeared in *London Society* in 1862 (95.23). One item which might conceivably contain additional illustrations by Millais — the Christmas Number of *Once a Week*, 1868 — was unavailable for examination. For convenience, all of Millais' collected illustrations (except *The Cornhill Gallery* [90.7]) have been included in the following list. For Millais' contributions to jointly illustrated volumes see 90.1 to 90.5, 90.7, 90.9 to 90.11, and 90.13.

*   *   *

95.1 Collins, Wilkie. *Mr. Wray's Cash-Box; or The Mask and the Mystery: A Christmas Sketch.* London: Bentley, 1852.
One illustration. A frontispiece.

95.2 Moore, Thomas. *Irish Melodies.* London: Longmans, 1856.
One illustration. "When First I Met Thee" (84).

95.3 *Lays of the Holy Land: From the Ancient and Modern Poets.* With Illustrations from Photographs and Drawings. London: Nisbet, 1858.
One illustration. The Finding of Moses (51), illustrating two poems, "The Birth of Moses" by Cawood and "Moses on the Nile" by Grahame.

95.4 Mackay, Charles, ed. *The Home Affections Portrayed by the Poets.* London: Routledge, 1858.

Two illustrations, "There's nae Luck about the House" (245), poem by William Julius Mickle; "The Border Widow" (259), anonymous poem.

95.5 *Once a Week.* Vol. I, 1859.
Eight illustrations. "Magenta" (10), poem by Tom Taylor; "The Grandmother's Apology" (41), poem by Tennyson; "On the Water" (70), poem by Memor; "La Fille bien gardée" (306), poem by S.B.; "The Plague of Elliant" (316), poem by Tom Taylor; "Maude Clare" (382), poem by Christina Rossetti; "A Lost Love" (482), poem by R.A.B.; "St. Bartholomew" (514), poem by H.E.E.M.

95.6 ——— Vol. II, 1860.
Five illustrations. "The Crown of Love" (10), poem by George Meredith; "A Wife" (32), poem by A.; "The Head of Bran" (132), poem by George Meredith; "Practis-

ing" (242), poem by Shirley Brooks; "Musa" (598), poem by E.M.B.

95.7 —— Vol. III, 1860.
Seven illustrations. "Master Olaf" (63), poem by L.B. from the German; "Violet" (140), poem by Arthur J. Munby; "Dark Gordon's Bride" (238), poem by B. S. Montgomery; "The Meeting" (276), poem by G[eorge] M[eredith]; "The Iceberg" (407, 435), two-part story by A. Stewart Harrison; "A Head of Hair for Sale" (519), anonymous anecdote.

95.8 *The Cornhill Magazine.* Vol. I, 1860.
Three illustrations. "Unspoken Dialogue" (194), poem by R. Monckton Milnes; two for *Framley Parsonage* by Anthony Trollope, appearing April and June.

95.9 —— Vol. II, 1860.
Three illustrations. "Last Words" (513), poem by Owen Meredith; two for *Framley Parsonage*, appearing August and October.

95.10 [Mulock, Dinah M]. *John Halifax, Gentleman* (Standard Library). London: Hurst and Blackett, [1861].
One illustration. A steel-engraved frontispiece entitled Ursula March.

95.11 —— *Nothing New* (Standard Library). London: Hurst and Blackett, [1861].
One illustration. A steel-engraved frontispiece entitled Jean Dowglas.

95.12 Stretton, Julia Cecilia. *The Valley of a Hundred Fires* (Standard Library). London: Hurst and Blackett, [1861].
One illustration. A steel-engraved frontispiece entitled Mrs. Leslie.

95.13 *The Cornhill Magazine.* Vol. III, 1861.
Three illustrations. Temptation (229), "Horace Saltoun," anonymous serialized tale; two for *Framley Parsonage*, appearing January and March.

95.14 Trollope, Anthony. *Framley Parsonage.* 3 vols. London: Smith, Elder, 1861.
Six illustrations. Reprints — see 95.8, 95.9, 95.13.

95.15 *Once a Week.* Vol. IV, 1861.
Two illustrations. "Iphis & Anaxarete" (98), poem by Mary C. F. Münster; Thorr's Hunt for His Hammer (126), poem by G.W.D.

95.16 —— Vol. V, 1861.
Two illustrations. "Tannhauser" (211), ballad, translated by L.D.G.; "Swing Song" (434), anonymous poem.

95.17 *Passages from Modern English Poets.* Illustrated by the Junior Etching Club. London: Day, 1862.
One illustration. Summer Indolence (10).

95.18 Trollope, Anthony. *Orley Farm.* 2 vols. London: Chapman and Hall, 1862.
Forty illustrations.

95.19 *The Cornhill Magazine.* Vol. V, 1862.
One illustration. "Irene" (478), poem by R.M.

95.20 —— Vol. VI, 1862.
Five illustrations. "The Bishop and the Knight" (100), anonymous poem; four for *The Small House at Allington* by Anthony Trollope, appearing monthly, September through December.

95.21 *Good Words.* 1862.
Fourteen illustrations. Twelve to "Mistress and Maid," by the author of *John Halifax* [Dinah M. Mulock], appearing monthly, January through December; Olaf (25), "Olaf the Sinner and Olaf the Saint," story by H.K.; Highland Flora (393), anonymous poem.

95.22 *The Illustrated London News.* 1862.
One illustration. Christmas Story Telling (672), independent illustration.

95.23 *London Society.* Vol. II, 1862.
Two illustrations. 'Ah me! She Was a Winsome Maid' (181 [A Lady with Hounds; "The Border Witch"]), "The Border Witch," poem by T.W.; 'Yes, Lewis,' she said, 'quite satisfied' (65 [also known by title of story]), "The Christmas Wreaths of Rockton," anonymous story. Concerning the latter illustration see the Introduction to Millais and 90.9.

95.24 *Once a Week.* Vol. VI, 1862.
Twelve illustrations. "Schwerting of Saxony" (43), poem, "translated from the German of Ebert," by A.D.; The Fair Jacobite (239), independent illustration; "Sir Tristem" (349), poem by [Robert] Williams Buchanan; "The Chase of the Siren" (630), a Doric legend by Walter Thornbury; five for "Sister Anna's Probation" by Harriet Martineau, three appearing in March and two in April; one each to "The Battle of the Thirty" (155), "The Crusader's Wife" (546), and "The Drowning of Kaer-is" (687 ['I'll win the key from my father's side']), all Breton ballads translated by Tom Taylor from Hersart de Villemarqué.

95.25 ———— Vol. VII, 1862.
Eleven illustrations. "Margaret Wilson" (42); five for "The Anglers of the Dove," serialized story by Harriet Martineau, two appearing in July and three in August; "Maid Avoraine" (98), poem by R. Williams Buchanan; The Mite of Dorcas (224), independent illustration; "The Spirit of the Vanished Island" (546), poem by Mrs. Acton Tindal; "The Parting of Ulysses" (658), from Pope's *Odyssey*; "Limerick Bells" (710), poem by Horace Mule.

95.26 Tytler, Sarah [= Henrietta Keddie] *Papers for Thoughtful Girls: With Illustrative Sketches of Some Girls' Lives.* 4th ed. London: Strahan, 1863.
Four illustrations. Ciss Berry's Arrival (frontis.); Our Sister Grizel (10); Dame Dorothy (190); Herr Willy Kaenig (268).

95.27 *Wordsworth's Poems for the Young.* London: Strahan, 1863.
One illustration. A title-page vignette.

95.28 *The Churchman's Family Magazine.* Vol. I, 1863.
Two illustrations. 'Let that be, please!' (15), and 'You will forgive me, won't you?' (221), "The New Curate. A Tale in Nine Chapters," anonymous.

95.29 *The Cornhill Magazine.* Vol. VII, 1863.
Six illustrations. All for *The Small House*
at Allington, appearing monthly, January through June.

95.30 ———— Vol. VIII, 1863.
Six illustrations. All for *The Small House at Allington*, appearing monthly, July through December.

95.31 *Good Words.* 1863.
Twelve illustrations. A series illustrating *The Parables*, "read in the light of the present day," by Thomas Guthrie, appearing monthly, January through December: The Leaven (1); The Ten Virgins (81); The Prodigal Son (161); The Good Samaritan (241); The Unjust Judge (313); The Pharisee and the Publican (385); The Hid Treasure (461); The Pearl of Great Price (533); The Lost Piece of Money (605); The Sower (677); The Unmerciful Servant (749); The Labourers in the Vineyard (frontis., from p. 821). See 95.37.

95.32 *Once a Week.* Vol. VIII, 1863.
Eleven illustrations. "Endymion on Latmos" (42), poem by R.N.S.; Ten for *The Hampdens* by Harriet Martineau, three appearing in February, four in March, and three in April. See 95.73.

95.33 ———— Vol. IX, 1863.
Nine illustrations. "Hacho the Dane; or The Bishop's Ransom: A Legend of Llandaff" (504), poem by C.H.W.; eight for "Son Christopher," an historiette by Harriet Martineau, two appearing in October, four in November, and two in December.

95.34 *Punch.* 1863.
One illustration. "Mokeanna; or, The White Witness" (115 ['It is the chapeau blanc, the white witness']), a parody by F. C. Burnand.

95.35 Collins, Wilkie. *No Name.* London: Sampson, Low, Marston, 1864.
One illustration. A steel-engraved frontispiece. See Michael Sadleir, *XIX Century Fiction: A Bibliographical Record* (Cambridge University Press, 1951), Vol. 1, 94.

95.36 Browne, Matthew. *Lilliput Levee.* London: Strahan, 1864.

Three illustrations. Reprints. One title-page vignette — see 95.27; "Prince Philibert" and "Polly" — see 95.42.

95.37 *Parables of Our Lord.* London: Routledge, [1863, dated] 1864.
Twenty illustrations. Twelve reprints — see 95.31. New illustrations: The Tares, The Wicked Husbandman, The Foolish Virgins, The Importunate Friend, The Marriage Feast, The Lost Sheep, The Rich Man and Lazarus, The Good Shepherd. All twenty illustrations are reprinted in 95.80. The volume was later reprinted by the S.P.C.K.

95.38 Trollope, Anthony. *Rachel Ray.* London: Chapman and Hall, 1864.
One illustration. A frontispiece. In the cheap edition only.

95.39 *The Cornhill Magazine.* Vol. IX, 1864.
Two illustrations. Both for *The Small House at Allington*, appearing January and February.

95.40 Trollope, Anthony. *The Small House at Allington.* 2 vols. London: Smith, Elder, 1864.
Eighteen illustrations. Reprints — see 95.20, 95.29, 95.30, 95.39.

95.41 *The Cornhill Magazine.* Vol. X, 1864.
Two illustrations. An Old Song (facing 434) and a vignette (434), "Madame de Monferrato," anonymous story.

95.42 *Good Words.* 1864.
Five illustrations. "Oh! the Lark is Singing" (65), poem by R.B.R.; "A Scene for a Study" (161), poem by Jean Ingelow; "Polly" (248), anonymous poem; "The Bridal of Dandelot" (304), poem by Dora Greenwell; "Prince Philibert" (481), anonymous poem.

95.43 *London Society.* Vol. VI, 1864.
One illustration. "Knightly Worth," illustrating "The Tale of a Chivalrous Life," anonymous. In the British Museum copy, the illustration appears as a frontispiece (193) to the September issue; the tale begins on p. 238.

95.44 Hugo, Victor. *Les Miserables.* 6th ed. (Standard Library). London: Hurst and Blackett, [1864–1865].
One illustration. A steel-engraved frontispiece entitled Cosette.

95.45 *Dalziel's Illustrated Arabian Nights' Entertainment.* The Text Revised and Emendated Throughout by H. W. Dulcken. London: Ward, Lock, [1864, dated] 1865.
Two illustrations. Zobeidè Discovers the Young Man Reciting the Koran (97), "The History of Zobeidè"; Aminè and the Lady (105), "The History of Aminè."

95.46 Leslie, Henry D. *Little Songs for Me to Sing.* London: Cassell, [1865].
Seven illustrations. There are also two vignettes and several border decorations. A later, enlarged edition of this volume, entitled *Songs for Little Folk* (London: Cramer, n.d.), adds a frontispiece, St. Agnes' Eve.

95.47 Taylor, Tom. *Ballads and Songs of Brittany.* Translated from the "Barsaz-Breiz" of Vicomte Hersart De La Villemarqué. London: Macmillan, 1865.
Four illustrations. Reprints. "The Drowning of Kaer is" (35), "The Crusader's Wife" (74), and "The Battle of the Thirty" (128) — see 95.24; "The Plague of Elliant" (64) — see 95.5.

95.48 Sullivan, John. *Wace, ses oeuvres, sa patrie.* n.p., n.d.
Unavailable for examination. The nature of this publication is uncertain. It may have been a pamphlet. Millais' illustration was probably for the 2nd edition, published sometime after 1865. A proof of the drawing, a portrait of Wace, engraved by Swain, is in the Prints Room in the British Museum.

95.49 *Punch's Almanacks.* Second Series. 1865.
One illustration. Mr. Vandyke Brown and His Lay Figure (n.p. [Mr. Vandyke Brown's sons thrashing the lay figure]).

95.50 Defoe, Daniel. *Robinson Crusoe.* Edited by J. W. Clark. London: Macmillan, 1866.

One illustration. A title-page vignette. In the Golden Treasury series.

95.51 [Ingelow, Jean]. *Studies for Stories from Girls' Lives*. London: Strahan, 1866.
Two illustrations. A frontispiece illustrating "The Cumberers" and a second (309) illustrating "The Stolen Treasure" — the latter the same as Pick-a-Pack in 95.52.

95.52 *Millais's Illustrations: A Collection of Drawings on Wood by John Everett Millais* [Cover title: *Millais's Collected Illustrations*]. London: Strahan, 1866.
Eighty illustrations. All are reprints from periodicals and books with the exception of Watching (plate 61) and possibly Pick-a-Pack (plate 79) — see 95.51.

95.53 *The Argosy: A Magazine for the Fireside and the Journey*. 1866.
One illustration. "The Sighing of the Shell" (64), poem by George MacDonald. A steel wash.

95.54 *A Thousand and One Gems of English Poetry*. Selected and Arranged by Charles Mackay. London: Routledge, 1867.
One illustration. A reprint. "Edward Gray" (501) — see 90.3.

95.55 *Twenty Nine Illustrations by J. E. Millais, Designed for "The Cornhill Magazine," with Extracts Descriptive of Each Picture*. London: Smith, Elder, 1867.
Reprinted from the *Cornhill Gallery* (90.7).

95.56 *St. Paul's Magazine*. Vol. I, 1867–1868.
Six illustrations. All for *Phineas Finn the Irish Member* by Anthony Trollope, one appearing monthly, October through March.

95.57 Goethe, Wilhelm. *Egmont: A Tragedy*. Translated from the Original German by Arthur Duke Coleridge. London: Chapman and Hall, 1868.
One illustration. A frontispiece showing Egmont asleep in prison, while Freedom, as an angel, hovers over his shoulders.

95.58 *Once a Week*. n.s. I, 1868.
One illustration. Death Dealing Arrows (79), independent illustration.

95.59 —— Christmas Number, 1868.
One illustration. Taking His Ease (65).

95.60 *St. Paul's Magazine*. Vol. II, 1868.
Six illustrations. All for *Phineas Finn*, one appearing monthly, April through September.

95.61 Cholmondeley-Pennell, Harry. *Puck on Pegasus*. 6th ed. London: Hotten, 1869.
One illustration. The Fire Brigade (140).

95.62 *St. Paul's Magazine*. Vol. III, 1869.
Six illustrations. All for *Phineas Finn*, appearing monthly, October through March.

95.63 —— Vol. IV, 1869.
Four illustrations. All for *Phineas Finn*. Two reprints from Vol. III (95.62); two new illustrations appearing April and May.

95.64 Trollope, Anthony. *Phineas Finn, The Irish Member*. 2 vols. London: Virtue, 1869.
Twenty illustrations. Reprints — see 95.56, 95.60, 95.62, and 95.63.

95.65 Leslie, Henry. *Leslie's Musical Annual*. London: Cassell, 1870.
One illustration. A Reverie. A line drawing.

95.66 Heaton, Mrs. Charles. *Routledge's Album for Children*. London: Routledge, 1871.
One illustration. A reprint. "The Father's Departure" (73) — see 95.4, "There's nae Luck about the House."

95.67 *Little Lily's Picture Book*. With 96 Pages of Pictures by John Gilbert, J. E. Millais, J. D. Watson, Frederick Walker, W. Small, J. Wolf, Harrison Weir, and Others. London: Routledge, [1872].
One illustration. A reprint. "The Father's Departure" (73) — see 95.4 and 95.66, "There's nae Luck about the House."

95.68 Garrett, Mrs. Semple. *Our Little Sun-*

beam's *Picture-Book: Tales & Sketches*. London: Routledge, [1877].

Two illustrations. One reprint. "Tommy's Swing" (25) — see 95.16, "Swing Song" and 95.69; "In the Fields" (78).

95.69 Frith, Henry. *Little Valentine and Other Tales*. London: Routledge, [1878].

One illustration. A reprint. "Swinging" (20), anonymous poem — see 95.16, "Swing Song" and 95.68.

95.70 *Good Words*. 1878.

One illustration. "Macleod of Dare" (651), serialized story by William Black.

95.71 *The Magazine of Art*. 1878.

One illustration. Two Fair Maidens (50). Described as an original drawing on wood, but probably a reprint.

95.72 Thackeray, William M. *Barry Lyndon*. London: Smith, Elder, 1879.

Four illustrations. Unavailable for examination. Reid refers to one of the illustrations, "The Last Days," as "the most realistic and the most terrible design Millais ever made." (p. 79)

95.73 Martineau, Harriet. *The Hampdens: An Historiette*. London: Routledge, 1880.

Ten illustrations. Reprints — see 95.32. An interesting variant of this volume is in the collection of W. E. Fredeman. The book is a small octavo, containing a half-title page, title page, table of contents, list of illustrations, pages 161–177 of the text, six pages of advertisements, and all ten illustrations. Whether the variant was simply accidental or issued after 1880 to dispose of surplus copies of the set of plates, I have been unable to determine.

95.74 *Good Words*. 1882.

One illustration. "Kept in the Dark" (365), serialized story by Anthony Trollope. Photograph from the original drawing on wood.

95.75 Trollope, Anthony. *Kept in the Dark: A Novel* (Piccadilly Novels). London: Chatto and Windus, 1882.

One illustration. A frontispiece. Presumably a reprint of 95.74.

95.76 *The Sunday Magazine*. 1882–1883.

One illustration. These Twin Girls (756), "The Two Sisters," story by Mrs. Toulmin Smith.

95.77 [*A Series of Woodcuts After J. E. Millais, R.A. Cut by Swain & Dalziel*. London: n.p., n.d.].

Fifty-nine proof woodcut illustrations. Reprints. There is no title page. The information provided appears on the copy in the Prints Room in the British Museum, the receipt stamp of which is dated 1885.

95.78 Harrison, Major Stewart. *The Queen of the Arena and Other Stories*. London: Unwin, 1886.

One illustration. A reprint. "The Iceberg" (205) — see 95.7.

95.79 *The Magazine of Art*. 1896.

One illustration. A reprint. A Reverie (xiv), a line drawing — 95.65.

95.80 *Twenty India Paper Proofs of the Drawings by Sir John Everett Millais . . . to the Parables of Our Lord, Engraved on Wood by the Brothers Dalziel: With 20 Facsimile Letters . . . from Millais to the Dalziels during the Progress of the Work*. London: Issued privately from the Camden Press by Charles Dalziel, 1902.

Less than fifty copies were printed. See 95.37.

Section 96

DANTE GABRIEL ROSSETTI

[Reid (88.9), pp. 44–46]

Rossetti's illustrations are not numerous; half of them have already been enumerated in section 90. A perfectionist — and a dilatory one at that, as his letters to Allingham (24.6) dealing with "The Maids of Elfen-Mere" clearly indicate — Rossetti is at his best in illustration when he can "allegorize on [his] own hook," without reference to the text he is supposed to be illustrating. In fact, Rossetti's designs seldom contain more than the merest suggestion of their source. Yet it is precisely because of this characteristic, and because he consciously chose subjects which would allow him complete imaginative freedom, that his designs are so distinctive and that they seldom degenerate into the sentimental banality of so many of the illustrations of Hughes and Millais. Rossetti's illustrations for the Moxon *Tennyson* (90.3) are all interesting and impressive, if not outstanding; and his drawing for "The Maids of Elfen-Mere" is, together with Sandys' *"Amor Mundi"* and Millais' "The Lost Piece of Silver," one of the most remarkable and beautiful wood engravings of the entire period. Burne-Jones, writing in *The Oxford and Cambridge Magazine*, called it, not without justification, "the most beautiful drawing for an illustration I have ever seen." (72.4, p. 60)

Beyond the scope of the present survey, but deserving of mention, are Rossetti's designs for book covers. Besides those for his own poems, he designed among others the covers for Hake's *Parables and Tales* (48.6) — his most complex cover decoration — for Maria Rossetti's *A Shadow of Dante*, for Swinburne's *Atalanta in Calydon* and *Songs Before Sunrise*, and for Christina Rossetti's *The Prince's Progress*. Many photographic reproductions of Rossetti's works have appeared in various periodicals and books, but, with two exceptions (96.4 and 96.5), these have no relevance here. Rossetti never allied himself with the famous illustrated journals to which Millais and Hughes contributed so profusely, and his fame as an illustrator rests entirely on ten engravings for four books, all published between 1855 and 1866. For Rossetti's contributions to jointly illustrated volumes see 90.2 and 90.3.

*   *   *

96.1 Rossetti, Dante Gabriel. *The Early Italian Poets*. London: Smith, Elder, 1861.

A single design intended for the title page of this volume was never published. Two impressions, both of which were formerly owned by Fairfax Murray, were made from the plate. One of these is now in the Fitzwilliam Museum, Cambridge. See 96.5.

96.2 Rossetti, Christina. *Goblin Market and Other Poems*. London: Macmillan, 1862.

Two illustrations. 'Buy from us with a golden curl' (frontis.); 'Golden head by golden head' (title page).

96.3 ———— *The Prince's Progress and Other Poems*. London: Macmillan, 1866.

Two illustrations. 'You should have wept her yesterday' (frontis.); 'The long hours go and come and go' (title page). Items 96.2 and 96.3 were issued together with the four illustrations in 1875.

96.4 Sharp, William. *Dante Gabriel Rossetti:*

A Record and a Study. London: Macmillan, 1882.

One illustration. A photographic reproduction of the unpublished design for an engraving, 'A Sonnet is a Moment's Monument' (frontis.).

96.5 *The English Illustrated Magazine*. 1883–1884.

One illustration. This previously unpublished design was intended for the title page of Rossetti's *Early Italian Poets* (23.3 and 96.1). The reproduction accompanies an article by J. Comyns Carr, entitled "Rossetti's Influence on Art" (30.10).

96.6 Allingham, William. *Flower Pieces*

and Other Poems. London: Reeves and Turner, 1888.

Two illustrations. One reprint. "The Maids of Elfen-Mere" (frontis.) — see 90.2; "The Queen's Page (189).

96.7 Jackson, Richard C. *The Risen Life: Hymns and Poems for Days and Seasons of the Christian Year*. 3rd ed. London: Elkins, 1889.

One illustration. "Hymn to Jesus in the Blessed Sacrament of the Altar" (9). Also used as cover design. It is not known when and for what purpose this design was made. This design was published as "Design for Sculptured panel: Pelican with Young. By the Late D. G. Rossetti, Artist," in *Building World*, 2 January 1888.

Section 97

FREDERICK SANDYS

[Reid (88.9), pp. 55–64]

Sandys' earliest illustrations were two series of designs, one depicting birds of Norfolk and another dealing with the antiquities of Norwich. Almost without exception, Sandys' engravings are uniformly good, reaching a high level in both conception and execution. Especially fine, and probably the best known, is *"Amor Mundi"*; others of almost equal quality are "Until Her Death," "Rosamund, Queen of the Lombards," "The Advent of Winter," "The Old Chartist," and "The Little Mourner."

Several items included below appeared in connection with a pair of articles on Sandys as a designer (Pennell [89.11] and Gray [89.10]) and are not, strictly speaking, illustrations. Not listed below are the collected edition of Sandys' wood engravings (89.13) and *The Nightmare* (82.2), the famous parody of Millais' *Sir Isumbras*, which was engraved on zinc and issued as a broadsheet. The most Pre-Raphaelite drawing by Sandys, "Morgan Le Fay," is also not included; it appeared as a supplement to *The British Architect* in October 1879, and was used as the frontispiece in Gleeson White's study (88.3). For Sandys' contributions to jointly illustrated volumes see 90.6, 90.7, 90.9, 90.10, and 90.12.

* * *

97.1 *The Cornhill Magazine*. Vol. I, 1860.

One illustration. "The Portent" (617), story by George MacDonald. Reprinted *Cornhill Gallery* (90.7), p. 94.

97.2 *Once a Week*. Vol. IV, 1861.

Two illustrations. "Yet Once More on the Organ Play" (350), a poem "from the Ger-

man of Uhland" by Julia Goddard; "The Sailor's Bride" (434), poem by Marion E. James. Another illustration, "The Dying Heroes," is wrongly attributed to Sandys.

97.3 —— Vol. V, 1861.

Three illustrations. "From My Window" (238), poem by Fred H. Whymper; "The

Three Statues of Aegina" (491 [Chiron's Ghost]), poem by Walter Thornbury; "Rosamund, Queen of the Lombards" (631), poem by C.S.E.

97.4 *Cornhill Magazine*. Vol. VI, 1862.
One illustration. "Manoli" (346), poem by W. M. Call. Reprinted *Cornhill Gallery* (90.7), p. 95.

97.5 *Good Words*. 1862.
One illustration. "Until Her Death" (312), poem by Dinah M. Mulock.

97.6 *Once a Week*. Vol. VI, 1862.
Three illustrations. "The Old Chartist" (183), poem by George Meredith; "The King at the Gate" (322), poem by Walter Thornbury; "Jacques De Caumont" (152), story by S. Baring-Gould.

97.7 —— Vol. VII, 1862.
Three illustrations. "Harold Harfagr" (154 [The Valkyrie and the Raven]), poem by George Borrow; "The Death of King Warwulf. A Norse Legend" (266), poem by Walter Thornbury; "The Boy Martyr" (602), poem by T.W.

97.8 *The Churchman's Family Magazine*. Vol. II, 1863.
One illustration. The Waiting Time (91), "The Hardest Time of All," poem by Sarah Doudney concerning an incident of the Lancashire cotton famine. See 90.9, "Lancashire Lesson."

97.9 *Good Words*. 1863.
One illustration. "Sleep" (589), anonymous poem (see 90.10). Another illustration, Sheep and Goats, by J. D. Watson, is wrongly attributed to Sandys.

97.10 Meredith, George. *The Shaving of Shagpat*. London: Chapman and Hall, 1865.
One illustration. A steel-engraved frontispiece illustrating "Bhanavar the Beautiful."

97.11 *The Shilling Magazine: A Miscellany of Literature, Social Science, Fiction, Poetry, Art*. 1865.
One illustration, *"Amor Mundi"* (193), poem by Christina Rossetti. Reproduced in

photogravure from an early impression from the block.

97.12 [Mulock, Dinah M.]. *Christian's Mistake* (Standard Library). London: Hurst and Blackett, [1866].
One illustration. Christian (frontis.). A steel-engraving. This illustration and the one for *The Shaving of Shagpat* (97.10) are line engravings by J. Saddler after drawings by Sandys.

97.13 *The Argosy*. 1866.
One illustration. "If" (336), poem by Christina Rossetti. The drawing also appears as a vignette on the title page.

97.14 *The Cornhill Magazine*. Vol. XIV, 1866.
One illustration. "Cleopatra" (331), poem by A. C. Swinburne.

97.15 *Once a Week*. n.s. Vol. I, 1866.
One illustration. "Helen and Cassandra" (454), poem by Alfred B. Richards.

97.16 *The Quiver: An Illustrated Magazine of Social, Intellectual, & Religious Progress*. 1866.
One illustration. "The Advent of Winter" (201 ['Yet she was all so queenly in her woe'; "October"]), poem by Thomas Hood.

97.17 *Idyllic Pictures*. London: Cassell, 1867.
One illustration. A reprint. "October" (61), poem by Thomas Hood — see 97.16.

97.18 Thornbury, Walter. *Historical and Legendary Ballads and Songs*. London: Chatto and Windus, 1876.
Nine illustrations. Reprints. Many strangely and inappropriately retitled. All reprinted from *Once a Week*.

97.19 *The Art Journal*. 1884.
One illustration. A photographic reproduction of an unpublished drawing. Tears (76). The illustration accompanies J. M. Gray's article (55.1). Five of Sandys' engravings are reprinted in the article: "If," "The Old Chartist," "Harold Harfagr," "The Advent of Winter," and "The Death of King Warwulf."

97.20 *The Century Guild Hobby Horse.* n.s. III, 1888.

Two illustrations. Miranda (41), a photogravure; Danae in the Brazen Chamber (147). Accompanying an article by J. M. Gray (89.10). Intended for *Once a Week*.

97.21 *The English Illustrated Magazine.* 1891.

One illustration. Proud Maisie (frontis., p. 561). Engraved by W. Spielmeyer from a drawing. According to J. M. Gray (89.10),

the drawing was first reproduced in *Pan* in 1881, but this must be an error. According to Gleeson White, it was first reproduced in *Cassell's Family Magazine* in 1881, but it is not to be found there either.

97.22 *The Quarto: An Artistic, Literary, & Musical Quarterly.* 1896.

One illustration. The Spirit of the Storm. An unfinished drawing accompanying Pennell's article, "An English Illustrator" (89.11).

Section 98

WILLIAM BELL SCOTT

William Bell Scott, often in collaboration with his brother David, executed so many engravings that no attempt has been made to list them all. The majority are not worthy of mention, and many of his designs are not illustrations at all, but decorations. In general, Scott's illustrations are crude in execution and they often exemplify a groping towards the pseudomystical which is not infrequently grotesque and ludicrous. With the exception of *Hades*, the two etchings for which are in some ways Scott's most imaginative illustrations, no work of his before 1850 has been included in the present listing. For Scott's contribution to jointly illustrated volumes see 90.8.

* * *

98.1 Scott, William Bell. *Hades; or, The Transit: and The Progress of the Mind. Two Poems.* London: Renshaw, 1838.

Two illustrations. Etchings illustrating *Hades; or, The Transit.*

98.2 *Chorea Sancti; or, Steps in the Journey of Prince Legion.* London: Bell, 1851.

Twelve illustrations.

98.3 Scott, William Bell. *Poems.* London: Smith, Elder, 1854.

Three illustrations. A frontispiece with the title *Poems by a Painter*, the title which appears on the spine of the volume; Rosa Munda (54), "Woodstock Maze"; St. Cuthbert (219), "Four Acts of St. Cuthbert."

98.4 Bunyan, John. *The Pilgrim's Progress.* With 65 Original Illustrations by David and William B. Scott; A Life of the Author by the Rev. J. M. Wilson.. And Explanatory Notes Abridged from the Rev. Thomas Scott. London: Fullarton, 1858.

Twenty-five illustrations. Published in two parts. All of W. B. Scott's designs are in part II. David Scott had 40 designs in part I.

98.5 *The Juvenile Verse and Picture Book.* London: Warne, 1866.

One full-page illustration to "Edwin, A Fairy Tale" (81), an unsigned poem; two half-page illustrations (83, 84), and a tailpiece.

98.6 *The Poetical Works of Samuel Taylor Coleridge.* Edited with an Introductory Memoir and Illustrations by William B. Scott. London: Routledge, [1874].

Five illustrations. The works illustrated are "The Ancient Mariner," "Christabel," and "Wallenstein."

98.7 *The Poetical Works of John Keats.* Edited with an Introductory Memoir and Illustrations by William B. Scott. London: Routledge, [1874].

Six illustrations. The works illustrated are

"La Belle Dame Sans Merci," "Endymion," "Isabella," "Hyperion," and "Ode to a Nightingale."

98.8 *The Poetical Works of Letitia Elizabeth Landon.* Edited with an Introductory Memoir and Illustrations by William B. Scott. London: Routledge, [1874].

Six illustrations. The works illustrated are "Sappho's Song," "The Troubador," "The Golden Violet," "A Legend of Tintagel," and "A Ruined Castle."

98.9 Scott, William Bell. *Poems: Ballads,*

Studies from Nature, Sonnets, Etc. Illustrated by Seventeen Etchings by the Author and L. Alma-Tadema. London: Longmans, 1875.

Thirteen illustrations. Two are engraved from a design and a painting by David Scott; another is from a painting by Alice Boyd; one, Recreating Genii, illustrating "Music of the Spheres," is a reprint from 98.1.

98.10 ——— *A Poet's Harvest Home: Being One Hundred Short Poems, with an Aftermath of Twenty Short Poems.* London: Elkin Mathews, 1893.

One illustration plus a title-page vignette and an endpiece.

Section 99

FREDERIC JAMES SHIELDS

[Reid (88.9), p. 208]

The reputation of Frederic Shields as an illustrator rests solely, but securely, on two works, Bunyan's *Pilgrim's Progress* and Defoe's *History of the Plague of London.* That Shields took infinite care in his illustrations and that he regarded the art of illustration seriously is clearly evident from his studies for *Pilgrim's Progress* in the Victoria and Albert Museum. All of his drawings have a high degree of finish and a quality of excellence; often they are overpowering, as in the case of his best known and most often reproduced engraving, Vanity Fair. Not included below are some drawings of famous paintings which Shields executed on wood for *The Art Treasures Examiner* (1857). For Shields' contribution to jointly illustrated volumes see 90.10.

*   *   *

99.1 Ormewood, Oliver. *A Rachde Felley's Visit to the Greyt Eggshibishun.* 3rd ed. Manchester: Heywood, 1856.

Fourteen illustrations. Shields' earliest and crudest work.

99.2 *The Illustrated London News.* 1859.

One illustration. The Holly Gatherers (or Christmas Eve).

99.3 *Once a Week.* Vol. IV, 1861.

One illustration. "An Hour with the Dead" (491), poem by Louisa Crow.

99.4 ——— Vol. V, 1861.

One illustration. "The Robber Saint" (378), poem by S.

99.5 Defoe, Daniel. *The History of the Plague of London* (The Shilling Entertainment Library. Edited by J. S. Laurie). London: Longman, 1863.

Six illustrations. The Decision of Faith (frontis.); The Plague-Stricken House (1 [The Death of the First-Born]); Imprisoned Family Escaping (54); Dead-Pit (62 [The Plague-Pit; The Plague Cart]); Fugitive Found Dead by Rustics (98); Solomon Eagle Denouncing the Impenitent (101). Reid is doubtful that 1863 is the first edition and refers to an undated, privately owned copy in Harold Hartley's collection (now in the Boston Museum of the Fine Arts) bearing the imprint of "John Marshall & Co., Simpkin & Co., Hamilton, Adams & Co., and H. S. King

& Co." This is one of the rarest of all the illustrated books of the period.

99.6 *Illustrations to Bunyan's Pilgrim's Progress.* London: Simpkin, 1864.

According to a letter from Shields (quoted in 58.7), the artist "got near sixty designs to do for *Pilgrim's Progress.*" The number finally printed, however, was only nineteen. Although this volume is missing from the collections of both the British Museum and the Victoria and Albert Museum, a copy in the possession of Mrs. Geoffrey Dennis was available for examination. The designs published in the volume are as follows: a frontispiece portrait of Bunyan; two initial letters for parts I and II; Christian Reading; The Vision of Judgment; Christian at the Cross; Christian, Sloth, Simple, &c.; Hill Difficulty; Apollyon; Giant Pope; Faithful and Wanton; Moses and Faithful; Vanity Fair — one of Shields' finest drawings and unquestionably the most magnificent illustration in the volume; Hill of Caution; The River of Death; Mercy Fainting; The Muck-Rake; Mercy Making Garments; The Good Shepherd; Turn-Away at the Cross. Included among the drawings, studies, and prints for *Pilgrim's Progress* in the collection of the Victoria and Albert Museum are two which do not figure in the published volume: Christian and Faithful in Vanity Fair, and The Valley of the Shadow of Death.

99.7 *Once a Week.* Vol. X, 1864.

One illustration. "Tuberville, and the Heiress of Coity" (378), poem by C.H.W.

99.8 *The Sunday Magazine.* n.s. II, 1866.

One illustration. "Even as Thou Wilt" (33) poem by [Isa] C[raig].

99.9 *Once a Week.* n.s. III, 1867.

One illustration. "Hide a Stick in a Little Hole" (572), anecdote by F. J. S[hields].

99.10 *Good Words.* 1868.

One illustration. "Among the Corn" (441), poem by Isabella Fyvie. This illustration is signed simply "S," and is attributed in the Index to "F. Shield." Its canonicity is questionable. No reference to it occurs in White, Reid, or Ernestine Mills (58.7). The drawing is without distinction and might have been done by anyone.

99.11 *Punch.* 1875.

One illustration. " 'Tis An Ill Wind Blows Nobody Good" (239 ['Want your door swep' mam?']). Reproduced by Ernestine Mills (58.7, p. 150), who comments that Shields did other illustrations for *Punch.*

Section 100

SIMEON SOLOMON

[Reid (88.9), pp. 103–104]

With two exceptions, all of Simeon Solomon's thirty-five illustrations treat religious subjects, especially incidents from Hebraic lore. Stylistically, however, as Forrest Reid has pointed out, Solomon's work falls between the two extremes of the Pre-Raphaelite method of his Biblical designs and the "impressionism of his studies of contemporary Jewish life." Certainly, most of his designs are far removed from those characteristics generally associated with the revival of engraving in the 1860's. Because the latest of Solomon's designs is 1871, his illustrations escape the nebulous and soporific mysticism of his later drawings and paintings. Only his last illustration, two dreamy heads for Swinburne's "The End of a Month," gives any indication of those qualities which were finally so disastrous to Solomon's art. For Solomon's contributions to jointly illustrated volumes see 90.5 and 90.12.

*   *   *

100.1 *Good Words*. 1862.

One illustration. "The Veiled Bride" (592), poem by William Robertson.

100.2 *Once a Week*. Vol. VII, 1862.

Two illustrations. The Marriage Ceremony (192); Lighting the Lamps, Eve of the Sabbath (193), "Jews in England," an article on Jewish customs by G.L.

100.3 *The Leisure Hour: A Family Journal of Instruction and Recreation*. 1866.

Ten illustrations. The Feast of Dedication (73); Initiation into the Tribe of Abraham, or The Circumcision (168); Celebration of the Passover (217); The Marriage Ceremony (329); The Eve of the Jewish Sabbath (377); The Fast of Jerusalem (476); The Day of Atonement (540); The Feast of Tabernacles (604); The Rejoicing of the Law (654); The Week of Mourning (824). All are illustrations in a series entitled "Illustrations of Jewish Customs," appearing monthly, February through December, excepting November. Two of these illustrations are practically identical with those in 100.2.

100.4 *The Dark Blue*. I, 1871.

One illustration. "The End of a Month" (217), a poem by A. C. Swinburne.

100.5 Fox, A., ed. *Art Pictures from the Old Testament*. London: S.P.C.K., 1894.

Twenty illustrations, six reprints — see 90.12. Abraham's Sacrifice; Abraham and the Three Angels; The First Offering of Aaron; The Feast of the Tabernacles; The Passover; Ruth and Naomi; And David Took an Harp; Jewish Women Burning Incense; Shadrach, Meshach, and Abednego; Offering the First-Fruits of the Harvest; The Burnt Offering; 'Righteousness and Peace Have Kissed Each Other'; 'He Shall Order the Lamps'; Offering Incense.

ADDITIONS

The following have come to the author's attention since completion of the manuscript.

8.8 *Ford Madox Brown, 1821–1893* [Catalogue of the Exhibition]. Liverpool: Walker Art Gallery, 1964.

With a Preface by Ben Shaw and an Introduction by Mary Bennett, who organized the exhibition and prepared the catalogue. Detailed notes are provided for each of the 89 works shown. The catalogue contains eight pages of reproductions.

16.27 (annot.) For further notices see Allen F. Staley, "Radical Romantics," *Art News*, LXIII (May 1964), 32–34; Stuart Preston, "Pre-Raphaelites in New York," *Apollo*, LXXIX (June 1964), 512–513; S. Tillim, "Pre-Raphaelite Retrospective at the Gallery of Modern Art," *Arts*, XXXVIII (September 1964), 58–60.

27.109 Pedrick, Gale. *Life with Rossetti.* London: Macdonald, 1964.

An intimate history of Henry Treffry Dunn's twenty-year association with Dante Gabriel Rossetti, drawing on a mass of family materials including a number of unpublished letters from Rossetti to Dunn.

43.181 Wilson, Arnold. "More from Morris and Company," *Apollo*, LXXX (July 1964), 57–59.

A cabinet designed by Philip Webb with painted panels by William De Morgan and a set of tiles illustrating *Beauty and the Beast*, by Burne-Jones, both in the William Morris Gallery, Walthamstow.

44.94 (annot.) Critical reaction to this volume has been lively and varied. Among the reviews see: Graham Hough, "The Pre-Raphaelite Vestal," *Spectator*, 3 April 1964, p. 453; V. S. Pritchett, "A Hushed Life," *New Statesman*, LXVII, no. 1724 (27 March 1964), 491–492; Morse Peckham, "Who Inspired her Imagery?," *Saturday Review*, 28 December 1963, p. 41; "Who Made her Heart Gladder?," *TLS*, no. 3241 (9 April 1964), p. 292 — for interesting follow-up correspondence on this review, from Mrs. Packer, H. F. Rossetti, Lucy M. O'Conor, Mrs. Janet Camp Troxell, Mrs. Virginia Surtees, and Signora Rossetti Angeli, see *TLS*, 23 April, 7, 14, 21 May, 2, 9 July 1964 — Paull Franklin Baum, in *Modern Language Quarterly*, XXV (June 1964), 224–226; W. E. Fredeman, in *Victorian Studies*, VIII (September 1964), 71–77; and R. H. Super, in "Recent Studies in Nineteenth-Century English Literature," *Studies in English Literature*, IV (Autumn 1964), 680–682.

50.10 (annot.) Reprinted with some variation in *Celebrities: Little Stories about Famous Folk*. London: Hutchinson, 1923.

51.25 Paden, W. D. "Arthur O'Shaughnessy in the British Museum; or, the Case of the Misplaced Fusees and the Reluctant Zoologist," *Victorian Studies*, VIII (September 1964), 7–30.

A most carefully researched article on O'Shaughnessy's scientific and personal ineptitude as a Senior Assistant, Second Class in the Department of Zoology of the British Museum, and of his inadvertent involvement in the transfer of the Departments of Natural History to South Kensington. A thoroughly documented and humorously written account.

62.40 Lang, Cecil Y., ed. *New Writings by Swinburne, or Miscellanea Nova et Curiosa: Being a Medley of Poems, Critical Essays, Hoaxes and Burlesques*. Syracuse University Press, 1964.

87.18. Gaunt, William. "Slight Sketch of a Wonderful Man," *The Saturday Book*, n. 5, edited by Leonard Russell. London: Hutchinson, 1945.

On Charles Augustus Howell.

Author's Note: Harold L. Weatherby (27.108) is wrongly cited as David . Clarence Gohdes (38.11) is wrongly cited as Ghodes.

PRB	Pre-Raphaelite Brotherhood
PRism	Pre-Raphaelitism
PRite (s)	Pre-Raphaelite (s)
ACS	Algernon Charles Swinburne
CGR	Christina Georgina Rossetti
DGR	Dante Gabriel Rossetti
EBJ	Edward Burne-Jones
FGS	Frederic George Stephens
FMB	Ford Madox Brown
JEM	John Everett Millais
WHH	William Holman Hunt
WMR	William Michael Rossetti

INDEX

An item in parentheses indicates that it is a duplication of the immediately preceding item. Italic entry numbers indicate that the item contains a complete annotation.

Abbott, Claude Colleer, 86.20, 26
Adolph, R. E., 36.54
Adrian, Arthur A., 24.24; 31.37
Aesthetic Movement: pp. 16–17, 19, 20 and items 43.52; 71.10, 14; 77.15 (33.27; 43.98); 78.2
Agnew, Thomas, & Sons, 9.2; 11.3; 18.23
Agresti, Antonio, 32.9; 33.3; 66.14
Agresti, Olivia Rossetti, 14.11; 19.37; 36.53; 44.43
Aitken, Charles, 18.14
Aitken, James, 41.30
Alden, J. E., 66.26
Aldington, Richard: p. 5 and item 43.33
Alexandre, Arsene, 42.73
Alford, Dean Henry, 90.6
Allen, James, 4.1
Allen, Josephine L., 75.35
Alleyn, Ellen, CGR's pseudonym in *The Germ*, p. 176
Allingham, Helen, 46.20–22, 24, 25
Allingham, William: section 46. MSS in public and private collections, 3.6; 4.3, 4. General: pp. 14, 15, 34, 186–187, 193, 275 and items 4.5; 20.3; 24.6; 27.33; 42.1; 44.74; 69.11, 15, 18, 19, 25; 84.1, 2, 7; 86.23; 88.9; 90.2
Alma-Tadema, Sir Laurence: p. 148 and items 21.15; 56.7 (98.9); 86.16
Alpine Club Gallery (London), 15.5
Alston, Rowland Wright, 63.11
Altick, Richard D., 25.93
Alton, John, 21.37
Alwyn, William, PRite collection, 19.39
Amaya, Mario, 16.28
American Church (Rome), EBJ's mosaics in, 42.29, 45
American PRite Movement: section 80 and pp. 10–13
American Settlers' Co-operative Association, p. 12
Anderson, Sir Colin, p. 55
Anderson Galleries (New York), 19.24, 26
Anderson, George K., 51.21
Anderson, John P.: p. 24 and items 25.11; 44.36; 75.18
Andrews, K., 78.26
Angeli, Signora Helen Rossetti: PRite collection at Woodstock, 4.1 and at Wightwick, 2.13. References: pp. 29, 303 and items 19.6, 25; 24.20; 25.89, 91; 30.31; 34.4; 41.24; 77.66; Howell letters acquired from, 3.8; on exhibition of DGR, 14.10; on WHH and DGR, p. 133; and Simeon Solomon, pp. 212–213

Ardagh, J., 25.60
Armes, William D., 33.1
Armfield, Maxwell, 70.37
Armstead, H. H., 88.9
Armstrong, C. B., 27.47
Armstrong, Martin, 42.105
Armstrong, Sir Walter: p. 133 and items 37.26, 29; 70.19
Arnault, Antoine Vincent, 28.18
Arnold, Sir Edwin, p. 289
Arnold, Matthew, 27.37, 42 (43.63); 33.6; 43.27, 174; 69.13; 81.2
Arnold, William Harris, 24.15
Arnot, R. Page, 43.26, 148
Aronstein, P., 30.33 (77.24)
Arrieta, R. A., 25.55
Art and Poetry, see The Germ
Art for Art's Sake: p. 16 and item 27.74
Art Nouveau, 16.28; 30.75; 71.15; 78.25
Art Workers' Guild, 8.3
Arts and Crafts Exhibition Society, 8.3; 13.2
Arts and Crafts Movement, and PRism: pp. 162, 164 and items 70.44; 78.13; 86.6
Arts Council of Great Britain, 13.12; 16.21, 22
Ashbee, C. R., 43.49 (45.13), 144
Ashbee, Charles B., 78.18
Ashley Library (in British Museum), 1.6; 2.2; 14.9; 24.20; 25.41; 28.5; 61.1. *See also* Wise, Thomas James
Ashmolean Museum (Oxford University): PRite collection, 2.8. General: 5.1; 16.6; 51.4. *See also* Combe Bequest
Association for Promoting the Free Exhibition of Modern Art (London): p. 8 and item 18.1
Athenaeum, The: on PRite exhibition, p. 15; review of ACS, p. 17; FGS as art editor of, p. 148; Watts-Dunton's association with, pp. 221–222; review of Morris, 43.11
Atkinson, J. Beavington, 21.15; 36.26; 75.9
Auction sales, section 19
Austin, Alfred, 29.8; 43.27; 62.14
Australia, State Art Galleries of, 16.25
Avery Architectural Library (Columbia University), 13.13
Axmann, M., 74.6

Bachschmidt, Friedrich Wilhelm, 32.19
Baildon, H. B., 32.5
Bailey, Philip James, 28.15; 90.9
Baille Gallery (London), 17.6
Baker, C. H. Collins, 42.107 (70.28)